COPTIC STUDIES

ZAKŁAD ARCHEOLOGII ŚRÓDZIEMNOMORSKIEJ
POLSKIEJ AKADEMII NAUK

STUDIA KOPTYJSKIE

Prace na Trzeci Międzynarodowy Kongres Studiów Koptyjskich

Warszawa, 20—25 sierpnia 1984 roku

Pod redakcją
Włodzimierza Godlewskiego

PWN —PAŃSTWOWE WYDAWNICTWO NAUKOWE

Warszawa 1990

CENTRE D'ARCHÉOLOGIE MÉDITERRANÉENNE
DE L'ACADÉMIE POLONAISE DES SCIENCES

COPTIC STUDIES

Acts of the Third International Congress
of Coptic Studies

Warsaw, 20—25 August, 1984

Edited by
Włodzimierz Godlewski

PWN —ÉDITIONS SCIENTIFIQUES DE POLOGNE

Varsovie 1990

COUVERTURE ET JAQUETTE DU LIVRE
Henryk Białoskórski

RÉDACTEURS
Maria M. Berger, Danuta Wilanowska

LA COMPOSITION GRAPHIQUE
Maria M. Modrzewska
Maryla Broda

Imprimé dans l'imprimerie
Zakład Graficzny Wydawnictw Naukowych w Łodzi

COPTIC STUDIES

Contents

6

Preface

The present volume of Coptic Studies contains sixty three papers read during the 3rd International Congress of Coptic Studies held in Warsaw on August 20—25, 1984. Other congress presentations have already been published in scholarly journals.

More than 120 scholars answered the invitation of the late Professor Kazimierz Michałowski issued at the plenary meeting of the International Association for Coptic Studies held in Rome on September 26, 1980, during the 2nd International Congress of Coptic Studies, to attend the next congress in Warsaw. Only thanks to such a large attendance was it possible to present a sufficiently complete picture of the newest research done in the fields of Coptic Egypt and Christian Nubia and to discuss directions to be taken by future studies.

Once again the great inspirational and coordinative role of the International Association for Coptic Studies, created in 1976 in Cairo, was made apparent.

The 3rd International Congress of Coptic Studies in Warsaw accentuated the complementary character of Coptological and Nubiological studies, and the great contribution of the Egyptian Antiquities Organization to the preservation of Coptic cultural heritage. The latter found expression in the address by Dr Ahmed Kadry, President of the EAO, and in the resolution adopted by the IACS.

Special thanks are due to the PWN publishers and its editors Mrs Maria M. Berger and Mrs Danuta Wilanowska, who prepared this volume for print.

Włodzimierz GODLEWSKI
National Museum in Warsaw

Karol MYŚLIWIEC
Polish Academy of Sciences

The Third International Congress of Coptic Studies
Warsaw, 20–25 August, 1984

Honorary Committee

Prof. JAN KAROL KOSTRZEWSKI — President of Polish Academy of Sciences

Prof. JULIUSZ BURSZE — Director of National Museum in Warsaw

Prof. KAZIMIERZ DOBROWOLSKI — Rector of Warsaw University

Prof. STANISŁAW LORENTZ — Prof. of Warsaw University and former Director of National Museum

Prof. JERZY ŁANOWSKI — President of the Committee for Antique Studies of Polish Academy of Sciences

Organizing Committee

Dr WŁODZIMIERZ GODLEWSKI — Congress Secretary of IACS, National Museum in Warsaw

Prof. TITO ORLANDI — Editor and Treasurer of IACS, University of Rome

Prof. KAROL MYŚLIWIEC — Research Centre for Mediterranean Archaeology of Polish Academy of Sciences

Dr STEFAN JAKOBIELSKI — Research Centre for Mediterranean Archaeology of Polish Academy of Sciences

Miss BOŻENA ROSTKOWSKA — Research Centre for Mediterranean Archaeology of Polish Academy of Sciences

Prof. ZOFIA SZTETYŁŁO — Institute of Archaeology, Warsaw University

Prof. EWA WIPSZYCKA — Institute of History, Warsaw University

Mrs KRYSTYNA POLACZEK — Polish Centre of Archaeology of Warsaw University, Cairo

Prof. WINCENTY MYSZOR — Academy of Catholic Theology

COPTIC STUDIES

List of Participants

Dr MAHMUD ABDEL RAZEK
Egyptian Antiquities Organization, Cairo, Egypt
Prof. GONZALO ARANDA PÉREZ
Facultad de Teologia, Universidad de Navarra, Pamplona, Spain
Miss PASCALE BALLET
IFAO, 37 Sheich Aly Yousef, Mounira, Cairo, Egypt
Prof. ABOU-EL-YOUN BARAKAT
College of Arts, University of Sohag, Egypt
Prof. THEOFRIED BAUMEISTER
Joh. Gutenberg-Universität, Saarstrasse 21, 6599 Mainz, BRD
Miss NATHALIE BEAUX
39, rue des Vignes, 75016 Paris, France
Prof. WALTER BELTZ
1147 Berlin-Mahlsdorf 1, Kiekemaler Str. 6, DDR
Dr DOMINIQUE BÉNAZETH
6, rue Faustin-Hélie, 75116 Paris, France
Prof. MARIA LUDWIKA BERNHARD
ul. Długa 36 m. 7, 00-238 Warszawa, Poland
Dr HANS-GEBHARD BETHGE
1409 Mühlenbeck, Birkenwerderstr. 4, DDR
Mr MIRRIT BOUTROS GHALI
Société d'Archéologie Copte, 222 Sharia Ramses, Abbasiya, Cairo, Egypt
Mr JEAN-LUC BOVOT
Musée du Louvre, Département des Antiquités Égyptiennes, 75041 Paris Cedex 01, France
Prof. KENT S. BROWN
122 JSB Brigham Young University Provo, UT 84602, USA
Prof. GERALD M. BROWNE
Department of Classics, University of Illinois, 4072 FLB 707 South Mathews Ave., Urbana, Illinois 61801, USA
Dr WOLFGANG BRUNSCH
Demotisches Namenbuch, Institut für Ägyptologie, Julius-Maximilians Universität, Residenzplatz 2 — Tor A, 8700 Wurzburg, BRD
Dr ANTONELLA CAMPAGNANO
41 Via Sesto Fiorentino, 00146 Roma, Italy
Mr MAREK CHŁODNICKI
Archaeological Museum, ul. Wodna 27, 61-787 Poznań, Poland
Dr ELVIRA D'AMICONE
Soprintendenza al Museo delle Antichità Egizie, via Accademia delle Scienze 6, 10123 Torino, Italy

Dr WIKTOR A. DASZEWSKI
ul. Fałata 6 m. 41, 02-534 Warszawa, Poland
Dr ALBERTYNA DEMBSKA
ul. Leszczyńska 8 m. 11, 00-339 Warszawa, Poland
Mr LÉO DEPUYDT
Stationsstraat 35A, 8158 Merkam, Belgium
Prof. SERGIO DONADONI
Via di Novella 22, 00199 Roma, Italy
Prof. TADEUSZ DZIERŻYKRAY-ROGALSKI
ul. Kasprowicza 91, 01-823 Warszawa, Poland
Dr LORETTA DEL FRANCIA
Viale Don Pasquino Borghi 192, 00144 Roma, Italy
Mr STEPHEN EMMEL
304 Aldenave, apt. 2, New Haven, CT 06515, USA
Dr WOLF-PETER FUNK
Paul-Robeson Str. 19, 1071 Berlin, DDR
Dr ABDEL-SAYED GAWDAT GABRA
The Coptic Museum, Old Cairo, Egypt
Dr CLAUDIO GIANOTTO
74, Corso Vercelli, 10015 Ivrea, Italy
Prof. SØREN GIVERSEN
Pileallé 16, 2840 Holte, Denmark
Dr WŁODZIMIERZ GODLEWSKI
ul. Kielecka 21 m. 6, 02-550 Warszawa, Poland
Dr DEIRDRE GOOD
363 S. Candler St., Decatur, Georgia 30030, USA
Prof. WILFRED C. GRIGGS
153 JSB Brigham Young University Provo, Utah 84602, USA
Dr PETER GROSSMANN
Botschaft Kairo–DAI, Postfach 1148, 5300 Bonn 1, BRD
Dr CHARLES HEDRICK
Department of Religious Studies, Southwest Missouri State University, Springfield, Missouri 65802, USA
Mr SØREN HERMANSEN
Bøstrup praestegard, 5953 Tranekaer, Denmark
Dr JÜRGEN HORN
Seminar fur Ägyptologie und Koptologie der Universität Prinzenstr. 21, 3400 Göttingen, BRD
Dr EL HUSSEIN IBRAHIM HASSAN ABOU-EL-ATTA
Graeco-Roman Museum, Alexandria, Egypt
Mr KAREL INNEMÉE
Hooikade 48, 2514 BK The Hague, Holland
Dr STEFAN JAKOBIELSKI
ul. Spacerowa 31, 05-805 Otrębusy, Poland

Dr AHMED KADRY
  Egyptian Antiquities Organization, Abbasiya, Cairo, Egypt
Prof. LÁSZLÓ KÁKOSY
  Pesti Barnabás u 1 Eötvös University, Budapest V, Hungary
Dr FARID ISAAC KAMAL
  9, Abdel Hamid Abu Heif Str., Heliopolis, Cairo, Egypt
Prof. RODOLPHE KASSER
  4 bis, rue Pestalozzi, 1400 Yverdon, Switzerland
Dr ANNA KASSER-DI BITONTO
  4 bis, rue Pestalozzi, 1400 Yverdon, Switzerland
Dr HUBERT KAUFHOLD
  15 Brucknerstr., 8000 München, BRD
Dr ZSOLT KISS
  Centre for Mediterranean Archaeology, Polish Academy of Sciences, PKiN, 00-901 Warszawa, Poland
Miss SUSANNE KLEPPER
  Bismarckallee 47/25, 4400 Münster, BRD
Dr JACEK KOŚCIUK
  ul. Sowińskiego 10 m. 4, 51-685 Wrocław, Poland
Prof. MARTIN KRAUSE
  Melcherstr. 30, 4400 Münster, BRD
Dr ALEKSANDRA KRZYŻANOWSKA
  ul. Broniewskiego 91 m. 101, 01-716 Warszawa, Poland
Prof. MUNEHIKO KUYAMA
  12–20 Heiwa-cho, Chigasaki, Japan
Prof. PAHOR LABIB
  12 Sharia Dr. Handoussa, Garden City, Cairo, Egypt
Dr GINETTE LACAZE
  18, rue du Vertbois, 75003 Paris, France
Miss LUCIA LANGENER
  Sternstrasse 48, 44 Münster, BRD
Prof. BENTLEY LAYTON
  Department of Religious Studies, Box 2160, Yale Station, New Haven, CT 06520, USA
Dr JADWIGA LIPIŃSKA
  ul. Gąbińska 9 m. 105, 01-703 Warszawa, Poland
Dr ANTONIO LOPRIENO
  Via Strozzacapponi 163, 06071 Castel del Piano, Italy
Mrs EWA LORENTZ
  ul. Krasińskiego 40 m. 15, 01-779 Warszawa, Poland
Dr ELISABETTA LUCCHESI-PALLI
  Rürstenbrunnstr. 7, 5020 Salzburg, Austria
Prof. ERICH LÜDDECKENS
  Schillerstr. 10, 8707 Veitschöchheim, BRD
Dr ADAM ŁUKASZEWICZ
  Zakład Papirologii, Uniwersytet Warszawski, Krakowskie Przedmieście 26/28, 00-927 Warszawa, Poland
Dr LESLIE S. B. MACCOULL
  2800 Wisconsin Ave., N.W.Ap't 702, Washington, D.C. 20007, USA
Dr ELŻBIETA MAKOWIECKA
  National Museum, Al. Jerozolimskie 3, 00-495 Warszawa, Poland
Dr GIANCARLO MANTOVANI
  Via Circonvallazione 22, 03011 Alatri, Italy
Dr MAŁGORZATA MARTENS-CZARNECKA
  ul. Puszczy Solskiej 5 m. 73, 01-390 Warszawa, Poland
Prof. FRANCISCO JAVIER MARTINEZ
  Federico Rubio 186, Madrid 20, Spain
Dr STANISŁAW MEDEKSZA
  Polish Centre of Archaeology, 14 Baron Empain Str., Cairo-Heliopolis, Egypt

Mrs KRYSTYNA MICHAŁOWSKA
  ul. Kwiatowa 20, 05-807 Podkowa Leśna, Poland
Mr MOHAMMED ABD EL-HADY
  ul. Zwycięzców 6a m. 2, 03-941 Warszawa, Poland
Prof. GAMAL EL-DIN MOKHTAR
  16, Sahab Street, Pyramids' Avenue, Giza, Egypt
Miss NICOLE MORFIN
  18, rue du Delta, 75009 Paris, France
Mr MOUNIR BASTA
  Coptic Museum, Old Cairo, Egypt
Dr CHRISTA MÜLLER
  Weserstr. 36, 3400 Göttingen, BRD
Dr WINCENTY MYSZOR
  ul. Słowiańska 21, 05-820 Piastów, Poland
Prof. KAROL MYŚLIWIEC
  ul. Janowskiego 54 m. 8, 02-784 Warszawa, Poland
Prof. PETER NAGEL
  Martin-Luther Universität Emil-Abderhalden-Str. 9, 4020 Halle, DDR
Dr CLAUDIA NAUERTH
  Karl-Poppstr. 30, 6748 Bad Bergzabern, BRD
Dr KINGA OLGYAY-STAWIKOWSKA
  ul. Spalska 3 m. 4, 02-934 Warszawa, Poland
Prof. TITO ORLANDI
  Via F. Civinini 24, 00197 Roma, Italy
Dr ALI OSMAN
  Department of Archaeology, University of Khartoum, Sudan
Dr LOUIS PAINCHAUD
  1216 Avenue Joseph-Vézina, Sillery, GIT 2K9 Québec, Canada
Dr LUCIA PAPINI
  Via della Piazzola 103, 50133 Firenze, Italy
Mr PIOTR PARANDOWSKI
  National Museum, Al. Jerozolimskie 3, 00-495 Warszawa, Poland
Prof. BIRGER A. PEARSON
  Dept. of Religious Studies, University of California, Santa Barbara, California 93106, USA
Prof. J. MARTIN PLUMLEY
  13, Lyndewode Road, Cambridge, CB1 2HL, Cambs., Great Britain
Mr KRZYSZTOF PLUSKOTA
  ul. Sobieskiego 109 m. 2, 00-763 Warszawa, Poland
Mrs KRYSTYNA POLACZEK
  ul. Olbrachta 62 m. 46, 01-111 Warszawa, Poland
Prof. ELŻBIETA PROMIŃSKA
  ul. Kasprowicza 91, 01-823 Warszawa, Poland
Dr DOROTHEE RENNER
  Akademie der Wissenschaften und der Literatur, Koptische Textilien, Geschwister-School-Str. 2, 6599 Mainz, BRD
Dr JOHANNA RIJNIERSE
  Groenoord 136, 2401 AH Alphen/Rhine, Holland
Prof. MICHEL ROBERGE
  9310, Avenue Veuillot, Charlesbourg, Québec, Canada GIG 3G6
Dr MARIAN ROBERTSON
  3631 Wellington St., Salt Lake City, Utah 84106, USA
Prof. JAMES M. ROBINSON
  Institute for Antiquity and Christianity, Claremont Graduate School, Claremont, CA 91711, USA
Dr MIECZYSŁAW RODZIEWICZ
  2, rue de Pharaons apt. 6, Alexandria, Egypt

Miss BOŻENA ROSTKOWSKA
Centre for Mediterranean Archaeology, Polish Academy of Sciences, PKiN,00-901 Warszawa, Poland

Dr MARIE H. RUTSCHOWSCAYA
Dept des Antiquités égyptiennes, Musée du Louvre, 75041 Paris, France

Dr BARBARA RUSZCZYC
ul. Marzanny 5 m. 35, 02-649 Warszawa, Poland

Mrs IDA RYL-PREIBISZ
ul. Bacha 30 m. 604, 02-743 Warszawa, Poland

Dr ASHRAF ISKANDER SADEK
19, rue Le Sueur, 87000 Limoges, France

Dr HELMUT SATZINGER
Rechte Bahngasse 12/17, 1030 Wien, Austria

Prof. TORGNY SÄVE-SÖDERBERGH
Kyrkogardsgatan 27, 75235 Uppsala, Sweden

Mr HEINRICH SCHATEN
Up'n Hoff 2, 4438 Heek, BRD

Mrs SOFIA SCHATEN
Up'n Hoff 2, 4438 Heek, BRD

Prof. HANS MARTIN SCHENKE
Leninallee 227, 1125 Berlin, DDR

Dr GESINE SCHENKE
Leninallee 227, 1125 Berlin, DDR

Prof. ERIC SEGELBERG
Dalhousie University, Dept. of Classics, Halifax, NS Canada

Prof. ADEL SIDARUS
Apartado Postal 34, 7001 Evora Codex, Portugal

Miss MARIE-FRANCE SŒURS
26, rue Jules Chatenay, 93380 Pierrefitte, France

Mr MAREK STEINBORN
ul. Białobrzeska 33 m. 8, 02-340 Warszawa, Poland

Miss EWA STELMACHOWSKA
Archaeological Museum, ul. Wodna 27, 61-781 Poznań, Poland

Dr HEIKE STERNBERG
Auf dem Lomberge 19, 3400 Göttingen, BRD

Prof. ZOFIA SZTETYŁŁO
ul. Brazylijska 3a m. 3, 03-966 Warszawa, Poland

Dr EINAR THOMASSEN
Universitetet i Bergen, Religionsvitenskapelig Institutt, Sydnesplass 9, 5000 Bergen, Norway

Dr BARBARA TKACZOW
ul. Wawelska 40 m. 2, 02-067 Warszawa, Poland

Dr LÁSZLÓ TÖRÖK
Inst. of Archaeology, Hungarian Academy of Sciences, 1014 Budapest, Uri utca 49, Hungary

Miss KATARZYNA URBANIAK
ul. Dickensa 19 m. 49, 02-382 Warszawa, Poland

Miss MIENEKE VAN DER HELM
Bazarstraat 46. a, 2518 AK Den Haag, Holland

Mr JACQUES VAN DER VLIET
Joh. Vermeerplantsoen 11, 2251 GP Voorschoten, Holland

Prof. PAUL VAN MOORSEL
Groencord 136, 2401 AH Alphen/Rhine, Holland

Prof. JEAN VERCOUTTER
25, rue de Trevise, 75009 Paris, France

Dr DEREK A. WELSBY
Dept. of Archaeology, University, Newcastle-upon-Tyne NE1 7RU, Great Britain

Dr EWA WIPSZYCKA
ul. Włościańska 14/46, 01-710 Warszawa, Poland

Mr MACIEJ WŁODARSKI
ul. Baśniowa 3 m. 67, 02-349 Warszawa, Poland

Miss BOŻENA WIŚNIEWSKA
National Museum, Al. Jerozolimskie 3, 00-495 Warszawa, Poland

Mr P.P.F.M. ZEEGERS
Bazarstraat 46a, 2518 AK Den Haag, Holland

Mrs CORNELIA E. ZIJDERVELD
Parnassiaveld 55, 1115 EE Duivendrecht, Holland

List of Contributions Read at the Congress *in absentia*

KRZYSZTOF BABRAJ, Jagiellonian University Library, Al. Mickiewicza 22, 530-069 Kraków, Poland, *La symbolique des lettres Γ et H dans l'abside de la Cathédrale de Faras et leur lien avec l'art copte*

JOHANNES DEN HEIJER, Institut Néerlandais d'Archéologie et d'Études Arabes, Le Caire, *Réflexions sur la composition de* l'Histoire des Patriarches d'Alexandrie: *les auteurs des sources coptes*

ALEKSANDER KAKOVKIN, ul. Lensovieta 66, apt 69, 196158 Leningrad, USSR, *L'art copte de l'Ermitage*

MARK MILBURN, Gernsheimerstr. 12, 6080 Gross-Gerau, BRD, *Nomads and Religion in the Context of Christian Nubia and Coptic Egypt: an Enquiry*

NATALIA POMERANTSEVA, Lomonovski Prospekt 18, apt 75, 117296 Moscow, USSR, *Spread of the Traditions of Ancient Egyptian Art on the Iconography of Coptic Ritual Sculpture (4th–6th centuries A.D.)*

MARGUERITE RASSART-DEBERGH, 30A, rue Lincoln, 1180 Bruxelles, Belgium, *Les peintures des Kellia (Missions de 1981 à 1983)*

List of Papers Read at the Congress but not Sent to Editors

ALBERTYNA DEMBSKA, *Some Remarks Concerning the Semantic Value of the Word* TWOYN

LÉO DEPUYDT, *The Coptic for "To Look" and "To See" in a Diachronic Perspective*

GAWDAT GABRA, *The Importance of the Site of Haǧar Edfu for Coptology and Nubiology*

SØREN GIVERSEN, *Psalm 136 in the Coptic Manichaen Psalmbook, part 1*

MOHAMMED ABD ELHADY, *The Role of Nubian Sandstone in the Ancient Buildings in Egypt*

CHARLES W. HEDRICK, *Beyond the Consensus: The Hid Treasure Parable in Matthew and Thomas*

SØREN HERMANSEN, *The Book of the Resurrection of Jesus Christ, by Bartholomew the Apostle*

JÜRGEN HORN, *"Da berief er alle Vorsteher der Klöster ein" (Vita prima Pachomii § 106). Zur Gliederung des pachomianischen Klosterverbandes in Jahr der Amtsenthebung Theodora*

JÜRGEN HORN, *Die Göttinger Surveys im XII oberägyptischen Gau. Aspekte eines spätantik-koptischen Ensembles*

JÜRGEN HORN, *Index textuum Sinuthianorum editorum*

EL HUSSEIN IBRAHIM HASSAN ABOU EL ATTA, *Some Coptic Objects from the Graeco-Roman in Alexandria*

STEFAN JAKOBIELSKI, *Documentation Project for Nubian Murals Files*

AHMED KADRY, *History and National Identity*

BENTLEY LAYTON, *A New Catalogue of Coptic Manuscripts in the British Library*

ELISABETTA LUCCHESI-PALLI, *Un motif ornemental de Baouît*

M. GAMAL EL-DIN MOKHTAR, *Coptic Egypt as Project for the Egyptian New Museum of Civilization*

TITO ORLANDI, *The Computer and Coptic Studies*

ALI OSMAN, *The National Society for Nubian Studies (Sudan)*

ELŻBIETA PROMIŃSKA, *Ancient Egyptian Tradition in Artificial Mummification in the Christian Period in Egypt*

DOROTHEE RENNER, *Lamellar Armoured Oriental Horsemen on Coptic Textiles*

JAMES M. ROBINSON, *The Fascimile Edition of the Nag Hammadi Codices: Final Report*

MIECZYSŁAW RODZIEWICZ, *Archaeological Evidence on Christian Alexandria and Its Environs*

BOŻENA ROSTKOWSKA, *Christian Paintings in the Nile Valley in the 4th–16th Centuries*

ASHRAF ISKANDER SADEK, *Quelques réflexions d'un égyptologue copte sur trois points concernant la coptologie*

HANS-MARTIN SCHENKE, *Summer Course in Coptology at Humboldt University in Berlin*

ERIC SEGELBERG, *Some Notes on the Gospel of Philip*

MAREK STEINBORN, *Remarks on the Economy of Medieval Nubia*

J. VAN DER VLIET, *Some Observations on Coptic Terms for "Demon"*

COPTIC STUDIES

Bentley Layton

The Future of Our Association
Presidential Address

I should like to begin on a personal note, by saying what a great pleasure it is to see so many good friends and colleagues gathered here in Warsaw, and such a wide representation of the many disciplines that make up the area of Coptic Studies. We have the honor to be guest of one of the world's great national academies, the Polish Academy of Sciences.

This is only the third International Congress of Coptic Studies—indeed, just the second to be sponsored by our Association. When the first International Congress was held in 1976, its sponsor was the Egyptian Antiquities Organization; the International Association for Coptic Studies was founded at that Congress as a result of the Egyptian effort to stimulate Coptic Studies at an international level, at the end of the UNESCO project to publish Nag Hammadi codexes. An important predecessor of the newly founded Association was the Cairo-based Société d'Archéologie Copte, whose president Mirrit Boutros Ghali became one of the first honorary presidents of our International Association. At the time of its founding, the Association acknowledged that whatever success it might achieve would be a continuation of the impetus and precedent already provided by the Société d'Archéologie Copte. Since our foundation, the Association and the Société have enjoyed a close and formally united relationship, which we expect to continue in a mutually beneficial way. I am happy to say that the Egyptian Antiquities Organization is represented at this Congress in the persons of His Excellency Dr Ahmed Kadry, Dr Gamal Ed-Din Mokhtar, Mr Mounir Basta, and Dr Abdel Sayed Gawdat Gabra, and that our honorary president Dr Boutros Ghali, president of the Société d'Archéologie Copte du Caire, is present here today.

After the Cairo meeting, we held a large and highly successful Congress of our own at the Università di Roma, the home base of our illustrious treasurer. The fact that now so many of us have been willing to make the demanding trip to Warsaw is, I think, a mark of the importance that scholars accord to the existence and activity of the Association, and the expectations that we have for its future.

The opening session of each Congress ought to provide an opportunity for the outgoing president to record his own personal observations about those future expectations. I shall therefore present, very briefly, my own assessment of the present state of the International Association for Coptic Studies, and the directions in which I think we must go in order to achieve the aims of the Association.

Certainly, in basic matters—membership, finances, and communication—the Association is sound. In July 1981, just after the Rome Congress, we had 179 members on our books. In the three following years, the overall number has hardly changed. Although death has robbed us of several members, we continue to gain new recruits at a slow but steady rate, so that the last published membership list carries 183 names—an overall increase of four.

There may be a few Coptic scholars or students of Coptic Studies in attendance at this Congress who are not yet members of the IACS. To you, let me say that we very much welcome your application for membership while you are here, and we hope you can join the Association. By our statutes, full voting membership requires a delay of at least nine months, and so will become effective at the next congress. You have only to speak to Prof. Tito Orlandi, our treasurer, to undertake the simple steps that are necessary.

At each Congress, the voting members of the Association hold a short business meeting, which hears reports from the officers, elects new officers, and transacts other business as necessary.

The business meeting at this Congress will be held on Saturday. According to the procedure of the Association, members wishing to introduce new resolutions at the meeting are required to contact the president one month in advance of this meeting, so the agenda can be prepared. The agenda of Saturday's meeting will be posted tomorrow. Anyone wishing to comment on the agenda should please contact Prof. Orlandi.

In questions of finance, our statutes specify that we must be a non-profit organization. I can safely report that we have not yet violated that stipulation in any serious way! Members will hear a formal treasurer's report at the business meeting next Saturday. Our very modest income derives entirely from members' dues and just barely covers printing, postage, and office expenses. Our Congresses do not figure in the regular budget of the Association, for they are subsidized by outside funds raised specifically for the occasion under the auspices of the Congress Secretary. In the past, our Congress funds have come from sources such as the Polish Academy and the Italian Consiglio Nazionale delle Ricerche. We have no endowment, nor any substantial balance with which the Association can undertake major scientific projects of its own. By agreement, five dollars from every member's dues subsidizes our twin organization the Société d'Archéologie Copte in Cairo, we have maintained a Cairo office on the premises of the Société; and in return for our modest financial contribution, our members also are to receive the *Bulletin* of the Cairo Société — though in recent years, printing conditions in Egypt have continued to threaten the *Bulletin's* future as an Egyptian publication.

The Association also publishes its own *Newsletter,* which, despite its very modest scope, is a valuable organ of information about Coptologists and their work, and about the Association. Thanks to the labor of our indefatigable treasurer Prof. Orlandi, the *Newsletter* is now going into its sixteenth number in a period of eight years — thus about two *Newsletters* per year from Rome, where our Association has its legal headquarters.

This is perhaps a good time to point out that the ongoing administration of the Association is mainly in the hands of the treasurer, who also edits the *Newsletter.* The success of the Association over these last six years is largely due to the enthusiasm and resourcefulness of Prof. Tito Orlandi, to whom we all owe a great debt of gratitude.

The Association holds Congresses at three or four year intervals. By statute they must be held at locations accessible to the whole membership. The concept of such a location is more an ideal than a reality, because our members come from such far-flung parts of the world. Therefore we have tried, in past years, to realize this ideal by rotating the Congress site among various parts of the world — Egypt, Italy, Poland.

So there can be little doubt that our Association has very well come through the period of its infancy — the "survival" period, if you like.

The next period of our development will be more difficult. In it, we must find the resources for more than mere survival: we must see to it that the International Association for Coptic Studies takes its rightful international place among other organizations and institutions with which it has common interest; that it finds more effective means to unite research in the quite diverse disciplines that form the area called Coptic Studies; and above all, that it promotes the very strict standards of high scholarship in all that it undertakes.

We must not forget that the fate of our Egyptian sister organization, the Société d'Archéologie Copte, is bound up with ours, and together we must consider what implications this will have for us both.

Looking to the difficult tasks that lie ahead, I should like to pass in review the purposes for which our Association exists, as found in our statutes. While our activities are not statutorily limited to these, they are a careful and intelligent statement of the ideal towards which we are striving:

1. to promote cooperation among individuals, organizations, and institutions,
2. to disseminate information,
3. to organize periodic congresses,
4. to promote full access to source materials,
5. to identify research priorities,
6. to encourage younger scholars.

How far has the Association come in achieving these aims? Despite notable successes, in many ways there is room for development. The reason for this is not simply our young age. Compared, say, to the great national academies, we also suffer from other disadvantages. Because our membership and Executive Board are truly international, concerted action is especially difficult in the interval between quadrennial Congresses, at least as we now operate. Probably in future years the

Executive Board will have to meet annually and assert a much more continuous and active leadership of the Association's affairs.

Furthermore, unlike an academy or even a well-founded society, we have no endowed funds that would enable us to sponsor and finance scientific projects or exert leverage in the question of academic standards.

Bearing in mind the six aims of the Association, I will quickly review some ways in which I believe we can hope to become more effective.

1. In promoting *cooperation among individuals,* the IACS has been outstandingly successful. Contacts made at Congresses and through membership have united scholars of the various disciplines that have a common interest in Coptic Studies. There is no clear sign of this than the ease with which Prof. Atiya's *Coptic Encyclopedia* has been able to proceed, using channels established by the IACS.

More difficult is the task of promoting *cooperation among institutions such as museums and libraries* that have Coptic holdings. With luck we shall soon be able to complete and publish the Association's worldwide checklist of institutions holding Coptic source materials. This publication should provide a new basis for institutional cooperation.

So far, we have done almost nothing to establish *liaisons with other organizations* that promote areas and disciplines related to ours. This is a task that remains for the future.

2 and 3. In the *dissemination of information,* so far the Association's efforts have been limited to short and somewhat random reports in the *Newsletter* and the publication of Congress proceedings, of which only the first Congress has appeared. The second is still in press, but there is hope we shall see it soon. I understand that the Research Center for Mediterranean Archaeology of the Polish Academy of Sciences is willing to undertake publication of the Warsaw Congress, and we look forward with gratitude to the speedy appearance of these proceedings.

I believe that in the future we ought to plan more deliberately in this area of our activity. Coptic Studies encompasses many quite different disciplines — linguistics, papyrology, classical philology, ancient history, history of literature, liturgics, history of religions, archaeology, architectural history, art history — and intersects with at least

three major areas, Egyptology, Patristics, and Islamics. In order to strengthen Coptic Studies as an area of learning, we must consciously develop dialogue, not only among ourselves, but also with the pure forms of these disciplines and areas.

I can imagine, for example, that everyone of our international Congresses ought, as a matter of course, to commission critical reports on all these disciplines and fields from major scholars in our Association. In these reports, a knowledgeable scholar would critically evaluate four years' progress as it related to Coptic Studies — thus, for example, on four-years' progress in Coptic linguistics, Coptic papyrology, Coptic philology, history of Coptic and Copto-Islamic Egypt, Coptic literature, Coptic liturgics, history of religions and its Coptic evidence, Coptic archaeology, Coptic architectural history, Coptic art history, and Coptic topics in Egyptology, Patristics, and Islamics.

While of course we are not in a financial position to reimburse the contributors of progress reports, it ought to be understood as a signal honor and important responsibility to receive such a commission; and the Executive Board or its delegate should make wise choices in selecting these scholars.

Not only would the reports give us all a detailed critical idea of recent work and priorities for research; but their publication would also give scholars outside our Association an up-to-date picture of Coptic Studies at four-year intervals, and open the way for exchange of ideas. Our Congress reporters might, for example, read the same papers at international conferences of linguistics, papyrology, philology, and so forth. We might also ask certain museums and libraries holding Coptic source materials to send representatives to our Congresses and to report to us on Coptic developments at those institutions.

There is nothing startling in these suggestions, I trust, but I personally believe we ought to make them a systematic part of the organization of future Congresses.

4. In the matter of *access to source materials,* members of the IACS have unanimously approved a resolution in which they renounce exclusive publication rights of texts, artifacts, and archaeological discoveries for longer than a period of five years. This resolution remains the official policy of the IACS and its members. It is extremely im-

portant to the rapid scientific development of Coptic Studies because its essential aim is to guarantee free access to all Coptic texts, artifacts, and source materials, and permit their study and use by all scholars in the general framework of scientific research. We can be proud to have such a policy on our books; it represents our dedication to pure, disinterested research and is a model for other organizations like ours. So far as I know, there have been no complaints of the violation of this resolution by members of the Association. Thus it would appear that the Association may have achieved its fourth aim as far as its own members go. Unfortunately, the policy of museums and libraries in this regard is not uniformly perfect, but it is beyond our control or influence.

5. *In identifying research priorities* the Association has so far followed the lead of individual members, who have come forward at the Business Meeting and proposed resolutions endorsing research projects that they were planning or already had under way. The projects that the Association has endorsed in this way have been worthwhile and important. Fortunately, our endorsement has never been given out willy-nilly; for example, we have rightly rejected some endorsement resolutions, on the grounds that their subject matter was not relevant to the scientific study of ancient Coptic language and civilization. However, the implications and procedure of project endorsement have not yet been carefully examined. I believe we must now adopt a more thoughtful and deliberate policy in this regard. In fact, the official endorsement of projects is our main opportunity to influence the standards of scholarship in Coptic Studies, and so we must be sure that every proposed project is fully examined before being approved. Furthermore, official endorsement will be meaningful only if it is given out carefully, and not too frequently. The Board should therefore establish a standard procedure for examining, some months in advance, any projects that will be submitted for IACS endorsement. A small advisory committee of scholars to carry out this examination ought to be appointed. Not only scientific quality, but also practical feasibility, ought to be examined. Only this committee should be empowered to introduce endorsement resolutions to the Business Meeting of the Association. Once a project is endorsed, the president and other

members of the Board should be obligated to lend their full support to the project director's efforts at fund-raising and other such problems. The publication of officially endorsed projects should also mention the fact of endorsement.

I have just described one proposal by which the IACS can become more actively involved in promoting the quality and effectiveness of scientific projects.

We must not forget the possibility for the Association actually to sponsor large projects. This possibility would be appropriate especially for projects of international dimensions, which depend on cooperation of institutions and scholars in several different countries. In such a case, the IACS could become the institutional recipient or coordinator of project funding from several national bodies such as the CNRS, NEH, DFG, or the national academies, for a project specifically directed by one of its members. In this kind of case the IACS would be able to function as a multinational umbrella guaranteeing the international character of the project and contributing not only its endorsement but also its ongoing help in the form of an official advisory committee, and the cooperation of several of its members. I hope our members will bear in mind such a possibility in the next few years.

Finally, it may be hoped that some day the Association will have a modest financial endowment at its own disposal. With this we could, for example, establish a prestigious quadrennial lectureship to be awarded at intervals to an outstanding Coptic scholar in one of the disciplines represented in the IACS; the lectureship could provide travel and living expenses at a Congress in return for a new major paper on some important topic. If the standard of lecturers were maintained, the Congress lectureship would indicate the Association's recognition of outstanding contributions to Coptic Studies.

I am optimistic that the Association will continue towards the full attainment of all the purposes for which it exists.

But we dare not forget that behind these individual purposes lies the more general aim of the Association, to promote Coptic Studies as a distinct area of scientific investigation. I hardly need to say that Coptic Studies does not possess a single, pure method of study, as do linguistics, archaeology, or textual criticism. It is an interdisciplinary area, and its students are held together by their common interest in ancient Coptic language and civilization. The area of Coptic Studies should thus be compared to other inter-disciplinary "areas" of the university, such as Classics or Egyptology.

The unity of Coptic Studies is more than an abstract construction. In *institutions,* such as museums, libraries, and archives, it is expressed physically by systematic collections of all kinds of physical data, which are fundamentally important to all the disciplines of our Association. Members of the IACS play active roles in the organizing, management, classification, and description of such collections, as well as in the archaeological field work that they presuppose.

In *human organization,* scholars who interpret these data are united not only in the IACS, but also in national and local organizations. World Congresses and local meetings provide a good framework for the live exchange of information and ideas across disciplinary boundaries.

But in the realm of publications, that is, in the exchange of scientific ideas through articles in journals, I deeply regret to say that we have almost completely failed our general aim, very much to the detriment of Coptic Studies as a distinct area. Scholars who wish to interpret the evidence for ancient Coptic language and civilization have, at this moment, almost no choice but to publish in discipline-oriented journals, such as the *Zeitschrift für Papyrologie und Epigraphik,* or in journals of a broader subject matter, such as *Le Muséon, Orientalia,* or *Enchoria.* There does not exist any outstanding journal of truly *international* character that is devoted solely to the inter-disciplinary area of Coptic Studies, even though Coptic journals of a more parochial character do indeed exist. Because Coptic Studies is still so young, we continue to be tempted by the danger of fragmentation back into our constituent method-ologies. I very much fear that until a good international journal of Coptic Studies is brought into existence, the unity of Coptic Studies will continue to be uncertain or even in danger.

What do we really need in such a journal?

First, its scope should be completely inter-disciplinary, embracing all the methodologies that we represent, in a balanced way. But its subject matter should be restricted to things that are essentially Coptic.

Second, it should be truly international, not domi-nated by one language or nationality.

Third, it should objectively maintain the highest scientific standards, accepting only articles of real importance and of the best quality that our area produces.

Fourth, it should be edited with insistence upon accuracy, good style, and high technical quality.

For such a journal to exist, everything rests upon the quality of the person who is editor. The editor would have to be someone of impeccable scholarship, someone with a good sense of organization, preferably with experience in edit-ing, and with a broad vision of the area of Coptic Studies. He would have to be aided by a very active and committed Board of Editorial Consultants representing various disciplines or methods of study; collectively, they would need the courage and independence to accept or reject contributions on a completely objective basis, without regard to the name of the author.

Only if the Coptic journal maintained a scientific standard equal to the very best, would it be able to compete successfully for articles, with more established journals such as *Orientalia* or *Le Muséon.*

Thanks to the revolution in computer printing, it is now possible for the editorial office of such a journal to be located anywhere in the world that computer word processing is available. By means of a personal computer, Coptic and Greek alphabets can now be composed alongside Roman without any special difficulty or cost. But the actual printing and publication of the journal could be done in a different part of the world: all that is needed is an offset printer and paper. This means that a journal of Coptic Studies could be edited and composed in Urbana, Illinois, or Paris, or Warsaw, but printed and published in Rome, or Halle, or Cairo.

It is possible that such a journal might have some official connection with the IACS. But that is by no means a necessity. The most important thing is that the journal exist, that it meet the standards I have just outlined, that leading members of the IACS should play an active role in editing it, and that scholars of Coptic Studies should be willing to publish their best articles there.

In any case, the IACS has no financial resources with which it could ever hope to found a new journal of its own. I lament this fact, but there is nothing at all that we can do to change it. Our only hope is that some great, dedicated, and visionary person will, of his own initiative, make it possible for this ideal to be realized.

I do not want to be more definite within a realm that is purely hypothetical. But if I were to hint at my own very personal feelings, I should say that there is probably no need to found an entirely new journal. There might also be the possibility that a more limited journal that already exists today would be willing to redefine itself in an entirely different way, and so to evolve into a great international journal of Coptic Studies, which can take its place with pride alongside the *Zeitschrift für ägyptische Sprache* and the *Journal of Egyptian Archaeology*.

If ever we can see this come to pass, then the IACS as an organization, and Coptic Studies as a scientific endeavour, will have reached the age of maturity.

Let me express, once again, my great joy in seeing this meeting assembled in Warsaw. I want to wish all the participants a stimulating, challenging, and enjoyable Congress of Coptic Studies.

COPTIC STUDIES

Gonzalo Aranda Pérez

Autour de la version sahidique du Nouveau Testament : s'agit-il d'une tradition textuelle unique ? Étude des manuscrits M 569 et Bodmer XIX

La version sahidique du Nouveau Testament est considérée jusqu'à présent comme un tout homogène qui représente le type du texte neutre, appelé aussi égyptien ou hésiquien. L'affinité parmi les manuscrits utilisés par Horner dans son édition monumentale, ainsi que leur caractère fragmentaire, ont fait que la question n'avait pas encore été posée avec rigueur méthodologique. Cependant, les éditions récentes des manuscrits complets ou presque complets, est une occasion de pouvoir nous interroger : y a-t-il des lignes diverses du texte dans la version sahidique ? Le Professeur H. Quecke dans l'édition des manuscrits PPalau magnifiquement faite, remarque les différences textuelles qui existent parmi ces manuscrits et le numéro 569 de la *Morgan Library*[1] pour ce qui est des Évangiles de Marc et de Luc. Le Professeur Tito Orlandi fait un pas en avant en établissant à grands traits l'affinité existante parmi quelques manuscrits du Monastère Blanc et ceux de la Collection PPalau ou Morgan[2]. Nous croyons cependant que la question mérite une étude plus approfondie.

Nous présentons ici les conclusions d'une analyse concernant l'Évangile de Saint Matthieu, qui a pour objet de déterminer dans les manuscrits sahidiques de cet Évangile l'existence des différences qui nous permettraient de constater des lignes textuelles diverses dans la version sahidique. Nous considérons à la base de cette étude le manuscrit de la Morgan (M 569) contenant le texte complet de

Matthieu, duquel nous avons préparé une édition critique, ainsi que celui de Bodmer XIX, édité par R. Kasser[3]. Nous avons tenu compte aussi des manuscrits procédant du Monastère Blanc d'accord avec l'édition de Horner et les fragments de Vienne. Nous étudions d'abord les caractéristiques textuelles de M 569 selon les lectures propres et exclusives à lui, c'est-à-dire celles qui le montrent tout différent des autres manuscrits sahidiques. Nous étudierons ensuite les lectures propres et exclusives à Bodmer XIX. Nous pourrons alors déterminer le type de texte qui est le plus proche de chacun de ces deux manuscrits.

1. Les caractéristiques textuelles de M 569

Les lectures exclusives de M 569 par rapport à tous les autres témoins sahidiques, et qui montrent quelque chose au-delà du style ou d'un simple caractère grammatical arrivent à une centaine environ. Elles appartiennent néanmoins à des genres très divers.

a) La plus grande partie est constituée par des *lectures variantes* qui changent quelque aspect de la phrase tout en gardant le sens fondamental, et qui n'ont pas de correspondance dans les manuscrits grecs. En général ces lectures manifestent quelque liberté de traduction du grec ou de transmission du texte sahidique. C'est le cas dans

---

[1] Cf. H. Quecke, *Das Markusevangelium saïdisch. Text der Handschrift PPalau Rib. Inv. Nr. 182 mit den Varianten der Handschrift M 569*, Barcelona 1972; *Das Lukasevangelium saïdisch Text der Handschrift PPalau 181 mit den Varianten der Handschrift M 569*, Barcelona 1977.

[2] Cf. T. Orlandi, Recensions aux éditions de H. Quecke, *Studia Papyrologica* 12(1973), 103-109; 17(1978), 118-121.

[3] Cf. R. Kasser, *Papyrus Bodmer XIX. Évangile de Matthieu XIV, 28–XXVIII, 20. Épitre aux Romains I,2–II,3 en sahidique*, Cologne–Genève 1962; G. Aranda Pérez, *El Evangelio de San Mateo en copto sahídico (Texto de M 569, estudio preliminar y aparato critico)*, Madrid 1984.

de *nombreuses omissions* qui simplifient le texte : le manque de pronoms personnels[4], possessifs[5] ou démonstratifs[6] qui se trouvent parfois dans tous les manuscrits grecs. D'autres mots sont omis, qui correspondraient cependant à une traduction littérale du grec[7], telle que le font les autres témoins sahidiques. De la même façon on pourrait considérer quelques additions exclusives du M. 569, qui nous permettent de concrétiser le sens ou renforcer la séquence narrative. Soit, par exemple, l'insertion du démonstratif au lieu de l'article déterminatif[8], l'usage des conjonctions de renfort tels que ON[9], ou ΓΑΡ[10], des prépositions[11] et des pronoms personnels[12]. Il y a aussi quelque addition due à l'influence d'autres passages parallèles, et qui n'offre pas de correspondance dans aucun autre manuscrit grec[13].

On observe tout de suite que les omissions sont plus nombreuses que les additions, ce qui permet de dire qu'il existe dans M 569 une tendance à simplifier le texte.

La liberté de traduction est découverte dans *quelques échanges* dans les prépositions[14], dans l'emploi de conjonctions diverses telles que ΓΑΡ par ΔΕ[15], ϬΕ par ΔΕ[16], dans l'usage de la forme verbale différente[17] et dans les constructions de la phrase au singulier ou au pluriel[18].

En très peu d'occasions, M 569 offre une traduction très littérale du grec par rapport au reste des manuscrits de la version sahidique. Ce sont quelques traductions respectant le pluriel[19] ou le singulier[20] et d'autres qui maintiennent ou pas la présence de ΚΑΙ[21], de ΔΕ[22] et de ON[23].

Toutes ces variantes parmi M 569 et le reste des manuscrits sahidiques de Matthieu nous donnent l'impression que le manuscrit de la Morgan représenterait la version sahidique déjà commune, mais retouchée sur la base d'un autre manuscrit originel grec (ou de plusieurs peut-être). Il est nécessaire d'analyser les lectures variantes exclusives de M 569 qui ont une représentation en grec pour en arriver à déterminer le type du texte de l'original grec supposé.

b) *Les variantes exclusives de M 569 avec représentation en grec* sont aussi du genre très divers, abondent surtout celles qui paraissent être l'effet de concordance avec d'autres passages. Quelques' unes viennent dans la plupart des témoins grecs, ce qui permet de les considérer assez communes, mais d'autres on peut seulement les mettre en relation avec quelques manuscrits grecs. Elles montrent purtant des rapports plus étroits parmi M 569 et le type du texte représenté dans ces manuscrits. Il

---

[4] Cf. l'omission de ΝΑϤ dans 4,7; de ΝΑΥ dans 16,15; 21,16.21; de ΝΗΤΝ dans 24,27; etc.

[5] Cf. l'omission de ΤΕΚ (M 569 ΝΤΚΕΤΕ , les autres ΝΤΕΚΚΕΟΥΕΙ l'autre dans 5,39; de ΝΕΝ dans 8,17; 23,30; de ΝΕΤΝ dans 11,29; etc.

[6] Cf. l'omission de ΜΜΙΝ ΜΜΟΝ dans 13,54; de ϨΩΩϤ dans 25,22; etc.

[7] Par ex. dans 16,12 la phrase ὅτι οὐκ εἶπεν προσέχειν ἀπὸ τῆς ζύμης τῶν ἄρτων ἀλλα ἀπὸ τῆς διδαχῆς est traduite par 'qu'il ne leur parlait pas du ferment du pain mais de l'enseignement...'; dans 17,1 on fait omission de καὶ ἀναφέρει αὐτούς; dans 23,20 ἐν πᾶσι τοῖς ἐπάνω αὐτοῦ est traduit par 'ce qui est posé sur lui' en correspondance avec 23,21 où le grec dit ἐν τῷ καθημένῳ ἐπάνω αὐτοῦ. Dans 26,61 on lit 'ce temple' au lieu de 'le temple de Dieu' par concordance avec Joh 2,19. Dabs 26,49 on omit καὶ εὐθέως par l'influence des parallèles (ainsi Mc 14,45 selon D θ 565 700 it; Lc 22,47).

[8] Cf. 6,5; 6,16; 15,33; 21,25. Cf. aussi 27,32 où on lit ΜΠΑΙ au lieu de ΜΜΟϤ .

[9] Cf. 4,7; 4,21.

[10] Cf. 10,24; 28,10.

[11] Cf. 21,33.

[12] Cf. 14,29; 19,28; 21,24; 21,27.

[13] Ainsi en 12,32 où on ajoute 'un mot' comme complément de εἴπῃ et en 26,28 où on introduit 'maintenant' par l'influence, peut être, de Mc 14,65 (selon quelques manuscrits : G φ sy^s) ou de Matth 27,43. Dans 25,41 on rencontre 'répondra et dira' au lieu de 'dira'. Cela, peut être, est dû à ce que la première phrase est une expression très courante. En 27,43 on explique le sujet de ῥυσάσθω : ΠΝΟΥΤΕ

[14] Par ex. ϨΝ et ΕΧΝ en traduisant εἰς. Cf. 10,27; 13,22

[15] Cf. 16,28; 23,8.

[16] Cf. 21,26. Cf. aussi ΝϬΙ par ϨΙΤΝ dans 28,14; mais ici il s'agit, peut être, d'une erreur de traduction.

[17] Cf. ΕϤΧΩ ΜΜΟ⳨ au lieu de ΠΕΧΑϤ en 25,26.

[18] Cf. 9,32; 15,12; 24,1; 26,58.

[19] Cf. ζιζάνια en 13,25 et οἱ ὄχλοι en 14,23.

[20] Cf. 'leur synagogue' en 13,54.

[21] Cf. 7,23.

[22] Cf. 11,12; 12,6.

[23] Cf. 7,23.

faut dire quand même qu'il pourrait s'agir simplement d'une liberté de traduction. Si l'on fait la classification des variantes selon le type du texte qu'elles représentent, nous arrivons aux résultats suivants:

— Nous ne trouvons aucun cas où M 569 coïncide exclusivement et seulement lui, avec des représentants grecs du type égyptien ou neutre. Les seules variantes qu'on pourrait présenter à cet égard consistent dans l'omission de οὐχί en 5,46, et la lecture concordatrice 'ce temple' au lieu de 'le temple de Dieu' dans 21,38 [24]. Nous trouvons par contre bien des lectures dans M 569 coïncidantes avec des témoins grecs représentants du type neutre ainsi que du césarien. Ainsi, la lecture πᾶσα ἡ devant Jérusalem dans 3,5 [25], l'omission de ὀπίσω μου dans 4,10 [26], l'addition de κύκλω dans 14,15 [27], l'omission de οἱ devant φαρισσαῖοι, dans 16,1 [28], et la lecture 'des cieux' au lieu de 'de Dieu' dans 19,24 [28bis]. Dans ce même groupe nous situons la lecture, insolite — compte tenu de l'ordre qui s'y donne — de 'aveugles, boiteux, muets, paralytiques' dans 15,30 [29] et la transposition dans 10,14 où M 569 lit: 'en sortant de la maison, ou de cette villa-là, ou du hameau', face à la tradition sahidique restante où l'on dit: 'en sortant de la maison, — de la ville, — de cet hameau-là'. Cette lecture, étrange dans M 569, nous permet l'hypothèse suivante: la lecture plus commune qui fait omission de 'le hameau' a été corrigée dans ce manuscrit particulièrement, par rapport aux autres qui disent: 'de ce hameau là'. Le reste des témoins sahidiques suit la lecture correcte de ces manuscrits [30].

— Fréquemment M 569 coïncide lui seul avec quelque autre manuscrit grec appartenant au type du texte césarien. En concret, l'addition de Ἰησοῦς dans 9, 27 [31], la lecture αὐτοῖς par αὐτῷ dans 11,3 [32], l'addition de ἐγένετο dans 13,4 [33], de γαρ dans 16,28 [34], de ταύτης après ἀμπέλου dans 26,29 [35], de τῶν ηροφητῶν après αἱ γραφαί dans 26,54 [36], l'omission de κατὰ τοῦ Ἰησοῦ dans 27,1 [37] et, probablement la lecture de 5,24 'ne l'éloigne pas de toi' au lieu de 'ne t'éloigne pas de lui' [38]. Il serait peut-être intéressant de constater que la plupart des témoins grecs appartient au type du texte designé C[1] dans l'édition de Merk, s'agissant d'habitude des variantes qui peuvent s'expliquer par concordance ou similitude avec d'autres passages.

Il y a d'autres cas, parmi lesquels M 569 coïncide uniquement avec des témoins grecs du type occidental, concrètement avec le *Codex Bezae* et quelques représentants de la version siriaque. Par exemple, dans 15,35 l'addition de αὐτῷ après εἶπον; dans 17,14 la lecture du singulier ἐλθών; dans 26,60: 'et vinrent beaucoup de faux témoins' au lieu de 'en venant beaucoup de faux témoins'. Une variante de M 569 est représentée dans des manuscrits grecs du type césarien et occidental à la fois, mais elle ne se trouve pas dans les manuscrits du type neutre. Il s'agit de 23,32 dont la lecture dit ἐπληρώσατε ('vous avez comble') [39].

Il nous semble moins important dans notre analyse les cas de M 569 coïncidant — face à tous les autres manuscrits sahidiques —, avec des témoins grecs appartenant au type du texte neutre, occidental et césarien ensemble. Ainsi la lecture de

---

[24] οὐχί est omis en S* sy[s], et 'ce temple' est omis aussi en S* sy[s].

[25] Πᾶσα ἡ est omis dans tous les manuscrits grecs excepté 892 λ 1242 517 *a l* Orig.

[26] Avec S B C* K P W Δ 0233 λ φ 565 700 892* *f k* vg sy[p] mae bo Orig.

[27] Avec C* θ 33 700 1010 1241 sy[hmg]

[28] Avec 33 λ 565, peu d'autres, et Orig.

[28bis] Avec Z 33, peu d'autres, *ff*[1] sy[sc].

[29] Avec 33 892 1241, quelques représentants de la *Vetus latina* et Orig.

[30] La lecture plus commune en grec est ἔξω τῆς οἰκίας ἤ της πόλεως ἐ κείνης. Mais S 892 893 348 et d'autres ont ἔξω τῆς οἰκίας ἤ τῆς πόλεως ἤ κώμης ἐκείνης. Le manuscrit de la Morgan (M 569) a introduit ἤ κώμης à la fin de la phrase.

[31] Avec Σ 399 047 1293.

[32] Avec le grec M.

[33] Avec 485.

[34] Avec K 238.

[35] Avec 251* *b gg* Clem. Chris. Iren.

[36] Avec Φ 1200 *b f ff*.

[37] Avec Φ 1424.

[38] C'est probable que la lecture de M 569 suive la lecture grecque (δανίσασθαι) ἀπὸ σοῦ μὴ αποστραφῇς de 047, au lieu de la lecture commune ἀπὸ σοῦ (δανίσασθαι) μὴ ἀποστραφῇς.

[39] Avec D 544 1675 7 4 1604 et d'autres, au lieu de πληρώσατε comme le reste de la tradition grecque (excepté B qui lit πληρώσετε).

20,13 ἐνὶ αὐτῶν εἶπεν au lieu de εἶπεν ἐνὶ αὐτῶν [40], l'omission de κύριε dans 20,30 [41] et l'inversion αὐτῶν κοινωνοί dans 23,30 [42]. Il en serait de même pour les lectures propres de M 569, représentées dans des manuscrits grecs appartenant à tous les types du texte: neutre, occidental, césarien et *koiné* [43].

D'ordinaire quand les grands manuscrits Vatican et Sinaïtique divergent, M 569 suit le Vatican. Il convient d'avertir aussi qu'une lecture exclusive de M 569 et coïncidant à la fois avec des manuscrits grecs du type *koiné* n'a jamais lieu.

On dirait, en conclusion, à la lumière de ces données, que même si M 569 représente le texte neutre et toute la version sahidique, pour ce qui concerne l'Évangile de Saint Matthieu, il offre cependant des lectures propres qui se trouvent dans le type du texte césarien et occidental. Donc, M 569 témoignerait que ces lectures variantes circulèrent aussi en Égypte antérieurement ou indépendamment des recensions du texte traditionnellement admises.

c) *D'autres variantes* se sont encore trouvées dans M 569 qui touchent au sens même du texte et qui n'ont pas de représentation dans la tradition grecque, mais toutes peuvent être expliquées par une erreur d'un copiste ou du traducteur. Nous pouvons attribuer au copiste ce qui concerne quelques omissions qui comptent le même nombre de lettres, semblable auquel il correspondrait une ligne dans les manuscrits coptes [44]. Comme erreur du traducteur, dans 24,30 il est dit: 'ils verront' au lieu de 'ils feront deuil'. Le traducteur, on ignore la raison, a lu de façon erronée ὄψονται par κόψονται. Cela pourrait indiquer qu'une traduction directe du grec est au dessous de M 569 bien que sur la base d'autres exemples sahidiques précédents.

En conclusion, M 569 représente une nouvelle preuve de la version sahidique, dont les aspects propres le font différent des autres témoins. Il suppose, à notre avis, une élaboration ou révision en suivant des lectures qui nous sont arrivées en grec dans les manuscrits dont le texte appartient au type césarien et occidental.

2. Caractéristiques textuelles de Bodmer XIX

Les lectures variantes que ce manuscrit nous présente par rapport aux autres témoins de la version sahidique sont aussi très nombreuses. La majorité cependant peuvent s'attribuer à la liberté de traduction ou de transmission et ne touchent pas proprement au sens du texte. D'autres lectures variantes, au contraire, pourraient être mises en rapport avec des originaux grecs différents des manuscrits suivis par le reste des témoins sahidiques.

Quant aux lectures premières, R. Kasser a réalisé dans son édition du Bodmer XIX un catalogue orientateur. Pour les autres —les lectures qui ont une correspondance dans les manuscrits grecs— qu'il soit d'abord dit que leur nombre est assez réduit par rapport à celles qui se trouvent dans M 569. D'ailleur il est douteux dans pas mal de cas que l'on puisse établir une relation avec des témoins grecs au lieu de les considérer comme un simple fait de traduction ou de transmission [45]. En principe, cela signifie que Bodmer XIX est plus proche de la version sahidique commune de Matthieu, représentée par les manuscrits du Monastère Blanc.

En distribuant les variantes de Bodmer XIX qui ont une représentation en grec selon les types divers du texte, voici les résultats:

—Bodmer XIX présente cinq fois la lecture plus commune en grec et témoignée par les manuscrits appartenant aux quatre types de texte, tandis que le reste de la version sahidique contient des lectures réservées à quelques'uns parmi les témoins grecs. Disons, par exemple, 17,12, où seulement Bodmer apporte la lecture: 'ils firent en lui tout ce qu'ils voulurent' qui traduit littéralement, quant à l'ordre même, le texte plus commun [46], tandis que

---

[40] ἐνὶ αὐτῶν εἶπεν est représenté en S D θ o85 700 sy[sc].

[41] Avec S D θ φ 565 700 it sy[c] et d'autres.

[42] Avec B D λ φ 700 et peu d'autres, au lieu de κοινωνοί αὐτῶν.

[43] Par ex. καί dans 7,23; ἔτι dans 12,46.

[44] On trouve une omission involontaire du copiste en 15,30 ('il les guérit'); en 16,24 ('qu'il me suive'); et en 21,38 ('lorsqu'ils virent le fils').

[45] Cf. par ex. 16,22; 23,13.

[46] Le texte le plus commun est ἐποίησαν ἐν αὐτῷ ὅσα ἠθέλησαν.

le reste des témoins sahidiques omettent ἐν pour suivre quelques manuscrits grecs [47] ou bien ils changent son ordre traduisant avec liberté: 'ils firent tout ce qu'ils voulurent en lui' [48]. Dans 18,16, l'ordre que Bodmer présente — 'prends avec toi un autre' coïncide avec toute la tradition grecque, excepté le *Codex Vaticanus* qui donne une lecture semblable en partie au reste de la tradition sahidique [49]. Dans 21,28 c'est uniquement Bodmer XIX qui apporte la traduction littérale de ἐν τῷ ἀμπελῶνι 'dans ma vigne', lecture commune en grec, face au reste des manuscrits sahidiques qui disent : 'à ma vigne' en suivant le *Codex Bezae* et un manuscrit du type césarien [50]. Dans 22,13 Bodmer donne la lecture : 'ses pieds et ses mains', commune à la majorité des textes grecs, face à l'inversion des termes 'ses mains et ses pieds' commune à la version sahidique et à quelques manuscrits du type césarien et *koiné* [51]. Disons, finalement, quoiqu'il s'agisse d'un cas assez douteux, la présence de Ϭⲉ au lieu de Ⲇⲉ dans 24,15 [52]. Ces données nous permettent de déduire que Bodmer est plus attaché à la tradition grecque commune que le reste des manuscrits sahidiques. Comme nous l'avons déjà vu, ceux-ci présentent des lectures témoignées dans des manuscrits grecs du type césarien et occidental qui n'ont eu aucune influence dans le texte de Bodmer XIX.

Il y a d'autres cas cependant, peu nombreux, où les lectures variantes d'une minorité de témoins grecs correspondent au texte de Bodmer XIX. L'omission de l'article οἱ devant φαρισσαῖοι dans 19,3 dans quelques manuscrits du type neutre, césarien et *koiné* [53] peut être au-dessous de la lecture de Bodmer XIX [54]. Dans trois occasions les variantes

qui se trouvent uniquement dans les manuscrits grecs du type neutre et césarien ont une correspondance plus ou moins exacte dans Bodmer : l'omission de κυλλοὺς ὑγιεῖς ('les paralytiques devennaient guéris') dans 15,31 [55]. Il est curieux d'observer que l'ordre d'insertion de cette phrase change parmi les manuscrits sahidiques [56]. Il nous semble que dans certains manuscrits, elle aurait été introduite plus tard en la mettant non pas en second lieu de la série, comme en grec, mais en dernier lieu. L'omission de ἑπτά dans 15,36 est peut-être due à l'influence de Jean 6,11 [57]. L'omission de ἐκεῖνος dans 18,28 — bien que témoignée dans deux manuscrits grecs [58] — pourrait être due simplement à une liberté de traduction. Or, les trois cas uniques qui permettraient le rapport de Bodmer XIX avec des variantes dans les manuscrits du type neutre ou césarien, n'ont pas de grand poids.

Il en est de même dans une des deux occasions où Bodmer XIX présente une certaine affinité avec des témoins du type césarien et *koiné*. Dans 22,13, la lecture : 'à ses serviteurs' est témoignée dans deux manuscrits grecs [59] face à la lecture commune sans αὐτοῦ traduite par 'servants' dans le reste de la version sahidique. Il est évident qu'il s'agit là d'une simple question de style. L'autre cas, 2,15 où Bodmer XIX suit la variante ἑστώς, masculin, au lieu de ἑστός, neutre [60], peut avoir effectivement un rapport parmi Bodmer XIX et les témoins grecs du type césarien et *koiné* [61]. Le rapport de Bodmer XIX avec des témoins grecs du type césarien pourrait aussi se prouver par deux variantes existantes uniquement dans des manuscrits de ce type et apportées aussi dans Bodmer XIX. L'une

---

[47] Omettent ἐν S W D 700 372 28 544 13 1424 517 348 U 213 1071 2145 047 1295 1604 F et quelques témoins de la version latine et syriaque.

[48] Cf. les manuscrits sahidiques 8 42 52 119.

[49] Au lieu de παράλαβε μετὰ σοῦ ἔτι ἕνα (...) *Codex Vaticanus* lit παράλαβε ἔτι ἕνα (...) μετὰ σεαυτοῦ. La tradition sahidique —excepté Bodmer— lit 'prends un autre avec toi...'.

[50] Bodmer lit Ϩⲛ ⲠⲀⲘⲀ ; tous les autres manuscrits sahidiques ⲈⲠⲀⲘⲀ; les grecs D 1424 εἰς τὸν ἀμπελόνα.

[51] Ainsi 565 1424 M et beaucoup d'autres.

[52] Dans la plupart des manuscrits grecs on lit οὖν, mais dans Sᶜ 1 157 syᶜ on lit δέ.

[53] Ainsi dans B C L W Δ λ φ 33 565 etc., mais l'article est dans les manuscrits du type occidental.

[54] Bodmer lit ϨⲉⲘϥⲀⲢⲓⲥⲀⲓⲟⲥ tandis que toute la tradition sahidique lit ⲚⲈϥⲀⲢⲓⲥⲥⲀⲓⲟⲥ

[55] Avec S 892 700 1 1582 22 1216 beaucoup de latins et syriaques.

[56] Les manuscrits sahidiques M 16 73 111 présentent cette phrase en second lieu de la série; les manuscrits 13 20 42 et un fragment de Vienne le présentent en dernier lieu.

[57] Omettent ἑπτά aussi les grecs 892 659 713 291 998 et quelques latins.

[58] B 245.

[59] 1675 du type césarien, et 1200 du type *koiné*.

[60] Dans Bodmer ⲈϥⲀϨⲈⲢⲀⲧⲩ̄ ; dans les autres manuscrits sahidiques ⲈⲤⲀϨⲈⲢⲀⲧⲉ̄ en concordance avec ⲦⲂⲟⲦⲉ .

[61] Bᶜ 1241 124 346 M 71 V 665 etc. et les représentans *koiné*.

consiste en l'inversion de πρὸς αὐτόν après ἡ γυνή dans 27,19 [62] et l'autre dans l'omission de ἐμπαίζοντες ('se moquant') dans 27,41 [63].

Finalement nous remarquerons un cas où Bodmer XIX coïncide uniquement avec le *Codex Bezae*: l'omission de μαρτύρων dans 18,16. C'est uniquement la seule fois que Bodmer présente une variante commune et exclusive avec le type du texte occidental. Mais, étant donné le caractère d'une telle omission, celle-ci ne constitue pas un argument suffisant pour établir une relation entre Bodmer et le type occidental du texte. Il en faudrait dire autant au sujet de l'omission de ἕως les deux fois qu'il arrive dans 18,22 et que nous trouvons aussi dans un manuscrit du type *koiné* [64].

Les données qui se sont exposées nous permettent de conclure que Bodmer XIX constitue un témoin très estimable de la version sahidique, compte tenue de son antiquité, et qui est plus uniforme que M 569 par rapport à la majorité des manuscrits sahidiques. L'influence que d'autres types de texte, le neutre excepté, auraient pu exercer en lui est mineure, c'est pourquoi il ne peut guère être considéré comme un témoin des lectures differenciées du texte grec appelé égyptien.

---

[62] Comme dans 1402 245.

[63] Avec le grec 348.

[64] C'est le 1573.

COPTIC STUDIES

Krzysztof Babraj

La symbolique des lettres Γ et H dans l'abside de la Cathédrale de Faras et leur lien avec l'art copte*

Aperçu général sur les études et essai de l'interprétation

L'intérêt porté à la symbolique des lettres sur les vêtements sacerdotaux date de 1605. A cette époque-là a été écrit par A. Joanne l'Heureux l'ouvrage intitulé: *Hagioglypta sive picture et sculpturae sacrae antiquiores praesertim quae Romae reperiuntur explicatae*[1] édité à Paris en 1865. Dans le chapitre De picturis Ecclesiarum et Coemeteriorum[2] l'auteur parle des lettres grecques I, H, X sur la peinture des catacombes et dans les mosaïques paléochrétiennes. Et les lettres Π, Θ l'auteur les a trouvées sur le vêtement d'une femme qui, dans le traité de Boethius *De Consolatione Philosophiae,* personnifiait la philosophie. L'auteur de cet ouvrage représente la philosophie en tant que femme parée d'un vêtement somptueux dont les deux côtés opposés ont des lettres brochées — supérieure Θ et inférieure Π.

L'Heureux tâche de prouver, sans grand succès, un rapport hypothétique entre le texte de Boethius et les lettres figurant sur les vêtements, sur la peinture et dans la mosaïque. Dans sa conclusion, il se réfère à l'opinion du pape Grégoire IX qui met les lettres évoquées au même niveau que les attributs des saints.

Antonio Bosio se posait des questions concernant la signification des lettres T, I, H, X. Dans l'ouvrage intitulé *Roma sotterranea*, édition posthume de 1632, dans le chapitre Delle Lettere nel Vesti il a constaté que l'explication de leur signification symbolique chez les Pères de l'Église restait pour lui mystérieuse[3].

Bosio ainsi que l'Heureux essaie d'interpréter le passage concernant les lettres T et P, provenant du traité de Boethius *De Consolatione Philosophiae* supposant que l'explication de leur signification peut être utile à interpréter la symbolique des lettres sur les vêtements.

Selon Bosio la lettre X — xύ[4] signifiait *crux decussata* et Goropius, dans l'ouvrage *Hierogliphica*[5], cité par Bosio, a voulu qu'elle signifiât la disponibilité à accueillir le Saint Esprit.

Cependant I — ιότα[6] chez les Grecs, constituait le début du nom de Jésus Christ, et le signe du nombre dix. L'auteur rapporte ici les mots de Clément d'Alexandrie, qui dans l'ouvrage intitulé παιδαγωγός[7] dans le second livre, traitant de Decachordum trouve que le nombre dix était la désignation la plus juste du nom de Jésus Christ.

La lettre H[8] était, aussi selon Bosio, l'abréviation du nom de Jésus Christ, tandis que Goropius déjà cité, trouvait qu'elle symbolisait « la sublimation

---

* Je voudrais remercier sincèrement Monsieur le Professeur Tadeusz Dobrzeniecki de son aide dans la préparation de cet article.
[1] A.J. L'Heureux (Macario), *Hagioglypta sive picture et sepulcturae sacre antiquiores presentim quae Romae reperiuntur explicatae*, Lutetiae Parisiorum 1856; cette œuvre écrite en 1605, a été éditée seulement en 1856, grâce aux soins de Raphaël Garrucci; elle est considérée comme premier manuel d'iconographie chrétienne.
[2] Ibid., pp. 26–28.
[3] A. Bosio, *Roma Sotterranea opera postuma di Antonio Bosio Romano Antiquario Ecclesiasto Singolare de'Svoi Tempi x Compita disposta, accresciuta. Dal M. R. D. Giovanni Severani da S. Severino Sacerdote della Congregatione dell'Oratorio di Roma. ...,* Roma 1632, libro IV, caput XXXVIII, p. 638.
[4] Ibid., p. 638.
[5] J. Goropii (Becani), *Hierogliphica*, Antverpiae 1580, p. 147.
[6] Bosio, *Roma Sotterranea...*, p. 638.
[7] Clemens Alexandrinus, παιδαγωγός, liber II, PG, 8, col. 444.
[8] Bosio, *Roma Sotterranea...*, p. 638.

des choses terrestres au niveau de celles supérieures ».

Le terme *gammadiae* (singulier *gammadium*) — forme latinisée de la désignation de la lettre grecque gamma avait un emploi, à partir de 1677, différent de celui admis a présent, c'est-à-dire, on l'a employé pour désigner le signe en forme soit d'un seul gamma, soit composé de quelques gammas. Il lui appartient la croix à branches égales composée à l'aide de quatre gammas (*crux gammata* ⊹ [9]. Ce terme a été employé pour la première fois par Macri dans l'ouvrage édité en 1677 intitulé *Hiero-Lexicon, sive dictionarium sacrum* [10], à l'occasion de la description de la chasuble sur laquelle se trouvait un signe en forme d'un gamma Γ, L soit en forme d'une croix ⊹

Les ouvrages scientifiques plus anciens ne connaissaient pas la notion de *gammadiae* mais employaient la désignation « les lettres sur le vêtements ».

Gaetano Moroni, auteur d'un ouvrage volumineux *Dizionario di Erudicione Storico-Ecclesiastica* traite aussi le problème de *gammadiae* [11]. Il sépare nettement les *gammadiae* des autres lettres apparaissant sur les vêtements des saints parmi lesquelles il distingue les lettres I et H, les considérant comme lettres initiales du nom du Sauveur. Au sujet de gamma il dit « ... che rappresenta la lettera Gamma, per significare Cristo pietra angolare... ». Il faut supposer que la ressemblance de la lettre, qui par sa forme rappelle la pierre biblique angulaire de temple, a fait naître cette association. Le fondement de cette conception demeure dans les textes relatifs de l'Ancien et du Nouveau Testament (Esaïe 28, 16; Psaumes 118, 22; Actes des Apôtres 4, 11; Première Epître aux Corinthiens 3, 10–11; L'Épitre aux Ephésiens 2, 20 à 22). Goblet d'Alviella dans son ouvrage intitulé *The Migration of Symbols* [12], sous le nom *gammadium*, comprend la *swastica* de différentes formes. J. A. Martigny, dans l'ouvrage intitulé *Dictionnaire des Antiquités Chrétiennes* édité en 1865, emploie le nom « gammadiae vestes » [13] sans essayer de les interpréter.

E. H. J. Reusens publie en 1871 un ouvrage en deux volumes intitulé *Éléments d'Archéologie Chrétienne* où il présente l'opinion que la signification des lettres simples et des monogrammes figurant dans les œuvres d'art n'est pas expliquée. Parmi les lettres T, I, H, X, il mentionne aussi le gamma mais il n'emploie pas le terme « gammadiae » le remplaçant par le mot « signe » [14].

F. X. Kraus, l'auteur de *Real-Enzyklopädie der Christlichen Alterthümer*, est le premier à constater qu'il ne faut pas associer *gammadium* [15], (comme le désigne *crux gammata* déjà mentionnée) à une seule lettre gamma.

Cependant, nous pouvons remarquer qu'on a cherché une signification qui soit propre seulement à cette lettre. Parmi d'autres lettres apparaissant sur les vêtements par ex. I, T, H, X, ce n'est que le gamma qui a été distingué par son propre terme *gammadium* (se rapportant aussi à *crux gammata*) et on en a parlé à part bien qu'il n'ait été mentionné dans les articles concernant la question des lettres grecques sur les vêtements.

J. A. Martigny trouve que les chercheurs ne sont pas du même avis sur l'interprétation des notions attribuées à ces lettres. Il associe la signification des lettres sur les vêtements aux nombres [16] symboliques sans étudier la question de la lettre gamma dans ce contexte. Établissant le rapport entre les lettres et la symbolique des nombres, il l'illustre par l'exemple des lettres H et Ξ pour prouver leur sens symbolique. Il trouve que les artistes exécutant les mosaïques ainsi que les peintures employaient les nombres représentés par les lettres correspondantes, ayant le sens analogiques à ceux-ci employées dans la parabole du Semeur (Matthieu 13, 8). Les Pères de l'Église ont doté les nombres d'une signification symbolique. Cette constatation est illustrée par l'auteur d'un rare exemple d'un signe apparaissant sur le vêtement de Sainte Agnès dont un pan est orné d'une

---

[9] F.X. Kraus, *Gammadia, RealEnzyklopädie der Christlichen Alterthümer*, Freiburg 1882, Bd. I, p. 548; aussi J.A. Martigny, *Gammadiae, Dictionnaire des Antiquités Chrétiennes*, Paris 1865, p. 285.

[10] Marci, *Gammadiae, Hiero-lexicon, sive dictionarium sacrum*, Romae 1677, p. 185.

[11] G. Moroni, *Gammadia, Dizionario di erudizione storico-ecclesiastica da S. Pietro sino ai nostri giorni*, Venezia 1844, vol. XXXVIII, p. 160.

[12] G. D'Alviella, *The Migration of Symbols*, New York 1894, pp. 32–83.

[13] Martigny, *Gammadiae...*, p. 285.

[14] E.H.J. Reusens, *Éléments d'Archéologie Chrétienne*, vol. I, Aix-La-Chapelle 1871, p. 272.

[15] Kraus, *Gammadia...*, p. 548.

[16] Martigny, *Gammadiae..., Nombres sur les vêtements*, p. 440.

lettre. Il trouve que chez les Grecs cette lettre représentait le nombre huit et d'après différents témoignages il est le symbole de la vie éternelle, de la béatitude et de la Résurrection.

F. X. Kraus voit le problème de la façon pareille : pour lui les signes qui sont l'objet de notre étude sont nommés « Buchstaben auf Kleidern » [17] ou « Monogramme und Figuren auf Kleidern » [18]. L'auteur n'établit pas de relations entre la lettre gamma et d'autres lettres. Il distingue parmi *vestes litteratae vestes gammadiae* où se trouve *crux gammata* et il l'associe à *crux immissa* dont il désigne l'apparition fréquente par le terme *polystauria*.

Des opinions présentées proviennent des rédactions lexicographiques concernant l'art et la liturgie chrétiens. Les auteurs des articles en parlant des vêtements liturgiques traitent aussi le problème des signes qui y figurent. Mais pourtant, ils ne remontent pas aux sources pour chercher la génèse de ce phénomene, mais ils formulent des hypothèses qui ne sont appuyées que par de pareilles opinions exposées antérieurement, sans précision des notions.

La nouvelle étape des études sur les *gammadiae* se limite à deux chercheurs : Klaus Wessel et Antonio Quacquarelli [19]. Toutefois Wessel [20] est seulement auteur d'un article monographique détaillé tandis que Quacquarelli fait des recherches systématiques dans ce domaine.

La peinture dans l'abside de la Cathédrale de Faras et les analogies de l'Égypte copte

Dans l'abside de la Cathédrale se trouvent plusieurs peintures interposées de différentes périodes, datant probablement du VIIIe au XIIe siècles (fig. 1). L'abside a été repeinte à maintes reprises. Mais le Collège des Apôtres et la Sainte Vierge sont restés, pendant tout le temps de la célébration de la liturgie, à la Cathédrale. Cette peinture a persisté sans aucun changement. Les origines de la scène qui nous intéresse proviennent du style nommé

« violet ». Alors la représentation était comme suit : au milieu figurait la Theotokos ayant six apôtres à sa droite et six à sa gauche qui se tenaient debout. Ils ne sont pas identifiés par des inscriptions. Sur leurs vêtements de dessus — *himation* apparaissent les *gammadiae*. Les *gammadiae* apparaissent déjà sur la peinture du VIIIe siècle. Ce sont deux lettres majuscules de l'alphabet grec : $H - \eta\tau\alpha$, $\Gamma - \gamma\alpha\mu\mu\alpha$.

La scène de l'abside de Faras, du point de vue de la composition, rappelle le schéma des peintures dans la chapelle XVII (fig. 2) et chapelle VI (fig. 3) datant du VIe au VIIe siècles du monastère d'Apollon à Baouît. Dans la partie inférieure de la scène est représentée la Theotokos-Orans entourée du Collège des Apôtres. Tous ces Apôtres ont, sur leurs vêtements, chacun une lettre gamma.

Sur la voûte de la niche est représentée *Maiestas Domini* de la vision d'Eséchiel. Le Christ sur le trône tient dans la main gauche un livre ouvert où $\alpha\gamma\iota\sigma\varsigma$ est répété trois fois. Dans la main droite levée la disposition des doigts est pareille à celle qui montre actuellement le nombre trois : pouce, index, doigt majeur plus ou moins redressés, au contraire — doigt annulaire et petit doigt courbés. Ce geste symbolise l'ogdoade et exprime le nombre huit [21]. Parmi les lettres, la lettre H est son équivalent. « Gest flexio digitorum du nombre huit et la lettre H étaient la même chose » [22]. Ce geste a indiqué la Résurrection du Christ le huitième jour, la béatitude éternelle, la félicité, la transition de la sphère terrestre à celle céleste.

Le schéma pareil représente la composition en mosaïque qui se trouve dans l'abside de la chapelle de San Venanzio le Battistero Lateranense (fig. 4). Dans la partie inférieure de la mosaïque figure, au milieu, la Sainte Vierge-Orans entourée entre autres des Apôtres Paul, Jean Evangéliste et Jean Baptiste, ces deux derniers ont sur leurs *himation* une lettre H. Dans la zone supérieure de la scène figure le Christ en Majesté en buste « avec le geste d'ogdoade » adoré de deux Anges, eux aussi en buste, ayant sur les vêtements chacun une lettre H. La mosaïque est datée des années 640–652.

---

[17] Kraus, *Gammadia...*, p. 176.

[18] Ibid., p. 419.

[19] J'adresse mes remerciements à Monsieur le Professeur Antonio Quacquarelli de L'Université de Roma d'avoir l'amabilité de m'envoyer ses articles et livres concernant les problèmes dont je m'occupe.

[20] K. Wessel et M. Restke, *Gammadia, Reallexikon zur Byzantinische Kunst*, Stuttgart 1966, Bd. II, cols 615–620.

[21] A. Quacquarelli, « L'ogdoade patristica e suoi reflessi nella liturgia e nei monumenti », *Quaderni di Vetera Christianorum* 7, (Bari 1973), p. 89.

[22] A. Quacquarelli, « Il monogramma cristologico (Gammadia H) », *Vetera Chistianorum* 16, (Bari 1979), 14.

1. Dessin de la peinture de l'abside de la Cathédrale de Faras

2. Monastère d'Apollon à Baouît, XVIIᵉ chapelle. La Theotokos-Orans entourée des Apôtres—partie inférieure; l'Ascension du Christ de la vision d'Eséchiel—partie supérieure (d'après K. Wessel, *L'art copte*, Bruxelles 1964, fig. 99)

3. Monastère d'Apollon à Baouît, VIᵉ chapelle. La Theotokos entourée des Apôtres — partie inférieure; l'Ascension du Christ de la vision d'Eséchiel — partie supérieure (d'après A. Grabar, *Byzantium from the Death of Theodosius to the Rise of Islam*)

4. Baptistere Lateranense, la chapelle San Venanzio. La Theotokos-Orans — partie inférieure; Christ en Majesté — partie supérieure (d'après G. Mathie, *Mosaici Medievali delle Chiese di Roma*)

On peut supposer que la mosaïque dans la chapelle de San Venanzio a servi de modèle à la chapelle XVII du monastère d'Apollon à Baouît [23].

Dans les catacombes de Commodilla (fig. 5), à Rome se trouve la fresque représentant la Theotokos avec l'Enfant sur la main entourée des Saint Félix et Saint Aucte datée entre le VIe et le VIIe siècles. La ressemblance de la figure de la Theotokos à celle qui se trouve dans la chapelle VI du monastère d'Apollon à Baouît est ici visible.

Le schéma des peintures dans les chapelles VI et VIII à Baouît est le même, une différence essentielle se voit dans la représentation de la Theotokos qui, dans la chapelle VI figure en tant que la Sainte Vierge en Majesté à l'Enfant, et dans la chapelle XVII—en tant que Marie-Orans se tenant debout. Il y a aussi la différence dans l'emploi des *gammadiae*. Dans la chapelle VI le gamma apparaît deux fois—sur *himation* de Saint Pierre et de Saint Philippe. Sur la voûte de la niche est représenté le Christ en Majesté « avec le geste d'ogdoade » et avec un livre ouvert où apparaît Trisagion.

Dans les exemples cités, on a employé seulement deux lettres—le gamma (Baouît) et le gamma et le êta (Faras).

Des lettres successives de l'alphabet grec ont leurs propres valeurs numérales. La lettre gamma a sa valeur établie du nombre trois, la lettre êta—du nombre huit. Les chrétiens ont pris les lettres grecques pour leur signification symbolique. Antonio Quacquarelli trouve qu'elles ont appartenu *ad genus dicendi* de ces abréviations, qui ont été employées à chaque époque pour transmettre les notions connues de tous [24]. Cette constatation se rapporte aussi à l'église nubienne.

La signification du nombre trois se répand sans interruption dans tout l'univers antique jusqu'à nos jours dans les mythes puissants ainsi que dans les croyances populaires. Son emploi a une longue tradition dans l'Ancien Testament et dans l'Antiquité. Le nombre trois est de sa nature clos parce qu'il a son début, son milieu et sa fin. On lui a attribué une force magique. Dans le système des Pithagoriciens, il était le plus parfait parce qu'ils y

ont vu la première liaison des principes fondamentaux de toutes les choses, il associait l'unité —*monas* à la duplicité —*dyas*. Aristote a vu dans ce nombre l'union du début, du milieu et de la fin. Saint Augustin a désigné le nombre trois en tant que *Numerus quo significatur perfectio*. Il y a même une œuvre dédiée à la perception du nombre trois —*Carmen de ternarii Numeri Excellentia*— dont Saint Ambroise est présumé auteur [25]. Le nombre trois, à l'égard du Christ, signifiait la Résurrection, car si l'on compte le jour du Crucifiement, Il a ressuscité le troisième jour.

Le nombre trois avait une importance particulière pour les chrétiens. Il était le symbole de la supérieure vérité révélée énonçant que Dieu existait dans sa nature en tant que *Trinitas*, alors la triplicité apartenait à l'existence absolue. L'existence créée était aussi marquée d'une empreinte de triplicité, parce que l'activité de Dieu *ad extra* est commune à trois personnes divines et en même temps elle est activité de chacune d'elles. On peut dire que le dogme de la Trinité peut être la source de la symbolique des autres lettres. Il faut comprendre d'autres lettres dans son activité. Voilà pourquoi ce nombre, dans la conscience chrétienne, a été doté d'une particulière importance sacramentale. Le nombre trois a son équivalent en lettre gamma qui symbolisait *Trinitas*. Et justement, elle figure dans ce sens symbolique à la Cathédrale de Faras. Pour que cela ait pu se produire, Dieu avait dû être révélé en Trois Personnes. Les fidèles, en voyant cette lettre, l'associaient d'une façon univoque à la Trinité omniprésente.

L'idée trinitaire du nombre trois est exprimée dans l'Hymne Liturgique de Soir de Grégoire de Nazianze [26].

Τριττοῦ φωτὸς εἰς μίαν
Δόξαν ἀθροιζομένου
Ὃς ἔλυσας τὸ σκότος,
Ὃς ὑπέστησας τὸ φῶς,
Ἵν ἐν φωτὶ τὰ πάντα κτί-
σῃς...

[23] C. Davis-Weyer, « Die Mosaiken Leos III und die Anfange der Karolingischen Renaissance in Rom », *Zeitschrift für Kunstgeschichte* 29 (München–Berlin 1966), 113; l'auteur trouve pourtant que la mosaïque de Théodore Ier à San Venanzio a eu son modèle dans les projets outre-romains et que ses rapports postérieurs sont à remarquer dans les fresques des monastères à Baouît et Saqqara.

[24] A. Quacquarelli, « Il monogramma cristologico (Gammadia Z) », *Vetera Christianorum* 15 (Bari 1978), 5.

[25] J.M. Szymusiak et, M. Starowieyski, *Ambroży, Słownik wczesnochrześcijańskiego piśmiennictwa*, Poznań 1971, p. 30.

[26] Gregorius Nazianzenus, *Hymnus Vespertinus XXXII*, PG 37, cols. 511–514.

5. Catacombe de Comodilla à Rome. La Theotokos entourée de Saints Felix et Adaucte (d'après
Propyläen Kunstgeschichte, Byzanz und der Christliche Osten, Bd 3)

Triduum sacrum est associé au dogme de la Résurrection du Christ. Saint Ambroise voit l'annonce de la Résurrection du Seigneur le troisième jour, dans le fragment de l'Évangile de Sᵗ Luc : « Quand il eut douze ans ». (2, 41–50), en écrivant : « A duodecimo anno, ut legimus, dominicae sumitur disputationis exordium, hic enim praedicandae fidei evangelisantium numerus debebateur. Nec otiose inmemor suorum secundum carnem parentum, qui secundum carnem utique sapientia dei implebatur et gratia, post triduum repperitur in templo, ut esset indicio quia post triduum triumphalis illius passionis in sede caelesti et honore divino fidei nostrae se resurrectures offerret, qui mortuus credebatur » [27].

Dans la niche de la chapelle XVII du monastère d'Apollon à Baouît [28], la scène de la Theotokos--Orans représente *intercessio* (une grande prière pour l'intercession). Dans la liturgie copte *Epiclesia* est suivie de la partie appelée *Intercessio* dans le cadre de laquelle on a trois fois chanté « Saint » [29]. Dans la partie supérieure de cette

---

[27] Ambroise de Milan, « Expositio Evangelii Secundum Lucam II, 63–64 », *Sources Chrétiennes* 45, 100.

[28] La situation analogique survient dans la chapelle VI. T. Dobrzeniecki polémise avec l'opinion d'André Grabar prétendant que les chapelles à Baouît servaient au culte eucharistique. Il trouve que la niche richement ornée servait à garder l'eucharistie et non pas à célébrer la liturgie : T. Dobrzeniecki, « *Maiestas Domini* w zabytkach polskich i obcych z Polską związanych », *Rocznik Muzeum Narodowego w Warszawie* XVII(1973), 46, 47. Je trouve que cette scène a eu rapport avec l'aucharistie ce qui est attesté par la triplication se trouvant dans un livre ouvert tenu par le Christ. Dans la liturgie copte pendant l'Anaphore dans la prière eucharistique « saint » apparaît trois fois : (selon : E. Hammerschmidt, *Kultsymbolik der Koptischen und Äthiopischen Kirche*, Symbolik der *Orthodoxen und Orientalischen Christentums*, Stuttgart 1962, p. 198).

[29] Ibid., p. 198, l'auteur dit que « saint » a été trois fois chanté dans la liturgie de Cyrille d'Alexandrie pendant *intercessio*.

scène, le Christ tient dans la main gauche un livre ouvert où nous voyons ces paroles qui expliquent la symbolique du nombre trois. A l'aide de ces mots, trois fois répétés, on a exprimé *Trinitas*. *Trisagion* provient de l'Apocalypse de Saint Jean (4,8) – « Saint, Saint, Saint, le Seigneur, le Dieu tout puissant ». Cela était chanté par les Séraphins. Denys l'Aréopagite dans l'œuvre de *L'Hiérarchie Céleste* trouve que la hiérarchie supérieure des Anges figure dans les trois triades qui sont divisées en neuf chœurs. La première et la plus élevée triade embrasse Séraphins, Chérubins et « Trônes » [30]. Les Anges qui restent autour du trône de Dieu en priant sans cesse et en chantant « Saint, Saint, Saint » et la lumière éternelle rayonne aussi sur eux.

Romanos Melodes, diacre d'origine syrienne, était auteur des hymnes liturgiques appelés *kontaktia*, *tropariony*, *hirmoi* [31]. Ils ont été très en vogue entre le VIe et le VIIe siècles en Égypte. L'un de ces hymnes qui commence par les mots Δεῦτε Πάντες comprend dans la première partie dediée au Christ et à la Sainte Trinité l'idée trinitaire du nombre trois.

ὅν ὑμνοῦσιν ἀγγέλων τα τάγματα,
ἀσωμάτων οἱ δήμοι δοξάζουσιν,
ἐκ πυρίνων γλωσσῶν ἀνακράζουσι,
τρισαγίαις φωναῖς ἀναμέλπουσι,
τὸν τρισάγιόν ὕμνὸν ἐξάδοντες
ἐπινίκιον αἶνον προσφέροντες
τὸν πατέρα ὑμνοῦσι καὶ κύριον,
τὸν υἱόν συν τῷ πνεύματι σύνθρονον [32].

La seconde partie de l'hymne cité (les strophes 5–9) c'est *teotokion*, c'est-à-dire la prière dédiée à la Theotokos. Dans la dernière strophe, il y a une demande adressée à la Sainte Marie de l'intercession chez son Fils [33]. A son tour, le thème de l'intercession de la Theotokos-Orans est exprimé par exemple sur la peinture déjà mentionnée dans la chapelle XVII du monastère d'Apollon à Baouît et dans l'Évangéliaire syriaque de Rabula, (fig. 6) (586) où deux des Apôtres entourant Marie-Orans ont sur leurs *himation* une lettre H et dans la partie supérieure il y a la figuration du Christ de la vision d'Eséchiel.

Dans la nef sud de la Cathédrale de Faras, sur la paroi est, il y a la scène représentant *Maiestas Domini* et trois figures divines du Christ entourées des Apôtres. Ce n'est pas la seule scène à Faras où on a employé la triplicité des personnes divines. La scène pareille a été trouvée sur le pilastre de la nef nord de la Cathédrale de Faras (actuellement cette peinture se trouve au musée à Khartoum) et à l'Église près de Rivergate. Alors on voit que le nombre trois était en vogue dans les scènes de différent caractère.

Un autre problème à traiter est la signification symbolique du nombre huit dont la lettre H était équivalent. Dans l'abside de la Cathédrale de Faras, la lettre H apparaît vingt fois sur les vêtements des Apôtres et la lettre Γ seize fois.

La symbolique du nombre huit est très significative dans la région chrétienne et implique différentes idées. Dans le système des Pithagoriciens ce nombre était l'image de la perfection, de l'éternité, de la paix, le symbole de l'harmonie céleste, de la forme parfaite, de la justice. Huit était le nombre des sphères qui tournent autour de la Terre. Πάντα ὀκτώ – dit un proverbe antique. Les chrétiens lui ont attribué un sens nouveau. La conscience de la Résurrection du Seigneur le huitième jour, en tant que fait historique qui s'est déroulé dans le temps déterminé, constitue la raison la plus importante du sacré de ce nombre. Au sujet du huitième jour parle aussi Barnabé de Chypre, appelé aussi Joseph Halevi (ou le Lévite). C'est la première source se rapportant au huitième jour. On date la lettre où Barnabé parle du Sabbat entre l'année 70 (la destruction du temple de Jérusalem) et 138 (la mort de l'empereur Hadrien).

En employant les mots:

πέρας γέ τοι λέγει αὐτοῖς· Τὰς νεομηνίας ὑμῶν καὶ τὰ σάββατα οὐκ ἀνέχομαι. ὁρᾶτε πῶς λέγει· Οὐ τὰ νῦν σάββατα ἐμοὶ δεκτά, ἀλλὰ ὁ πεποίηκα, ἐν ᾧ καταπαύσας τὰ πάντα ἀρχὴν ἡμέρας ὀγδόης ποιήσω, ὅ ἐστιν ἄλλου κόσμου ἀρχήν. διὸ καὶ ἄγομεν τὴν ἡμέραν τὴν ὀγδόην εἰς εὐφροσύνην, ἐν ᾗ καὶ ὁ Ἰησοῦς ἀνέστη ἐκ νεκρῶν καὶ φανερωθεὶς ἀνέβη εἰς οὐρανούς [34].

Barnabé trouve que le huitième jour où la Resurrection du Seigneur a eu lieu est le début du monde nouveau, il est le temps de la joie. Il y a eu un rapport étroit entre le nombre huit et dimanche,

---

[30] H. Schmid et M. Schmid, *Die vergessene Bildersprache christlicher Kunst*, München 1982, p. 128.

[31] T. Schermann, *Ägyptische Abendmahlsliturgien des ersten Jahrtausend*, Paderborn 1912, p. 216.

[32] P. Maas, *Frübyzantinische Kirchenpoesie. I Anonymen Hymne des V–VI Jahrhunderts, Kleine Texte... 52/53*, Berlin 1931, p. 14.

[33] A. Bober, *Antologia patrystyczna*, Kraków 1966, p. 514.

[34] *Barnabae epistula XV, 8–9, Patrum Apostolicorum Opera*, Lipsiae 1878, p. 66.

6. Evangéliaire de Rabula. La Theotokos-Orans entourée des Apôtres — partie inférieure;
l'Ascension du Christ de la vision d'Eséchiel — partie supérieure (d'après A. Grabar, *Byzantine
Painting*)

Constantin le Grand en 321 confirme ce status quo par le décret à la lumière duquel dimanche reste le jour du repos. Les fidèles, avant cette date, célébraient ce jour en tant que jour du repos [35].

Saint Basile le Grand voit un rapport entre dimanche et Pâques. Selon lui le huitième jour est une image de la future sphère traitée comme symbole de la nouvelle vie [36]. Saint Grégoire de Nysse traite ce problème d'une façon différente se rapportant au texte de huit bénédictions dans le contexte du nombre huit. Il trouve qu'il a rapport avec les huit bénédictions et d'une façon parti-

culière se réfère à la huitième bénédiction qui est l'apogée des autres. Selon le commentaire de W. Swierzawski « le huitième jour, sauf qu'il est symbole de la Résurrection, exprime aussi le retour de l'homme sali à la pureté, le rejet du vieil homme. Ainsi la huitième bénédiction se réfère à ceux qui libérés de l'esclavage et renés... sont passés au Royaume [37]. »

Le nombre huit porte toutes les notions citées se rapportant au huitième jour.

Au sujet de l'ogdoade parle aussi Saint Athanase, d'une façon brève et expressive :

---

[35] A. Quacquarelli, « Il monogramma cristologico... », *Vetera Christianorum* 16, (Bari 1979), 10.

[36] W. Swierzawski, *Dynamic « Memory » of the Lord. Eucharistic Anamnesis of the Paschal Mystery and Its Existentional Dynamics*, Kraków 1980, p. 88.

[37] Ibid., p. 89.

Ὀγδοή ἐστί ἡ τοῦ Χριστοῦ ἀναστάσιμος ἡμέρα, καθἣν τῶν ἡμετέρων κόπων απολήψόμεθα καρπούς [38].

L'école théologique d'Alexandrie, très puissante, au cours des premiers siècles de son développement, exerçait une grande influence sur d'autres centres. Saint Ambroise appartenait à ces théologiciens qui restaient sous l'impression des allégoristes alexandrins. L'interprétation allégorique de la Bible et l'exégèse arithmologique étaient sous une évidente influence des écoles citées. Cela prouve, avec force, le texte du Baptistère de Sainte Thècle à Milan et le traité de l'Évangile de Saint Luc. Ce texte de l'inscription d'Ambroise, gardé dans la copie est un exemple de l'adoration du nombre huit. Il souligne sa grandeur et son importance pour les chrétiens. Le sens le plus significatif se rapporte au jour de la Résurrection du Seigneur.

Et voici l'inscription composée de huit distiques:

octachorum $\overline{scos}$ templum surrexit in usus,
    octagonus fons est munere dignus eo.
hoc numero decuit sacri baptismatis aulam
    surgere, quo populis uera salus rediit
luce resurgentis $\overline{Xρι}$, qui claustra resoluit
    mortis et e tumulis suscitat exanimes
confessosq. reos maculoso crimine soluens
    fontis puriflui diluit inriguo.
hic quicumq. uolent probrosa ⟨e⟩ crimina uitae
    ponere, corda lauent, pectora munda gerant.
huc ueniant alacres: quamuis tenebrosus adire
    audeat, abscedet candidior niuibus.
huc $\overline{sci}$ properent: non expers ullus aquarum
    $\overline{scs}$, in his regnum est consiliumq. $\overline{di}$,
gloria iustitiae. nam quid diuinius isto,
    ut puncto exiguo culpa cadat populi? [39]

Cette inscription glorifie le nombre huit en tant que puissance du salut (verset 2) se manifestant par le baptême. La symbolique de ce nombre avait une influence sur le plan des baptistères élevés sur le plan octogonal.

La Résurrection du Seigneur eut lieu après sept jours de la semaine – c'est-à-dire le huitième jour. Le Christ par sa Résurrection a sanctifié ce jour. Donc le nombre huit se rapporte à la Résurrection et il est identifié avec le Christ lui-même [40]. Le baptême constitue une circoncision spirituelle, le début de la nouvelle vie, la résurrection [41], voilà pourquoi huit constitue le symbole de la résurrection par le baptême pour la vie éternelle qui commence dans l'eau [42]. Saint Ambroise concevait la semaine de sept jours et le sabbat en tant que symbole de nos jours qui seront suivis de l'éternelle béatitude de l'octave [43].

Dans son traité sur l'Evangile de Saint Luc, en commentant perycope (Luc 9, 10–17) Saint Ambroise dit: « Ét fortasse si primum quinque panes sensibiliter manducaueris, audebo et dicam: post quinque panes et septem tertio in terra non manducabis panem, sed supra terram manducabis octo panes, sicut qui sunt in caelestibus; sicut enim septem panes panes quietis, ita octo panes panes sunt résurrectionis. Ergo isti qui septem aluntur panibus triduo perstiterunt et fortasse integram resurrectionis futurae fidem et constantiam consecuti » [44].

Dans les paroles citées, le nombre huit signifie le temps à venir c'est-à-dire l'ogdoade, alors que le nombre sept appartient encore à l'Ancien Testament où il symbolisait la Loi. La convergence entre le nombre 7, 8, 3 apparaît ici très nettement. Il y a aussi un rapport entre la Transfiguration du Seigneur sur le Mont Thabor et la symbolique des lettres. Clément d'Alexandrie, dans son œuvre *Stromates*, à l'aide d'une interprétation arithmologique déchiffre la symbolique des nombre 6, 7, 8 dans cette scène.

ταύτη τοι ὁ κύρεος τέταρτος ἀναβὰς εἰς τὸ ὄρος ἕκτος γίνεται καὶ φωτὶ περιλάμπεται πνευματικῷ τῆς δύναμιν τὴν ἀπ᾽ αὐτοῦ παραγυμνώσας εἰς ὅσον οἷον τε ἦν ἰδεῖν τοῖς ὁρᾶν ἐκλεγεῖσι, δι᾽ ἑβδόμης ἀνακηρυσσόμενος τῆς φωνῆς υἱος εἶναι θεοῦ, ἵνα δὴ οἱ μὲν ἀναπαύσωνται

---

[38] Athanase d'Alexandrie, « Expositiones psalmorum 6,1 », PG 27, 76, selon: Quacquarelli, « L'ogdoade patristica... », 54.

[39] Selon: O. Perler, « L'inscription du baptistère de Sainte-Thècle à Milan et de sacramentis de Saint Ambroise », *Rivista di Archeologia Christiana* 27(1951) 146; ci-joint un commentaire philologique détaillé.

[40] Quacquarelli, « L'ogdoade patristica... », 37.

[41] « Misterium Sakramentów », wybór i wstęp A. Bober, dans: *Sakramenty wiary*, Kraków 1970, p. 139.

[42] H. Rahner, *Griechische Mythen in Christlicher Deutung*, Zürich 1945, p. 110.

[43] Quacquarelli, « Il monogramma cristologico... », *Vetera Christianorum* 16, 7 trouve que la raison décisive du sacré de ce nombre était la conscience de la Résurrection du Seigneur conçue comme fait réel et concret placé dans l'histoire. Cette conscience de l'existence du Christ implique au nombre 8 l'existence autonome et distingue parmi d'autres conceptions en Occident et en Orient.

[44] Ambroise de Milan, *Expositio Evangelii Secundum Lucam VI*, 80, *Sources Chrétiennes* 45, p. 258.

7. Église dediée à Hagia Sophia à Thessaloniques. Ascension du Christ (d'après *Propyläen Kunstgeschichte, Byzanz und der Christliche Osten*, Bd 3)

πεισθέντες περὶ αὐτοῦ, ὁ δὲ διὰ γενέσεως, ἣν ἐδήλωσεν ἡ ἑξὰς ἐπίσημος, ὀγδοὰς ὑπάρχων φανῇ, θεὸς ἐν σαρκίῳ τὴν δύναμιν ἐνδεικνύμενος ἀριθμούμενος μὲν ὡς ἄνθρωπος, κρυπτόμενος δὲ ὃς ἦν [45].

« Après six jours » (Matthieu 17, 1), le Christ monte sur le Mont Thabor avec Pierre, Jean Jacques. Le Sauveur est alors « quatrième personnage » « τεταρτός » – c'est-à-dire qu'il a trois compagnons. Leur nombre s'accroît par l'arrivée d'Élie et de Moïse et alors le Christ devient « ἕκτος ». Le septième personnage est représenté par la voix qui le déclare « Fils de Dieu », « Celui-ci est mon Fils bien-aimé, celui qu'il m'a plu de choisir. Écoutez-le ». Par le fait que Jésus était entouré de la lumière spirituelle qui est le nombre sept, Il a dévoilé à ses compagnons sa

nature divine. Jésus déclaré Fils de Dieu devient dans cet événement le huitième personnage. Dieu révèle sa puissance, jusqu'alors il s'était tenu caché dans l'humanité. Ce Dieu appelé l'ogdoade [46] c'est encore Jésus, il est identifié avec les trois nombres 6, 7, 8 – ainsi aux nombres déjà cités est joint le nombre trois.

Πάντα οκτώ ce proverbe antique se rapporte aux huit sphères qui tournent autour de la Terre. On peut rencontrer la même symbolique des nombres, par exemple chez Orygène qui dit:

Ὥσπερ ἡ ὀγδόη σύμβολον ἐστὶ τοῦ μέλλοντος αἰῶνος, δύναμιν ἀναστάσεως περιέχουσα, οὕτω καὶ ἡ ἑβδόμη σύμβολόν ἐστι τοῦ κόσμου τούτου [47].

La scène de l'Ascension du Christ de l'Église dédiée à Hagia Sophia (fig. 7) à Thessalonique peut

---

[45] Clemens Alexandrinus, « Stromates VI », PG 9, cols 368–369, selon; A. Delatte, *Étude sur la littérature Pythagorienne*, Paris 1915, p. 237.

[46] Delatte, *Étude...*, p. 237.

[47] Origenes, *Selectorum in Psalmos* 118, vol. XIII, ed. C.H.E. Lommatzsch, Berlin 1842, p. 102, selon: F.J. Dolger, « Zur Symbolik des altchristlichen Taufhauses », *Antike und Christentum* IV (1934), 177.

8. Tissu copte — le Père Silvane (d'après Coptic Textiles, Collection of Coptic Textiles State Pushkin Museum of Fine Arts in Moscow)

illustrer ces paroles. La mosaïque date du début du Xᵉ siècle et se trouve dans la coupole. Elle présente le Christ en Majesté sur l'arc-en-ciel sur fond des sphères célestes. A sa droite, le nombre des sphères est huit et symbolise la Résurrection, le monde à venir. La main droite du Christ exprime le geste christologique et symbolise le nombre six[48].

Tandis qu'à sa gauche, il y a sept sphères. Cette quantité fait penser au nombre sept et symbolise ce monde terrestre. Dans la scène décrite, la symbolique de la transition du nombre sept au nombre huit par six est visible. Le nombre six a été identifié par exemple avec le Christ par égard à la quantité des lettres figurant dans le nom Ιηςόυς[49].

[48] A. Quacquarelli, « Ai margini dell'actio: la loquela digitorum », *Vetera Christianorum* 7 (Bari 1970), 207, fig. 6.
[49] Delatte, *Étude...*, p. 238.

9. Tissu copte d'Akchim – la fuite en Égypte (d'après *Lexikon für Theologie und Kirche*, Bd 6, tabl. Koptische Kunst II)

10. Église Panagia Angeloktistos de Kitttion en Chypre. La Theotokos entourée des Archanges Michel et Gabriel (d'après *Propyläen Kunstgeschichte, Byzanz und der Christliche Osten*, Bd 3)

Orygène traite le huitième jour comme un type de nouvelle vie. Dans son commentaire du 118 Psaume qui est comme suit : « Voici le jour que le Seigneur a fait », il dit :

Τι γὰρ τῆς ἡμέρας ταύτης ἴσον γένοιτο ἄν, ἐν ᾗ καταλλαγὴ θεοῦ πρὸς ἀνθρώπους ἐγένετο, καὶ ὁ χρόνιος κατελύθη πόλεμος, καὶ οὐρανὸς ἀπεδείχθη ἡ γῆ, καὶ οἱ τῆς γῆς ἀνάξιοι ἄνθρωποι τῆς βασιλείας ἐφάνησαν ἄξιοι, καὶ ἡ ἀπαρχὴ τῆς φύσεως τῆς ἡμετέρας ὑπεράνω τῶν οὐρανῶν ἀνηνέχθη, καὶ παράδεισος ἠνοίγη, καὶ τὴν ἀρχαίαν ἀπελάβομεν πατρίδα, καὶ κατάρα ἠφανίσθη, καὶ ἡ ἁμαρτία ἐλύθη; Εἰ γὰρ καὶ πάσας τὰς ἡμέρας ἐποίησεν, ἀλλ᾽ ἐκείνην ἐξαιρέτως, ἐπειδὴ τὰ μέγιστα ἐν αὐτῇ τῶν οἰκείων μυστησίων ἐπλήρωσε [50].

La compréhension de ce mystère était toujours vive en Orient et en Occident. Ce qui a impliqué une très bonne connaissance de la symbolique du nombre huit. Orygène distingue, parmi d'autres nombres, le nombre huit. H. Rahner nomme le fragment cité du commentaire du 118 Psaume « l'hymne de l'adoration » [51] qui indique dimanche en tant que le huitième jour. L'idée de ce mystère pénétrait toute la vie chrétienne et était connue de tous les croyants de la communauté chrétienne. Les lettres H figurant sur les vêtements étaient déchiffrées correctement. Il n'y avait pas de crainte que les croyants pussent mal interpréter leur signification.

La symbolique des nombres discutés était connue dans chaque centre de l'Orient et de l'Occident chrétiens. Le nombre était l'élément de l'exégèse biblique pour les chrétiens [52]. Pour exprimer de profondes idées de toute la sphère spirituelle, l'homme se sert d'abréviations et de symboles. Les *gammadiae* appartiennent à ces formes. La somptuosité des nombres 8 et 3 a été l'objet de la contemplation incessante qui accompagnait les fidèles toute leur vie terrestre durant. Le prélude de la vie éternelle se fait sur la terre tandis que la béatitude de l'octave n'a pas de bornes et elle est la gloire éternelle où l'on aboutit par le baptême selon ce que dit Saint Ambroise dans l'inscription du Baptistère de Sainte Thècle. La connaissance de ce fait a demeuré dans tout *Orbis Christianus Antiquus*.

Comme exemple de la présence de la lettre H sur le tissu copte de la fin du Ve – début VIe siècle peut servir l'image du Père Silvane (fig. 8) : le tissu se trouve actuellement au musée des Beaux-Arts Pouchkine à Moscou. Sur le *himation* de l'abbé, les lettres H répétées trois fois sont visibles; il est dans l'attitude de l'orant entouré de trois croix à branches égales. Une relation entre le nombre huit et trois est à remarquer. Les lettres H placées sur son *himation* rappellent la disposition des lettres sur les vêtements des Apôtres dans l'abside de la Cathédrale de Faras.

Le tissu suivant avec des *gammadiae* provient d'Akchmim. Deux lettres H accompagnent la scène de la « Fuite en Égypte » (fig. 9).

Dans l'art de l'Orient byzantin, les exemples des *gammadiae* sont peu nombreux parce que la plupart des scènes de cette époque ont disparu. La mosaïque de l'église Panagia Angeloktistos (fig. 10) de Kittion en Chypre mérite d'y porter l'attention. Sur les vêtements de l'Archange Gabriel qui avec l'Archange Michel entoure la Theotokos, figurent les lettres H et Γ donc les mêmes que dans l'abside de la Cathédrale de Faras.

L'itinéraire que la religion chrétienne a suivi pour parvenir en Nubie, permet d'établir les origines des *gammadiae* de la Cathédrale de Faras dans les catacombes romaines, d'où, à travers la Byzance et l'Égypte copte, ces motifs ont été transmis en Nubie. Il y a un grand écalage de temps entre les premiers signes des catacombes (IIe–IVe siècles) et les *gammadiae* de Faras (VIIe siècle). Il est difficile de ne pas voir leurs ressemblances principales — les uns et les autres se caractérisent par la simplicité des formes qui imitent les lettres majuscules de l'alphabet grec.

A la Cathédrale de Faras, les signes figurent dans la scène placée dans l'abside, donc à l'endroit le plus important du point de vue liturgique. Leur fréquence prouve que les notions qu'ils véhiculaient, étaient d'une grande importance dans le contexte du programme iconographique de toute la peinture de l'abside.

---

[50] Origenes, *Selectorum in Psalmos*..., p. 65.

[51] Rahner, *Griechische Mythem*..., p. 109.

[52] Quacquarelli, « L'ogdoade patristica... », 4.

COPTIC STUDIES

Pascale Ballet

La céramique des Kellia. Fouilles récentes de l'Institut Français d'Archéologie Orientale

Cette communication a pour but de présenter un bilan préliminaire relatif à la céramique provenant des ermitages fouillés par l'Institut Français d'Archéologie Orientale, sous la direction de M. René-Georges Coquin, depuis 1979, et de poser quelques problèmes touchant à l'origine géographique du matériel céramique trouvé aux Kellia. Il importe, grâce aux bases typologiques dont nous disposons actuellement, de tenter de restituer l'ensemble de cette documentation à l'échelle de l'Égypte copto-byzantine et d'évoquer quelques faits d'artisanat et de commerce [1].

Les Kellia (*Cellules*), découverts en 1964 par A. Guillaumont, sont situés dans le Delta occidental, plus précisément dans la Beheira (province de Damanhūr), à l'ouest d'Al-Dilingat. Ce site monastique fut fondé par Saint Antoine et l'Abbé Amoun, d'après les Apophtegma Patrum, vers 335, sur la piste allant de Nitrie (Al-Barnūdji) à Scété (Wādi Natrūn); la durée d'existence de la communauté semble attestée jusqu'à la fin du VIIIᵉ siècle [2]. Plus de mille cinq cent ermitages ont été dénombrés.

A partir de l'automne 1965, le site fut divisé en deux concessions, l'une suisse, l'autre française, celle-ci comprenant les Quṣur Al-Rubāʿiyyāt et Qaṣr Al-Waḥayda, à l'ouest du site. Les travaux de défrichements consécutifs à la réforme agraire et l'établissement de la voie ferrée Le Caire–Alexandrie, à partir de 1977, ont incité les archéologues à reprendre d'urgence les travaux, interrompus de 1969 à 1975 à cause de la guerre [3].

Depuis décembre 1979, l'Institut Français a mené cinq campagnes de fouilles, par ordre chronologique des travaux, le kôm 34 (Qaṣr Al-Waḥayda), partiellememnt fouillé précédement, les kôms 167, 171, 166 et 88, sur les Quṣūr Al-Rubāʿiyyāt [4].

Les études céramologiques menées aux Kellia sont fondées sur l'ouvrage de M. Michel Egloff, base typologique et chronologique de référence, complété par le corpus du Survey de la Mission Suisse d'Archéologie Copte (MSAC), enrichissant celui d'Egloff de formes nouvelles [5].

Un point peu satisfaisant, par lequel je commencerai, concerne les faibles progrès en matiere de datation par la céramique, sur laquelle repose,

---

[1] Nous remercions Madame Paule Posener-Krieger, Directeur de l'Institut Français d'Archéologie Orientale du Caire, et Monsieur René-Georges Coquin, chef de la mission des Kellia, de nous avoir permis de présenter cette communication. Principales abréviations bibliographiques:

Bulletin de Liaison = *Bulletin de Liaison du Groupe International d'Étude de la Céramique Égyptienne*; IFAO, Le Caire.

Egloff, *Kellia* = M. Egloff, *Kellia. La poterie copte. Quatre siècles d'artisanat et d'échanges en Basse-Égypte*, Recherches Suisses d'Archéologie Copte III: Georg, Genève 1977.

Hayes, LRP = J.W. Hayes, *Late Roman Pottery. A Catalogue of Roman Fine Wares*, The British School at Rome, Londres 1972.

Rodziewicz, *La céramique romaine tardive* = M. Rodziewicz, *La céramique romaine tardive d'Alexandrie I*, Varsovie 1976.

[2] F. Daumas et A. Guillaumont, *Kellia I. Kôm 219. Fouilles exécutées en 1964 et 1965*, FIFAO 28, Le Caire, 1969, 2 s.; A. Guillaumont, « Histoire des moines aux Kellia », : *Aux origines du monachisme chrétien. Pour une phénomenologie du monachisme*, Spiritualité Orientale 30, (1979), 151: Abbaye de Bellefontaine, Bégrolles en Mauges.

[3] Sur l'historique des travaux menés aux Kellia, G. Andreu, G. Castel et R.-G Coquin, BIFAO 80 (1980), 347 s.

[4] Ces ermitages ont été l'objet de rapports préliminaires; le kôm 34 (Qaṣr al-Waḥayda), G. Andreu, G. Castel et R.-G. Coquin, BIFAO 80 (1980), 350–368; le kôm 167, première campagne, G. Andreu et R.-G. Coquin, BIFAO 81 (1981), 159–188; le kôm 167, seconde campagne, et le kôm 171, R.-G. Coquin, BIFAO 82 (1982), 363–377; les kôms 166 et 88, première campagne, ASAE 70 (1984–1985).

[5] Egloff, *Kellia*; id., *Survey archéologique des Kellia (Basse-Égypte). Rapport de la campagne 1981*, Louvain 1983, pp. 423–461, pls CXLVI – CXLXIII.

parfois, la chronologie des Kellia; les questions de méthodologie ont déjà été évoquées [6]; les contextes archéologiques ne favorisent guère une appréciation plus affinée de la chronologie : absence de stratigraphie, effondrement des voûtes livrant ainsi les tessons ayant servi au calage des briques, se superposant généralement (ou s'entremêlant parfois) aux céramiques des niveaux d'abandon (ou derniers niveaux d'utilisation); encore faut-il signaler que les tessons de calage peuvent avoir été puisés dans les dépôtoirs voisins et peuvent être très antérieurs à la construction même de l'ermitage. Les bases les plus sûres sont les dépôtoirs, situés dans les cours et à l'extérieur des kôms; dans ce cas, il est cependant nécessaire de disposer d'autres données fournissant à la céramique des dépôtoirs une valeur chronologique indicative.

Les bases de datation restent, dans leur grandes lignes, celles qu'a proposées Michel Egloff, et dont la cohérence interne n'a pas été mise à l'épreuve de résultats postérieurs contradictoires.

Les principaux groupes céramiques de fabrication égyptienne, provenant des ermitages 167, 171, 166 et 88, sont les suivants :

—la céramique fine locale (égyptienne) est constituée de bols, d'assiettes et de plats du groupe K (pl. I, 2) (selon la terminologie de Rodziewicz = *Egyptian B* de Hayes) [7], à pâte brun-rouge, micacée, et du groupe 0 (idem = *Coptic Red Slip A* de Hayes) [8], à pâte rose-orangé, comprenant de nombreuses petites inclusions minérales. Les formes les plus fréquentes sont les types Egloff 76-77 en ce qui concerne le groupe K, les types Egloff 33-35 pour le groupe 0;

—parmi les récipients de cuisson, on trouve des plats à fond arrondi (pl. I, 3), type Egloff 90, à pâte brun-rouge micacée, et des marmites à pâte micacée et fortement sableuse; les marmites les plus caractéristiques sont à rebord biseauté et à anses horizontales (types Egloff 115-116) ou à col légèrement marqué, assorti d'anses verticales (pl. I, 4);

—les plats de grande taille, appelés selon la terminologie morphologique plats creux et jattes, sont définis par un fond plat, des parois évasées à section épaisse et une pâte grossière à dégraissant végétal abondant; un type à rebord évasé et festonné, portant sur sa surface interne des cannelures horizontales parallèls, est fréquent (type *Survey archéologique des Kellia* n° 137);

—la majeure partie des vases à eau comprend des gargoulettes (pl. II, 1), à pâte rougeâtre micacée et sableuse, décorées de motifs floraux ou géométriques peints (types Egloff 212-217); signalons un décor rare de quadrillage brun-noir sur l'épaule d'une gargoulette trouvée dans le kôm 166; quelques pichets à pâte claire, la panse excisée de cannelures verticales, sont considérés comme une production d'Abou Mina [9];

—les amphores égyptiennes sont de types divers : *les amphores-obus,* à pâte orangé-brun, comprenant de nombreux petits nodules blanchâtres, sont généralement encastrées horizontalement dans les murs; il s'agit, dans ce cas, du type Egloff 182; dans la cour du kôm 88, elles ont servi de canalisations; *les amphores effilées* (pl. II, 4), de couleur brune, à pâte micacée, sont relativement nombreuses dans les kôms 88 et 167; ici, le type tardif (Egloff 173-175) prédomine et fut trouvé en abondance dans le Qaṣr de l'ermitage 88; ces amphores contenaient des résidus noirâtres organiques dans le fond (elles sont considérées comme des produits vinaires); le Qaṣr fit probablement fonction de magazin;

les amphores ovoïdes ou sphéroïdes à pâte rouge, (pl. II, 3), constituée de dégraissant végétal, entre autres inclusions (type Egloff 187), sont abondantes dans les niveaux d'abandon (sols, réfections des bas de murs, etc.);

quelques amphores sphéroides, à pâte claire (type Egloff 186), sont des produits fabriqués à Abou Mina [10];

—parmi les céramiques à usage spécifique et rare, on notera la présence de calices à encens et de tuyaux de canalisation, ceux-ci étant inconnus aux Kellia jusqu'à la fouille du kôm 88, qui en livra deux types [11].

La céramique importée est constituée de quelques exemplaires de *Late Roman B* (= *Sigillée Claire D,* pl. I, 1, d'assiettes du *Late Roman D* (= *Cypriot*

---

[6] Egloff, *Kellia,* pp. 29–39; id., *Survey archéologique...,* pp. 46–55.

[7] Rodziewicz, *La céramique romaine tardive,* pp. 50 s.; Hayes, LRP, pp. 397 s.

[8] Rodziewicz, *La céramique...,* pp. 54 s.; Hayes, LRP, pp. 387 s.

[9] Egloff, *Kellia,* pp. 134 s.

[10] Ibid., pp. 117–118; elles auraient pu être expédiées avec les pichets à cannelures verticales excisées, mais leur datation respective ne coïncide par parfaitement aux Kellia.

[11] P. Ballet, *Bulletin de Liaison* VIII (1983), fig. p. 3.

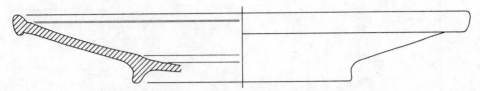

1. Assiette du *Late Roman B* (sigillée–Claire D) – kôm 167 (échelle 1:3)

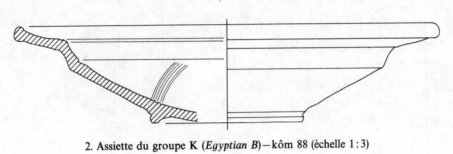

2. Assiette du groupe K (*Egyptian B*) – kôm 88 (échelle 1:3)

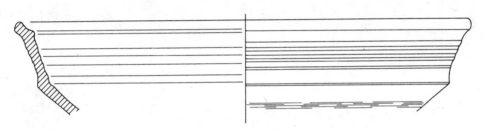

3. Plat de cuisson – kôm 167 (échelle 1:3)

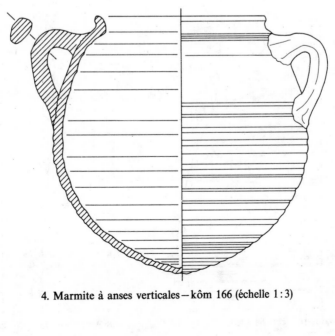

4. Marmite à anses verticales – kôm 166 (échelle 1:3)

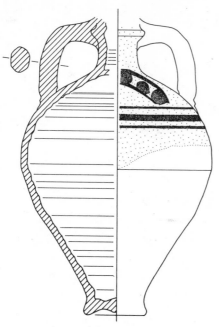

5. Gargoulette – kôm 88 (échelle 1 : 3)

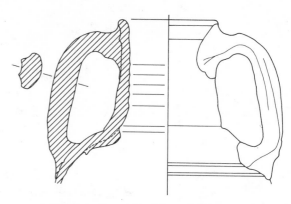

6. Col d'amphore 164 – kôm 166 (échelle 1 : 3)

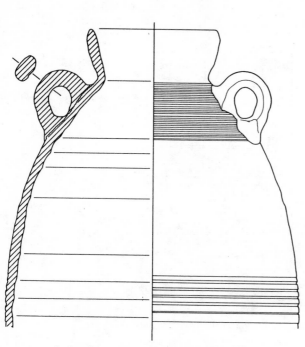

7. Amphore 187 – kôm 167 (échelle 1 : 3)

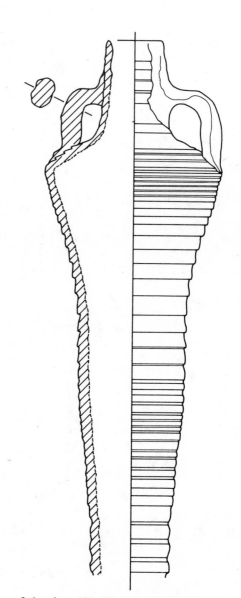

8. Amphore 173–175 – kôm 88 (échelle 1 : 4)

Red Slip) et d'amphores à pâte claire (pl. II, 2), caractérisée par de multiples petites inclusions minérales (type Egloff 164), dont l'origine géographique est incertaine[12]; les deux derniers groupes, tout particulièrement l'amphore claire, sont essentiellement représentés par des tessons de construction; les cols d'amphores 164 sont aussi utilisés comme tuyaux acoustiques entre deux pièces et comme éléments de canalisation dans les cours.

Un certain nombre d'éléments militent en faveur d'une datation tardive, du moins en ce qui concerne les dernières utilisations (occupations et abandons) des ermitages 88, 166 et 167:

—l'absence de matériel, à quelques exceptions près qui ne sont pas représentatives, daté de la seconde moitié du IVe siècle au VIe siècle inclus, encore que la céramique du VIe siècle soit mal connue aux Kellia;

—la majorité des types identifiés correspondent aux exemplaires les plus récents du site, datés par M. Egloff du début VIIe à la première moitié du VIIIe siècles: il s'agit des bols, assiettes et plats de la céramique fine égyptienne (groupes K et O), des amphores ovoïdes rouges (type Egloff 187) et de la variante tardive des amphores brunes (types Egloff 173-175); ces groupes d'amphores apparaîtraient aux Kellia à partir du milieu du VIIe siècle. Un dépôtoir, aménagé dans la cour du kôm 167, comprenait un ensemble de marmites et d'amphores appartenant à la même fourchette chronologique[13].

Les attestations les plus tardives de la céramique coïncident avec « l'étranglement » économique progressif des ermitages au cours du VIIIe siècle; les relations de voyageurs arabes signalent l'abandon presque définitif des Kellia à partir du début du IX[a] siècle; des preuves littéraires et archéologiques manquent à partir de cette période, à l'exclusion de quelques occupations sporadiques[14].

La documentation céramique permet d'entrevoir quelques aspects du fonctionnement économique des ermitages, par le biais de la recherche des centres de production de la poterie. En d'autres termes, les ermitages furent-ils producteurs et/ou importateurs de céramique?

En dehors des importations identifiées sur l'ensemble du site (*Late Roman A, Late Roman B, Late Roman C, Late Roman D,* quelques *spatheion* et les amphores 164, dont j'ai souligné précédemment l'incertitude de la localisation), en nombre limité, à l'exception du dernier groupe d'amphores, la céramique est majoritairement de fabrication égyptienne.

Toutefois, alors que les Apophtegmes et quelques données archéologiques attestent que les moines vaquaient aux activités de vannerie et peut-être de tissage[15], aucun élément, dont l'absence de fours de potiers et la rareté des rebuts de cuisson sur le site, ne permet d'affirmer que la poterie fut fabriquée, même partiellement, aux Kellia.

L'atelier actuel d'Al-'Imāra, village situé sur la rive orientale du canal de la Nūbārīya, à proximité des Quṣūr Al-Rubā'iyyāt, importe, aux dires du potier, l'argile rouge d'autres localités du Delta (dont Kafr Al-Zaiyat) et la blanche du Saïd, l'argile locale étant trop sableuse. C'est en effet une des caractéristiques des briques crues employées à la construction des ermitages, seul matériau prélevé localement[16]; la brique cuite (?), la pierre et la chaux sont importées[17].

[12] Elles sont extrêmement répandues en Égypte et en Nubie, mais aussi dans tout le bassin méditerranéen; d'après certains *dipinti* grecs inscrits sur des amphores de ce type à Saqqara, elles pourraient avoir été fabriquées en Égypte, J. Gascou, *Bulletin de Liaison* III (1978), 24–27; les caractéristiques pétrographiques de la pâte semblent exclure l'Égypte comme lieu d'origine; elles correspondraient davantage, entre autres sites de la Méditerranée orientale, à la région d'Antioche, M.G. Fulford et D.P.S. Peacock, *Excavations at Carthage: The British Mission,* Vol. I, 2. *The Avenue du Président Habib Bourguiba, Salambô: The Pottery and Other Ceramic Objects from the Site,* The British Academy, Sheffield 1984, pp. 20–22.

[13] P. Ballet, *Bulletin de Liaison* VII (1982), 2–3.

[14] Sur l'extinction des Kellia. J.-C. Garcin, dans: F. Daumas et A. Guillaumont, *Kellia I. Kôm 219...,* pp. 125–126, et les causes économiques de l'appauvrissement des ermitages, E. Wipszycka, « Les aspects économiques de la vie de la communauté des Kellia », *Le site monastique copte des Kellia. Sources historiques et explorations archéologiques,* Colloque de Genève, 13 — 15 août 1984, Louvain. Quant aux apports et aux limites de la céramique concernant la fin des Kellia, P. Ballet, *Céramique tardive des Kellia et présence islamique,* ibid.

[15] E. Wipszycka, « Les aspects économiques... » et E. Makowiecka, « The Interpretation of the Room of RI XIV at Q. el-Izeila », *Le site monastique copte des Kellia...*

[16] Les briques crues sont façonnées à partir du caliche, encroûtement salin des anciennes dunes et des sédiments sous-jacents, comprenant des limons, des sables et des argiles de provenance fluviatile; des prétraitements destinés à éliminer le sel étaient probablement effectués dans les fosses d'extraction, *Survey archéologique des Kellia,* pp. 1–3, 71 s.

[17] Ibid., p. 72.

La poterie des ermitages est elle-même un indice révélant la dépendance des Kellia, en matière d'approvisionnement céramique; elle appartient aux principales productions connues en Égypte pendant la période copto-byzantine et les premiers temps de l'occupation arabe: en particulier, la céramique fine et les amphores ont des parallèles précis dans d'autres régions, parallèles fondés sur la morphologie, certes, mais aussi sur les pâtes et les techniques de fabrication.

Dans certains cas, l'origine de ces produits est connue, du moins pressentie avec de fortes vraisemblances. C'est le cas du groupe O (*Coptic Red Slip A*) qui aurait été fabriqué dans la région d'Assouan; sa diffusion a atteint tant la Basse et la Haute Nubie qu'Alexandrie [18]. La groupe K (*Egyptian B*) serait originaire du Delta ou du Fayoum d'après la littérature archéologique, si l'on considère la répartition de ces produits, principalement attestés dans ces deux régions [19]. Les céramiques à pâte claire, amphores, pichets et jattes, sont envoyées aux Kellia par les ateliers d'Abou Mina [20]; on notera, cependant, la rareté de la pacotille religieuse, fabriquée aussi à Abou Mina, ampoules à eulogies, figurines de terre cuite, aux Kellia, alors que la diffusion des produits utilitaires soit assurée.

Les centres de production des gargoulettes, des jattes et des plats creux, des marmites et des amphores brunes restent inconnus, bien que l'aspect des pâtes les apparente aux *Nile silt*, dites encore « pâtes limoneuses » [21]. La recherche de ces ateliers paraît justifiée, non seulement à l'échelle des Kellia mais aussi de toute l'Égypte.

Il existe donc des réseaux d'approvisionnement, fournissant les ermitages des Kellia en céramique, à l'instar de certains matériaux de construction: ils peuvent mettre en relation des régions parfois éloignées les unes des autres et suppléent ainsi à l'insuffisance des ressources locales et peut-être au mode de vie des moines. On ne sait rien de l'organisation des échanges, commandes, quantité de céramiques expédiées par un atelier, importance et fonctionnement des centres de fabrication. D'après l'existence de groupes et de types céramiques bien caractérisés et la connaissance partielle de quelques lieux producteurs, signalés précédemment, plusieurs ateliers, localisés dans différentes régions, ont fourni simultanément les ermitages des Kellia, selon les besoins en produits céramiques divers, répondant chacun à un usage précis.

La connaissance des voies commerciales et de la distribution de la céramique est incertaine; on sait cependant que les Kellia sont une étape traditionnelle de la route monastique allant d'Alexandrie aux monastères du Wādi Natrūn, itinéraire qu'emprunta le patriarche Benjamin au début du VIIe siècle, selon *l'Histoire des Patriarches* [22]; les moines écoulaient probablement à Alexandrie le fruit de leur activité artisanale, la vannerie.

Alexandrie a pu jouer un rôle de redistributeur pour certaines catégories de produits, par exemple la céramique fine du groupe O, expédiée d'Assouan et bien attestée à Alexandrie, ainsi que la *Late Roman D* (*Cypriot Red Slip*), originaire de Chypre. Les importations massives de ce groupe à Alexandrie, fin VIe–début VIIe siècles, connu cependant avant cette date, et sa répartition limitée essentiellement au Delta occidental (Alexandrie, Abou Mina, les Kellia) témoigneraient du rayonnement économique d'Alexandrie sur des centres religieux et monastiques peu éloignés [23]. Il est un

---

[18] Sur l'origine du Groupe O, T. Ulbert, MDIAK 27 (1971); 235–242; W. Adams, *Études Nubiennes,* Colloque de Chantilly, 2–6 juillet 1975, Rd'E 77 (1978), 5-7.

[19] Hayes, LRP, pp. 397–399; Rodziewicz, *La céramique romaine tardive,* pp. 50–51.

[20] Cf. supra notes 9–10; lors d'une récente visite du site, j'ai pu en effet constater la présence de ces pâtes calcaires dans le secteur des fours, à l'est de la grande basilique.

[21] Sur ces classifications généralement adoptées pour la céramique d'époque pharaonique, D. Arnold, *Keramik*, LÄ III, cols 394–399; J. Bourriau, *Umm el-Ga'ab. Pottery from the Nile Valley before the Arab Conquest,* Fitzwilliam Museum, Cambridge 1981, pp. 14–15.

[22] Garcin, dans: F. Daumas et A. Guillaumont, *Kellia I. Kom 219...*, p . 126 et Guillaumont, *Histoire des moines aux Kellia,* p. 163.

[23] Hayes, LRP, p. 385 remarque la présence de la *Late Roman D* dans les sites du Delta, dont Abou Mina, et sa rareté dans le sud de l'Égypte; pour Rodziewicz, *La céramique romaine tardive,* pp. 44–45, elle est concentrée à Alexandrie et peu fréquente dans le reste de l'Égypte, bien qu'elle atteigne Assouan. Cependant, j'en ai vu à Tanis et Janine Bourriau m'en a signalé dans la région thébaine. Toutefois, elle reste prédominante quantitativement dans le Delta.

fait que, dans son ensemble, la céramique des Kellia, égyptienne et importée, présente de nombreux points communs avec celle d'Alexandrie [24].

La céramique provenant des ermitages fouillés par l'Institut Français appartient à la phase tardive d'occupation du site (VIIe – VIIIe siècles). Les Kellia apparaissent importateurs de céramique, certains centres de production étant connus, d'autres encore non identifiés; ils s'intègrent aussi, dans une certaine mesure, à la sphère économique du Delta occidental.

---

[24] Par exemple, Alexandrie reçoit aussi des produits d'Abou Mina. On peut se demander si cette similitude du matériel céramique n'est pas due au fait que la poterie d'Alexandrie est accessible à notre connaissance grâce aux publications de M. Rodziewicz.

COPTIC STUDIES

Theofried Baumeister

Der aktuelle Forschungsstand zu den Pachomiusregeln

Bekanntlich hat Hieronymus im Jahr 404 eine Reihe von Schriften der frühen Pachomianerväter, darunter vier Stücke, die man die Regel oder die Regeln des Pachomius nennt, ins Lateinische übertragen. Zu Beginn der Praefatio berichtet er über die Umstände dieser Unternehmung [1]. In der Trauer über den Tod der Paula (Anfang 404), die ihn in seinen Arbeiten lähmt, hat er durch Vermittlung des Presbyters Silvanus, der als *homo Dei* charakterisiert wird und deshalb selbst wohl Mönch war, die genannten Schriften erhalten, die diesem aus Alexandrien, doch wohl aus dem gleich darauf erwähnten pachomianischen Kloster Metanoia in Kanopus zugeschickt worden waren. Dort wie auch in der Thebais lebten lateinische Pachomianer, die der ägyptischen und griechischen Sprache nicht mächtig waren, *quo Pachomii et Theodori et Orsiesii praecepta conscripta sunt* [2]. Heinrich Bacht hat aus dieser Wendung geschlossen, daß dem Hieronymus bewußt gewesen sei, daß die Pachomiusregel nach und nach unter Mitarbeit mehrerer Verfasser entstanden sei [3]. Doch dürfte » praecepta « hier nicht allein die Pachomiusregel, sondern auch die anderen von Hieronymus übersetzten Schriften wie die Epistula Theodori und den Liber Orsiesii mit ihren

Mahnungen meinen. Die Boten, der Presbyter Leontius *et ceteri cum eo fratres,* drängen Hieronymus, so daß dieser einem herbeigerufenen Schreiber die ihm in griechischer Übertragung vorliegenden Texte in lateinischer Übersetzung diktiert [4]. Die hier interessierenden Stücke tragen die Titel *Praecepta* [5], *Praecepta et Instituta* [6], *Praecepta atque Iudicia* [7] und *Praecepta ac Leges* [8]. Im folgenden werden sie Praecepta, Instituta, Iudicia und Leges genannt. Die inzwischen bekannten Reste des sahidischen Urtextes hat 1956 L.Th. Lefort vorgelegt [9]. Heinrich Bacht hat gezeigt, daß ein von Lafort einer Katechese des Horsiese zugewiesenes Stück [10] in Wirklichkeit das Proömium der Instituta darstellt [11]. Damit haben wir das sahidische Original für Praecepta 88–130, wobei 126 fehlt und 130 unvollständig ist, und fast die gesamten Instituta. Von den Iudicia und Leges fehlt bislang ein koptisches Zeugnis. Die von Hieronymus benutzte griechische Übersetzung ist verlorengegangen. Erhalten blieben die sog. *Excerpta graeca,* für eine andere monastische Welt bestimmte Auszüge aus den Praecepta und in einem Fall aus den Instituta, deren Edition Lefort als Anhang zu Boons *Pachomiana latina* beigesteuert hat [12].

---

[1] A. Boon, » Pachomiana latina «, *Bibliothèque de la Revue d'Histoire Ecclésiastique* 7 (Louvain 1932), 3–5.

[2] Ebd., 4,7f.

[3] H. Bacht, » Das Vermächtnis des Ursprungs. Studien zum frühen Mönchtum 2. Pachomius — Der Mann und sein Werk «, *Studien zur Theologie des geistlichen Lebens* 8 (Würzburg 1983), 42 u. 73, Anm. 10.

[4] 4,14/5,1 Boon: accito notario, ut erant de aegyptiaca in graecam linguam uersa, nostro sermone dictaui.

[5] Boon, 13–52.

[6] Ebd., 53–62.

[7] Ebd., 63–70.

[8] Ebd., 71–74.

[9] L.Th. Lefort, » Œuvres de S. Pachôme et de ses disciples «, CSCO 159, Script. Copt. 23 (Louvain 1956), 30–36; französische Übersetzung: CSCO 160, Script. Copt. 24, 30–37. Vgl. auch die folgende Anmerkung.

[10] Ebd., 80,23-33; Übersetzung: 80, 1–14.

[11] H. Bacht, » Ein verkanntes Fragment der koptischen Pachomius-Regel «, *Muséon* 75 (1962), 5–18.

[12] Boon, 169–182. Die ebenfalls im Anhang befindliche Edition und Übersetzung der koptischen Fragmente durch Lefort wurde abgelöst durch die Anm. 9 genannte Ausgabe von 1956. Zur äthiopischen Übersetzung der Excerpta graeca s. Boon, XLVI, Anm. 3.

In meinem Referat über die Forschung der letzten Jahre möchte ich beginnen mit den Bemerkungen, die Charles de Clercq zu Anfang seines Aufsatzes » über den Einfluß der Regel des hl. Pachomius im Westen « gemacht hat [13]. Er konstatiert: Die Instituta und die Leges richten sich an die Oberen, die Iudicia bilden ein Strafgesetzbuch (code pénal). In den Praecepta erkennt er kleinere Einheiten, die jeweils formelhaft am Ende von 7 (besser: mit dem Anfang von 8), 14, 22, 48, 103, 144 abgeschlossen werden und in denen er sukzessiv gemachte Zufügungen sieht. Die ersten 14 Praecepta sind seiner Ansicht nach die ältesten; sie behandeln summarisch verschiedene Themen, die darauf dann wieder aufgenommen werden. Von 104 an dürfte es sich um ergänzende Praecepta handeln, unter denen einige vorher schon gegebene Regeln wieder aufnehmen oder entfalten. Von Strafen ist an verschiedenen Stellen der Praecepta die Rede; ihre Grade werden in den Iudicia präzisiert. Mehrere Regeln, die in den Instituta und Leges zum Gebrauch der Oberen formuliert sind, finden sich bereits in den Praecepta. Da zu den Iudicia und Leges bisher keine koptischen und griechischen Stücke gefunden wurden, neigt de Clercq zu der Ansicht, daß diese beiden Dokumente nicht zum ursprünglichen pachomianischen Bestand gehört haben. Ein Strafbuch kann sich gut erst später entwickelt haben, da die Praecepta schon häufig von Strafen handeln. Die Leges berühren sich mit den Instituta. De Clercq rechnet mit der Möglichkeit unterschiedlicher Redaktionen in verschiedenen Pachomianerklöstern, was auch leichte Widersprüche zwischen den Texten etwa in den Ämtern erklären könnte.

M. van Molle, die in vier Aufsätzen [14] ihre Sicht der Entstehungsgeschichte der pachomianischen Regeln und damit der gesamten Pachomianergeschichte vorgelegt und für die Fragen der Gegenwart fruchtbar machen wollen, hat m.E. die Beobachtungen de Clercqs und die Ansichten anderer zu leichtfertig beiseite gestoßen [15]. Ihr geht es darum, die ursprüngliche Gestalt des pachomianischen Mönchtums zu ermitteln und abzuheben von dem Prozeß der Verrechtlichung, als dessen Endergebnis sie die Praecepta begreift. Das älteste Dokument sind nach ihr die Iudicia, die einen Blick auf die noch wenig organisierten Anfänge des Gemeinschaftslebens gestatten. Sie handeln von den Vergehen gegen die Harmonie des brüderlichen Lebens und gegen den Geist des Evangeliums. Die Maßnahmen gegenüber dem Sünder sind die, welche das Neue Testament an die Hand gibt: mit Geduld ermahnen und, wenn es notwendig ist, durch Ausschluß zeigen, daß die Gemeinschaft ein bestimmtes Verhalten nicht akzeptieren kann [16]. In der Folgezeit macht sich das Bedürfnis genauerer Regelungen bemerkbar. Die Entwicklung verläuft nach van Molle über die Instituta, die noch der Zeit zuzuweisen seien, in der die Brüder in einem Haus zusammenwohnten, über die Leges zu den Praecepta, in denen die Autorin die Reglementierung eines bis in die Einzelheiten uniformen Gemeinschaftslebens sieht [17]. Die hier knapp skizzierte Hypothese gibt Anlaß zur Skepsis, insofern in ihr das öfter in der Kirchengeschichts- und Ordensgeschichtsschreibung begegnende Klischee von den reinen Ursprüngen und dem folgenden Verfall unterschiedlicher Art entdeckt werden kann. Doch darf diese Skepsis nicht ausschlaggebend sein. Eine Hypothese gilt so viel wie die beigebrachten Argumente, die in diesem Fall von Adalbert de Vogüé und von Fidelis Ruppert einer eingehenden Überprüfung unterzogen worden sind, die hier nicht wiederholt werden kann [18]. Vor allem ist der Ausgangspunkt zu subjektiv. Die Autorin streicht in den nur lateinisch vorliegenden Iudicia die Wörter *monasterium* und *regula monasterii* als nicht ursprünglich. Dort wo man den koptischen

---

[13] Ch. de Clercq, *L'influence de la règle de saint Pachôme en occident, Mélanges d'histoire du moyen âge dédiés à la mémoire de Louis Halphen*, Paris 1951, S. 169–176, hier 169–171.

[14] M. van Molle, » Essai de classement chronologique des premières règles de vie commune connue en chrétienté «, *Supplément de la Vie Spirituelle* 21 (1968), 108–127; dies., » Confrontation entre les règles et la littérature Pachômienne postérieure «, ebd., 394–424; dies., » Aux origines de la vie communautaire chrétienne, quelques équivoques déterminantes pour l'avenir «, ebd., 22 (1969), 101–121; dies., » Vie commune et obéissance d'après les institutions premières de Pachôme et Basile «, ebd., 23 (1970), 196–225.

[15] Van Molle, » Essai de classement... «, 109.

[16] Ebd., 119 f.

[17] Ebd., 126 f.

[18] A. de Vogüé, » Les pièces latines du dossier pachômien «, *Revue d'Histoire Ecclésiastique* 67 (1972), 26–67; F. Ruppert, » Das pachomianische Mönchtum und die Anfänge klösterlichen Gehorsams «, *Münsterschwarzacher Studien* 20 (Münsterschwarzach 1971), 240–262.

Text mit der Hieronymusübersetzung vergleichen kann, begegneten diese Begriffe nämlich ohne koptisches Äquivalent nur im lateinischen Text, dem die vorausgehende griechische Übersetzung entsprochen haben soll. Doch zeigt Ruppert, daß den lateinischen Wörtern sehr wohl entsprechende koptische Wendungen zugrundeliegen. Zudem kennt auch der koptische Text der Instituta bereits das pachomianische System der Häuser [19]. Die Verfasserin hätte beachten müssen, daß die Texte verschiedene Adressaten haben und daß sich in ihnen selbst, vor allem in den Praecepta, ein Wachstumsprozeß vollzogen haben kann. Welchen Eindruck die Iudicia auch erwecken können, zeigt folgendes Zitat aus Rupperts Studie: » Es mutet auch etwas seltsam an, daß ausgerechnet das älteste Regeldokument einer ganz aus dem Evangelium lebenden Gemeinschaft ein detaillierter Katalog von Strafvorschriften sein soll « [20]. Die genannten Strafen sind doch z.T. gravierend.

Unabhängig von van Molle hat sich zu etwa gleicher Zeit Armand Veilleux mit der Kritik der pachomianischen Quellen befaßt [21]. Beim Vergleich der sahidischen Fragmente mit dem lateinischen Text gelangt er zum Urteil, daß Hieronymus im allgemeinen treu übersetzt, sich aber im einzelnen auch Freiheiten erlaubt hat [22]. Auf die kodikologischen Überlegungen, nach denen möglicherweise der koptischen Überlieferung Horsiese als Autor der Praecepta und Instituta gegolten haben könnte [23], soll hier nicht weiter eingegangen werden. Hans Quecke hat auf die nicht seltenen koptischen Kodizes hingewiesen, » in denen die darin kopierten Werke je für sich paginiert waren « [24]. Die sahidischen Fragmente der Praecepta gehörten zu einem solchen Kodex, die der Instituta möglicherweise ebenso. Veilleux ist denn auch in der Einleitung zu seiner englischen Übersetzung der Regeln nicht wieder auf dieses Thema zurückgekommen [25]. In der

Analyse der vier Regelgruppen verfolgt er die Linie von de Clercq. Zu den Instituta präzisiert er dessen Beobachtung. Sie richten sich an den Hebdomar, d.h. den Hausoberen, der mit den Mönchen seines Hauses beauftragt war, die Synaxis einzuberufen, dort die gemeinsame Arbeit zu organisieren etc., und schöpfen aus den Praecepta und Iudicia [26]. Es handelt sich also um eine spätere Zusammenstellung, die wohl wegen der unterschiedlichen Terminologie der Ämter aus einem anderen Milieu als die Praecepta stammen. Die Iudicia sind eine Art Paenitentiale; einige ihrer Elemente finden sich bereits in den Praecepta. Die Leges enthalten die Regeln für die Synaxis in den einzelnen Häusern und handeln von den Verantwortlichkeiten des Hausoberen. In der Einleitung zur oben erwähnten englischen Übersetzung bemerkt Veilleux zu den Praecepta, daß diese wahrscheinlich, wenigstens ursprünglich, das Buch des Klosteroberen waren, die zuerst von allem handelten, was die morgendliche Zusammenkunft aller Brüder betraf [27]. In diesem Zusammenhang geht Veilleux auch kurz auf die Studien von van Molle ein. Ihrem Postulat einer sukzessiven Entstehung der vier Regeltexte hält er entgegen, daß sie verschiedene Absichten verfolgen und daß die Annahme wahrscheinlicher ist, daß sie Paralleltexte sind, die zur gleichen Zeit im Verlauf der Entwicklung der Koinonia in verschiedenen Kontexten entstanden. Veilleux rechnet mit einem pachomianischen Kern der Vorschriften, die nach ihm ergänzt worden sind. Er weist sodann auf die sog. » Règlements « des Horsiese [28] hin, die von einem Autor später als Horsiese stammen dürften und die das Bild der pachomianischen Gesetzgebung komplettieren. Sein abschließendes Urteil: » Es scheint uns, daß die pachomianische Gesetzgebung als lebendige Realität erwachsen ist aus einigen, von Pachomius selbst verfaßten Vorschriften und daß sie periodisch den Notwendigkeiten neuer Situationen angepaßt wurde. Die vier als Regel des

---

[19] Ebd., 256.

[20] Ebd., 259, Anm. 501.

[21] A. Veilleux, » La liturgie dans le cénobitisme Pachômien au quatrième siècle «, *Studia Anselmiana* 57 (Rom 1968), 9–158, zu den Regeln S. 116–132.

[22] Ebd., 120–122.

[23] Ebd., 123–6, 123–126.

[24] H. Quecke, Rez. zu F. Ruppert, » Das pachomianische Mönchtum und die Anfäge klösterlichen Gehorsams «, *Enchoria* 3 (1973), 161–163, hier 162.

[25] A. Veilleux, » Pachomian Koinonia 2. Pachomian chronicles and rules «, *Cistercian Studies Series* 46 (Kalamazoo 1981), 7–13.

[26] Veilleux, » La liturgie... «, 127.

[27] Veilleux, » Pachomian Koinonia 2... «, 10.

[28] Lefort, CSCO 159, 82–99. Übersetzung: 160, 81–99.

Pachomius bekannten Serien und die anderen, bekannt als Regelungen des Horsiese, sind in ihres Gesamtheit Zeugnisse des Standes der Gesetzgebung Ende des 4. Jahrhunderts « [29].

Gegen diese Spätdatierung der Regel des Pachomius hatte de Vogüé schon 1972 Stellung bezogen [30]. Für ihn ist es entscheidend, daß der Liber Orsiesii an den Stellen, an denen er Parallelen zur pachomianischen Regel enthält, fast immer *expressis verbis* auf eine schon bestehende Gesetzgebung verweist, die er mehrere Male Pachomius selbst zuweist. De Vogüé ist deshalb der Ansicht, daß die unter dem Namen des Pachomius überlieferte Gesetzgebung, insbesondere der Praecepta und der Instituta, auf die sich der Liber Orsiesii deutlich bezieht, zumindest im großen und ganzen auf den Gründer der coenobia zurückgeht. Damit will er nicht ausschließen, daß die Nachfolger des Pachomius hier da ihre eigenen Vorschriften eingefügt hätten. Das könne etwa in Praecepta 1–8 der Fall sein, da die » Règlements « des Horsiese ihnen so sehr entsprechen, ohne sich jemals explizit auf sie zu berufen. Doch meint er, daß man die Zuweisung der vier Sammlungen an Pachomius, so wie sie in den Titeln vorgenommen werden, ernst nehmen muß [31]. Die Reihenfolge der vier Gruppen war schon in dem Hieronymus vorgelegten griechieschen Text die künstliche Gruppierung nach abnehmender Länge. Die Praecepta sind am längsten; es folgen die Instituta, sodann die Iudicia; am kürzesten sind die Leges [32]. Placide Deseille verweist in der 2. Auflage von » L'esprit du monachisme Pachômien « zustimmend auf de Vogüé [33]. Vorsichtiger äußert sich Heinrich Bacht in seinem wertvollen Kommentar zur Pachomiusregel. Er referiert die Positionen von van Molle, Veilleux und de Vogüé, ohne sich im letzten festzulegen [34]. Doch dürfte es m.E.

feststehen, daß die Hypothese von van Molle nach der Kritik von Ruppert und de Vogüé nicht mehr aufrechtgehalten werden kann. Als Ergebnis der genannten Studien möchte ich festhalten: Die Regel des Pachomius ist entsprechend den Notwendigkeiten der Gemeinschaft oder der Gemeinschaften allmählich gewachsen. Die vier Stücke haben unterschiedliche Adressaten; sie dürften etwa gleichzeitig entstanden und gewachsen sein. Abzulehnen ist für den Moment eine Globallösung. Vielmehr muß durch geduldige Kleinarbeit versucht werden, den Redaktionsprozeß, soweit es geht, zu rekonstruieren. Strittig ist die Frage der Chronologie und der Authentizität. Es ist davon auszugehen, daß der vollständige Text des Hieronymus den Zustand Ende des 4. Jahrhunderts bezeugt. Man hat sicherlich nicht für Hieronymus eigens eine griechische Übersetzung angefertigt, sondern er hatte die Texte vor sich, die im Metanoia-Kloster für die dortigen Bedürfnisse bereits vorhanden waren. Gleichzeitig tut man gut daran, nicht nur für einen kleinen Kern, sondern für einen beträchtlichen Teil pachomianische Autorschaft zu vermuten. Nur ist es im einzelnen schwer, hier zu Klarheiten zu kommen. Es scheint, daß man sich am besten zunächst damit begnügt, Einzelstudien zu einzelnen Bestimmungen und Themenkreisen durchzuführen. Dann kann man sich später fragen, ob sich die Ergebnisse zu einem Gesamtbild vereinigen lassen. Um das Gesagte zu veranschaulichen, möchte ich den Themenkomplex » Klosterpforte « herausgreifen, der mich seit längerem beschäftigt und auf den mich einige Seiten von de Vogüé [35] und Bacht [36] erneut aufmerksam gemacht haben.

Praeceptum 1 spricht vom Neuling (rudis), den der Pförtner von der Klosterpforte einführt und dem

[29] Veilleux, » Pachomian Koinonia 2... «, 12 f.

[30] A. de Vogüé, » Les pièces latines du dossier pachômien «, 47–56; vgl. auch ders. » Saint Pachôme et son œuvre d'après plusieurs études récentes «, *Revue d'Histoire Ecclésiastique* 69 (1974), 425–453, hier 442–445.

[31] De Vogüé, » Les pièces latines... «, 52 f.

[32] Ebd., 31 f.

[33] Pl. Deseille, » L'esprit du monachisme Pachômien, suivi de la traduction française des Pachomiana Latina par les moines de Solesmes «, *Spiritualité Orientale* 2 (Bégrolles-en-Mauges ²1980) Vf., XXXIX f. R. De Coster, in: » Regels van de heilige Pachomius. Het boek van Orsiesius «, *Monastieke cahiers* 23 (Bonheiden 1983), 9–11, nennt die entsprechenden Studien. Vgl. auch die polnische Übersetzung des Hieronymustextes, in: » Starożytne reguły zakonne «. Przekład zbiorowy. Wybór, wstępy, opracowanie: ks. Marek Starowieyski; Opracowanie redakcyjne: ks. Emil Stanula, *Pisma starochrześcijańskie pisarzy* 26 (Warszawa 1980); s. K.S. Frank, *Theologische Revue* 78 (1982), 122.

[34] H. Bacht, » Das Vermächtnis des Ursprungs... «, 45–47, bes. 45. Im einzelnen übt er sehr wohl Kritik an van Molle, vgl. 240,– Anm. 33 u. 244, Anm. 78.

[35] De Vogüé, » Les pièces latines... «, 58–61.

[36] Bacht, » Das Vermächtnis des Ursprungs... «, im Kommentar zu den im folgenden genannten Stellen.

er einem vorläufigen Platz in der Versammlung der Brüder zuweist, bis ihm der Oikiakos den endgültigen gibt [37]. Es fällt auf, daß diese Bestimmung in beiden Versionen der *Excerpta graeca* fehlt, wohl aber findet sich die griechische Entsprechung zum Praeceptum 49, das sich mit 1 berührt, aber sehr viel ausführlicher ist. In 49 wird bestimmt: » Wenn einer zur Klosterpforte kommt mit dem Willen, der Welt zu entsagen und sich der Zahl der Brüder anzuschließen, so soll er nicht die Freiheit haben einzutreten, sondern er soll zuerst dem Vater des Klosters gemeldet werden und einige Tage draußen vor der Pforte bleiben, und man soll ihn das Harrengebet lehren und Psalmen, soviel er lernen kann, und er soll sich gewissenhaft ausweisen, ob er nicht etwas Böses begangen und für eine Zeit von Angst erschüttert davongelaufen ist, oder ob er unter irgendjemandes Gewalt steht, und ob er seinen Eltern entsagen und seinen eigenen Besitz verachten kann. Wenn sie ihn zu alldem geeignet ansehen, dann sol man ihn auch in den übrigen Klostervorschriften unterrichten, was er tun und wem er dienen muß, sei es in der Collecta aller Brüder, sei es im Haus, dem er zuzuweisen ist, sei es in der Tischordnung, damit er 〉 wohlunterrichtet und zu jedem guten Werk gerüstet 〈 (2 Tim 3,1) den Brüdern beigesellt werde. Dann sollen sie ihm die weltliche Kleider ausziehen und ihm das Gewand der Mönche anlegen, und er soll dem Pförtner übergeben werden, damit dieser ihn zu Zeit des Gebetes vor alle Brüder führe. Und er soll sich an den Ort setzen, der ihm zugewiesen wird. Die Kleider aber, die er bei sich hatte, sollen diejenigen, die dafür zuständig sind, nehmen und in die Aufbewahrungskammer bringen, und sie sollen dort unter der Verfügung des Klostervorstehers bleiben « [38].

Es ist nun zu einfach gedacht, die knappere Bestimmung müsse stets die ältere sein und die ausführlichere die jüngere. Doch muß man in diesem Fall den Grund dafür suchen, daß Praeceptum 1 im Griechischen fehlt, Praeceptum 49 aber in beiden Versionen in jeweils anderer Gestalt vorliegt [39]. Die griechischen Excerpta sind sicher für ein entwickeltes Klosterwesen redigiert worden. In beiden griechischen Versionen ist an dieser Stelle keine Rede vom Pförtner. Das läßt vermuten, daß man mit Praeceptum 1 nichts anfangen konnte. Für einen Pachomianer, der sowohl 1 als auch 49 kennt, widersprechen sich die beiden Abschnitte nicht. Wenn man jedoch 1 ohne 49 für sich interpretiert, muß man zu der Auffassung gelangen, daß der Neuling ohne besondere Zeit eines Postulats ins Kloster geführt wird. Der Pförtner ist zuständig für das Hineingeleiten, der Hausobere für die endgültige Praezedens. Einen Reflex dieser Praxis enthält 49, erweitert um neue Bestimmungen. Dabei ist der Wechsel von *ianitor* in Praeceptum 1 zu *ostiarius* in Praeceptum 49 nicht von Belang, weil es sich hierbei sicher um einen Ausdruck der Variationsfreude des Übersetzers handelt [40].

Praeceptum 1 bildet den Anfang einer in 8a abgeschlossenen Einheit, die de Vogüé » le petit directoire du postulant « genannt hat [41]. Die Wendung: » Haec sunt praecepta uitalia nobis a maioribus tradita « ist nicht Überschrift zum Folgenden, sondern faßt, wie es das Verständnis des Griechen nahelegt [42], das vorher Gesagte zusammen. Dieser Satz wird so kaum von Pachomius stammen. Nun enthalten sie sog. » Règlements « des Horsiese im Kontext einer Ermahnung zum rechten Beten einen deutlichen Bezug zumindest zu Praecepta 3 und 7, ohne das ausdrücklich zu sagen [43]. Man könnte meinen, wie de Vogüé im Anschluß an Veilleux erwägt [44], daß die Ermahnungen, die Horsiese in den » Règlements « an alle Mönche richtet, ihm dazu gedient zu haben, in einer verdichteten Form dieses schon erwähnte kleine Direktorium des Postulanten zu redigieren. Hierzu ist zu sagen, daß die Autorschaft des Horsiese für die sog. » Règlements « erschlossen und nicht sicher ist, sie ist also nicht überliefert. Erst Lefort hat diesen sicher pachomianischen Text, der zuvor Schenute

[37] Boon, 13.

[38] Ebd., 25 f.; vgl. H. Bacht, » Das Vermächtnis des Ursprungs... «, 92 f.

[39] Boon, 174 f.

[40] Vgl. A. de Vogüé, » Les noms de la porte et du portier dans la règle de Pachôme «, *Studia Monastica* 17 (1975), 233–235.

[41] De Vogüé, » Les pièces latines... «, 48.

[42] 170, Z. 19: ταῦτα γάρ... Vgl. de Vogüé, » Les pièces latines... «, 36.

[43] Lefort, CSCO 159, 84, Z. 15 u. 85, Z. 5 f. Übersetzung: CSCO 160, 83, Z. 24 f. u. 84, Z. 13 f.

[44] De Vogüé, » Les pièces latines... «, 48.

zugeschrieben wurde, Horsiese zugewiesen [45]. Da der Verfasser nicht so eindeutig feststeht, kann man nicht vom Lieber Orsiesii aus argumentieren und sagen, daß Horsiese sich wie im Liber so auch in den » Règlements « *expressis verbis* auf Pachomius berufen hätte, wenn ihm Praecepta 1–7 als Text des Gründers vorgelegen hätte. Vielmehr erscheint es mir wahrscheinlich, daß der Verfasser der » Règlements « die schon bekannten und geltenden Regeln moralisierend einschärfen will. Es wird nicht etwas Neues eingeführt, sondern Altes wird den Mönchen neu ans Herz gelegt [46]. So beginnt der Gebetsabschnitt in folgender Weise [47]:

ⲈⲦⲂⲈⲠⲀⲒ ⲘⲀⲢⲚ̄ⳈⲀⲢⲈⳈ ⲈⲢⲞⲚ ⳈⲚ̄ⳈⲰⲂ ⲚⲒⲘ ⲀⲨⲰ
Ⲛ̄ⲦⲚ̄ⲠⲢⲞⲤⲈⲬⲈ ⳈⲚ̄ⲞⲨⲘⲚ̄ⲦⲀⲔⲢⲒⲂⲎⲤ ⲈⲚ̄ⲔⲀⲚⲰⲚ
Ⲙ̄ⲠⲈⲰ̄ⲗⲎⲗ...

(deswegen hüten wir uns in jeder Sache und beachten wir mit Sorgfalt die Regeln des Gebets!). In dieser Weise kann man aber doch von den Kanones des Gebets nur reden, wenn sie bereits existieren. Im Folgenden werden diese Regeln dann entfaltet. Es spricht also sehr viel dafür, daß Praecepta 1–7 ein altes Stück ist, dem später Praeceptum 8a angehängt worden ist [48]. Es kann gut dem Neuling in die Hand gegeben worden sein, oder es diente der Unterrichtung derer, die ihn einzuführen hatten. Später hat man dann ein eigenes Postulat von mehreren Tagen an der Pforte eingerichtet. Diese Bestimmungen stehen am Anfang eines Teiles, der vor allem von der Pforte handelt: Praecepta 49–57. Die darin enthaltenen Regeln über Außenkontakte leiten über zum Abschnitt, der die Arbeit außerhalb des Klosters regelt (Praecepta 58–66).
Die 3. Katechese des Theodor handelt von dem Fall, daß jemand ins Kloster eintreten will, der schon einen Bruder dort hat [49]. Dieser soll sich einen Monat an der Pforte aufhalten und sein Bruder soll ihn dort nur einmal in der Woche besuchen. Die Weisungen betreffen das Verhalten des Mönches gegenüber dem Postulanten, der sein Bruder ist. Das einmonatige Postulat dürfte kein Spezifikum für diesen Fall, sondern zur Zeit des Theodor allgemeine Praxis gewesen sein. Das würde zeigen, wie man zu dieser Zeit die Wendung Praeceptum 49: » et manebit paucis diebus foris « verstanden hat. Man hat den Regeltext also nicht geändert und präzisiert.
Praeceptum 139 betrifft nicht, wie Bacht schön gezeigt hat, die Zeit des Neulings an der Pforte, sondern die Zeit nach der Einkleidung, wenn dieser schon ins Kloster eingetreten ist [50]. Er soll in dem unterwiesen werden, was er zu beobachten hat, und er soll Teile der hl. Schrift auswendig lernen und, wenn er nicht lesen kann, Unterricht bekommen [51]. Daran schließt sich die allgemeine Bestimmung Praeceptum 140 an, daß es grundsätzlich niemanden im Kloster geben soll, der nicht lesen lernt und etwas aus der Schrift auswendig weiß [52]. Vorausgeht die Aufforderung in Praeceptum 138, das in der Katechese Gehörte miteinander zu wiederholen und durchzugehen [53]. Das Gemeinsame der drei Abschnitte ist also das Lernen. Im Vergleich zu den zuvor genannten Themenkomplexen Pforte und Arbeit außerhalb des Klosters ist diese Untergruppe klein. Der Eindruck entsteht, daß in diesem Teil der Praecepta verschiedene Dinge wie unter dem Stichwort Verschiedenes zusammengestellt sind. Die hier besprochenen Stücke sind zu kleine Basis, als daß man darauf eine Hypothese bauen könnte. Zudem müßten die anderen Stellen zum Thema Pforte hinzugezogen werden [54]. Doch läßt sich immerhin begründeterweise vermuten, daß es eine Entwicklung von Praeceptum 1 nach Praeceptum 49 gegeben hat. Wahrscheinlich hat man verschiedene Sammlungen zum Komplex der heute vorliegenden Praecepta zusammengearbeitet.

---

[45] Vgl. Veilleux, » Pachomian Koiononia 2... «, 11 f.

[46] De Vogüé hält auch eine solche Deutung für möglich; » Les pièces latines... «, 48 f.

[47] Lefort, CSCO 159, 83, Z. 27 f.

[48] Zum Ausdruck praecepta uitalia, der auch schon bei Pachomius begegnet; s. de Vogüé, » Les pièces latines... «, 36.

[49] CSCO 159, 47 f. Übersetzung: CSCO 160, 47 f.

[50] Das Vermächtnis des Ursprungs 2, 220 f. Anm. 608 stimmt allerdings nicht. Zu Praeceptum 49 haben wir natürlich griechische Parallelen (174 f. Boon).

[51] Boon, 49 f.

[52] Ebd., 50.

[53] Ebd., 49.

[54] Vgl. auch D. Gorce, » Die Gastfreundlichkeit der altchristlichen Einsiedler und Mönche «, *Jahrbuch für Antike Christentum* 15 (1972), 66–91, bes. 75 f.

COPTIC STUDIES

Walter Beltz

Zur Morphologie koptischer Zaubertexte

Eine Morphologie koptischer Zaubertexte ist noch ein Desiderat der Koptologie. Besonders seit Erscheinen der Untersuchungen von Biedenkopf-Ziehner [1] zum kop. Briefformular wird das Fehlen einer für die Gattung der koptischen Zaubertexte entsprechenden Untersuchung sinnfällig.

Kropps epochales opus [2] hatte seinerzeit die Aufgabe zu erfüllen eine Systematik der koptischen Zaubertexte zu formulieren. Sie liefert die Grundlage für Arbeiten an koptischen Zaubertexten noch heute. Seither erfolgte Publikationen koptischer Zaubertexte [3] begnügen sich mit der philologischen und religionsgeschichtlichen Kommentierung der Texte, wie sie sich auch in anderen Editionen finden [4].

Im Rahmen eines Kongreßbeitrages kann nur der Versuch unternommen werden, neben der Postulierung einer Morphologie koptischer Zaubertexte und ihrer Begründung, eine Versuchsskizze zu entwerfen und zur Diskussion zu stellen.

Zur Begründung ist zunächst anzuführen, daß bei jeder Inventarisierung koptischer Handschriften auch die Gattung des Textes zu bestimmen ist. Es gibt nun zahllose Beispiele, nicht nur in der Berliner Sammlung [5], wo der Gattungscharakter nicht eindeutig festzustellen ist, weil der fragmentarische Charakter eines Stückes mehrere Deutungen zuläßt. Wenn z.B. ein biblischer Text, sofern nicht durch Schriftform und — duktus eindeutig eine Zuschreibung zu einer Handschrift biblischer Texte möglich ist, bislang als Schüler- oder Schreibübung deklariert wurde, so kann doch auch ein solches Fragment ein Amulett gewesen sein, und würde dann der Gattung der Zaubertexte zuzuweissen sein. Denn es gibt zahlreiche Beispiele für den Gebrauch von Bibelzitaten als Amulett [6]. Zum anderen sind auch Briefe frommer Väter als Reliquien mit apotropäischer Wirkung verwendet worden. Solche Amulette gehören dann zumindest sekundär zur Gattung magischer Texte, auch wenn sie primär zur Briefliteratur zu zählen sind [7].

Drittens ist die klassische Trennung zwischen weißer und schwarzer Magie in der koptischen magischen Literatur nicht ohne Schwierigkeiten vorzunehmen, weshalb man sie besser nicht vornimmt [8]. Schwarze Magie wurde und wird immer noch verstanden als Teil der Subkultur einer Epoche, während weiße Magie immer noch den Bereich des Kultisch-Rituellen umfaßt, also etwa die kirchliche Segens- und Reliquienpraxis. Die Schwierigkeiten sind größer als bei lateinischen

---

[1] A. Biedenkopf-Ziehner, » Untersuchungen zum koptischen Briefformular, unter Berücksichtigung ägyptischer und griechischer Parallelen «, in: *Kopt. Studien*, Bd. 1, Würzburg 1983.

[2] A. M. Kropp, *Ausgewählte koptische Zaubertexte*, Bd. I–II, Brüssel 1931, Bd. III, Brüssel 1930.

[3] V. Stegemann, *Die koptischen Zaubertexte der Sammlung Papyrus Erzherzog Rainer in Wien, Sitzungsberichte der Heidelberger Akademie der Wissenschaften*, phil.-hist. Klasse, 1. Abh. Jahrg. 1933/34;' W. Brunsch, » Ein koptischer Bindezauber «, *Enchoria* VIII, 1(1978), 151 – 157.

[4] Vgl. etwa D. Wildung, Jahresgabe 1984, *Freundeskreis der Ägypt*, Sammlung München, E.V. 1984, Sonderdruck des Münchener Jahrbuches der bildenden Kunst 1983, Prestel-Verlag München, S. 6791–6793. Oder: W. Brashear, ZPE 50 (1983), 106–110 und M. Marcowich, ebenda 155; G. M. Brown, ZPE 52 (1983), 60.

[5] Vgl. W. Beltz, » Katalog der koptischen Handschriften der Papyrus-Sammlung der Staatlichen Museen zu Berlin «, APF 27 (1980), 198.

[6] G. Viaud, *Les 151 Psaumes de David dans la magie copte*, Paris 1977; ders., *Magie et coutumes populaires chez les Coptes d'Égypte*, Paris 1979.

[7] Ein solcher Fall liegt z.B. vor in Berlin, P. 20 982, der von mir mit anderen in APF 31, 1985, ediert wird.

[8] Vgl. dagegen T. Orlandi, » Rassegna di Studi Copti N. 7 «, *Vetera Christianorum* (1981), 215.

und griechischen Texten, weil die nach 540 in Ägypten feststellbare Aufspaltung der koptischen Kirche in die einzelnen Diözesen, Gemeinden und Klöster auch Folgen für den Glaubensstand der jeweiligen Gemeinschaft hatte[9]. Nicht zuletzt ist der Textbestand der koptischen Zaubertexte ein gewichtiges Argument. Wie keine andere koptische Literaturgattung bieten koptische Zaubertexte orthographische und grammatische Schwierigkeiten, denn die Autoren solcher Texte und ihre Schreiber gehörten offensichtlich nicht zu den Gebildeten ihrer Gesellschaft.

Eine Morphologie koptischer Zaubertexte muß davon ausgehen, daß das Modell für einen koptischen Zaubertexte auch die Modellstruktur zeitlich vergleichbarer Zaubertexte gewesen ist. Ein solches Grundmodell ist dreigliedrig:

A — Anrufung,
B — Beschwörung,
C — Beteuerung.

Das Grundmodell ist variabel, insofern die Glieder vertauschbar in ihrer Reihenfolge sein können. Es können auch Glieder fehlen. Häufig fehlt die Beteuerung. Das kann objektiv damit zusammenhängen, daß naturgemäß die Enden für jede Zerstörung eines Textes anfälliger sind als Mitte oder Anfang. Dabei spielt die Natur des Schriftträgers, organisch wie bei Holz, Pergament, Papyrus oder Papier, unorganisch wie bei Stein oder Blei, kaum eine Rolle. Wir gehen aber davon aus, daß zu einem vollständigen koptischen magischen Text die drei Elemente gehören. Eine Ausnahme bilden die Amulette und die Reliquien mit Schriftelementen.

Aufgabe einer Morphologie koptischer Zaubertexte ist es, das Spezifische dieser drei Elemente, die Akzidenzien, zu fixieren und zu prüfen, ob und wann ein Gestaltwandel erfolgt ist und welche Ursachen diesem zugrunde liegen. Dabei entfällt für die Zaubertexte als Gliederungselement, was bei dem Briefformular möglich war, nämlich die Gliederung nach bestimmten Verben. Diese fehlen häufig. Und es drängt sich ohnehin der Verdacht auf, daß ihr Vorkommen dafür spricht, daß diese

Texte Lehrcharakter haben. Das betrifft vor allem die Verben αιτι μ παρακαλι.

Spezifica sind also Appositionen und Attribute innerhalb der drei Grundelemente, wodurch sich die koptischen von griechischen und lateinischen unterscheiden, also christianisierte und christliche ägyptische Elemente, die zwar auch in griechischen Zaubertexten[10] auftauchen können, aber zusammen mit dem koptischen Sprachbestand den unverwechselbaren Charakter der koptischen Zaubertexte bilden. Diese bestimmen vor allem Inhalt und Form der Glieder A und C. Das Mittelglied B, die eigentliche Beschwörung, ist wesentlich nicht von gleichzeitigen anderssprachigen Zaubertexten zu unterscheiden, weil die Inhalte der Beschwörungen allgemeinen Typs sind. Es gibt apo- und epipompische Iatromantik, Binde- und Lösezauber, Amulette oder Reliquien gegen allgemeinmenschlichen Gefährnisse.

Dabei ist folgendes festzustellen:

1. In der Epiklese haben koptische Zaubertexte die Namen von ägyptischen Göttern, gnostischen Gottheiten, biblischen Gestalten, christlichen Heiligen und Märtyrern und in ganz vereinzelten Fällen auch Personen der Trinität[11].

2. Dem entspricht, daß die magischen Legenden denselben religionsgeschichtlichen Traditionen entspringen, denen die Namen in Anrufung und Beteuerung entlehnt sind. Es werden also altägyptische Mythen, gnostische, biblische und apokryphe Mythen verwendet[12]. Diese magischen Legenden können in allen drei Gliedern des Grundgerüsts auftauchen, gesondert oder vermischt. Allerdings kommen sie in den Verfluchungs- oder Bekräftigungsformeln unter C, der Beteuerung, nur selten vor[13].

3. Die dekorativen Elemente sind dem Gestaltungswandel der koptischen Kunst unterworfen und ihrerseits ungeeignet, etwas zur Morphologie koptischer Zaubertexte beizutragen, zumal sie in keinem sachlichen Zusammenhang mit den jeweiligen magischen Texten stehen. Um das Gesagte zu demonstrieren, möchte ich aus den Berliner magischen koptischen Texten einige Beispiele anführen,

---

[9] B. Spuler, » Die koptische Kirche «, HdO I/8, 2. Abschnitt, Leiden (1961), 284–285.

[10] Dazu sind bei Preisendanz beliebige Beispiele zu finden.

[11] Dazu siehe die weiter unten im Texte aufgeführten Beispiele aus der Berliner Sammlung.

[12] Ägypt. Mythen und Legenden enthalten P. 5565 u. P. 8314, Gnostika enthalten P. 5531, P. 5735, P. 8320, P. 8321, P. 8324, P. 15990, P. 9074, P. 20911. Biblische Motive enthalten P. 5527, P. 8318, P. 8326, P. 8328, P. 10587, P. 11330, P. 15870. Apokryphe Motive finden sich in P. 8105, P. 8314, P. 8326, P. 8328, P. 8322, P. 8503, P. 5535, P. 5537.

[13] Hier überwiegen die Namenreihen und die Vokalreihen, die *Ephesia Grammata*. Es versteht sich von selbst, daß mit Hilfe von Paläographie, Literaturwissenschaft und Religionsgeschichte die einzelnen Elemente bestimmt werden müssen.

die zeigen können, welche Formen und Elemente in koptischen Zaubertexten enthalten sind[14]. Da alle diese Texte 1985 ediert vorliegen werden, erübrigt es sich, an dieser Stelle den Text zu zitieren.

Adressaten magischer Texte aus dem altägyptischen Pantheon enthalten die Nr. P. 3289, 5565, 8314.

An gnostische Götterwesen adressiert sind die Texte Nr. 5527, 5735, 8320, 8321, 8325, 8503, 9074, 1057, 15990.

Biblische Adressaten haben P. 8105, 5531, 11350, 15878, 11918, 20911.

An christliche Heilige werden die Texte P. 8317, 8322, 8324, 8330, 8332 und 5535 gerichtet, während an Personen der Trinität P. 5744, 8314, 8318, 8327, 5537, 5684, 8828, 15931, 20910 gerichtet sind.

Die für magische Texte charakteristische Reihung der Namen[15] ist also als Indiz zu sehen, daß bei ähnlichen Vorkommen, vor allem, wenn der übrige Text schwer oder kaum lesbar ist, mit relativer Sicherheit auf einen magischen Text geschlossen werden kann. Die philologische und paläographische Untersuchung dieser Texte wirft allerdings manche interessante Frage auf. Denn es sind nicht die ältesten Texte, die sich auf altägyptische Götter besinnen, und die gnostischen Dämonennamen tauchen auf Stücken aus dem 8. Jahrhundert auf. Lediglich die topographische Untersuchung läßt erkennen, daß die rein christlichen Texte vor allem aus Unterägypten kommen, während die oberägyptischen Texte mehr pagane Einflüsse bewahrt haben. So liegt in P. 8314 ein Text vor, dessen Legende nur durch ein vorgesetztes » Jesus « den anschließend erwähnten Horus christianisiert, den ägyptischen Mythos aber unverändert gelassen hat. Der aus dem Fajum stammende P. 5527, der in das 8. Jahrhundert zu datieren ist, bezeichnet Maria » als Mutter des vollkommenen Menschen Jesus « und macht somit deutlich, daß in der Magie des Fajum der Protest gegen das Nicänum noch im 8. Jahrhundert erhoben wird.

Inhaltlich liegt insofern ein Gestaltwandel vor, als nicht nur bei den Berliner Stücken die iatromantischen Texte, sowohl des apowie des epipom-

pischen Typs langsam zurückgehen, während die Zahl der Amulette zunimmt. Das Amulett als ubiquitär wirkendes Pharmakon ersetzt offensichtlich die konkreten iatromantischen Texte. Das hängt vielreicht mit dem Wiederaufleben der kopt. medizinischen Literatur seit dem 7. Jahrhundert zusammen. Die Binde- und Lösezaubertexte, die klassische Form der Magie, bleiben in der Relation konstant, vermutlich weil die Sozialstruktur der ägyptischen Gesellschaft bis zur wollständigen Islamisierung Ägyptens relativ unverändert geblieben ist.

Ein Vergleich des Umfanges der einzelnen Texte ergibt, daß nicht die Gattung maßgeblich gewesen ist, sondern andere Kriterien für Umfang und Länge ausschlaggebend gewesen sein müssen. Sie sind in der Situation der Rezipienten zu suchen. Ein vermögender Rezipient erwarb vermutlich weitläufig formulierte und qualitätsvollere Texte oder Amulette aus Metall, Pergament und Papyrus, während der minderbemittelte sich mit kürzerem Text und auch schlechterer Qualität begnügte, auf Ostraka, Holz oder Papier geschrieben.

Für die Bestimmung als magischer Text weniger wichtig ist auch die Beobachtung, daß ägyptische Legenden und Mythen in den koptischen Zaubertexten relativ selten sind, während Anleihen bei gnostischen Quellen zahlreicher nachzuweisen sind. Dabei fällt auf, daß im 8. Jahrhundert in Oberägypten noch ägyptische Mythen verwendet werden, nachdem schon jarhhundertelang die christlichen Motive vorherrschten. Da die koptische Kirche auch die apokryphe Literatur im liturgischen Gebrauch hatte, empfiehlt es sich, keine Trennung zwischen Bibel und Apokryphen vorzunehmen. Die biblischen Anspielungen sind keine Zitate, abgesehen von einigen Amuletten, sondern freie Assoziationen. Das gilt auch von den apokryphen Themen.

Die Gattung der magischen Texte, also Binde- oder Lösezauber oder iatromantischer Text, sind ohne Bedeutung für die Auswahl der magischen Legenden gewesen. Magische Legenden für sich allein bieten deshald keinen Anhaltspunkt für die jeweilige Gattung des magischen Textes. Darin gleichen die koptischen den griechischen und lateinischen Quellen.

---

[14] Die koptische Zauberpergamente der Berliner Sammlung erschienen APF 30 (1984), 83–104. Die Zauberpapyri erschienen APF 29 (1983), 59–86. Die Ostraka, die zuerst in den *Halleschen Beiträgen zur Orientwissenschaft* 2, Halle 1980, 59–75, erschienen waren, werden mit den übrigen Texten in APF 31 (1985) ediert. Die Register für alle Teilpublikationen werden in derselben Zeitschrift 1986 erscheinen.

[15] Magische Vokalreihen sind keine Besonderheit koptischer Zaubertexte. Sie kommen in koptischen gnostischen Texten wie in ägypt. magischen oder auch in griechischen magischen Texten vor.

COPTIC STUDIES

Dominique Bénazeth

Tôd : historique du site et des fouilles

Le Musée du Louvre a réouvert le chantier de Tôd en 1979. Les fouilles, qui se poursuivent, ont principalement mis au jour des vestiges d'époque copte. Certains objets figurent maintenant parmi les collections du Musée du Louvre. Il convenait de vous faire part de ces récentes découvertes (exposé de Mme Rutschowscaya). J'essaierai tout d'abord de retracer l'histoire du site, particulièrement à l'époque copte, à la lumière des premières prospections et des fouilles antérieures.

Typonyme

» Tod « ou Taoud est le nom arabe. Les Romains l'appelaient » Tuphium « et les Égyptiens de l'époque ptolémaique : » Djerty «.

Localisation

Localité de Haute-Égypte, Tôd est situé sur la rive droite, à 25 km au sud de Louxor. A l'époque pharaonique, c'était l'un des quatre grands sanctuaires de Montou qui protégeaient Thèbes, les trois autres étant Karnak-Nord, Médamoud et Ermant.

Disposition du site: Le village actuel (environ 15.000 habitants) recouvre et déborde le kôm antique. Il est situé à la limite des terres cultivables. Un petit quartier copte se groupe autour d'un ancien deir, qui sert maintenant d'église. La zone désertique cache des nécropoles de toutes époques, aussi bien païennes que chrétiennes ou musulmanes.

La maison de fouilles, construite en 1933, offre toute commodité aux archéologues (logement, labo photo, salles de travail pour les architectes, topographes et fouilleurs).

Le chantier: Le monument principal est un temple pharaonique dédié à Montou, dont il reste le pronaos ptolémaïque. A l'arrière, une esplanade correspond au sanctuaire, plus ancien, démoli par les Coptes. C'est là qu'ils édifièrent une église. A l'avant s'étalent les vestiges d'un pylone démoli, un dromos et un quai-embarcadère. Du côté est se trouvent un lac sacré avec kiosque d'époque romaine et une chapelle-reposoir de la barque du Nouvel-Empire. Ces éléments ont été dégagés du kôm et le chantier forme une cuvette au milieu du village. Sur le côteau ouest se trouve la mosquée.

Histoire du site

Époque pharaonique

Le plus ancien vestige est un pilier de granit portant le nom d'Ouserkaf, pharaon de la Ve dynastie. Un temple de Montou, existant au moins à la XIe dynastie, fut reconstruit en calcaire et granit par Sésostris I (Moyen-Empire). C'est dans ses fondations que fut trouvé le célèbre Trésor de Tôd, en 1936. Il se compose d'objets étrangers (coupes d'argent, lingots, sceaux-cylindres, lapis-lazuli) contenus dans quatre coffres de bronze. Il fut partagé entre les Musées du Caire et du Louvre. Le Nouvel-Empire fut one période de constructions dont seule subsiste une chapelle-reposoir édifiée par Touthmosis III et des blocs réutilisés dans les constructions ultérieures. A signaler des blocs remployés dans le deir et quelques talatats amarniennes trouvées en fouilles. De cette époque datent aussi quelques tombes.

Époque gréco-romaine

Les Grecs remodelèrent le téménos en adjoignant à l'ancien temple un grand pronaos en grès, le dromos et la tribune du quai, qui devait donner sur un canal. Ils reconstruisirent les enceintes.

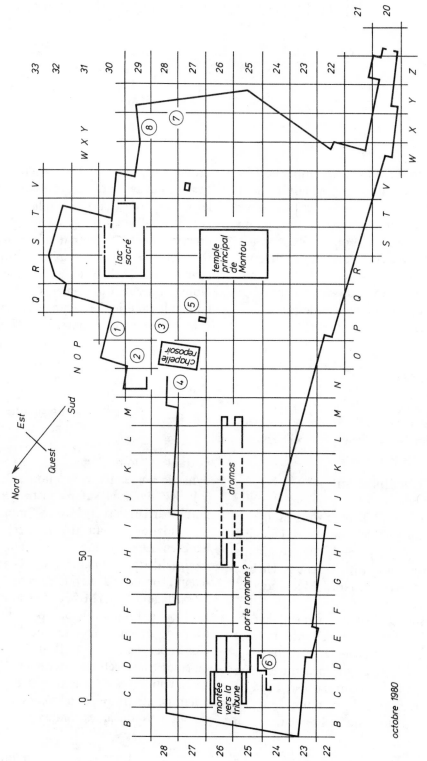

Nord
Est
Quest
Sud

lac
sacré

temple
principal
de
Montou

chapelle
reposoir

dromos

porte romaine ?

montée
vers la
tribune

0   50

octobre 1980

1. Topographie du chantier

2. Conque (fouilles F. Bisson de la Roque). Actuellement au Louvre (E 14758) (phot. Chuzevine)

3. Relief (fouilles F. Bisson de la Roque). Actuellement au Louvre (E 14759) (phot. Chuzevine)

4. Élément de frise (fouilles F. Bisson de la Roque). Actuellement au Louvre (E 14749)

Les Romains poursuivirent ces travaux en achevant la décoration du temple (Antonin le Pieux) et en creusant le lac sacré, près duquel ils édifièrent un petit kiosque. Les premiers vestiges urbains décelés à Tôd datent de cette époque : ce sont des thermes, dont une partie seulement put être dégagée, à cause de la limite de la concession. Construits en briques cuites, dalles de grès, de granit ou de gypse, ils présentent des bassins, des piscines et des conduites en poterie.

Les fondations d'une constructions, en briques cuites bien appareillées, furent récemment dégagées à l'arrière du reposoir de Touthmosis III. Faisait-elle partie du téménos ou était-ce une maison d'habitation qui le jouxtait ?

Des inscriptions en latin indiquent qu'aux IIe et IIIe siècles de notre ère, Tôd possédait une garnison de soldats romains. Enfin des tombes romaines, à superstructure de briques crues, sont encore visibles dans le désert.

Époque chrétienne

La christianisation de l'Égypte n'entraîna pas l'abandon du site de Tôd, qui devint au contraire un important centre religieux, en face de l'évêché d'Ermant. Le synaxaire nous apprend qu'il possédait un monastère et une stèle funéraire, comme de nombreux ostraca, mentionnent des religieux vivant à Tôd. Ce couvent n'a pas été retrouvé, mais on peut l'imaginer à l'emplacement du deir actuel, qui semble remonter au Moyen Age.

Les Coptes transformèrent radicalement le téménos, à l'histoire déjà millénaire. D'après l'étude de F. Bisson de la Roque, il y aurait eu plusieurs étapes d'occupation.

Dès l'abandon des cultes païens, l'enceinte fut démontée, ainsi que la partie ancienne du temple, en calcaire. Certains blocs furent réutilisés pour la décoration d'une église (colonnettes, chapiteaux,

5. Chapiteau (fouilles F. Bisson de la Roque). Actuellement au Luovre (E 14757)

frises, conques). Les autres furent probablement envoyés dans les fours à chaux. Le pronaos de grès fut occupé, comme en témoigne le martelage de certaines figures païennes et le crépi recouvrant d'autres parois. Les bains romains furent transformés en habitations. Les Coptes commencèrent à s'installer dans l'ancienne aire sacrée, où l'on a retrouvé en plusieurs endroits des dallages, des vestiges de murs, des fours et des puits. Plus tard (probablement vers le VIIIᵉ siècle), une église fut édifiée à l'emplacement de l'ancien sanctuaire, tandis que le pronaos servait peut-être d'édifice public, devant lequel s'ouvrait une vaste esplanade dallée.

L'église ne semble pas avoir été achevée. Son plan était de type basilical, à abside rentrante. La séparation des nefs n'existe plus, mais correspond sans doute aux fondations d'une cloison destinée à isoler les femmes. Des banquettes de grès bordaient les murs. Le chœur, surélevé, était orné d'un socle en gypse supportant six colonnettes ornementales. De petites pièces de part et d'autre correspondaient au prothésis et au diaconicon. L'église fut détruite probablement au XIᵉ siècle. Les habitations envahirent progressivement l'esplanade et le pronaos. Lors de la découverte du site, il ne dépassait des maisons que quelques sommets de murs ptolémaïques.

Histoire des fouilles

Dès 1766, Tôd fut identifiée avec la Tuphium de géographe Ptolémée, par Bourguignon d'Anville. Lors de la campagne d'Égypte, les savants s'y arrêtèrent et découvrirent les affleurements ptolémaïques au milieu des maisons. Ils visitèrent aussi la mosquée, où ils reconnurent que les colonnes étaient antiques, empruntées aux Coptes, qui les avaient retaillées dans des obélisques ou piliers présentant encore quelques hiéroglyphes. En 1829, Champollion identifia les dieux vénérés dans l'ancien temple.

G. Maspéro prospecta le site en 1881–83 [1]. Il mentionne dans son rapport une basilique chrétienne où il aurait trouvé une croix de bronze et une stèle coptes. De quoi voulait-il parler? L'église dégagée par F. Bisson de la Roque n'était pas visible à cette époque. La stèle fut déposée au Musée de Boulaq [2]. Maspéro explora aussi la nécropole. Il y trouva des cadavres bien conservés, enveloppés de vêtements colorés. Parmi ceux-ci se distinguait une robe de laine pourpre ≫ brodée ≪ — dit-il-de lin ou de soie, avec une calotte ronde décorée d'animaux fantastiques et d'une grande rosace représentant la Vierge entre deux saints accompagnés de leurs noms. Malheureusement aucune illustration n'accompagne cette description et les objets sont perdus.

En 1915, Legrain parvint à dresser le plan du pronaos et attira l'attention sur la nécessité d'exproprier des habitations pour commencer l'étude de ces vestiges.

Ce projet aboutit en 1933, lorsque le Musée du Louvre décida de financer des fouilles a Tôd. La direction en fut confiée à F. Bisson de la Roque. De 1934 a 1936, il dégagea les couches coptes avec l'église et découvrit le fameux trésor du Moyen--Empire. Son rapport de fouilles [3] est très précieux pour nous. Ne négligeant pas l'époque copte, il y publia entre autres, les structures des villages, la sculpture et quelques objets, et proposa une re-constitution historique. De 1937 à 1940 il élargit son chantier, trouvant le lac sacré et le dromos. La guerre interrompit les fouilles jusqu'en 1946; F. Bisson de la Roque était alors secondé par des pensionnaires de l'IFAO, parmi lesquels J. Vercoutter et P. Barguet, qui publièrent quelques rapports dans le BIFAO [4]. C'est en 1949 que Vercoutter fit une intéressante découverte: en pratiquant un sondage dans le kôm, près de la mosquée, mais en dehors de la concession, il trouva une église dont le dallage et les bases de colonnes étaient en place, les fûts et les chapiteaux gisant à côté, ainsi que des frises sculptées et quelques bois intacts. Il fut malheuresement contraint à tout réenterrer.

Ces fouilles s'arrêtèrent en 1950 pour ne recommencer qu'en 1980. Le Musée du Louvre en prit la décision en décembre 1978, et en confia la direction à Mme Desroches-Noblecourt. Après une mission de reconnaissance en 1979, les fouilles s'échelonnèrent au rythme de deux campagnes par an [5]. Mlle Letellier, conservateur au Département des Antiquités Égyptiennes, en est maintenant la responsable et s'apprête à conduire l'équipe de fouilleurs en octobre prochain.

Cet historique met en évidence certains problèmes qui se posent à nous: les fouilles n'ont pas eu lieu de manière suivie par une seule équipe et sur un même terrain. La concession a sans cesse été élargie grâce aux expropriations de maisons modernes, ce qui a entraîné une fouille par parcelles. Les rapports antérieurs sont partiels et aucune synthèse n'a pu être encore réalisée. Une autre difficulté, d'ordre géographique, se présente à nous: jusqu'à la mise en eaux du barrage d'Assouan, le site fut chaque année inondé; cela a occasionné des glissements de terrain, voire d'objets, et les vestiges de briques crues, régulièrement noyés, sont difficiles à déceler.

En dépit de ces difficultés, qu'aucun chantier archéologique n'ignore, le travail se poursuit, apportant toujours de nouvelles découvertes à inscrire dans le domaine copte.

---

[1] G. Maspero, ≫ Trois années de fouilles ≪, MMAF I, 181.

[2] A. Gaayet, ≫ Les monuments coptes du musée de Boulaq ≪, MMAF III, pl. XXII.

[3] F.B.R., Tôd (1934 à 1936), FIFAO XVII (1937).

[4] J. Vercoutter, ≫ Rapport succinct des fouilles: Tôd (1946–1949) ≪, BIFAO L (1952), 69–87; P. Barguet, ≫ Rapport préliminaire des fouilles 1950 ≪, BIFAO LI (1952), 80–110.

[5] Comptes rendus dans Orientalia 51 (1982), 85 et 457; C. Desroches-Noblecourt, ≫ Les fouilles de Tôd, égyptologie et mécénat ≪, La revue du Louvre (Juin 1980), 192–197; idem, ≫ Les nouvelles fouilles de Tôd ≪ BSFE 93 (1982), 5–20.

COPTIC STUDIES

Hans-Gebhard Bethge

Zu einigen literarischen, exegetischen und inhaltlichen Problemen der » Epistula Petri ad Philippum « (NHC VIII, 2)

Die ursprünglich in griechischer Sprache abgefaßte und auf das 2./3. Jahrhundert zu datierende, auch außerhalb der koptischen Texte von Nag Hammadi überlieferte Schrift » Der Brief des Petrus an Philippus « (EpPt) läßt als ein den neutestamentlichen Apokryphen zuzuordnendes Dokument ein Stück Wirkungsgeschichte von Teilen des Neuen Testaments sichtbar werden. EpPt gehört darüber hinaus in den größeren und äußerst komplexen Zusammenhang Neues Testament — frühes Christentum — Gnosis.

EpPt weist, vor allem in Bezug auf den Rahmen, gewisse Ähnlichkeiten mit solchen Texten auf, die von Begegnungen der Jünger mit dem auferstandenen Jesus Christus handeln, z.B. Freer-Logion in Mk 16, 14, Lk-Schluß/Anfang der Apg, Epistula Apostolorum und — mit teilweise bemerkenswerten inhaltlichen Parallelen — Fragen des Bartholomäus, sowie von den koptisch-gnostischen Texten SJC, EpJac, ferner im anfänglichem Rahmen von PistSoph. Die bemerkenswerteste Parallele sind jedoch die Petersburger Fragmente von Philippus-Akten, die — zusammen mit Bruchstücken des gleichen Werkes nach Borgianischen Handschriften — O. v. Lemm im Jahre 1890 veröffentlicht hat. Sie sind in mancher Hinsicht ein Schlüssel zum Verständnis einiger Probleme in EpPt.

Jesus erscheint dort den versammelten Aposteln auf dem Ölberg und erteilt ihnen den Missionsbefehl. Er fordert zur Aufteilung der Missionsgebiete nach dem Los unter die zwölf Apostel auf, gibt ihnen den Frieden und entweicht. Insoweit geht EpPt in sehr vielen Punkten parallel. Was in den Fragmenten dann aber weiter geschildert wird, gibt uns einen Hinweis darauf, was im vorliegenden Text von EpPt nur teilweise oder gar

nicht enthalten ist. Philippus wird durch das Los für Phrygien bestimmt. Er macht sich unter Begleitung des Petrus, den er — unter Berufung auf Jesus — dazu ausdrücklich auffordert, sogleich auf. Unterwegs erscheint ihnen Jesus, der ihnen Leiden, endlich aber Ruhe verheißt und wieder in den Himmel zurückkehrt. Daraufhin gehen Petrus und Philippus weiter » in der Kraft Christi «. Wenn auch in EpPt vieles anders ist, so gibt es doch bei diesen Partien in einzelnen Punkten deutliche Parallelen zum vorliegenden Text von EpPt. Dann aber folgen, ohne daß es dafür irgenwelche Entsprechungen in EpPt gibt, Taten der Apostel. So heilt Petrus einen Mann mit einem Wahrsagergeist, veranlaßt eine Säule, sich herabzusenken und wieder zu erheben, und die beiden Apostel gehen gegen die göttliche Verehrung eines Sperbers vor und bringen Menschen jener Stadt zum Glauben. Danach enden die Fragmente.

Diese Philippus-Akten bestätigen uns in unserer bereits früher geäußerten Vermutung, daß wir in EpPt nur einen Teil eines Werkes vor uns haben und zeigen, in welcher Richtung eine ursprünglich wohl vorhandene Fortsetzung denkbar erscheint. Wir vermuten nun allerdings zum einen, daß EpPt nicht einfach aus technischen Gründen so endet und zum anderen, daß der Schluß nicht als auf gleicher Ebene liegend anzusehen ist wie das Ende, z.B. von SJC oder EvMar oder gar des späteren Nachtrages von PistSoph. Die Fragmente der koptischen Philippus-Akten sind darüber hinaus bemerkenswert in Bezug auf die Rolle, die Petrus dabei spielt, allein als autoritativer Führer der Apostel, darin mit der Apg und anderen Zeugnissen der ur- und frühchristlichen Petrustradition übereinstimmend, aber auch zusammen mit

Philippus bei dessen gleichzeitiger Subordination. Sie zeigen schließlich, daß es höchst verschiedene Philippus-Akten gab, denn mit den bekannten ActPhil haben die genannten Fragmente und auch EpPt nichts zu tun.

Wenn nun EpPt in der uns vorliegenden Form bezüglich des Rahmens bei einem direkten Vergleich trotz aller Nähe zu den Fragmenten der koptischen Philippus-Akten doch auch beträchtliche Unterschiede aufweist, insbesondere hinsichtlich der Fortsetzung des Handlungsablaufes, so hängt dies damit zusammen, daß EpPt u.E. das Resultat eines mehrstufigen literarischen Prozesses ist, den wir uns — in Aufnahme und Fortführung unserer früheren Erwägungen — etwa so vorstellen können.

1. Stufe: Am Beginn stehen apokryphe Philippus — oder andere Apostel-Akten, ähnlich den erwähnten Fragmenten der koptischen Philippus-Akten. In ihnen spielen Mission und Verkündigung, sicher auch Taten, aber auch Widerstände und Bedrohung eine Rolle.

2. Stufe: Es kommt zu verschiedenen Einschaltungen.
a) Zum Zwecke einer ätiologischen Erklärung und gleichzeitigen Bewältigung einer aktuellen Bedrohungssituation wird eine längere Passage eingeschoben. Dies betrifft den überwiegenden Teil des Lehrgespräches p. 134, 18–137, 13 + 137, 13–138, 3, das in seinen mythologischen Passagen an einer bestimmten, nicht distinktiv sethianischen, Form des Sophia-Mythos orientiert ist. Dieser Einschub zeigt in seiner uns vorliegenden Form anfänglich kaum christliche Spuren, ist später aber in zunehmendem Maße von christlicher Tradition geprägt.
b) Einschaltung der einer christlich-gnostischen Apostelgeschichte entnommenen Partie p. 139, 9–140, 1, die die Passion Jesus Christi mit der Leidenssituation von Autor/Redaktor und Lesern in Verbindung bringt. Diese Apostelgeschichte trug möglicherweise den Namen des Petrus im Titel, muß deswegen aber nicht identisch mit dem Werk sein, von dem wir mit NHC VI, 1 oder BG 4 jeweils einen Teil vor uns haben.
c) . . . . Weitere mögliche Einschal-
d) . . . . tungen, die auf Grund der
e) . . . . Verkürzungen (3.Stufe) nicht
     mehr oder nicht mehr sicher
etc.   erkennbar vorhanden sind.

Ob diese Einschaltungen das Werk *eines* Autors sind und zeitlich auf der gleichen Ebene liegen oder in mehreren Schüben erfolgten, muß offen bleiben.

3. Stufe: Durch Kürzungen am Anfang und vor allem am Schluß sowie durch redaktionelle Überarbeitungen entsteht eine Art Epitome, die das Werk inhaltlich im Wesentlichen auf die Leidensthematik konzentriert. Ein von Petrus an Philippus gerichteter Brief, dessen Inhalt ein Geschehen voraussetzt, das in einem früheren Stadium des Werkes wohl enthalten war, kommt dabei an den Anfang. Wir können uns vorstellen, daß dies alles im Prinzip in einem Zuge erfolgte.

4. Stufe: Dieses Werk, das nun den Titel » Brief des Petrus an Philippus « hat, wird aus dem Griechischen ins Koptische übersetzt und verbreitet, u.a. durch Aufnahme in Nag-Hammadi-Codex VIII.

Was den zeitlichen Aspekt betrifft, so wird man für die Stufen 1–3 am ehesten an den Zeitraum von Ende des zweiten bis zur Mitte des dritten Jahrhunderts denken können und müssen. Es ist die Zeit einerseits der Entstehung vieler apokrypher Apostelgeschichten und andererseits größerer Christenverfolgungen. Bei einer wesentlich späteren Datierung des Prozesses würde der Zeitraum zwischen der dritten Stufe, der danach erfolgten Übersetzung ins Koptische und der Verbreitung der EpPt, bis hin zur Aufnahme auch in NHC VIII, zu knapp bemessen sein.

Auf Grund des Entstehungsprozesses ist EpPt in Bezug auf die Gattung ein insgesamt die Acta-Literatur repräsentierendes Dokument, ohne daß dabei formal wie inhaltlich ein einheitliches Werk vorliegt. Auf Grund des inhaltlich dominierenden Rahmens ist EpPt trotz der gnostischen Einschübe und der damit gegebenen inhaltlichen Akzente insgesamt nicht als ein genuin gnostisches Werk anzusehen. Die inhaltlichen Aussagen werden von unterschiedlichen bzw. heterogenen Traditionen bestimmt. EpPt ist dabei formal wie inhaltlich — und das ist längst erkannt — an Teilen neutestamentlicher Überlieferungen orientiert, vor allem an den Evangelien und der Apostelgeschichte, und steht gleichzeitig in der Tradition der apokryphen Apostelgeschichten des zweiten und dritten Jahrhunderts.

Unter der Voraussetzung, daß EpPt ein Text ist, der von seinen Adressaten und nicht nur von seinem Schöpfer verstanden werden konnte bzw.

mit dessen Inhalt sich die Leser auch identifizieren konnten, sind diese nicht nur wie andere Christen von der allgemeinchristlichen Tradition geprägt, sondern haben darüber hinaus Gedankengut der Gnosis gekannt und bis zu einem gewissen Grade, dabei aber nicht prägend und wirklich dominierend, anerkannt, wobei allerdings eine bestimmte Schulrichtung nicht zu erkennen ist.

Das Leiden und die Bedrohung, der sich in EpPt artikulierenden, in gleicher Lage befindlichen und von ihnen angesprochenen Christen, sind Anlaß und zentrales Thema der uns vorliegenden Schrift. Beides gehört, wie einerseits schon in dem früheren Stadium des Textes unter Berufung auf neutestamentliche Traditionen hervorgehoben wird, notwendigerweise zur christlichen Existenz. Andererseits wird in den Passagen, durch deren Einführung bereits der frühere, EpPt vorausgehende, Text inhaltliche Neuakzentuierungen erfuhr, die in EpPt nun infolge des Epitome-Charakters in starker Weise hervortreten, das Leiden als Folge der ΠΑΡΑΒΑСΙС der Eva sowie unter Rückgriff auf Elemente einer Form des auch in Zeugnissen der sethianischen Gnosis begegnenden Sophia-Mythos letztlich als Werk der Archonten und als anthropologische Grundbefindlichkeit angesehen.

Bereits in den Teilen von EpPt, die den Rahmen bilden und nicht erkennbar gnostisch sind, spielt eine Bedrohungssituation eine Rolle. Die aktuelle Verschärfung dieser Problematik bis hin zur Tötungsabsicht seitens nicht identifizierbarer Gegner soll mit Hilfe der Einschübe bewältigt werden. Der Schöpfer von EpPt will mit der Konzentration auf dieses Thema den Adressaten helfen, die Leidenssituation in richtiger Weise zu erkennen, zu erklären und durchzustehen.
Der Bewältigung des Leidens im Gehorsam gegenüber Jesus Christus dient neben der ätiologischen Erklärung auch die einer christlichgnostischen Apostelgeschichte entnommene, in einen vorgegebenen Rahmen eingefügte und in EpPt in konzentrierter Form gebotene, Bezugnahme auf die Passion Jesu Christi. Er nahm diese Passion real, dabei aber nicht notwendigerweise, sondern um der Erlösung willen und vorbildlich im Hinblick auf die Christen auf sich, also um ihret-, nicht um seinetwillen und dabei auch nicht als Sühne- oder stellvertretendes Leiden. Im Unterschied zu Jesus Christus — er ist in Bezug auf ΠΕΪΧΙ ΜΚΑϨ ein ϢΜΜΟ (u.E. entspricht dies einem ἀλλότριος) — müssen die Christen notwen-

digerweise — die wichtigsten Aussagen dazu finden sich schon in p. 138, 19 f. 23 ff. — leiden.
Die zentrale Aussage ΕΤΒΕ ΠΑΪ (sc. ΠΑΡΑΒΑСΙС ΝΤΜΑΑΥ [Eva]), ΑϤΕΙΡΕ ΝϨWΒ ΝΙΜ (sc. das Leiden) ΚΑΤΑ ΟΥΕΙΝΕ ϨΡΑΪ ΝϨΗΤΝ (p. 139, 24 f.) verstehen wir so, daß wir hinter dem ΕΙΝΕ ein ὁμοίωμα vermuten, was Distanz und Nähe zugleich ausdrückt, und daß hinter ϨΡΑΪ ΝϨΗΤΝ ein ἐν ἡμῖν oder εἰς ἡμᾶς steht. Diesem Satz könnte folgender griechischer Wortlaut zugrunde liegen: καὶ διὰ τοῦτο ἐποίησεν πάντα καθόμοίωμα ἐν ἡμῖν (bzw. εἰς ἡμᾶς). Für den Schöpfer von EpPt gehören dieser Satz und das ΑϤΧΙ ΜΚΑϨ ΕΤΒΗΗΤΝ von p. 138,18 zusammen. Hinter dem ΕΤΒΗΗΤ steht dabei wohl am ehesten die Präposition διὰ oder ein ἕνεκεν.
Konkrete Anhaltspunkte über nähere Umstände, Ort und Zeitpunkt des Leidens, der Verfolgung und Bedrohung liefert der Text von EpPt nicht. Man wird diese zentrale Thematik im Kontext der Situation sehen müssen, in der nicht nur der Schöpfer und die Adressaten von EpPt, sondern auch andere Christen im zweiten und dritten Jahrhundert stehen. EpPt ist also, ganz anders als etwa 2LogSeth, kein Werk, das in einer auch theoretischen Auseinandersetzung, etwa zwischen gnostischem und kirchlichem Christentum, steht, sondern will mit dem Bezug auf die Passion Jesu Christi in einer durch Leiden und Bedrohung verursachten existentiellen Gefährdung hilfreich wirken.
Die in EpPt dominierende Leidensthematik läßt ein Wechselverhältnis zwischen erfahrenem und zu erwartendem Leid und dem Selbstverständnis der sich Artikulierenden und Angesprochenen sichtbar werden. Die ΜΝΤΚΟΥΕΙ von p. 138, 20 läßt dabei an entsprechende Aussagen in der ApcPt oder die οἱ μικροί des Matthäus-Evangeliums denken, wobei freilich der historische Kontext ein ganz anderer ist.
Die im Dienste der Soteriologie stehenden christologischen Aussagen von EpPt sind neben dem inhaltlich nicht entfalteten traditionellen und dabei an verschiedenen, nicht nur neutestamentlichen Überlieferungen orientierten Gebrauch von christologischen Titeln (ΑΡΧΗΓΟС, ΡΕϤСWΤΕ, СWΤΗΡ, ΦWСΤΗΡ, ΧС, ϢΗΡΕ) vor allem durch die mehrfache Hervorhebung der Bedeutung der Wirksamkeit des irdischen Jesus, insbesondere dessen Verkündigung und Passion, bestimmt. In den gnostischen Passagen wird darüber hinaus eine christologische Konzeption

sichtbar, wie sie auch in der mutmaßlichen Tradition, die dem johanneischen Prolog zugrunde liegt, enthalten ist. Die Soteriologie von EpPt ist im Hinblick auf die zu Erlösenden nicht *a priori* exklusiv oder partikularistisch, sondern universalistisch ausgerichtet. Das Heil Jesu Christi gilt der ganzen Welt, bedarf aber im Einzelfall des Glaubens an den Namen Jesu. Um dies zu bewirken und zu fördern, ist Missionsarbeit erforderlich. Ähnlich wie bei manchen gnostischen, z.B. sethianischen, Texten wird auch in EpPt an einigen Stellen innerhalb der gnostischen Partien eine Verchristlichung einer ursprünglich nichtchristlichen soteriologischen Konzeption sichtbar, während die Soteriologie ansonsten weithin genuiun christlich ist oder christlich-gnostisch eingefärbt erscheint.

Die Individual-Anthropologie, in EpPt nur Thema des gnostischen Dialogs in Form eines Lehrgespräches, ist dualistisch: in dem von den Archonten erschaffenen Körper befindet sich der wesensmäßig zu Erlöser gehörende » innere Mensch «, im Munde der Erlösers auch ⲡⲱⲓ (p. 136,23) genannt. Die stark verkürzte Anthropogonie, in EpPt nur enthalten in der von einer ursprünglich nichtchristlichen Gnosis geprägten Passage im Zusammenhang mit der Beantwortung der an ExcTheod 78,2 erinnernden Grundsatzfragen, basiert auf der auch in vergleichbaren Zeugnissen der Gnosis ausführlicher enthaltenen Uminterpretation von Gen 1 und 2, ohne daß dies aber in EpPt den Charakter einer Auseinandersetzung bekommt.
Die entsprechende Partie lautet:

ⲁⲩⲱ ⲁϥⲟ[ⲩ]ⲱ[ϣ] ⲉ̄ⲧⲁⲙⲓⲟ ⲛ̄ⲛⲟⲩϩⲓⲕⲱⲛ ⲉⲡⲙ[ⲁ
ⲛ̄ⲛⲟⲩϩⲓⲕⲱⲛ] ⲙ̄ⲛ ⲟⲩⲙⲟⲣⲫⲏ ⲉⲡⲙⲁ ⲛ̄ⲛⲟⲩⲙ[ⲟⲣ]ⲫⲏ
ⲁϥⲧⲱϣ ⲇⲉ ⲛ̄ⲛⲓϭⲟⲙ ϩⲣⲁⲓ̈ ϩ̄ⲛ ⲧⲉϥⲉⲝⲟⲩⲥⲓⲁ ϫⲉ
ⲉⲩⲉⲡⲗⲁⲥⲥⲁ ⲛ̄ϩⲉ[ⲛ]ⲥⲱⲙⲁ ⲉⲩⲙⲟⲟⲩⲧ ⲁⲩⲱ ⲁⲩϣⲱⲡⲉ
ⲉⲃⲟⲗ ϩ̄ⲛ ⲟⲩⲙ̄ⲛ̄ⲧⲁⲧⲉⲓⲛⲉ ⲉⲃⲟⲗ ϩ̄ⲛ ϯⲉⲓⲇⲉⲁ
ⲉⲧⲉⲁⲥϣⲱⲡⲉ (p. 136, 8-15).

Dieser Text wirft eine Vielzahl von Fragen auf, die im Rahmen eines Kurzbeitrages unmöglich zu klären sind. Dennoch soll bei einigen Punkten angedeutet werden, wie diese Passage verstanden werden kann.
Problematisch ist das Verhältnis von ⲉⲓⲕⲱⲛ und ⲙⲟⲣⲫⲏ Auch wenn man es nicht einfach identifizieren sollte, so darf man doch damit rechnen, daß hier eine Art Hendiadyoin vorliegt, daß wir

zwei Bezeichnungen für den gleichen Vorgang haben. ⲉⲓⲕⲱⲛ und ⲙⲟⲣⲫⲏ stehen auch sonst gelegentlich in enger Beziehung zueinander, ja ⲉⲓⲕⲱⲛ kann im Sinne von » Gestalt «, gebraucht werden. In dem ⲙⲛ̄ würden wir dann das Äquivalent eines ⲕⲁⲓ epexegeticum bzw. explicativum sehen. Vielleicht wird der Begriff ⲙⲟⲣⲫⲏ aber überhaupt nur wegen des dann folgenden πλάσσειν gebraucht. Im letzten oben zitierten Satz geht es offensichtlich darum, daß etwas Unvollkommenes entsteht. Das zeigt sich zum einen in dem ⲙⲛ̄ⲧⲁⲧⲉⲓⲛⲉ ,dem u.E. ein ἀνομοιότης zugrunde liegt, zum anderen aber auch in einer ganz bestimmten, auch aus anderen Texten bekannten Verwendung des ja an sich nicht gnostischen Ur-/Vorbild-Abbild-Gedankens. ⲉⲓⲇⲉⲁ setzen wir nicht einfach mit einem anderen Begriff gleich, sondern verstehen es im üblichen Sinne, also als » Gestalt «, » äußere Erscheinung «. Es geht um die Sichtbarkeit der ⲉⲓⲕⲱⲛ , nicht um diese selbst. Gemeint wäre dann : Die Leiber, die sich als tot erweisen, entstanden nicht καϑ'ὁμοίωσιν, auch nicht κατ' εἰκόνα, sondern lediglich κατ' ἰδέαν. Bei dieser Textauffassung verstehen wir das ⲉⲃⲟⲗ ϩⲛ im Sinne von κατά. Wenn dies hier nicht deutlich zum Ausdruck kommt, so kann das auch mit einer unkorrekten Übersetzung des Textes aus dem Griechischen zusammenhängen, wo der Text vielleicht so lautete : καί ἐγένοντο οὐ κατ' εἰκόνα μέν κατ' ἰδέαν δέ. Der vorliegende koptische text könnte dann dadurch entstanden sein, daß die Negation des einen Ausdrucks an falscher Stelle erscheint, d.h. κατ'οὐ εἰκόνα statt οὐ κατ' εἰκόνα.

In Bezug auf die Menschheit ist in EpPt im Kontext der missionarischen Tätigkeit ein faktischer anthropologischer Dualismus erkennbar, dabei aber eher vorausgesetzt als entfaltet. Jesus ist Erlöser für alle, aber nicht alle werden erlöst. Es gibt Christen, wie Jesus Christus als ⲫⲱⲥⲧⲏⲣ bezeichnet, und » tote Menschen «, womit sich eine Zweiteilung ergibt.

Trotz gewisser paränetischer Formulierungen entwickelt und enthält EpPt, vielleicht auch — ebenso wie bei anderen Sachverhalten — resultierend aus der Verkürzung, bei der Hervorhebung der Leidensthematik und ihrer Bewältigung keine spezielle und auch keine indirekte Ethik. Die für viele Apostel-Akten und auch einige Nag-Hammadi-Texte typische asketische Tendenz fehlt.
Im Gegensatz zur Leidensthematik und der damit im Zusammenhang stehenden mythologischen

Ätiologie samt Christologie, Soteriologie und Anthropologie ist EpPt auf Grund des Hauptanliegens an der Darlegung anderer grundsätzlicher Sachverhalte nur insoweit und daher mehr indirekt interessiert, als dies im Zusammenhang mit der Hauptproblematik steht. So ist z.B. die Eschatologie mit Ausnahme der Nennung von ⲘⲦⲞⲚ als eschatologischem Gut kein Thema für EpPt.

EpPt ist in der Ekklesiologie, die — bewußt oder infolge des Epitome-Charakters — ebenfalls nicht thematisiert wird, eher traditionell orientiert. Dabei fehlen Ämter ebenso wie Strukturen, andererseits wird eine offene Missionsarbeit der als ⲤⲈⲚⲪⲰⲤⲦⲎⲢ Wirkenden gefordert. Ein innerkirchliches Leben der die EpPt repräsentierenden Gruppe ist mit Ausnahme der Hervorhebung des Gebets und der Andeutung liturgischer Einzelheiten kaum erkennbar.

Mit der betonten Sonderstellung des Petrus liegt EpPt auf der Linie der lukanischen Apostelgeschichte und verschiedener Zeugnisse der urchristlichen Petrustradition, die gerade auch Verfolgung und Martyrium einschließen. Die den Inhalt nicht dominierende Erwähnung des Philippus ist ein Hinweis auf die Schilderung seiner Wirksamkeit in den in EpPt nicht mehr enthaltenen Partien des dieser Schrift vorausgehenden und zugrunde liegenden Werkes.

Der mehrfach begegnende missionarische Aspekt ist nicht nur erzählerisches Moment in EpPt, sondern hat inhaltliches Gewicht: Missionarische Verkündigungstätigkeit ist Bestandteil der Bewältigung des Leidens und gehört zugleich ganz wesentlich zum antiarchontischen Kampf. Dennoch ist EpPt kein literarisches Dokument, das selbst missionarisch wirken will und soll, sondern möchte der missionarischen Zurüstung dienen.

COPTIC STUDIES

Kent S. Brown

A Communiqué: Microfilming the Manuscripts of the Coptic Orthodox Church in Egypt

Four years ago at our meeting in Rome, I announced a plan to preserve on microfilm the manuscripts which belong to the Coptic Orthodox Church in Egypt. At that time, it was only a hope, a dream. At this moment that plan is on the verge of becoming a reality. In this connection, it gives me pleasure to note that His Excellency, Dr Ahmed Kadry, President of the Egyptian Antiquities Organization, has kindly consented to review personally our request for the required permit which will allow us to begin microfilming these precious manuscripts. Let me describe briefly the most important facets of this effort and how we have arrived at this point. [1]

As many are aware, the Coptic Orthodox Church was dealt a stunning blow when, in March 1979, in Old Cairo, the Church of the All-Holy Virgin Mary was razed by fire. Virtually everything was lost, including ancient icons and most of the 122 precious manuscripts stored there. [2] As a result Coptic authorities decided to act to preserve their precious heritage so that fire and insects could no longer destroy it.

About two months after the fire, I had the pleasure of meeting His Grace, the late Bishop Samuel, who had begun to organize an appeal for assistance in conserving the Copts' significant heritage which is composed of the art treasures and ancient manuscripts of the Church.

In the intervening years, authorities of the Church and officers of Brigham Young University have arranged a joint enterprise to preserve the documents located in Egypt (the conservation and recording of the icons and other artistic works have yet to be arranged. [3] Upon receiving the cooperation of the Egyptian Antiquities Organization, we anticipate completing this cooperative task within a period of three years.

Our most important job is to preserve, with archival quality photographs, the 3.5 million pages of manuscripts belonging to the Church. By good fortune, we have been able to obtain the most sophisticated equipment and technology through the Genealogical Society of Utah, the largest microfilming agency in the world. It is important that, for storage, we shall have access to specially excavated vaults in the mountains of Utah, USA, which, because of the natural features of the subterranean rock, will keep the microfilm at the optimum temperature and humidity for long-term storage. In fact, the length of storage is indefinite. By contrast, if we were to keep the rolls of microfilm, say, in a bank vault, they would last only 100 years before deterioration of the film begins. In the facility in Utah, it will be at least 5000 years before anyone will need to deal with such problems.

Concerning quality control, because we have access to the best equipment, we therefore possess technology which will aid our project in producing archival quality film. Moreover, the Genealogical Society of Utah has kindly put its experienced personnel at our disposal for the duration of our effort. In fact, Mr Eric Erickson has already

[1] An interim report, detailing progress and difficulties occurring before 1983, was published by S. Kent Brown in "Microfilming Coptic and Arabic Manuscripts in Egypt". *Coptologia* 5 (1984), 63–67.

[2] The 122 documents are inventoried in the publication by Antoine Khater and O. H. E. Khs-Burmester: *Catalogue of the Coptic and Christian Arabic Manuscripts Preserved in the Library of the Church of the All-Holy Virgin Mary, Known as Qasrîat ar-Rihân at Old Cairo, Bibliothèque de Manuscrits*, vol. II, Cairo 1973.

[3] Copies of this agreement were signed on April 2, 1982, by Professor Dr Neal E. Lambert, Associate Academic Vice-President of Brigham Young University, and were co-signed on April 29, 1982, by His Grace Anba Gregorios, Archbishop of the Coptic Orthodox Church who has charge of the Bishopric of Higher Theological Studies, Coptic Culture, and Scientific Research.

assisted us greatly in organizing and setting up the project in a manner appropriate to obtaining the best possible results.

In terms of personnel, we are ready to train two camera operators—both Coptes—to aid our efforts. Our supervisor of the project in Egypt is to be Mr Steven W. Baldridge, a former employee of the Genealogical Society who has microfilmed in various places: the Middle East, the Far East and the Pacific Islands. We are fortunate indeed to have a person with Mr Baldridge's qualifications and experience to oversee the work.

The matter of financing the project, of course, is crucial to its success. After receiving from His Grace, Bishop Gregorios, a letter commissioning us to work cooperatively with the Church and to assist in organizing the project, we set about immediately to find sources of revenue. [4] Naturally, one must reckon the kind assistance both from the Coptic Orthodox Church and from Brigham Young University, since much of the expense of organizing and setting up the project has been borne by these two organizations. In addition, the project has received a major award from the National Endowment for the Humanities. In addition to an outright grant, NEH has made allowance that, as we raise monies from private sources, these funds will be matched on a one-for--one basis. In this connection, the project has received generous help from the Mormon Archaeology and Research Foundation, organized by Mr and Mrs Wallace O. Tanner of Scottsdale, Arizona. This organization has so far provided substantial help toward the initial expenses of the project and has committed itself to raise further significant amounts. Moreover, the development officer of the American Research Center in Egypt, Dr Mary Ellen Lane, is also assisting our efforts.

Concerning the plan of the work, we shall center the project in Cairo. His Holiness, Pope Shenouda III, has graciously given to the project a suite of rooms in his residence next to the cathedral of St Mark in Abbasiya, a northern suburb of Cairo. In addition to our storage areas, our processing and evaluating equipment are to be set up there. Naturally, as long as we are filming in the archives in and near Cairo, transporting the film and developing it will present little difficulty. But there are several archives which are far away from the headquarters. In those instances we shall rely upon couriers to transport the exposed film from outlying monasteries and churches to our developing facility in Abbasiya.

In the agreement between Brigham Young University and the Coptic Orthodox Church, it is affirmed that two copies of the microfilm will remain in the possession of the Church. Further, if such copies are damaged or destroyed, they will be replaced without cost. Using these positive and negative copies, the Church plans a microfilm storage and reading facility for use by members of the Church and interested scholars. Moreover, one copy will be placed in the hands of the Egyptian Antiquities Organization for its own reference and work.

As the manuscripts are microfilmed, a descriptive inventory will be drawn up which will contain essential data concerning the manuscripts: e.g., date, name of copyist or author, place of composition, language of the text, and content. [5] We shall begin this phase of the work in Egypt but the bulk will be done from the microfilmed rolls themselves at Brigham Young University. Dr William F. Macomber, an experienced cataloguer of oriental manuscripts at the Hill Monastic Manuscript Library in Collegeville, Minnesota, will produce the inventory which will later serve as the basis for a thorough catalogue. The inventory will be shared in a continually updated format with other centers, universities and individuals who are interested in such manuscripts. [6]

---

[4] Dated 30 April 1982, Bishop Gregorios wrote: "You are kindly requested to pursue the matter (of the microfilming project) on behalf of the Patriarchate with the circles concerned, especially the National Endowment for the Humanities in America; and please keep us informed about the development".

[5] For some archives, catalogues already exist. But during our preliminary period of training the camera operators at the Patriarchal library in Azbakiya, Dr William F. Macomber has discovered omissions and deficiencies in the published inventories compiled by Georg Graf (*Catalogue de Manuscrits arabes chrétiens conservés au Caire* [Vatican City 1937]) and by Marcus Simaika Pasha and Yassa ʿAbd al-Masih (*Catalogue of the Coptic and Christian Arabic Manuscripts in the Coptic Museum, the Patriarchate, the Principal Churches of Cairo and Alexandria and the Monasteries of Egypt*, 2 volumes in 3, Cairo 1939 ff.

[6] Both during and following the 2nd International Congress of Coptic Studies, Professor Dr Tito Orlandi of the University of Rome has begun to organize centers, which have interest in things Coptic, to form a consortium of photographic archives. This consortium will consist of at least fifteen institutions located in Europe, the Middle East, and the United States. See Orlandi's circular letter dated 29 January 1981 and sent to the relevant centers.

In our initial survey of the various archives in Egypt, Mr Roy Holton of the Genealogical Society of Utah and I determined in 1980 that approximately 3.5 million pages of manuscript exist in the known archives throughout the Nile Valley, the deserts, and the Delta. [7] But in a meeting with interested Egyptians in May 1984, many of those present began to recall that, in the Churches where they had lived as children, the priests had old manuscripts in desks or cupboards. Consequently, at an appropriate moment during the project, it now appears that we shall need to send a small team to Upper Egypt and the Delta to microfilm the additional manuscripts located in the ancient Churches. It is not impossible, in fact, that we shall microfilm nearly four million pages of manuscript before the project is finally completed.

The primary beneficiaries of this effort, of course, are the people of Egypt. It is their heritage which we seek to preserve. Since an extensive part of Egypt's history involved the Copts and their culture, it is thus Egyptians in general and Copts in particular who will profit from conserving this treasury. The second group to be benefited by this project will be the world's scholars. And access to such documents will provide important resources to the growing number of students interested in Egypt in Late Antiquity.

The various subjects of the manuscripts to be microfilmed will become material for study by scholars interested in Coptic and/or Arabic paleography, the development of Christian worship, the history of ancient science, textual criticism of the Bible, the development of religious institutions in the Orient, and the history of Egypt from the Byzantine Empire to the present.

Concerning the nature of manuscripts themselves, we note that approximately 50% contain the liturgical services of the Church. The remaining texts are biblical, theological, dogmatic, historical, hagiographical, and legal in character. In addition, there are important commentaries on the Bible as well as important theological treatises. Concerning the language of the texts, the majority are written in Arabic. While the number is substantial, it is a minority written in Coptic. A number are polyglots with both Coptic and Arabic. We are already aware of a few Ethiopic and Syriac texts. Doubtless there will be other surprises which we shall meet during the course of the work.

It appears that our overall plan — the best equipment, high quality, duplicate copies in Egypt, storage of the master negative in one of the world's best facilities, creating an inventory of this rich literary heritage — is one of the best that can be arranged. Without a doubt, it will benefit and preserve the rich heritage of Egypt's Christians in such a way that disasters and insects can never harm these records again.

---

[7] Published reports of the survey include: S. K. Brown, "Microfilming Coptic Records in Egypt: Report of a Research Development Trip", *Newsletter of the American Research Center in Egypt* 114 (Spring 1981), 11–17, and "Microfilming", *Bulletin d'Arabe chrétien* V, 1–3 (1981), 79–86. A report is also to appear in the published proceedings of the 2nd International Congress of Coptic Studies.

COPTIC STUDIES

Gerald M. Browne

An Old Nubian Version
of the *Liber Institutionis Michaelis**

The parchment leaf here edited for the first time was unearthed at Qasr Ibrim by the Egypt Exploration Society in 1964, when Professor J. Martin Plumley was in charge of the excavations. I transcribed the text in July 1983 through the kindness of Professor Plumley, to whom I am also grateful for permission to publish it here.

The leaf presents part of an Old Nubian translation of the so-called *Liber Institutionis Michaelis,* [1] a work which elsewhere survives only in Coptic. The Coptic text, in both a Sahidic and a Fayumic version, is found in two separate codices in the Pierpont Morgan Library. In 1962, Professor C. Detlef G. Müller published an exemplary edition of both Coptic versions as well as a similar text dealing with the installation of Gabriel: *Die Bücher der Einsetzung der Erzengel Michael und Gabriel* (CSCO 225–226 [Copt. 31–32]), and it is on this edition that I rely for information about the Coptic.

The Nubian fragment is to be set within what Müller designates as Section 6 of the book: in response to the query of the apostles, Jesus describes the expulsion from heaven of the evil Mastema and the installation of Michael in his place.

In general and often in detail, the Old Nubian matches the Coptic, especially the fuller treatment provided by the Sahidic, and the latter is helpful in clarifying much that would have otherwise remained obscure in the Nubian. At times, however, we find material which is in neither of the Coptic versions. Most interesting are the references to the ⲥⲟⲅⲟⲃ– in i 1, ii 5–6 and 12–13; these are treated in full in Part II (forthcoming) of this paper. The other passages displaying an expanded

text are set forth and discussed in the commentary that follows the transcription and translation. Only a fragment of the Old Nubian version survives, and one must be careful in extracting general conclusions from its evidence, but what we have suggests that the Nubian reflects a stage of textual transmission anterior to the Coptic (see especially i 19–20n.) and free of the latter's interpolations (see ii 11–13n.). Here it is appropriate to recall Müller's observations on the transmission of the *Liber Institutionis Michaelis;* after discussing some lost sources of the work, he writes: "Das Buch selbst ist gut durchkomponiert. Der Leser erfährt alles Wissenswerte über den behandelten Fragenkreis. Wir stehen also am Endpunkt einer Überlierferungskette, die sicher erst über mehrere Zwischenglieder zu dieser Vollkommenheit führte" (Einleitung, Trans. Vol., IV).

A paleographic feature of the Old Nubian text should here be noted: the scribe has consistently used red ink for the name Michael. In the transcript that follows, I have underlined all these occurrences.

13.3 × 12.7 cm

i Flesh Side

ⲣ̅ⲉ̅

ⲗⲟ· <u>ⲙⲓⲭⲁⲗ̈ⲓⲛⲁ</u> ⲧⲁⲣⲓⲟ ⲥⲟⲅⲟⲃⲁ ⲇⲁⲩⲣⲁⲅⲁ
[ⲅ]ⲟ̈ⲫⲧⲁⲕⲉⲥⲛ̄ⲛⲁ ⲕⲟⲉⲕⲟⲛ· ⲧⲁⲣ ⲁⲫⲟ̅ⲗⲗⲟ ⲧⲁⲛ
[ⲁ]ⲡⲟⲥⲧⲟⲗⲟⲥⲅⲟⲩⲕⲁ ⲉⲓⲁⲣ̅ⲗ̅ⲅⲁⲣⲣⲁ ⲡⲉⲥⲗ̅·
ⲉ ⲁⲛ ⲡ̄ⲧⲁ ⲁⲡⲟⲥⲧⲟⲗⲟⲥⲁⲅⲟⲩⲉⲕⲉ· ⲁⲕⲉⲛⲇⲁⲛ
5 ⲕⲉ ⲟⲩⲣⲟⲩ ⲏⲛ ⲃⲙ̄ⲗ̄ⲅⲟⲩⲕⲁ ⲡⲉⲱⲱⲓⲕⲓ
ⲃⲁⲣⲟⲩⲗⲱ· ⲁⲩⲟⲩⲧⲁⲕⲟⲛⲁ ⲙⲁⲛ ⲧⲁⲩ
ⲕⲗⲱ· ⲡⲁⲡⲓⲛⲁ ⲅⲁⲣⲙⲗⲟ ⲧⲁⲣⲁ ⲉⲓⲧⲣⲉⲡ̄

---

* Although they have freely consulted with one another, Gerald M. Browne is responsible for Part I, Bożena Rostkowska for Part II.

[1] The title is adapted from that used by H. Hyvernat, *Liber institutionis s. Michaelis archangeli*: see *Bibliothecae Pierpont Morgan codices coptici photographice expressi ...*, Rome 1922, vols 23 and 34.

κ⳿ⲇⲉⲥ⳿ⲗ⳿ ⲁ̄ⲑ̄ⲩ̄ⲣ· ⲥⲟⲩⲁⲉⲓⲗⲁ ⲅⲛ̄ⲕⲉⲣⲟⲩ
ⲧ̣ⲛ̄ ⲇⲓⲡⲁ ⲡ̄ⲗ̄ⲗⲁⲇⲇⲗ̄ ⲇⲓⲙⲉⲇⲟⲩ ⲟⲩⲉⲓⲧⲓⲛⲛ̄ ᵗⁱᶜ
10 [ⲡⲁⲡⲗ̄] ⲕⲉⲗⲉⲩⲉⲣ̄ⲥⲛⲁ· ⲁⲅⲅⲉⲗⲟⲥⲁ ⲙ̄ⲩ̄ⲩ̄ⲁⲛ
  [ⲅⲟⲩⲕⲁ̣] ⲧ̄ⲙ̄ⲙⲁⲛⲛⲁⲥⲁ· ⲟⲩⲉⲣⲟⲩⲉⲣⲇⲁ·
  [   ]ⲅ̣ⲛ̄ⲛⲓⲁ ⲑⲣⲟⲛⲟⲥⲛ̄
  [   ]ⲗ̄ ⲅⲁⲓⲉⲓⲛⲁ
  [   ]ⲙⲟⲩⲣⲧⲱ ⲉ
15 [ⲙⲓⲭⲁ]ⲏⲗⲓⲕⲁ ⲧⲁ .
  [   ]ⲥ̣ⲁⲅⲉⲛ̄ ⲑⲣⲟⲛⲟⲥ
  [   ]ⲙⲁⲥⲧⲓⲙⲁ
  [   ]ⲙⲟⲣⲫⲟⲥ [(.)]
  [±9   ⲙⲓⲭ]ⲁⲏⲗⲓⲕ[ⲁ ⲧⲣ̄]ⲥⲛⲁ ⲇ̣[±2]
20 [±6 ⲡⲓⲕ]ⲧⲛ̄ⲗ̄· ⲙⲓⲭⲁⲏ[ⲗⲓ]ⲅ̄ⲗ̄ⲗⲉ[ⲗⲱ]
  [ⲧⲓⲇ̄ⲧ̄ⲧⲁⲕⲥⲛⲁ]· ⲧⲣⲁⲧⲟⲩ· ⲡⲗ̄ⲗ̄[ⲗ̄ ⲙⲓⲭⲁⲏⲗⲓⲛ]

ii Hair Side

          ϙ̄ⲅ̄
ⲟⲩⲇⲇⲟⲗⲟ ⲟⲩⲥⲕⲣ̄ⲧⲁⲕⲟⲛⲁ ⲥⲟⲩⲇⲇⲟⲩ ⲙⲉⲇ̣
ⲇⲕ̄ⲕⲧⲓⲛⲁ ⲅⲟⲩⲉⲓⲟⲩ ⲉⲥⲕⲓⲟ̄ⲣⲉⲛⲛⲗ̄·
<ⲕⲟⲥ> ⲙⲟⲥ [ⲛ̄]
ⲧⲟⲩⲇ̣ⲅⲓⲧⲓⲛⲗ̄ ⲁⲡⲟⲕⲁⲗⲁⲗⲗⲟⲛ ⲧⲱⲕⲛ̄
ⲣ̄ⲗ̄ⲅ̄ ⲛⲁⲅⲉⲛⲗ̄· ⲙⲓⲭⲁⲏⲗⲓⲅ̄ⲗ̄ⲗⲉⲗⲱ ⲧⲓⲇ̄ⲧ̄ⲧⲁⲕ
5 ⲥⲁⲛⲁ· ⲟ̄ⲁⲣ ⲟⲩⲁⲧⲧⲟⲕⲟⲛ ⲥⲟⲅⲟ66ⲓⲛ ⲕⲧ̣̄
  ⲧⲗⲱ ⲇⲟⲩⲧⲗ̄ ⲟⲩⲁⲗⲓⲥⲟ· ⲡ̄ⲗ̄ⲗⲁⲇⲇⲗ̄ ⲅⲓⲅⲁ·
  ⲁⲑ̄ⲩ̄ⲣ ⲥⲟⲩⲁⲉⲛ̄ ⲇⲓⲙⲉⲇ ⲟⲩⲉⲓⲧⲓⲛⲛ̄·
  ⲕⲟⲥⲙⲟⲥ ⲕⲟⲗⲟⲧⲛ̄ ⲡ̄ⲥ̄ⲕⲁⲛⲉⲗⲇⲱⲉⲓⲟⲛ
  ⲅⲟⲫⲧⲁⲕⲥⲛⲁ ⳽ⲁⲣⲙ̄ⲗ̄ⲇⲱⲛⲓⲅⲟⲩⲛⲁ· ⲟⲛ
10 ⲥⲕⲧ̄ⲗ̄ⲇⲱⲛⲓⲅⲟⲩⲛⲁ· ⲅⲟⲩⲗ ⲟⲩⲁⲙⲛ̄ⲛⲁ̣ⲛ̣
  ⲙⲁⲩ̣ⲁⲗⲟⲥⲕⲗⲱ ⲡ̄ⲗ̄ⲟⲛⲛⲟⲛ ⲙⲁ̣[ⲩⲁⲛ ⲧⲁ]
  ⲣⲁⲧⲗⲱ ⲙⲓⲭⲁⲏⲗⲓⲕⲁ· ⲥⲟⲅⲟⲃⲁ̣ [ⲇⲁⲩⲣⲁ]
  ⲅⲣⲁ ⲅⲟⲩⲫⲓⲙ· ⲱ[
  ⲗ̄ⲛ̄ ⲧⲟⲩ[
15 ⲇⲟⲩⲕⲕ[
  ⲕⲉⲗⲉⲩⲉⲣ̄ [ⲥⲛⲁ
  ⲁⲅⲅⲉⲗⲟⲥⲅⲟ̣ⲩ‐
  ⲙⲓⲭⲁⲏⲗⲓⲕⲁ[ⲙⲓⲭⲁ]
  ⲏⲗⲓ̈ ⲁⲫⲟ̄ⲛ̄ [ⲡⲟⲧⲟⲧⲕⲁ
20 [(.)].ⲛⲟⲛⲛⲟⲛ[±4   ] ·ⲁ̣.[
  [. . .].ⲗⲁ ⲟⲩ.[1-2]ⲗ̄ⲗⲉ ⲡ̄ⲣ̄ⲣⲁ .[
  [   ]ⲗⲁ̣[1-2]ⲉⲕⲕ̄ⲗ̄ⲇⲁⲕⲓⲧⲁ̣[
  – – – – – – – – – – – – – – – – – –

Translation

(i 95) ... And the Savior himself caused his apostles to know the power in which Michael was established as great *soňoj*, saying: 'O my chosen apostles, blessed are you when you will go and judge all these. It happened at that time, when the Father was about to go forth and send (Mastema) from heaven, manifestly on the twelfth (*sic*) day in the evening of the second Wednesday (?) in the month of Hathyr, the Father ordered all the angels to assemble with one another ... in order that he might see ... the throne ... on this side (?) ... in command (?) ... Michael ... the throne of the hateful one ... Mastema ... -form ... he gave to Michael. [The chariot] of light was given to Michael. The shining crown (ii 96) was placed on the head of Michael. The victorious shield of the staff of readiness, which is the security of the world, and the shoes of peace were given to Michael. And adorning him in the garment of the *soňoj* for the entire night, we spent the morning manifestly rejoicing on the twelfth day of the month of Hathyr. And to the joy of the seven worlds was he established, as those in heaven and those upon the earth rejoiced and danced (?). And at the hour when the sun appeared in the east, establishing Michael as great *soňoj* ... worship ... he ordered ... angels ... Michael ... And when Michael [sounded] the trumpet of life ... came forth ...'

Commentary [2]

i

1–3 These lines do not correspond to the Coptic, which has merely ⲁϥⲟⲩⲱ̄ⲩ̄ⲃ ⲛ̄ϭⲓⲡ̄ⲥⲱⲧⲏⲣ ⲡⲉⲭⲁϥ
1 ⲥⲟⲅⲟ6‐: see Part II.
2 [ⲅ]ⲟ̣ϥ‐: modelled on ii 9 (see n. ad loc.); cf. also ii 13. ⲕⲟⲉ‐: cf. M. *kō* 'der Herr' (Lepsius) and ⲕⲟⲁⲛⲧⲣⲉ̣ⲅⲟⲩⲛⲁ in WN 17 ('wohl "die Vorfahren"' — Zyhlarz, 'Sprachdenkmäler' 192, but the original notion of 'master' is still present); ⲕⲟⲉ‐ (in which -ⲉ is an abstract-forming suffix [§23.a])

[2] N.B. I cite texts and secondary literature in accordance with my practice in SC (= *Chrysostomus Nubianus* ... [Rome–Barcelona 1984]); the Stauros-Text (St.) is cited on the basis of my revision published in StudPap 22 (1983), 75–119. In quoting from Müller's Coptic text (of which — unless I indicate otherwise — I use only the Sahidic), I have replaced his somewhat awkward editorial signs with those employed by papyrologists.

means 'power.' ⲧⲁⲣ: cf. K. 21.12 ⲧⲁⲣⲟⲩ ⲅⲟⲇⳑ- ; and for the loss of -ⲟⲩ see NON XI.B(8).

3 -ⲅⲁⲣⲣⲁ: see ONVS §27.c.

4 ⲉ ⲁⲛ ⲡⳠⲧⲁ ⲁⲡⲟⲥⲧⲟⲗⲟⲥⲁⲅⲟⲩⲉⲕⲉ: = Coptic ⲱ̄ ⲛⲁ ⲥⲱⲡ⳦ [sic] ⲛⲁⲡⲟⲥⲧⲟⲗⲟⲥ (16.33–34); cf. St. 5.9 ⲉ̄ ⲁⲛ ⲡⳠⲧⲁ (= Coptic ⲱ ⲡⲁⲥⲱⲡ⳦ and see my note ad loc.

4–6 ⲁⲕⲉⲛⲇⲁⲛⲕⲉ --- ⲡⲉⳛⳡⲓⲕⲓⳝⲁⲣⲟⲩⲗⲱ: = Coptic ⲛ̄ⲧⲱⲧⲛ ⲅ̄ⲙⲙⲁⲕⲁⲣⲓⲟⲥ ⲭⲉⲉⲧⲉⲧ̄ⲛ̄ⳛⲓⲛⲉ ⲛ̄ⲥⲁⲛⲁ̈ⲓ ⲧⲏⲣⲟⲩ (16.34; Müller reads ⲛ̄ⲧⲉⲧ̄ⲛ- , but the plate in Hyvernat's facsimile edition suggests that the text has the expected ⲉⲧⲉⲧ̄ⲛ- [Present II]; cf. also the Fayumic, which likewise uses Present II: ⲭⲉⲁⲧⲉⲧⲉⲛⳛⲓⲛⲓ ⲛⲥⲁⲛⲉⲓ ⲧⲏⲣⲟⲩ [17.30]). For -ⲕⲓ- 'come' cf. SC 7.16 and n.; -ⲁⲣⲟⲩ- = -ⲁⲣⲣⲟⲩ- (cf. ONVS §5).

6–7 ⲁⲩⲟⲩⲧⲁⲕⲟⲛⲁ ⲙⲁⲛ ⲧⲁⲩⲕⲗⲱ: cf. Coptic, which has merely ⲁⲥⳛⲱⲡⲉ ⲇⲉ (16.35).

7–8 ⲡⲁⲡⲓⲛⲁ --- ⲕⳠⲇⲉⲥⳑ: cf. Coptic ⲛ̄ⲧⲉⲣⲉⲛⲛⲟⲩ ⲭ ⲙ̄ⲡⲇⲓ̈ⲁⲃⲟⲗⲟⲥ ⲉ̄ⲃⲟⲗ ⳟ̄ⲛⲧⲡⲉ (16.35). The Nubian restricts the subject and omits the object. I analyse it as: ⲉⲓⲧⲓⲣⲉⲓ- (cf. SC 22.23–24 ⲕⲁⲥⲓ ⲡⲁⳝ-; for ⲓ instead of ⲟⲩ see NON XI.B introd.) -ⲡⲓ(ⲗ)- (cf. SC 8.11–12 ⲕⲓⲡⳑⲗⲁⲛ) -ⲕⲓ (ⲣ)- 'come' -ⲇⲉⲥⳑ Future Preterite II infinitive (cf. ONVS §§26–27, though note that here we are dealing with an action imminent in the past ['was about to ...']; the instances in ONVS loc. cit. designate unreal apodoses ['would have' ...]; comparable is the Coptic Imperfectum Futuri [cf. Till, *Koptische Grammatik* §318]).

8–9 ⲁ̄ⲑⲩ̄ⲣ --- ⲟⲩⲉⲓⲧⲓⲛⲛ̄: this is an expansion of the Coptic, from which it also differs as to the date and the time of day (see below, n. to ⲇⲓⲙⲉⲇⲟⲩ ⲟⲩⲉⲓ ⲧⲓⲛⲛ̄): ⳟ̄ⲣⲁ̈ⲓ ⲇⲉ ⲛⲥⲟⲩⲙ̄ⲛ̄ⲧⲥⲛⲟⲟⲩⲥ ⲛ̄ⳟⲁⲑⲱⲣ ⲙ̄ⲡⲛⲁⲩ ⲙ̄ⲡⲟⲩⳝⲉⲓⲛ (16.36).

8–9 ⲁ̄ⲑⲩ̄ⲣ --- ⲅ̄ⲛⲕⲉⲣⲟⲩⲧⲛ̄: cf. WN 16 ⲧⲁⲡⲟⲧⲛ̄ ⲥⲟⲩⲇⲁⲉⲓⲗⲁ ⲅⲓⲛⲕⲉⲣⲟⲩⲉⲓⲧⲁ (*sic legi*) ⲁ̄ⲡⲟ ⲙⲁⲣⲧⲩⲣ ⲓⲟⲛ--- ;ⲟⲩⲧ- in the present text = ⲟⲩⲉⲓⲧ- in WN and means 'second' (cf. M. *uwitti* 'der zweite' [Lepsius 52] and below, 9 and ii 7); for ⲟⲩ instead of ⲟⲩⲉⲓ cf. e.g. SC 4.5 ⲟⲩⲥⲕⲓⲧⲓⲛⲓⲛ- with 13 ⲟⲩⲉⲥ̄ⲕⲧⲉⲓⲛⲛ̄. Regarding ⲅⲓⲛⲕⲉⲣ-, I suggest that ⲅⲓⲛ-is cognate with K.D. *kina* 'klein'(Lepsius) and that -ⲕⲉⲣ- is a reduced form of ⲕⲟⲣⲉ- 'feast, sacrament' (Griffith 103); the expression may be comparable to Coptic ⲧⲕⲟⲩⲓ ⲛ̄ⲛⲏⲥⲧⲓⲁ 'das kleine Fasten' = 'Mittwoch' (Till, *Koptische Grammatik* §180).

9 ⲇⲓⲡⲁ: i.e. ⲇⲓⲡⲡⲁ from ⲇⲓⲡⲧ-ⲗⲁ; cf. M. *dib* 'der Abend' (Lepsius).

ⲡⳑⲗⲁⲇⳑ̄: literally 'going to appear', the word

here and in ii 6 seems to mean little more than 'manifestly'; cf. M. 10.15 ⲡ̄ⲗⲁⲁⲁⲗⲗⲟ and K. 31.1 ⲡ̄ⲗⳑⳑⲇⲟ, both of which mean 'clearly, manifestly, openly'.

ⲇⲓⲙⲉⲇⲟⲩ ⲟⲩⲉⲓⲧⲓⲛⲛ̄: 'it being the twelfth' (sim.: ii 7); cf. *dimeruwitti* 'der zwölfte' (Lepsius 52). In the Coptic, Mastema is cast out of heaven on the evening of 11 Hathor (16.23–25), and Michael is appointed in his place on the following morning (16.36; cf. also 18.10–11). The Old Nubian, however, reports in the present passage that Mastema is about to be thrown out of heaven on the evening of 12 Hathor, while in ii 7 we read that Michael's installation occurs in the morning of the same day. We should probably emend ⲇⲓⲙⲉⲇⲟⲩ ⲟⲩⲉⲓⲧⲓⲛⲛ̄ to ⲇⲓⲙⲉⲇⲟⲩ *ⲟⲩⲉ<ⲣ>ⲓⲧⲓⲛⲛ̄ 'it being the eleventh'; the form proposed is not attested in Old Nubian but is cognate with M. *dimeweritti* 'der elfte' (Lepsius 52); cf. also ⲟⲩⲉⲣ- 'eins' (§113).

10–11 Cf. Coptic ⲁ̄ⲡⲁⲉⲓ̈ⲱⲧ ⲕⲉⲗⲉⲩⲉ ⲛ̄ⲛⲉⲁⲅⲅⲉⲗⲟⲥ ⲉⲧⲣⲉⲩⲉⲓ̈ --- (16.37).

10 ⲕⲉⲗⲉⲩⲉⲣ̄-: = ⲕⲉⲗⲉⲩⲉ in Coptic; cf. SC 18.10, where ⲕⲉⲗⲉⲩⲁ̄ⲣⲁ renders ὁρίσας. The word is borrowed from Greek, and I erred in giving it an enchoric etymology in SC loc. cit.

10–11 ⲙ̄ⳝⳛⲁⲛ [ⲅⲟⲩⲕⲁ]: no correspondence in the Sahidic, but cf. the Fayumic: ⲁⲩⲓ ⲛ̄ⳝⲓⲛⲉⲁⲅ ⲅⲉⲗⲟⲥ ⲧⲏⲣⲟⲩ (19.).

11 ⲧ̄ⲙⲙⲁⲛⲛⲁⲥⲁ: i.e. ⲧ̄ⲙⲙⲁⲣ-ⲁⲛⲁ-ⲥⲁ , as in SC 18.17 (see n. ad loc.).

ⲟⲩⲉⲣⲟⲩⲉⲣ-: 'each other'; see SC 11.14n.

-ⲇⲁ: i.e. -ⲇⲁⲗ 'with', as in Nauri 3–4 ⲓ̈ⲥⲟⲩⲅ ⲁⲇⲁ ⲕⲟⲩⲥⲥⲓ and NI 78/76 i 9–10 [ⲁⲅⲅ]ⲉⲗⲟⲥ ⲅ̄ⳓ ⲥⲓ ⲧⲓⲧⲟⲩⲣⲓⲅⲟⲩⲇⲁ· [ⲟⲛ ⲁⲅⲅ]ⲉⲗⲟⲥ ⲟⲩⲣⲁⲛⲓⲅⲟⲩⲇⲁ· ('with myriads of holy angels and with archangels').

12 ⲅ̄ⲛ̄ⲛⲓⲁ 'in order that he might see'; there is no exact correspondence in the Coptic, which reads (after the passage guoted in 10–11n) ⲙ̄ⲡⲉ ⲩⲉⲙⲧⲟ ⲉ̄ⲃⲟⲗ ⲛ̄ⲥⲉⲁ̄ⳍⲉⲣⲁⲧⲟⲩ ⲙ̄ⲡⲉⲙⲧⲟ ⲉ̄ⲃⲟⲗ ⲙ̄ⲡⲉⲩⲑⲣⲟⲛⲟⲥ ⲛ̄ⲥⲁⲡ̈ⲓⲥⲁ ⲙ̄ⲛ̄ⲥⲁⲡⲁ̈ⲓ ⲙ̄ⲙⲟ ⲩ (16.37–18.2). Perhaps the Nubian should be reconstructed as ⲧⲉⲕⲕⲁ] ⲅ̄ⲛ̄ⲛⲓⲁ ⲑⲣⲟⲛⲟⲥⲛ̄ [ⲧⲁⲩⳟⲗⲟ ⲅⲟⲛⳝⲉⲣⲁⲛ 'in order that he might see them standing under his throne'; cf. St. 12.7–8 ⲧⲁⲩⳟⲗⲟ ⲅⲟⲛ6ⳑ , and for -ⲛ ⲧⲁⲩⳟ(ⲗⲟ) cf. §213; for the subjunctive see ONVS §66 (especially K. 28.5–7, there quoted).

13 ⲅⲁⲓⲉⲓⲛⲁ: perhaps for ⲅⲁⲣ-ⲉⲓⲛ-ⲗⲁ 'on this side' (Coptic: ⲛ̄ⲥⲁⲡ̈ⲓⲥⲁ ⲙ̄ⲛ̄ⲥⲁⲡⲁ̈ⲓ ; for replacement of /r/ with /i/ see NON XI.C.

14–16 Here the Coptic has ⲛⲧⲉⲩⲛⲟⲩ ⲁ̄�981ⲁ ⲁⲙⲁ �013ⲧⲉ ⲛⲟⲩⲛⲟ6 ⲛⲁⲅⲅⲉⲗⲟⲥ ⲛ̄ⲭⲱ̄ⲣⲉ, ⲉⲩⲙⲟⲩⲧⲉ ⲉ̄ⲣⲟ ⲩ

ⲭⲉⲙⲓ̈ⲭⲁⲏⲗ, ⲁ̄ⲩⲕⲁⲑⲓ̄ⲥⲧⲁ ⲙ̄ⲙⲟⲩ ⲉ̄ⲭⲉⲙⲡⲉⲑⲣⲟⲛⲟⲥ
ⲉⲡⲙⲁ ⲙ̄ⲡⲁⲣⲭⲏⲡⲗⲁⲥⲙⲁ (18.3–5). In 14 ⲙⲟⲩⲣⲧⲱ
may be connected with the verb ⲙⲟⲩⲣⲧ–
'command' (see SC 18.9n.). In 16 ⲥ̣ⲁⲩⲉⲛ̄ invites comparison with M.K.D. *saui* 'schmutzig,
hässlich' (Lepsius; the word is Arabic *sū'*); if the
comparison is valid, ⲥ̣ⲁⲩⲉⲛ̄ ⲑⲣⲟⲛⲟⲥ– will mean
'the throne of the hateful one', a reference to
Mastema, whose name in Coptic is linked with
ⲙⲟⲥⲧⲉ 'hate': see Müller, *Engellehre* 77 n. 590.
17–19 These lines appear to correspond to the
sequel to the Coptic quoted in 14–16n. :ⲁⲩⲱ ⲡⲉ
ⲟ̄ⲟⲩ ⲧⲏⲣ̣ⲩ̣ ⲛⲧⲁⲩⲅ̈ⲓ̈ⲧⲩ ⲛⲧⲟⲟⲧⲩ̄ ⲙ̄ⲙⲁⲥⲧⲏⲙⲁ ⲁⲩⲧⲁⲁⲩ
ⲙ̄ⲙⲓ̈ⲭⲁⲏⲗ (18.5–6). In 18]ⲙⲟⲣⲫⲟⲥ– may be part
of an attributive (missing in the Coptic) to the glory
given to Michael (e.g. εὔμορφος).
19–20 ⲁ̣[±2]/[±6 ⲡⲓⲕ]ⲧ̄ⲛ̄ⲗ: this is presumably
the chariot of light which is found in the Fayumic
version as the second of the items given to Michael:
ⲡⲅ̄ⲁⲣⲙⲁ ⲧⲉ ⲟ̄ⲣⲏⲡⲓ ⲙ̄ⲡⲗⲉⲱⲓ ⲁⲩⲧⲉⲓⲥ ⲅⲓ̄ⲭⲉⲛⲧⲉⲃⲁⲡⲏ,
ⲛⲟⲩⲁⲓⲛ ⲁⲩⲧⲉⲓ ⲉⲙⲓⲭⲁⲏⲗ, ⲡ̄ⲃⲁⲣⲱⲙ ⲙ̄ⲡⲥⲁⲩⲧⲉⲛ
ⲁⲩⲧⲉⲓⲃ ⲙ̄ⲙⲓ̈ⲭⲁⲏⲗ (19.5–7). The Sahidic omits
the chariot, and its remaining items are
arranged as in the Nubian: ⲧⲉⲟ̄ⲣⲏⲡⲉ ⲛⲟⲩⲟ̄ⲉⲓ̈ⲛ
ⲙ̄ⲡ̄ⲣⲁⲱⲉ ⲁⲩⲧⲁⲁⲥ ⲉ̄ⲭ̄ⲛⲧⲁⲡⲉ ⲙ̄ⲙⲓ̈ⲭⲁⲏⲗ, ⲡ̄ⲟ̄ⲣ
ⲱⲃ ⲙ̄ⲙⲉ ⲁⲩⲧⲁⲁⲩ ⲙ̄ⲙⲓⲭⲁⲏⲗ, ⲡ̄ⲧⲟⲟⲩⲉ ⲛ̄ⲧⲡⲏ
ⲛⲏ ⲁⲩⲧⲁⲁⲩ ⲉ̄ⲛⲉⲟⲩⲉ̄ⲣⲏⲧⲉ ⲙ̄ⲙⲓ̈ⲭⲁⲏⲗ (18.6–8).
Doubtless the Nubian reflects an earlier text with
four items, and the Coptic versions, each of which
deletes a different item, come from a later stage in
transmission.

19 ⲡⲓⲕ]ⲧ̄ⲛ̄ⲗ: i.e. ⲡⲓⲕⲧ̄– 'light' + genitival –ⲓⲛ
21 [ⲧⲓⲁ̄ⲧⲧⲁⲕⲥⲛⲁ]: restored on the basis of ii 4–5.
ⲧⲣⲁⲧⲟⲩ· ⲡⲗ̄ⲗ̄[ⲗ̄: cf. ⲧⲉⲟ̄ⲣⲏⲡⲉ ⲛⲟⲩⲟ̄ⲉⲓ̈ⲛ ⲙ̄ⲡ̄ⲣ
ⲁⲱⲉ / ⲧⲉⲟ̄ⲣⲏⲡⲓ ⲙ̄ⲡⲗⲉⲱⲓ (cited above, 19–20n.).
There is no room after ⲡⲗ̄ⲗ̄[ⲗ̄ for the Nubian
equivalent of ⲙ̄ⲡ̄ⲣⲁⲱⲉ; comparable is the omission of ⲛⲟⲩⲁⲓⲛ in the Fayumic.

ii
1–2 ⲥⲟⲩⲁ̄ⲁ̄ⲟⲩ – – – ⲉⲥⲕⲓ̄ⲟⲣⲉⲛⲛⲁ̄: cf. ⲡ̄ⲟ̄ⲣⲱⲃ
ⲙ̄ⲙⲉ / ⲡ̄ⲃⲁⲣⲱⲙ ⲙ̄ⲡⲥⲁⲩⲧⲉⲛ (cited above, i 19–20n.),
of which the Nubian is an expansion.
1 ⲥⲟⲩⲁ̄ⲁ̄–: translates βακτηρία in St. 19.11.
1–2 ⲙⲉⲁ̄ⲁ̄ⲕ̄ⲕⲧⲓⲛⲁ: ⲙⲉⲁ̄ⲁ̄– 'be full' + ⲕ̄ⲕⲧⲓⲛⲁ,
genitive of an abstract noun in –ⲓⲧ (§29) of the

verb ⲓⲕⲕ–/ ⲉⲕⲕ– (see SC 4.16–17n.); for the association of the two verbs note SC 8.6–7
ⲙⲉⲁ̄ⲁ̄ [ⲗ̄ⲅ] ⲟⲩⲥⲁⲛⲕⲁ ⲁ̣ⲣⲓ̣ⲁ̣ⲇⲉⲕⲕⲁ and St.
30.5–6 ⲙⲉⲁ̄ⲁ̄ⲗ̄ [ⲅⲓⲥ] ⲁ [ⲛ̄]ⲕⲁ ⲁⲁⲁ̄ⲕ̄ⲕⲁ; the noun
will therefore mean something like 'readiness,
preparedness'.
2 ⲅⲟⲩⲉⲓ–: 'shield' vel sim.; cf. SC 15.8n.
ⲉⲥⲕⲓ̄ⲟⲣⲉⲛⲛⲁ̄: cf. SC 15.1 ⲁ̣ⲓ̣ⲅⲉⲗ ⲉⲥⲕⲓ̄ⲟⲣⲉⲣⲁⲗⲱ
(νῖκος [sc. ἐστίν]); probably the complex is to
be analysed as ⲉⲥⲕⲓ̄ⲟⲣ(ⲁ) ⲉⲓⲛⲛⲁ̄ 'being victorious' (ONVS §41).
2–3 <ⲕⲟⲥ> ⲙⲟⲥ [ⲛ̄] ⲧⲟⲩⲁ̄ⲅⲓⲧⲓⲛⲁ̄: cf. St. 24.7–8
ⲅⲁⲣⲕⲉⲙⲥⲟⲛⲛⲁ ⲧⲟⲩⲁ̄ⲅⲓⲧⲁⲗⲟ (οἰκουμένης ἀσφά-
φάλεια [sc. ἐστίν]).
3–4 ⲁⲡⲟⲕⲁⲗⲁⲗⲗⲟⲛ ⲧⲱⲕⲛ̄ⲛⲁⲅⲉⲛⲗ̄: cf. ⲡⲧⲟⲟⲩⲉ
ⲛ̄ⲧⲣⲏⲛⲏ (cited above, i 19–20n.). The Vorlage may
have read ὑποδήματα καλά, subsequently cor-
rupted to ⲁⲡⲟⲕⲁⲗⲁⲗ–.
4 What the marginal reference to 136 means I
cannot say.
4–5 ⲧⲓⲁ̄ⲧⲧⲁⲕⲥⲁⲛⲁ: cf. Rev 8:2 and 3 (ined.)
ⲧⲓⲁ̄ⲧⲧⲁⲕⲓⲥⲛⲁ *bis* (ἐδόθησαν ... ἐδόθη); probably ⲧⲓⲁ̄ⲧ– is assimilated from ⲧⲓⲁ–ⲣ̄–
'kommen lassen, begegnen lassen,' for which see
BanG III 5.1.
5–7 Here the Coptic has (continuing from the
quote in i 19–20n.) ⲁⲩⲕⲟⲥⲙⲉⲓ̈ ⲙ̄ⲙⲟⲩ ⲛ̄ⲧⲉⲩⲱⲏ
ⲛ̄ⲥⲟⲩⲙⲛ̄ⲧⲥⲛⲟⲟⲩⲥ ⲛ̄ⲅⲁⲑⲱⲣ, ⲁⲩⲧⲁⲅⲟⲩ ⲉ̄ⲣⲁⲧⲩ̄
ⲅⲓ̈ⲭⲙ̄ⲡⲕⲟⲥⲙⲟⲥ ⲛⲟⲩⲟ̄ⲉⲓ̈ⲛ ⲅ̄ⲛ̄ⲧⲡⲉ ⲁⲩⲱ ⲅⲓ̈ⲭ̄ⲙⲡ
ⲕⲟⲥⲙⲟⲥ[3] ⲛ̄ⲥⲟⲩⲙⲛ̄ⲧⲥⲛⲟⲟⲩⲥ ⲛ̄ⲅⲁⲑⲱⲣ (18.8–11),
with the time of day mentioned later (see below,
11–13n.).
5 ⲟ̄ⲁⲣ–: cf. Rev 14:11 (cited in SC 19.8n.).
ⲥⲟⲣⲟⲟ̄ⲟⲓⲛ ⲕ̄ⲧ̄ⲧⲗⲱ: for this phrase, absent
in the Coptic, see Part II. Presumably
ⲥⲟⲣⲟⲟ̄– = ⲥⲟⲣⲟ̄–: cf. SC 24.20n.
6 ⲁ̄ⲟⲩⲧ–: = ⲕⲟⲥⲙⲉⲓ̈; the same verb also renders κοσμέω in SC 18.5 (if—as I suggested in my
note ad loc.—it is connected with F.M. *ded*
'sammeln' (Reinisch), it has shifted semantically in
passing from Old Nubian to the modern dialects).
ⲟⲩⲁⲗⲓⲥⲟ: I connect this with F.M. *wallo* 'mor-
gen' (Reinisch) and assume that it is a verb, 1st pers.
pl. Pret. II: 'we spent the morning': cf. Coptic
ϣⲱⲣⲡ̄ 'be early' (verb) and 'morning' (noun); see
Crum, *Dictionary* 586b.

---

[3] Müller translates: 'und über die Welt (scil. die irdische)' (Trans. Vol., p. 21). Corresponding to the passage cited in the
commentary, the Fayumic reads: ⲁⲩⲕⲱⲥⲙⲓ ⲙ̄ⲙⲁⲩ ⲛⲧⲉⲩⲱⲏ ⲛⲥⲟⲩⲓ̄ⲃ ⲛⲅ̄ⲁⲑⲱⲗ, ⲁⲩⲧⲁⲅⲁⲃ ⲉⲗⲉⲧⲩ ⲅⲓ̈ⲭⲉⲛⲡ
ⲕⲟⲥⲙⲟ<ⲥ> ⲙ̄ⲡⲟⲩⲁ̄ⲓⲛ (19.7–9). This suggests that the words ⲅ̄ⲛ̄ⲧⲡⲉ ⲁⲩⲱ ⲅⲓ̈ⲭ̄ⲙⲡⲕⲟⲥⲙⲟⲥ ⲛ̄ⲥⲟⲩⲙⲛ̄ⲧⲥⲛⲟⲟⲩⲥ
ⲅ̄ⲱⲑⲁ̄ⲅ̄ⲛ̄ belong to a different strand of text and should be deleted.

ⲡⲗⲗⲁⲆⲆⲗ: cf. on i 9; there is no correspondent in the Coptic.

ⲅⲓⲅⲁ: cf. F.M. *gig* 'lachen' (Reinisch); if the comparison holds, the meaning here will be 'rejoicing' vel sim. The word corresponds to nothing in the Coptic.

7 Cf. on i 9.

8–10 This section is somewhat similar to the Coptic in a later passage: ⲁⲩⲱ ⲁ̄ⲡⲉⲅⲥ̄ⲧⲛⲟⲩϥⲉ ⲙⲟⲩⲅ ⲙ̄ⲡ̄ⲙⲉⲅⲥⲁϣϥ̄ ⲛⲉⲱⲛ ⲙ̄ⲡⲟⲩⲟ̄ⲉⲓ̈ⲛ. ⲇ̄ⲡⲁⲉⲓ̈ⲱⲧ ⲟⲩⲛ<ⲟⲩ> ⲁⲩⲣⲁϣⲉ --- ⲁ̄ⲡⲉⲇⲟⲩ ⲙ̄ⲛⲛⲉⲇⲩⲛⲁⲙⲓ̈ⲥ ⲭⲱⲣⲉⲩⲉ --- ⲁⲩⲥ̄ⲙⲟⲩ ⲉⲧⲃⲓ̄ⲛⲧⲁⲅⲟ ⲉ̄ⲣⲁⲧⲩ̄ ⲙ̄ⲙ ⲓ̈ⲭ̄ⲁⲏⲗ, ⲉ̄ⲣⲉⲛⲉⲙⲡⲏⲩⲉ̄ ⲣⲁϣⲉ ⲉⲩⲉⲣϣⲁ (18.21––26).

8 ⲕⲟⲥⲙⲟⲥ ⲕⲟⲗⲟⲧⲛ̄: 'of seven worlds'; the Coptic ⲙ̄ⲡ̄ⲙⲉⲅⲥⲁϣϥ̄ ⲛⲉⲱⲛ suggests that this is corrupt for ⲕⲟⲥⲙⲟⲥⲛ̄ ⲕⲟⲗⲟⲧⲓⲧⲛ̄ (cf. Rev 8:1 [ined.] ⲧⲣⲁⲡⲁⲧⲛ̄ ⲕⲟⲗⲟⲧⲓⲧⲕⲁ [τὴν σφραγῖδα τὴν ἑβδόμην]).

9 ⲅⲟⲩⲧⲁⲕⲥⲛⲁ: 'he was established,' literally, 'he was built,' if this is the same verb that appears in SC 11.4 ⲅⲟⲩϥⲓⲣ[ⲉ (οἰκοδομήσω), IC b 14 ⲅⲟⲩϥ- and below in line 13, ⲅⲟⲩϥ-; cf. F.M.K.D. *goñ* 'bauen' (Reinisch); the alternation of ⲟ and ⲟⲩ is attested: see §18.1.c.

10 ⲥⲕⲧ-: the expected stroke over ⲥ was not written; sim.: K. 20.11, Rev 6:8 and possibly Ben 20 (ⲥⲕ̄ⲧ-).

ⲅⲟⲩ-: cf. F.M.K.D. *gur* 'sich freuen, fröhlich sein, lachen' (Reinisch).

ⲟⲩⲁⲙⲛ̄ⲛⲁⲛ̄: if this corresponds to ⲉⲩⲉⲣϣⲁ (see above, ii 8–10n.), I have no cognate; possibly it is related to K.D. *bān* 'tanzen' (Almkvist), for which cf. ⲭⲱⲣⲉⲩⲉ in the same passage. The form is subjunctive, 3rd pers. pl., used as a circumstantial (cf. ONVS §66).

11–13 Here the Nubian somewhat closely follows the Coptic, which—after a statement (possibly an interpolation) about Mary's giving birth to the whole world on 29 Choiak (18.12–13)[4]—continues with the narrative at the point where we stopped quoting in ii 5–7n.: ⲅ̄ⲛ̄ⲧⲉⲩⲛⲟⲩ ⲉ̄ⲧⲙⲙⲁⲩ ⲁⲡⲛⲟⲃ ⲛ̄ⲥⲓ̈ⲟⲩ ϣⲁ ⲅ̄ⲛ̄ⲧⲁⲛⲁⲧⲟⲗⲏ. ⲛ̄ⲧⲉⲩⲛⲟⲩ ⲟⲛ

ⲉ̄ⲧⲙⲙⲁⲩ ⲁⲩⲧⲁⲅⲟ ⲉ̄ⲣⲁⲧⲩ̄ ⲙ̄ⲙⲓ̈ⲭⲁⲏⲗ, ⲉ̄ⲧⲉⲡ̄ ⲛⲁⲩ ⲙ̄ⲡⲟⲩⲟ̄ⲉⲓ̈ⲛⲡⲉ (18.13–15).

11–12 ⲙⲁ [ϣⲁⲛ ⲧⲁ] ⲣⲁⲧⲗⲱ: cf., e.g. SC 18.7 and L. 106.11 (with n.).

12–13 ⲥⲟⲅⲟⲃⲁ̣ [Δⲁⲩⲣⲁ]ⲅⲣⲁ: 'making (Michael) great *soñoj*'; for the phrase, absent in the Coptic, see Part II.

13 ⲅⲟⲩϥⲓⲙ: this may be a mistake for ⲅⲟⲩϥⲓⲗⲟ (cf. SC 13.18n.), itself equivalent to ⲅⲟⲩϥⲓⲗ-ⲗⲟ (cf. Mk 11:9 ⲧⲁⲣⲟⲩⲥⲁⲛⲗⲱ̄ = ⲧⲁⲣⲟⲩ-ⲥⲁⲛⲓⲗ-ⲗⲱ; cf. my note ad loc. in ZPE 44 [1981] 164).

15–16 Cf. Coptic ⲙ̄ⲛ̄ⲛ̄ⲥⲱⲥ ⲁ̄ⲡⲁⲉⲓ̈ⲱⲧ ⲟⲩⲉⲅⲥⲁ ⲅ̄ⲛⲉ ⲛ̄ⲛⲉⲁⲅⲅⲉⲗⲟⲥ ⲉⲧⲣⲉⲅⲉⲓ̈ ⲛ̄ⲥⲉⲟⲩⲱϣⲧ̄ ⲙ̄ⲙⲓ̈ⲭⲁⲏⲗ (18.16–17).Possibly restore ⲁⲅⲅⲉⲗⲟⲥⲅⲟⲩⲕⲁ]Δⲟⲩⲕⲕ [ⲁⲛⲁⲥⲁ (for the syntax cf. SC 18.14 ⲁ̄ⲙⲁⲛⲅⲟⲉⲓⲅ ⲟⲩⲕⲁ ⲙⲓⲇⲁⲛⲁⲥⲁ).

17–18 Cf. Coptic: ⲛ̄ⲥⲉⲁⲥⲡⲁⲍⲉ ⲙ̄ⲙⲟⲩ ⲁⲩⲱ ⲛ̄ⲥⲉ ⲙⲟⲩ ⲛ̄ⲙⲙⲁⲩ ⲉ̄ⲡⲉⲇⲟⲩ ⲉⲧⲭ̄ⲏⲕ ⲉ̄ⲃⲟⲗ (18.17–18), but if the Nubian reflects this passage, it has altered it by specifying the subject (ⲁⲅⲅⲉⲗⲟⲥⲅⲟ[ⲩⲗ?]) and the object (ⲙⲓⲭⲁ̄ⲏⲗⲓⲕⲁ).

18–20 Cf. Coptic: ⲁⲩⲱ ⲁ̄ⲙⲓ̈ⲭⲁⲏⲗ ⲥⲁⲗⲡⲓ̈ⲍⲉ ⲛ̄ⲧⲥⲁ ⲗⲡⲓ̈ⲅⲝ̄ ⲙ̄ⲡⲱⲛⲅ̄ (18.18–19).The restoration ⲡⲟⲧⲟⲧ ⲕⲁ is modelled on Rev 8:6–8 (ined.), where we find the following expressions: ⲡⲟⲧⲟⲧⲕⲁ ⲟⲩϣⲉⲛⲟⲩⲅ̄ (ἵνα σαλπίσωσιν), ⲡⲟⲧⲟⲧⲕ ⲟⲩϣⲟⲩⲛⲟⲛ- (ἐσάλπισεν), and ⲡⲟⲧⲟⲧⲕⲁ ⲟⲩϣⲛⲟⲩⲛⲟⲛ (ἐσάλπισεν).[5] In the present text, the space is too short for this verb, however it was spelled, but it may have been preceded by an adjunctive; note that the verb ends in line 20.

21 ⲡ̄ⲣ̄ⲣⲁ: cf. SC 19.9–10 ⲃⲓⲙⲙⲗ̄ⲅⲟ[ⲩ]ⲗ ⲡ̄ⲣ̄ⲣⲁ 'all things came forth' (see my note in STB 5 [1983] 3). Cf. the Coptic: ⲙ̄ⲡⲉⲟⲩⲁⲅⲅⲉⲗⲟⲥ ⲛⲟⲩⲱⲧ ⲃⲱ ⲅ̄ⲛ̄ⲧⲡⲉ ⲙ̄ⲛ̄ⲍⲓ̈ⲭⲉⲙ̄ⲡⲕⲁⲅ ⲟⲩⲇⲉ ⲅ̄ⲙ̄ⲡⲡⲁⲣⲁⲇⲓ̈ⲥⲟⲥ, ⲉⲓ̈ⲙ ⲛ̄ⲧⲉⲓ̈ ⲛ̄ⲧⲁⲅⲉⲓ̈ ⲧⲏⲣⲟⲩ (18.19–20).

22]ⲉⲕⲕⲗ̄Δⲁⲕⲓⲧⲁ̣[: this may be connected with ⲉⲕⲕⲗ̄Δⲁⲧⲧ- 'prophet' discussed in SC 4.16–17n. At this point there is no obvious association with the Coptic, which reads: ⲁⲅⲁⲥⲡⲁⲍⲉ ⲙ̄ⲙⲓ̈ⲭⲁⲏⲗ ⲉ̄ⲣⲉⲛⲉⲅⲥ̄ⲧⲛⲟⲩϥⲉ ⲅ̄ⲛ̄ⲛⲉⲩⲃⲓⲭ· ⲁⲩⲱ ⲁ̄ⲡⲉⲅⲥ̄ⲧ ⲛⲟⲩϥⲉ ⲙⲟⲩⲅ ⲙ̄ⲡ̄ⲙⲉⲅⲥⲁϣϥ̄ ⲛⲉⲱⲛ ⲙ̄ⲡⲟⲩⲟ̄ⲉⲓ̈ⲛ (18.20–22: cf. above, ii 8–10n.).

---

[4] Here the Coptic reads: ⲛ̄ⲧⲉⲩⲛⲟⲩ ⲛ̄ⲧⲁⲅ̄ⲡⲁⲣⲑⲉⲛⲟⲥ ⲉ̄ⲧⲟⲩⲁⲁⲃ ⲙⲁⲣⲓ̄ⲁ ⲭ̄ⲡⲟ ⲙ̄ⲡⲱⲛⲅ̄ ⲙ̄ⲡⲕⲟⲥⲙⲟⲥ ⲧⲏⲣϥ̄, ⲛ̄ϣⲱⲣⲡ̄ ⲛ̄ⲥⲟⲩⲭⲟⲩⲧⲯⲓ̈ⲥ ⲛ̄ⲭⲟⲓ̈ⲁⲅⲕ.

[5] In the last two instances, the Old Nubian renders ἐσάλπισεν by a subordinating subjunctive; for other instances of this phenomenon, see my remarks on Mk 11:6 in ZPE 44 (1981), 160 (ad 3–4).

COPTIC STUDIES

Wolfgang Brunsch

Bitte um Mitteilung der bibliographischen Daten koptisch-philologischer Publikationen für die AEB und PEB

Mr President, sehr geehrte Damen und Herren!

Für den Jahrgang 1980 noch zum Teil und von 1981 an allein habe ich das Referat des Koptischen als verantwortlicher Mitautor in der Annual Egyptological Bibliography (AEB) übernommen. Dem vorgegebenen Rahmen entsprechend soll in der AEB in stärkerem Masse als bisher über Veröffentlichungen koptischer Philologie referiert werden, was auch Publikationen koptischer Texte miteinschließt, sofern sie philologisch kommentiert sind.

Nun hat sich im Zusammenhang mit den allgemeinen Sparmaßnahmen die Bibliotheksituation in Würzburg seit 1981 erheblich verschlechtert. Für die Beschaffung von koptologischen Monographien und entlegeneren Zeitschriften hänge ich folglich fast ganz von der Hilfe auswärtiger Bibliotheken ab. Des weiteren bin ich aber auch auf die Unterstützung der Fachgenoßen angewiesen, wenn grössere Lücken in meinem Referat vermieden werden sollen.

Um diese Unterstützung in einem meines Erachtens für uns alle wichtigen Unternehmen, wie es die AEB darstellt, möchte ich Sie bitten. Konkret denke ich mir diese Ihrerseits wie folgt: Mitteilung der bibliographischen Daten neu erschienener Monographien und Aufsätze an meine Würzburger Institutsadresse. Bei Aufsätzen wäre ich für Sonderdrucke oder Xerokopien besonders dankbar. In diesem Zusammenhag darf ich Sie darauf hinweisen, daß entsprechende Monographien oder Sonderdrucke, die zum Zwecke der Aufnahme in AEB direkt nach Leiden geschickt werden, in den Besitz der dortigen Universitätsbibliothek übergehen, für mich also (zunächst einmal) unzugänglich sind.

Ihre Mitteilungen sollten möglichst bald nach Erscheinen erfolgen, damit eine rechtzeitige Aufnahme der jeweiligen Titel bereits in die Preliminary Egyptological Bibliography (PEB), die Nachfolgerin der Egyptology Titels, gewährleistet ist.

Herzlichen Dank!

COPTIC STUDIES

Elvira D'Amicone

A Stele of a "Follower of Isis" in the Egyptian Museum of Turin

The stele under study is Number 18110 in the Egyptian Museum of Turin (photo). According to the museum's archives, it was acquired on the antiquities market, just as other examples of the same category of document which appeared on the market at the end of the 1950s.[1] The indicated place of origin was referred to as Antinoe, and since no considerations contrary to such origin were proposed during the study of the extant examples, this attribution has remained and continues to remain, notwithstanding doubts and uncertainty. The period of datation is 3rd–4th century A.D.; the typological and cultural reference is to the category of funerary stelae whose particular iconography seems to refer to the Isis cult (represented by the figure of the young boy Harpocrates). In this connection, an evident element of reference is the figure of the child-god painted on a wooden tablet conserved in the Egyptian Museum of Cairo: the god is depicted semi-reclining on a pillow with a cluster of grapes in the left hand; he is flanked on the right by a small dog in a playful position. This object is examined by Müller in his second study dedicated to this category of documents, and the image doubtless constitutes a precise reference point.[2] The more general works of Parlasca and Wessel, together with the catalogues of exhibitions and collections enlarge and enrich the documentary repertoire relative to this category of material, offering a unitary and stylistically modulated panorama.[3]

And now let us look at the typology of the stele. Inside a niche, hardly characterized from the architectonic point of view,[4] there is the figure of a

child sculpted in high-relief, almost completely in the round, either standing or kneeling on a pillow. The child is usually depicted wearing a simple tunic, which in some examples still conserves traces of the original colours; only a single example exists with a rich, decorated form of the tunic,

[1] H. W. Müller, "Grabstele eines Isismysten aus Antinoe", *Pantheon* XVIII (1960), 267–271; id., "Stele eines Jünglings mit christlichen Kreuz", in: *Die Sammlung W. Esch-Duisburg*, München 1961, pp. 35–39, figs 23–27.

[2] Müller, "Stele...", p. 38, fig. 26.

[3] K. Wessel, *L'art copte*, Bruxelles 1964, pp. 97–101; K. Parlasca, *Mumienporträts und verwandte Denkmäler*, Wiesbaden 1976, pp. 204–206; H. D. Schneider and M. J. Raven, *De Egyptische Oudheit*, Leiden 1981, n. 161.

[4] On the subject of funerary stele with a similar architectonic frame, cf. Schneider-Raven, nos 158–159.

having *clavi* and *orbiculi*. In this example, the *orbiculus* decorating the neck-opening reproduces a fairly characteristic element of juvenile clothing, the *bulla*, a circular pendant with apotropaic value present on many of the stelae under examination. Usually the young boy is depicted grasping a dove or a little dog in one hand, and a cluster of grapes in the other. There exists a single example of a boy holding a cross in his right hand, while in two other examples, the arms are represented closely flanking the boy's body. On a stele in the Grand collection in Zurich, a frog is represented near the pillow, the frog having an auspicious value related to renewal and rebirth. The measurements of the stele vary from 40 to 50 cm in height, and from 20 to 30 cm in width. As for the colours conserved, there is documented a fairly consistent use of red and greenish-blue. The iconography of the young boy's face shows the elements characteristic of Late Antique portrait art, amply documented in Egypt by both mummy-masks and portraits: large eyes, ears frontally depicted, and a hairstyle with short locks arranged in a parallel fashion in order to frame the face, almost in a "page-boy style". The example conserved in Turin demonstrates a very rude and simplified production of a typology which in other cases is more precise and rich in details, succeeding even in representing the decoration of the column capitals in the niche, and that of the embroidered bands on the child's tunic[5].

Notwithstanding the difficulties and queries posed by the stele under observation, I would have nothing to add to the study of Müller taken up and redefined by Parlasca and others, if not for the fact that during a visit to the Museum of Oriental Art in Rome, I came across a singular document, in which the figure of the young boy with the dove and the cluster of grapes in his hands reappears in a completely different context. In this case we are dealing with a limestone slab employed as a burial niche closure, typical of the artistic production of Palmyra. The object is worked in high-relief, with the figure of a richly ornamented female bust flanked by a young boy standing; he holds a cluster of grapes in his right hand and a dove in his left hand. Two Aramaic texts are incised, with the name of the dead person, their patronym, and the exclamation of mourning to the left of their faces respectively. Although not specified by the inscriptions, a mother–son relationship is not to be excluded, encouraged by reference to other similar examples where such attestation is clearly documented. Acquired by the Italian government in 1971 during the sale of the Sangiorgi collection, the stele was attested on the antiquities market since the end of the 1800s, just as the majority of the Palmyrean stelae present in European and American collections. The image of the young boy, similar in many aspects to that on the stele studied by Müller and Parlasca (attributes, hairstyle, typology of the ears) is, however, different with regard to the more triangular shape of the face, the oval eyes, and the clothing (short tunic worn over trousers). These attributes lead us to a Syrian environment heavily imbued with Parthian influences.[6]

The search for other possible references and links between the Syrian city of Palmyra (important centre for sorting out the destination of various merchandise and stopping-place for long-distance trade from the Far East to Africa and Europe) and the cities of Roman Egypt led me to retrieve a work of Reinach from 1913. This work included, among the artifacts brought to light during the excavation of the city of Coptos, numerous limestone slabs with highrelief busts of the Palmyra-type.[7] The documentation confirmed the presence of communities of Palmyreans, among whom were archers, attested in Egypt as well as in other provinces of the Roman Empire during the Antonine Period.[8] It is interesting to note that on some stelae, the dead persons are depicted with an arrow in their hands. In some examples, they are also shown as having a garland folded in their hands, this too being a typical element of Late Period funerary iconography and subject to repeated attempts at exegetic reconstruction. The

---

[5] Parlasca 1966, tab. Ib.

[6] P. Callieri, "Il rilievo palmireno di Btmlkw e Hyrn nel Museo Nazionale d'Arte Orientale di Roma", in: *Museo Nazionale d'Arte Orientale 6, Arte Orientale Italia* V, Roma 1980, 5–18.

[7] A. Reinach, *Catalogue des Antiquités égyptiennes recueillies dans les fouilles de Koptos 1910–1911*, Chalon sur Saône 1913, pp. 46–56.

[8] J. Lesquier, "L'armée romaine d'Égypte d'Auguste à Dioclétien", MIFAO XLI, 97, 282; H. Zaloscher, "Quelques considérations sur les rapports entre l'art copte et les Indes", Suppl.ASAE 6 (Le Caire 1947), 54–70.

connection Coptos–Palmyra is not unexpected, from the commercial point of view, since both cities are located along the mercantile route which, crossing the Negev, reached the Red Sea und subsequently the Nile Valley. Such a connection reproposes the problem of cultural exchanges and of the presence of foreign colonies in cities particularly important in ancient times for caravan traffic. In this respect, I think it opportune to open an excursus which, although it proposes again the theme of relations and influences, shows how the innovations could only be accepted where the environment was particularly susceptible to such a transplant as well as how these phenomena acquire particular connotations according to the period in which they occur.

In 1941 in his annual report on the excavations at Palmyra, Seyrig published a fragmentary document (an altar) whose frontal surface was decorated with a radial element indicating a solar reference, and an imperial eagle, which contains weighty connotations of an auspicious and solar nature.[9] The scrutiny (unfortunately not yet completely systematic) of the Palmyra excavation reports led me to another example of this decorative scheme in a fragmentary naos discovered in 1960 by Michałowski.[10] The obvious solar characters and the same decorative system can be noted in another area and period, however, following an identical reproposition, i.e. the Upper Egyptian area, to be exact the sites of Luxor--Esna-Edfu.[11] Direct connections between the Red Sea ports, where ships loaded with merchandise from the important caravan cities landed, and the centre of Edfu already existed in the Antonine Period by way of Berenice.[12] Thus it is no surprise that there could have been exchanges and influence between an area like that of Upper Egypt with the strong character of its sun-cults, and the city of Palmyra, where a local cult of Helios was likewise formly established.

That these influences were accomplished by means of the figure of the Roman imperial eagle is a sign of the times, just as we owe the exegesis of another element of Late Period religious-funerary iconography to the particular spiritual atmosphere: the cluster of grapes, which when related to images of adults is often transformed into a cup of wine. In all of the ancient societies, this beverage plays a particular role both in the sectors of daily life and of religious events, due to its evident references to the experience of the divine and of the sacrifice and for its specific qualities which provoke a condition of intoxication superior to that caused by beer, another drink common in ancient times.[13] The presence and the role of wine in Egypt are very old, but the importance of the beverage grew progressively greater following Egypt's ever-widening contacts with the Middle East, where wine must have had a doubtlessly greater importance and role in both the profane and religious fields. Many syncretisms and assimilations connected with the figures of the divinities and of the cults referring to wine were already present at the end of the Hellenistic period. During the political unification of the ancient world attempted by Rome, such an operation becomes still more extensive, rendered necessary by the need to create a religious language common to all. In this koiné the cup of wine and the cluster of grapes are widely propagated, accompanying the dead person during his passage into another dimension. It is not improbable that the wide-reaching diffusion of such iconography during the profound spiritual crisis which characterizes the Late Antique Period refers to the sacrificial experience and thus to the primary re-acquisition of the divinity.

During the exegesis of attributes of the funerary repertoire which likewise characterize the documentary repertoire of the stele herein under examination, the figure of the dove must not be neglected. Local folklore and the peasantry generally connected the dove with fertility; mythology assigned it to Aphrodite, perhaps

[9] Seyrig, Syria XXII (1941), tab. III.

[10] K. Michałowski, Palmyre 1960, Paris 1962, pp. 122–130.

[11] S. Sauneron et R. R. Coquin, "Catalogue provisoire des stèles funéraires coptes d'Esna", in: Livre du centenaire 1880–1980, Le Caire 1980, pp. 239–280.

[12] Lexicon der Ägyptologie I, s.v. "Berenike".

[13] V. Lanniello, "Il sangue dell'uva", in: F. Vattioni (ed.), Sangue e Antropologia Biblica nella Patristica, Roma 23–28 agosto 1981, Roma 1982, pp. 241–269; E. D'Amicone, La coppa di vino ed il grappolo d'uva nell'iconografia funeraria di età tardoantica (in press).

Aphrodite Libitina, the protectress of the dead [14] who was often assimilated with the funerary Isis both in Egypt and in the areas demonstrating a strong diffusion of Egyptian cults. It is not by change that the dove appears as an attribute of a young boy on an object found at Ostia, clearly depicted according to the iconography of the child-god Harpocrates, i.e. the presence of the braided sidelock.[15]

Egyptian traditions, assimilations with other religious speculations, new cultural exigencies, and iconographic languages having polyvalent meanings make up the complex panorama of the deep-seated intellectual tension present in the Late Antique Period, of which the so-called "Followers of Isis" stele constitute an example at the popular level.

---

[14] *Realencyclopedie PW, s.v.* "Taube".
[15] *Enciclopedia dell'Arte Antica Classica ed Orientale* V, Roma, fig. 958.

COPTIC STUDIES

Wiktor A. Daszewski, Hassan el Sheikh, Stanisław Medeksza

An Unknown Christian Complex in Alexandria

In the summer of 1981 construction work for a new residential building was carried out on the plot of land belonging to a certain Mr Abdel Haleem Hamouda in the area of Miami-Sidi Bishr in the eastern part of modern Alexandria. The plot, situated some 800 m south of the seashore, lies between Gamal Abdel Nasser street to the south, 1007 street to the west, 1006 street to the north and 56 street to the east. The Ras el Soda sanctuary is to be found a short distance to the south-east, the El Mandara district and El Montaza Gardens lie further to the east.[1]

During foundation digging for a new house on the said plot traces of ancient walls and a large water cistern were spotted. This casual discovery induced Dr Youssef Cheriani, Director of the Graeco-Roman Museum in Alexandria, to intervene and delegate Mr Hassan el Sheikh to conduct brief rescue excavations. Dr W. A. Daszewski accompanied by Dr S. Medeksza and Mr Z. Doliński of the Polish Centre of Archaeology was invited to cooperate briefly in the execution of documentation.[2] At present, that is in August 1984, nothing remains of the ancient structures. By the time the rescue operation was begun much of the ancient constructions had already been destroyed by modern development. Only the outlines of walls remained in the sections of the foundation trenches. The total area in question covered some 7000 m², out of which less than 500 m² were summarily investigated. The remainder was surveyed in order that all visible traces of ancient remains would be registered. Following are the results obtained. In the western part of the plot a large structure oriented NW–SE was found. Excavated were only the northern section of this structure and a few spots to the south. The central part of the structure, damaged already in antiquity, was uncovered during construction work. It appears to be rectangular in plan (cf. plan I). Its northern wall, some 0.60 m large, stood to a height of about 1.25 m. It was made of partly dressed limestone blocks of medium and small size, set upon lime mortar and plastered with white lime plaster. Also preserved were the northern part of the west wall and a small fragment of the east wall. The latter has been damaged by modern foundation digging. In the southern end of the structure parts of a wall, which may perhaps have also belonged to the building in question, were visible in a foundation trench. This part of the plot has not been excavated, however. The entire structure measured from east to west 15 m; its length (N–S) remains uncertain.

The only wall (mentioned above) found to the south at a distance of 21 m from the north wall had a slightly different orientation being more inclined towards NE. It was, however, similar in character to the other walls of the building. Either this wall belonged to an adjacent structure situated further to the south or it formed part of our building. Had it belonged to the building, its entire length would have then been 21 m. The existence of a large water cistern under the structure may also perhaps be instrumental for our calculations. The cistern was situated on the NE side of the building (cf. plan I). Its outer wall formed the foundation for the E wall of the building. It is not to be precluded that the S wall of the cistern had supported the S wall of the upper building. If the latter is true, the length of the building would have approximated 15.5 m suggesting an almost square plan.

In the middle of the N wall and adjacent to it on the south there was found a large podium provided

[1] Cf. *Guide Blue Egypte* (1956), plan on p. 32.

[2] The present paper is the result of this joint effort.

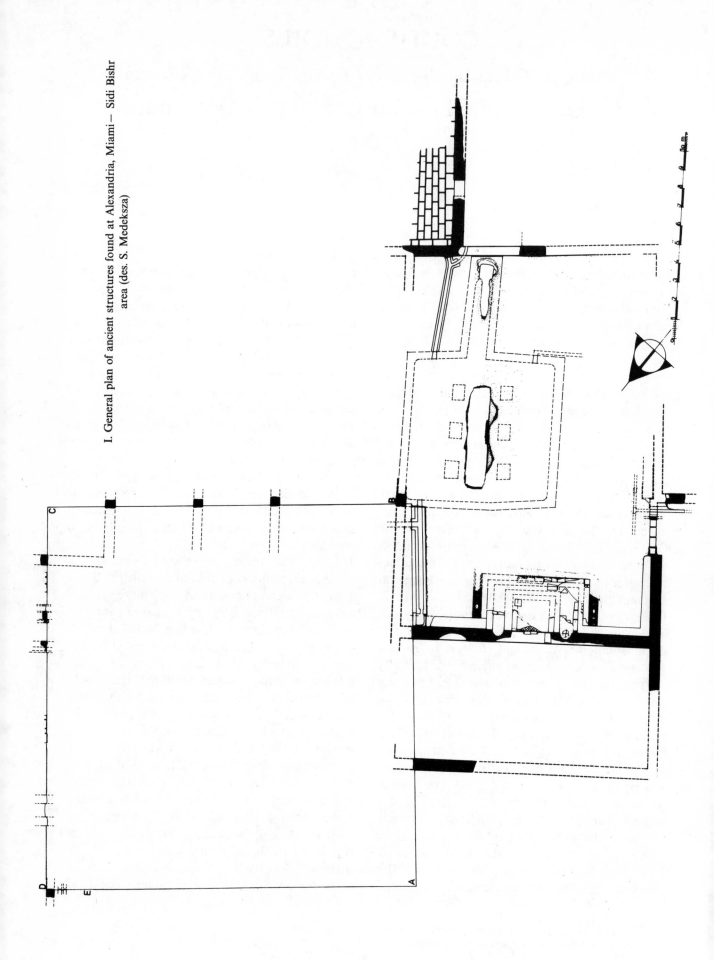

I. General plan of ancient structures found at Alexandria, Miami – Sidi Bishr area (des. S. Medeksza)

1. Large podium adjacent to the north wall of the main structure. Painted decoration of the floor visible alongst the lower step. View from the south-west

with six steps on all three sides (fig. 1). The dimensions of the steps are as follows: step 1 — H: 14 cm; W: 26 cm; step 2 — H: 14 cm; W: 26 cm, step 3 — H: 9.5 cm; W: 32 cm; step 4 — H: 22 cm; W: 32 cm; step 5 — H: 16 cm; W: 31 cm. They were made of small limestone blocks revetted with limestone slabs 5 cm thick and 40 cm long set in lime mortar. Some of the steps were strengthened at the corners with rectangular blocks 0.40 m long. The steps led to an almost square platform (1.70 m × 1.75 m) which bore traces of revetment in *opus sectile*. Lozenge-shaped slabs of greyish marble were set in a mortar of lime mixed with ashes. In the N wall, on the level of the third (wider) step of the podium there were found two semi-circular brick-built niches approximately 0.71 m large. The niches, which faced south, were decorated on either side with pilasters of limestone covered with white plaster. The pilasters supported two rectangular blocks from which sprang an arch of bricks. The bricks were 0.12 m long and 0.045 m high. The arch was embellished with stucco reliefs in the form of a meander with swastikas and rosettes inscribed within the squares alternating with the swastikas.[3] Small fragments of this decoration as well as of dentils were found in this area [4] (fig. 2a–e). The W niche revealed two pavements. The earlier one was made of limestone slabs. At some later date the slabs were covered with a 2 cm thick layer of lime plaster.

The floor of the building, better preserved in its northern part especially near the stairs of the podium, was made of fired bricks covered with a thick layer of lime plaster. Alongst the lowest step of the podium, on both sides of it, there was a painted geometric decoration applied to the floor upon the uppermost thin layer of clean lime (cf. plan I). It had the form of a wide band 0.43 m wide, of red-claret colour upon which there showed in white a row of alternating one big and two or three small lozenges. On both sides of the broad band there were two narrow stripes of red-claret and

---

[3] For similar decoration see a limestone relief stele, now in Dumbarton Oaks, showing an old saint in monk's dress, cf. K. Wessel, *Koptische Kunst,* Recklinghausen 1963, p. 47 and fig. 62.

[4] For similar decoration see fragment of the pediment of a niche, cf. J. Strzygowski, *Koptische Kunst,* Wien 1904, pp. 32 f., no 7288; another fragment now in Berlin K.F.M. 1106, id. 33, fig. 39, assigned to 4th/5th centuries A.D.

a

c

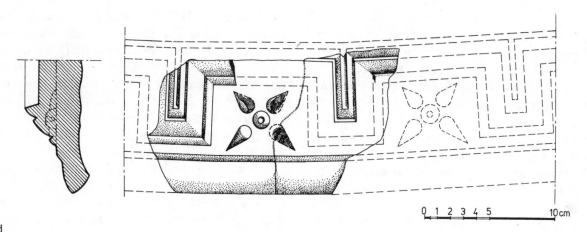

d

e

0 1 2 3 4 5   10 cm

2. Fragments of stucco decorations of the niches flanking the podium
a) meander with swastikas and squares; b) graphic reconstruction of the meander; c) dentils; d) graphic reconstruction of the dentils;
e) stylized egg and tongue pattern

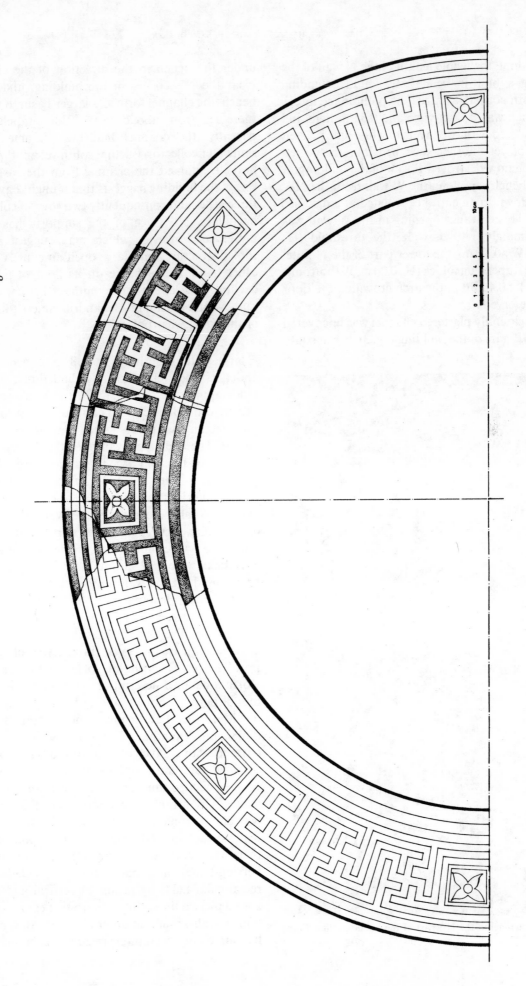

b

white. Along the whole length of the N wall of the building a built-in bench was found extending from both corners towards the podium (cf. fig. 1). The bench was 0.52 m wide and 0.33 m high and was plastered with two layers of white lime plaster. Traces of yet another such bench were spotted along the now destroyed E wall of the building. A similar bench ran along the W wall from the NW corner down to an entrance situated at a distance of 4 m. This entrance opening in the W wall was approximately 1.40 m wide; the threshold (H: 0.14 m; W: 0.36 m), the lower part of the N lintel and one trapezoidal block (H: 0.20 m; W (bottom): 0.26 m; L: 0.46 m) of the arch crowning the door were preserved.

A small carefully plastered channel was uncovered in the NE part of the building (fig. 3). It ran south

3. Water channel in the NE part of the building. View from the south

under the bench in the direction of the cistern. Near the NE corner of the building, under the bench, the channel formed a larger basin to which there led from above east a side branch. Apparently, the channel had the character of a rainwater collector. Further south yet another side branch adjoined the channel from the east. The size of the building suggests that it might have had three aisles and consequently two rows of columns or pillars. No trace of the supports has been preserved, however, which may suggest not a roofed structure, but a large open-air court. On the other hand, the presence on its floor of painted decoration weakens this hypothesis in view of the rainy winter season in Alexandria, unless this part of the court was roofed.

A large water cistern (8.5 m × 8.25 m) was found under its floor (cf. plan II). It had three vaulted aisles (approx. H: 2.65 m; L: 7.70 m; W-side aisles: 2.25 m; central aisle: 2 m) divided by two rows of three rectangular pillars joined together by arches (fig. 4). The walls and vaults of the cistern were made of red bricks. Large interstices were filled in with lime plaster mixed with sand and some powdered bricks. The size of the bricks in the walls and the vaults differed. In the walls they were 0.23 m long, 5 cm high; in the upper parts of the arches they were shorter and thicker. In the vaults the bricks were 0.22 m long and 5 cm high. The bricks used for the wall on top of the arches and vaults, i.e. the lower courses of the floor of the upper structure, were 0.22 m long, 0.10 m wide and 6 cm high. The outer surface of the walls was covered with two or even three layers of water-proof plaster. The technique of laying the plaster is worth a detailed description here since it is to be found, perhaps not always in such an elaborate form, in other Late Roman and Byzantine buildings in Alexandria. The brick wall was first covered with a layer of lime mixed with coarse--grained terracotta and brick powder in which were embedded small chips of marble and of other stones. Upon this layer, about 2 cm thick, there was laid in some places a pink red layer of lime with terracotta and brick powder upon which there were scratched designs in the form of rows of herring-bone and palm leaves divided into rectangular fields by means of vertical and horizontal incised lines. This "decorative effort" of the builders, also found in other places in Alexandria, has sometimes been interpreted as deliberate wall

II. Water cistern found under the floor of the main structure with the podium (des. S. Medeksza)

4. Central aisle of the water cistern. View from the south

decoration.[5] At Sidi Bishr it obviously played the role of support (just like the embedded stones) for the uppermost layer of very fine waterproof plaster, pink-red in colour, carefully smoothed or polished on the surface. In some instances, for example in the central aisle of the cistern, the layer containing stone gravel was missing, but the designs of palm leaves were visible in the places where the surface layer had fallen off the wall. From the south of the cistern a large passage 5 m long and 1.05 m wide led towards the main aisle of the reservoir (cf. plan II). The passage was entered through a deep vertical shaft semicircular in shape, with steps cut into the side walls and reveted with marble (fig. 5).[6]

South of the building with podium and cistern (or adjacent to it?) there was found part of yet another large chamber of which the north and west walls (0.51 m and 0.53 m wide) were partly preserved (fig. 6). They were all made of limestone and reveted with two layers of lime plaster. The lower layer bore traces of painted decoration: a horizontal stripe, ca. 1 cm wide, of red colour, running 4 cm above the floor. The upper layer was plain

[5] For instance in Late Roman houses at Kom el-Dikka, cf. M. Rodziewicz, *Études et Travaux* 9 (1976), 169 ff.; also E.M. Rodziewicz, *Études et Travaux* 11 (1979), 205.

[6] For a similar arrangement see a newly discovered cistern at Sultan Hussein str., under El Manaara School, cf. W.A. Daszewski, "Alexandriaca I", in: *Mélanges G.E. Mukhtar*, I; Le Caire 1985, pp. 177–185; for older examples, A. Bernand, *Alexandrie la Grande*, Paris 1966, pp. 42 ff., esp. 44 (description by Saint Genis). See also Mahmoud Bey (el Falaki), *Mém. sur l'antique Alexandrie*, Copenhague 1876, pp. 29 ff.; G. Botti, BSAA 2, (1899), 15 ff.; J. Strzygowski, ByzZeit 4 (1885), 92; E. Breccia, *Alexandrea ad Aegyptum*, Bergamo 1914, pp. 68 f.

Most of the Alexandrian cisterns were supplied with water from the main canals by means of underground channels. Isolated examples had special wells from where water was brought up to the cistern. The cistern at Sidi Bishr probably belonged to this last type, although it obviously had arrangements to collect rain water also.

5. Passage to the cistern. Steps reveted with marble

6. Floor of rectangular slabs of limestone south of the main building

white. The floor was made of fine rectangular slabs of limestone with smoothed surface (0.815 m × 0.380 m; 0.830 m × 0.380 m). The channel ran from under the NW corner of the room towards the cistern. A door (W : 1.10 m) in the west wall with a well-preserved threshold opened to the west.

Traces of yet different structures adjoining the main building were found to the west, north and east. To the west, near the arched entrance, a fragment of a wall 0.51 m wide was found running west and a channel running east. To the north, a large room (L : ca. 14 m; W : 6.5 m) was identified. It had two successive floors (cf. plan III, section 1). The lower one of lime mortar set upon small stones was about 10 cm thick; it corresponded with the painted floor of the main building. The upper floor, situated some 93 cm higher, was 7 cm thick and made of lime mortar mixed with ashes; its level corresponded with the level of the marble revetment on top of the podium.

To the east there were limestone walls usually 0.51–0.52 m wide. These walls point to the possibility of the existence of at least three more rooms (plan III, section 2). Only an approximate width (E–W) of these rooms could be established (room 1 − 6.5 m; room 2 − 3.75 m; room 3 − 4.5 m). Two of the rooms were provided with floors consisting of lime mortar spread upon small stones (fig. 7). In room 2 the space in between the E and W walls was filled with small stones and mortar (fig. 8). There was no floor, but in the upper part of the fill there were found remains of two rectangular "boxes" or niches (would thus the fill be what remained of the S wall?). The "boxes" were plastered from inside with white lime plaster.

Yet another set of three walls, all of them seen in section in a large foundation trench dug by bulldozer, were spotted on the far east of the plot at a distance of nearly 20 m from the main building (cf. plan III, section 3). Two of the walls adjoined channels made of terracotta pipes. A floor of lime mortar mixed with ashes showed in the profile south of the southernmost wall. The level of this and all other floors mentioned above corresponded exactly with the level of the floor of the main building with podium. Still further to the east of the plot a curious oblong structure was spotted. It resembled in section a bathtub and appeared to have been some kind of large channel or basin (fig. 9). Its sides were of low brick-and-stone walls which were not vertical, but opening towards the top. They were plastered with waterproof plaster, reddish in colour, 2 cm thick. Added later upon this layer was a thin layer of clean lime about 1 cm thick. Within the "basin" there were built two parallel vertical walls forming a sort of rectangular box covered at the top with a limestone slab about 5 cm thick. This slab was in turn covered with a thin layer of earth (3 cm), upon which lay another slab about 5 cm thick. This slab formed the floor of another small box (a channel seen in section?). Inside these two rectangular conduits whose function remains obscure there were found sherds of broken amphorae and sand. Further NW of the remains described above yet another limestone wall was found. It was accompanied by a channel cut in clean sand and plastered with waterproof plaster. Many small shells of all kinds were found under the channel (cf. plan III, section 4).

All the structures enumerated above appear to have belonged to one big complex which was erected at one time upon virgin soil and underwent at a certain moment of its existence some alterations.

The complex was located atop a small hillock about 12–15 m above sea level dominating the whole area now known as Sidi Bishr. It provided a very privileged location for the building. The excavator, Mr Hassan el Sheikh expressed the opinion that: "the complex at Sidi Bishr could be connected with one of the resthouses which were known from the mentions in Strabo's work and repeated by Mahmoud el Falaki. They had existed between the city of Alexandria and Canopus. Such a building at Sidi Bishr was re-used in the Christian period as a religious complex. This is proved by the fact that the lower parts of the walls are different from the upper ones, the blocks being regular in the lower and irregular in the upper parts. When a fragment of the podium was removed, we found that the mortar in the removed part also differed from the upper part".

The analysis of architectural remains — two layers of plaster on the walls, two floors within the room north of the podium, traces of alterations within the podium, two floors in the niche — have proved that the observations concerning two periods in the existence of the complex are correct. However, neither the technique of construction [7] nor the

---

[7] See the way the cistern was made and plastered.

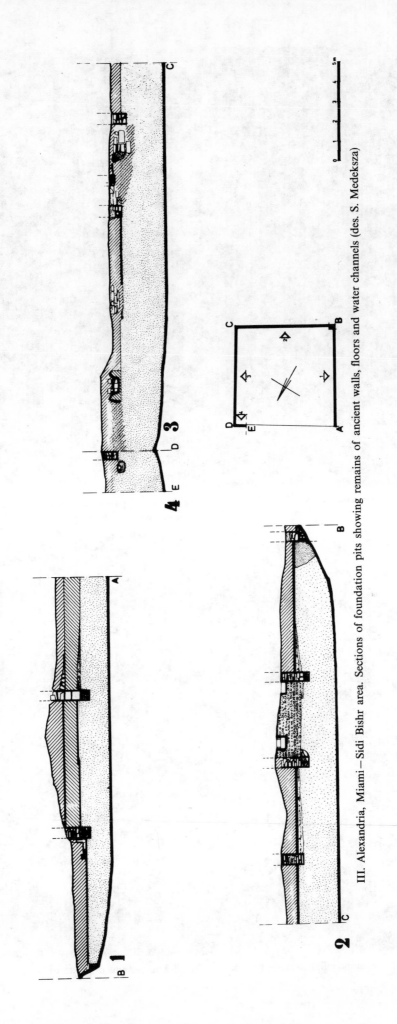

III. Alexandria, Miami—Sidi Bishr area. Sections of foundation pits showing remains of ancient walls, floors and water channels (des. S. Medeksza)

7. Traces of rooms with floor of lime mortar visible in the castern part of section 2 of the foundation pit. View from the north-west

8. Stone filling in central room of section 2 with remains of plastered "box"

9. Fragments of a water basin with inbuilt later constructions visible in section 3 of the foundation pit.
View from the west

architectural decoration[8] and moveable objects[9] advocate an early dating. There was virtually nothing that would allow for dating the first stage of the complex to a period earlier than the very end of the fourth or the first half of the fifth century A.D. The plot itself seems to have been unoccupied until late antiquity. This observation is not astonishing, since the whole countryside east of ancient Alexandria along the seashore had never been densely populated. Things began to change only after modern development started in the late 19th century spurred by a railroad, later changed to a tramway line, built in the late 1870. Nevertheless, the entire area comprising such modern districts as Mustafa Pasha, Bulkeley, Ramleh, Sidi Bishr, El Mandara up to El Montaza Gardens was

not as void and deserted in ancient times as one is led to believe on the ground of 19th century descriptions. The Ptolemaic necropolis at Mustapha Pasha is too well known to be mentioned here in detail.[10] The finds at Bulkeley have also been discussed at length in scholarly literature.[11] In the nearer vicinity of our site several important discoveries have taken place. In 1936 remains of a small sanctuary of the Roman period (end of 2nd–3rd century A.D.) with several marble statues were found at the locality Ras el Soda.[12] In 1940 a great number of Hellenistic terracotta grotesque figurines, Egyptian style amulets and statuettes of faience, objects of bone, limestone and marble, pottery vessels and bones of big animals were found in a layer of clean sand.[13]

[8] Above, notes 3–4.

[9] Below, notes 23–30.

[10] A. Adriani, "La Necropole de Mustapha Pasha", *Annuaire du Musée Gréco-Romain d'Alexandrie* 1933–35 (1936); id., *Repertorio* C I, 129 ff.

[11] Adriani, *Repertorio* C I, 127, no 81, with bibliography.

[12] Adriani, *Annuaire...*, 1935–39 (1940), 136 ff.; id., *Repertorio* C I, 100 f., no 56.

[13] Adriani, *Annuaire...*, 1940–1950 (1952), 28 ff. and plates; id., *Repertorio* C I, 101.

In 1959, during restoration work being carried out in the sanctuary at Ras el Soda, a mosaic floor was uncovered east of the temple.[14] From the nearby region of Siouf, situated SW of Sidi Bishr, comes an important inscription of the time of Ptolemy III.[15] Finally, in 1973, in the area between Gamal Abdel Nasser street and Sidi Bishr Station a cache of marble sculptures was found during construction work.[16] There were statues of Harpocrates, Asklepios, Hygieia, Mars, Baby Dionysos, Aphrodite fastening her sandal, a standing young woman as Ceres, another standing female statue headless, a reclining Nile, head of a young woman, a standing Isis or priestess of Isis, Egyptian sphinx, table support in the form of an animal's leg with a lion's head.[17] At least some of the statues suggest an Alexandrian provenance. Most of them could be tentatively assigned to the late second or early third century A.D.

Casual discoveries are corroborated by literary sources. Strabo (17,1,16–17) writes that in the countryside along the canal branch leading from Alexandria to Canopus [18] (i.e. further south from our site) there were located beautiful gardens of rich Alexandrians, enclosed with walls and often containing the family tombs of the owners. Near the canal there were also to be found resthouses and taverns where all sorts of agreable if not always decent services were offered to pilgrims proceeding from Alexandria to Canopus which was famous for its miraculous sanctuary of Sarapis, its pleasant climate and joyful life.[19] The state of things from Strabo's day changed much in later times. The last decades of the third century brought to Alexandria and to its vicinity destruction caused by the military expeditions of the belligerent Zenobia, queen of Palmyra, and by the sieges of the town by Aurelian and Diocletian. Perhaps more profound changes, especially in the way of life, occurred under the influence of triumphant Christianity. After the edict of Theodosius II the old shrines were closed, destroyed or transformed into churches.[20] Persecution of pagans increased.[21] In the neighbourhood of Alexandria a new element — the ever more numerous monastic settlements and their often fanatic inhabitants began to play an important role.[22]

The ruins yielded various objects. Notable were the sherds of various types of imported Late Roman tableware such as: a fragment of an undecorated dish of Cypriot Red Slip Ware, form 1 with sloping wall and plain thickened rim, rounded on the outside, datable to the late fourth till third quarter of the fifth century A.D.[23]; fragment of a dish of Cypriot Red Slip Ware, form 9 with flaring wall and thickened incurved rim, convex on outer face and projecting from wall to bottom (fig. 10c) datable to the second half of the sixth and early seventh century A.D.[24]; fragment of a thick-walled Cypriot Red Slip basin of form 7 with heavy rectangular rim, grooved on top and marked off on outside by an angular offset, one row of ruletting (fig. 10a) and a flat handle attached at bottom of rim [25], datable to the second half of the sixth or early seventh century A.D.; fragment of

---

[14] Id., *Repertorio* C I, 101.

[15] E. Breccia, *Inscrizioni greche e latine*, Cairo 1911, 6, no 10; also P. Fraser, *Ptolemaic Alexandria* I, Oxford 1972, p. 194.

[16] B. Gąssowska, „Depozyt rzeźb z Sidi Bishr w Alexandrii", in: *Starożytna Aleksandria w badaniach polskich*, Warszawa 1977, pp. 99 ff.

[17] All the sculptures are now in the Graeco-Roman Museum in Alexandria, mostly on display.

[18] The Canopus branch of the canal detached itself from the canal leading from Schedia to Alexandria near the place now called Hagar el Nawatieh in the south-eastern part of modern Alexandria.

[19] See remarks by Seneca, Ep. Luc. 51, 3–4; also Ovid, Metam. XV, 828; Am. II, 13; Juvenal. Sat. VI, 82–4; XV, 45–46.

[20] Sozomenus, HE VII, 15; Rufinus, HE XI, 22–24.

[21] Cf. J. Marlowe, *The Golden Age of Alexandria*, London 1971, pp. 288–89; also E. Wipszycka, „Świeckie bractwa w życiu religijnym chrześcijańskiego Egiptu", *Przegląd Historyczny* LIX (1968), 3, 458.

[22] In the 6th century there were 600 monasteries at Ennaton (i.e. probably in the area of modern Dakheliah, just west of Alexandria. The situation east of the town should not have been very much different, cf. Hist. Patr., PO I, 208–209. For explanation of the Mount Thabor, mentioned there, cf. G. Wiet, in: J. Maspero, *Histoire des Patriarches d'Alexandrie*, Paris 1923, p. 279, note 3 (Thabor = bātārūn = πατερων = Monastère des Pères). For Ennaton cf. Crum, Breccia, BSAA 9 (1907), 3–12. For monasteries at Canopus, cf. Faivre, Canope, Meneuthis, Aboukir, SAA 1917, 25–31; also Ladeuze, *Étude sur le cénobitisme pâchomien*, pp. 201 ff.; J. Maspero, "Papyrus grecs d'époque byzantine", in: Cat. Gen. Ant. Egypt. 3, Le Caire 1916, pp. 25–26.

[23] J. Hayes, *Late Roman Pottery* (henceforth LRP), London 1972, pp. 372 ff.; also M. Egloff, *Kellia. La potterie Copte* I, Genève 1977, pp. 87, type 68 and 72, pl. 43,2,6.

[24] Hayes, LRP, pp. 379 ff.; also Egloff, *Kellia...*, p. 78, type 28, pl. 39, 6.

[25] Hayes, LPR, pp. 377 ff. Mr Hayes (379) considers the presence of a flat handle attached to rim as an exceptional feature. He quotes one example only, from Paphos.

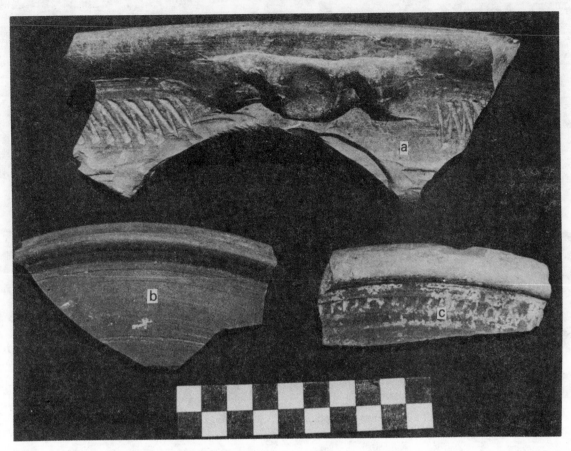

10. Fragments of imported Late Roman table-ware:
a) Cypriot Red Slip basin (Hayes form 7); b) Late Roman C Ware (Hayes form 3, type F); c) Cypriot Red Slip (Hayes form 9)

dish or bowl of Late Roman C Ware, form 3, type F, with flaring wall, curved vertical rim incorporating a flange (fig. 10b). Our sherd is particularly close to example no 19 from Athens Agora P 19629 coming from a deposit of the second quarter of the sixth century.[26] Surprisingly enough, no Egyptian Red Slip or "Egyptian Sigillata" was found. Local pottery was represented by a few sherds of painted Coptic pottery (fig. 11) among which one fragment of coarse light-red clay can be compared with bowls with painted decoration round the body and upon the rim of the type found at Karanis.[27] Apart from tableware there were fragments of ribbed amphorae of light-brown-pinkish clay with an inscription in ochre in the Byzantine cursive script (fig. 12a-b).

These amphorae are paralleled by very similar finds from Kellia and Qasr Ibrim assigned to the period from the end of the fourth to the sixth century A.D.[28]

Together with the pottery sherds a fragment of a votive figurine was found (H: 0.11 m; W at bottom: 0.06 m) (fig. 13). It represents a standing woman clad in a long white dress upon which a brown belt around the waist and a garland-like ornament near the bottom edge of the dress are indicated in painting. Above the garland a large dark-brown circle is depicted. The woman holds a child upon her left hand; it touches her breast with its hand. Similar figurines have been found at Abu Mina and at Kom el-Dikka in Alexandria. They are usually assigned to the late fifth and the sixth

---

[26] Hayes, LRP, pp. 329 ff., esp. 334 and 338.

[27] Although examples from Fayum seem to be slightly earlier, cf. B. Johnson, *Pottery from Karanis,* 1981, p. 35 pl. 16, no 18, assigned to the 4th century A.D.

[28] For Kellia, see Egloff, *Kellia...,* pp. 111, 113, type 169, pl. 4; 58, 2; 19, 2–3; 62, 5; Qasr Ibrim, A.J. Mills, *The Cemeteries of Qasr Ibrim* (55 Excav. Mem. Egypt Explor. Society, London 1982(58), grave 193, 121, pl. LXI; for other parallels, see L.P. Kirwan, *The Oxford Univ. Excavations at Firka,* London: Humphrey, Milford 1939, p. 22, fig. 4 (5th cent. A.D.); R. Mond, *Temples of Armant, a Preliminary Survey,* London 1940, p. 82, pl. 63, nos 878 and 88 (Gl).

11. Fragments of Coptic pottery with painted decoration

12 a–b. Inscribed fragments of ribbed amphorae

13. Terracotta figurine of a standing woman clad in white dress with brown belt, holding a child upon her left arm

14. St Menas bottle of the type datable to the end of the sixth and the early seventh cent. A.D

century A.D.[29] Of interest was yet another find, namely a bottle of St. Menas (fig. 14) of the type datable to the end of the sixth and the early seventh century A.D. just before the Persian invasion.[30] Among the stuccoed architectural decorations of particular importance were fragments of what seems to be a large cross painted in imitation of an incrustation of precious stones (fig. 15 a-b). Similar crosses painted upon the walls were found in the monastic settlements of Kellia.[31] The presence of the cross together with some of the small finds mentioned above suggest that we have here a Christian complex of some kind. Its main part, namely the hall with podium and the underground cistern, cannot be easily identified. There is practically no evidence that it had been a church. This must be stated in spite of the fact that several rectangular church buildings without an apse are known from North Africa, e.g. Djemila, Zana, Henchir Tikouba, Timgad, Lixus[32] and probably

from Egypt — at Mahura, west of Taposoris Magna.[33] Nor is the orientation of decisive importance. It is enough to compare some North African churches, for instance at Anouna, Henchir el Atech, Kherbet Guidra (cf. Ponsich, op. cit., fig. 34) to notice how different was their orientation. The character of the hall, as has been stated already, does not exclude the possibility that it had been a court from which stairs of the podium led to another chamber situated to the north. Its second, upper floor corresponded with the top of the podium. Nevertheless, taking all the observations and facts into consideration and bearing in mind the shortness and the insufficiency of research done on the spot, it seems more advisable to see the building at Miami-Sidi Bishr as an indefinite religious complex, most probably of monastic character one of many hundred such establishments, though perhaps of better quality than the average,[34] known to have been erected in Late

---

[29] We wish to thank for this information Mr P. Parandowski who is preparing for publication a catalogue of such figurines from the Polish excavations at Kom el-Dikka. For comparison see a figurine from Kom el-Dikka no SM 1102/68. See also such figurines from Abu Mina in the Graeco-Roman Museum in Alexandria, Inv. nos 18967, 18968.

[30] Cf. Z. Kiss, *Études et Travaux* 7 (1973), 146 ff., esp. nos 23–24. Dr Kiss has kindly confirmed this dating after examining the piece.

[31] R. Kasser et al., "Kellia 1965", in: *Rech. Suisse d'Archéologie Copte* I, Genève 1967, p. 30, fig. 27; p. 32, fig. 36.

[32] M. Ponisch, "Lixus, le Quartier des Temples", *Études et Travaux d'Archéologie marocaine* IX (1981), 113 ff. and figs 32 and 33; N. Duval, "La basilique de Zana", MEFRA 89 (1977), 2, 847–873; S. Gsell, *Les monuments antiques de l'Algérie* II, liv. III (1901), chap. Édifices du culte chrétien, pp. 124, 157 ff.

[33] P. Grossmann and H. Jaritz, MDIK 36 (1980), 225 ff. We wish to thank dr P. Grossman for this information.

[34] Perhaps of the type of Qousour Isa at Kellia, cf. Kasser et al., *Kellia 1965*, Egloff, *Kellia...*, pp. 11 ff. and pl. 117.

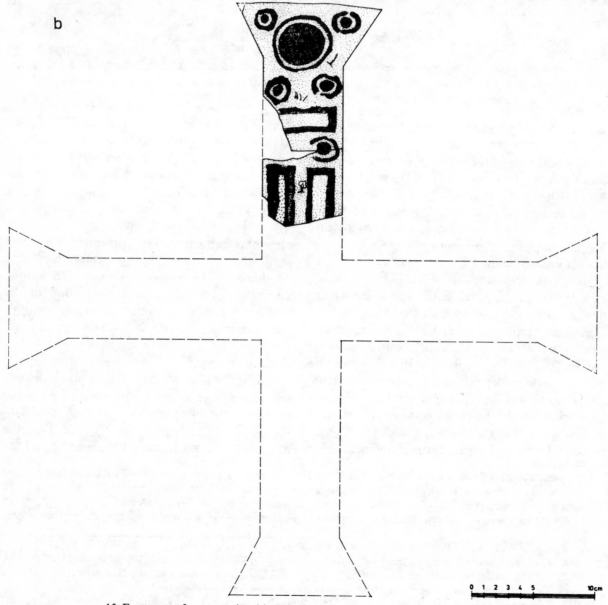

15. Fragments of a cross painted in imitation of an incrustation of precious stones

Antiquity in the desert areas east and west of Alexandria.[35] This complex should have been founded sometime at the very end of the fourth or in the early fifth century A.D. and must have existed for about two centuries. Its end should probably be connected with the well-known destruction of monastic settlements near Alexandria by the Persian troops of Chosroes in the early seventh century A.D.[36] Such an imposing complex as the one described above would have been a primary target for plundering. When Moslem Arabs conquered Alexandria in 641 A.D. the complex at Sidi Bishr thus lay in ruins already covered by a thick layer of sand blown from the nearby seashore. This explains well the lack of any evidence of early Arab presence among the finds of the excavations.

[35] The total number of monasteries near Alexandria was estimated at six hundred only on the area of Ennaton (west of Alexandria). On the east there must have been yet other monasteries. Cf. above note 22.

[36] Hist. Patr., PO I, 221 (Persian troops destroy monasteries of Ennaton; see also Hist. Part. PO I, 223). Persians spare the monastery at Canopus.

COPTIC STUDIES

Johannes den Heijer

Réflexions sur la composition de l'*Histoire des Patriarches d'Alexandrie* : les auteurs des sources coptes *

L'*Histoire des Patriarches d'Alexandrie* [1] est un texte arabe dont l'importance en tant que source pour l'histoire ecclésiastique et politique de l'Égypte est bien connue. Cependant, le processus de sa composition impose encore des recherches approfondies et ardues, afin d'éclaircir, non seulement l'identité de ses sources grecques et coptes, mais également la façon dont celles-ci ont été traduites et utilisées dans la rédaction arabe qui nous est parvenue.

Il convient de signaler tout d'abord, que l'*Histoire des Patriarches* peut se caractériser comme une tradition historiographique : à différentes époques, des auteurs coptes ont entrepris d'enregistrer des événements touchant à leur Église. Ainsi, le premier de ces historiographes a dû écrire au Ve siècle. Puis, chaque période a connu un continuateur de cette tradition, jusqu'au XXe siècle même, mais avec de fréquentes interruptions. Pourtant dans cette communication, nous nous limiterons à la première partie, c'est-à-dire à la rédaction arabe, faite à la fin du XIe siècle, et basée sur les textes grecs et surtout coptes rédigés entre le Ve et le XIe siècles.

Encore une remarque préliminaire : dans les observations qui vont suivre, nous ferons souvent appel à la recension primitive de l'*HP*. Il s'agit ici de la recension des 47 premières biographies de patriarches, transmises dans un manuscrit de Hambourg, daté en 1266 de notre ère, et édité par Seybold en 1912. Nous avons pu constater que c'est bien à cette recension initiale, plutôt qu'à celle connue comme la Vulgate, et éditée par Evetts et aussi par Seybold, qu'il faut avoir recours pour de nombreux passages révélateurs de la composition du texte [2]. En outre, nous avons montré que la recension primitive connaît une continuation dans le manuscrit Paris arabe 303 — ce que Seybold

---

* Cet article constitue la version provisoire et abrégée d'un chapitre d'une monographie en cours de préparation, intitulée *Mawhūb Ibn Manṣūr Ibn Mufarrig, historiographe copte du XIe siècle. Étude philologique sur les biographies arabes des patriarches Aḫristūdulūs (1047–1077) et Kīrillus (1078–1092)*. Nous sommes en mesure de réaliser ce projet grâce à une subvention de l'Organisation Néerlandaise pour le Développement de la Recherche Scientifique (ZWO), pour les années 1984–1985.

[1] Pour renvoyer à cet ouvrage, et aux éditions qui en ont été faites, nous suivons les abréviations de K. Samir, « Un traité inédit de Sévère b. al- Muqaffaᶜ (10e siècle :) 'Le Flambeau de l'Intelligence' », *Orientalia Christiana Periodica* 41 (1975), 150–168, notamment p. 150. Nous les reprenons :

HP   = l'*Histoire des Patriarches*, en général;

HPS   = C.F. Seybold, *Severus Ben al-Muqaffaᶜ, Historia Patriarcharum Alexandrinorum*, (*Corpus Scriptorum Christianorum Orientalium*, Scriptores arabici, textus, ser. III, tome 9, fasc. I–II), Beyrouth–Paris 1904–1910.

HPE   = B. Evetts, « History of the Patriarchs of the Coptic Church of Alexandria ». Arabic text edited, translated and annotated, *Patrologia Orientalis* I, 99–214; I, 381–619; V, 1–215; X,357–551, Paris 1904–1915.

HPSH   = C.F. Seybold, *Severus ibn al-Muqaffaᶜ. Alexandrinische Patriarchengeschichte von S. Marcus bis Michael I (61–767)*, nach der ältesten 1266 geschriebenen Hamburger Handschrift im arabischen Urtext herausgegeben, Hamburg 1912.

HPC   = *History of the Patriarchs of the Egyptian Church, known as the History of the Holy Church*, edited, translated by :
         II i   Y. ᶜAbdal-Masīḥ, O.H.E.-Burmester;
         II ii–iii A.S. Atiya O.H.E. KHS-Burmester;
         III i–iii A. Khater, O.H.E. KHS-Burmester;
         IV i–ii   A. Khater, O.H.E. KHS-Burmester.

[2] Nous avons exposé nos arguments pour ce point de vue au IIe Symposium d'Études arabes chrétiennes, au mois de septembre dernier, à Oosterhesselen (Pays-Bas). Voir aussi notre article intitulé « L'Histoire des Patriarches d'Alexandrie, recension primitive et Vulgate », à paraître dans le *Bulletin de la Société d'Archéologie Copte* 27 (1985).

avait déjà suggéré brièvement — qui couvre les *Vies* des patriarches 49 à 65, et dans le manuscrit du Caire, Patriarcat copte, hist. 12, manuscrit de 1275, qui contient les *Vies* 66 à 72 [3].

Pour ce qui est des personnes auxquelles nous devons la composition de l'*HP,* il nous paraît opportun de consacrer en premier lieu quelques mots au rédacteur du texte arabe. Traditionnel-lement, le grand théologien du Xe siècle, Sévère (Sawīrus) Ibn al-Muqaffa'[4], a été assimilé à ce rédacteur. Si les chercheurs ont correctement observé que Sawīrus ne peut être considéré comme l'auteur de l'*HP,* ils lui concèdent néanmoins le rôle d'initiateur du projet: c'est lui qui aurait collectionné les sources coptes et qui les aurait fait traduire en arabe. Un siècle plus tard, le notable alexandrin Mawhūb Ibn Manṣūr Ibn Mufarriğ aurait repris les notices laissées par Sawīrus, en les compilant dans un ouvrage ordonné [5]. Cependant, l'examination scrupuleuse de la recension pri-mitive nous a portés à dénier à Sawīrus toute contribution à la composition de l'*HP* [6]. Nos arguments principaux pour rejeter le rôle attribué à Sawīrus sont, d'une part, l'absence totale des mentions de ce personnage dans la recension primitive — recension qui conserve bien, par ailleurs, les indications d'ordre rédactionnelle — et d'autre part, les similitudes fort remarquables entre la préface traditionnellement attribuée à Sawīrus et les notices de Mawhūb. Bref, c'est à ce dernier que nous proposons d'attribuer la recher-che et la compilation des documents coptes, autant que leur rédaction arabe. Mawhūb mentionne souvent ses collaborateurs, particulièrement le diacre Abū Ḥabīb Mīḫā'īl Ibn Badīr ad--Damanhūrī, qui l'a aidé en traduisant les textes coptes an arabe [7].

Quant aux sources coptes, la rédaction arabe contient des passages qui permettent d'identifier plusieurs auteurs des textes coptes ayant servi de source. Il s'agit de notices que ces auteurs ont intégrées au texte et dans lesquelles ils rendent compte des circonstances et des motifs de leurs contributions, souvent en renvoyant aux auteurs qui les ont précédés. D'autres notices sont dues à Mawhūb, le rédacteur du texte arabe. Notamment dans la préface de sa biographie de Christodoulos (Aḫrisṭūdulūs), le 66e patriarche, il indique assez nettement dans quels monastères il avait retrouvé les séries de biographies qui lui ont servi de base. La recension primitive contient de nombreuses notes attribuables à Mawhūb, qui touchent à la génèse de la rédaction arabe [8].

C'est à D. W. Johnson que revient le mérite d'avoir dressé la liste des cinq auteurs, et d'avoir délimité les tranches dues à leurs plumes [9]. Cette répartition nous paraissant tout à fait pertinente, nous voudrions pourtant proposer ici quelques pro-blèmes non encore signalés, et ajouter certains détails, qui ne manquent peut-être pas d'im-portance.

1. La première série de biographies est la seule à avoir reçu beaucoup d'attention de la part des coptisants. La raison en est que des fragments coptes en ont été retrouvés, et c'est grâce aux efforts d'O. von Lemm, de W.E. Crum, de T. Orlandi, et de D.W. Johnson, que nous disposons aujourd'hui du texte copte d'une *Histoire de l'Église* [10]. Si cette *Histoire* se termine par la 26e biographie, celle de Timothée Elure, l'*HP* arabe finit sa première série par la 24e, celle de Cyrille: au lieu d'une 25e *Vie,* de Dioscore, le lecteur trouvera une brève esquisse biographique, sans doute due à

---

[3] Sur ce manuscrit, voir notre étude intitulée « Quelques remarques sur la deuxième partie de l'*Histoire des Patriarches d'Alexandrie* », *Bulletin de la Société d'Archeologie Copte* 25 (1983), 107–124.

[4] Sur lui, voir Samir, Or. Chr. Per. 41 (1975), 150–168, et G. Graf, *Geschichte der christlichen arabischen Literatur,* Città del Vaticano 1944–1958, II, pp. 300–317.

[5] Cf. Graf, GCAL II, 300–301; Samir, Or. Chr. Per. 41 (1975), 156–157; D.W. Johnson, « Further Remarks on the Arabic History of the Patriarchs of Alexandria », *Oriens Christianus* 61 (1977), 103–116, notamment 108, 115–116; R.-G. Coquin, *Livre de la consécration du sanctuaire de Benjamin,* Le Caire 1975, pp. 24–25.

[6] Nous avons eu l'occasion de présenter nos observations sur cette question dans un article qui est actuellement sous presse et qui paraîtra en 1985 dans *Bibliotheca Orientalis* 41 (1985), et dans notre monographie en préparation.

[7] Cf. Samir, Or. Chr. Per. 41 (1975), 156–157.

[8] Pour les références, voir notre article dans BiOr (cf. note 6).

[9] « Further Remarks... » voir note 5.

[10] O. van Lemm, *Koptische Fragmente zur Patriarchengeschichte Alexandriens* = *Mémoires de l'Académie des Sciences de St. Pétersbourg* 7,36,11 (1888); W.E. Crum, « Eusebius and Coptic Church Histories », *Proceedings of the Society of Biblical Archaeology* 24 (1902), 68–84; T. Orlandi, « Le fonte copti della Storia dei Patriarchi di Alessandria », *Studi Copti,* Milano–Varese 1968, pp. 53–66; id., *Storia della Chiesa di Alessandria. Testo copto, traduzione e commento,* I. *Da Pietro ad*

Mawhūb, qui y explique l'absence d'une véritable biographie de Dioscore (*HPSH*, p. 75; *HPS*, pp. 83–84; *HPE* I, pp. 443–444). A remarquer que la recension primitive diffère ici de la Vulgate: selon cette dernière, l'historiographie aurait été empêchée par les conséquences de Chalcédoine, tandis que la recension primitive précise qu'un autre ouvrage comporte déjà une biographie de Dioscore. Les autres notices de rédaction concernant la délimitation de la première série distinguent assez vaguement une série qui va » jusqu'à Dioscore « (voir ci-dessous). Ce décalage entre l'*Histoire* copte se terminant par la 26ᵉ *Vie*, et la première série de l'*HP* arabe finissant par la 24ᵉ, pourrait s'expliquer par le fait, signalé par Crum, que la rédaction arabe a dû se fonder sur une autre version que le manuscrit copte fragmentaire qui nous est parvenu.

Nous ne reprendrons pas ici la discussion sur la question de savoir si les fragments coptes représentent deux ouvrages distincts, tous les deux utilisés par la rédaction arabe, comme le voulait Orlandi, ou bien une seule *Histoire,* ce qui fut l'opinion de Brakmann et de Johnson [11]. Il nous suffit de rappeler qu'Orlandi avait proposé un argument fort intéressant, non pas mentionné par ces opposants: il s'agit des doublures dans le texte arabe, qui suggèrent l'emploi de deux sources coptes alternatives [12].

Ce qui nous concerne ici, c'est que l'*Histoire de l'Église* ne constitue pas nécessairement la seule source dont Mawhūb s'est servi. Orlandi a déjà signalé les parallèles avec certains textes de caractère légendaire ou hagiographique [13], et il faudra encore un dépouillement systématique de la littérature copte et arabe chrétienne avant que l'on ne puisse avoir une idée complète des sources que Mawhūb a pu employer. Or, les notices de rédaction dans le texte arabe confirment l'idée que plusieurs textes ont dû servir de sources à notre texte arabe. Il est vrai que ces notices mentionnent

— comme Johnson le dit — un certain Mennas (Mīnā) comme l'auteur de l'*Histoire* copte, mais elles font également référence à plusieurs auteurs israélites, puis à Jules l'Africain, à Eusèbe de Césarée, et à Sozomène. Puisque Crum a montré convenablement le rapport entre l'*HP* et l'*Histoire Ecclésiastique* d'Eusèbe [14], il faudrait aussi étudier les éventuelles parallèles avec les autres écrivains qui figurent dans ces notices. Les indications que Mawhūb fournit quant à ses sources suggèrent aussi une diversité de textes, bien que ses paroles ne contiennent pas la distinction si nette entre textes historiographiques et hagiographiques qu'Orlandi y voit [15]: Mawhūb dit seulement avoir eu recours aux *Histoires* — l'arabe emploie le mot emprunté *'isturiyyāt* — aux traditions (*al-aḥādīt*), et aux renseignements (*al-aḫbār*), et cela dans une préface que nous pensons attribuée à tort à Sawīrus Ibn al-Muqaffaʿ (*HPSH*, pp. 1–2; *HPS*, pp. 5–6; *HPE* I, pp. 114–117).

Dans l'une des notices sus-mentionnées, Johnson a vu un renvoi à un livre particulier, ayant un statut différent de celui des auteurs classiques, et cela d'après la Vulgate, qui dit, dans la traduction d'Evetts: « This is shown to us by that book which begins with the names of the patriarchs as far as... Dioscorus... » (*HPSH,* p. 152; *HPS*, p. 161; *HPE* V, p. 90) [16]. Pourtant, le passage correspondant dans la recension primitive est à interpréter ainsi: « Comme nous l'ont montré les écrivains dont nous avons commencé par mentionner les noms », phrase qui renvoie, dans le contexte concerné, clairement à Eusèbe, à Jules l'Africain, et à Sozomène.

Ailleurs, le scribe Mennas est, effectivement, mis à part des trois auteurs classiques, mais quelques lignes plus loin, les événements contemporains à Cyrille, le 24ᵉ patriarche, sont attribués à « ceux dont nous avons mentionné les noms » (*HPS*, p. 218; *HPE* X, p. 360). De nouveau, il s'agit des trois auteurs connus, que nous avons mentionnés, aussi

Atanasio, II. *Da Teofilo a Timoteo* II°, Milano–Varese 1968–1970; H. Brakmann, « Eine oder zwei koptische Kirchengeschichten? », *Le Muséon* 87 (1974), 129–142; D.W. Johnson, « Further Fragments of a Coptic History of the Church: Cambridge OR. 1699 R. », *Enchoria* 6 (1976), 7–17; cf. aussi F.R. Farag, « The Technique of research of a tenth-century Christian Arab writer: Severus Ibn al-Muqaffa », *Le Muséon* 86 (1973), 37–66.

[11] Voir les études desdits auteurs, citées ci-dessus (note 10).

[12] Orlandi, *Studi,* pp. 63–64.

[13] Orlandi, *Storia* I, pp.73–100, 113–121, II, 95–121; *Studi,* pp. 64–66, 69–71.

[14] Crum, *Proc. Soc. Bibl. Arch.* 24 (1902), 68–84.

[15] Orlandi, *Storia* I, p. 127, *Studi,* pp. 57–58.

[16] Johnson, *Or. Chr.* 61 (1977), 114.

bien que de Mennas. Dans la notice de Mawhūb qui sert à remplacer la *Vie* de Dioscore, Mennas ne figure pas parmi les auteurs cités.

2. D'après deux notices étudiées par Johnson, un archidiacre nommé Georges (Ǧirǧah) est responsable de la deuxième série de *Vies* (*HPSH*, pp. 151–153; *HPS*, pp. 160–162; *HPE* V, pp. 88–92; *HPS*, pp. 217–218; *HPE* X, pp. 259–360). Johnson a observé que ce Georges était le secrétaire du 42ᵉ patriarche, Simon, et le père spirituel du 44ᵉ, Cosmas II, qui règnait en 730 et 731 [17]. Nous pouvons encore ajouter que Georges se présente une fois, au cours de la biographie du 40ᵉ patriarche, Jean III, à la première personne, en disant qu'il est le fils spirituel de ce patriarche (*HPSH*, p. 120; *HPS*, p. 129; *HPE* V, p. 20). Remarquons enfin que, dans la *Vie* d'Alexandre, le 43ᵉ patriarche, un moine Georges, représentant du patriarche, intervient, mais à la troisième personne (*HPSH*, p. 138; *HPS*, p. 147; *HPE* V, p. 59). Quoi qu'il en soit, il y a tout lieu de décrire l'archidiacre Georges comme un personnage assez proche des patriarches dont il écrivit les biographies.

Le début de sa contribution pose problème dans la mesure où l'auteur de la première des notices en question, reclame aussi la paternité de la 24ᵉ biographie (celle de Cyrille). Une explication possible de cette ambiguïté serait que Georges aurait écrit une autre version de cette biographie-là.

La fin de sa contribution nous est donnée dans la même notice, qui indique que le travail de Georges s'est étendu jusqu'à la disparition du calife umayyade Sulaymān Ibn 'Abd al-Malik (en 717), point historique qui se situe dans la 43ᵉ *Vie* (*HPSH*, p. 143; *HPS*, p. 152; *HPE* V, p. 71) [18]. Georges aurait ainsi composé les *Vies* 24 à 42, et le début de la *Vie* 43. Cependant Mawhūb, dans sa préface (Ms. Patr. copte, hist. 12, ff. 1r–3r; *HPC* II ii, pp. 159–161), relève une première série se consituant de 42 *Vies*. En plus, il finit la 42ᵉ *Vie* par une notice qui marque clairement la fin d'une unité de rédaction (*HPSH*, p. 132; *HPS*, p. 141; *HPE* V, pp. 47–48). Hypothétiquement, l'on pourrait croire que l'auteur de la troisième série, dont nous parlerons dans un instant, avait, avant de compléter la 43ᵉ *Vie*, recopié son début, de sorte que toute la 43ᵉ *Vie* appartenait, aux yeux de Mawhūb, à cette troisième série.

Remarquons encore que le principe d'Orlandi, selon lequel il faudra prendre en considération l'emploi d'autres textes, non historiographiques, pour la rédaction de Mawhūb, se confirme par le *Livre de la consécration de Benjamin*. R.-G. Coquin a montré de manière très pertinente comment ce texte copte a été résumé dans le texte arabe de la *Vie* du patriarche Benjamin [19].

3. L'auteur de la troisième série s'appelle Jean (ar. *Yūḥannā* ou *Yuḥannis* ou *Yu'annis*); nous l'indiquerons, d'après Johnson, par Jean I. Celui-ci se présente, dans une notice de sa main, comme le continuateur de la *Vie* 43, et comme l'auteur des biographies 44 et 45, portion qui constitue le chapitre (ar. *Sīrah*) 16. Puisque son successeur, Jean II, commence sa rédaction par la 18ᵉ *Sīrah*, ce que nous allons voir ci-dessous, Jean I est à considérer comme l'auteur de la *Sīrah* 17, correspondant à la *Vie* 46. Il faut lui attribuer donc la deuxième partie de la *Vie* 43 et les *Vies* 44, 45, et 46. Pour ce qui est de la personnalité de ce Jean I, tout ce que Johnson mentionne, est qu'il était le fils spirituel de Moïse, l'évêque de Wasīm [20]. Effectivement, en mentionnant cet évêque, Jean I manque rarement de souligner son rapport personnel avec lui. Mais il montre aussi souvent qu'il est très proche du 46ᵉ patriarche, Khaël (Ḥā'īl). Il joue un rôle actif dans un conflit qui oppose ce patriarche aux Melkites (*HPSH*, p. 169; *HPS*, p. 177; *HPE* V, p. 127), fait qui suggère qu'il est un personnage important dans l'hiérarchie. Notre auteur est emprisonné avec le patriarche, et avec son père spirituel Moïse (*HPSH*, p. 174; *HPS*, p. 181; *HPE* V, p. 136); plus tard, il les accompagne en voyage (*HPSH*, p. 175; *HPS*, p. 183; *HPE* V, p. 139). Une grande partie de sa biographie de Khaël est consacrée aux jours qui marquent l'effondrement du califat umayyade, et l'avènement des Abbasides. Dans sa panique, le dernier calife umayyade, Marwān, et ses gouverneurs, commettent de grandes cruautés contre la patriarche, et notre auteur Jean, aussi bien que l'évêque Moïse, ne le quittent pas (*HPSH*, pp. 190–196; *HPS*, pp. 197–205; *HPE* V, pp. 170–188). Ainsi, Jean décrit avec l'autorité d'un témoin oculaire tous les événements qui arrivèrent au patriarche. Vers la fin, Jean nous donne progressivement une image un peu plus claire de son identité. A plusieurs occasions, ce

---

[17] Ibid., 113–114.
[18] Ibid., 113.

[19] Voir note 5.
[20] Johnson, Or. Chr. 61, 112–113.

ne sont que lui et Moïse de Wasīm qui soutiennent le patriarche; ailleurs, ils se trouvent entourés d'autres évêques. Dans un cas, Jean porte l'habit d'un moine, « bien que je ne le mérite pas » (*HPSH*, p. 189; *HPS*, p. 197; *HPE* V, p. 171). Postérieurement, il se qualifie de diacre, « sur lequel le patriarche avait mis ses saintes mains, sans que je ne le mérite » (*HPSH*, p. 192; *HPS*, p. 201; *HPE* V, p. 179). Lorsqu'une communauté de moines adhère à la vielle hérésie mélétienne, c'est bien Jean qui va les admonester. Certains d'entr'eux étaient de vieux amis à lui, qu'il avait connus lorsqu'il était encore laïc (*HPSH*, p. 201; *HPS*, p. 210; *HPE* V, p. 200). Peu après, il rappelle sa jeunesse, à Gizah — la Vulgate dissimule ce détail, en lisant « dans la vie », ar. *fī l-ḥayāh* au lieu de *fī l-Ǧīzah* (*HPSH*, p. 203; *HPS*, p. 212; *HPE* V, p. 203). Le maximum de renseignements vient vers la fin de la biographie, où Jean est chargé de recevoir deux métropolites syriens qui visitent l'Égypte. Moïse et un autre évêque l'envoyent, parce qu'il est « l'un de leurs membres ». Habillé en moine, il étonne les Syriens par son éloquence. Mais les deux évêques expliquent cela en décrivant Jean comme étant « au niveau d'un évêque ». Quand les Syriens lui demandent combien d'enfants sa diocèse compte, Jean répond qu'elle contient « dix villages, chacun peuplé de dix adultes » (*HPSH*, p. 206; *HPS*, pp. 214–215; *HPE* V, pp. 209–211), ce qui nous permet de conclure qu'il était effectivement évêque, pourtant d'un siège peu important, et dont le nom ne nous est pas relevé.

A côté de Jean I, Johnson signale la mention de deux écrivains tous les deux nommés Macaire (Maqārah), qui figurent dans l'une des notices (*HPS*, p. 218; *HPE* X, p. 360)[21]. Il remarque fort bien que la répartition des séries entre les auteurs identifiés ne laisse pas de biographies à attribuer à ces deux personnages. Pourtant, il convient de rappeler le principe selon lequel plusieurs auteurs ont pu couvrir les mêmes périodes. Il n'est néanmoins pas possible de déterminer si Mawhūb a connu les textes de ces deux Macaires.

4. La quatrième série est due à un certain Jean II, qui a laissé trois notices de rédaction. Dans l'une d'elles, il raconte comment son père spirituel, le moine Ammūnah, avait prédit qu'il deviendrait l'auteur de la 18ᵉ *Sīrah* (chapitre), à l'époque de

« celui dont le nom commence par dix-huit » (Ms. Par. ar. 303, ff. 70r–71r; *HPS*, pp. 293–294; *HPE* X, pp. 531–532). Après sa mort, le moine lui apparaît dans une vision, pour lui expliquer que « celui dont le nom commence par dix-huit », est le 55ᵉ patriarche, Schenoute, dont le nom (en grec Σινοῦθιος) commence par la 18ᵉ lettre de l'alphabet (Ms. Par. ar 303, ff. 120v–122r; *HPC* II i, pp. 34–35). Ainsi, la contribution de Jean II comprend les chapitres 18 à 20, ainsi que la période jusqu'à la fin de la *Vie* de Schenoute. La 18ᵉ *Sīrah* correspond à la 47ᵉ biographie, celle de Mennas I. Johnson signale que l'édition *HPE* assimile la 47ᵉ *Vie* à la 19ᵉ *Sīrah*, ce qui contredirait la numérotation alphabétique du moine Ammunah[22]. Cependant cette interprétation d'Evetts se fonde sur une correction qui n'est guère justifiée si l'on considère la recension primitive. Cette recension écrit au début de la 43ᵉ *Vie* : « *Sīrah* 27 » (*HPSH*, p. 132). C'est une erreur manifeste, puisque les biographies précédentes appartiennent à la 16ᵉ *Sīrah*. Malheuresement, la Vulgate a corrigé 27 en 17 (*HPS*, p. 141; *HPE* V, p. 48). Puisque la « vraie » *Sīrah* 17 correspond à la *Vie* 46 (début : *HPSH*, p. 151; *HPS*, p. 160; *HPE* V, p. 88), la Vulgate contient ainsi deux chapitres dits « *Sīrah* 17 », ce qui a amené Evetts à changer systématiquement 17 en 18, 18 en 19, et 19 en 20. Le fait que la Vulgate a aussi deux chapitres 20 — à la différence de la recension primitive — a permis à Evetts de reprendre la numérotation des manuscrits, en rejetant le titre « *Sīrah* 20 » en tête de la *Vie* 49 (*HPE* X, p. 402; cf. *HPS*, p. 237), et en le laissant au début de la *Vie* 51 (*HPE* X, p. 475; cf. ms. Par. ar. 303, f. 38r; *HPS*, p. 270).

Les biographies rédigées par Jean contiennent d'autres éléments autobiographiques, en plus du fait qu'il était le disciple du moine Ammūnah. Son identité de moine se confirme par un passage où il précise avoir écrit « afin que tous les frères moines sachent que Dieu choisit celui qui Lui sert par ses intentions sincères » (Ms. Par. ar. 303, f. 44v; *HPS*, p. 275; *HPE* X, p. 485). Johnson a raison de dire que Jean II était le scribe du patriarche Schenoute I, mais le passage qu'il cite dans ce but, n'est pas très bien choisi. Le fait qu'un certain scribe Jean figure à la 3ᵉ personne, dans une phrase — faisant d'ailleurs défaut dans la recension primitive — (Ms. Par. ar. 303, f. 141v; *HPC* II i, p. 52), nous oblige à tenir compte qu'il peut s'agir d'un autre

---

[21] Ibid., 114.

[22] Ibid., 112.

secrétaire, d'autant plus que quelques lignes plus loin, Jean parle à la première personne : « moi, l'auteur... ». D'autres passages démontrent que Jean n'était, dans tous les cas, pas le seul secrétaire de Schenoute; celui-ci avait tout un groupe de scribes qui recopiaient des livres (Ms. Par. ar. 303, f. 150v; *HPC* II i, p. 63). Quoi qu'il en soit, il est intéressant de noter que Jean II n'était pas seulement très proche du 55ᵉ patriarche, Schenoute I, mais également de ses trois prédécesseurs. Dans les *Vies* des patriarches 47 à 51, l'on cherchera en vain des traces autobiographiques, mais dès le début de la biographie de Joseph, le 52ᵉ, il est présent. Il se trouve en prison avec ce patriarche-ci (Ms. Par. ar. 303, f. 77r; *HPE* X, p. 543), dont il est évidemment aussi le scribe : à une occasion, il raconte comment Joseph lui ordonne de prendre papier et encrier, afin d'écrire une lettre (Ms. Par. ar. 303, ff. 71v–72r; *HPE* X, p. 533–534).

Ce que nous voudrions encore ajouter aux observations de Johnson quant à la contribution de Jean II, c'est bien l'année dans laquelle il l'écrivit : l'année 582 des Martyrs, ce qui correspond à 252 de l'Hégire, ou à 865–866 après J.-C. (Ms. Par. ar. 303, f. 118r; *HPC* II i, p. 31). L'on remarquera que cette date tombe avant la mort de Schenoute I, disparu en 880. En effet, la fin de la biographie de ce patriarche, qui relève son décès, n'apparaît pas dans la recension primitive (Ms. Par. ar. 303, f. 156r; *HPC* II i, p. 68). Nous avons donc de très bonnes raisons de croire que la Vulgate contient ici une addition plus tardive.

La période couverte par Jean II s'accorde parfaitement avec la série que Mawhūb décrit dans sa préface, et qui comporte également les biographies 47–55.

5. Michel (dans la recension primitive il s'appelle Khaël — Ḫā'īl —, dans la Vulgate Mīḫā'īl), évêque de Tinnīs, montre dans une préface (Ms. Par. ar. 303, ff. 160r–161r; *HPC* II ii, pp. 79–80), et dans d'autres passages, sans équivoque, qu'il est l'auteur de la cinquième série, c'est-à-dire des *Vies* 56 à 65. Il précise la date de sa rédaction : 1051 après J.-C., — selon la recension primitive, c'est sept ans plus tard

— (Ms. Par. ar. 303, f. 251v; *HPC* II, ii, p. 137). Mawhūb confirme la délimitation de la contribution de Michel à plusieurs reprises (Ms. Patr. copte hist. 12, ff. 1v, 13v, 16r–16v; *HPC* II iii, pp. 160–161, 171–172, 174). Les observations de Johnson sur Michel sont tout a fait correctes [23]. Toutefois, nous avons un détail saillant à ajouter : la recension primitive contient une note de Mawhūb, omise dans la Vulgate, qui précise, sans aucune équivoque, que Michel a rédigé sa série de biographies en langue copte, et que le collaborateur de Mawhūb, Abū Ḥabīb ad-Damanhūrī, l'a traduite en arabe d'après l'autographe (Ms. Par. ar. 303, f. 160r; *HPC* II ii, p. 69). Le fait que Michel écrivit encore au XIᵉ siècle ses biographies des patriarches en copte, nous semble digne d'être signalé. A ce propos, il est intéressant de rappeler que le même Michel est connu comme le traducteur arabe des *Canons* coptes attribuées à Athanase [24]. Cependant, le passage qui a amené les éditeurs de ces *Canons* à croire cela [25], ne permet pas, en réalité, de voir s'il a vraiment traduit le texte en arabe, ou bien s'il l'a seulement transcrit, laissant autrui le traduire. Notre doute est causé par l'emploi du verbe ambigu *naqala*, qui, dans l'*HP*, a parfois le sens de « traduire », mais plus fréquemment celui de « transcrire », ou « recopier » [26].

Ce que la recension primitive nous apprend encore, c'est que plusieurs passages du texte de Michel sont en fait des additions de Mawhūb. Les phrases par lesquelles il les introduit, ont disparu dans la Vulgate (par ex. Ms. Par. ar. 303, ff. 220v–221v; *HPC* II ii, pp. 114–115; Ms. Par. ar. 303, f. 269r; *HPC* II ii, p. 148).

Pour ce qui est des donnés autobiographiques de Michel, Johnson résume les points les plus importants, à savoir qu'il fut diacre d'abord, et que le patriarche Schenoute II le recruta comme scribe, et l'ordonna prêtre [27]. Bien qu'il ait été proche de ce patriarche, il lui reproche cependant sa pratique de la simonie dans de nombreux cas (Ms. Par. ar. 274v; *HPC* II ii, p. 155). C'est le 66ème patriarche, Christodoulos, qui consacre Michel évêque de Tinnīs. Il raconte en détail sa mission au patriarcat d'Antioche, épisode qui appartient en fait au

---

[23] Ibid., 110.

[24] W. Riedel and W.E. Crum, *The Canons of Athanasius of Alexandria. The Arabic and Coptic Versions edited and translated with Introduction, Notes and Appendices*, London 1904; cf. Graf, GCAL I, pp. 605–606.

[25] Crum, Riedel, *The Canons...*, ix, 69.

[26] Cf. les remarques de Johnson, Or. Chr. 61, 109; dans notre monographie en cours de préparation, nous donnerons un aperçu de cette terminologie.

[27] Johnson, Or. Chr. 61, 110.

patriarcat de Christodoulos, non pas aux *Vies* de la main de Michel (Ms. Par. ar. 303, ff. 261r–270r; *HPC* II ii, pp. 142–148).

Conclusion. Nous avons essayé de reconstituer, autant que possible, les personnalités des auteurs auxquels nous devons les biographies coptes des patriarches, que Mawhūb, aidé de son traducteur Abū Ḥabīb, nous a transmises dans sa rédaction arabe de l'*HP*. Nous avons vu que ces renseignements, plus ou moins cachés dans le texte, permettent d'ajouter des données intéressantes concernant la datation ou la composition, à celles fournies par les notices de rédaction. D'autre part, nous n'avons pas relevé ici les particularités stylistiques de chaque auteur[28]. Certes, l'on trouvera certaines expressions ou figures de style plus fréquemment chez l'un des auteurs que chez les autres. Ainsi, Jean II insère très régulièrement des citations bibliques de sensibilité prophétique, afin d'illustrer les événements racontés. Cependant, il ne faut pas oublier que ces textes sont des traductions, faites par une seule personne; une analyse stylistique ne sera dons possible qu'après une étude systématique sur la méthode de traduction, fondée sur la comparaison du texte arabe avec les fragments coptes que nous possédons. Nous pensons pouvoir présenter cette étude dans notre monographie en préparation.

---

[28] Johnson, ibid., 116 signale l'intérêt d'une telle étude stylistique.

COPTIC STUDIES

Tadeusz Dzierżykray-Rogalski

Living and Environmental Conditions of the Bishops in Pachoras-Faras

It can be assumed that during the 600–700 years of the duration of the bishopric at Faras the climatic and environmental conditions in this place did not undergo any considerable transformations. The bed of the Nile was, most probably, further away from the south-east side of the Kom on which the Cathedral and the buildings surrounding this, stood. It should be borne in mind that this entire centre which, in any case, according to the notions of those times, was an urban complex, was situated on an island. From the south-east side of this there ran the main stream of the Nile separated from the walls of the Cathedral and the monastery buildings by quite a steep bank. On the north-west this complex was encircled by an additional tributary of which up to recent times, despite the progressive aridity of the desert there, remained a separate lake. Thus, the North and South Churches (F_1 and F_2) in the desert, had their own separate water supplies. Presumably even the heaviest Nile floods did not reach the gardens which had probably surrounded the Cathedral and the Monasteries. Admittedly, the definite traces of water in the graves of the bishops and the collapse of the South Church near the Cathedral (so far attributed to an earthquake), could also have been caused by some heavier Nile flood, which undermined an even partly washed away the escarpment on which the South Church stood, but this could also have been caused by some extraordinarily heavy rainfalls, which has recently been accepted as being a more feasible explanation for this phenomenon.

As for the island, apart from buildings, there must have also been many gardens on it, and, on the north-west side of it in particular, cultivated fields. Here, there were no swamps nor thickets of wild coastal plants. The construction of the First Aswan Dam raised the bed of the river and thus brought this nearer the Cathedral complex. The remains of the plantations and the walls sur-

rounding this part of the town must have disappeared under the waters of the Nile, but all this must have come to pass when the Cathedral hill and the remains of the buildings on it were under the wind-blown sands of the desert which created an extensive Kom in this place, but this happened a few hundred years after the destruction of the Cathedral and the Islamization of Nubia.

Living conditions in the times of the Pachoras–Faras Bishopric must have been very favourable. The proximity of the Nile provided a convenient communications system and with this, contact with even the remotest urban centres and the facile transportation of commodities and food-stuff. The inhabitants of Faras were probably not short of the latter. Of course here there were none of the swamps which form nesting grounds for the countless birds along the Nile, but the river must have provided fish and the neighbouring desert (which was at that time, partly savanna--land), abounded in game. In the monastery gardens fruit and vegetables were cultivated (and no doubt also, the date and dum palms which survived in this region up to the time when they were inundated by the waters of Lake Nasser). Food was also provided in the form of offerings and gifts by the people of the adjacent villages and settlements as well as by the pilgrims from more remote places.

It can be assumed that the monks, apart from their religious duties, also cultivated the crops and gardens and it is reasonable to suppose that even the bishops themselves participated in these chores. This supposition seems to be attested by the visible on their bones, scars left by the injuries although these injuries might also have occurred in their younger days. Their way of life must have been austere and modest, but adequate for their needs. Nonetheless they suffered from the degenerative diseases common in this part of the world, although these could also have been due to the advanced ages they lived to.

More can be said about the housing conditions of the Faras priests. It is known that these were extremely modest and that their dwelling and monastery accommodation consisted of small rooms to which a dark, narrow passage gave access. Furthermore, no traces of any sanitary systems or bathrooms were discovered during our excavations.

No luxury articles, interior decorations or personal adornments had survived at Faras. It can, therefore, be assumed that there simply could not have been any of these, for the rich liturgical and cult objects survived in a very good condition and are evident in the preserved murals. An analogy to the living conditions in the monasteries of those times is to be found in the Christian monasteries existing in present-day Egypt, such as, for instance, at Wadi Natrun, in which despite the technical progress attained in the world, life based on manual labour goes on austerely and modestly. It is probable that the Faras monks did not travel too far from their monasteries, with the exception of the bishops of course who had to journey beyond their diocese. This could be borne out by the death of bishop Marianos which occurred at Qasr Ibrim quite possible when he was making a diocesian visit to this place.

To sum up, it can be said that the way of life of the Faras priests, their stabilized material conditions, the abundance of food-stuffs and moderate physical labour, were all conducive to the longevity in spite of the illnesses that suffered from differentiated diseases the representatives of the ecclasiastical hierarchy of Faras. Their modest housing conditions did not apparently greatly effect their health. In any case, in this climatic zone, life goes on outdoors, but the summer months and in particular, from May to September, were very arduous ones.

I have already mentioned that this region is one of the hottest ones in Africa and this is why the deaths of older people and of the priests occurred during this unbearable and unsalubrious period. To what extent they pestered by the namitta fly or mosquitoes, is obscure, but in all probability, these insects were unknown here in those times. This could be explained by the fact that there were no cisterns of stagnant waters or any of the swamps which were prevalent in the parts of Egypt along the mainstream of the Nile.

As has been previously mentioned, the bishops of Pachoras-Faras, irrespective of their origin or even their race, lived to a ripe old age. This is known to us from objective sources such as the definitions based on the preserved bones and the epitaphs on the stelae located by individual graves. At this point, attention should be drawn to a still vital fact that the ages defined by us by means of anthropological methods concur with those appearing in the epitaphs, which is one more highly significant fact in support of their authenticity.

In a similar way, we were able to confirm the concordance existing between the portraits preserved in the Faras Cathedral and the skeletons of individual bishops.

These modern objective analyses fully support and corroborate the veracity of transmissions of the historical type.

An entirely new element is my confirmation of the effect of water (rainfalls?) on the state of preservation of the graves and the skeletons of the bishops. From the description of the course of their exploration, it emerges that the bodies of the bishops had survived in a mummified condition and that they began to decompose under the influence of water. This would also explain the certain mixing up of the skeletons remaining from the mummies as well as the paucity and even the lack of any grave furnishings, robes or even the shrouds in which the bishops had most probably been wrapped in.

COPTIC STUDIES

Wolf-Peter Funk

How Closely Related Are the Subakhmimic Dialects?

PUBLISHED IN: *ZEITSCHRIFT FÜR ÄGYPTISCHE SPRACHE* 112 (1985)

Abstract

This paper aims at a well-founded classification of those Coptic dialects that are usually joined under the name "Subakhmimic" (or "Lycopolitan"). To this end, a comparison of idiolectal usage has been made, involving a selection of 50 features (reduced to 47 for calculation procedures) of a phonological, morphophonological or morphosyntactic nature, which have been specified for each of 15 texts and text groups, regarded as "idiolects", from the Akhmimic/Subakhmimic area (including all major extant manuscripts). Similarity coefficients have been calculated for each pair of idiolect specimens and used to establish a classification by cluster analysis applying the "complete linkage" method. The classification has been exhibited by means of three diagrams, which visibly show that groups of almost identical idiolects can be established, which are clearly distinct from one another and vary in their closeness to Akhmimic, depending on the level of linguistic analysis chosen for the comparison.

This result seems to be sufficient evidence that neither a uniform treatment of "Subakhmimic" as one dialect nor the denial of any particular norm (i.e., the assumption of exaggerated idiosyncrasy) in this area is justified. It rather suggests that the manuscripts should be considered as more or less representative of three dialects (the dialect of the Manichaean MSS, the dialect o the Subakhmimic Nag Hammadi texts plus the Heidelberg Acts of Paul, and the dialect of Thompson's Gospel of John), each of which can be reasonably defined in terms of essential features as well as limited fluctuations.

COPTIC STUDIES

Gawdat Gabra

Patape (Bīḍābā), Märtyrer und Bischof von Koptos (ca. 244–ca. 312): Ein Vorbericht über sein arabisches Enkomium

Es ist bekannt, daß uns viele koptische Literaturwerke nur in arabischer Übersetzung überliefert sind.[1] Daher lohnt es sich, wichtige Texte dieser Art bekannt zu machen. Ich möchte hier die wichtigsten Angaben von Teilen einer Sammelhandschrift des Koptischen Museums übersetzen und kurz kommentieren; von dieser Hs. wurden schon die Folios 112r–119v behandelt.[2] Die unmittelbar davor stehenden Folios (71r–111v) handeln von Patape, Märtyrer und Bischof von Koptos.[3] Auf einen weiteren unveröffentlichten arabischen Text über Patape im Antonius-Kloster hat R.-G. Coquin hingewiesen.[4] Der Vergleich dieses jüngeren Textes mit der hier besprochen Hs. zeigt, daß sie — von unbedeutenden Varianten abgesehen — fast wörtlich miteinander übereinstimmen (der Text des Antonius-Klosters wird im folgenden mit A abgekürzt). Daß es einen Märty-rer und Bischof von Koptos dieses Namens gegeben hat, war seit mehr als einem Jahrhundert bekannt.[5] Spätestens seit dem 17. Jahrhundert wird ein Kloster Patapes (Bīḍābā) im Gebiet von Nag'Ḥammadi erwähnt.[6] Auch eine Kirche des Merkurius-Klosters in Ḥiğāza — etwa 12 Kilometer von Qus entfernt — trägt seinen Namen.[7] Eine nach ihm benannte Kirche wird auf koptischen Ostraca genannt; sein Name und der seines Gefährten Andreas stehen auf einen Diptychon.[8] Wir wissen über ihn nichts, außer diesen Angaben, die zugleich zeigen, daß er eine bedeutende Persönlichkeit gewesen sein muß. Wie wir sehen werden, wurde er um 244 geboren. Mit 15 Jahren zog er sich als Anachoret zurück und er wurde um 309 vom Patriarchen Petrus zum Bischof von Koptos geweiht. Um 312 erlitt er das Martyrium. Wie zu erwarten, ist unser Text in einem Mischstil

[1] Siehe z.B. M. Krause, » Koptische Literatur «,: *Lexikon der Ägyptologie* 3. Wiesbaden 1980, sp. 714 und Anm. 244, 247, 259, sp. 715 und Anm. 287.

[2] G. Gabra, » Zu einem arabischen Bericht über Pesyntheus, einem Heiligen aus Hermonthis im 4.–5. Jh. «, BSAC 25(1985), 53 ff.

[3] G. Graf, » Catalogue de manuscrits arabes chrétiens conservés au Caire «, *Studi e Testi* 63 (Vatikanstadt 1934), Nr. 138 (Hist. 275: IV); M. Simaika, *Catalogue of the Coptic and Arabic Manuscripts in the Coptic Museum, the Patriarchate, the Principal Churches of Cairo and Alexandria and the Monasteries of Egypt.* Bd. 1, Kairo 1939, Serial Nr. 101 (Hist. 275: 3); G. Graf, » Geschichte der christlichen arabischen Literatur « 1, *Studi e Testi* 118 (Vatikanstadt 1944), 532.

[4] R.G. Coquin, » Le Synaxaire des Coptes: Un nouveau témoin de la recension de Haute Égypte «, *Analecta Bollandiana* 96 (1978), 326.

[5] S.C. Malan, *The Calender of the Coptic Church* (translated from an Arabic MS.), London 1875, S. 35 und Anm. 25; siehe auch J. Forget, » Synaxarium alexandrium «, CSCO 67 (1912), 332 und 90 (1926), 227 (Übersetzung); H. Delehaye, » Les martyrs d'Égypte «, *Analecta Bollandiana* 40 (1922), 107; De L. O'Leary, *The Saints of Egypt*, London 1937, p. 106; O. Meinardus, » A Comparative Study on the Sources of the Synaxarium of the Coptic Church «. BSAC 17 (1963–1964), 194.

[6] Claude Sicard: » Œuvres « III (présentation et notes de S. Sauneron et M. Martin), *Bibliothèque d'Études* 85 (1982), 194 f., 197; siehe auch L.Th. Lefort, » *Les premiers monastères pachômiens* « *Le Muséon* 52 (1939), 400 f.; S. Timm, *Christliche Stätten in Ägypten*, TAVO: Beih.: Reihe B, Geisteswiss. Nr. 36. Wiesbaden 1979, S. 83 und Anm. 1; S. Adli, » Several Churches in Upper Egypt «, MDAIK 36 (1980), 12.

[7] O. Meinardus, *Christian Egypt: Ancient and Modern*, Kairo 1965, S. 306 f.

[8] W.E. Crum, *The Monastery of Epiphanius at Thebes* 1, New York 1926, S. 117 und Anm. 7, 8.

von hoch- und umgangsarabischen Schreibungen abgefaßt.[9]

Fol. 71 r:

"نبتدى بعون الله وحسن توفيقه بشرح ميمر وضعه الاب المكرم القديس الطاهر المختار الا اسقف الفاضل القديس ابينا انبا تاوفيلس[10] اسقف كرسى قفط يشرح فيه كرامة الاب الفاضل القديس العظيم والشهيد المكرم الاسقف المكرم بكل نوع ابينا بيضابا الذى تفسيره الجوهرى اسقف الكرسى المذكور هذا الذى اكمل جهاده المكرم فى اليوم التاسع عشر من ابيب وتكريز بيعته المقدسه الذى بنيت له على اسمه فى الموضع الذى كان منفرد فيه فى اليوم الثالث عشر من كيهك..."

'Wir beginnen – Gott gewähre uns Hilfe und gutes Gelingen – mit der Ausführung einer Homilie, die der ehrwürdige Vater verfaßte, der reine auserwählte Heilige, der vorzügliche Bischof, der Heilige unser Vater Anba Theophilus (sic *tāwfīlbus*), Bischof von Koptos zur Verehrung des vorzüglichen Vaters, des großen Heligen, des vornehmen Märtyrers, des in jeder Weise verehrungswürdigen Bischofs, Anba Patape (Bīdābā), was übersetzt »Juwelier« heißt, des Bischofs der obengenannten Diözese. Dieser, der seinen verehrungswürdigen Kampf am 19. Epep vollendete; und dessen heiligen Kirche, die auf seinem Namen an der Stelle gebaut wurde, wohin er sich Zurückgezogen hatte, am 13 Chojahk ihren Weihetag hat...'

Theophilus, Bischof von Koptos, dürfte der direkte Nachfolger Patapes gewesen sein. Er muß bereits vor dem Jahre 325 verstorben sein; denn sowohl ein Melitianer namens Theodor[11] als auch ein Teilnehmer am Konzil von Nicaea, namens Arianus,[12] waren Bischöfe von Koptos. Am Tag der Weihe seiner Kirche (13 Chojahk) wird nach einer unveröffentlichten Rezension des saidischen Synaxars Patapes gedacht.[13]

Fol. 72r:

"...ان تفتحوا سماع اذانكم وتفهموا بعقولكم ما اتلوه عليكم انا المسكـين تاوفيلس[14] الجالس على كرسى الاسقفيه كما اخبرنى صديقه الاب القس المكرم اندراوس لما سالته ان يخبرنى بقليل من فضايل هذا الاب وما عمل من النسك والجهاد وما ناله من الاتعاب الى ان اكمل سعيه المبارك وجهاد ه الحسن واخبار والد يه وبلد ه وما جرى له منذ صباه بسلام من الرب امين . قال كان ابو هذا القديس رجل خايف من الله اسمه مينا وكانت امـه وام القد يس اندراوس اخواة وكانا سالكين فى مرضاة الله عاملين بنواميسه وكانا من مدينة فى الصعيد تسما ارمنت ..."

'..., daß ihr eure Ohren öffnet und mit eurem Verstand begreift, was ich euch vortrage; ich, der Geringste, Theophilus (sic *tāwfīlbus*), der auf dem bischöflichen Stuhl sitzt. (Ich erzählte es euch), wie es sein Freund, der Vater und ehrwürdige Priester Andreas, mir mitteilte, als ich ihn darum gebeten hatte, mir etwas von den Tugenden dieses Vaters mitzuteilen wie auch von Askeseübungen, die er verrichtete und von dem Kampf, den er ausgeführt und von den Mühen, die er auf sich genommen hatte, bis er seinen gesegneten Lauf und seinen guten Kampf vollendete; auch die Nachrichten über seine (d.h. Patapes) Eltern, seine Herkunft und über das, was seit seiner Jungenzeit erlebt hatte; mit dem Heil vom Herrn, Amen. Man sagte: Der Vater dieses Heiligen war ein gottesfürchtiger Mann, namens Mena. Seine Mutter (d.h. des Patape) und die Mutter des Heiligen Andreas waren Schwestern. Sie (d.h. die Eltern Patapes) wandelten in dem wohlgefallen Gottes und handelten sich nach seinen Satzungen. Sie stammten aus einer Stadt in Oberägypten namens Hermonthis (Armant)...'

Es fällt auf, daß Pesyntheus, Bischof von Koptos auch aus Hermonthis stammt.[15] Im Gegensatz

---

[9] Auch die Orthographie gleicht der anderer Texte dieser Art. ت wird immer für ث geschrieben: Z.B. الثالث für التالت (71r, zl. 11), ثم für تم (73r, zl. 2); د wird immer für ذ geschrieben: Z.B. هذا الذى für هذا الدى (95v, zl. 6). Statt eines *Hamza* steht in der Wortmitte ein *Alif*: Z.B. امراة für امرأة (77v, zl. 7; 96r, zl. 13); oder ein *Wāw*: Z.B. البناوون für البناون (81r, zl.8); oder die beiden Pünktchen des *Yā*: Z.B. ليلا für لئلا , عجايب für عجائب (99v, zl. 1). *Alif maqsūra* wird oft mit *Alif* geschrieben: Z.B. تسما für تسمى (72r, zl.13; 95v, zl.13), اعطا für اعطى (93r, zl. 11), صلا für صلى (86v, zl. 12; 91v, zl. 7), القا für القى (79v, zl. 12). *Tā'awīla* wird manchmal mit *Tā'marbūta* wiedergegeben und umgekehrt: Z.B. قواة für بواسطت (106v, zl. 9), انت für انة (106v, zl.3), كنت für كنة (88v, zl. 10), كانت für كانة (86v, zl. 5), قوات für بواسطة (87r, zl. 8), انية für انيت (93r, zl. 7), بقوة für بقوت (106v, zl. 11). غ wird manchmal für ق geschrieben: Z.B. يغضى für يقضى (85r, zl. 9), تغربوا für تقربوا (85v, zl. 10).

[10] Im A (1r) تاوفيلس

[11] H. Munier, *Recueil des listes épiscopales de l'église copte.*, Kairo 1943, S. 2, zl. 9 der Liste.

[12] J. Muyser, » Contribution à l'étude des listes épiscopales de l'église copte «, BSAC 10 (1944), 141.

[13] Coquin, » Le Synaxaire... «, 361 f.

[14] Im A (2r) تاوفيلس siehe oben, Anm. 10.

[15] Gawdat Gabra Abdel-Sayed, *Untersuchungen zu den Texten über Pesyntheus, Bischof von Koptos (569–632)*, Bonn 1984, S. 308.

zum Anfang des Textes wird hier neben Bischof Theophilus ein Freund Patapes namens Andreas als Quelle für das Enkomium genannt. Im folgenden Textteil (95r–95v) begegnen wir aber Andreas allein als Erzähler in der 1. Person.

ولما بلغو حد القـامـه وصاروا رجال فصاروا يصوموا يومين يومين ...

ولما كانوا فى بعض الايام وهم جالسين قالا لبعضهما ليس يمكننا ان نخلص نفوسنا ونحن مقيمين عند اهالينا بل نمضى ونجلس فى مكان وحدنا ثم انهم خرجوا من المـدينه بامر الاسقف وجاءو الى الجبل الشرقى فوجدوا القـديس انبا ايساك فى الموضع الذى تعبد فيه بعده القـديس انبا بلامون فعزاهم وقواهم وقال لهم ليس يمكن ان تكونوا عندى بل امضوا وانفردوا وبارك على القـديس انبا بيضابا وقال لهلابد لك كان ترعى قطيع المسيح وتنال اتعاب كثيره على اسمه وانت يا اندراوس لك اكليل معد معه وباركهم ودعا لهما وخرجوا من عنده واتوا الى البر الغربى وابتنوا لهم قلاية وسكنوا هناك وكانت صناعتهم نسخ الكتب المقـدسه ... فسمع بخبرهم اسقف تلك البلاد فاتى اليهم وجعل القـديس بيضابا شماسا وكانوا يمضوا الى بيعته بالقرب منهم ويتقربوا فى كل اربعين يوم مره ففى بعض الايام دخلوا البيعه فوقف القـديس بيضابا يسمع الكتب المقـدسة وكان الاب الاسقف جالس على كرسيه فنظر الى وجه القـديس بيضابا واذ امتلا مجدا واكليلا على راسه فامر الاسقف بان ياتوا بالقـديس بيضابا ورفيقه اندراوس فجعل القـديس بيضابا قسا واندراوس شماسا وقال لهما تكونوا عندى فاما القـديس بيضابا فابا ان يمكث عنده وقال له يا ابى صلاتك تكون معى وتعيننى فاخذ القـديس اندراوس معه الى قلايته ليكون عنده واما القـديس بيضابا رجع الى قلايته وصار يبكى بكاً مراً وقال اطلب اليك ياسيدى يسوع المسيح ان يكون هذا الموضع يذكر فيه اسمك الى الابد ومضى وانفرد الى الجبل وبعد زمان يسير ارسل الاسقف يطلبه فلم يجده فبنى الاسقف فى ذلك الموضع بيعة على اسم القـديس بيضابا وكرزها فى اليوم الثالث عشر من شهر كيهك ...

'... Nun möchte ich damit anfangen, euch ein wenig von den Wundern zu offenbaren, die Gott durch die Hand dieses Vaters tat; ich, der Geringste, Andreas: Der Vater, der Bischof, Anba Theodor nahm mich und ließ mich in der Zelle dienen, die er bei der Kirche erbaute, die (d.h. die Kirche) er auf den Namen des heiligen Patape errichtete. Er machte mich zum Diakon und danach zum Priester, (und ich blieb da) bis mein Vater, der Bischof, der heilige Patape nach ihm die Diözese von Koptos übernahm. Da schickte er zu mir, daß ich bei ihm bliebe. Daraufhin kam ich zu ihm. Ich, der Geringste (erzählte euch), was ich mit meinen Augen sah und mit meinen Ohren hörte, als ich bei ihm war. Und sie (d.h. die Wunder) sind überall erkennbar. Ich möchte euch dieses Wunder erzählen, das durch meinen Vater, Anba Patape geschah...'

Diese Aussagen erinnern stark an die Verfasserangaben der Texte über Pesyntheus, Bischof von Koptos.[16] Hinzu kommt, daß Andreas nach dem Text mit Patape das Martyrium erlitt, wie wir sehen werden. Nicht selten ist die Zuschreibung koptischer Literaturwerke problematisch.[17] Mit Patape, seinem schon genannten Nachfolger Theophilus und seinem Vorgänger Theodor werden uns drei Bischöfe der Diözese Koptos im frühen 4. Jahrhundert bekannt.

Fol. 72v–74r:

" ... ولما كان القـديس انبا بيضابا له من العمر عشر سنين تعلم ساير العلوم الروحانيه وكان يوميذ عمر القـديس اندراوس اثنى عشر سنة ....

'... Als der Heilige Patape (Bīdābā) zehn Jahre alt war, lernte er alle geistlichen Wissenschaften; damals war das Alter des Heiligen Andreas zwölf Jahre... Als sie erwachsen waren und Männer wurden, begannen sie, je zwei Tage zu fasten. Als sie einees Tages zusammensassen, sagten sie zueinander: » Wir können unsere Seelen nicht retten, solange wir bei unseren Leuten wohnen, wir wollen weggehen und uns an irgendeinem Ort allein für uns bleiben «; Dann verließen sie mit der Erlaubnis des Bischofs die Stadt und kamen zum östlichen Gebirge. Da fanden sie den Heiligen Anba Isaak an derselben Stelle, an der sich Anba Palamon nach ihm (d.h. Isaak) dem Dienste Gottes widmete. Er tröste-te, bestärkte sie und sagte zu ihnen: » Ihr könnt nicht bei mir bleiben, vielmehr geht und kehrt zurück «. Und er segnete den heiligen

---

[16] Ibid., S. 267 ff.
[17] Ibid., S. 268 und Anm. 16, S. 269 und Anm. 17.

Anba Patape (Bīdābā) und sagte zu ihm: »Es ist dir unvermeidlich, daß du die Herde Christi hütest und viele Mühen um seinen Namens willen auf dich nimmst«. (Er sagte zu Andreas): »Und dir Andreas, ist schon eine Krone bei ihm (d.h. bei Christus) bereitet«. Er segnete sie und sprach ihnen Segenswünsche aus; und sie gingen von ihm, kamen zum westlichen Ufer, bauten sich eine Zelle und wohnten dort; ihre Beschäftigung war das Abschreiben der heiligen Bücher... Der Bischof dieses Gebietes hörte von ihnen, kam zu ihnen und machte den Heiligen Patape zum Diakon. Sie (d.h. Patape und Andreas) gingen fortan zu seiner (d.h. des Bischofs) Kirche in ihrer Nähe und empfingen alle vierzig Tage die Kommunion. Eines Tages gingen sie in die Kirche hinein; der Heilige Patape stellte sich hin, um (den Text) der heiligen Bücher zu hören, während der Vater, der Bischof, auf dem Thron saß. Er erblickte das Gesicht des Heiligen Patape, wie es von Herrlichkeit voll war, und auf seinem (d.h. Patapes) Kopf eine Krone. Der Bischof befahl, den Heiligen Patape und seinen Genossen Andreas zu ihm zu bringen. Er machte den hl. Patape zum Priester und Andreas zum Diakon. Er sagte zu ihnen: »Bleibt bei mir!« Der hl. Patape lehnte es aber ab, bei ihm zu bleiben. Er sagte zu ihm: »Vater, möge dein Gebet bei mir sein und mir helfen«. Und so nahm er (d.h. der Bischof) den hl. Andreas mit sich zu seiner Zelle, um bei ihm zu sein. Der hl. Patape kehrte aber zu seiner Zelle zurück, weinte bitterlich und sagte: »Ich erbitte von dir, o mein Herr, Jesus Christus, daß dein Name für immer an dieser Stelle genannt wird«. Und er begab sich ins Gebirge und lebte als Anachoret. Nach kurzer Zeit wollte der Bischof ihn holen; er fand ihn aber nicht. Da erbaute er eine Kirche an dieser Stelle auf dem Namen des hl. Patape und er weihte sie am 13. Chojahk...'

Wie wir sehen werden, zog sich Patape als Anachoret im Alter von 15 Jahre zurück (um 259). Mit der Erlaubnis des »Bischofs« verließ Patape die »Stadt«. Handelt es sich um einen Bischof von Hermonthis, woher Patape stammt?. Der »Bischof« dieses Gebietes—in dem Palamon lebte—ernannte Patape zum Diakon. War es

der Bischof von Diospolis Parva (Hu) oder von Koptos?[18] In jedem Falle haben wir hier einen Hinweis auf Bischöfe im 3. Viertel des 3. Jahrhunderts tief im Süden Oberägyptens; Palamon kann nur der geistliche Vater Pachoms sein, bei dem er 313/320 gewesen war.[19] Der Einsiedler Isaak, als Bewohner des später von Palamon bewohnten Ortes, ist m.W. nicht an anderweitig belegt. Nach dem Text wurde der Anachoret Patape vom Bischof zum Diakon und dann zum Priester geweiht. Die Anachoreten Patape und sein Genosse Andreas empfingen die Kommunion alle 40 Tage in der Kirche. Wir müssen annehmen, daß Pachom von Patape und seiner Beziehung zur Kirche gehört hat.[20]

Fol. 86r.:

”... فبعد زمان قليل اجتمعوا الشعب الى الاب الاسقف انبا تادرس اسقف تلك البلاد وسالوه قايلين نسالك يا ابانا ان تحضر لنا القديس بيضابا لنتبارك منه ويقيم عندنا فاجاب الى سوالهم وكتب اليه وارسل له اثنين كهنة فاحضروه الى بلدة تسمى بهجوره ...“

'... Nach kurzer Zeit versammelten sich die Leute bei dem Bischof Anba Theodor, dem Bischof dieses Gebietes, und baten ihn: »Wir bitten dich, unseren Vater, daß du den hl. Patape zu uns bringst, damit wir von ihm gesegnet werden und er bei uns bleibt«. Er kam ihrer Bitte nach, schrieb an ihn und schickte zwei Priester zu ihm. Sie brachten ihn zu einer Stadt namens Bahğūra...'

Es sei darauf hingewiesen, daß nach einer noch nicht veröffentlichten Rezension des saidischen Synaxars die Kirche Patapes in der Nähe von Bahğūra liegt.[21] In unserer Zeit führt ein Priester von »al-Gharbî Bahgura« den Gottesdienst im Patape-Kloster durch.[22]

Fol. 87r–88r

”... ولماكان يوم الاحد والشعب مجتمعين فى البيعة فقال الاب الاسقف قد موا الى القديس بيضابا فعند ما قد موه اليه وضع اليد عليه وجعله قمص[23] ولما تقربوا الشعب وانصرفوا

---

[18] Jeder Bischof kann nach den Kanones nur Weihungen (zu Diakonen und Priestern) in *seiner* Diözese vornehmen: M. Krause, *Apa Abraham von Hermonthis*, Dissertation, Berlin 1956, II, 1, S. 42 und Anm. 62 ff.

[19] Siehe H. Bacht, *Das Vermächtnis des Ursprungs*, Bb. 2 (*Pachomius – Der Mann und sein Werk*), Würzburg 1983, S. 21 ff, 293. (A [3r] bezeichnet Palamon als den »großen« Heiligen); siehe auch Meinardus, *Christian Egypt...*, S. 305.

[20] Bacht, *Das Vermächtnis...*, S. 21 und Anm. 81; siehe auch P. Pius Tamburrino, »Koinonid. Die Beziehung 'Monasterium'-'Kirche' im frühen pachomianischen Mönchtum«, *Erbe und Auftrag* 43 (1967) 5, ff.

[21] Coquin, »Le Synaxaire...«, S. 362 und Anm. 1.

[22] Meinardus, *Christian Egypt...*, S. 302.

[23] Im A (17v) »ايغومانس« (=ἡγούμενος), siehe Graf, *Verzeichnis arabischer kirchlicher Termini*, CSCO, subs. 8, 1954, 93.

بسلام فمكث عند الاب الاسقف تسعة ٢٤ ايام وان القديس
توجه الى الجبل وفيها هو متوجه استقبله اربعة رجال ارسلوا اليه
لكى يحضر الى عندهم بنواحى قوص ونقاده ... فتوجه مع الرجال
الى نواحى الصعيد فلما قرب من نقاده قبله اهلها بفرح عظيم ...
واقمنا هناك ثلاثة ايام عند رجلا صالحا فى تد بيره مزين بكل
فضيلة اسمه مويساس وخرج من عنده فتلقا ه رجال وعدوا به
الى البر الشرقى واقام هناك سبعة ايام فصنع عجايب كثيرة ...″

'... Als die Leute am Sonntag in der Kirche beisammen waren, sagte der Vater, der Bischof: » Führt den heiligen Patape zu mir «. Als sie ihn zu ihm führten, legte er ihm die Hand auf und machte ihn zum Hegumen. Nachdem die Leute die Kommunion empfangen hatten und in Frieden weggegangen waren, blieb·er bei dem Vater, dem Bischof, neun Tage. Der Heilige begab sich ins Gebirge. Während er weiterging, kamen ihm vier Männer zum Empfang entgegen, die zu ihm geschickt worden waren, damit er zu ihnen—in die Gegenden von Quṣ und Naqada—komme... Er begab sich mit den Männern nach Süden. Als sie sich Naqada nährten, empfingen ihn die Einwohner mit großer Freude... Und wir blieben drei Tage dort bei einem Mann namens Moses (Mwīsās) mit gutem Lebenswandel und versehen mit jeder Tugend. Als er (d.h. Patape) von ihm wegging, nahmen sich einige Leute Seiner an und setzten ihn zum östlichen Ufer über. Er blieb dort sieben Tage und tat viele Wunder...'

Dieser Textteil zeigt, daß der Anachoret Patape mit Bewohnern der Gegenden von Naqâda und Quṣ in Kontakt kam, bevor er ein Bischof von Koptos wurde.[25]

Fol. 89v–91r:

″... وبعد ذلك لما تنيح الاسقف اعنى اسقف قفط اجتمعوا
اهالى البلاد واشتوروا على احد يقيموه اسقف على الكرسى
فكتبوا تزكية ٢٦ للاب البطريرك انبا بطرس التاسع عشر ٢٧
من عدة البطاركة ان يرسل ياخذ القديس بيضابا ليجعله اسقفا
عليهم ... واذ بالقصاد ٢٨ حضروا الى الاب البطريرك وعرضوا
عليه التركية فلما قراها ارسل اربعة كهنة من عند ه صحبة

القصاد الذ ى حضروا له بالتزكية ... فاخذوه الرسل ونزلوا فى
المركب وباراد ة الله تعالى وصلوا الى الاب البطريرك ... حينذا
اخذ ه الاب البطريرك وقد مه بحضرة اهل كرسيه وقسمه اسقفا
وطقسه على الكرسى المذكور وهو قايل اكسيوس ثلاثة مراة
وفيها هو يقول هكذا واذا صوتا من السا يقول بحضرة ها هنا
يقول الشعب كله

ⲁⲅⲓⲟⲥ ⲁⲅⲓⲟⲥ ⲁⲅⲓⲟⲥ (ⲁⲅⲓⲟⲥ) ⲁⲃⲃⲁ ⲡⲓⲧⲁⲡⲏ ⲡⲓⲁⲡⲓ
ⲥⲕⲱⲡⲟⲥ (ἐπίσκοπος) [29]

وكان جميع السامعين يقولوا مستحق مستحق مستحق ... وان
الاب البطريرك بارك على الاسقف وعلى شعبه واذ نهم يسافروا
الى بلاد هم ...″

'... Als danach der Bischof entschlief, nämlich der Bischof von Koptos, versammelte sich die Bevölkerung des Gebietes und beriet, wen sie als Bischof über die Diözese einsetzen könnten. Und so schrieben sie ein Protokoll (tazkiya) an den Vater, den Patriarchen, Anba Peter, den Neunzehnten[30] in der Liste (wörtl. Zahl) der Patriarchen, damit er den heiligen Patape holen lasse, um ihn zum Bischof über sie zu ernennen... Und siehe, die Delegierten kamen zum Patriarchen und legten ihm das Protokoll vor. Nachdem er es gelesen hatte, schickte er vier seiner Priester mit den Delegierten, die zu ihm (d.h. dem Patriarchen) mit dem Protokoll gekommen waren... Und die Boten nahmen ihn (d.h. Patape), stiegen in das Schiff ein und kamen—entsprechend dem Willen des erhabenen Gottes—beim Patriarchen an... Dann nahm der Vater, der Patriarch ihn, ordinierte ihn in Anwesenheit der Leute seiner Diözese, weihte ihn als Bischof und verlieh ihm den (bischöflichen) Rang (τάξις) über die genannte Diözese, in dem er drei mal sagte: » Aksiyus (ἄξιος: d.h. er ist würdig «. Während er dies sagte, erscholl eine Stimme vom Himmel: Hier sollen alle Leute in Ehrfurcht sagen: » ἄξιος ἄξιος ἄξιος (ἄξιος) ⲁⲃⲃⲁ ⲡⲓⲧⲁⲡⲏ ⲡⲓⲁⲡⲓⲥⲕⲱⲡⲟⲥ (ἐπίσκοπος) « Alle Zuhörer sagten: » (er ist) würdig, würdig, würdig «... Der Vater, der Patriarch, segnete der Bischof und seine Gemeinde und er erlaubte ihnen, in ihre Heimat zu reisen...'

Gehen diese Einzelheiten auf einen koptischen Text zurück, wird die Rolle der Gemeinde bei der

---

[24] Im A 17v » سبعة «.

[25] Zu Bischöfen, die zeurst zu Diakonen oder Priestern ernannt wurden, siehe Crum, *The Monastery...*, S. 226 und Anm. 12.

[26] Zu *tazkiya* siehe O.H.E. Burmester, » The Canons of Cyril III Ibn Laḳlaḳ, 75th Patriarch of Alexandria, A.D. 1235–1250 «, BCAS 12 (1946–1947), S. 105 und Anm. 4; R.G. Coquin, » Saint Constantin, évêque d'Asyūt «, *SOC Collectanea* 16 (1981), S. 160 und Anm. 5.

[27] Im A (19v) » السابع عشر « der siebzehnte', was historisch korrekt ist. Die arabischen Grapheme für 7 und 9 werden of rezwechselt/vertauscht.

[28] Im A (20r) » الرسل «.

[29] Im A (20v) steht nur » αξιος: αξιος: αξιος «.

[30] Vgl. G.W.H. Lampe, *A Patristic Greek Lexicon*, Oxford 1961, 167. s.v. ⲕⲕ ξιος.

Bischofsauswahl aufgezeigt.[31] Die Ordination des Anachoreten Patape zum Bischof geschah schon lange, bevor Athanasius Mönche aufforderte, sich zu Bischöfen weihen zu lassen.[32]

Fol. 99r–99v:

„... هوذا هولاء قلنا هم لمحبتكم على قدر عقلي وما قد رايته بعيني من ابينا الطاهر الاب الاسقف انبا بيضابا وتركت عيني عجايب كثيره لم اقو لهم ... لنعرفكم ما قد نال هذا القديس من العذاب والاتعاب على اسم السيد المسيح له المجد الى الابد امين فلما كان فى مملكة دقلاديانوس ومكسيمانوس الاعزا الاقويا الذى تباعدوا من المسيح كان اريانا والى الصعيد ... فمضى الى الصعيد وقبض على المسيحيين فى كل بلد الى ان وصل الى مدينه اسنا ...‟

‚... Seht, wir erzählten Eurer Liebenswürdigkeit dieses entsprechend meiner Geistesgabe und dem, was ich mit meinen Augen von unserem tugendhaften Vater, dem Bischof, Anba Patape gesehen habe. Meine Augen haben viele Wunder nicht gesehen, die erzähle ich nicht..., damit wir euch mitteilen können, was diesem Heiligen an Qual and Mühe wegen des Namens des Herrn Christus — ihm gebührt der Ruhm bis in die Ewigkeit der Ewigkeiten, Amen — zugefügt wurde. Es geschah während der Regierungszeit der Mächtigen und Starken Diokletian und Maximin, die Christus mieden, daß Arianus den Gouverneur von Oberägypten (wörtl. des Süden) war... Er ging nach Süden (d.h. Arianus) und nahm die Christen in jeder Stadt fest, bis er die Stadt Esna erreichte...'

Wie in vielen anderen Märtyrerberichten wird diese Periode der Christenverfolgung (303–311) mit den Namen der zwei Kaiser Diokletian und Maximin verbunden,[33] sowie mit dem Namen des Arianus, des Praeses der Thebais, den unser Text als Gouverneur Oberägyptens (oder des Südens) bezeichnet.[34]

Fol. 102r–102v:

„... حينئذا تجهز الاب الى السفر وخرج من البلد ومضى الى مدينة اسنا فتبعه القديس العظيم الاب المكرم القس

اندراوس والاب المكرم القس الفاضل انبا اخرستوضولوا الذى من دمقرات ... فساروا فى الطريق واذا بالقد يس بنيامين ملاقيهم ... ومشوا مع بعضهم الى حين دخلوا مدينة اسنا ...‟

‚... Dann machte der Vater (d.h. Patape) sich für die Reise bereit. Er verließ die Stadt und begab sich nach der Stadt Esna. Der große heilige, der ehrwürdige Vater, der Priester Andreas und der ehrwürdige Vater, der tugendhafte Priester, Anba Christodulus, der aus Dimuqrat stammte, folgten ihm... sie begaben sich auf den Weg; da begegnete ihnen der heilige Benjamin... Sie gingen miteinander, bis sie in die Stadt Esna eintraten...'

Esna als Märtyrerort wird oft erwähnt.[35] Ein Märtyrer-Kloster steht noch in Esna.[36]

Fol. 105v:

„... وللوقت صرخوا القد يسين اعني القديس اندراوس ورفقته الاثنين عند ما نظروا القد يس افتضح ايها الوالى واخزى لانه ليس اله الا الهنا يسوع المسيح وللوقت امر باخذ روسهم ونالوا الاكليل الشهاده ...‟

‚und sofort schrien die Heiligen, nämlich der heilige Andreas und seine zwei Genossen (d.h. Christodulus und Benjamin), als sie den Heiligen (d.h. Patape) erblickten. Und sie sagten: » Du sollst beschämt werden, Gouverneur und verächtlich dastehen, denn es gibt keinen Gott außer unserem Gott, Jesus Christus. « Sogleich befahl er, sie zu enthaupten. Und sie empfingen die Krone des Märtyrertums...'

Wir haben gesehen, daß Andreas als Erzähler in der 1. Person spricht; daß sein Martyrium in derselben Zeit geschah (wie wir gleich sehen werden), läßt sich mit der Aussage über die Zuschreibung des Textes nicht erklären.[37]

Fol. 109v–110r:

„... فقال المخلص تعزى يا حبيبى بيضابا ... ان كلمن ياتى الى البيعة الذى بنيت على اسمك ويعطى قربان على اسمك انا ابارك ... والذى لا يعمل شغل يوم تذكارك انا ابارك فى كده

---

[31] Vgl. Gawdat Gabra Abdel-Sayed, *Untersuchungen...*, S. 311 f. und Anm. 248 auf S. 312.

[32] Siehe H. Bacht, *Das Konzil von Chalkedon* 2, Würzburg 1953, S. 303.

[33] Vgl. Cl. Vandersleyen, *Chronologie des préfets d'Égypte de 284 à 395*, Bruxelles 1962, S. 86, 91.

[34] Vgl. ibid., S. 87 und Anm. 6.

[35] Siehe z.B. H. Leclercq, » Esneh «, *Dictionnaire d'archéologie chrétienne et de liturgie*, Bd. 5/1, Paris 1922, 398 ff.; S. Sauneron, *Quatre campagnes à Esna*, Kairo 1959, S. 32.

[36] Leclercq, » Esneh «, 401 ff.; R.G. Coquin, » Les inscriptions pariétales des monastères d'Esna: Dayr al-Šuhadā – Dayr al-Faḫūrī, BIFAO 75 (1975), 241.

[37] Siehe oben S. 2, 3, 4 und Anm. 16, 17.

واعـوض ذلـك فى ملكـوت السمـوات وكلمن كان فى شد ه
اوضيقة وطلب المعونة منى باسمك انا اخلصه من شد ته ...."

'... Der Soter sagte: » Tröste dich, meinen
geliebter Patape... Wer zu der auf deinem
Namen gebauten Kirche kommt und auf
deinen Namen Opfergaben darbringt, den
werde ich segnen... Wer am Tag deines
Gedächtnisses nicht arbeitet, dem werde ich
seinen Fleiß segnen und ihn stattdessen im
Himmelreich entschädigen. Wer in Unglück
oder Not geriet und mich in deinem Namen um
Hilfe bittet, den rette ich aus seinem
Unglück... «'
Dieser Abschnitt zeigt den Ruf Patapes in der
Nachwelt; nämlich daß er u.a. als Fürsprecher galt.

Fol. 110v–111r:

".... وان القـد يس انبـا بيضابـا فاضـرب رقبته بالسيف ونال
اكليل الشهاد ة الغـر مضمحل فى اليوم التاسع عشر من شهر
ابيب المبارك وكان عمره ثمانية وستين سنة منها فى بيت ابيه
خمسة عشر سنه ومنها وهو فى النسك تسعة واربعين سنه ونصف
واقام على كرسى قفط فى الاسقفية ثلاثة سنين ونصف وكان
تكريزه اسقف فى عاشر سنة من رياست الاب انبا بطرس رييس
اساقفة الاسكندريه ....."

'... Der heilige Anba Patape wurde mit
dem Schwert enthauptet und er empfing am 19.
Tag des gesegneten Monates Epep die unver-
gängliche Krone des Märtyriums. Er war 68
Jahre alt; 15 Jahre davon war er im Hause
seines Vaters gewesen, 49 1/2 Jahre in der
Askese, als Bischof von Koptos 3 1/2 Jahre.
Seine Ordination zum Bischof war im 10. Jahre
der Regierungszeit des Vaters, Anba Pater, des
Patriarchen (wörtl. Erzbischof) von Alexan-
drien...'
Die am Anfang des Artikels genannten Angaben
über die Daten Patapes [38] basieren auf dieser
Stelle; die Inthronisation des Patriarchen Petrus

wird von Wissenschaftlern mit einer Differenz von
ein bis zwei Jahren datiert (300–302).[39] Es sei
darauf hingewiesen, daß solche biographischen
Daten auf Stellen von Bischöfen in Nubien belegt
sind [40] und ebenso in koptischen [41] und arabischen Texten.[42]

Der Text über den Märtyrer und Bischof
Patape enthält viele Wunder, die auch in anderen
Werken dieser Literaturgattung noch vorkom-
men.

Die besondere Bedeutung dieses arabischen
Textes, der sicher auf einen koptischen Text
zurückgeht, liegt im folgenden:

1. Wurde der ursprüngliche koptische Text
vom Bischof Theophilus abgefaßt, der ein direkter
Nachfolger Patapes gewesen sein dürfte, so ent-
stand der Text vor dem Jahre 325.[43] Es würde sich
um eine *Vita* handeln, die in südlichen Teil von
Oberägypten niedergeschrieben wurde, mehrere
Jahrzehnte bevor Athanasius die *Vita Antonii*
verfaßte.[44]

2. Er bietet Informationen über die Lage der
Kirche, die Beziehung zwischen Anachoreten und
der Kirche und das Leben von Anachoreten jenes
Gebiets und jener Zeit, kurz bevor sich
Pachom — der Begründer des koinobitischen
Mönchtums — dort niedergelassen hat.

3. Der Text handelt von einem Bischof des
Binnenlandes, der den größten Teil seines Lebens
im 3. Jahrhundert verbrachte und im frühen 4. Jh.
als Bischof tätig war, was bisher nicht so ausführlich in anderen koptischen oder arabischen Texten
überliefert ist.[45] Darüber hinaus werden in ihm
viele andere geschichtliche Personen erwähnt,
darunter Bischöfe dieser Zeit.

Das zeigt, daß sich die vollständige Herausga-
be dieses arabischen Textes ohne Zweifel lohnt.

---

[38] Siehe oben S. 1.

[39] Siehe z.B. B. Evetts, » History of the Patriarchs of the Coptic Church of Alexandria «, PO 1 (1904–1906), 383 ff.; E.R. Hardy, *Christian Egypt: Church and People*, New York 1952, S. 42; B. Spuler, » Die koptische Kirche «, *Handbuch der Orientalistik* 8, 2 (1961), 272; A.S. Atiya, *A History of the Eastern Christianity*, London 1968, S. 31, 479; M. Roncaglia, *Histoire de l'église copte* 2, Beirut 1969, S. 249; B. Altaner–A. Stuiber, *Patrologie*, 8. Auflage, Freiburg–Basel–Wien 1978, 212. Iris Habib al Masri hat ohne Begründung das Jahr 285 und das Jahr 293 als das seiner Inthronisation genannt (*The Story of the Copts*, Kairo 1978, 76, S. 563).

[40] Siehe Krause, » Die Formulare der christlichen Grabsteine Nubiens «, in: *Nubia. Récentes Recherches*, Warschau 1975, S. 82 und Anm. 93.

[41] Siehe z.B. L.Th. Lefort, » S. Pachomii vitae sahidice scriptae «, CSCO, script, copt. 9 und 10, 1933, 96.

[42] Siehe z.B. R. Basset, » Le synaxaire arabe jacobite «, PO 3 (1909), 505 (=429).

[43] Siehe oben S. 2 und Anm. 11.

[44] Zur Datierung der *Vita Antonii* siehe L. Barnard, » The Date of S. Athanasius' *Vita Antonii* «, *Vigiliae Christianae* 27 (1974), 169 ff.; B. Brennan, » Dating Athanasius' *Vita Antonii* «, *Vigiliae Christianae* 30 (1976), 52 ff.

[45] Vgl. z.B. die von T. Orlandi (*Elementi di lingua e letteratura copta*, Mailand 1970, S. 72 f.) genannten Angaben über den Märtyrer Psote, Bischof von Psoi, der ein Zeitgenosse Patapes war.

COPTIC STUDIES

Włodzimierz Godlewski

The Cruciform Church at Old Dongola (Sudan). Some Comments

After the last season of excavations in Old Dongola in 1984, 70 per cent of the inner space of the Cruciform Church was uncovered. Only the northern part of the building is still under sand.[1] The state of preservation of the walls of this edifice varies from one part of the building to another. There are parts of the walls preserved up to 4 m high but also some fragments of the edifice are razed to the platform on which whole building was founded. Some vertical stone elements as columns are also preserved in situ but the majority of the architectural elements were found laying on the pavement of the Cruciform Building or were re-used in very late Christian and post-Christian constructions.

On the basis of detailed analysis of remnants of the building as well as of material which was found during the excavation, we can say that the Cruciform Church in Dongola was built, most probably, in the 9th century and was later twice rebuilt.

During the first reconstruction of the building the southern arm was elongated by a small addition, a kind of vestibule. Most probably similar annexes were also added to the ends of the northern arm and perhaps to the western one as well.[2]

The second reconstruction of the Cruciform Building was connected with the destruction of the monument at the end of the 13th century or at the beginning of the 14th, most probably during the campains of the Mameluke army against Nubia. All constructions of this period are in mud brick and are easy to recognize. At that time the building was only partly rebuilt and was intended for celebration of the liturgy. Some parts of the monument were left in ruins. The Cruciform Building was abandoned at the end of the 14th century.

The main core of the Cruciform Church in Old Dongola is central square bay (14×14 m) which is closed from each side by two-column portico (triforium). The cross was formed by arms radiating outward from the central part. Each arm of the Dongolese building is composed of two parts. The identical inner parts of the arms are wider (7.15 m) and open by portico to the central bay. The outside parts of the arms are narrower (3.40 m) and differ in size as well as in function.

In the southern arm there is an entrance to the building with some remnants still preserved, for example jambs, threshold, inner threshold, the place where the door could be opened and closed, a hole in the pavement where the door could be blocked. In the western arm there was also entrance but arranged in a different way, so that it could be only a passage from the western room, still unknown, to the western arm of the building. The eastern arm was longer (7.5 m) and separated by a wall from the remaining part of the building. In this wall there is a small doorway beside the southern wall of the arm and, because this arm was closed from the east, the doorway permitted access.

The northern arm of the building, now still under the sand, was most probably similar to the southern part of this edifice.[3] The Cruciform Building in Old Dongola belongs to the well--known group of the cruciform martyria and commemorative buildings from Palestine, Syria

---

[1] During the season in 1985 the northern part of the Cruciform Church was completely uncovered.

[2] The northern entrance to the building was also rebuilt but not alongated as the excavations in 1985 proved.

[3] During the excavations in 1985 the monumental stair-case leading from the lower level outside of the building to the interior of the church, was uncovered.

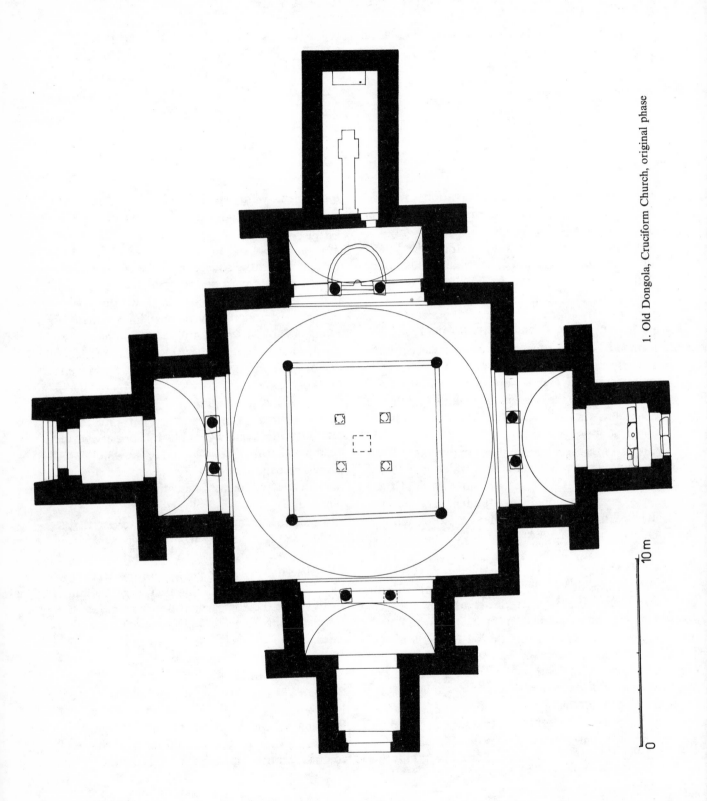

1. Old Dongola, Cruciform Church, original phase

10 m

0

and Asia Minor.[4] All of these buildings of "croix libre" are earlier than the Dongolese edifice and are connected either with a tomb of a martyr or with a holy place. But it is easy to show some differences between the Cruciform Building in Dongola and martyria from the Byzantine *koiné*. The differences concern the arrangement of the arms inside the Dongolese building, with two--column portico in its wider part. The plan of the Cruciform Building in this sense is unique, as far as I know, and we need more studies designed to establish links between this building and Byzantine monuments because it is hard to believe that the Cruciform Building in Dongola was an original Nubia attainment.

If the plan of the Cruciform Building in Dongola is more or less established, the reconstruction of the building itself is much more difficult and controversial. It is possible now to give only some general ideas. As a basis for understanding the reconstruction of this edifice from Dongola we have besides the general plan only thick walls (1.10 m) in some parts preserved up to 4.00 m high and several vertical elements (columns) still standing in situ. Some significance also attaches to the remains of buttresses outside of the wider parts of the arms. But most useful is the reconstruction of the southern portico.[5] A theoretical reconstruction of this type was possible owing to the preservation in situ of the lower part of this portico, here I am thinking of the great basalt bases and shafts of grey granite columns. Also significant is the localization of the architectural elements uncovered on the pavement in this part of the building. There were found not only great capitals but also smaller bases, lower columns and smaller capitals of red granite. In such a situation it is possible to propose a theoretical reconstruction of this triforium as two level portico, of which lower part comprised the grey granite elements and reached a hight of 6.30 m, but the upper part, which is much smaller (2.70 m) consisted of the red granite elements. The wooden beams which our reconstruction places between both parts of the portico are of course controversial but in the Nubian tradition we find

that the stone monolithic supports were used only for a flat wooden roof and never for arches or barrel volts. We can adore a very similar example on the arrangement of the portico originating from Constantinople, inside the Church of Holy Sergius and Bacchus from the age of Justinian.[6]

In our opinion all porticos inside the Cruciform Building were similar to the southern one, but it is very probably that the upper parts of the triforia on the east–west axe of the building were somewhat higher because the red granite shafts assigned to these porticos were also higher.

On the bases of such reconstruction of the porticos it is possible to establish that the total height of the walls of the central bay Dongolese building was about 14 m. It is also possible to suppose that the arms of the Cruciform Building in Dongola were covered by barrel volts and that the square part was under the dome, and in such a case the total height of the building could be ca. 28 m. Of course such a reconstruction is only one of the possible solutions. Another possibility is that the central part of the building was a courtyard but opposed to such a conclusion are remnants, of the structures which were uncovered inside the building on the pavement of the central bay as well as the symbolic significance of the entire building.

Coming back to the interior of the Cruciform Building in Dongola, we should analyse the preserved remnants of the furnishings. It is possible to show that some of them belong to the original equipment of the edifice.

In the middle of the eastern side of the central bay, between the two bases of the eastern portico, we have a partly preserved structure of red brick, semicircular from the outside and with two steps in the front. This is most probably the lower part of the synthronon much more Greek in shape than Nubian,[7] but the strange appearance of this structure results by its being located between two high bases. Such a location of the synthronon on the eastern side of the central square inside Cruciform Building is confirmed in the Church of Holy Apostles in Constantinople and inside the Church of St John in Ephesus.

---

[4] S. Lewis, "The Latin Iconography of the Single-Naved Cruciform Basilica Apostolorum in Milan", *The Art Bulletin* LI, 3 (September 1969), 205–219; P.M. Gartkiewicz, "The Central Plan in Nubian Church Architecture", in: *Nubia. Récentes Recherches*, Varsovie 1975, pp. 49–64.

[5] W. Godlewski, S. Medeksza, "The Southern Portico of the Cruciform Church at Old Dongola. The Theoretical Reconstruction", *Études et Travaux* XVI.

[6] C. Mango, *Byzantinische Architektur*, Stuttgart 1975, pp. 98–107, figs 109–110.

[7] T. F. Mathews, *The Early Churches of Constantinople; Architecture and Liturgy*, London 1971, p. 109.

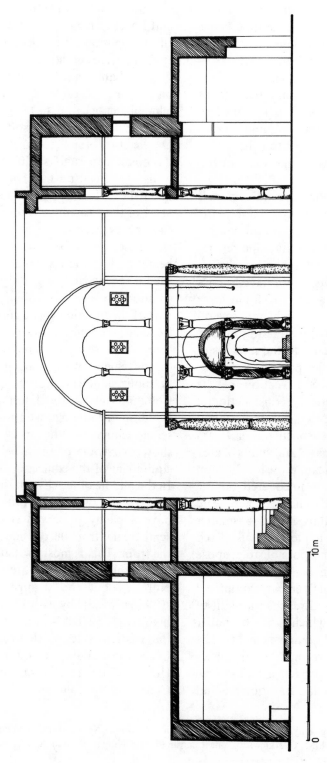

2. Old Dongola, Cruciform Church, cross-section E–W, with open central court. Sketch

0   10 m

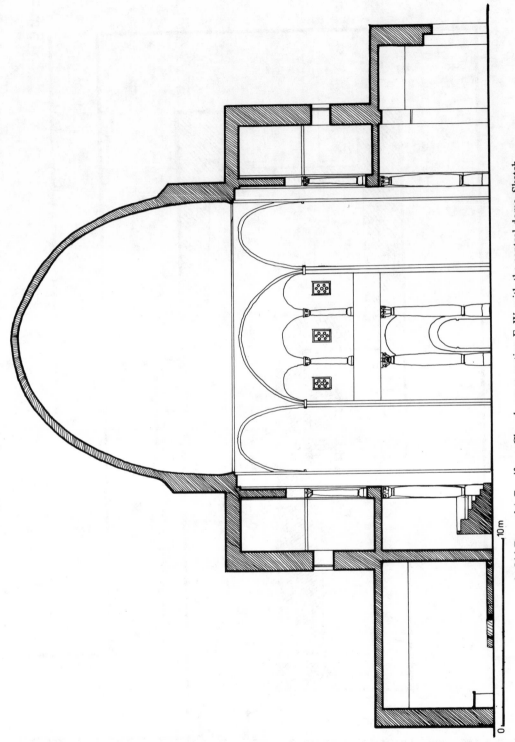

3. Old Dongola, Cruciform Church, cross-section E–W, with the central dome. Sketch

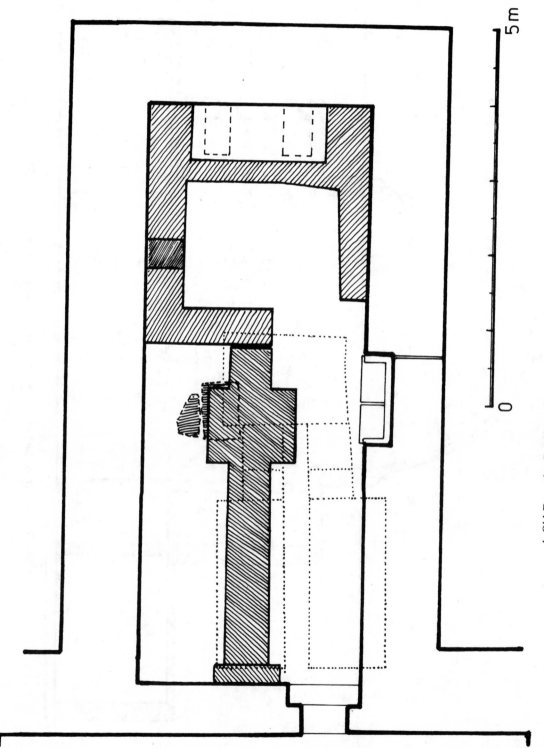

5 m

0

4. Old Dongola, Cruciform Church, the Eastern arm of the building

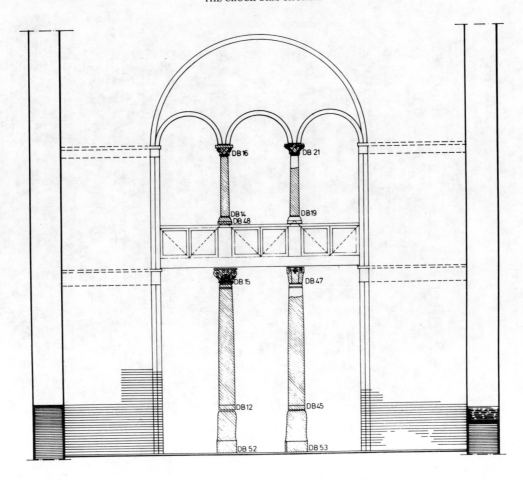

5. Old Dongola, Cruciform Church, the reconstruction of the Southern portico (des. S. Medeksza)

In the Cruciform Church in Old Dongola were found remnants of the wooden barrier which separated the eastern part of the building, i.e. the wider part of the eastern arm, from the rest of the interior. This barrier, most probably not very high, was between pilasters of the walls and bases of the eastern triforium.

On the central square there are more elements which belong to the original inner-dress of the building. All these elements support our attaching importance to the middle of the central bay. One can see four columns, in the strange construction, in corners of the central square. Each of these columns was composed of a high base, 2.15 m, above the pavement (this base is a shaft of a column sunk in a deep pit) and a normal column of red granite with capital. All these columns, ca. 6.60 m high, without any structural links with porticos or walls of the building have no

significance in the construction of the roof but were connected most probably with the function of the central part of the square bay. Perhaps on top of these columns there were wooden beams on which lights were hang.

In the middle of the central square of the building was most probably a great stone ciborium, but we have no proper evidence for the exact place of this structure. Several architectural elements from this ciborium were found during the excavation. All these elements (bases, shafts of columns and capitals) are different in size from the architectural elements which were used in construction of triforias and corner columns.

More remnants of the original furnishings were uncovered inside the eastern room in the arm of the building. Nearby the east wall were found red brick remnants of a structure whose dimensions and location show that it was, most probably, one

6. Cruciform Church, general view of interior from the north (phot. J. Kucy)

7. Old Dongola, Cruciform Church, general view of interior from the south (phot. J. Kucy)

8. Old Dongola, Cruciform Church, the northern part of the central square (phot. J. Kucy)

of the two supports of stone slab, a kind of table. On the red brick pavement of the room were found remains of an elongated low structure in the form of a Latin cross extending from the west wall to the middle of the room.

Proceeding to the functional analysis of the Cruciform Building in Dongola together with furnishings which were connected with the original form of this building, first we should underline the architectural division of the whole interior of the edifice in two parts. The eastern arm of the monument was separated by a wall from the rest of the building. Furnishings uncovered in both parts of the interior also confirm the functional and ideological division of the interior. At the beginning of this analysis we should mention the general notion underlining all cruciform martyrias in the East... in the Eastern martyrias the main core of the structure is constituted by a central square or octogonal unit, an independent shrine, to accommodate the martyrs' tomb or holy place as focal point of veneration.[8] According to this definition one can easy perceive which part of the Cruciform Building in Dongola played a basic role in the ideological sense. But first we should try to explain the function of the Eastern room of the building because this part, according to our present knowledge, though secondary in ideological importance, had a long local tradition of veneration. Under the pavement of this room there are two crypts and over the top of the northern one Latin cross was built on the floor. Both crypts are the oldest construction at this place and were parts of two earlier buildings: the so-called Building X — from the 6th century (whose structure is now only partly recognized) and the Church of Stone Pavement — dated to the 7th century. In such a situation we can interpret the eastern arm of the building as a commemorative chapel with an altar nearby the eastern wall and superstructure in the form of a Latin cross over the northern crypt. Unfortunately, we do not know who was buried in

---

[8] Lewis, "The Latin Iconography...", 211.

this crypt. After examination of the skeleton which was found in the northern crypt it is possible to say that he was a man over sixty years old.[9]

The location of the tombs in the eastern arm of the Cruciform Building suggests that the main reason for the foundation of this edifice should be sought in the central square bay. Around the middle of this part of the building we have also a concentration of the furnishings, but, unfortunately, we have no material evidence for the centre-piece that was the object of veneration. Most probably under the ciborium, in the middle of the central place there was not altar which would be too far from the synthronon, but in fact an important object of veneration which was the reason for the foundation of the whole building.

Gathering all possible evidence which can have links with this exceptional building in Old Dongola we should take into consideration some perhaps important information in Arabic, Christian and Muslim, sources:

First we should mention information about the foundation by King Zacharias of a church in Dongola as an expression of his thanks to God for a safe and successful return af his son Georgios from Baghdad.[10]

During the first Mameluke campain against Nubia in 1276 the largest church in Dongola was partly destroyed and from this building were taken objects of great value, among them a large silver cross.[11]

According to the same sources this church was called Usu or Isu. In other words the Church was dedicated to Jesus.

This same church was next rebuilt so that the emirs who commanded the next campain against Nubia in 1284 could be received inside the largest church in Dongola.[12]

We have no certainty that all these above-said pieces of information concern the Cruciform Building but in our opinion some coincidences are significant. The date of the foundation as well as the destruction and rebuilding of the Cruciform Building are more or less close to the dates which we have from the sources. It is very likely that the Cruciform Building was the largest church in Dongola. The commemorative character of the Dongolese building need not be discussed. And so it is very interesting to take into consideration the solution that the Cruciform Building in Dongola was founded as a place of veneration of the holy cross. Such a foundation could have a connection with the journey of King Georgios to Baghdad.[13] During this journey he visited Egypt, Palestine and Syria. He was, most probably, in Jerusalem, but we have no mention of this fact in Arabic sources. There he most probably visited not only the great Memoria but also the church on the rock of Golgotha inside of which the holy cross was venerated. All that we know of this church comes from a drawing from a Psalter dated to the 9th century.[14] According to the opinion of A. Grabar this sketch is a representation of the church which existed on the rock before Arculf' visit in Jerusalem, But Arculf' quadrangulata church could be only the central part of this cruciform church on the rock of Golgotha. This same building could have inspired King Georgios. From Latin sources we know of several foundations of churches in Europe built on the basis of drawings, descriptions and even measurements of the Jerusalem Memoria.[15]

From Nubia we have evidence of the foundations of crosses as symbols of the christianization of the country. An inscription from Dendur dated to the 6th century speaks about such a foundation of the cross.[16] Some remnants, probably of the base of such a holy cross, were uncovered also in Faras,

[9] S. Jakobielski, "Polish Excavations at Old Dongola, 1973 and 1974 Seasons", in: Études Nubiennes, Chantilly 2, Juillet 1975, Le Caire 1978, pp. 134–136. The interpretation of the crypts as simultaneously built with the Church of Stone Pavement is misleading. T. Dzierżykray-Rogalski, E. Promińska, "Tombeaux de deux dignitaires chrétiens dans l'Église Cruciforme de Dongola", Études Nubiennes..., pp. 91–93, pls XXIV–XXVI.

[10] G. Vantini, Oriental Sources Concerning Nubia, Heidelberg–Warsaw 1975, p. 331.

[11] Ibid., pp. 472, 475, 534, 536.

[12] Ibid., pp. 546, 689.

[13] G. Vantini, "Le Roi Kirki de Nubie à Bagdad: Un ou deux voyages?", in: Kunst und Geschichte Nubiens in christlicher Zeit, Recklinghausen 1970, pp. 41–48.

[14] A. Grabar, "Quelques notes sur les psautiers illustrés byzantins du IXᵉ siecle", Cah. Arch. XV (1965), 70–75.

[15] L. Grodecki, L'architecture ottonienne, Paris 1968, p. 160.

[16] A. Mallon, "Coptica II. Inscriptions de Nubie", Mélanges de la Faculté Orientale, Beyrouth V, 1912, pp. 129–130.

close to the Cathedral.[17] The same habit is known also in different countries but most interesting for us is an example from Georgia where such a holy cross founded in 4th century by St Nino in Mchata[18] was next surrounded by a cruciform church at the end of 6th or at the beginning of the 7th century. The holy cross itself was located on the central octagon under the dome.

From Nubia we have several examples of venera-tion of the holy cross as a symbol of Jesus Christ. First should be mentioned numerous murals with the representation of the crosses.[19] Some paintings have under the cross the head of Adam,[20] this has significant links with the rock of Golgotha. Very significant is also a translation in Old Nubian of a Greek homily Ps.-Chrisostom, *In venerabilem crucem sermo.*[21]

[17] K. Michałowski, "Polish Excavations at Faras, Third Season 1962–63", Kush XII (1964), 197; id., *Faras. Die Kathedrale aus dem Wüstensand,* Zürich–Köln 1967, p. 54.

[18] H. L. Nickel, *Kirchen, Burgen, Miniaturen. Armenien und Georgien während des Mittelalters,* Berlin 1974, pp. 40–50 and 54.

[19] T. Dobrzeniecki, "Maiestas Crucis in the Mural Paintings of the Faras Cathedral (now in the National Museum in Warsaw). Some Iconographical Notes", *Bulletin du Musée National de Varsovie* XV, 1–2 (1974), 2–20; P. van Moorsel, "Une théophanie nubienne", *Rivista di archaeologia cristiana* XLII (1966), 297–316.

[20] Rivergate Church in Faras or Church in Wadi es Sebua Temple.

[21] G. M. Browne, "Chrisostomus Nubianus: An Old Nubian Version of PS.-Chrisostom, *In venerabilem crucem sermo*", *Papyrologia Castroctaviana* 10, Rome–Barcelona 1983.

COPTIC STUDIES

Deirdre J. Good

Sophia in Eugnostos the Blessed and the Sophia of Jesus Christ (NHC III, 3 and V, 1; NHC III, 4, and BG 8502,3)

Sophia (Greek: Wisdom) is a divine female figure that is found in later books of the Hebrew Bible, in Hellenistic Jewish literature, in early Christian speculation on Christology and Theology and in Christian art of both the east and west.[1] In each of these cases, Sophia has been the subject of separate investigation by different scholars of the period, but rarely has a history of Sophia herself been attempted. This is in part due to the question of Sophia's autonomy—at what point in the history of interpretation can Sophia be said to exist as an independent entity rather than a personification of a divine attribute (wisdom)? When Sophia's autonomous existence is not in doubt, how is Sophia to be understood in relation to God, especially in the case of Biblical material? In discussing Biblical texts, the question of how to regard the personified Sophia is also caught up with the question of how to regard Wisdom material. For a long time, Israelite history was reconstructed largely without reference to the Wisdom books of the Hebrew Bible; these books were then regarded as evidence of the influence of foreign literature. Given such a judgement, it is easy to see how the content of this material, especially if it suggested autonomous female divinity, would be regarded as suspect. More recently, however, scholars have begun to re-shape conceptions of Israel's religious and literary history to take account of the presence not only of a large corpus of Wisdom material within the Hebrew Bible itself, but of features of Wisdom literature found in legal, historical and prophetic books themselves.[2]

Thus figure of Sophia has not been the subject of a happy consensus. Some scholars continue to regard this figure entirely without significance for an understanding of Christology in the pre-Christian era, while others take the opposite view.[3] There is no agreement over the subject of her autonomous existence in any scholarly discussion of the Biblical texts. However, in a discussion of texts from the Nag Hammadi Library, or in Patristic investigations of Gnosticism, Sophia is a divine female aeon whose autonomous existence is never in question (although it may be questionable). Two texts from the Nag Hammadi Library are the subject of the present investigation.

Scholars are generally agreed that behind the portrait of Sophia in Gnostic texts lies that of the Wisdom figure in the Wisdom of Solomon, I Enoch, the Book of Proverbs and Sirach 24.[4] Two interrelated assumptions also seem to govern scholarly research on this figure in Gnostic

---

[1] For a general introduction to the figure, see B. Lang, *Frau Weisheit*, Düsseldorf; Patmos, 1975; M. Hengel, *Judaism and Hellenism*, Philadelphia: Fortress, 1974, 1, pp. 153–175; M. Küchler, *Frühjüdische Weisheitstraditionen*, Göttingen; Vandenhoeck and Ruprecht, 1979. On the Iconography of Sophia, see U. Mielke, "Sapientia", in: E. Kirschbaum (ed.), *Lexikon der christlichen Ikonographie*, Freiburg–Basle–Vienna: Herder, 1972, 4, 39–43.

[2] R.B.Y. Scott, "The Study of Wisdom Literature", *Interpretation* 24 (1970), 20–45; D.F. Morgan, *Wisdom in the Old Testament Traditions*, Atlanta: John Knox, 1981; D. Bergant, *What Are They Saying about Wisdom Literature?*, New York: Paulist, 1984.

[3] For the former, see J.D.G. Dunn, *Christology in the Making*, Philadelphia: Westminster, 1980, pp. 170, 210. For the latter, see R. Bultmann, *The Gospel of John*, Philadelphia: Westminster, 1971, pp. 22–23; J. Painter, "Christology and the History of the Johannine Community in the Prologue of the Fourth Gospel", *New Testament Studies* 30, 3 (1984), 460–474.

[4] G. MacRae, "The Jewish Background of the Gnostic Sophia Myth", *Novum Testamentum* 12, 2 (1970), 86–101; K. Rudolph, "Sophia und Gnosis: Bemerkungen zu Problem 'Gnosis und Frühjudentum'", in: K.W. Troeger (ed.), *Altes Testament–Frühjudentum–Gnosis*, Berlin: Akademie Verlag, 1980, pp. 220–237.

texts—that she plays a central role in Gnostic self-understanding and that this role is specifically to be understood as a "fall" from the divine realm which occasions the disastrous origins of material creation. The world Gnostics inhabit has come into being by a fault which must be known in order that it may be overcome. Several scholars speak of "the Sophia Myth" as a "fall"[5] and see this myth as a central element in the composition of Gnostic material. The Sophia Myth is seen as central to Gnostic self-understanding[6] and in some way it represents a development of the descent of the soul into a human body.[7]

It is my contention that such interpretations rest on a partial investigation of Gnostic texts in which Sophia plays an important role and that there are other texts in the Nag Hammadi Library and in Patristic material which necessitate a revision of this well-nigh universal scholarly consensus. Rudolph has already drawn attention to texts in which Sophia is understood as Consort to other divine entities in the Pleroma and in this position, she is not censured for her independent conduct, nor for the disastrous genesis of material creation. Eugnostos the Blessed and the Sophia of Jesus Christ are two such texts.[8] In these documents, Sophia is described as Mother, Genetress, and Consort to a number of divine beings and only in one version of SJC is her action independent of her consort regarded as culpable. As Mother, Genetress and Consort, Sophia is the female manifestation of the highest God (Anthropos) whose male aspect can be called Mind or, subsequently, Anthropos. Without the Immortal Anthropos, creation would not take place for it can only occur from the harmony of male and female entities. From this harmony, subsequent manifestations of divine male–female beings occur, all of whose female aspects are called Sophia, and out of whose plurality a multiform creation results. Eugnostos, in which this development is seen most clearly, is a document that answers the old philosophical problem of deriving the multiplicity of creation from the singleness of divinity. Eventually, the number of 360 powers is reached and this number is regarded as a type of the 360 days of the year. SJC, essentially an expansion of Eugnostos, adds to this material a dialogue between the risen Jesus and his disciples (including women) and an appended account of Sophia's independent activity. It is possible to regard these two documents as an indication of the scope of Gnostic thought about Sophia and to begin to chart the course of its development and elaboration in a way that has not previously been attempted.

Texts

All the texts are accessible in the facsimile edition of the Nag Hammadi Codices. The Berlin Codex was the first to be published by Till and this text has been re-edited by Schenke. Three editions of these texts are in preparation by the Laval project (under Professor Anne Pasquier), the Nag Hammadi Codices series (under Professor Douglas Parrott) and the Berliner Arbeitskreis (under Professor Hans-Martin Schenke). Professor Parrott generously made his texts and translations accessible to me prior to their publication. In order to facilitate access to the text, a synopsis of all four versions of the text has been compiled and used as the basis of the present discussion. All the translations however, are my own.

The four versions of the text under discussion will be known as A (NHC V,1), B (NHC III,3), C (NHC III,4) and D (BG 8502,3). The present status of scholarship regards A and B as independent recensions of the underlying Greek text. A offers a text with frequently divergent readings while B's text is much closer to that of C and D. On typological grounds, A and B precede C and D—the priority of Eugnostos having been estab-

---

[5]P. Perkins, *The Gnostic Revelation Dialogue*, New York: Paulist, 1980, pp. 60–66; J.E. Göhring, "A Classical Influence on the Gnostic Sophia Myth", *Vigiliae Christianae* 35 (1981), 16.

[6]K. Rudolph, *Gnosis*, San Francisco–New York: Harper and Row, 1983, p. 57 (quoting the Messina Colloquium's definition in 1966); Göhring, "A Classical Influence...", 16.

[7]J. Dillon, "The Descent of the Soul in Middle Platonic and Gnostic Theory", in: B. Layton (ed.), *The Rediscovery of Gnosticism*, Leiden: Brill, 1981, pp. 357–364.

[8]Eugnostos the Blessed (Eugnostos) and the Sophia of Jesus Christ (SJC); NHC III, 3 and V, 1; NHC III, 4 and BG 8502, 3. Perkins seems to have changed her mind about some aspects of the Sophia Myth in a recent article, "Sophia and the Mother–Father: The Gnostic Goddess", in: C. Olson (ed.), *The Book of the Goddess Past and Present*, New York: Crossroad, 1983, pp. 97–109, 100.

lished by Krause in 1964.[9] While previous editions and translations of the text have used one or other of the versions to fill in the missing pages of either A or B's version, this tendency will be avoided in the present discussion since unwarranted harmonisation can result. Extensive lacunae, especially the case with the poorly preserved text of A, will be left unrestored. A more extensive discussion of the differences between the versions can be found elsewhere.[10]

All texts go back to a Greek original nothing of which remains. However, part of a Greek version of SJC, P. Oxy. 1081, has been published by Professor Harold Attridge which appears to display affinities with C's text.

Sophia in Eugnostos

As far as A is concerned, the text has at least four sections each of which can be form–critically identified by the word "beginning" ἀρχή. Material prior to the word "beginning" forms similar concluding statements: "His whole kingdom is full of ineffable glory that was never heard of or known among all the worlds... and aeons. Afterward, another beginning came from..." In the fifth case, the concluding statement ends the document. The formal observation that "beginning" functions as a demarcation for a new section can be substantiated by content. The "beginning of knowledge" (A 4.7–8) consists of an explanation of the expansion from the unity of divinity into multiplicity achieved in several stages. In the first place, the appellation "Forefather" is, according to the text, correctly applied to the highest entity in the Pleroma, the Lord of the All.[11] The term "Father–/Parent" (ⲡⲓⲱⲧ) is thought more appropriate to the subject under discussion "for the Father is the beginning of those that are to come through him".[12] Father is a generative term, whereas Forefather is

not. "Beginning" thus implies the expansion of divinity into form. Generation in each of the four sections is made explicit by way of nomenclature. In the first section, as has been observed, the Parent is "the beginning of those that are to come"; in the second, the androgyny of Immortal Anthropos is named the Genetor Nous (male) and Ennoia the Genetress of the Sophias (female). The third passage begins by calling Immortal Anthropos "self–perfected Genetor"[13] while the fourth designates the male name of the Saviour "Genetor of all things".[14]

In B, the word "beginning" appears only twice to function as a demarcation of a new section although like A, the words prior to "beginning" form a conclusion. In both cases the word "beginning" is modified by the word "knowledge" (γνῶσις). In A, "beginning" has to do with successive revelation of the same divinity while in B, it forms two statements about the correct way of perceiving. The first section in B describes the revelation of the Self-father as self-contained since it concludes with a multitude "of the place over which there is no kingdom"[15] while the second section contains the revelation of Immortal Anthropos (male and female) and Son of Anthropos (male and female). The contents of this revelation extend to the rest of the document and include a description of the 360 days of the year.

The first occurrence of the femaleness of Immortal Anthropos is termed in A "the Ennoia, the one belonging to all the Sophias, the Genetress of the Sophias"[16] and in B "All-wise Genetress Sophia."[17] A speaks of androgyne in terms of a male and female aspect whereas B speaks of male and female names. In C and D, Sophia is unambiguously called the consort of Immortal Anthropos who is not described as an androgyne, but rather as a male aeon with a spouse. Since all texts are strikingly divergent at this point, an attempt will be made at the end of the discussion to account for the textual variations.

---

[9] M. Krause, "Das Literarische Verhältnis des Eugnostosbriefes zur Sophia Jesu Christi", in: A. Stuiber and A. Hermann (eds), *Mullus: Festschrift Theodor Klauser; Jahrbuch für Antike und Christentum* I, Münster: Aschendorff, 1964, pp. 215–23.

[10] "Sophia as Mother and Consort: Eugnostos the Blessed (NHC III, 3 and V, 2) and the Sophia of Jesus Christ (NHC III, 4 and BG 8502, 3)", Harvard University, 1983.

[11] A 4.8–14.

[12] A 4.11–12.

[13] A 8.27–30.

[14] A 10.9–10.

[15] B 75.17–19.

[16] A 6.7–9.

[17] B 77.2–3.

Material from other Gnostic texts supports the description of the interrelatedness of Sophia and Ennoia; the Second Logos of the Great Seth speaks of Ennoia as the sister of Sophia.[18] What is significant here is that no Gnostic text attributes a "fall" to Ennoia. Thus, were Sophia is connected to Ennoia, she cannot be a fallen aeon. The Apocryphon of John attests the position of Ennoia at the highest level of divinity: she is "the power which was before all of them... the first Ennoia, his image, she became the womb of everything for she is prior to them all, the Mother/Father, the first Anthropos, the Holy Spirit, the thrice-male, the thrice-powerful, the thrice-named androgynous one, and the eternal aeon among the invisible ones and the first to come forth".[19] If Sophia and Ennoia are connected in A, this is at the highest level of divinity. It is interesting to note support from Wisdom Literature for the connection between Ennoia and Sophia, namely, the Greek text of Proverbs 24:7 "Sophia and good Ennoia are in the gates of the wise."[20]

The second appearance of Sophia in Eugnostos is as follows: "When he (Immortal Anthropos) received the consent of his consort Great Sophia, – revealed that First Begotten Son of God. His female aspect is First Begotten Sophia, Mother of the Universe, whom some call Agape".[21] B is lacunal; C and D read as follows: "He (First Authority) reflected with Great Sophia his consort and revealed his First Begotten androgynous Son. His male name is called First Genetor Son of God (BG: who is Christ), his female name First Genetress Sophia, Mother of the Universe. Some call her Love".[22] Traces of Christian influence are apparent in C and D; C, for example, continues the above passage "Now First Begotten is called Christ". This would mean that for readers of C and D, Christ is one of the male names or the consort of Sophia, Mother of the Universe.

In comparing A with C and D, the small but significant difference between the (conjectured) temporal of A: "when he received the consent..." and the first perfect of C and D: "he reflected with the Great Sophia" should be observed. In A, Sophia's assent is required while in C and D, an action is simply recorded. A implies the autonomy of Sophia. Occurences of this same verb at 10.6,14 confirm that in A, maleness needs the consent of femaleness to create. The six androgynous beings create mutually at 11.6. C and D simply do not explain why androgynes do not always create mutually; they simply record that the male element "reveals". Thus, it is difficult to account for the textual variations although their function can be detected. A's text leaves open the possibility that both male and female reveal as the verbal preface indicating number of persons has been lost. One direction of elaboration has become clear: the autonomy of Sophia was not maintained.

The description of Sophia as Love (ἀγάπη) in the above text is also found at B 82.24–5. It also occurs in Origen's account of the Ophite diagram which Welburn plausibly reconstructs.[23] Within the circle, Pronoia of Sophia is a smaller circle labelled "Love" which Origen's account does not explain further. We may assume that it had something to do with Sophia.

In C and D, Sophia is called First Genetress which is a variant of Genetress ([†pεϥ]ϫпо) at A 6.8–9 and All-Genetress at B 82.5,22. Each of these terms are the counterparts of the terms First Genetor at C 104.16, B 81.10–11; Genetor (пρεϥϫпо) at C 104.9 and Genetor of All Things at A 10.10–11 and parallels. Genetor means quite simply "Father", but more specifically "Sire", with a specific reference to the Father's generative capacity. The English language, perhaps preserving notions of Aristotelian biology, has no word that can translate the Greek word γενέτειρα other than "mother". The German language offers "Erzeugerin". In order to preserve the Greek, the word Genetress has been used in the present discussion.

The background of this term in Eugnostos is quite probably the later Wisdom literature. It is striking to observe that in early Wisdom books such as Proverbs, Sophia does not display overtly maternal characteristics. Subsequently, she is infrequently recognised to have children (Sirach 4:11; 24:18). The growing importance of this notion is recognised by the Wisdom of Solomon 7:12 "I (Solomon) rejoiced in (all good things)... but I did

[18] The Second Logos of the Great Seth (NHC VII, 2) 59.12–13.

[19] The Apocryphon of John (NHC II, 1; III, 1; IV 1 and BG 8502, 2) II 4.26–5.11.

[20] The Greek text (LXX) here differs markedly from the MT.

[21] A 8.31–9.6.

[22] C 104.10–20; D 99.1–4.

[23] A. J. Welburn, "Reconstructing the Ophite Diagram", Novum Testamentum 23, 3 (1981), 262–287.

not know that she (Sophia) was their Mother". The word loosely translated here by "Mother" is γενέτιν, the feminine form of γενέτης, a begetter, father or ancestor, attested here for the first time. The author of the Wisdom of Solomon frequently forms feminine substantives such as this. Thus, the association between Sophia as generative mother in the Wisdom of Solomon is unmistakably connected with Sophia as Genetress in Eugnostos.

Geneteira, however, is a word widely attested in Greek literature from Pindar's Nemian Odes (485 BCE) to the Orphic hymns. In the former, the Goddess of birth is the "Genetress of children" and in the latter, Aphrodite is the "Divine Genetress".[24] The choice of this term to describe Sophia in Eugnostos makes her preeminent position explicitly clear.

The notion of Sophia as Consort (σύζυγος) is particularly prominent in Eugnostos. In fact, a multiplicity of Sophias are consorts to almost every aeon described in the document. B, more than any other text, emphasises Sophia in this role. At 77.6 and 89.9, Sophia is described as Consort where in the parallel texts of A, this is not the case. Once again later Wisdom literature, especially the Wisdom of Solomon, provides a background for this designation. In 8:3, Sophia lives with God and is loved by him; she is co-occupant of God's throne at 9:4. While in these passages links with Eugnostos are established conceptually rather than verbally, there is a peculiar use of the term "consort" that seems to be unique to Eugnostos. Since it invariably occurs after the term "male–female", it is used explicitly to explain androgyny as male and female consorts. Again, the direction of elaboration can be seen by referring to the first appearance of Sophia/Ennoia cited at the beginning of this paper. In A, Ennoia is not described as a consort but simply juxtaposed with her male counterpart. In B, C and D, Sophia is called a consort, either of Immortal Anthropos or because she is like her brother. This serves to draw attention to a peculiar feature of the description of Sophia and her counterparts in comparing the four versions of Eugnostos and SJC. Initially, in A and B, the Immortal Anthropos is revealed in a male and female aspect, the female aspect of which is usually designated Sofia. Gradually, during the course of A and B, it becomes clear that Sophia's male consort becomes Immortal Anthropos who thus no longer has a male and female aspect. All documents can speak of Sophia as "his consort" at the conclusion when it is said that "the aeons and their heavens were completed for the glory of Immortal Anthropos and Sophia, his consort".[25] This shift from an Anthropos containing male and female elements to an Anthropos who stands for the male aspect alone and who thus becomes Sophia's partner is explained, in part, by the association of Sophia and Immortal Anthropos found in Wisdom and Apocalyptic texts such as I Enoch 48–50, the Book of the Secrets of Enoch, Job 15:7 and the Wisdom of Solomon 10. This association may have been too strong for the author of Eugnostos to carry through what the initial appearance of Immortal Anthropos suggested, namely, that Immortal Anthropos contained both male and female aspects. A comes the closest to this since it does not habitually call Sophia "his consort" like B, but rather "his Sophia" (A 15.18) or "a companion" (A 6.23). Eugnostos, in its depiction of Sophia, represents the unsuccessful fusion of two strains in the tradition about Sophia, both of which the author seems to have known. Sophia was associated with Anthropos/Son of Anthropos, but she was also independent of either. A expresses both these strains while B, C and D express first the former (by describing Sophia as Consort) and subsequently the latter (in C's and D's special material). When separated from her consort, one tradition viewed her independent action as reprehensible. Other Gnostic traditions besides Eugnostos knew of Sophia's original isolation and that conceiving of her in syzygial relations was inaccurate since it would not achieve redemption.[26]

Conclusion

The focus of the present work on Sophia as Genetress, Mother and Consort restores the myth of Sophia's folly to its proper place—a derivative

---

[24] Pindar's Nemian Odes 7,3; The Orphic Hymns 55,2.

[25] A 16.15–24; B 89.7–15. Cf. C 113.11–19.

[26] Irenaeus' Adversus Haeresus I.21.5; The First Apocalypse of James (NHC V, 3) 35.5–27.

one – while the notion of a plurality of Sophias enables passages such as the Codex II version of the Apocryphon of John 28.13 "... and they committed adultery with each other's Sophia" to be seen not as anomalous or a late accretion but rather as the trace of an older idea adapted to serve the purpose of a different mythical structure.

It is also suggested here that Christian Gnosticism was not exclusively preoccupied with the culpable activity of a Sophia. To be sure, the fate of Sophia came to occupy a prominent position in certain Gnostic circles and in the minds of several Gnostic interpreters but a survey of Eugnostos, SJC and related texts indicate that it was not always so.

COPTIC STUDIES

C. Wilfred Griggs

Excavating a Christian Cemetery Near Seila, in the Fayum Region of Egypt

Mr Chairman, Ladies, and Gentlemen:

May I begin this report with an expression of gratitude to Dr Ahmed Kadry, Dr Ali Kholy, Mr Mutawe Balboush, and other officers and members of the Egyptian Antiquities Organization, for generous interest and support for Brigham Young University in its excavation work at the site of Seila. The excavation staff members express heartfelt gratitude to the Mormon Archaeology and Research Foundation and its director, Mr Wallace O. Tanner, and to Brigham Young University and its administrators for temporal and financial support for the Seila excavation project. The archaeological site of Seila, taking its name from a nearby Egyptian village close to the eastern edge of the Fayum depression (see fig. 1, a map showing the site in relationship to the Fayum depression), is comprised of numerous components representing the entire scope of Egyptian history. Brigham Young University began work at the site in 1980, working jointly with the University of California at Berkeley that year, and having sole responsibility for the excavation since 1981.

The oldest monument in the concession is the four-step pyramid of Seila constructed in the early 3rd Dynasty atop the Gebel el Rus and situated on a line directly east of the 4th Dynasty Meidum pyramid. What relationship may exist between the later Meidum pyramid, the southernmost of the pyramids along the so-called Pyramid Row of the western edge of the Nile valley, and the earlier Seila pyramid, built on a ridge at the eastern edge of the Fayum depression and visible from both the Fayum and the Nile valley, is yet to be determined. During the 1980 season the BYU-Berkeley team removed the sandy debris from about one half of the exposed portion of the pyramid. Beneath the dust and sand accumulated over five millenia was a weathered and eroded surface, but some lower portions of the walls were protected from weathering by the aeolian sands, and there the limestone blocks are in quite good condition, measuring, on the average, $1 \times 0,5 \times 0,5$ meters. Much work yet remains to be done, both to uncover the pyramid totally and to place it accurately in the early historical and religious context of the 3rd Dynasty. Approximately two kilometers northwest of the pyramid and adjacent to the Abdallah Wahbi canal, which borders the cultivated land on the east of the Fayum is an ancient cemetery which now bears the name Fag el Gamus (Way of the Cow). A large limestone stele was erected on the western edge of the cemetery, not far from the canal (probably adjacent to the road leading south from Philadelphia, about 5 km north of the cemetery), and perhaps was intended to be an identification marker or dedicatory monument relating to the entire area. The stele is so badly weathered, however, that no markings remain on it which would assist in determining its function. The cemetery itself, covering approximately 300 acres (125 hectares), is almost entirely unplundered, though repeated digging fot interment of bodies and later subsidence of the burial shafts have left the entire area in a very disturbed condition. A few very deep shafts, ranging from 15 to 23 meters in depth, have horizontal shafts and burial chambers leading from the base of the vertical shafts, and these date probably from the Middle Kingdom. One unfinished burial chamber, beginning with a large room (ca. 3×3 meters) hewn from a limestone ridge running east–west in the cemetery continues north in a shaft for approximately 4–5 meters before turning east in an unfinished burial chamber. Other rectangular shafts approximately one meter square in size and hewn into the small hills and mounts of the cemetery area angle downward and appear to turn

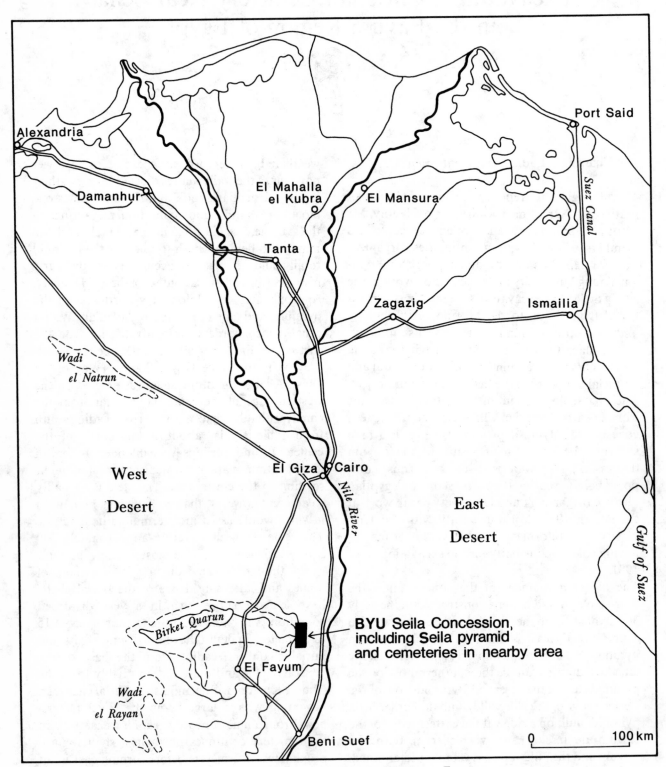

Alexandria

Damanhur

El Mahalla
el Kubra

El Mansura

Port Said

Suez Canal

Tanta

Zagazig

Ismailia

Wadi
el Natrun

West

Desert

El Giza Cairo

Nile River

East

Desert

Gulf of Suez

Birket Quarun

BYU Seila Concession,
including Seila pyramid
and cemeteries in nearby area

El Fayum

Wadi
el Rayan

Beni Suef

0   100 km

1. Map of the Fayum depression and the Lower Egypt

horizontally left or right to burial chambers, but these have not yet been excavated, and firm dates cannot be assigned to them.

The BYU team has concentrated in an area of the cemetery which dates from the 1st century B.C. through the 8th century A.D., based on artifact analysis, including pottery, coins, textiles, and jewelry.

Within the portion of the cemetery excavated to the present time, two patterns of interment can be distinguished. The first consists of shafts hewn through the limestone bedrock to varying depths for burial. The most shallow are approximately one meter deep, into which were placed shrouded remains partially or wholly enclosed in wooden sarcophagi. Some of the shafts contained a narrower burial pit at the bottom, in which the burial was placed, and dressed rocks were placed over the body, resting on the rock shelves formed when the burial pit was cut into the base of the shaft. Gypsum plaster was then poured over the rocks, sealing the burial in its tomb. The shaft was then filled to ground level with rocks, sand, and miscellaneous debris. Other shafts extended to a depth of as much as four meters, then branching horizontally into burial chambers of varying sizes and degrees of sophistication in construction (i.e., with rooms, doorways with rock thresholds, and dressed, though undecorated, walls).

In all of the shaft burials hewn through the limestone bedrock, the decomposition of the remains and related organic artifacts was virtually complete. Sealing in the moisture and the atmosphere of the burial by means of the gypsum plaster caps prevented the desiccation of the body, and the artifact recovery from this portion of the cemetery has been limited to pottery, jewelry, and skeletal remains. A small amount of gold, including an amulet, two nuggets, and a gold-filled tooth, also came from burials in the rock-shaft tombs. Burials ranged in number from one in the shallow shafts to twelve in the deep shafts with burial chambers branching off horizontally from the shaft. We cannot determine whether the large number of burials in one shaft-tomb represented a family burial, opened repeatedly as different members of the family died (both children and adults were buried in the multiple-burial tombs), or whether some catastrophe in the village or family resulted in a mass common burial effort.

After excavating some seventeen rock-shaft burial chambers, the team moved across a small wadi (approximately 100 meters north) to excavate in an area comprised of aeolian sands and sedimentary lakeshore sands and gravels. Burials were encountered near the surface, and within the first 5×5 meter area 22 bodies were recovered between the surface and the depth of 1.5 meters. Because the normal factors of Egyptian desert geography and climate (sand and low humidity) played their roles in this region of the cemetery, the condition of recovered artifacts was considerably better than in the limestone shaft burials. In addition to pottery and jewelry, burial wrappings were often well-preserved, and textiles have been recovered in great abundance. During the 1981 season, the excavators recovered some mummiform burials which had articles of clothing neatly wrapped and placed on the face of the deceased. When the corpse was wrapped for burial, after being clothed in linen garments overlaid with an embroidered robe worn like a serape, the extra clothing on the face made the shrouded corpse appear deformed at the head. Of the 123 burials excavated in 100 square meters during the 1984 season, none had the extra clothing wrapped upon the face, although various articles of clothing were placed in close proximity to a body. There were, however, numerous burials which had linen or palm-fiber rope folded to many thicknesses or intertwined into woven designs and placed upon the face just as the articles of clothing were in some of the burials found in 1981. We are quite certain that this aspect of the burial technique found often in the cemetery has religious significance, but we have not yet ascertained its meaning. Many head coverings have been excavated, including a number of hooded robes associated with both males and females, children and adults. The quality of cloth ranges from very coarse material to finely-woven linen, and there are many samples of embroidered designs. Some designs are geometric and others are symbolic, including a design resembling the Egyptian *Wedjet eye* and some sacerdotal symbols, and there is also some representational art, including one piece of cloth adorned with brightly colored ducks. Some cloth is hemmed and other pieces have fringed edges, with some of the fringe up to 25 cm long. Most of the burials were wrapped with linen ribbon, averaging a little more than 1 cm in width, and containing simple geometric designs in red, black, or white. These ribbons were wrapped in geometric crisscrossing patterns over the shrouded body, often with numerous wraps about the feet and neck areas. Although there is much similarity in clothing and wrapping techniques, individual differences from body to body show that each family (or whoever assumed responsibility for burials) was free to modify slightly the general methods and customs. The jewelry associated with the burials consists mostly of necklaces, bracelets, and earrings. The materials used in fabricating the pieces include copper, bronze, tin, silver, and a slight amount of gold, as mentioned before. There are also some ceramic bracelets, and a few necklaces and bracelets were made of polished semi-precious stones, held together by single-strand fiber twine or a fabric string. Wire clasps are common for all kinds of jewelry, and one pair of earrings consists of 4 pendant pearls on each earring, connected to a wire clasp for wearing in pierced earlobes. The jewelry is found mostly with female burials, both children and adults. The observations that most burials do not have jewelry associated with them, and that the artifacts are made from relatively inexpensive and commonly available materials (with a very few notable exceptions which, if anything, tend to emphasize the mean quality of the rest), lead us to the conclusion that burial jewelry in the excavated portion of the cemetery had a sentimental value for the families associated with burying the deceased, rather than religious or commercial value. This may be an argument for the generally low economic status of the people associated with the cemetery, but one may also suggest that religious beliefs precluded the necessity of burying much of worldly value with the dead. The quality and amount of textiles buried with many of the bodies demonstrates that care was taken to ensure that the deceased were properly prepared for interment, and if this world's goods were thought to be necessary in the post--mortal existence, more such artifacts would be expected to appear in the excavation.

Virtually all the burials in the cemetery are buried on an east–west axis, with variations that correspond to the sun's amplitude at different seasons of the year. The fracture lines of the limestone bedrock happen to run in the same directions, and one could account for east–west burial shafts in that portion of the cemetery by assuming that it was easier to dig shafts along those fracture lines than across or against them. That supposition does not hold in the sandy areas of the cemetery, however, where digging grave shafts would have

been equally easy in any direction, and the burials still fall in the east–west axis. We conclude, therefore, that direction of burial was important for reasons beyond those associated with ease of digging, and we further surmise that one might determine the season of digging the shaft by noting where on the sun's amplitude the axis falls. This would be valid only for the first burial in the shaft, since later burials would be added to the reopened shaft without attempting to align the body with the seasonal amplitude of the sun's rising. In the shafts dug in the sandy portion of the cemetery, there are as many as five burials from near the surface to the bottom of the shafts, each shaft having an average depth of about three meters (see fig. 2, sketch illustrating burial patterns in the sandy portions of the cemetery). However, the burials are not evenly spaced in depth, but sometimes one is touching the next above or below, and at other times the burial layers are a meter apart. In some instances children and adults are clustered, as if in family units, in other instances there seem to be no connection between burials in the same shaft. Bundles of reeds used as head markers, pottery, and other artifacts were placed as markers in strata well beneath the surface of the ground, where it would be impossible to see them after the shaft was filled. The reasons for placing such markers beneath the ground have not yet been determined. The burial technique for the first burial, at the bottom of the shaft, differed in most instances from the later (and higher) interments. Angling slightly to the north or south of the vertical shaft the diggers fashioned a burial chamber with dressed stones or mud bricks, often leaning them at an angle from the floor to the wall of the shaft. Only rarely did burials of the upper strata exhibit the same protective measures, and then large amphora sherds were used as often as the dressed rocks or mud bricks. In addition to the added effort made for burials at the base of the shafts, one especially noteworthy difference from all other layers must be mentioned. All of the burials from upper layers were placed with the feet at the east and head at the west, suggesting that the person would arise in a resurrection facing east. The bottom layer burials, however, almost always reverse the direction, having the head to the east and feet to the west. Such a significant and total change of technique in one of the most conservative and pervasive ritual activities of man can best be accounted for by a major cultural upheaval in the area. Because the

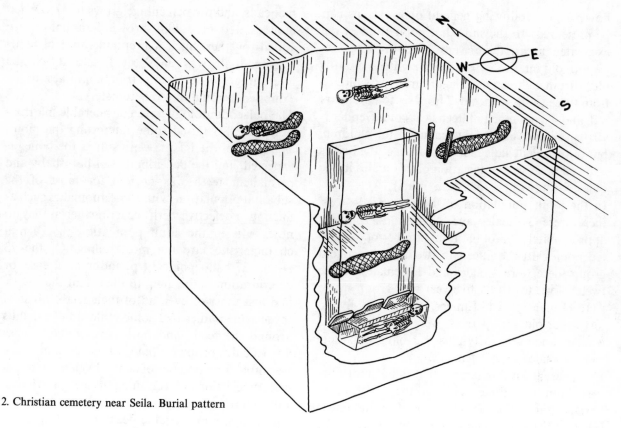

2. Christian cemetery near Seila. Burial pattern

pottery of all strata above the bottom layer dates from the 2nd century A.D. and later (the pottery is often mixed because of disturbances caused by reopening shafts), and because the pottery from the bottom layers of shafts dates from the first centuries B.C. and A.D., we propose that the cultural change occurred around the end of the 1st century A.D. The discovery of two terra-cotta figurines of robed figures, one complete and one broken (an angel, the Virgin Mary?) in the burial level just above the bottom of the shafts, the late 1st century—erly 2nd century A.D. pottery associated with these burials, and a consistency in burial techniques from that level to the present *terminus ad quem* of the 8th century A.D. at the surface level of the cemetery, lead to the further suggestion that the cultural change which occurred in this area around the end of the 1st century or the early part of the 2nd century and was dominant for at least the next six or seven centuries was the arrival and widespread adoption of Christianity. Of course this hypothesis must remain somewhat conjectural until inscribed materials or other similarly indisputable artifacts of early Christianity are recovered, but it is at present the best explanation for such a remarkable shift in burial direction, and it also accords with

the fact that Christianity became the dominant religion in Egypt for the succeeding centuries. One would thus not expect another major change in burial techniques after the arrival of the Christian faith, and none occurs. The argument for an early arrival and spread of Christianity within Egypt can be made from literary sources, but this may well be one of the first archaeological sources to support that proposition.

As mentioned above, the team excavated 123 burials in 100 square meters during the 1984 season (some had to be left *in situ* until a future season because they were in the baulk between areas), and the pathology of the bodies done by the three palaeopathologists on the staff yielded considerable information regarding gender, age, stature, and general health. Cranial analysis, including palaeodontology, bone development, especially in the epiphyses of the humerus, femur, and tibia, and determination of pubic width, subpubic angle, and the presence or absence of a lateral recurve were among the field activities of the pathologists in determining anthropological data. Of the 123 burials, 8 were so close to the surface of the ground and so badly preserved or so fragmentary that no meaningful data could be obtained from them. From the remaining 115, however, the following general observations can be presented: In the sub-adult population of the excavated areas, there were 7 newborn to six-month old infants, 7 from six to eighteen months old, 1 from eighteen months to three years old, 16 from three to six years old, 7 from six to nine years old, and 4 from nine to fifteen years old. Gender is virtually impossible to determine in the children, but the excellent state of preservation of the bodies allowed positive identification of two males in the oldest group (nine to fifteen years).

In the adult population of the excavated areas, there were 31 males and 42 females, totalling approximately 2/3 of the total number of excavated bodies. In the fifteen to twenty-five-year-old group there were 4 males and 13 females; in the twenty-five to thirty-five-year-old group there were 11 males and 17 females; in the thirty-five to forty-year-old group there were 7 males and 5 females; and in the forty-plus year-old group there were 9 males and 7 females.

It appears from this sample that infant mortality was about three times as high to the age of six (31 burials) as it was between the ages of six and fifteen (11 burials), and female mortality during the child-bearing years (fifteen to thirty-five) was just double that of males of the same age group (30 to 15). The difference in male and female mortality rates for those older than thirty-five years was negligible (16 to 14), according to this sample. Of course, further excavation in the cemetery will enhance or modify these observations, but they are offered for the four random sample areas excavated in the cemetery.

Not all of the burials had preserved head and body hair, but the characteristics of those which did are rather striking. Eight of the adult males had facial hair, i.e. mustaches and/or beards, and two of the adults had quite curly hair. Four of the adult females had very long hair, and two of those had the hair braided and the braids were wrapped over the ears and around the back of the head. Of the thirty-seven adults whose hair was still preserved, the most interesting observation relates to the hair color. There were four redheads, sixteen blondes, twelve with light or medium brown hair, and only five with dark brown or black hair. 54% of those whose hair was preserved are thus blondes or redheads, and the percentage grows to 87% when blondes, red, and light-brown hair colors are added together. Such a preponderance of light-colored hair was unexpected, and it will be interesting to see if this trait continues to be exhibited throughout the cemetery.

The palaeodontology gave considerable information and also raised some interesting questions. The teeth of the infants were still in the bone, as expected, and the development of both baby and permanent teeth was normal for most of the subadult population, with some anomalies such as missing or defective teeth occurring then as they do now. It is in the adult population that dental characteristics are the most telling. Of the 73 adults, 37 had significant periodontal disease, or deterioration of the gum, to the extent that many had lost most or even all of their teeth. Most of those same bodies had some build-up of calculus around the teeth, and both periodontal disease and calculus problems point to the fact that there was little or no practice of dental hygiene, either in dietary selection or by cleaning the teeth and gums. Interestingly, however, there were only 14 adults who had any measurable decay in existing teeth, and most of that decay was minimal, often only one cavity per person. This lack of decay suggests little sugar in the diet, among other possible reasons. 10 adults had extremely good teeth, mostly females, and further analysis must precede conclusions regarding the wide disparity in dental conditions of the adults. The same is true for attrition in the teeth, which ranges from little wear to attrition to the root tips. At present it does not seem adequate to assign the difference in wear patterns totally to dietary causes, such as sand in breads, etc. Some scientists have offered to help in this matter by performing an isotopic analysis of bone fragments in order to determine individual diets more certainly.

This brief survey of the BYU excavation of the Fag el Gamus cemetery in the Fayum leaves many questions unasked and others unanswered, but as the excavation continues in succeeding seasons, the data gleaned from burials and artifacts will yield increased understanding concerning the Roman–Christian period of Egyptian history, especially in the Fayum.

COPTIC STUDIES

Peter Grossmann

Typologische Probleme der nubischen Vierstützenbauten

Im Zuge der Arbeiten zur wissenschaftlichen Erfassung der durch den inzwischen existent gewordenen Stausee in Nubien dem Untergang geweihten Baudenkmälern wurde u.a. eine große Anzahl von christlichen Kultbauten aufgedeckt. Mehrere Veröffentlichungen beschäftigen sich mit der Klassifizierung dieser Bauten. Zu nennen sind vor allem die Arbeiten von W.Y. Adams und M.P. Gartkiewicz. Ersterer hat bereits 1965 eine Klassifizierung erarbeitet, die weit über alle älteren Versuche dieser Art hinausgeht.[1] M.P. Gartkiewicz ist in mehreren Beiträgen den gegenseitigen Abhängigkeiten der in Nubien vertretenen Bautypen und ihren architekturgeschichtlichen Wurzeln nachgegangen.[2]

Ich selbst möchte heute die Aufmerksamkeit auf die Vielzahl der nubischen Vierstützenbauten lenken. Bereits W.Y. Adams hat diese drei verschiedenen Typen zugewiesen: den Typen 2b, 3b, und 3c. Andererseits sind in seiner Typologie noch eine Reihe von Unregelmäßigkeiten und Überschneidungen enthalten. Es ist daher zu prüfen, inwieweit eine etwas abweichende Gruppierung günstiger ist.

Als Kriterium der Klassifizierung möge die im Bereich des Naos der betreffenden Kirchen vorliegende Raumgestalt gelten. Diese wird durch die Anordnung und formale Ausbildung der Stützen und vor allem durch die Art der Überwölbung entscheidend geprägt. Insbesondere ist bei baulich derart wenig strukturierten Bauten wie den nubischen Kirchen häufig nur an der Gewölbeführung zu erkennen, ob die Erbauer ihnen eine

mehr längsgerichtete oder eine im Zentrum betonte Baugestalt zu geben beabsichtigten. Zwar hat sich gerade die Überwölbung nur in den wenigsten Fällen erhalten, doch sind in der Beziehung der Stützen untereinander und zu den umgebenden Wänden in der Regel genügend Hinweise enthalten, um wenigstens die Grundstruktur der Wölbung noch einigermaßen sicher zu rekonstruieren. Aussichtslos ist dieses Unterfangen erst in den Fällen, in denen sich keine Hinweise auf die Art der Stützen und deren Anordnung erhalten haben. Glücklicherweise gilt das jedoch nur für sehr wenige Beispiele: die Zentralkirche von Iḥmīndi (Nr. 26) und bis zu einem gewissen Grade auch die Exterior Church von Abkanarti (Nr. 96).

Nur summarisch erwähne ich hier die Gruppe der mit vier Winkelpfeilern ausgestatteten Umgangsvierstützenbauten, da ich diese bereits an anderer Stelle eingehend behandelt habe.[3] Wie sich an der spezifischen Gestalt ihrer Pfeiler erkennen läßt, wird in die diesen Bauten aus dem Gesamtraum des Naos ein überkuppelter Zentralraum ausgeschieden. Hingewiesen sei jedoch auf zwei weitere Beispiele dieses Typus, die Kirchen von Aïn Färah bei Dafūr[4] und — mit gewissen Einschränkungen — die Kirche 16-E-19 von Samna-West (Nr. 108), auf die später noch zurückzukommen sein wird. Bei letzterer haben die Pfeiler einen im Prinzip quadratischen Querschnitt, an den an den Außenkanten kurze, jeweils zu den Nachbarpfeilern weisende Vorlagen angefügt sind. Die entwicklungsmäßig älteste Gruppe der übri-

[1] N.Y. Adams, JARCE 4 (1965), 67 ff.

[2] P.M. Gartkiewicz, BABesch 55 (1980), 137 ff.; sowie ders., *Nubia Christiana* 1 (1982), 43 ff.

[3] » Elephantine II «, AV 25 (1980), 104 ff.

[4] A.J. Arkell, Kush 7 (1959), 115 ff.

gen Vierstützenbauten möchte ich als » Verkürzte Longitudinalbauten « bezeichnen.[5]
Typologisch scheint diese Gruppe aus den frühmittelalterlichen Basiliken hervogegangen zu sein, die zunächst noch mit einer größeren Zahl von Stützen versehen waren. In den verkürzten Beispielen hat sich diese Zahl dann zu einer gewissermaßen kanonisch gewordenen Vierzahl reduziert. In der gleichmäßigen Reihung der Stützen und vielfach auch in dem oblongen Querschnitt der Pfeiler lassen sie deutlich eine Längsbetonung erkennen, wie sie jenen Basiliken ebenfalls eigen war. Und zwar gilt das auch dann, wenn die Gesamtausdehnung des Naos gegenüber seiner Breite bereits erheblich reduziert war. Diese Bauten waren in allen Schiffen ausschließlich tonnengewölbt. Das Mittelschiff war zudem in fast allen Fällen in der Breite und Höhe leicht betont, und damit decken sie sich weitgehend mit dem Typus 2b der Klassifizierung von W.Y. Adams. Allerdings möchte ich — abweichend von Adams — den » Verkürzten Longitudinalbauten « meiner jetzt vorzuschlagenden Klassifizierung nur diejenigen Bauten zuweisen, die mit Sicherheit nicht mit einer das Zentrum betonenden Kuppel versehen waren. Letztere gehören vielmehr zu einer weiteren Gruppe, auf die später zurückzukommen sein wird.
Die älteren Beispiele jener » Verkürzten Longitudinalbauten « besitzen betont oblonge Pfeiler. Zudem folgen diese in einer streng gleichmäßigen Reihung aufeinander. Beide Eigentümlichkeiten sind baukünstlerische Mittel, die Längsachse der Bauten zu betonen, auch wenn die Raumproportionen selbst verkürzt sind. Darüber hinaus schließt diese Betonung der Längsachse aus, daß das Mittelschiff an irgendeiner Stelle mit einer Kuppelwölbung versehen war. Sonst weisen die

genannten Bauten — abgesehen von der etwas problematischen Kirche von ad-Duma (Nr. 34) — sämtlich die für den mittelalterlichen Kirchenbau in Nubien charakteristischen Merkmale auf. Entsprechend ihrer verhältnismaßig frühen zeitliche Stellung fehlt der Mehrzahl von ihnen der sonst in Nubien sehr verbreitete östliche Quergang, der die beiden Seitenräume des Sanktuariums miteinander verband. Nach W.Y. Adams tritt dieser, mit Ausnahme von einigen Frühformen, erst im späten 8.Jh. auf.[6]
Neben diesen gewissermaßen ordentlichen Vertretern der » Verkürzten Longitudinalbauten « gibt es noch eine kleine etwas jüngere Gruppe von Beispielen, in denen die gleichmäßige Reihung der Stützen zugunsten einer Betonung des mittleren Interkolumniums aufgegeben wurde. Wegen der starken räumlichen Verkürzung haben bei einigen Bauten zudem die Pfeiler ihren betont oblongen Querschnitt verloren (Nr. 18. 64). Gleichwohl sind aber auch diese noch voll und ganz zum Typus der » Verkürzten Longitudinalbauten « zu zählen, denn auch für diese war eine zentrale Kuppelwölbung — wenigstens nach dem bisher bekannt gewordenen Denkmälerbestand — niemals vorgesehen. Ein charakteristisches Beispiel bildet die Kirche von Sināsra (Nr. 40), bei der der von U. Monneret de Villard festgehaltene Erhaltungszustand[7] deutlich die Ergänzung einer Kuppel ausschließt. Darüber hinaus haben die Pfeiler bei der Mehrzahl der Bauten noch eine oblonge Ausbildung. In der sog. Mastabakirche von Faras (Nr. 64) wurden sie nachträglich zu solchen verlängert. Ferner stimmt die Bemessung der Pfeiler mit der Außenwände in der Regel ziemlich genau überein, was ebenfalls erkennen läßt, daß man ihnen die zusätzliche Belastung, wie sie im Fall einer Kuppelwölbung auftreten würde, nicht zuzu-

---

[5] Die beigeschriebenen Zahlen entsprechen der Numerierung von W.Y. Adams. Grundrisse, die in etwa einen ähnlichen Entwicklungsstand erkennen lassen, wurden nebeneinandergesetzt. Die der Zusammenstellung zu Grunde liegenden Pläne wurden den jüngsten mir zugänglichen Publikationen entnommen. Sie wurden optisch auf denselben Maßstab gebracht. In mehreren Publikationen sind jedoch die den Grundrissen beigefügten Skalen derart kurz und unsauber gezeichnet, daß eine exakte Übertragung kaum möglich ist. Dadurch entstandene etwaige Fehler bitte ich, nicht mir anzukreiden. Ferner mußte in der Rekonstruktion gelegentlich über die in den vorliegenden Veröffentlichungen angebotenen Vorschläge hinausgegangen werden. Ich hoffe jedoch, alles richtig gemacht zu haben. Nicht verstanden habe ich den Plan von Abdallah Nirqi Süd (Nr. 53a), da von diesem Bau zwei sich widersprechende Aufnahmepläne vorliegen, vgl. L. Barkoczi–A. Salomon, Acta Arch. Hung. 26 (1974), 313 f. Abb 46 f, sowie G. Hajnóczi, ebenda 358 ff. Abb. 7. Keinem der beiden Pläne ist zu entnehmen, welche Partien nun der jüngeren Bauphase zuzuschreiben sind. Ebenso ist meine Ergänzung der Kirche von Mainarti (Nr. 85) noch äußerst hypothetisch. W.Y. Adams bestätigte mir, daß es für die hier vorgeschlagene Auflösung der inneren westlichen Querwand in Winkelpfeiler und vermauerte Bodendurchgänge, keinerlei Hinweise gebe. Eine andere Möglichkeit wäre, die gesamte Westpartie als eine spätere Erweiterung anzusehen, womit der ursprüngliche Plan etwa dem der Kirche von ad-Duma (Nr. 34) entsprechen würde.

[6] Adams, JARCE 4, 93 f.

[7] U. Monneret de Villard, *La Nubia medioevale* I, Kairo 1935, S. 120 f. Abb. 97 f.

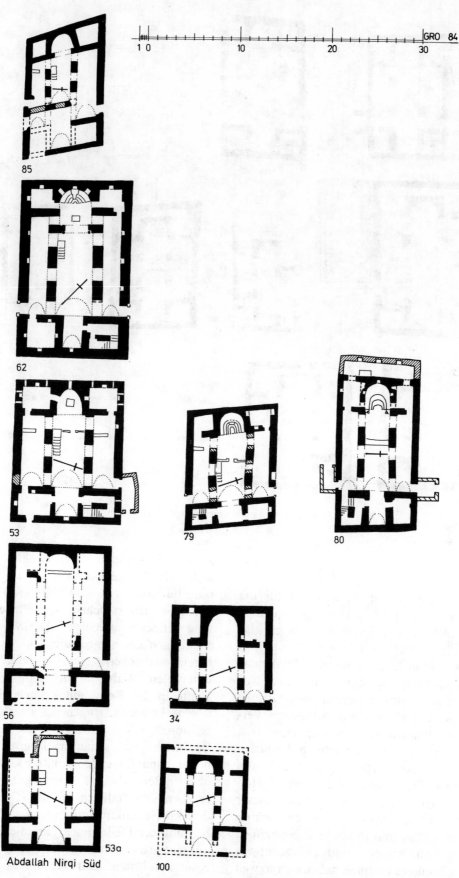

GRO 84

85

62

53

79

80

56

34

Abdallah Nirqi Süd

53a

100

1. Verkürzte Longitudinalbauten

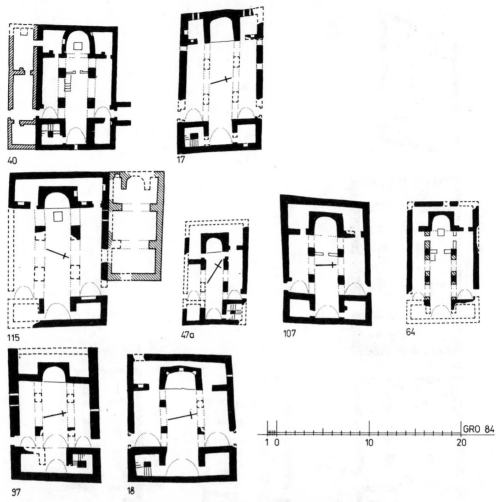

2. Zentrumsbetonte verkürzte Longitudinalbauten

muten beabsichtigte. Schließlich ergibt sich das Fehlen einer Kuppelwölbung auch aus der Unmöglichkeit, zwischen den Pfeilern ein für die Ergänzung einer Kuppel notwendiges quadratisches Raumfeld zu schaffen. Und zwar gilt das sogar noch für die stark verkürzte Südkirche von Sabagūra (Nr. 18), in der alle erhaltenen Pfeiler nur einen quadratischen Querschnitt aufweisen. Zur Unterscheidung von der zuerst genannten Gruppe seien diese Bauten als » Zentrumsbetonte Verkürzte Longitudinalbauten « bezeichnet.

Einen gegenüber den vorher genannten Beispielen gänzlich andersartigen Typus repräsentieren nun diejenigen Vierstützenbauten, die ich als » Hallenkirchen « charakterisieren möchte. Dieser Typus ist wesentlich jünger und zeichnet sich im Gegensatz zu jenem nun durch eine bevorzugte Verwendung von Kuppel- und Hängekuppelgewölbe aus. Mehrere Beispiele haben sich so weit erhalten, daß über ihr ursprüngliches Wölbungs-

schema keinerlei Zweifel besteht. Allen voran stehen die Raphaelskirche von Tamit (Nr. 48) und die Flußkirche von Kaw (Nr. 45). In beiden von ihnen wurde zwischen den Pfeilern und den umgebenden Wänden eine Anzahl von Gurt- und Jochbogen geschlagen, die den gesamten Naosbereich in neun etwa gleich große Kompartimente unterteilen. Während die seitlichen Kompartimente in der Regel mit flachen Hängekuppeln überdeckt waren, trugen die jeweils im Zentrum befindlichen Raumfelder — wie sich bei beiden Beispielen noch sicher nachweisen ließ — eine höher hinaufragende Vollkreiskuppel. Bei den übrigen Beispielen, die weniger gut erhalten waren, ergeben sich Indizien für die Zugehörigkeit zu diesem Hallenkirchentypus vor allem aus der Stellung der Pfeiler im Raum, die einen Verzicht auf eine grundrißmäßige Betonung des Zentrums erkennen lassen. Darüber hinaus besitzen die Pfeiler auch selbst gelegentlich eine kreuzförmige

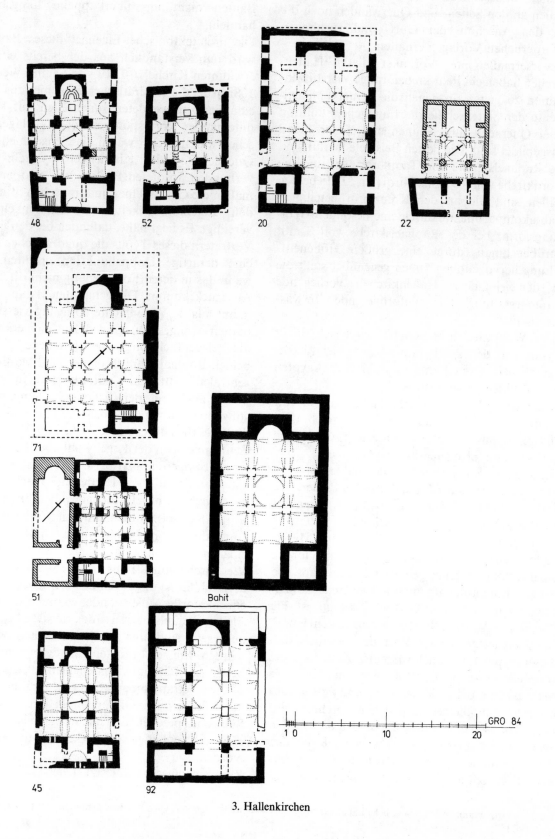

48 52 20 22

71

51 Bahit

45 92

3. Hallenkirchen

Gestalt, und schließlich haben sich in mehreren Fällen an den Seiten- und Querwänden noch die für den Anschluß der Gurt- und Jochbogen erforderlichen Vorlagen erhalten.

Gewissermaßen als Vorläufer dieser Hallenkirchen haben ein Paar kreuzförmige Vierstützenbauten zu gelten, in denen die Mittelkompartimente der Seitenschiffe die räumliche Funktion einer Querachse übernehmen und entsprechend ausgebildet sind. Die besten Beispiele hierfür sind die Raphaelskirche von Tamit (Nr. 48) und die Nordkirche von Abdallāh Nirqi (Nr. 52). In beiden Fällen sind die an der Kreuzform beteiligten Raumkompartimente durch eine besondere Wölbungsform, bei der Raphaelskirche von Tamit darüber hinaus durch eine größere Höhenentfaltung hervogehoben. Ihnen gegenüber stellt die in den einfachen Hallenkirchen vorliegende Raumgestaltung eine uniformierende Verwässerung dar.

Aller Wahrscheinlichkeit nach leitet sich dieser Typus von den spätbyzantinischen Vierstützenbauten her, deren Kenntnis wohl über Ägypten nach Nubien gelangt ist.[8]

Schließlich gibt es noch eine kleine Anzahl von Bauten, die sich weder dem einen noch dem anderen Typus zuordnen lassen. Sie ist zugleich die mit Abstand problematischste Gruppe.

Die in Frage kommenden Bauten haben sämtlich bemerkenswert starke quadratische Pfeiler, die darüber hinaus jeweils ein betontes, genähert quadratisches Mittelfeld umschreiben. Letzteres dürfte daher mit gutem Grund einst eine Mittelkuppel getragen haben. Hingegen kommen für die Überdeckung der übrigen Partien des Naos wie bei den Longitudinalbauten nur einfache Tonengewölbe in Betracht. Ein Schlüsselbau ist die Kirche von Abū Sīr (Nr. 88). Sie zeigt in dem von F. Cailliaud festgehaltenen Zustand[9] deutlich, daß dieser Typus tatsächlich mit einer Zentralkuppel versehen gewesen ist.[10] Ferner sind bei der Mehrzahl der Beispiele die östlich und westlich des zentralen Mittelfeldes befindlichen Abschnitte des Naos unterschiedlich tief ausgebildet. Sie wurden also von den Erbauern — abweichend von den dem basilikalen Schema verpflichteten » Verkürzten Longitudinalbauten « — nicht als gleich

wertig angesehen. Folglich kann es sich bei diesen Bauten nicht um überkuppelte Längsbauten handeln.

Die architektonische Eigenart dieses Bautyps wird nun verständlich aus der bereits eingangs erwähnten Kirche 16-E-19 von Samna-West (Nr. 108), in der die quadratischen Pfeiler jeweils an den einander zugewendeten Innenseiten mit kleinen miteinander korrespondierenden Vorlagen versehen waren. Sicher waren diese einst auch in der Querrichtung der Kirchenachse durch Bogen verbunden. In diesen Pfeilern war also gewissermaßen die Gestalt einer quadratischen Stütze mit den Eigentümlichkeiten eines Winkelpfeilers vereinigt. Es liegt nahe, daß auch bei den übrigen Vertretern dieses Typus die quadratischen Pfeiler eine derartige Doppelfunktion erfüllten, auch wenn das in deren Formgebung nicht direkt zum Ausdruck kommt. Die genannten Bauten dürfen damit als » Vereinfachte Umgangsvierstützenbauten « angesehen werden. Zugleich erklärt das die gelegentlich ungleiche räumliche Tiefe der beiden Raumabschnitte östlich und westlich des zentralen Mittelfeldes. Sie kommt in gleicher Weise auch bei den geläufigen Umgangsvierstützenbauten vor (Nr. 30, 84, 98 und Philae). Wie diese besaßen die etwas vereinfachten Vertreter im Zentrum eine in der Regel wohl über Eckbrücken (sog. Trompen) konstruierte Vollkreiskuppel und waren in den übrigen Partien des Naos ebenfalls ausschließlich mit Tonnengewölben überdeckt.

Von allen bisher bekannt gewordenen Vierstützenbauten in Nubien bleibt mithin nur ein einziger nicht klassifizierbarer Bau übrig: die Westkirche von Kalâbša (Nr. 15). Dieser Bau ist atypisch. Er ist ungewöhnlich klein, besitzt jedoch enorm starke Aubenwände, während die inneren Pfeiler, die üblicherweise der stärksten Belastung ausgesetzt sind, nur ziemlich schwach bemessen wurden. Meines Erachtens handelt es sich daher bei diesem Bau um einen ehemaligen, als allseitig offenen Tetrapylon ausgeführten Grabbau, wofür auch die großen Öffnungen in der Nord- und Südwand sprechen. Erst nachträglich ist er dann in eine mehrschiffige Pfeilerkirche umgewandelt worden.

Zusammenfassend ist festzustellen : Die nubischen

---

[8] P. Grossmann, » Mittelalterliche Langhauskuppelkirchen und verwandte Typen in Oberägypten «, ADIK kopt. 3 (1982), 198 f.

[9] Abgedruckt auch bei Monneret de Villard, *La Nubia...*, II Taf. 95.

[10] Der Grundriß dieses Baues in Taf. 4 folgt einer mir von W.Y. Adams dankenswerterweise zur Verfügung gestellten Neuaufnahme.

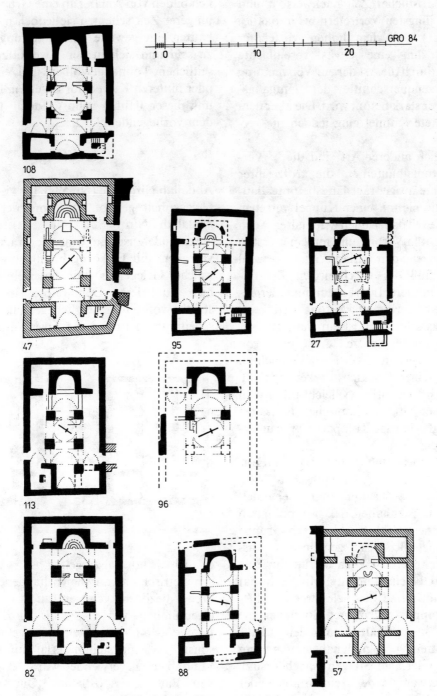

GRO 84

108

47

95

27

113

96

82

88

57

4. Vereinfachte Umgangsvierstützenbauten

Vierstützenbauten lassen sich nach drei grundsätzlich verschiedenen Typen ordnen. Der in
architekturgeschichtlicher Hinsicht wichtigste
Typus ist der Umgangsvierstützenbau. Er ist
bereits in frühchristlicher Zeit nachweisbar und
reicht in seinen jüngsten Vertretern bis in das 13.
Jahrhundert A.D. Seit dem hohen Mittelalter
besteht neben ihm eine etwas vereinfachte
Variante, in der durch die Art der zur Verwendung
gelangten Stützenquerschnitte der Umgangs-
charakter weniger stark betont wird. Die über dem
Zentrum errichtete Kuppel ging jedoch nie verloren.

Von grundsätzlich anderer Art sind die » Verkürzten Longitudialbauten «, die trotz ihrer
räumlichen Kürze ausgeprägt längsbetonte Bauten sind, und die nie mit einer Kuppel versehen
waren. Es gibt sie seit dem frühen Mittelalter. Auch
dieser Typus steht in Verbindung mit einer erst in
jüngerer Zeit auftretenden Variante, in der — wohl
unter dem Einfluß der gleichzeitigen Zentral-
bauten — das mittlere Interkolumnium der inneren Stützenreihe geringfügig betont wird.

Der dritte Typus schließlich ist ein charakteristi-
scher Repräsentant der Spätzeit. Ausgehend von
einem Bautypus, der einen gewissen Versuch zu
der Einführung einer Querachse erkennen läßt,
wird aus ihm sehr schnell — vielleicht unter dem
Einfluß der gleichzeitigen islamischen Baukunst
— eine in neun gleichartige Kompartimente unter-
teilte Hallenkirche.

Zum Abschluß noch eine grundsätzliche Fest-
stellung. Auch wenn wir die nubischen Vierstützenbauten hier im Zusammenhang behandelt
haben, so ist doch festzuhalten, daß sie typologisch
keineswegs zu einer in sich geschlossenen Gruppe
gehören. Die allen Beispielen gemeinsame Ausbildung mit vier inneren Pfeilen betrifft nur eine
rein äußerliche Übereinstimmung. Mit Recht hat
auch W.Y. Adams seine Beispiele zwei verschiedenen Hauptgruppen zugeordnet. So stehen die
» Verkürzten Longitudinalbauten « den ordentlichen Längsbauten typologisch näher, auch wenn
diese mit sechs oder acht Stützen versehen sind.
Die nächsten Verwandten der kreuzförmigen oder
einfachen Hallenkirchen sind unter einigen Bauten

mit nur einem Stützenpaar — wie z.B. der kleinen
Kirche von Arminna West (Nr. 44) — oder den
Bauten, denen überhaupt alle Stützen fehlen, zu
suchen. Die Umgangsvierstützenbauten schließlich bilden von Anfang an eine Gruppe für sich. In
jüngerer Zeit scheinen sie jedoch mit den Längsbauten eine gewisse Verschmelzung eingegangen
zu sein und sich in den Zweistützenbauten mit
seitlichen Tonnengewölben und einer vorderen
oder hinteren Kuppel fortzusetzen. Die Besprechung dieser Bauten gehört jedoch nicht mehr zu
dem vorliegenden Thema.

Nachträge:

Abdallah Nirqi Süd (Nr. 53a): Inzwischen habe ich
Gelegenheit gehabt, mich mit der Kirche von
Abdallah Nirqi Süd (Nr. 53a) etwas weiter
auseinanderzusetzen. Einzelne Fragen konnte ich
vor allem mit L. Török brieflich besprechen, bei
welcher Gelegenheit mir dieser ein Paar weitere,
nich publizierte Detailphotos zur Verfügung
stellte, wofür ihm herzlich gedankt sei. Danach
scheint die ursprüngliche Apsiskrümmung — wie

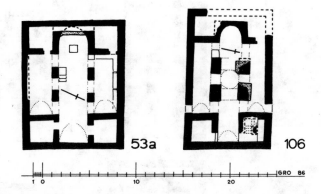

es auch als normal zu gelten hat — einigermaßen
symmetrisch und auf die vorhandene Mittelschiff-
breite bezogen gewesen zu sein.[11] Sie war
eigentümlicherweise — wie auch die Pfeiler der
Kirche — aus Bruchsteinen aufgeführt, während
sonst das Bruchsteinmaterial nur mehr in den
Fundamenten verwendet wurde. Als man später
den Bau eines östlichen Querkorridors für
notwendig fand, wurde die Apsis verkürzt.

---

[11] Dasselbe geht auch bereits aus dem Text von G. Hajnóczi a.O. 360 Zeile 6 u. 7 hervor. Die Krümmung ist jedoch
merkwürdigerweise in beiden publizierten Plänen, s.o. Anm. 5, erheblich verzeichnet, was vielleicht damit zu erklären ist, daß
der Scheitel der Krümmung nicht von Anfang an sichtbar war.

Eine weitere Besonderheit dieser Kirche ist die breite Vorlage vor der südlichen Apsiswange. Nach dem Ziegelverband, der deutlich auf Taf. 41,1 der Acta Archaeologica 26, 1974 zu erkennen ist, gehört sie unzweifelhaft zum originalen Bestand, ist aber sonst — zudem auch nur auf einer Seite — bei keinem weiteren Bau im Niltal belegt. Ebenso ist sie bautechnisch nicht vonnöten, zumal die Gegenseite ohne eine solche Vorlage auskommt. Eine Erklärung vermag ich nur in den etwas merkwürdigen Ruhebänken auf der Südseite des Naos zu erkennen, die offenbar zum ursprünglichen Bestand der Kirche gehören.[12] Die entlang der Ostwand des südlichen Seitenschiffs geführte Ruhebank scheint nun — aus welchem Grunde auch immer — eine Vorlage am Apsiseingang verlangt zu haben. Sie ist damit mehr als ein einfacher Ambo, der ohnehin üblicherweise erst nachträglich aufgebaut wird. Es bleibt jedoch fraglich, ob die Vorlage in voller Höhe, bis zum Bogenansatz der Arkaden hinaufgeführt war. Die allgemeine bauliche Struktur der Kirche wird durch diese Vorlage derart gestört, daß wir sie uns nur bis zu einer mittleren Höhe — etwa einer Brüstung entsprechend — hinaufgeführt vorstellen mögen. Auch die wohl einer ähnlichen Bestimmung dienende mittlere Vorlage an der Westwand des westlichen Mittelraumes dürfte nur bis auf Brüstungshöhe hinaufgereicht haben.

Samna Süd (Nr. 106): Ferner wurde kürzlich ein neuer Grundriß der Kirche von Samna Süd (Nr. 106) publiziert.[13] Er tritt an die Stelle der alten Aufnahme von R. Lepsius[14] und erlaubt eine Zuweisung der Kirche zum Typus der vereinfachten Umgangsvierstützenbauten (Taf. 4). Über dem Zentrum hat sich eine Kuppel erhalten, die Seitenzonen trugen Tonnengewölbe. Charakteristisch ist ferner der verhältnismäßig geringe Abstand der beiden westlichen Pfeiler von der westlichen Naoswand. Apsis soll erst später ausgeführt worden sein. Sonst ist jedoch die Gestalt der Pfeiler im Zuge zahlreicher Reparaturen vielfältig verändert wordeu. Das gleiche gilt für die Rundung der Apsis. Das Mauermassiv in dem südwestlichen Eckraum ist als Unterbau für die Treppe anzusehen.

---

[12] Bemerkenswerterweise sind sie auch vor den Türen entlang gezogen, so daß man nicht umhin konnte, beim Betreten der betreffenden Räume über sie hinwegzusteigen. Die Zwischenlehne vor dem Eingang in das südliche Pastophorium (sog. Baptisterium) ist demzufolge gänzlich niedergetreten.

[13] L.V. and J.J. Zabkar, JARCE 19, 1982, 5ff. Plan 1.

[14] Publ. bei Monneret de Villard a.O. I 231f. Abb. 221. G. Haeny, der seinerzeit den Bau vermessen hat, bin ich für weitere Auskünfte und die Überlassung der Aufnahmepläne verpflichtet.

COPTIC STUDIES

Karel C. Innemée

Relationships between Episcopal and Monastic Vestments in Nubian Wall–painting

So far little is known about liturgical vestments in Nubia as represented in wall-paintings, especially those from Faras, where numerous bishops were depicted. As written sources concerning Nubian liturgical dress are still lacking, information might be obtained from comparison with Coptic, Byzantine and Syrian vestments, about which we have both pictorial and literary sources.

Nubian bishops were most probably consecrated from Alexandria.[1] Although the Nubian episcopal vestments and their decoration differ in details from the contemporary Coptic ones, we may assume that the ritual of consecration was the Coptic one and we may therefore apply the information that we get from these rituals concerning the vestments equally to the Nubian episcopal costume. The Coptic higher clergy, starting from bishops was supposed to have the monk's status, like still is the case in eastern churches in general. In practice, however, it seems to have been difficult to find candidate–bishops meeting this requirement and for this reason most of the versions of the ordination–rituals provide a preceding ceremony for the monk's profession for the case that the candidate did not have the monastic status. During this profession either the complete monastic costume was given or the most characteristic pieces, the cxhma and the (black) monk's cap.[2] About the interpretation of the word cxhma confusion exists. It occurs in Coptic texts with the meaning of "monastic costume", "monk's scapular" or as a synonym of

the Greek ἀνάλαβος, a complex of interwoven leather strips, worn crossed over back and breast. In the case of the formal profession preceding the bishop's consecration it seems that the scapular was given. In wall–paintings in the church of St Athony's monastery near the Red Sea, bishops and patriarchs are depicted, wearing both the scapular (and sometimes the ἀναλαβος as well) and the monk's cap.[3] In the Syrian episcopal costume we even find a headdress with the name of eskīmō, which in shape is derived from the monk's cap and in name is related to the Coptic ECKIM (= cxhma).[4]

Considering these facts, it is not illogical to suppose vestments of monastic origin in the portraits of bishops from Faras. In the portraits of Petros I (Warsaw no 33), Ioannes III (Warsaw no 19), Marianos (Warsaw no 45) and Merkurios (Khartoum inv. no 57) we find a vestment that in the catalogue of the National Museum in Warsaw is called epigonation.[5] The shape, however, does not remind of the epigonation which is a lozenge-shaped attribute. It looks like a rectangular strip of cloth, hanging from the neck under the epitrachelion and could be identified as the scapular (fig. 1). This could also mean an identification for the red collar appearing from under the phelonion which could be the collar of the scapular, which is of the same colour. In representations of Byzantine monks the scapular can appear in a similar way from under the cape (fig. 2).

[1] W.Y. Adams, Nubia, *Corridor to Africa*, London 1977, pp. 471–2.

[2] V. Mistrih (ed.), Jûhannâ ibn Abi Zakariâ ibn Sibâ⁽, *Pretiosa Margarita de Scientiis Ecclesiasticis*, Cairo 1966, p. 511.

[3] P. van Moorsel, *La Peinture Murale chez les Coptes III, Les peintures du monastère de St Antoine* (in preparation).

[4] A.A. King, *Liturgie d'Antiochie*, Paris 1967, pp. 58–9; J. Assfalg and P. Krüger, *Kleines Wörterbuch des christlichen Orients*, Wiesbaden 1975, p. 240.

[5] K. Michałowski, *Faras, Die Wandbilder in den Sammlungen des Nationalmuseums zu Warschau*, Warschau–Dresden 1974, p. 50.

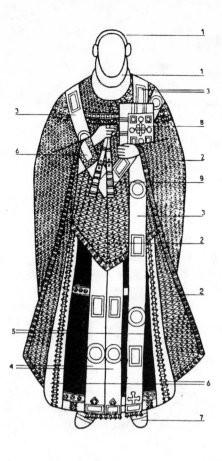

1. Scapular (after K. Michałowski, *Faras. Die Wandbilder in den Sammlungen des Nationalmuseums zu Warschau*, p. 50): 1 — Schamla, 2 — Phelonion, 3 — Omophorion, 4 — Epitrachelion, 5 — Epigonation, 6 — Sticharion (Alba), decorated with Potamoi, 7 — Shoes, 8 — Book, 9 — Maniple

2. St Euphrosinos, after a 16th–century wall-painting in the monastery of St Nicholas in Meteora (Greece)

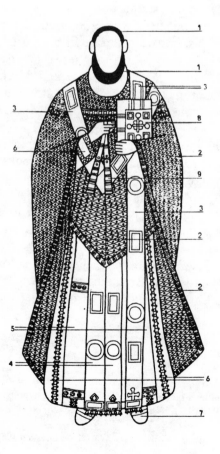

3. Monk's cap (?) (after K. Michałowski, *Faras. Die Wandbilder in den Sammlungen des Nationalmuseums zu Warschau*, p. 50): 1 — Schamla, 2 — Phelonion, 3 — Omophorion, 4 — Epitrachelion, 5 — Epigonation, 6 — Sticharion (Alba), decorated with Potamoi, 7 — Shoes, 8 — Book, 9 — Maniple

4. St Mattheos (?), wall-painting from Deir al-Fakhoury, Esna (after J. Leroy, *La peinture murale chez les Coptes. I. Les peintures des couvents du Desert d'Esna*, Cairo, 1975, Pl. 66)

The second vestment that might be of monastic origin is the headdress, called shamla in the Warsaw catalogue. The shamla is a Coptic priestly vestment that can be worn like a shawl or turban draped around head, neck and shoulders. The headdress of the bishops of Faras does not resemble the shamla and moreover, the shamla was not worn by Coptic bishops. If we assume that the tight cap, covering the head and the part covering the neck are one and the same vestment, it is difficult to identify it (fig. 3). Nevertheless there exists a similar example in Coptic wall-painting, the portrait of a monk in Deir-al-Fakhoury near Esna, who wears a similar headdress (fig. 4). If we only consider the tight cap, leaving the ears out, it bears similarity with the above-mentioned Syrian eskīmō.

Although a specific identification remains uncertain, there are indications that the headdress that we find with some of the bishops of Faras is of monastic origin. If not the ⲕⲟⲩⲗⲗⲁ, that must have been of a rather pointed model, it could be the cap called ⲕⲗⲁⲫⲧ.

More detailed study is required in this matter, but it seems likely that the costumes of the bishops Petros I, Ioannes III, Marianos and Merkurios in the paintings from Faras express the monastic status of these bishops like in certain cases of Coptic and Syrian episcopal vestments, be it *pro forma* or not.

COPTIC STUDIES

Stefan Jakobielski, Stanisław Medeksza
The North-West Church at Old Dongola

To the north of the town of Old Dongola on a flat ground at the edge of sand dunes area bordering the Polish Concession limits from the western side, ca. 240 metres west from the North Church, situated half way between the town centre and the modern village el-Ghaddar and about half a kilometre north from the site Suburbs another church named North-West was discovered and excavated by the Polish Expedition in 1983 field season. Additional archaeological works were also carried out at this site in 1984.[1]

Although the surroundings of the edifice are not yet fully examined, one may state that the church was a free-standing building, like the North Church located, at a certain distance from the settlement. Before excavations started, the site looked like a small elevation of the ground (fig. 1). The removal of a thin layer of blown sand from its surface permitted discovery of remnants of the building's walls which were razed to the level of only 25 cm higher than the pavement. The floor was covered with a layer of rubble containing crushed mud-brick, mud mortar and collapsed pieces of plaster, some with traces of mural paintings. The top of this layer, corresponding exactly with the height of the preserved walls, formed with them a kind of levelled hard surface. The overall appearance and compact consistency may be a proof that the site remained for a time under water.[2] It was extremely difficult to remove this stratum, hard as it was, because of the necessity of

extracting from it several hundred small pieces of painted plaster for preservation (fig. 2).

The state of preservation of the edifice seems to prove that the building itself had been purposely dismantled, and that most of the building material obtained in this way had been removed from the site.

The church is almost totally constructed of mud-brick [3] except for at least some arches or vaults in between spans in the nave and aisles and arches over door-heads to sacristies; there were fragments of such arches jointed with lime mortar found in the church's rubble stratum. The floor composed of small pottery tiles laid on a thin layer of sand,[4] was found nearly intact except for the western portion of the church where it had been partly removed.

The church was founded directly on a sand dune in the western part, while in the eastern one it was built on the top of a layer of rubble originating from the earlier structures which generally can be dated to the Classic Christian period. These structures had been previously nearly totally dismantled and levelled throughout. Only remains of the last two courses of bricks were observed as well as fragment of a mud-brick wall running east to west. We should note that, on the basis of the uncovered remains, one can identify a large edifice, built of mixed types of bricks, extending to the north and east of the church. Its plan, which can partly be reconstructed out of the building as an

---

[1] An archaeological report concerning these field seasons will appear in "Chronique des fouilles", ET XV.

[2] This fact found unexpected confirmation from the villagers of el Ghaddar; they reported that sometime in the first quarter of this century the whole of the low area was flooded for a certain period permitting the use of boats, and also that in the early fifties, as a result of heavy rainfall, the water stayed on the surface for about a week.

[3] The standard mud-brick used in the walls is $27 \times 15 \times 6$ cm in size. However, we also find occasionally much bigger (re-used?) bricks of $33.5 \times 17.5 \times 7$ and $39 \times 18 \times 7$.

[4] The floor tiles are on the average $27 \times 16 \times 3.5$ and are similar to those used in the North Church; also the technique of paving is identical in both churches.

1. Site of the North-West Church before the excavations (phot. Z. Doliński)

2. Fragments of painted plaster disinterred in the interior of the North-West Church (phot. Z. Doliński)

earlier church because of the existence of a wall orientated north–south and running through the buildings. Its traces were observed in a row of trial-pits under the Haikal and the North Sacristy of the North-West Church (fig. 3).

Curiously enough, in spite of the lack of firm ground as a building platform for erection of the North-West Church, its walls have no distinctive foundation and the footing level falls only 16 cm lower than the actual level of pavement. The lack of foundation has been compensated for, by the unusual thickness of walls (the outer ones being 1.60 m in breadth, the inner ones about 1.30 m). The North-West Church, with overall dimensions of 19.25 × 15 m, is orientated nearly precisely as on east-west axis. Its plan can generally be classified as a cross within a rectangle or rather in this case "cross over rectangle", since four apses, ending the individual arms of the cross, slightly project outside the main outline of the building. The main east-west axis of the edifice is nevertheless emphasized by the elongation to the west of the vertical arm of the cross and two massive piers in the centre (1.80 × 1.65 m) seem to divide the church into a nave (slightly over two metres in width) and two shorter aisles of the same breadth (plan I).

The church was accessible by two parallel doorways leading from the south and north sides to the westermost spans of the aisles. Their location emphasizes an additional transversal axis of the building (fig. 4).

The eastern part of the church contains the usual arrangement of three rooms (fig. 5); the Haikal (Sanctuary) contained within an extra span added to the main nave and closed by an apse of the same width, distinguished from the rest of the interior only by raised level of pavement, as is the case with the other apses. Traces of a mud-brick substructure for the altar were found here close to the edge of the elevated pavement. Two doors led from the Haikal to two small Sacristies (each 2 × 2 m). None of the inner furnishings of the interior of the eastern part has been found; nor do we even have the baptismal basin in the South Sacristy which presumably served as the Baptistry Room as usual in Nubia.[5] The only preserved element of the inner furnishings in the other part of the church was the

3. Remains of an earlier building underneath the North-West Church. View from the north (phot. Z. Doliński)

pulpit (ambo) located in the passage-way from the nave to the northern apse.[6]

The western part of the church also preserved a tripartite division, the only novelty being the western apse. Both sides of the apse are typical corner rooms. But the North-West Room is accessible only from the North Aisle, while the door to the Staircase, located as usual in the southwestern corner of the building, led from the Main Nave. The Staircase, divided by a thin wall, in place of a central newel, apparently contained two flights of steps anchored in its outer walls and based on rubble filling, whose remnants were still observed

---

[5] Cf. Godlewski, *Faras* VI, passim.

[6] The pulpit might have been accessible from the north side where the pavement shows traces of extensive use and repairs. In the last phase of usage of the church some additional flooring tiles were laid here on the pavement thereby possibly reducing the height of the supposed first step leading to the pulpit.

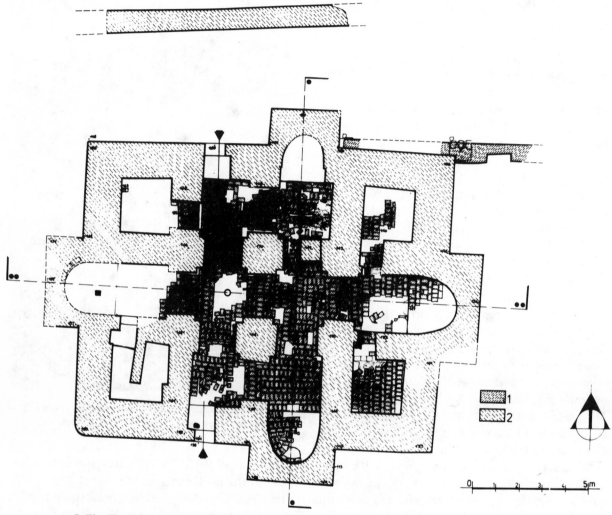

I. The North-West Church. Plan of uncovered remains (original phase) elaborated by S. Medeksza

4. General view of the North-West Church from the south (phot. Z. Doliński)

5. Central part of the North-West Church seen from the north (phot. Z. Doliński)

in situ. A platform landing connecting the two flights must have been situated in the south side of the room. Even if we accept the fact that the unpreserved steps (maximum 20 in number) were rather high (19–20 cm), the stairs permitted attaining only a height of some four metres; this gives us an idea about the possible height of the vaulting over the westernmost span in the Nave, as well as, in all probability, the height of other rooms in the interior which most probably were barrel vaulted. The direction of barrel vaults which can easily be deduced, put very strong stress on the cruciform layout of the building. Only two spans, one at intersection of "the arms of the cross" and the other at the intersection of the main axis of the building with the axis of the entrances, must have been covered with domes of considerable height [7] (plan II). Such a solution would allow also proper lighting of the interior, where the quantity of light provided by windows (if any) might have been greatly reduced by the thickness of walls.

The interior of the North-West Church was only once plastered with a kind of gravel-lime plaster with a considerable addition of mud and covered with a thick layer of whitewash, and it must have been reachly decorated with murals. Fragments of painted plaster were found everywhere except in all four of the corner rooms; most of the remaining part of the interior provided almost a thousand pieces which can be identified as originating from at least 11 compositions. This material, however, does not allow reconstruction of the individual paintings nor even their parts; it may be used only as a source of information about the style and painting technique used. The whole decoration was obviously done by the same painter. His basic palette of colours comprised red, purple, yellow, white, blue-grey and black; but by superimposing layers of paint he obtained other hues, like brown, orange, dark violet etc. One of the characteristics of his style is that the individual compositions have one of the basic palette as the predominant colour. The style of paintings does not correspond strictly to any of the known ones from Nubia (for instance thin contour lines are never used here) but there are characteristic ornaments and details which can

be compared with those used in the multicoloured II and III styles from Faras [8] from the end of the 11th and 12th centuries respectively (cf. fig. 2). There are preserved only two fragments, each containing a few letters of the legends written in grey paint in a late, so-called "Nubian hand"; it is probable that the text is in Old Nubian.

Except for the plan of the church, another unusual feature was observed during the excavations. Before the time of constructing the church large pots and some building materials were intentionally placed at the foundation level which most probably served for the demarcation of axes and positioning of walls. Most of them were later destroyed or removed, perhaps by robbers searching for a treasure; one of the pots, however, put in the centre of the church on the main axis was found apparently intact and containing only clean gravel; another pot, placed under the southern apse, had been partly removed and thrown out nearby; it obviously had been once filled with *jir* (local material for whitewash). Under the main (eastern) apse, there were found fragments of a large *qulla* for wáter (fig. 6); under the western one there were two burnt bricks and at the intersection of the naves a nodule of mud was found. Whether these findings also have some symbolic meaning in the ceremony of founding the church remains still an open question.

Fragments of at least 25 local amphorae, bearing different monograms, most probably dated to the Late-Christian period, were found to the north of the church on the level of utilization of the building as well as inside the church on the pavement (fig. 7). They must have been destroyed during the time of demolition of the church. Potsherds from the same type of vessels were found also in the levelling stratum beneath the churches pavement. This circumstance as well as the lack of any rebuilding, renovation or re-plastering of the church's interior except for repairs in parts of two doorways and occasionally of the paving, seem to indicate a fairly short period during which the church was used. Further indications for dating can only be obtained on the basis of examining structural and architectural features of the edifice. The North

---

[7] All barrel vaults must obviously have been of a so-called "Nubian type" (skew vault), inclined towards the two central spans; in such an arrangement one may see the intention to strengthen the bases of domes erected over both these spans. Similar disposition occurs also in the North Church in Old Dongola. On vaultings used in Nubian buildings cf. Gartkiewicz, Nub. Chr. I, pp. 66 f., and Grossmann, *Kuppelkirchen,* pp. 239 ff.

[8] Cf. Martens-Czarnecka, *Faras* VII, pp. 89 ff (Styles G, H).

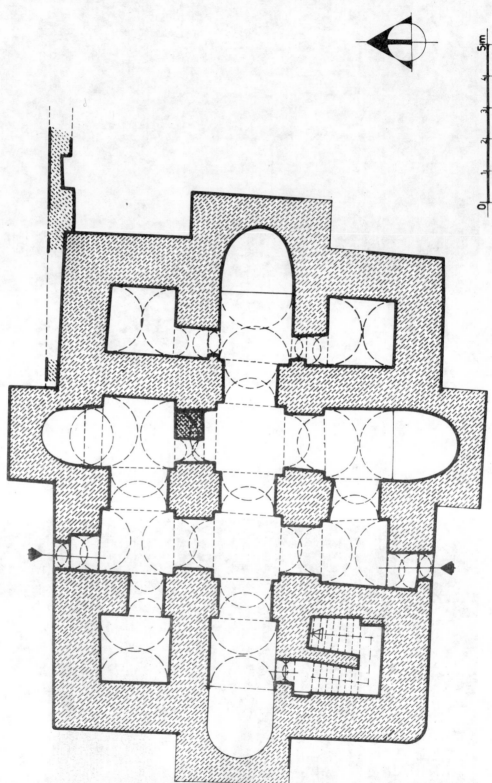

II. The North-West Church. Plan with reconstructed vaultings elaborated by S. Medeksza

6. The Eastern Apse with fragments of a *qulla in situ* and the remains of an altar in the foreground (phot. Z. Doliński)

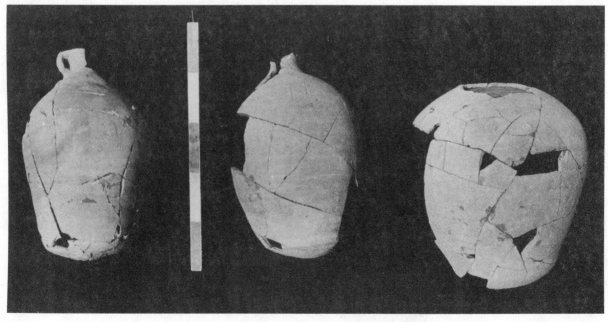

7. Examples of amphorae found in and nearby the Church (phot. Z. Doliński)

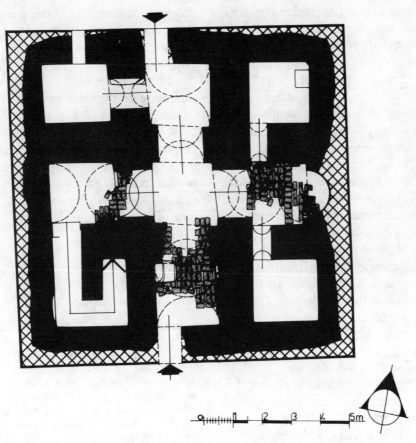

III. The North Church in Old Dongola. Plan and sections elaborated by
J. Dobrowolski, M. Rostworowski and S. Medeksza

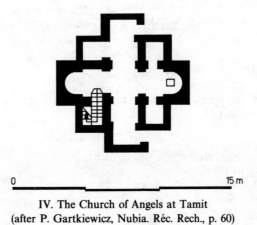

IV. The Church of Angels at Tamit
(after P. Gartkiewicz, Nubia. Réc. Rech., p. 60)

Church in Dongola (plan III), located nearby, excavated in 1981 and dated on archaeological grounds as not earlier than the 13th century, can serve here as an analogy especially as regards the construction. The building is of a cruciform plan, i.e. a cross-in-square, with overall dimensions of 11.5 × 11.5 m; it was built entirely of mud-brick and had massive walls 1.30 m thick. All rooms are here of the same dimensions as in the North-West Church, but the architectural programme of the interior has here been considerably reduced. Both buildings have similar paving consisting of pottery tiles laid in a similar manner. There are also similarities in the construction of the staircase as well as in the type of plaster used. No doubt both edifices belong to the same building tradition, and the plan of the North Church was obviously inspired by the shape of the North-West Church, which therefore cannot be more than a century earlier.

As another analogy from Nubia concerning spatial arrangement, we should certainly mention the Church of Angels at Tamit.[9] Except for similarities in the general architectural concept, we should pay special attention here to the layout of the eastern and western parts of the church; its arrangement is similar to our example in every detail (plan IV). The dating of the Tamit church is still a matter of debate. According to William Adams[10] and also Eda Bresciani[11] the building took place between 1150 and 1400 A.D. The late dating seems to be supported also by Przemysław Gartkiewicz, who in his so-called "development of spatial concept" places it in Period III, type c, 3 in the time span 10th/11th–14th centuries.[12] Peter Grossmann, in his latest elaboration of Upper Egyptian churches[13] seems to be inclined to follow the earlier opinion of Ugo Monneret de Villard in accepting the 9th century as the date for the building. It is perhaps worth adding that the painted decoration in the Tamit church speaks definitely in favour of a later date. If one examines the murals in the Tamit church[14] in terms of the styles established on the basis of Faras paintings one may deduce that they cannot be earlier than the 11th century.

Summing up the archaeological and architectural arguments we propose the 12th century as the most probable date of the erection of the North-West Church. The building itself adds to the series of architectural Nubian creations: it is a further example of the development of cruciform design so readily accepted by the church authorities of Old Dongola.[15]

Abbreviations

Adams, JARCE 4 = W. Y. Adams, "Architectural Evolution of the Nubian Church, 500–1400 A.D.", *Journal of the American Research Center in Egypt* IV (1965), 87–139.

Gartkiewicz, BABesch = P. M. Gartkiewicz, "New Outline of the History of Nubian Church Architecture", *Bulletin Antieke Beschaving* 55, 1 (1980), 137–160.

Gartkiewicz, Nub. Chr. = P. M. Gartkiewicz, "An Introduction to the History of Nubian Church Architecture", *Nubia Christiana* I, Warszawa 1982, pp. 43–133.

Gartkiewicz, Nubia Réc. Rech. = P. M. Gartkiewicz, "The Central Plan in Nubian Church Architecture", *Nubia. Récentes Recherches, Actes du Colloque Nubiologique International au Musée National de Varsovie 1972*, Warszawa 1975, pp. 49–64.

Godlewski, *Faras VI* = W. Godlewski, *Faras VI, Baptistères nubiens*, Warszawa 1979.

Grossmann, *Kuppelkirchen* = P. Grossmann, *Mittelalterliche Langhauskuppelnkirchen und verwandte Typen in Oberägypten, Abhandlungen des Deutschen Archäologischen Instituts Kairo. Koptische Reihe 3*, Glückstadt 1982.

Martens-Czarnecka, Faras VII = M. Martens-Czarnecka, *Faras VII, Les éléments décoratifs sur les peintures de la Cathédrale de Faras*, Warszawa 1982.

Monneret de Villard, Nub. Med. = U. Monneret de Villard, *La Nubia Medioevale* I–IV, Le Caire 1935–57.

Tamit 1964 = *Tamit 1964. Missione Archaeologica in Egitto dell' Università di Roma* (ed. S. Donadoni), Roma 1967.

ET = *Études et Travaux*.

---

[9] Cf. Monneret de Villard, Nub. Med. I, pp. 154 ff; Adams, JARCE 4, 100, 128, no 49; Gartkiewicz, Nubia Réc. Rech., pp. 60, 61, 64; Grossmann, *Kuppelkirchen*, pp. 81 f.

[10] Adams, JARCE 4, no 49.

[11] E. Bresciani, in: *Tamit 1964*, p. 35.

[12] Gartkiewicz, BABesch, figs 18, 22; id., Nub. Chr. I, pp. 74, 97–98.

[13] Grossmann, *Kuppelkirchen*, pp. 81 f.

[14] Monneret de Villard, Nub. Med. IV, pls CLVII–CLXV.

[15] On one of the most important structures of this kind cf. W. Godlewski, *Cruciform Church at Old Dongola*, supra in this volume.

COPTIC STUDIES

László Kákosy

Survivals of Ancient Egyptian Gods in Coptic and Islamic Egypt

The suppression of the pagan cults in the temples under Theodosius (391) put an end to the official form of ancient religions [1] (for political reasons, the cult in the temple of Philae survived up to the reign of Justinianus). Nevertheless, the heathen gods, regarded by the Christians as frightful demons (cf. the LXX translation of psalm 96.5), did not disappear from the popular mind with the closing of their temples.

The Nile God. Under emperor Mauricius (in 600 A.D.) an alleged miracle generated great excitement in Egypt. [2] Two gigantic creatures of human form emerged from the Nile, one resembling a man, the other a woman. The story represents a remarkable re-emergence of heathen mythology (Nile-God and Euthenia). Even the sacrifice of a young virgin seems to have been considered at the time of the Arab conquest. [3] Also the custom of the "bride of the Nile" of modern times should be mentioned here. [4]

Isis. The type of Isis giving suck to her son Horus is generally taken to represent the prototype of the Madonna with the bambino. Since such pictures were current in the Graeco-Roman Period, there is no reason to reject this possibility. [5] The adoption is chronologically well possible and also Solomon, the bishop of Basra spoke later of Isis and Horus as the prefiguration of Mary and Christ. [6] At any rate, individual monuments must be carefully examined. Thus a stela with mother and child was used as a funerary monument, [7] that is, in this case, a human mother and not the Virgin was modelled after Isis.

In the Middle Ages Isis was still looked on as mistress of the Nile. A statue of a woman with a child near el-Muᶜ llaqa church in Old Cairo was endowed with supernatural power over the Nile in popular belief. It was expected to protect the district from being submerged by the flood. [8]

In several Coptic magical texts Isis appears in her ancient role as mother-goddess healing her son. The child Horus may by afflicted either by illness or by the passion of unrequited love. [9] In a magical text the illness and the recovery of the young god is related in an elaborate mythological story. [10] The news of the stomach ailment of Horus is brought to his mother by a demon of marvellously quick march. Also the goddess *Nepthys* can come to his assistance. [11] Another Coptic magical text which may have had a Greek original, speaks of the consecration of the holy oil with the aim to win the love of somebody. This is the holy oil "That flows under the throne of Sabaoth, the oil with which Isis anointed the bones of *Osiris*". [12] In a Greek

---

[1] W. Ensslin, "Die Religionspolitik des Kaisers Theodosius des Gr.", SBAW 1953, (Heft 2), 77; L. Kákosy, "Das Ende des Heidentums in Ägypten", in: *Graeco-Coptica. Griechen und Kopten im byzantinischen Ägypten,* Halle (Saale) 1984, pp. 61 ff.

[2] Theophylactos Symocattes, Oic. hist. VII. 16; *The Chronicle of John, Bishop of Nikiu* translated from Zotenberg's Ethiopic Text by R. Charles, Oxford 1916, pp. 160 f. (XCVIII 34–37).

[3] E.W. Lane, *Manners and Customs of the Modern Egyptians,* London 1860, reprint 1954, p. 500.

[4] Ibid.

[5] V. Tran Tam Tinh, "Isis lactans", EPRO 37 (Leiden 1973), 40 ff. Cf. Kl. Wessel, SAK 6 (1978), 185 ff.

[6] J. Bidez and Fr. Cumont, *Les mages hellénisés* II, Paris 1938, p. 130.

[7] E.g., A. Effenberger, *Koptische Kunst,* Leipzig 1975, pl. 12, Staatliche Museen Inv. 4726.

[8] U. Haarmann, *Saeculum* 24 (1978), 376 ff.

[9] A.M. Kropp, *Ausgewählte koptische Zaubertexte* II, Bruxelles 1931, pp. 6 ff.

[10] Ibid., pp. 9 ff.

[11] Ibid., p. 13.

[12] W.H. Worrell, *Orientalia* 4 (1935), 184, 186.

incantation in the same Coptic text the goddess is invoked as "great Isis ruling in the absolute blackness".[13] The Osiris-Isis pair plays a prominent part also in Old-Coptic love charms, such as the Papyrus Schmidt and the Coptic mythological section of the Greek Magical Papyrus in Paris.[14] Since both of them are products of a still decidedly pagan environment, they can be counted as survivals only to a limited extent.

The well-known relief in the Louvre (prob. 5th century) of the falcon-headed equestrian figure stabbing a crocodile with his spear[15] may be interpreted as Horus killing *Seth* in a crocodile--form or as a Christian saint, probably Saint Theodor the General, subjugating the dragon.[16] It may have had an ambiguous meaning even to the contemporary mind. Iconographically it may be derived from the equestrian representations of Horus in the Roman Period which probably had an influence on the type of equestrian saints in Coptic art.[17]

Anubis appears in the Old Coptic Pap. Schmidt,[18] *Amun* and *Thot* in a text from the Fayum.[19] Amun shows features alien to his nature in ancient Egyptian religion. He is said to ride a horse, and he is carrying the books of Thot. It is well known that the cult of *Amun* has a yearly revival in present-day Luxor in the boat procession in honour of the Moslem patron saint Abu el-Haggag.[20]

While not assuming distinct mythological functions, *Seth* seems to have played the role of an evil demon. His name was used in compound magical words. The pictures of the ass-headed demons in the late parchment manuscript from Edfu (10th cent.?) probably derive from the representations of this god.[21]

Bes had a dual character in the Christian Period. In a legend he figures as a wicked demon haunting in the vicinity of his old temple at Abydos, and causing illness to the people living around. He had to be combated by Apa Moyses and his monk--brothers.[22] On the other hand, a picture on a papyrus points to a fusion of Christ and Bes in Coptic magic.[23]

The frog-goddess *Heqet,* a helper of child-birth in Pharaonic religion, is not attested by name but the so-called frog-lamps with the inscription "I am the resurrection" bear witness to the tenacious adherence to this ancient symbol of new life.[24]

The god *Petbe* was a product of the latest centuries of the ancient religion. The name (p3 *Db3*) represented a deification of the idea of (divine) reward, retaliation and revenge.[25] In a Coptic magical text (prob. 7th cent.) in which we find also *Artemis, Apollon, Athene, Kronos, Moira, Pallas, Aphrodite, Eos, Serapis* and *Uranos,* he reappears as a compound being.[26] In details, however, this latest form differs from the earlier one. He bears the face of a lion, while the back of his face is that of a bear. This god whose body extends over all the cosmos, might have influenced the gnostic concept of Christ. In a papyrus the gnostic Iao-Christos--Pantocrator is imagined with the forepart of a lion and his back as a forepart of a bear.[27]

The name Petbe appears also in a non-magical text. A letter of Shenute gives evidence that not

[13] Ibid., 18, 29.

[14] H. Satzinger, JARCE 12 (1975), 37 ff.; PGM IV, 94 ff.

[15] J. Vandier, *Musée du Louvre. Le Département des Antiquités Égyptiennes,* Paris 1973, pl. XXVIII, 1; *Koptische Kunst. Christentum am Nil,* Essen 1963, Kat. 77.

[16] De Lacy O'Leary, *The Saints of Egypt,* London 1937, pp. 262 ff.

[17] Effenberger, *Koptische Kunst,* p. 47.

[18] Satzinger, p. 40, line 16, cf. J. Quaegebeur, *Studia Aegyptiaca* 3 (Budapest 1977), 119 ff.

[19] Worrell, pp. 20, 30 f.; that also in PGM IV, 96 ff.

[20] G. Legrain, *Louqsor sans les pharaons,* Bruxelles–Paris 1914, pp. 47 ff.

[21] E. Drioton, *Le Muséon* 59 (1946), Mélanges Lefort, pp. 479 ff.

[22] W. Till, "Koptische Heiligen- und Martyrerlegenden", *Orientalia Christiana Analecta* 108 (1936), 52 ff.; L. Kákosy, *Acta Antiqua Hung.* 14 (1966), 185 f. (Reprint in *Studia Aegyptiaca* 7 (1981), 119 ff.

[23] Kropp III, § 9.

[24] Cf. Ev. John. XI: 25; C. Ristow, Fuß 3–4 (1961), 60 ff.; H. Wrede, JAC 11–12 (1968–1969), 83 ff.; J. Leclant, "La grenouille d'éternité des pays du Nil au monde méditerranéen", (*Hommages à M.J. Vermaseren* II), Leiden 1978, p. 566.

[25] LÄ IV, 992 f. (Petbe, H. Brunner); I.A. Elanskaja, in: *Drevnij Vostok i mirovaja kultura,* Moscow 1981, pp. 133 ff.

[26] H.O. Lange, *Ein Faijumischer Beschwörungstext* (Studies presented to F.Ll. Griffith), Oxford 1932, pp. 161 ff.

[27] Kropp I, 25, lines 81–91, II, p. 158.

only the name of this god was familiar to him but he knew that *Kronos* was regarded as the Greek equivalent of *Petbe*. [28] *Shai,* the personified Fate was also known to Shenute, he mentions it, among other remains of paganism, as a demon of the village and the house. [29] He refers also to the practice of paying homage to the *Sun* and the *Moon* by some peoples. [30]

The name *Kothos* for a deity, unknown both in Egyptian and Greek mythology, appears in a story about the destruction of a pagan temple. [31]

There are clear signs of Egyptian influence on the iconography of the archangels. On gems the figure of Anubis is associated with the name of Michael or Gabriel. [32] Both Anubis and Michael had a psychopompous function which prompted their fusion in the time of religious syncretism. On an Anubis-gem the names Uriel, Suriel, Gabriel and Michael can be read. [33] Michael merged with Thot and *Chnumis* as well. [34] Apart from Anubis, Michael was linked with a compound syncretistic god, a crocodile with falcon-head. [35]

It was suggested that the dog (jackal)–headed Anubis survived in the representations of Saint Christophorus. This may be true but we do not yet have decisive proof for a direct connection between the Egyptian god and the saint. [36] A late icon in the Coptic Museum in Cairo with two dog-headed figures, called Ahraqas and Oghani cannot be an illustration of the Christophorus legend. They may depict the cynocephalus servants of Saint Mercurius. [37]

The prohibition of the cult was not necessarily accompanied by the disappearance of the belief in the numinous power of a place. Thus the healing centre of Menuthis continued to exist in a christianized form. Under patriarch Cyrillus the relics of the Martyrs Cyrus and Johannes were transferred here. [38] Yet, even after that, a secret heathen cult remained alive in Menuthis up to the end of the 5th century. [39]

Another instance of continuity can be seen in Deir el-Bahari where the sanatorium of Imhotep and Amenhotep-Son-of-Hapu was replaced by the monastery of Phoibammon, again a place of healing. [40]

The cult of *trees* is a common feature in the folk religion of both the ancient Egyptians and the Copts. The persistence of cults of this kind is best exemplified in the Virgin's Tree at Mataryeh at ancient Heliopolis. [41] This tree, associated in Christian times with the visit of the Holy Family to Egypt, originates in one of the tree-cults at Heliopolis. [42] As a possible survival of *animal--worship*, the still existing cult of snakes can be mentioned. [43]

All this evidence points to the fact that while the masses broke with the religion of their ancestors in the 4th century, several centres of paganism survived up to the Arab conquest.

---

[28] A. Erman, ZAS 33 (1895), 47.

[29] G. Zoega, *Catalogus codicum Copticorum...*, p. 457; J. Quaegebeur, *Le dieu égyptien Shai,* Leuven 1975, pp. 39, 161.

[30] Zoega, *Catalogus...*, p. 457.

[31] A. Mallon, *Grammaire copte,* Beyrouth 1956, Chrestomathie 89.

[32] C. Bonner, *Studies in Magical Amulets, Chiefly Graeco-Egyptian,* Ann Arbor 1950, pp. 31 f.; A. Delatte and Ph. Darchain, *Les intailles magiques gréco-égyptiennes,* Paris 1964, p. 102; Z. Ameisonowa, *Journal of the Warburg and Courtauld Institutes* 12 (1949), 44 f.

[33] Delatte-Derhain, *Les intailles...*, pp. 95 ff., no 116.

[34] G. Lanczkowski, MDAIK 14 (1956) Fs. Kees, 117 ff.; D. Wortmann, *Bonner Jahrbücher* 166 (1966), 102f.

[35] P. Perdrizet, MonPiot 34 (1934), 106, fig. 4.

[36] J. Doresse, *Des hiéroglyphes à la croix...*, Instanbul 1960, p. 45; E.N. Maksimow, *Obras Khristophora kinokephala* (Drevnij Vostok Sbornjik 1 k semidesjatpjatpjatiletiju akademika M.A. Korostovtseva), Moscow 1975, pp. 76 ff. (summary 310); P. Saintyves, *Saint Christophe, successeur d'Anubis, d'Hermès et Héraclès,* Paris 1936.

[37] A. Piankoff, BSAC 12 (1040), 57 ff. (inv. no 3375).

[38] R. Herzog, *Der Kampf um den Kult von Menuthis* (Pisciculi. Studien zur Region und Kultur... F.J. Dölger dargeboten), Münster 1039, pp. 117 ff.; Sophronius, *Laudes in SS. Cyrum et Joannem* 27 (Th. Hopfner, *Fontes,* p. 732).

[39] Zacharias Scholastikos, "Vie du Sevère", *Patrologia Orientalis* 2 (Paris 1907), 17 ff.

[40] Doresse, *Des hiéroglyphes...*, pp. 31 f., A. Bataille, *Les inscriptions grecques du temple de Hatsepsout à Deir el-Bahari,* Le Caire 1951; E. Laskowska-Kusztal, "Le sanctuaire ptolémaïque de Deir el-Bahari", dans: *Deir el-Bahari* III, Varsovie 1984.

[41] Doresse, *Des hiéroglyphes...*, p. 27. Cult of a tree at Hermopolis, p. 28.

[42] Sacred trees at Heliopolis: LÄ II, 1112 (Heliopolis, L. Kákosy).

[43] Sheikh Heridi and Th. Hophner, "Der Tierkult der alten Ägypter", DAWW 57, 2 (1913), 142.

COPTIC STUDIES

Aleksander Kakovkin

L'art copte de l'Ermitage

La collection des monuments d'art copte à l'Ermitage (Léningrad) compte plus de 5.500 objets. Les premiers monuments coptes ont paru au musée au début des années 1880. Les œuvres apportées par le conservateur de l'Ermitage W. de Bock (W.G. Bock) de ses deux expéditions en Égypte (1888–89 et 1897–98) ont constitué la base de la collection. En 1920–30 on a complété la collection de l'Ermitage en y ajoutant les monuments coptes de l'ancien musée de l'École d'art de dessin technique du baron A. Stiglitž (plus de 500 étoffes achetées à son temps chez le marchand Th. Graf de Vienne), les collections des académiciens Boris Turaev (étoffes, papyrus, sculptures, ostracons, objets d'art appliqué), Ivan Tolstoy (étoffes, parchemins) et Nicolas Likhatchev (stèles funéraires, plaques avec inscriptions, ostracons, papyrus, parchemins). Des rentrées peu considérables ont eu lieu dans les années d'après (dons, acquisitions des collections privées).

L'Ermitage est fier de sa collection d'étoffes coptes. Actuellement on en compte plus de 3.000. Les objets de la collection permettent de se faire une idée du degré du développement du tissage en Égypte pendant presque un millénaire (IVᵉ–XIIIᵉ siècles), de faire la connaisance de tous les procédés du tissage, de divers espèces d'étoffes et d'objets, nombreuses images et scènes de la mythologie antique et chrétienne, d'une quantité interminable d'arabesques. La plupart des objets sont faits de lin et de laine dans la technique dite gobelin, plus d'une centaine de spécimens en laine pure, près de trois dizaines de soieries, quelques broderies. La collection comprend plus d'une dizaine de tuniques (IVᵉ–IXᵉ siècles) dont la moitié sont celles d'enfants. Les objets de grandes dimensions ne sont pas nombreux et, en général, ils ne sont pas en bon état : une tenture représentant une colonne, deux arbres et les trois têtes de femmes dans les médaillons, Vᵉsiècle (nº 11660); l'autre aux images

de Nikas, Vᵉ–début VIᵉ siècles (nº 11643); et la troisième qui représente la scène de chasse exécutée en technique de toile imprimée, IVᵉ–Vᵉ siècles nº 11658.

Outre les étoffes célèbres avec les sujets antiques (dont la plupart ont été étudiées dans les publications de W. de Bock, M. Mathieu, X. Liapounova) et représentant la déesse de la Terre Gê, IVᵉ siècle (nº 11440), Dionysos avec sa suite, IVᵉ–VIᵉ siècles (nᵒˢ 11334, 11335, 11337 et autres), Aphrodite et Eros, Vᵉ siècle (nº 11620), Douze Travaux d'Hercule, Vᵉ siècle (nº 11337), le Jugement de Pâris, Vᵉ siècle (nº 11507), Orphée, Vᵉ et VIᵉ–VIIᵉ siècles (nᵒˢ 11158, 11159), Ganimède donnant la becquée à l'aigle, Xᵉ–XIᵉ siècles (nº 18582), les scènes de l'Histoire de Phèdre et Hippolyte, IVᵉ–Vᵉ siècles (nº 13139), les saisons personnifiées, VIIᵉ–IXᵉ siècles (nᵒˢ 11645, 11356, 8870, 12942a); les étoffes aux images qui continuent les traditions de l'Ancienne Égypte, tels que les nombreux sujets nilotiques (nᵒˢ 11437, 12535, 12734 et autres), les spécimens à « l'œil de Horus » (l'œil–oudjat), les saintes fleurs de lotus, Vᵉ–VIIIᵉ siècles (nᵒˢ 11647, 11642, 11447 et autres), et enfin, l'étoffe reproduisant l'ancien signe hiérogliphique – ânkh, signifiant « la vie », Vᵉ siècle (nº 11590), sont aussi très intéressantes.

Les étoffes aux images chrétiennes constituent une partie considérable. Parmi elles on peut noter près d'une dizaine de spécimens représentant les épisodes de l'histoire du patriarche Joseph, VIIᵉ–IXᵉ siècles (nᵒˢ 11552, 11176a,b, 12519, 12893 et autres). Les épisodes de l'histoire de David, VIIIᵉ siècle (nᵒˢ 9031, 11547, 11641, 13122a,b et autres), sont reproduits sur quelques étoffes.

Sur un des spécimens est représenté Daniel dans le fossé de lion, IXᵉ siècle (nº 13127). Parmi les sujets du Nouveau Testament on peut souligner une étoffe unique montrant la scène de martyre de la Sainte Thècle, VIᵉ siècle (nº 9094), et les spécimens

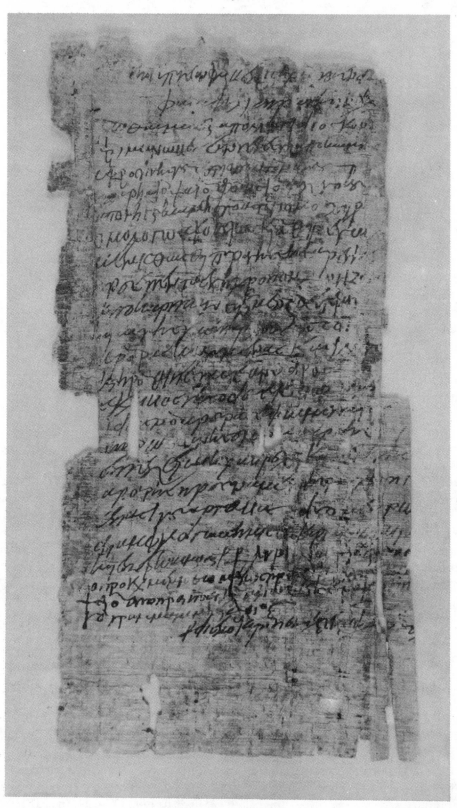

1. Papyrus inv. nº 13428

2. Fragment d'un coffret inv. nº 13221

aux scènes de l'Annonciation, VIIᵉ–VIIIᵉ siècles (nᵒˢ 9025, 12930), et de la Nativité de Christ, VIIIᵉ siècle (nº 11177). Les images des croix, des monogrammes du Christ (des chrismes), des swasticas, et des autres symboles chrétiens sont nombreux. Un tiers d'étoffes sont garnies de divers ornements d'ordre végétal et géometrique.

Nous croyons que la plupart des images sur les étoffes sont liées à la foi au salut, à l'espoir et à la vie éternelle.

La sculpture de la collection de l'Ermitage est bien représentée par les objets en pierre, en bois, en ivoire et en os dont le nombre monte à 120. Ce sont des détails du décor architectural, des stèles funéraires, des plaques avec inscriptions, des parties des meubles démontables, des décorations des petits objets de ménage. La collection se compose des parties de valeurs différentes. Tout de même, elle donne la possibilité de se faire une idée générale sur les tendances principales du développement de l'art plastique copte.

Les détails architecturaux, les stèles funéraires, les plaques avec des images et des inscriptions sont éxecutés, pour la plupart, de calcaire et de grès, quelques spécimens sont de diorite et de marbre.

Notons les spécimens les plus intéressants : une plaque d'espèce d'Ahnas reproduisant la tête d'homme entourée d'une couronne et de branches d'acanthe, Vᵉ siècle (nº 11090), une partie de pilastre qui représente la scène de chasse et le cep, Vᵉ siècle (nº 11076), des reliefs du Vᵉ siècle reproduisant la lutte des bêtes (nº 11090 a) et la lionne nourrissant son lionceau (nº 11091).

Les spécimens à des sujets proprement chrétiens sont peu nombreux mais ils excitent un intérêt évident : le fragment d'une stèle de calcaire datée de la fin du IVᵉ siècle reproduisant Daniel dans le fossé de lion (nº 11151), une partie de plat en marbre avec une inscription du VIIIᵉ siècle et des images des personnages bibliques (David, Saul[?] et autres), IVᵉ–Vᵉ siècles (nº 11106), quelques monuments du Vᵉ siècle : une plaque représentant le sacrifice d'Isaac (nº 11090a), un relief d'un vase flanqué de deux oiseaux (nº 11089), une tête d'ange (nº 5505), une plaque avec une croix à monogramme en relief au milieu d'une couronne (nº 11077).

Plus d'une demi-centaine de spécimens sont des stèles funéraires dont le tiers sont garnies d'images et portent des inscriptions. D'habitude, ils sont

3. Plaque d'Ahnas inv. nº 11090

datés VIᵉ–VIIᵉ siècle. Les autres, ayant des inscriptions, proviennent en général de l'époque arabe.

Plusieurs stèles avec des inscriptions ont été analysées dans les publications (B. Turaev, P. Ernstedt, A. Elanskaija), celles aux images sont moin célèbres.

On peut considérer les monuments de la période transitoire, c'est-à-dire, ceux du IIᵉ au IVᵉ siècles, comme prédécesseurs des stèles coptes. Parmi ces spécimens, comparativement rares, on trouve une stèle représentant le buste d'un décédé, acheté par W. de Bock à Coptos (nᵒ 5701). Ce monument a des analogies (Le Caire, Berlin) et est daté fin du IIᵉ–début du IIIᵉ siècles et témoigne des liens variés entre l'Égypte et la Syrie. Une plaque avec une inscription grecque consacrée à Démètre et à Core (nᵒ 8859) se rapporte au début du IIIᵉ siècle.

Les stèles de la fin du IIIᵉ–début du IVᵉ siècles provenant de Kom Abou Billou (dont la plupart sont gardées à Michigan et au Caire) composent un groupe intéressant. Il y a trois monuments de ce genre à l'Ermitage (nᵒˢ 5702, 5703, 5704).

« La stèle de Pétosyris, moine et médecin », VIᵉ(?) siècle (nᵒ 11074) et une plaque de fragments avec le reste d'une inscription (nᵒ 11075) se rapportent à des monuments funéraires en marbre rare.

Une plaque avec une inscription en mémoire du presbytère et du moine Patermoutius est datée de 574–575 (nᵒ 11115).

Les éléments du décor des stèles les plus répandus sont : croix = ânkh (nᵒˢ 11080, 11081, 11085, 11086, 13292), croix (nᵒˢ 11078, 11079, 11082, 13290), portique du temple (nᵒˢ 11080, 11082, 11108, 11109, 11110, 11112 et autres), parfois avec une ouverture-porte (nᵒ 11094). Les images d'orantes (nᵒˢ 11105, 11110, 11111, 11112) et d'oiseaux personnifiant les âmes des décédés sont assez fréquentes (nᵒˢ 11107, 11108, 11109).

La stèle « en mémoire de l'abbé Moïse » est datée de 795 (nᵒ 2955).

La plupart des stèles de l'Ermitage sont composées de plaques en fragments avec le reste des inscriptions qui sont difficiles à lire et, en cette raison, difficiles à dater.

Les monuments de sculpture en bois sont peu nombreux. Le plus célèbre d'entre eux est un grand panneau en bois représentant les scènes de paysage nilotique sculptées et peintes en peintures de cire, IVᵉ–Vᵉ siècles (nᵒ 10296). Excitent l'intérêt : une planche avec un demi-cercle flanqué de deux couples de bêtes, VIᵉ–VIIᵉ siècles (nᵒ 10292), un tableau représentant un temple au fronton appuyé sur deux colonnes et une croix là-dedans, VIᵉ–VIIᵉ siècles (nᵒ 8675) et un détail de meuble reproduisant un cerf, Vᵉ siècle (nᵒ 4977). La collection comprend deux peignes, l'un du VIᵉ siècle (nᵒ 10299) et l'autre de VIIIᵉ–IXᵉ siècles (nᵒ 13255).

La collection des sculptures en ivoire comprend deux dizaines de spécimens et est très variée en thèmes. On y trouve des objets d'ouvrage alexandrin qui sont étroitement liés par leur technique d'exécution et leur sujets aux traditions hellénistiques : Eros (nᵒˢ 2433, 10331), danseuses (nᵒ 10330), guerrier s'appuyant contre le pavois (nᵒ 5067), homme avec un poisson (nᵒ 10329), créature fantastique reproduisant un demi-homme demi-oiseau (nᵒ 10332), plaques aux ornements végétaux (nᵒˢ 10335, 10337, 10338), des lamelles aux images des scènes de chasse (nᵒˢ E 761, E 762, E 763) et des oiseaux (nᵒˢ E 758, E 760, E 764, E 765, E 766); un groupe de soi-disant « poupées » —amulettes que les femmes utilisaient comme un moyen pour avoir des descendants (nᵒˢ 5068, 6356, 10364–10370).

Trois médaillons d'ivoire exécutés en technique primitive représentent des cavaliers (nᵒˢ 10357, 10358, 10360) dont nous trouvons de nombreuses analogies sur les étoffes, sur les objets en métaux, dans la peinture.

La collection des objets en métaux de l'Ermitage compte plus de 450 exemplaires d'objets de ménage et d'église. Elle est représentée par les objets d'art en bronze, en laiton, en fer, en plomb datés de la fin du IIIᵉ–XIIIᵉ siècles. La destination des objets est très variée : flambeaux, candélabres, cassolettes, toutes sortes de vases, clochettes, petites figures de bêtes et d'oiseaux, petits autels, diadèmes, médaillons, croix etc. Il faut mettre un accent particulier sur le revêtement de laiton d'un coffret en bois sur lequel sont représentés Dionysos avec une suite s'égayante, IVᵉ siècle (nᵒ 13221), un vase de bronze à l'encens, Vᵉ siècle (nᵒ 10647) décrit dans une publication de W. de Bock et une cassolette de bronze reproduisant un cheval, VIIᵉ–VIIIᵉ siècles (nᵒ 11619). Les candélabres coptes de l'Ermitage (nᵒˢ 10578, 10581–10590) ont été étudiés par N. Križanovskaja.

La collection des céramiques coptes de l'Ermitage n'est pas grande mais elle est assez intéressante. Elle consiste, essentiellement, en vases de différentes destinations, entiers ou en fragments, en flambeaux aux reliefs de grenouilles, croix, chrismes, inscriptions chrétiennes; cachets à apposer des scelles sur les vases; on y trouve toutes les formes de soi-disant ampoules de Saint Ménas. Particulièrement intéressants sont: un vase avec le portrait de femme (n° 10195) et un fragment de la croix en argile avec les poisson peints en couleurs, VIᵉ siècle (n° 10211). L'étude de M. Matthieu a montré qu'en céramiques coptes les anciennes traditions s'embrouillent étroitement aux sujets chrétiens.

La colletion des monuments de la peinture de chevalet copte de l'Ermitage n'est pas grande. Outre neuf fragments des portraits de Fayoum (n°ˢ 2949–2951, 2964, 2965a,b, 2966, 5051, 8855) étudiés dans une publication de A. Strelkov elle comprend: portrait funéraire d'homme, exécuté en détrempe, IVᵉ–Vᵉ siècles (n° 8684) dont les analogies sont faussement considérées comme les détails de meubles ou les ornements de plafonds; deux monuments de la peinture d'encaustique de la fin du VIᵉ–début du VIIᵉ siècles, le battant droit d'un triptique représentant un guerrier debout devant son cheval (n° 10297) et une icône avec le buste d'un guerrier (n° 18348). Il faut aussi y classer un fragment en détrempe exécuté sur la toile et représentant la scène du « Baptême », Xᵉ–XIᵉ siècles (n° 11257). Malheureusement, ces œuvres sont en mauvais état.

En outre, la collection comprend: verre (vases, vaisselles, flacons à parfums et à médicaments), cuir (ceintures, souliers, croix etc.), nacre (croix), etc.

Grâce aux publications de O. von Lemm, G. Zereteli, P. Ernstedt, O. Krüger, les spécialistes connaissent bien la collection de l'Ermitage qui compte plus de 700 numéros et qui comprend

4. Fragment de céramique copte

5. Fragment de croix en argile inv. n° 10211

6. Fragment de plat

7. Étoffe copte inv. n° 11642

8. Icône inv. n° 18346

papyrus, parchemins, ostracons représentant des documents administratifs, économiques et privés, des textes littéraires et liturgiques.

Le nombre de monuments coptes de l'Ermitage, la diversité des matériaux et des techniques d'exécution qui y sont représentés, l'ample diapason chronologique de ses monuments leur attachent beaucoup d'importance artistique et historique et les placent au même rang avec les collections les plus importantes du monde.

La plupart des monuments de la collection de l'Ermitage ne sont analysée dans aucune publication. Presque toutes les œuvres de la peinture ont été publiées, celles de céramique ont été étudiées passablement, on a édité des travaux sur près de la moitié de monuments écrits tels que papyrus et parchemins, ostracons, quelques spécimens de sculpture et d'objets en métal, et seulement la cinquième partie de la collections d'étoffes. C'est pourquoi il y a un vaste champ d'activité pour les savants.

La bibliographie des publications des savants russes et soviétiques sur les thèmes coptes jusqu'à 1976 (y compris des travaux sur les monuments de l'art copte de l'Ermitage) a été éditée par docteur P. Nagel (Halle).

Malheureusement, à cause du manque de locaux la collection est gardée dans les dépôts du musée, depuis plusieurs années.

COPTIC STUDIES

Rodolphe Kasser

A propos des caractéristiques lexicales des dialectes coptes dans divers textes bibliques

Les dialectes coptes (y compris leurs principaux subdialectes) ont été étudiés jusqu'ici presque toujours sur le plan de la phonologie (considérée comme suffisamment connue par leur orthographe) : priorité rendue légitime par les nécessités pratiques, puisque là, même des fragments de textes relativement petits peuvent être classés avec un degré de certitude acceptable.

Cependant, on a répété avec raison que l'analyse interdialectale ne pouvait être réduite à une approche orthographico-phonologique. Chaque fois que c'est possible, elle doit s'étendre aussi aux domaines de la lexicologie et de la morphosyntaxe. Mais, hélas, c'est possible beaucoup moins souvent que pour l'orthographe, car ces approches-là exigent de textes beaucoup plus longs, homogènes, de bonne qualité [1], et ils sont relativement rares...

L'espace qui nous est accordé ici est limité, ce qui nous oblige à limiter aussi, sévèrement, notre sujet. Nous nous en tiendrons donc au seul domaine lexical. La question qui s'y pose est la suivante : les dialectes coptes sont-ils caractérisés, entre autres, par quelques particularités lexicologiques ? Ce que nous enseigne la dialectologie générale nous fera présupposer, raisonnablement, que tel pourrait bien être le cas; cela du moins à certaines condi-tions, qui font partie des conditions d'existence des dialectes eux-mêmes. Pour vérifier cet a priori, il faudra bien, un jour, effectuer cette recherche d'une manière plus systématique et globale que cela n'a été fait jusqu'ici.

Toutefois, le seul domaine lexical, sur lequel nous fixons notre attention dans ce travail, est encore tellement vaste, que nous devrons nous contenter d'en envisager un seul secteur : le vocabulaire de la Bible copte. Cela non seulement pour respecter les limites d'espace qui nous sont fixées ici, mais encore pour un motif de méthodologie. En effet, l'analyse interdialectale est faite avant tout de comparaisons, et en bonne méthode, ne peuvent être comparés que des éléments de nature assez proches pour être comparables. Or si l'usage, ou non, de tel lexème, peut caractériser tout un idiome, il peut dépendre de beaucoup d'autres facteurs encore; d'abord il sera évidemment fonction du genre littéraire, et du sujet traité; et si l'on constate que la Bible est attestée, au moins en quelque passage, dans tous les principaux dialectes coptes (sinon dans tous leurs subdialectes), aucun des autres secteurs de la littérature copte (au sens le plus large) n'est aussi complètement attesté [2]. En outre l'usage, ou non, de tel lexème, sera aussi

[1] Les textes en trop mauvais état n'offrent à l'analyse, dans ce domaine, qu'une base fort incertaine (ainsi par.ex. le papyrus *M* de Milan, éd. Orlandi–Quecke 1974, quelle que soit la qualité de l'édition): une lacune malencontreusement placée (« trou » du à une détérioration du manuscrit) peut facilement dissimuler un élément essentiel, et fausser ainsi l'appréciation d'ensemble qu'on croit pouvoir porter sur un texte donné.

[2] Un rapide examen de la question (en ne tenant compte ici que des dialectes « chefs de groupes » et en divisant grosso modo le domaine des écrits coptes en cinq genres littéraires seulement: Bible, littérature chrétienne [au sens le plus large], gnose, manichéisme, textes non littéraires) donne ceci : *A* Bi., Lchr.,−,−,−; *L* (avec *İ* etc.) Bi., Lchr., Gn., Ma., nlitt. (mais il y a un important subdialecte pour Bi., un autre pour Lchr. et Gn., un troisième pour Ma. ! [cf. *infra*, note 4]); *M* Bi., Lchr., −, −, nlitt. ?; *F* Bi., Lchr.,−,−, nlitt.; *S* (avec *P*) Bi., Lchr., Gn.,−, nlitt.; *B* Bi., Lchr., −,−, nlitt. Ce sujet mériterait évidemment d'être examiné d'une manière moins sommaire, en soumettant le champ des écrits coptes à une analyse plus subtile, génératrice d'une subdivision plus diversifiée; et il serait nécessaire de distinguer aussi les dialectes « chefs de groupes » de leurs principaux subdialectes (spécialement à l'intérieur de *L*); faute d'espace, nous ne pouvons pas le faire ici. Mais la présentation succincte ci-dessus, jointe à l'estimation du volume des attestations textuelles dans chaque dialecte (infra, note 4) suffit aux modestes besoins de la présente étude, et fait en tous cas apparaître comme vraisemblable que probablement nous connaissons la totalité du vocabulaire d'aucun de ces idiomes : pas même de *S* (env. 90 % du tout), qui est hélas totalement absent du domaine de Ma., où la densité et richesse du vocabulaire est exceptionnelle (ce qui compense un peu, pour *L*, la relative brièveté de l'attestation textuelle totale).

fonction des goûts personnels de l'auteur (auteur de la version copte d'un texte grec le plus souvent). Ces facteurs non dialectaux, facilement capables de rendre inopérante l'analyse lexicale interdialectale, ne peuvent être rendus assez innofensifs que si quelques conditions très favorables sont réunies : analyse comparative limitée aux mots d'usage relativement banal, utilisés en dehors de toute spécialisation (trop étroitement liée à quelque domaine littéraire particulier), et peu susceptibles d'attirer l'attention d'un auteur soucieux de l'efficacité ou de la beauté de son style; ou s'il s'agit malgré tout de mots d'un usage un peu spécialisé (vocabulaire théologique, hagiographique, etc.), existence d'importantes sections hétérodialectales de versions du même texte (l'idéal, probablement inaccessible, étant évidemment que ces versions soient du même auteur)[3], ce qui (d'où notre choix dans le présent travail) existe certes, mais n'existe guère que pour certaines sections (les plus lues) de la Bible, et dans certains dialectes seulement. Pourquoi donc?... alors que l'immense majorité des textes coptes est biblique ou de culture chrétienne (ce qui devrait nous garantir les conditions d'analyse les plus favorables possibles)? Parce que la quantité de texte attestant les divers dialectes coptes présente d'énormes et désastreuses disproportions[4]. Si l'on se rapelle que chaque auteur s'exprime dans son propre idiolecte, dont le stock lexical est l'une des composantes majeures[5], on pourra certes négliger le facteur idiolectal en lexicologie dans un dialecte (par.ex. S) richement attesté, par plus de cent textes importants et issus d'auteurs différents. Mais que dire d'un idiome tel que M par exemple ?... où, à part quelques bribes insignifiantes en ce qui concerne la présente recherche, on est en présence de trois stocks lexicaux idiolectaux seulement (et encore est-ce une chance qu'ils appartiennent tous à la Bible, et même au Nouveau Testament) : celui de l'évangile de Matthieu, celui des Actes des apôtres, et celui du papyrus de Milan, des épîtres pauliniennes (malheureusement criblé de lacunes, ce qui le désavantage gravement). Ces conditions fort aléatoires font qu'on peut certes connaître un petit nombre des caractéristiques lexicales de M (par.ex. l'usage de ⲧⲣⲟⲩⲣ 'hâte', ⲍⲛⲧⲟⲩⲟⲩ 's'installer pour manger', ou l'adverbe ⲉⲡⲟⲁⲛ 'en bas'). Mais combien d'autres nous échappent dans l'état actuel de notre documentation !... car la totalité des textes M n'atteint pas même le deux-centième de la totalité des textes S[6].

---

[3] Très rares seront sans doute les cas où l'analyse du texte de tel et tel livres (ou selections de livres) de la Bible copte permettra de conclure qu'ils sont sortis de la plume d'un même auteur (cette analyse restant d'ailleurs encore à faire), encore que les différences de style entre ces auteurs divers aient pu être atténuées dans une certaine mesure par les procédés de révision auxquels furent vraisemblablement soumis les textes primitifs devant former ce monument officiel qu'est la version saïdique classique (et de même la version bohaïrique classique). Nous disposons néanmoins d'un avantage (d'importance secondaire quoique non négligeable) en ce que tous les textes bibliques connus en A et L (sans parler de P proto-S et de Í7 proto-L), et en outre un texte F au moins (Ephésiens et Philippiens dans Engelbreth 1811), appartiennent manifestement à la version saïdique classique, qu'ils en soient un stade préparatoire (comme on sera tenté de le supposer a priori pour P et Í7 dialectalement très archaïques), ou qu'ils aient été traduits directement de S pour les besoins de la mission chrétienne dans certaines campagnes où S était mal compris au IVe siècle (comme c'est vraisemblablement le cas pour A et L, éventuellement F en partie). La comparaison lexicale S vs A, S vs L, etc. en est grandement facilitée et rendue beaucoup plus sûre.
[4] En évaluant la longueur de ces supports textuels dialectaux en unités d'un « millier de lettres » de texte (mlt), une estimation très sommaire de toute la littérature copte attestée en manuscrits du IIIe au XIIIe siècle nous donne grosso modo un total qu'on peut situer autour de 40.000 mlt. Dans ce total, S se taille la part du lion, entre 30.000 et 40.000 mlt, fixons arbitrairement ce nombre à 36.000 (???) mlt (=90 % du tout). Les autres idiomes n'ont pour eux que des miettes : grosse miette pour B avec ses 3000 (??) mlt (7,5 %); petites miettes pour tous les autres (où nous divisons le « lycopolitain » ou « subakhmîmique » dans ses trois branches principales : L6, appelé précédemment L, est l'idiome des textes gnostiques (non S) de Nag Hammadi, et encore, des Acta Pauli de Heidelberg (Schmidt 1905); L5 est l'idiome de l'évangile de Jean (Thompson 1924), etc. (mss. inédits); L4 est l'idiome des textes manichéens (Allberry 1938, Böhlig 1966, Polotsky 1934c, [Schmidt ...] 1940) : A 235 (0,5 %), Í etc. 1,5(!), L6 140 (0,3 %), L5 55 (0,1 %), L4 430 (1 %), M 155 (0,4 %), V 25 (0,05 %), F 135 (0,3 %), H 15 (0,03 %), F7 40 (0,1 %), B 74 130 (0,3 %), G 1,5 (!), P 40 (0,1 %). Si donc l'on peut s'attendre, a priori, à connaître à peu près tout le vocabulaire de S (cf. cependant supra, note 2), cette connaissance est déjà beaucoup plus aléatoire en ce qui concerne B, et elle reste tout à fait insuffisante en ce qui concerne les autres idiomes coptes : si (à part quelques mots d'usage tout à fait banal et courant) tel ou tel lexème n'apparaît pas dans les trop brefs et rares textes qui attestent tel ou tel de ces dialectes, cela ne prouve en aucune manière qu'il n'a jamais fait usage de ce lexème, et que cette absence, systématique, est l'une de ses caractéristiques proprement dialectales.
[5] « L'idiolecte est au départ la seule réalité que rencontre le dialectologue » (Dubois 1973, idiolecte, 249b).
[6] Cf. supra, note 4.

*

En limitant au domaine de la Bible copte notre étude lexicale interdialectale, nous assurerons à sa base textuelle une homogénéité appréciable [7]. Reste à savoir, cependant, si une même qualité d'homogénéité existe entre les divers « dialectes » coptes pris en considération ici [8]; question essentielle pour celui qui voudra utiliser les résultats de cette étude pour situer géographiquement les idiomes coptes les uns par rapport aux autres [9]. Négligeons provisoirement le problème que peut poser en soi l'énorme disproportion d'attestation de ces idiomes [10]. Il reste que, si nous nous en tenons à notre schéma de géographie dialectale copte le plus récent (Kasser 1982c: 68–71), schéma basé essentiellement sur l'étude des voyelles toniques, et qu'il sera tout à fait indiqué de confronter aux quelques réalités que nous révèlera la présente analyse lexicale (limitée, cf. supra), et en laissant de côté ici tous les protodialectes [11], métadialectes et mésodialectes [12] et subdialectes [13] divers (leur assise textuelle est le plus souvent très maigre et pauvre), même ainsi, parmi les idiomes coptes vraiment importants [14], il convient d'opérer une distinction de qualité (tous ne sont pas de même rang). Certains sont de vrais « dialectes » (avec le plein sens particulariste qu'implique ce terme) en tant qu'idiomes *locaux* restés tels pendant toute leur existence, ainsi d'une part A, M et F (relativement peu neutralisés), éventuellement

aussi V (fayoumique sans lambdacisme, ou fayoumique le plus neutralisé [ayant peut-être tendu à devenir, mais sans grand succès apparement, la langue véhiculaire de la Moyenne–Égypte ?]). Et d'autre part nous avons des idiomes à vocation supradialectale; dialectes locaux aussi à leur origine (vraisemblablement), ils ont progressivement envahi les régions dialectales voisines, dont ils sont devenus peu à peu (partiellement ou totalement) la langue véhiculaire, se neutralisant eux-mêmes de plus en plus par les contacts interdialectaux intenses provoqués par ce processus. Ainsi probablement l'une ou l'autre des trois variétés principales [15] de L (où deux d'entre elles, ou toutes les trois ensemble, chacune en sa section de la Valée du Nil), cela cependant seulement à l'aube du copte littéraire, puisque très tôt S, immigré depuis le nord, est venu jouer dans la même région le même rôle, evec plus de succès encore (il en est résulté l'extinction de L avec A et M, et V sans doute aussi). Ainsi certainement encore S et B, devenus respectivement la langue véhiculaire la plus puissante, puis la langue littéraire unique, de la Vallée du Nil (avec le Fayoum) d'une part, du Delta d'autre part [16].

Ici, nous ne nous occuperons pas de B *langue* du Delta, puisque nous ne connaissons pas les « dialectes » locaux (ont-ils existé ?) que cette « langue » a pu dominer, puis étouffer [17].

Mais si l'on considère la Vallée du Nil, dont la

[7] Certes, nous savons tous que la Bible n'est pas *un* ouvrage, écrit par *un* auteur, mais une bibliothèque de « livres » en tous points fort diverse. Ils sont unis cependant par des liens spirituels indéniables, qui donnent *grosso modo* au style de la Bible et aux sujets qu'elle aborde une certaine unité. Nous devrons bien, ici, nous en contenter.

[8] Cf. supra, note 4.

[9] Déduction tout à fait légitime et prévisible; on a fait très souvent le même usage des résultats de l'analyse phonologique comparée des dialectes coptes (par.ex. Worrell 1934, 63–82; Kahle 1954, 193–257, Vergote 1973a, 53–59.

[10] Cf. supra, note 6.

[11] Kasser 1980–1 (I), 63; etc.

[12] Ibid. 60; etc.

[13] Ibid. 67; etc.

[14] « Dialectes » dits « chefs de groupes », Kasser 1980–1 (III), 117.

[15] Cf. supra, note 4.

[16] À propos de cette division géographique bipartite de l'Égypte, remontant à la plus haute tradition pharaonique, et sensible même aujourd'hui dans l'Égypte moderne, il faut observer qu'on a affaire, là, à deux parties sensiblement égales et comparables (en ce qui concerne les surfaces cultivables, le nombre d'habitants, etc.). Nous tenons à remercier ici G. Haeny qui nous l'a confirmé lors de notre conversation du 26 juillet 1984.

[17] Cette ignorance provient sans doute en très grande partie de l'extrême rareté des manuscrits coptes anciens qui ont pu être récupérés dans le Delta : le sol de cette région est trop humide; il y pleut en hiver même sur les déserts voisins des terres cultivées (déserts pratiquement toujours secs ailleurs et capables de ce fait de conserver les papyrus et parchemins qu'on y a enfouis). Si l'on compare la proportion des textes S et de ceux d'autres dialectes trouvés dans la Vallée du Nil (environ 45 contre 1 de tous les autres ensemble), on ne s'étonne guère de n'avoir, pour cette vaste région, que des documents B(à l'exception des miettes textuelles G, dont l'origine géographique n'est pas assurée, cf. Kasser 1975d). On se demandera d'autre part si la configuration géographique du Delta est favorable à une division de la langue en parlers locaux, dialectes et subdialectes : vaste plaine

langue est partout *S*, recouvrant *L* quasi-
« langue » aussi environ d'Achmounein[18] à
Assouan, *S* seul (d'Achmounein au Caire ?) ou *S* et
L (plus au sud) recouvrant ensemble tous les
dialectes locaux de ces 800 km d'étroit territoire
linguistique, on peut y pressentir l'existence de
rapports interdialectaux extrêmement complexes,
ayant des implications sur le plan social aussi
(comme nous le verrons plus loin). Ces rapports ne
peuvent trouver une place satisfaisante et suffisante en quelque concept trop idéalement simple
et linéaire d'une succession géographique d'idiomes a−b−c−d−e, b étant à situer entre a et c
parce qu'il leur ressemble plus qu'à d ou e, c étant
entre b et d parce qu'il leur ressemble plus qu'à a et
e, lesquels sont aux deux bouts de la file parce que
c'est eux qui ont, entre eux, le moins de points
communs; etc. C'est vraisemblablement (avec tout
ce que ces contacts comportent d'influences et
d'interactions neutralisatrices réciproques) *L* en
contact à la fois avec *A* (et d'autres dialectes locaux
encore inconnus?) et *M* (et peut-être même avec *V*
et [à la limite] *B* [sous la forme de son subdialecte
méridional *B74*])[19], et *S* partout bien sûr; c'est *A*
en contact, au sud, avec quelque dialecte local
probablement assez semblable à lui, mais surtout
confronté à *L* (dialecte local puis quasi-langue
supradialectale) partout, et de même à *S*; c'est *M* en
contact avec *L* au sud et avec *V* au nord[20], avec *L*
peut-être partout, et surtout (dans tout le territoire
autochtone de *M*) avec *S*; c'est *F* (surtout sous la
forme de son subdialecte *V*) en contact avec *M* (et

peut-être aussi *L* septentrional) et avec *S* (dialecte
local puis langue supradialectale) partout; des
contacts *V-B74* peuvent raisonnablement être
envisagés[21]; c'est *S* enfin en contact avec tous les
autres dialectes[22] coptes, comme on a pu le voir
plus haut: *A*, *L*, *M*, *V* (et *F*), *B* (contacts frontaliers
seulement, puisque *S* n'a pu s'infiltrer substantiel-
lement dans le Delta, comme *B* n'a pu pénétrer
fortement dans la Vallée avant les périodes tardives où de toute manière l'ensemble de la langue
copte était près de s'éteindre[23].

Il faut en venir maintenant aux implications
sociales de l'existence, l'usage et l'interaction des
« dialectes » coptes. En effet, l'usage de tout
idiome n'est pas limité seulement dans le cadre de
la géographie; il l'est aussi dans le temps, et à
l'intérieur de la société où il existe, société où l'on
peut distinguer diverses couches, dont toutes ne lui
sont pas favorables. Un dialecte naît et meurt, sa
« mort » apparente n'étant souvent qu'une
métamorphose, par laquelle il survit cependant en
quelque autre forme linguistique, sous l'influence
contraignante de divers facteurs intérieurs et ex-
térieurs. Mais même pendant son existence, il est
utilisé par certaines couches de la population plus
que par d'autres. Le dialecte est en effet l'expression d'un particularisme se développant chez certains usagers que l'universalisme relatif de la
langue supradialectale intéresse peu, ou n'intéresse
pas; ou qui même considèrent cet universalisme
avec méfiance, comme un danger d'hégémonie
centralisatrice, se développant au détriment des

_____

ouverte, que ne fragmentent (un peu) que les deux bras principaux du Nil (en négligeant les bras secondaires et les canaux qui en
dérivent); toute autre est la Vallée du Nil, étroite et démesurément longue bande de terres cultivables enserrée entre deux
déserts: on doit naturellement s'attendre à y trouver divers idiomes se succédant le long du Nil, « comme les perles d'un
collier ».

[18] Ou même encore un peu plus au nord?

[19] Cf. Kasser 1980–1 (III), 93–94. Nous ne pouvons pas évoquer ici le problème très particulier posé par l'hypothèse du contact
de *L* primitif avec *P* à Thèbes ou dans ses environs, cf. Kasser 1982a.

[20] Éventuellement avec *B* (sous sa forme *B74*, cf. note 19) à travers *V*.

[21] Cf. notes 19 et 20.

[22] Au sens habituel du terme.

[23] On a bien sûr encore, coiffant tout cela, le grec en tant que langue véhiculaire administrative de toute l'Égypte, Delta y
compris (mais langue *étrangère* quant à son origine, régie par un système morphosyntaxique fondamentalement différent de
celui de l'égyptien, même copte, ce qui annihile l'interaction). Le grec d'Égypte fournit à la langue copte un très important
apport de termes techniques spécialisés: cela en dosages différents selon les dialectes, etc. semble-t-il, certains termes d'emprunt
étant préférés ici, évités là, en fonction des domaines littéraires, et des sujets abordés aussi, ou pour d'autres motifs (pour
pratiquement chaque terme copto-grec utilisé dans la langue copte, il existe un équivalent copte autochtone sémantiquement
acceptable, même s'il a été écarté parfois parce que, par.ex., la sensibilité copte, chrétienne orthodoxe, lui trouvait une
connotation dangereuse [païenne, hérétique, etc.]; inversement, le terme autochtone a pu être préféré localement au terme grec
parce que le second, bien que techniquement plus précis et paraissant rendre plus exactement [même en identité parfaite]
l'original de la version copte, paraissait trop difficile à comprendre pour le grand public copte). Dans la présente étude, nous ne
faisons que très parcimonieusement recours à l'usage dialectal des mots copto-grecs (d'autres paramètres s'ajoutant à ceux
régissant l'usage dialectal des mots autochtones, et nous ne pouvons traiter ce problème ici). On trouvera diverses indications à
ce sujet dans Böhlig 1958a (voir sa bibliographie pour les travaux plus anciens); Kasser 1966d; Funk 1982; Diethart-Satzinger
1983.

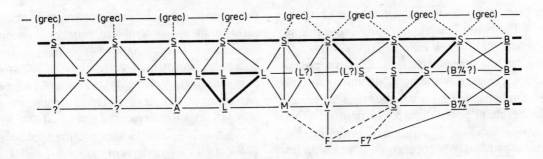

liberté dont jouissent les collectivités locales; d'où, souvent, la tendance à utiliser le dialecte comme langue semi-secrète propre à un groupe local ou régional, permettant à ses membres de communiquer entre eux, à l'abri des oreilles indiscrètes de ceux qui sont étrangers à ce groupe par leur origine, ou pour progresser dans leur carrière et élargir leurs horizons, se sont volontairement distancés de lui (ayant opté pour la centralisation et pour l'usage de la langue supradialectale). La vitalité du dialecte va donc avec la vitalité des forces centrifuges, et elle décroît à mesure que se renforce le courant centralisateur et unificateur. Le dialecte naît fréquemment du fractionnement d'une *koiné* (égyptienne autochtone en ce qui nous concerne ici), et ce fractionnement va de pair avec un affaiblissement cultural[24], avec la perte d'une partie du stock lexical; le niveau culturel de chaque zone dialectale baisse (la proportion des usagers du dialecte par rapport à ceux de la langue supradialectale augmente, au point que l'usage du dialecte pénètre même dans les couches supérieures de la population, celles qui sont aptes à produire des œuvres littéraires, et c'est ainsi que le dialecte peut en arriver à connaître, pour quelque temps, une existence littéraire). Or à cette baisse correspond un appauvrissement du stock lexical: on se contente d'un choix de mots plus restreint, choix qui varie d'une zone dialectale à l'autre, d'où le fait que tel dialecte est parfois le seul à avoir

conservé, du stock primitif, tel mot que tous les autres ont abondonné.

Puis il arrive que les forces centralisatrices reprennent le dessus, et voici que naît (généralement d'un dialecte particulièrement actif et favorisé par le développement économique de sa région) une nouvelle *koiné* (qui se forme progressivement, par neutralisation de ce dialecte au contact des principaux parmi ses voisins, éventuellement ses concurrents dans ce développement vers un rôle de langue véhiculaire, supradialectale). Dans les régions qu'envahit cette *koiné* copte (où le dialecte qui la devient peu à peu apparaît comme un dialecte immigré, sorti de la région dont il est le dialecte autochtone), son utilité (économique) reconnue fait qu'elle est adoptée par des couches de plus en plus larges de la population, au détriment du nombre des usagers du dialecte local, autochtone; en sorte que ce dernier, s'il a eu la chance d'être écrit pendant quelque temps, se met alors à dépérir, et en vient même à mourir sur le plan littéraire[25] (le seul qu'on puisse observer en copte, langue morte)[26].

Au cours de ce processus (à variantes multiples) se manifestent évidemment toutes sortes d'interactions réciproques (dont beaucoup transforment leurs protagonistes en les induisant à accepter des compris). Leur source énergétique réside avant tout dans le fait que la plus grande partie de la population de cette région parle à la fois, plus ou

---

[24] En Égypte, cet affaiblissement pourrait bien avoir eu l'une de ses causes principales dans les atteintes répétées et durables à l'identité égyptienne ayant suivi la perte de l'indépendance politique au VIᵉ siècle avant notre ère, sous diverses dominations étrangères successives; dont, dans les derniers siècles avant notre ère, l'hellénisation très poussée de l'administration du pays consécutive à sa conquête par Alexandre le Grand: désormais, les nouveaux pharaons de l'Égypte étaient de culture grecque plus qu'égyptienne. Tout le poids culturel qu'on ajoutait au grec en Égypte, on l'enlevait évidemment à la langue autochtone.

[25] Terme entendu ici dans son sens le plus large: toutes les manifestations *écrites* de la langue (y compris les textes dits « non littéraires », cf. supra, note 2).

[26] Il est évident que presque toujours une langue ou un dialecte que l'on n'écrit plus, continue à survivre de quelque manière (en évoluant bien sûr) en tant que moyen d'expression purement oral.

moins bien, aussi bien le dialecte que la *koiné* copte[27]. Pourquoi? ... par nécessité économique sans doute, car ce « bilinguisme » dialecte––koiné[28] (même trilinguisme là où *S* se superpose à *L* se superposant lui–même à quelque dialecte local) est indispensable à la collaboration de toutes les couches de la population participant à l'éffort économique commun[29]. Ainsi le dialecte local est contaminé par la *koiné* copte, qu'il contamine lui aussi, du moins localement. Pour jouer son rôle avec plus d'efficacité, et être comprise de tous, si possible, cette *koiné* tend à adopter régionalement (en les adaptant à sa phonologie) plusieurs lexèmes empruntés au dialecte local, lexèmes que, à l'origine, et avant cette contamination, elle n'utilisait pas, et que dans d'autres régions elle rejetterait en les considérant comme mal adaptés, désuets, ou inintelligibles pour quelque autre motif[30]. Ainsi ne s'étonnera-t-on pas de trouver en *S* surtout, mais aussi en *L*, et en *B* (à cause de ses tentatives de pénétrer dans le nord de la Vallée du Nil)[31], un stock lexical relativement grand et complet, tendant à devenir pan-copte; et de trouver dans ce

stock (en *S* ou en *B*) l'usage, rare mais attesté, de certains mots qui semblent propres à tel dialecte local ou à la « langue » voisine (où ils sont courants) plutôt qu'à cette *koiné* et « langue » coptes: ainsi *S* ⲙ̄ⲡϣⲁ 'beaucoup', terme appartenant plutôt au vocabulaire caractéristique de *A* et *L*(*S* dit normalement ⲉⲙⲁⲧⲉ, que n'ont ni *A* ni *L*); ou *S* ϯ ϫⲓ 'allaiter', terme typique de *B*, ϯ ϭⲓ (*S* dit normalement ⲧⲥⲛ̄ⲕⲟ [avec *L* et *F*], ou parfois ϯⲉⲕⲓⲃⲉ [expression en revanche typique de *A*]); ou *B* ⲙ̇ϩⲁⲗ *sic* 'serviteur, esclave', caractéristique de *S*, ϩⲙ̄ϩⲁⲗ ,avec *A L M* et probablement aussi *F* (*B* dit normalement ⲃⲱⲕ lexème apparaissant exceptionnellement aussi en *F*)[32].

Cela peut être aussi, bien sûr, le résultat individuel et accidentel du travail « hybride » d'un traducteur dont la langue maternelle était tel dialecte copte local, et qui inconsciemment s'y référait tout en croyant s'exprimer dans telle *koiné* copte à l'état pur; ou l'influence d'un original dialectal sur sa version en *koiné*; ou tout phénomène ponctuel de ce genre[33]. Mais ce peut être aussi la preuve de

---

[27] Seuls les moins doués et les plus ignorants ne parlent que le dialecte (exclusivement local). Et à l'opposé, il peut se trouver même, dans les couches supérieures de la population, une petite minorité d'intellectuels affectant de ne pas comprendre du tout le dialecte local. Cette minorité, et quelques autres, s'efforcera en outre de parler le mieux possible la *koiné* grecque, qui leur ouvre des horizons encore plus vastes que la *koiné* copte, curiosité d'autant plus légitime qu'avec l'avènement du christianisme et au moins jusqu'au concile de Chalcédoine (451) le principal centre de diffusion et de décisions de la nouvelle religion égyptienne se trouve hors d'Égypte, en plein pays hellénophone, entre les mains de Grecs ou de dignitaires profondément hellénisés.

[28] Cette sorte de « bilinguisme » à l'intérieur d'une même langue (l'égyptien) est sans doute facile à pratiquer; il est donc accessible même à des couches de la population médiocres, au niveau intellectuel plutôt bas, et c'est par lui sans doute que divers lexèmes de tel dialecte s'infiltrent dans tel autre, enrichissant son stock lexical. Radicalement différent est le bilinguisme égypto-grec (malgré l'enrichissement lexical qu'il a apporté au copte [non au grec local !... ou presque pas] par l'incorporation de nombreux mots grecs, devenus copto-grecs, dans la langue copte): dans ce bilinguisme-là, on a affaire à deux mondes, culturels et linguistiques, presque en tous points étrangers l'un à l'autre.

[29] L'interaction sera donc non seulement de tel dialecte local sur ses voisins, dans leurs territoires respectifs, mais encore de tel et tel idiome en tel phonateur d'un dialecte local voisin, immigré hors de la zone dont le dialecte est sa langue maternelle, et restant pendant un certain temps et dans une certaine mesure (inconsciemment) bidialectal. Cf. aussi, à ce sujet, Kasser 1980–1 (I), 79–80.

[30] Le lexème ainsi adopté régionalement et non partout, apparaît de ce fait comme *rare* dans l'ensemble de l'attestation textuelle de cette « langue » supradialectale. Mais dans les autres dialectes coptes (locaux), si pauvrement attestés, la rareté ou l'absence même d'un lexème est loin d'être aussi significative (cf. *supra*, p. 187). La prudence invite alors à admettre a priori que si le mot n'apparaît pas, c'est que l'occasion d'apparaître ne lui a pas été donnée dans les trop rares textes attestant cet idiome; ou encore, pour des motifs de style ou d'autres qui nous échappent aujourd'hui, l'auteur (dont le dialecte aurait permis de l'utiliser) a écarté ce mot, arbitrairement.

[31] Cf. supra, pp. 189–190.

[32] *B* a d'ailleurs fréquemment, à sa disposition, à la fois un mot tout à fait « régional », du Delta seul, et totalement inconnu des autres dialectes coptes; et un mot pan-copte ou presque, probablement propre à *B* aussi, quoique atypique sur le plan dialectal, lexème non emprunté au stock lexical de la Vallée du Nil. Ainsi par.ex. ⲁⲙⲟⲛⲓ 'saisir' à côté de ⲁⲙⲁϩⲓ (*S* etc. ⲁⲙⲁϩ(ⲧ)ⲉ etc.); ⲃⲁⲕⲓ 'ville' vs ⲡⲟⲗⲓⲥ ; ⲉⲣϣⲓϣⲓ 'pouvoir' vs ⲉϫⲟⲩⲥⲓⲁ; ⲕⲁϯ 'comprendre, savoir' vs ⲥⲱⲟⲩⲛ etc.; ⲙⲟⲕⲓ 'vase' vs ϩⲛⲁⲁⲩ; ⲙⲟⲛⲙⲉⲛ 'ébranler' vs ⲛⲱⲓⲛⲓ; ⲙⲉϣϣⲱⲧ 'campagne, champ, plaine' vs ⲕⲟⲓ; ⲥⲱⲟⲩⲃⲉⲛ 'herbe' vs ⲥⲓⲙ (ou ⲭⲟⲣⲧⲟⲥ); ϣⲗⲟⲗ) 'peuple' vs (ϩ)ⲉⲑⲛⲟⲥ; ⲩⲑⲉϩ 'place (de ville)' vs ⲡⲗⲁⲧⲓⲁ ou ϧⲓⲣ; ϩⲓ ⲡϩⲟ 'repousser, abandonner' vs ⲕⲱ ⲛ̄ⲥⲁ- ; ϫⲱⲟⲩ 'génération' vs ⲅⲉⲛⲉⲁ (ou *S* etc. ϫⲱⲙ).

[33] Selon Lefort 1931a, d'autres facteurs encore (textes massivement traduits de *S* en *B* au IXe siècle) ont pu favoriser (dans le domaine de la syntaxe au moins) l'apparition de phénomènes non bohaïriques dans certains manuscrits *B*; ont-ils pu aider aussi à l'adoption exceptionnelle de tel ou tel lexème n'appartenant pas au « vrai » *B*?

l'adoption régionale de tel mot dialectal dans telle *koiné* copte, pour répondre à certains besoins de communication que cette « langue » véhiculaire autochtone ne rencontrait pas ailleurs, où ce mot était inconnu des dialectes locaux eux aussi [34].

*

Il a été dit plus haut (p. 188) que le domaine de la Bible copte est particulièrement favorable à la comparaison du vocabulaire des différents « dialectes » coptes, encore qu'on n'y trouve jamais aucun passage, si bref soit-il (et il devrait même être long et homogène !) [35] attesté par tous ces idiomes à la fois [36]. Notre analyse (assez poussée quoique encore incomplète) [37] de ces textes nous a fait mettre en exergue environ 300 lexèmes [38] où quelque différence d'usage dialectal significative se manifeste avec une clarté suffisante (il arrive que telle ou telle différence de ce genre touche accessoirement au domaine copto-grec) [39].

Cette analyse comparative fait apparaître, comme on pouvait s'y attendre, le plus grand nombre de points d'accord entre *A* et *L*, le plus petit entre *A* et *B* (idiomes entre lesquels notre concept de géographie dialectale [40], déjà, ne postulait aucune possibilité de contact sur le terrain). Mais en outre, ce qui ressort le plus clairement de cette analyse, c'est une coupure nette, quoique non absolue (loin de là), entre *B* d'une part, et tous les autres dialectes coptes d'autre part; les résultats (en « pour--cents » d'accord sur le total attesté) sont, à cet égard, assez éloquents : *S A* et *S L* 77, *S M* 60, *S F* 70; *A L* 87, *A M* 69, *A F* 66; *L M* 66, *L F* 60, *M F* 67; mais *B S* 50, *B A* 36, *B L* 42, *B M* 40, *B F* 54. Ces résultats confirment, pour l'ensemble, la géographie dialectale basée sur l'analyse phonologique (cf. supra, p. 190). Ils pourraient toutefois inciter à modifier sur un point la répartition des idiomes coptes en six « groupes » (Kasser 1980–1 (III), 120–122) et trois « grands groupes » (Kasser 1982c, 68–71) dialectaux (cf. aussi Hintze 1984, 420–423), qui par d'autres voies arrive à des conclusions fort similaires), « grands groupes » correspondant à autant de « grandes régions ». La grande région III (basse Moyenne-Égypte et Delta) ne sera considérée comme telle que sur le seul plan phonologique. Sur le plan lexical, au contraire, on préfèrera s'en tenir simplement à l'existence de deux « collectifs » ou « ensembles », correspondant en fait aux deux « langues » véhiculaires, respectivement, des deux grandes subdivisions de L'Égypte : ce qui est dans le Delta et se trouve donc dans le domaine spatial de *B*; et ce qui est dans la Vallée du Nil (d'abord dans la basse Moyenne–Égypte puis ultérieurement dans toute la Vallée, du Caire à Assouan) et se trouve donc dans le domaine spatial de *S*. Plus précisément, on pourra, si on l'estime

---

[34] Cf. infra, note 40.

[35] Cf. supra, p. 188.

[36] La situation la plus favorable est celle de livres très appréciés et recopiés dans l'Église copte, où l'on peut trouver, dans le meilleur des cas, 6 idiomes en parallèle. Dans la première moitié du Livre des Proverbes, on a la chance de pouvoir comparer *S, P, A* et *B*; dans d'importants passages des Petits prophètes, on pourra comparer *S, A, B74* et *B*; de bonnes sections de l'évangile de Matthieu nous sont attestées à la fois par *S, M, F,* et *B*; mais surtout, la plus grande partie de l'évangile de Jean apparaît en *S, L5, B74* et *B*, certaines sections permettant même la comparaison de *S, L5, F, B74* et *B*, d'autres *S, L5, V, B74* et *B*, d'autres même *S, A, L5, V, B74* et *B*; notons encore quelques sections des Actes des apôtres en *S, M, F,* et *B*; de même I Cor., Eph., I Thess., Hébreux, et quelques bribes de l'épître de Jacques en *S, A, F,* et *M*. Tout cela parce qu'aucune des versions coptes de la Bible ne nous est parvenue complète, à ce jour, loin de là : on peut évaluer l'ensemble du texte biblique, approximativement, à 3400 mlt; or *S* (dialecte le plus favorisé) n'en atteste guere que 60 % aujourd'hui, *B* 55 %, puis (les miettes !) *A* 5 %, *M* 4 %, *F* 3 %, *L5* 2 %, *V* et *F7* 1 % environ. D'ailleurs, dans lequel de ces idiomes a-t-on jamais vraiment traduit la Bible en entier ? Certes on peut supposer raisonnablement qu'il a dû exister une version *S* complète. Mais en ce qui concerne les autres versions dialectales, rien n'est moins sûr (le même doute s'étendant à *B*). Il se pourrait fort bien qu'on n'ait traduit en *I* etc., *V, F7, B74, P,* que les portions de livres attestées aujourd'hui dans ces dialectes, ou à peine un peu plus : pour répondre à certains besoins précis, limités dans le temps et l'espace. La suprématie linguistique de *S* (étouffant tous les dialectes concurrents rencontrés sur son passage dans l'ensemble de la Vallée du Nil), a bientôt rendu inutile, d'abord l'extension de ces versions non *S* à d'autres livres de la Bible, puis la survivance même de l'usage de ces versions incomplètes. Cela, à l'exception de la version *B* (*S* n'ayant jamais réussi à s'implanter assez solidement dans le Delta).

[37] Elle a porté surtout sur les livres bibliques, ou certains passages d'entre eux, les plus favorables : tous ceux où l'on trouve *A* ou *L*, la majeure partie de ceux où apparaît *F* (ou *V*) ou *M*, plus d'importantes sections où seuls *S* et *B* sont face à face.

[38] Ce nombre est, à vrai dire, minime (3 % environ) par rapport à la totalité du vocabulaire copte (copto-grec y compris).

[39] Cf. supra, notes 23 et 31.

[40] Cf. supra, pp. 192.

utile, opposer ainsi l'ensemble supradialectal *A I L M V F H P S* ou ens*S*, à l'ensemble supradialectal *B G* ou ens*B* [41].

Abréviations

Allberry 1938 = C. R. C. Allberry, *A Manichaean Psalmbook...*, Stuttgart.

Böhlig 1958a — A. Böhlig, *Die griechischen Lehnworter im sahidischen und bohairischen Neuen Testament*, München.

Böhlig 1966 = A. Böhlig, *Kephalaïa, Zweite Hälfte* [Lief. 11–12], Stuttgart.

Diethart–Satzinger 1983 = J.M. Diethart et H. Satzinger, « Eine griechisch-koptische Wörterliste », dans : *Festschrift zum 100-Jährigen Bestehen der Nationalbibliothek, Papyrus Erzherzog Rainer* (*P. Rainer Cent.*), *Textband*, Wien, 206–213.

Dubois... 1973 = J. Dubois, M. Giacomo, L. Guespin, Ch. et J.-B. Marcellesi, J.-P. Mevel, *Dictionnaire de linguistique*, Paris.

Engelbreth 1811 = W.F. Engelbreth, *Fragmenta basmurico--coptica Veteris et Novi Testament quae in Museo Borgiano Velitris asservantur...*, Copenhague.

Funk 1982 = W.P. Funk, « Πόλις, πολίτης und πολιτεία im Koptischen, zu einigen Fragen des einschlägigen koptischen Lehnwortschatzes », dans : E.Ch. Welskopf (éd.), *Soziale Typen im alten Griechenland*, Berlin, 7, 283–320.

Hintze 1984 = Fr. Hintze, « Eine Klassifizierung der koptischen Dialekte », dans : *Studien zu Sprache und Religion Ägyptens, I, Sprache* (Zu Ehren von W. Westendorf...), Göttingen, 411–432.

Kahle 1954 = P.E. Kahle, *Bala'izah, Coptic Texts from Deir el-Bala'izah in Upper Egypt*, London.

Kasser 1966d = R. Kasser, « La pénétration des mots grecs dans la langue copte », *Wissenschaftliche Zeitschrift der Universität Halle-Wittenberg* 15; 419–425.

Kasser 1975d = R. Kasser, « L'idiome de Bachmour », BIFAO 75, 401–427.

Kasser 1980–1 (I), ... (II), ... (III) = R. Kasser, « Prolégomènes à un essai de classification systématique des dialectes et subdialectes coptes selon les critères de la phonétique, I, principes et terminologie », *Muséon* 93, 53–112; ... II, alphabets et systèmes phonétiques, *Muséon* 93, 237–297; ... III, systèmes orthographiques et catégories dialectales, *Muséon* 94, 91–152.

Kasser 1982a = R. Kasser, « Le dialecte protosaïdique de Thèbes », *Archiv für Papyrusforschung* 28, 67–81.

Kasser 1982c = R. Kasser, « Le grand-groupe dialectal de Haute-Ègypte » *Bulletin de la Société d'égyptologie*, Genève, 7, 47–72.

Lefort 1931a = L.Th. Lefort, « Littérature bohaïrique » *Muséon* 44, 115–133.

Orlandi–Quecke 1974 = T. Orlandi (avec H. Quecke), *Papiri della Università degli Studi di Milano* (*P. Mil. Copti*) V, *Lettere di San Paolo in copto ossirinchita*, Milano.

Polotsky 1934c = H.J. Polotsky, *Manichäische Homilien...*, Stuttgart.

Schmidt 1905 = C. Schmidt, *Acta Pauli aus der Heidelberg koptischen Papyrushandschrift* Nr. 1..., Leipzig.

[Schmidt...] 1940 = [C. Schmidt, H.J. Polotsky, A. Böhlig], *Kephalaia, 1. Hälfte Lief. 1–10*, Stuttgart.

Thompson 1924 = H. Thompson, *The Gospel of St. John According to the Earliest Coptic Manuscript*, London.

Vergote 1973a = J. Vergote, *Grammaire copte, tome Ia, introduction, phonétique et phonologie, morphologie synthématique* (*structure des sémantèmes*), *partie synchronique*, Louvain.

Worell 1934 = W.H. Worell, *Coptic Sounds*, Ann. Arbor.

---

[41] Le fait que sur le plan lexical *S* soit un peu plus proche de *L* et de *A* que de *F* et de *M* ne devra pas nous inciter à chercher à nouveau l'origine de *S* en Haute–Égypte, voire dans la région thébaine. Ce phénomène peut être expliqué par l'un ou l'autre des facteurs suivants : 1) L'interaction entre *S* et les autres idiomes de la Vallée du Nil est naturellement la plus active entre *S koiné* copte de cette vaste région et *L* semi-*koiné* copte de la plus grande partie de cette région (et l'on a noté les étroits rapports lexicaux entre *L* e *A*); l'interaction entre *S* et les dialectes locaux est moindre; elle est néanmoins remarquable entre *S* et *F* son voisin d'origine, et elle le serait encore plus si l'on ne tenait compte, en *F*, que de sa variante la plus neutralisée, *V*. 2) Si l'on admet que *P* soit un protosaïdique immigré très tôt en région thébaine, par voie fluviale et en « sautant » primitivement toute la région entre Thèbes et la basse Moyenne-Égypte, on a dès lors tôt (et en tous cas largement avant le IVe siècle de notre ère), un *S* devenu bipolaire, ayant un centre de rayonnement dans la région de Memphis, un autre dans celle de Thèbes, ces deux centres s'influençant mutuellement; celui du nord, confronté à des idiomes voisins culturellement plus vivaces et actifs (ils ont produit leurs versions bibliques indépendants [et plus ou moins complètes] *B*, *F* et *M*) en a été longtemps tenu quelque peu à distance, d'où moins d'emprunts lexicaux réciproques; l'autre centre au contraire, en plein sud culturellement plus faible, a pu y exercer aussitôt un rayonnement puissant, puis une activité missionnaire (et simultanément littéraire) chrétienne pratiquement sans concurrence (les traductions de la Bible en *A* et *L* sont à rattacher directement à la version *S*, à qui appartient aussi la traduction *P*, cf, supra, note 3; ce qui n'a pu que faciliter l'entrée massive de lexèmes *L* et *A* en *S*). 3) Le nombre de manuscrits *S* trouvés en Haute-Égypte (et surtout dans la région thébaine) dépasse sensiblement celui des mss. *S* trouvés en Moyenne-Égypte (surtout dans sa partie inférieure); on peut en déduire que la variété de *S* immigré en Haute-Égypte est, dans notre documentation actuelle, mieux représentée que *S* en son terrain d'origine ou *S* immigré dans les autres zones de la Moyenne-Égypte; et il paraît vraisemblable que *S* ait tenu à adopter localement une partie du vocabulaire typique de chacun des idiomes locaux auxquels il se superposait en tant que *koiné* copte (cf. supra, note 33).

COPTIC STUDIES

Zsolt Kiss

Évolution stylistique des ampoules de St Ménas

Une manifestation spécifique de l'art de l'Égypte chrétienne étaient les ampoules de St Ménas, ces petites miniatures de gourdes de pèlerin en argile [1]. Leur production massive près du sanctuaire de St Ménas dans la région du Mariout était liée au pèlerinage au tombeau du Saint. Elles renfermaient de l'eau miraculeuse de la source près du tombeau du Saint et les pèlerins sillonant l'Orient chrétien jusqu'à la conquête arabe les emportaient en guise de reliques. Ainsi elles aboutirent jusqu'aux confins du monde chrétien des IVe–VIIe siècles (par ex. on en a trouvé en Germanie [2], en Hongrie [3] ou en Roumanie [4]). Pour bien remplir leur fonction, ces ampoules devaient donc être « authentifiées ». Aussi leurs flancs comportaient imprimé en relief soit une « signature » : Eulogia tou Hagiou Mena, soit une image du Saint de schéma caractéristique.

Mais les images sur les ampoules de St Ménas étaient fort variées (bâteau, corbeille de pain, Ste Thècle, etc.) et les effigies de St Ménas en diverses variantes formelles. L'ensemble du répertoire fut recensé par K.M. Kaufmann [5], mais, malgré les fouilles menées sur le site d'Abou Mina, tout le matériel reçut en gros la datation : IVe–VIe siècles, sans aucune recherche de stratification chrono-

logique de ce matériel. Par conséquent également, malgré la grande disparité de style des images de St Ménas, il n'était guère possible d'étayer une évolution stylistique sur des critères autres que subjectifs.

Les prémisses d'une distribution chronologique furent fournies par les fouilles archéologiques polonaises à Kôm el-Dikka à Alexandrie. Actuellement, nous avons trouvé sur ce site plus de 130 ampoules de St Ménas ou fragments [6]. Dans l'attente d'une analyse du matériel des fouilles allemandes en cours à Abou Mina, il s'agit donc du plus abondant matériel existant, issu de fouilles archéologiques. En particulier, un sondage minutieux mené en 1967–1970 au Sud de la construction théâtrale à Kôm el-Dikka a permis de recueillir près de 80 fragments d'ampoules de St Ménas [7], dispersés en trois couches stratigraphiques (couche II haut, couche II bas et couche III de la classification de M. Rodziewicz) [8]. L'analyse de ce matériel a permis de tirer certaines conclusions sur la chronologie et sur une division formelle de l'iconographie sur les ampoules de St Ménas.

Sans nous apesantir sur les questions de chronologie, présentées ailleurs, on a pu en tirer les conclusions suivantes :

[1] Cf. K. Wessel, « Eulogia », *Reallexikon zur Byz. Kunst,* cols 427–433; Z. Kiss, « Ampoules coptes », dans: *The Coptic Encyclopaedia*, Salt Lake City (sous presse).

[2] G. Grimm, *Die Zeugnisse ägyptischer Religion und Kunstelemente im römischen Deutschland*, Leiden 1969, p. 174, n° 70, pl. 15,3; p. 203, n° 114; pp. 228-229, n° 140, pl. 15,2.

[3] L. Nagy, « I ricordi cristiano-romani trovati recentemente in Ungheria », dans: *Atti del III Congresso Internazionale di Archeologia Cristiana*, Roma 1934, pp. 293–310, fig. 12.

[4] R. Vulpe, I. Barnea, *Romanii la Dunara de Jos,* Bucuresti 1968, fig. 52.

[5] K.M. Kaufmann, *Zur Ikonographie der Menas-Ampullen*, Cairo 1910.

[6] Z. Kiss, *Alexandrie V.* Les ampoules de Saint Ménas découvertes à Kôm el-Dikke en 1961–1981, Varsovie 1989.

[7] Z. Kiss, « Les ampoules de St Ménas découvertes à Kôm el-Dikka (Alexandrie) en 1967 », *Études et Travaux* III, 1969, 154–166; id., « Nouvelles ampoules de St Ménas à Kôm el-Dikka », *Études et Travaux* V, 1971, 146–149; id., « Les ampoules de St Ménas découvertes à Kôm el-Dikka (Alexandrie) en 1969 », *Études et Travaux* VII, 1973, 138–154; id., « Les ampoules de St Ménas découvertes à Kôm el-Dikka (Alexandrie) en 1970 », *Études et Travaux* IX, 1975, 212–216.

[8] M. Rodziewicz, « Stratigraphie du sondage M XVI, 1 dans la partie Sud de Kôm el-Dikka, Alexandrie », *Études et Travaux* III, 1969, 133–145.

1. Dans la période d'environ 610–650 on constate un monopole presque sans faille d'un schéma de médaillon : St Ménas orant adoré par deux chameaux dans un pourtour de perles. C'est en général, également dans le matériel hors de Kôm el-Dikka, le schéma d'ampoule le plus répandu. Il en découle qu'en cette période la production fut massive et fortement uniformisée.

2. Dans la période d'environ 560–610, les représentations de St Ménas suivant le schéma connu ont une composition bien plus variée et une plus grande diversité de style. Mais le médaillon caractéristique pour la période la plus récente est ici inconnu.

3. La période précédente, d'environ 480–560, est assez faiblement représenté à Kôm el-Dikka. On pense naturellement à une producton plus modeste des ateliers céramiques du sanctuaire, mais il convient aussi de dire qu'à ce niveau la superficie de notre sondage fut également plus modeste. On a pu en particulier juste identifier ici l'apparition du médaillon avec St Ménas dans un pourtour de couronne de laurier, en particulier sur des ampoules de grandes dimensions.

Effectivement, de nombreux motifs recensés par K.M. Kaufmann sont absents de notre matériel (par ex. le bâteau, certains schémas de composition du médaillon avec St Ménas), mais à l'heure actuelle on peut avoir une forte présomption qu'il s'agit d'exemplaires remontant à la période 560–610 et surtout 480–560.

De ce fait, nous ne tiendrons compte ici que des images de St Ménas même sur les médaillons de ces trois périodes en essayant de saisir leurs caractéristiques stylistiques dans le cadre de la séquence chronologique dont nous disposons à l'heure actuelle.

Voilà un exemple de grande ampoule avec l'image de St Ménas dans un pourtour de couronne de laurier qui est rendue avec soin (fig. 1). Dans l'image de St Ménas observons le rendu extrêmement plastique encore des plis du vêtement, la forme presque naturelle du visage. Par contre, la position des chameaux en adoration est loin de la nature, sans parler de leur échelle purement conventionnelle. Mais il ne s'agit pas ici d'une maladresse, plutôt d'une nécessité de la composition et surtout c'est une manifestation de l'« hiérarchie d'importance » entre les éléments du schéma, bien caractéristique pour l'art de l'Antiquité tardive. Soulignons enfin l'inscription flanquant le Saint, élément qui disparaîtra plus

tard ou deviendra autonome. Tel était le style de l'image du Saint vers 480–560 (on ne peut malheureusement aujourd'hui préciser plus).

Quelle différence avec l'image du Saint sur une ampoule des années 560–610 (fig. 2). La taille un peu plus réduite ne justifie pas une telle « réduction » des éléments de l'image. Les proportions du corps de Ménas sont faussées : les jambes courtes, les bras trop longs. Les plis du vêtement sont réduits au bourrelet de la ceinture et deux rainures transversales sur la poitrine. Également l'artisan a renoncé à rendre les traits caractéristiques des chameaux : le fidèle avait plutôt une indication illisible de ces éléments dont, par ailleurs, il connaissait le sens. On constate donc un rejet du modelé plastique au bénéfice d'une réduction aux éléments essentiels, de manière déjà linéaire, mais non géométrisée.

Pourtant, il ne s'agit pas d'un courant d'évolution harmonieux. Voyons une seconde ampoule de cette même période 560–610 (fig. 3). Ici, l'évolution est allée en une autre direction. Les proportions sont mieux respectées, mais le style n'opère que par des masses sommaires. Le Saint est réduit à sa silhouette, tandis que les chameaux sont devenus des zigzags serpentins touchant à l'abstraction. On ne voit aucune trace de linéarisme, mais plutôt d'une approche décorative ramenant le schéma à une composition conventionnelle loin de toute réalité, même simplifiée.

Mais la période suivante, 610–650, de production massive des ampoules de St Ménas revient au schématisme linéaire (fig. 4). Le motif devient fortement rigide dans son aspect, par ex. toujours la représentation est desaxée : le chameau de gauche est plus tassé et plus petit, la croix de gauche est d'aplomb, celle de droite est en oblique. Ainsi le schématisme devient prépondérant et plus poussé. La tête est devenue un triangle surmonté d'une rangée droite de petites boules. Les bourrelets des plis prennent un rythme géométrisé, mais pas encore contraire à la nature.

Il convient pourtant d'introduire certaines corrections dans cette évolution stylistique. Une première correction découle de la chronologie formelle.

Sur les deux faces d'une ampoule de Kôm el-Dikka, nous rencontrons deux médaillons entièrement différents (figs 5–6). Sur une face, St Ménas est placé dans un cadre de couronne de laurier. Il est rendu avec une simplification, mais aussi un grand souci du modelé plastique dans les

1. Ampoule de St Ménas. Alexandrie, Fouilles Polonaises, inv. n° 3717
(phot. Z. Doliński)

plis du manteau, le nimbe. Sur l'autre face, par contre, figure le schéma caractéristique de St Ménas dans une bordure de grénetis. Le Saint est simplifié à l'extrême, son rendu est conventionnel. Malheureusement, l'état de conservation de cette face ne permet pas de tirer plus de conclusions sur le style. Il reste que si l'artiste ici obéit au schéma formel et au style des années 610–650, l'exécutant du premier médaillon trahit tous les traits d'un schéma et d'un style d'au moins 50 ans plus ancien ! En ce moment, il convient de dire que voilà une preuve tangible de ce qu'on ne peut parler du « style d'une époque ». Comme J.Ch. Balty l'a

brillamment démontré pour le portrait romain du IIIe siècle [9], il faut être conscient du fait qu'à un moment donné travaillent simultanément des représentants d'un style « ancien », des représentants du style « à la mode » et enfin des « novateurs ».

Par ailleurs, cette ampoule confirme également notre chronologie assez « serrée », dont les points extrêmes de contact se renferment en un demi-siècle.

Une seconde correction découle du style de représentations d'une simultanéité évidente, chronologique et formelle, mais avec nuances stylisti-

[9] J. Ch. Balty, « Style et facture, notes sur le portrait romain du IIIe siècle de notre ère », CA 1983, 301–315.

2. Ampoule de St Ménas. Alexandrie, Fouilles Polonaises, inv. nº SM/1532/70 (phot. W. Jerke)

3. Ampoule de St Ménas. Alexandrie, Fouilles Polonaises, inv. nº SM/1378/69 (phot. W. Jerke)

4. Ampoule de St Ménas. Alexandrie, Fouilles Polonaises, inv. n° Wl/2641/76 (phot. A. Bodytko)

5–6. Ampoule de St Ménas. Alexandrie, Fouilles Polonaises, inv. n° W1/2567/76 (phot. A. Bodytko)

7–8. Ampoule de St Ménas. Alexandrie, Fouilles Polonaises, inv. n°W1/3640/81 (phot. Z. Doliński)

9. Ampoule de St Ménas. Alexandrie, Fouilles Polonaises, inv. n° WI/2072/74 (phot. W. Jerke)

ques remarquables. Ainsi, voyons les deux faces d'une autre ampoule de Kôm el-Dikka avec St Ménas du schéma disons « canonique » dans une bordure de grénetis (figs 7–8). Sur une face, la représentation est « fermée ». Dans l'image simplifiée de St Ménas on observe pourtant une tendance à suggérer le modelé des plis d'un vêtement, à marquer les manchettes de la tunique. Enfin, les croix au-dessus des bras de Ménas sont à branches continues. Sur l'autre face, les croix sont « désagrégées » en quatre grains. Combien différente aussi est l'image de St Ménas ! Les vêtements sont réduits à un système de bourrelets. La tête atteint à un niveau de schématisme proche de l'abstraction. L'idée maîtresse de ce médaillon semble maintenant une réduction géométrique de l'image à des bourrelets et des grains.

La diversité d'approche, dirait-on d'esprit, est enfin illustrée par une dernière ampoule provenant de Kôm el-Dikka (figs 9–10). Sur une face, malgré les croix continues, l'image de St Ménas est menée à une simplification extrême : tous les éléments y sont, et sont ensemble, mais réduits à leur plus simple expression. Sur l'autre face, par contre, le type de géométrisation est entièrement différent :

les plis du vêtement sont fins et parallèles. Mais surtout on est frappé par le visage d'une conception géométrique audacieuse avec le « T » du nez et des sourcils encadré de deux grains des yeux et surmonté du bourrelet droit parallèle de la chevelure. Observons aussi le degré d'abstraction géométrique atteint par le chameau de gauche, qui devient une boule hérissée de pointes. Ici, on doit reconnaître un « novateur », car un tel mode de géométrisation n'apparaîtra dans la sculpture copte que bien plus tard.

Ces exemples démontrent suffisamment, j'espère, que dans le cadre d'un schéma formel très rigide des années 610–650 nous voyons s'exprimer une tendance générale à la schématisation, allant vers le géométrisme, mais en combien de degrés et combien de modes ! Ainsi, en dehors d'une ligne générale d'évolution, courante dans tout l'art de l'Antiquité tardive et copte, s'éloignant du modelé plastique réaliste, ou illusioniste si on préfère, on observe en une période, un centre et un groupe précis d'objets d'art mineur ce que L. Török avait souligné ici-même à notre Congrès : un pluralisme, une « polyphonie » stylistique [10].

---

[10] L. Török, « Notes on the Chronology of Late Antique Stone Sculpture in Egypt », dans ce volume.

COPTIC STUDIES

Martin Krause

Die ägyptischen Klöster.
Bemerkungen zu den Phoibammon–Klöstern
in Theben–West und den Apollon–Klöstern

Bei der zentralen Rolle, die das Mönchtum in Ägypten gespielt hat und noch spielt, ist es verwunderlich, daß zusammenfassende Arbeiten über die ägyptischen Klöster bisher fehlen. Für die Archäologie gibt es zwar seit 1974 in der Arbeit von C.C. Walters[1] eine erste, wenn auch unvollständige, Zusammenfassung.[2] Die Dissertation von J. Doresse[3] aus dem Jahre 1970 über die Klöster Mittelägyptens ist leider bisher nicht zugänglich. Der Stand der Erforschung der *schriftlichen* Quellen ist noch schlechter. Die wichtige Arbeit von Frau Barison[4] über die Klöster Ägyptens in der byzantinischen und arabischen Epoche basiert nur auf den bis 1938 veröffentlichten *griechischen* Urkunden. Sie müßte also weitergeführt werden, und es müßten auch die in den letzten 46 Jahren veröffentlichten griechischen Urkunden auf Nennungen koptischer Klöster durchgesehen werden.[5] Eine parallele Arbeit, die die in den *koptischen* Urkunden, Papyri und Ostraka, genannten Klöster einmal zusammenstellt, fehlt dagegen bisher völlig, obwohl A. Steinwenter[6] bereits vor mehr als 25 Jahren auf ihr Fehlen hingewiesen hat. Eine solche Arbeit erscheint mir umso dringlicher, weil in zunehmenden Maße vor allem jüngere Wissenschaftler aus den der Koptologie nahestehenden Disziplinen sich an der Publikation koptischer papyrologischer Quel-

len beteiligen wollen und dieses Hilfsmittel dringend benötigen — wie ich noch zeigen werde — um nicht länger zu falschen Zuweisungen zu kommen. Aber auch die Kollegen, die sich um die archäologische Erforschung koptischer Klöster verdient machen, benötigen dringend eine Arbeit, um die schriftliche Quellen für ihre Untersuchungen kennenzulernen und auszuwerten.
Um die Schwierigkeit einer solchen Arbeit, die wegen der Fülle bisher unveröffentlichter koptischer Ostraka und Papyri nur vorläufigen Charakter haben kann, bin ich mir bewußt. Dennoch muß sie einmal begonnen werden und ich möchte Ihnen an zwei Beispielen zeigen, wie lohnend ein solches Unternehmen ist.

1. Die Phoibammon-Klöster
in Theben-West

Frau Barison nennt drei in den griechischen Papyri vorkommende Klöster, die nach dem hl. Phoibammon genannt wurden: in Antinupolis,[7] Lykopolis[8] und in Theben.[9] Letzteres Kloster, mit dem wir uns befassen wollen, wird in dem griechischen Testament des Bischofs Abraham von Hermonthis, P. London I, 77, erwähnt. Die Ansetzung

---

[1] *Monastic Archaeology in Egypt,* Warminster 1974.

[2] Vgl. M. Krause, » Die Aussagen der Urkunden über die Verfassung koptischer Klöster «, *Le site monastique copte des Kellia,* Genève 1986, 41–52.

[3] J. Doresse, *Les anciens monastères coptes de moyenne Égypte (du Gebel el-Teir à Kôm-Ishgaou(d'après l'archéologie et l'hagiographie,* Diss., Paris 1970.

[4] P. Barison, » Ricerche sui monasteri dell'Egitto bizantino ed arabo secondo i documenti dei papiri greci «, *Aegyptus* 18 (1938), 29–148.

[5] Wie mir Frau A. Kasser mitteilt, soll eine Schülerin von Frau O. Montevecchi diese Arbeit vorbereiten.

[6] A. Steinwenter, » Aus dem kirchlichen Vermögensrecht der Papyri «, ZSS 75 (1958), 3 f.

[7] Barison, » Ricerche..., « 88(4).

[8] Ebd., 117(40).

[9] Ebd., 129(2)–131.

dieses Papyrus von Barison in das VIII. Jahrhundert [10] ist zu spät. Es dürfte vor 600, um 590 zu datieren sein. Barison nennt 2 Klöster in Theben-West, die nach ihrer Kenntnis der Sekundärliteratur mit diesem Kloster identifiziert werden könnten: Dêr-el Medine – wie Amelineau [11] glaubte – und Dêr-el Bahri – was Crum [12] vorschlug. Ein Hinweis auf die vielen *koptischen* Urkunden über dieses Kloster fehlt bei Barison, selbst der Hinweis auf das zwar koptische Testament Viktors, der Abraham als Klosterabt folgte, das aber 6 Zeilen griechischen Text [13] am Anfang aufweist, die u.a. die Datierung und den Ort der Errichtung der Urkunde sowie die Lage des Klosters nennen: ἐν τῷ τόπῳ τοῦ ἀθλοφόρου μάρτυρος ἀββᾶ Φοιβάμων τοῦ ὄρους Μεμνωνίου τοῦ νόμου Ἑρμώνθεως. [14]

Die alternative Identifikation des Klosters ist inzwischen zu Gunsten von Dêr el-Bahri entschieden. [15] Verwirrung stiftete vorübergehend die Ausgrabung eines dem Phoibammon gewidmeten Klosters, das 1948/49 von der Société d'Archéologie Copte am Ende eines Tales rund 8 km von Dêr el-Bahri entfernt ausgegraben wurde. Inzwischen kann als gesichert gelten, daß dieses Kloster ein weiteres, bisher unbekanntes, ebenfalls dem Phoibammon geweihtes Kloster ist. Griechische und koptische Urkunden erlauben es m.E., die Beziehungen zwischen den beiden Klöstern zu erhellen. Die Ausgrabung der Société d'Archéologie Copte hatte ergeben, daß es sich um ein nach dem 4. Jahrhundert gegründetes Kloster handelte, das im 7. Jahrhundert unter Mitnahme aller wertvollen Dinge verlassen worden war. Das Phoibammon Kloster in Dêr el-Bahri konnte leider archäologisch nicht untersucht werden, weil es Ende des letzten Jahrhunderts von Naville abgerissen worden war, ohne vorher untersucht worden zu sein. Vielleicht kann Herr Kollege Godlewski aus den unveröffentlichten Plänen von

Ägypten-Reisenden, vor allem von Robert Hay, archäologische Daten erheben.

Aus den schriftlichen Quellen, [16] von denen ich vor allem zwei Texte, von Crum als CO ad 59 und KRU 105 publiziert, nenne, ergibt sich für mich eine Beziehung zwischen den beiden Klöstern, die ich aber nur als Thesen vortragen kann, weil beide Texte nich vollständig erhalten sind. Während in CO ad 59 die Namen der Adressaten und Absender fehlen, fehlt in KRU 105 nur der Name des Adressaten. Die *Schrift* beider Texte – für KRU 105 danke ich meinem Schüler Gawdat Gabra Abdel Sayed für die Besorgung von Photos des im Koptischen Museum in Kairo aufbewahrten Papyrus – und ihr *Inhalt* setzen sie in die Zeit kurz vor 600.

Der Absender von CO ad 59, wohl der Bischof Abraham, sagt in seinem Schreiben, wohl an den Laschanen oder den Klerus von Djeme: » ihr wißt, es ist nicht unser Wunsch, daß wir unser Kloster verlassen, vielmehr auf Grund der Fürsorge unseres heiligen Vaters (d.h. des Erzbischofs Damian von Alexandria) und der Reisebemühung, die sie (d.h. die Überbringer seines Festbriefes) auf sich nahmen, um zu uns zu kommen «. Daraus schließe ich, daß der im Phoibammon-Kloster, und zwar in dem von der Société d'Archéologie Copte ausgegrabenen Phoibammon-Kloster residierende Bischof wegen der entlegenen Lage des Klosters auf Wunsch – oder Anordnung – des Erzbischofs [17] seinen ursprünglichen Wohnsitz verließ und ein neues, ebenfalls dem Phoibammon geweihtes Kloster in Dêr el-Bahri erbaute, in das er dann übersiedelte. Dieses, bei der Stadt Djeme in den Ruinen des Hatschepsuttempels neu erbaute Kloster war wesentlich leichter erreichbar als das ältere Phoibammon-Kloster. Da das Gelände der Stadt Djeme gehörte, mußte die Stadt ihm dieses überlassen. In KRU 105 wird Abraham und seinen Nachfolgern im Amte des Klosterabtes das

---

[10] Ebd., 129.

[11] Ebd., 129, A.4.

[12] Ebd., 129, A.4.

[13] KRU 77,2–7.

[14] KRU 77,5–7.

[15] M. Krause, » Zwei Phoibammon-Klöster in Theben-West «, MDIK 37 (1981), 261–266; Krause, » Die Beziehungen zwischen den beiden Phoibammon-Klöstern auf dem thebanischen Westufer «, BSAC 27 (1985) im Druck; W. Godlewski, » Remarques sur la création du monastère de St Phoibammon à Deir el-Bahari «, *African Bulletin* 31 (1982), 107–114; Godlewski, » Monastère nord au monastère St Phoibammon «, *Études et Travaux* 12 (1983), 94–98.

[16] Vgl. zum folgenden meinen, in BSAC 27 erscheinenden Aufsatz.

[17] Mein Kollege Godlewski bezieht CO ad 59 nicht in seine Untersuchungen ein. Er meint – in Übereinstimmung mit den Ausgräbern- daß ein drohender Erdrutsch der Anlaß zum Verlassen des Klosters gewesen sei. Außerdem meint er, Abraham have *vor* seiner Ernennung zum Bischof dieses Kloster verlassen.

Eigentum des um 590 neu erbauten Phoibammon-Klosters vom Laschanen von Djeme anerkannt. Wohl nur wenig später — ich hoffe, die Schrift des als KRU 108 [18] veröffentlichten Papyrus im Britischen Museum in Kürze auf ihr Alter untersuchen zu können [19] — schenkt die Stadt Djeme dem Kloster ein weiteres Grundstück, damit das Kloster von seinen Erträgen die Armen der Stadt unterstützen kann. Allgemein bekannt sind die Testamente der Äbte des Phoibammon-Klosters [20], die Kinderschenkungsurkunden [21] u.a. dieses Kloster betreffende Urkunden. Vor allem viele Ostraka aus diesem Kloster sind noch unveröffentlicht. Ich nenne stellvertretend für alle die von der Columbia Universität angekaufte Sammlung des Metropolitan Museum of Art New York, die aus Winlocks Ausgrabungen des von Naville angelegten Schutthügels von Dêr el-Bahri stammen. [22] Viele Texte lassen sich diesem Kloster zuweisen, weil uns eine große Anzahl der Klosteräbte, Klosterfunktionäre und auch der Mönche dieses Klosters bekannt sind. [23] Sie erlauben, eine Geschichte dieses bedeutenden Klosters über mehrere Jahrhunderte zu schreiben. [24]

2. Die Apollon-Klöster

Während Frau Barison nur zwei nach Apollo benannte Klöster bei Oxyrhynchos [25] und Aphrodito [26] in ihrer Liste der in den griechischen Papyri

belegten koptischen Klöster aufführt, ist in der Zwischenzeit in griechischen Urkunden ein weiteres Apollon-Kloster bezeugt [27] und vermehren die koptischen Papyri die nach Apollo benannten Klöster um zwei weitere: es ist einmal das allen Archäologen bekannte, vom Französischen Archäologischen Institut in Kairo zum großen Teil ausgegrabene Apollon-Kloster bei Bawit, [28] rd. 25 km südlich der Stadt Hermopolis gelegen, und das Apollon-Kloster bei Bala'izah, [29] südlich von Assiut. Peter Grossmann hat letzteres Kloster vermessen und wird eine Plan dieses Klosters bald publizieren. [30]

Die Urkunden bezeichnen das Apollon-Kloster von Bawit als ⲘⲞⲚⲀⲤⲦⲎⲢⲒⲞⲚ Ⲛ̄ⲠⲌⲀⲄⲒⲞⲤ ⲀⲂⲂⲀ ⲀⲠⲞⲖⲖⲰ Ⲛ̄ⲠⲢⲎⲤ Ⲛ̄ⲰⲘⲞⲨⲚ ⲦⲠⲞⲖⲒⲤ » Kloster des hl. Apollo, südlich der Stadt Hermopolis « [31] und das gleichnamige Kloster bei Bala'izah als ⲘⲞⲚⲀⲤⲦⲎⲢⲒⲞⲚ (ⲈⲦⲞⲨⲀⲀⲂ) Ⲛ̄ⲀⲠⲀ ⲀⲠⲞⲖⲖⲰ ϩⲘ̄ ⲠⲚⲞⲘⲞⲤ Ⲛ̄ⲤⲂϩⲦ ⲦⲠⲞⲖⲒⲤ » (hl.) Kloster, des Apa Apollo im Gau der Stadt Sbeht «. [32] Wir kennen aus den Urkunden bisher als fünf nach Apollo benannte Klöster. Bei Bekanntwerden neuer Texte muß daher geprüft werden, welches dieser fünf Apollon-Klöster gemeint ist, falls nicht noch ein weiteres Apollon-Kloster neu belegt ist.

Kürzlich hat W. Brunsch [33] einen Papyrus publiziert, der an den Abt eines Apollon-Klosters ohne Ortsangabe gerichtet ist. Er weist diese Urkunde

---

[18] Steinwenter, » Aus dem kirchlichen... «, 30f, setzt ihn ins 7. Jh. (?).

[19] Die im September 1985 durchgeführte Untersuchung bestätigte die Frühansetzung des Papyrus in die Zeit um 600.

[20] Vgl. dazu M. Krause, » Die Testamente der Äbte des Phoibammon Klosters in Theben «, MDIK 25 (1969), 57–67.

[21] A. Steinwenter, » Kinderschenkungen an koptische Klöster «, ZSS 42 (1921), 175–207.

[22] M. Krause, » Die Disziplin Koptologie «, in: *The Future of Coptic Studies* (hrsg. v. R. McL. Wilson), Leiden 1978, p. 12 f. (*Coptic Studies* I).

[23] W.C. Till, *Datierung und Prosopographie der koptischen Urkunden aus Theben*, Wien 1962 (Österr. Ak.d. Wissensch., phil.-hist. Kl. 240,1) passim; vgl. dazu auch M. Krause, » Das christliche Theben: Neuere Arbeiten und Funde «, BSAC 24 (1982), 21–33.

[24] Eine solche Geschichte wird von W. Godlewski vorbereitet.

[25] Barison, » Ricerche..., «, 77.

[26] Ebd., 100–102.

[27] M. Hombert et Cl. Préaux, » Les papyrus de la Fondation Egyptologique Reine Elisabeth «, CdE 41 (1946), 121–126. (SB 9051). Dieses Kloster liegt im Gau von Hermopolis in Titkois. Weitere zwei griechische Urkunden bei J. Gascou, » Documents grecs relatifs au monastère d'Abba Apollon de Titkois «, *Anagennesis* 1 (1981), 219–230. Es war schon durch P. London V, 1899 bezeugt (der Name war nicht erhalten) und wird von Barison, » Ricerche... «, 93(4) als namenloses Kloster: » il nome del monastero manca nel papiro « aufgeführt.

[28] M. Krause u. K. Wessel, Rbk I (1966), 568–83, s.v. Bawit (mit Lit.); H. Torp, » Le monastère copte de Baouît. Quelques notes d'introduction «, in: *Institutum Romanum Norvegiae. Acta ad archaeologiam et artium historiam pertinentia*, 9, Rom 1981, S. 1–8.

[29] P.E. Kahle, » Bala'izah. Coptic Texts from Deir el-Bala'izah in Upper Egypt «, London 1954, 2Bde.

[30] P. Grossmann, *Le site monastique copte des Kellia*, Genève 1986, 33–40.

[31] Z.B. BM Or 6203, 17–18.

[32] Kahle, » Bala'izah... «, I, 15.

[33] W. Brunsch » P. Würzburg Inv. Nr. 43 — eine koptische Verzichtserklärung «, ZÄS 108 (1981), 93-106.

dem Apollon-Kloster von Bala'izah [34] zu, ohne die vier anderen Apollon-Klöster zu nennen und seine Zuweisung zu diesem Kloster zu begründen. Da sein Ausatz sich durch eine Fülle von zitierter Sekulärliteratur, auch unnötiger, auzeichnet, muß man wohl annehmen, daß er die vier anderen Apollon-Klöster nicht kennt; denn er nennt weder die Arbeit von Barison [35] noch das Apollon-Kloster von Titkôis [36] und Bawit.[37] Ich kann und will hier nicht die vielen falschen Lesungen, die Übersetzungsfehler und die sich daraus ergebenden falschen Interpretationen besprechen. Wegen ihrer Vielzahl und dem großen Wert der Urkunde habe ich eine Neuausgabe des Papyrus vorgenommen, die sich im Druck befindet.[38]

Hier interessiert nur die Frage, zu welchem der fünf Apollon-Klöster die Urkunde wohl gehört. Wenig aussagekräftig sind moderne Angaben der Händler über die Herkunft der Papyri, da sie oft die wirkliche Herkunft der Papyri verschleiern und auch die Behörden auf eine falsche Spur lenken wollen. Mehr Vertrauen darf man alten Fundangaben schenken, weil damals der Verkauf von Papyri noch nicht unter Strafe stand. Grundsätzlich läßt sich bei fehlenden Ortsangaben sagen, daß — neben dem Dialekt koptischer Urkunden — m.E. *drei Kriterien,* allerdings von verschiedener Aussagekraft, die Zuweisung einer Urkunde zu einem bestimmten Kloster ermöglichen:

1) die *Bezeichnung* des Klosters,
2) die in den Texten belegten *Titel* der Klosterfunktionäre,
3) die Namen der in den Texten genannten Personen, bei Zeugen vor allem deren *Herkunftsangaben.*

Die ersten beiden Kriterien helfen bei der Lokalisierung von P. Würzburg 43 nicht weiter, denn:

ad 1) das Kloster wird als τόπος (Z. 1.2.7) bzw. μοναστήριον bezeichnet, ebenso wie das von Bawit, Titkôis, Bala'izah und Aphrodito; lediglich das von Oxyrhynchos heißt κοινόβιον [39];

ad 2) auch die in der Urkunde belegten Titel der

Klosterfunktioñare: ἀρχιμανδρίτης (Z. 2), ⲚⲞⳠ ⲚⳘⲚⲎⲨ (Z. 4), sowie der Verwaltungsrat, δίκαιον begegnen sowohl in Bawit, als auch in Bala'izah, das δίκαιον ist auch für Aphrodito bezeugt; der Abt des Apollon-Klosters von Titkôis trug den Titel προεστώς;[40]

ad 3) die Namen der im Papyrus genannten Mönche Isaak (Z. 1, 14. u. verso 2) und Jeremias (Z. 5,8 und 11) sind weit verbreitet und haben wenig Aussagekraft, ein Abt names Daniel ist in den übrigen vier Klöstern bisher nicht belegt.

Hier helfen nur die als Zeugen fungierenden Personen weiter, denn zwei von ihnen bezeichnen sich als Einwohner von Taposi (Z. 17) bzw. Senesla (verso Z. 2). Während Taposi m.W. bisher noch nicht belegt ist, kennen wir einen Ort Σενεσλαις, Σλεεσλαις und in anderen Schreibungen aus mehreren griechischen Urkunden des 3.–8. Jahrhunderts [41] und er ist — entgegen der Aussage von Brunsch [42] — auch in einem koptischen Papyrus der Eremitage in Leningrad [43] belegt. Er liegt im Grau von Hermopolis bei Sanabou, nur wenige Kilometer südlich von Bawit. Die Aussage des Protokometen Lazaros von Senesla, daß er » zufällig zur Zisterne kam « (verso Z. 1) zeigt, daß er in der Nähe tätig und dem Aussteller der Urkunde bekannt war, da er ihn bat, als Zeuge zu fungieren. Das spricht dafür, diese Urkunde dem der Ortschaft Senesla benachbarten Apollon-Kloster von Bawit zuzuweisen und nicht dem 80 km weiter südlich gelegenem gleichnamigen Kloster von Bala'izah, wie Brunsch meint.

Wir erfahren aus diesem Papyrus, deß Mönche dieses Klosters Grundstücke besitzen und einer von ihnen, weil er nicht imstande war, seine Steuern von den Erträgen seiner Grundstücke zu bezahlen, durch Vermittlung des Abtes ein Grundstück an einen anderen Mönch abtritt, der dafür die Steuern für beide Grundstücke bezahlt. Das bedeutet, daß in Bawit bereits am Anfang des 8. Jahrhunderts beim Eintritt ins Kloster keine ἀπόταξις vorgenommen wurde. Außerdem lernen

---

[34] Ebd., 93 u. A. 3; 104 A. 74.
[35] Vgl. A. 4.
[36] Vgl. A. 27.
[37] Vgl. A. 28.
[38] M. Krause, » Zur Edition koptischer nichtliterarischer Texte. P. Würzburg neu bearbeitet «, ZÄS 112 (1985) (im Druck).
[39] Barison, 77.
[40] Ebd., 93.
[41] M. Drew-Bear, » Le nome hermopolite. Toponymes et sites «, *American Studies in Papyrology* 21 (1979), 235 f.
[42] Brunsch, » P. Würzburg... «, 104a: » der Ortsname ⲤⲈⲚⲈⲤⲖⲀ war koptisch bisher ebenfalls nicht belegt «.
[43] P.V. Jernštedt, *Koptische Texte der Eremitage* (russ.), Moskau–Leningrad 1959, Nr. 3, Z. 6 und verso Z. 3.

wir einen uns bisher unbekannten Abt und einige Mönche dieses Klosters kennen. In das Apollon--Kloster von Bawit gehört auch der bereits genannte, von Jernstedt publizierte Papyrus 3 der Eremitage, eine Pachturkunde, in der Z.6 wieder Einwohner von Senesla genannt werden. Zwei Mönche des Apollon-Klosters shreiben an den Abt des Klosters namens Georgius, der bisher noch nicht in anderen Urkunden aus Bawit belegt ist. Aus BM Or 6201–6206, Urkunden des Apollon-Klosters von Bawit, kennen wir weitere Namen von Archimandriten dieses Klosters aus der 1. Hälfte des 9. Jahrhunderts, während die genannten und andere Urkunden bereits ins 8. Jahrhundert zu datieren sind. Sie befinden sich in verschiedenen Papyrussammlungen, z.B. in der British Library London, im Museum von Ismailija und in amerikanischen Sammlungen, letztere sollen von Frau MacCoull veröffentlicht werden.

Im 9. Jahrhundert, genauer in den Jahren 833 bis 850, erfahren wir aus Urkunden dieses Klosters, daß die διακονία Teile des Klosters an Mönche verkauft, und diese sich nach wenigen Jahren an andere Mönche desselben Klosters weiterverkaufen. Sie können ihren Besitz bei ihrem Tode aber nicht an Verwandte vererben, denn eine Klausel in den Kaufverträgen besagt, daß dann die gekauften Klosteranteile an die διακονία des Klosters zurückfallen.[44]

Auch die Geschichte dieses Klosters läßt sich — wenn auch lückenhafgter als die des Phoibammon-Klosters — nach der Zuordnung der vielen, meist noch unveröffentlichten Urkunden schreiben.[45]

Damit die Liste der in koptischen Urkunden genannten Klöster angesichts der vielen unveröffentlichten Urkunden nicht zu lückenhaft bleibt, möchte ich alle Bearbeiter koptischer Urkunden, in denen Klöster und Mönche genannt werden, bitten, mir eine Notiz zu senden, damit diese mit Nennung des Informanten in die Publikation aufgenommen werden kann.

---

[44] Vgl. M. Krause, » Zur Möglichkeit von Besitz im apotaktischen Mönchtum Ägyptens «, in: *Proceedings of the Second International Congress of Coptic Studies,* Rom 22.–26. September 1980 (im Druck).

[45] Vgl. vorläufig M. Krause, *Das Apa-Apollon-Kloster zu Bawit. Untersuchungen unveröffentlichter Urkunden als Beitrag zur Geschichte des ägyptischen Mönchtums.* Diss. Leipzig 1958.

COPTIC STUDIES

Aleksandra Krzyżanowska

Remarques sur la circulation monétaire en Égypte du IVᵉ au VIIᵉ siècles

Cette courte communication n'est qu'un supplément numismatique à l'exposé du dr Barbara Ruszczyc qui aura lieu demain, concernant les fouilles menées en 1969 et puis de 1979 à 1983 à Tell Atrib à Kôm Sidi Joussuf. Pendant ces fouilles furent trouvées environ cinq cents monnaies en bronze.

On peut y distinguer quelques groupes chronologiques. Le premier comprend les monnaies les plus anciennes d'époque ptolémaique et romaines impériales des trois premiers siècles de notre ère, frappées dans l'atelier grec d'Alexandrie. Ce groupe, quoique peu nombreux, prédomine nettement dans le secteur fouillé en 1969 où on a trouvé des installations balnéaires et dans les sondages au pied du Kôm, en particulier dans le secteur Z fouillé en 1981.

Un second groupe, également réduit, réunit les monnaies du règne de Constantin le Grand et de ses fils, formant à peine 7 % de l'ensemble. Elles apparaissent en même temps que celles du groupe suivant et peuvent être considérées ensemble, en raison de possibilité d'une circulation prolongée. Ensuite vient le groupe le plus nombreux — 50 % de l'ensemble du matériel trouvé — comprenant de petites monnaies en bronze dites « minimi », frappées à la fin du IVᵉ siècle, sous le règne de Theodose I, d'Arcadius et de Valentinien II. Si nous y ajoutons des exemplaires indéfinis, de forme et de taille analogues, frappés au Vᵉ siècle, nous obtenons 60 % de l'ensemble du matériel numismatique.

Le dernier groupe, second quant au nombre, englobe les monnaies d'époque byzantine, frappées depuis le règne de Justinien I jusqu'à celui d'Heraclius et de son fils Constant II. Hors de rares exceptions ce sont des *dodekanummia* en bronze provenant de l'atelier alexandrin.

Compte tenu non seulement de la période de frappe des monnaies mais aussi d'une certaine période de circulation, on peut encore élargir le cadre chronoloqigue de ces groupes. Les monnaies du IVᵉ siècle purent encore servir de petite monnaie au Vᵉ et peut-être aussi au VIᵉ siècles. Le second groupe de monnaies byzantines, par contre, put rester en circulation pendant la haute période arabe. Cette hypothèse est confirmée par la trouvaille en leur compagnie de quelques monnaies arabes imitant les émissions d'Héraclius, mais avec légende arabe.

Prenant en considération le problème de la circulation monétaire, en se basant sur les fouilles de Kôm Sidi Joussuf à Tell Atrib, nous pouvons essayer de présenter l'image suivante.

La politique financière de l'Égypte ptolémaïque était tout à fait différente de celle dans d'autres pays grecs et la circulation monétaire y était close. Ce phenomène est à observer pendant la domination romaine en Égypte. Parmi les trouvailles archéoloqiques des trois premiers siècles on constate le préponderance des monnaies provenant de l'atelier grec d'Alexandrie. L'activité de cet atelier s'était arrêtée à la fin de la Tetrarchie; alors des monnaies des autres ateliers impériaux se sont introduites en Égypte, suppléant des émissions, assez réduites en ce temps, de l'atelier romain d'Alexandrie. Nous connaissons de cette époque des cas où on avait fourni la solde pour les garnisons romaines éloignées en procurant même les moulages des monnaies romaines en circulation.

Le grand nombre de monnaies frappées à la fin du IVᵉ et au Vᵉ siècles découvertes à Tell Atrib démontre que la base de la masse monétaire en circulation était formée alors par ces petites unités en bronze, frappées en quantité énorme. Ce phenoméne fut beaucoup plus général et apparaissait dans tout l'empire, où la durée de leur circulation fut prolongée jusqu'au VIᵉ et même au VIIᵉ siècles. Il faut mentionner ici que, au point de vue du pouvoir d'achat, le grand nombre de ces minimi ne formaient pas la somme considérable. Les données provenant de l'Afrique du Nord nous renseignent qu'en ce temps-là le solidus d'or (poids 4 g env.) équivalait 14.000 de ces petites monnaies en bronze. Or la monnaie d'or ne servait que pour de grandes transactions et c'étaient les minimi qui étaient la petite monnaie quotidienne.

La constatation ci-mentionnée concerne aussi le groupe postérieur de monnaies byzantines. Parmi les 80 pièces trouvées à Kôm Sidi Joussuf quelques exemplaires à peine formaient une autre unité que *dodekanummium*, frappé uniquement à Alexandrie. Ce dernier, la petite monnaie du pays, ne présentait non plus un grand capital. L'ensemble même de 16 pièces découvertes auprès des restes du crâne humain, qualifié du point de vue numismatique pour un trésor, ne constituait pas une grande somme d'argent.

Si, en se basant sur les fouilles de Tell Atrib, nous voulions tirer des conclusions concernant la richesse des habitants, nous serions obligés de constater leur pauvreté. Cependant, toujours quand il s'agit des fouilles archéologiques, il faut tenir compte de la possibilité de pillage des objects de valeur, les monnaies d'or et d'argent y compris. En ce moment les excavations de Kôm Sidi Joussuf ne sont pas encore terminées. Avec la fin des travaux il sera possible de tirer des conclusions plus approfondies et mieux étayées.

COPTIC STUDIES

Pahor Labib

Some Aspects of Coptic Civilization

Ancient Egyptian civilization did not end with Pharaonic Egypt, for the Egyptian people carried on the Egyptian civilization, developing her linguistic, spiritual, religious, scientific and artistic fields into what we now call the "Coptic civilization".

Today I wish to discuss art. Coptic art is important not only because it links the Egyptian art of the Pharaonic and Graeco-Roman periods on the one hand with the Arab period on the other, but also because it is a reflection of monastic and ecclesiastical tendencies the purpose of which was strictly religious as well as a sincere portrayal of Egyptian daily life before and after the Coptic period. Finally, it is important because of its influence upon the early Arabic art of Egypt and upon the early arts of Mediaeval Europe.

The various forms of art are:

1. Architecture
2. Sculpture
3. Painting: a) frescoes or wall paintings, b) mummy portraits (Fayum), c) wooden palettes, d) icons
4. Industries: a) textiles, b) woodwork, c) metalwork, d) pottery, e) glass, f) ivory
5. Inscriptions: a) on papyri, b) on parchment, c) on ostraca (limestone or pottery)
6. Folk art.

1. Architecture

The Copts built the great monasteries[1] found throughout the Egyptian deserts, i.e. the monastery of St Paul and St Anthony in the Eastern desert near the Red Sea; the two monasteries of Shenute, known as the White and the Red Monasteries, near Sohag in Upper Egypt; the monastery of Abou Mina (or Saint Menas) in the Western desert; the monasteries of Wadi-el-Natrun and, especially, of Apa Makarios; that of the Virgin Mary known as Deir-es-Suryani, and another, of Anba Bishoi; the monastery of the Virgin Mary known as Deir-El-Moharrak, where the Holy Family lived in a place known as Quos-Quam near the modern Qosia; the monastery of Phakhuri and that of El Shuhada at Esna; the monastery of St Simeon at Aswan.

These monasteries display different features of Coptic architecture and the massive grandeur of Egypt's heritage. The style that the Copts developed, in architecture as in the other forms of art, was a style of their own, proof of the existence of Coptic civilization. There are marble columns with marble capitals ornamented with acanthus leaves, limestone capitals adorned with vine leaves and branches (a limestone capital of a column with bas-relief representing acanthus branches and leaves carved as if swayed by the wind), others still ornamented with bunches of grapes or palm leaves (St Jeremias Monastery at Saqqara) (fig. 1). The vine is a symbol of Christ ("I am the vine and you are the branches"), while the palm is a common symbol of victory or of welcome.

Convents for women or for nuns were erected in the cities as well as in the deserts. They are still to be found in Cairo. In the nuns' convent named after St George we find a high wooden door with 2 high shutters in the big hall preceding the Chapel of St George, with a floral decoration beautiful in its simplicity.

The Copts built churches as well, the high-vaulted arc with rounded top being one of the features of Coptic architecture. They were also the early inventors of the dome placed at the end of the church, above the altar.

---

[1] Monasticism has survived in Egypt and has given the Coptic Church an unbroken line of 116 patriarchs, beginning with St Mark. In a few years it had spread over the entire Christian world.

1. Limestone capital, Saqqara

The Coptic Museum in Old Cairo and many museums in Europe and in the USA possess a great deal of Coptic architectural fragments consisting of niches, columns, capitals, pilasters, lintels, sculptured stones, door jambs and window frames. We must not forget the pulpit of the 6th cent. A.D., now in the Saqqara hall of the Coptic Museum, made of limestone,[2] which led to the development of the Moslem mimbar made of wood. It is interesting to mention that pieces of a broken marble column capital ornamented with gold stripes have been found in the remains of the church of St Mary in Tell Atrib near Benha (excavated by Dr Barbara Ruszczyc of the Polish Centre of Mediterranean Archaeology of the University of Warsaw in Cairo in cooperation with the Coptic Committee). The Arabic historian El Makrizi[3] described these capitals decorated with gold when writing of this church.

2. Sculpture

Sculpture is another aspect of Coptic civilization. The Copts used to decorate their churches with different kinds of stone sculptured to form the figures of Saints (i.e. Saint Menas on a marble panel shown in relief, standing in between two camels, now in the Graeco-Roman Museum in Alexandria), plants, birds, or geometrical designs. Their houses were decorated with subjects from daily life, such as scenes representing the Nile (the life of Egypt in all periods ancient and modern), the land and plant life, i.e. the gathering of grapes in a vineyard.

3. Painting

The walls, domes and columns of the early Coptic churches and monasteries were decorated with paintings of a) Adam and Eve (fig. 2) or other subjects from the Old Testament, and b) Christian

---

[2] In the Hanging Church there is a pulpit of marble.
[3] Makrizi, *Al Khitat* XXV, 3,5.

subjects such as Christ, the Virgin Mary, the Disciples, Saints, Martyrs, etc. These mural frescoes were painted by Coptic artists. The Coptic Museum in Old Cairo contains a large number of paintings and frescoes from ancient Coptic churches and monasteries. One of the principal frescoes in the Coptic Museum is that of Bawit (fig. 3). The painting had been executed upon a layer of clay in a kind of niche. In the upper part there is a representation of Christ seated in majesty, surrounded by symbols of the four Evangelists of the Apocalyptic vision, flanked by the representations of the two archangels, one of a light face representing the sun, the other of a dark face representing the moon and the stars. In the lower part, there is the Madonna and Christ flanked not only by the twelve Apostles, but also by the two local saints of Egypt. It dates from the end of the 5th or the beginning of the 6th cent. A.D.

Another fresco is known from Saqqara. Its subject is the representation of the Virgin Mary nursing the infant Jesus in a way recalling Isis nursing the infant Horus. It dates to the 6th cent. A.D.

A third interesting polychrome fresco showing Adam and Eve before eating the forbidden fruit and then after the fall. It comes from Fayum and dates to the 10th cent. A.D.

Only recently have the relics of Christian Nubia (both Sudanese and Egyptian) been uncovered; it has been proved that there were churches and monasteries built along both banks of the Nile. Hundreds of frescoes have also been found. Some of these frescoes are now in the Khartoum Museum, others are in the Warsaw National Museum (Poland), still others in the Coptic Museum. Some of these Nubian Christian frescoes have been exhibited in the Coptic Art Exhibition in 1963 in Villa Hügel, Essen, West Germany.

From the 10th cent. A.D. on the Coptic painters collaborated with Nubian, Greek and Armenian artists and the mural paintings were replaced by icons. Some beautiful icons still remain *in situ* in the Abu Sarga church (or Saint Sergius Church) — an icon in the southern sanctuary representing the Flight of the Holy Family to Egypt — and the Abu Sifain in Old Cairo. Not only did the Copts follow

2. Mural from Kom el Baragat. Adam and Eve

3. An apse composition from Bawit

the accomplishments of their ancestors in this respect, but they also improved upon them. After the 10th cent. A.D. the Coptic icons came under the influence of Byzantine and Arabic art.

Some of these ancient churches preserving very early characteristics of architecture and painting are still to be found in the vicinity of the Coptic Museum in Old Cairo.

4. Industries

a) Textiles

Coptic textiles are of great importance to Egyptian history, since from the most ancient times the Egyptians were renowned for the manufacture of textiles. The earliest stuffs are fully pagan in character, such as the representation of Venus, others cover the period of transition from paganism to Christian art, still others are plainly Christian in character. The designs encompass also scenes from daily life, such as a player of musical instruments and dancing horses and similar ones. The Coptic textile industry has been attracting a great deal of attention, specimens of great beauty are on display in many museums. Even in Japan 10 big volumes on Coptic textiles have been published.

b) Woodwork

Coptic carpenters carried out their work with considerable taste and skill and had a profound knowledge of the different kinds of wood. For example, cedar wood inlaid with thin plates of ivory can be seen in the Hanging Church. They produced a considerable quantity of valuable work either for religious purposes, to be used in churches and monasteries, or for everyday use in houses (doors, cupboards, furniture).

The Coptic Museum possesses a rich collection of carved and painted items showing scenes connected with the Nile — boats, crocodiles, fish, lotus plants, birds, pigeons among them, etc. Other objects present religious scenes, for instance the long panel of the 5th cent A.D. once part of a door lintel, now in the Coptic Museum, with a representation of the Entry of Jesus into Jerusalem on Palm Sunday.

c) Metal work

As in the case of all the ancient arts, in this respect also the Copts inherited the great skill of their ancestors, the ancient Egyptians. The metal collections, exhibited in various churches, monasteries and museums, are remarkable for the diversity of the metal used: gold, silver, bronze, copper and iron.

Most of the metal objects were used for religious purposes (censors, chandeliers, crosses, silver boxes for the Bible ornamented with floral designs and Coptic relief inscriptions of the 6th cent. A.D.) (fig. 4). Objects of everyday use include jewels, rings, bracelets with snake heads, earrings of gold (fig. 5) and bronze oil lamps of different shapes (fig. 6).

d) Glass

Glass was produced in ancient Egypt from the most ancient times it seems, being apparently an Egyptian invention. In the Coptic period, the glass industry was one of the most important industries in Egypt. This is clear from the number of stained glass windows visible in the architecture of ancient churches and monasteries.

e) Pottery

The different museums of Egypt and abroad contain fine plates and pottery dishes, some of which are ornamented with animals, plants, birds and fish.

f) Ivory

The decoration of the doors of churches with ivory shows the keen taste of the Coptic artist for this field of production, a skill equally well visible in the

4. Silver box for the Bible

5. Two earrings, gold

6. Oil lamp, bronze

ornamentation of the small ivory objects such as boxes, hair combs, bracelets and other items for personal use.

5. Inscriptions

The Coptic inscriptions are written on different materials such as papyrus (the changing from the papyri rolls to the codices was one of the achievements of the Coptic period), parchment, ostraca (fragments of inscribed broken pottery or limestone) and paper. One of the limestone ostraca shows a sarcastic sketch of a man falling down off a palm tree.

Examples of Coptic literature are widespread in the libraries of monasteries and in the different museums of the world. Some of the Coptic manuscripts have figural illumination, others have multi-coloured geometrical designs or ornamentation.

6. Folk Art

Folk art is represented on Coptic textiles, e.g. the scene of the dancing horse shown in front of a figure playing a flute shown on a linen polychrome curtain now in the Coptic Museum. It should be noted that dancing horses have remained a folk entertainment till today.

Riding horses was a favoured entertainment in the Coptic period. This is illustrated in the Nag-Hammadi Codices, where a verse of Thomas the Evangelist explains that one cannot ride two horses at the same time.

Among the toys displayed in the Hannover Museum there is a metal figure of a man riding on horseback.

Bibliography

1. Marcus Simaika, *A Brief Guide to the Coptic Museum*, 1938.
2. Otto Meinardus, *Monks and Monasteries of the Egyptian Deserts*, 1961.
3. Pahor Labib, *The Coptic Museum and the Fortress of Babylon*, 1962.
4. Pahor Labib, *Coptic Gnostic Papyri in the Coptic Museum*, 1956.
5. Pahor Labib and Victor Girgis, *The Coptic Museum and the Fortress of Babylon*, 1975.
6. Villa Hügel, *Koptische Kunst Ausstellung*, 1963.

COPTIC STUDIES

Adam Łukaszewicz

Einige Bemerkungen zu den Asketen in den griechischen urkundlichen Papyri

Die Askese gehört zu den interessantesten Aspekten des religiösen und sozialen Lebens im spätantiken und koptischen Ägypten. Diese Erscheinung spiegelt sich in aller Mannigfaltigkeit in den griechischen und koptischen hagiographischen Quellen, die die wohl interessanteste Epoche der Geschichte des ägyptischen Christentums betreffen.

Wir finden jedoch auch in den urkundlichen Papyri einige Erwähnungen der ägyptischen Asketen. Der Zweck dieser Bemerkungen ist es, eine kurze Übersicht der griechischen Papyrusurkunden zu geben, die als Quelle zu diesem Thema benutzt werden können.

Selbstverständlich handelt es sich hier nicht um eine generelle Besprechung der Erscheinungen Askese und Eremitismus im spätantiken Ägypten, sondern um eine kurze Überlegung über den Quellenwert einer Urkundenkategorie. Aus den griechischen Papyrusurkunden können wir natürlich nur einen beschränkten Beitrag zur Geschichte des ursprünglichen, heroischen Mönchtums erwarten. Das ergibt sich aus der Natur der Urkunden, die ja ein Element des *weltlichen* Lebens waren. Unter Asketen verstehen wir hier nicht nur die Einsiedler, sondern auch einige Zönobiten oder Vertreter der Übergangsstufe des » kollektiven Eremitismus «, wie sie A.S. Atiya nennt. [1] Auf die weite Problematik des organi-sierten Mönchtums wollen wir hier jedoch nicht eingehen.

Henri Henne hat seinerzeit gesagt, es bestünde » un certain lien entre l'*anachôrésis* des papyrus administratifs, et l'*anachorèse* chrétienne, c'est--à-dire, l'état d'anachorète. « [2] Obwohl viele psychologische Gründe bestehen, die das Vergleichen beider Erscheinungen rechtfertigen (und zwar: die zivilisationsfeindliche Tendenz, der Wille zur Freiheit, das Bedürfnis nach innerer Ruhe und Unterlassung der *negotia saecularia* u.s.w.), kann man jedoch von einer direkten Verbindung nicht sprechen. Nur die Terminologie ist dieselbe.

Das Wort ἀναχωρέω ist schon sehr früh zu einem *terminus technicus* für die Flucht der mit Steuern überlasteten Bauern geworden, die als ἀνακεχωρεκότες bezeichnet wurden. [3]

Es bezeichnete später auch die Zuflucht zu einem christlichen heiligen Ort (so z.B. im Falle der entflohenen Rekruten, die im Kloster des Phoibammon Schutz suchten: εἰσκρύβωμεν κτλ. und ἀναχωροῦμεν εἰς ὧδε). [4] Das griechische Wort ἀναχωρητής, die übliche Bezeichnung eines Einsiedlers, ist nicht nur in den griechischen Papyrusurkunden vorhanden [5], sondern auch — und sogar häufiger — in den koptischen, die hier nicht besprochen werden [6], oft natürlich mit dem koptischen Artikel. [7] Der Artikel Π — erscheint

---

[1] Aziz S. Atiya, *A History of Eastern Christianity*, London 1968, S. 61.

[2] H. Henne, *Documents et Travaux sur l'anachôrèsis, Akten des VIII. Internationalen Kongresses für Papyrologie*, Wien 1956, S. 65.

[3] Vgl. z.B. A. Świderek, OI ΤΩΙ ONTI ANAKEΧΩΡΕΚΟΤΕΣ, *Festschrift zum 150-jährigen Bestehen des Berliner Ägyptischen Museums*, Berlin 1974, S. 425–429.

[4] Greek Graff. Phoeb. 2.

[5] P. Jews 1925.24–25 (IV); P.Herm.Rees 7.21 = Nald.82(IV); 10.2 = Nald.85 (IV); PSI XIII 1342.5,27 = Nald.86(V); P.Ant. III 202 b 9 (VI/VII); P. Lond. I 77.76, S. 235 (VI/VII).

[6] Z.B. Copt.O.Phoeb. 8.4; 38.5; Copt.Graff.Phoeb. 145; P.V. Jernštedt, *Koptskie teksty gos. Muzea Iz. Is.im. A.S. Puškina*, Moskwa 1959, Nr. 56.18; L. Mc.Coull, P.Freer 2–4 (Kommentar S. 50 mit Literatur- und Quellenangaben).

[7] Copt.O.Phoeb. 8.4; Copt.Graff.Phoeb. 145.

aber vor dem Wort ἀναχωρητής auch in einem griechischen Kontext des 4. Jahrhunderts.[8] Ein anderer Terminus, der einen Asketen bezeichnet, lautet ἀποτακτικός[9], bzw. ἀποτακτάριος[10] oder ἀποτακτήρ[11], ἀποτάσσομαι und ἀπόταξις sind übliche Bezeichnungen, die sich auf den Verzicht auf den κόσμος beziehen; in dem Sinne erscheinen sie häufig in der Literatur.[12] Zu ähnlichen Bezeichnungen gehören die Partizipial-formen von ἀσκέω und θρησκεύω.[13] Eine Urkunde aus dem 6. Jahrhundert erwähnt einen Styliten (στυλλίτης)[14]. Es fehlen aber Zeugnisse der Dendriten oder anderer besonderen Arten der Asketen.

Die in Frage kommenden Texte vertreten verschiedene Urkundenkategorien: Briefe, Rechnungen, Verträge, Quittungen, Steuerlisten. Sie kommen (soweit die Herkunft bekannt ist) aus: Theben (Dscheme)[15], Antinoupolis[16], Oxyrhyn-chos[17], Fayum[18], Hermopolis oder *nomos Hermopolites*[19].

Die meisten und auch inhaltlich wichtigsten Urkunden, in denen die Asketen erscheinen, sind jedoch Briefe. Wir verfügen über 2 kleine, Anachoreten betreffende Archive, wenn man die-ses Wort in Bezug auf sehr wenig umfassende Urkundengruppen benutzen darf. Das von H.I. Bell im Jahre 1924 veröffentlichte *dossier* des Anachoreten Papnuthios besteht aus 7 Urkunden unbekannter Herkunft, die nur paläographisch datierbar sind[20]. Die andere Gruppe besteht aus 4 Papyri aus dem Archiv des ἄπα Ἰωάννης. Diese Urkunden kommen aus Hermopolis[21]. Beide Urkundengruppen werden in das 4. Jahrhundert datiert. Der Herausgeber der P. Jews 1923–1929 will sie der Mitte des 4. Jahrhundert zuschreiben.

Die erste Frage, die sich im Zusammenhang mit diesen Texten stellt, ist, ob die Personen aus hagiographischen Quellen bekannt sind. Bell, der sich für die Identifizierung der in den von ihm edierten Urkunden erwähnten Personen mit his-torischen Persönlichkeiten stark eingesetzt hat, hat die Frage nach Identität des Papnuthios nicht lösen können[22]. In der Tat ist der Name Παπνούθιος zu banal, um ohne klare Hinweise in den Texten einen Identifizierungsversuch zu wagen. Auch im Falle des Ἰωάννης aus der Gegend von Hermopolis ist eine Identifizierung mit einem aus der Literatur bekannten Anachoreten wohl nicht möglich.

Außerdem sind folgende Personen bezeugt: P. Würzb. 16, die Gestellungsbürgschaft eines Diakons (10.Okt.349) wurde von Αὐρήλιος Ἀγαθὸς [ἀποτα]κτικὸς υἱὸς Συρίου [πρυτα]νεύσαντος geschrieben. Die Ergänzung [ἀποτα]κτικὸς von Wilcken passt gut zum Kontext, in dem auch ein Diakon und ein Pres-byter erwähnt werden. Wenn auch die andere Konjektur zu]νευσαντος richtig ist, hätten wir hier eine interessante Angabe über die soziale Abstammung, die auf einen Vertreter der städ-tischen Oberschicht in der Rolle eines ἀποτακτικός hinweist. P. Lips.28.7,27(381)enthält den Namen eines ἀποτακτικός Silvanus, Sohn des Petesios und der Teeus, aus der κώμη Ἄρεως (Fayum). Im hermopolitanischen P. Flor.I 71.722 (IV) wird Μακάριος ἀποτακτικός erwähnt.

Der Empfänger des PSI XIII 1342 (Anfang V. Jhdt.) = Nald.86 hieß ἄπα Σαβῖνος ἀναχωρητής (5,27).

In P.Oxy.X 1311 (V) wird Ἀνιανὸς πρ(εσβύτερος) μαρτυρ(ίου) Ἄπα Ἰούστου erwähnt.

---

8 P.Herm.Rees 10.2.

9 P.Herm.Rees 9.2 (IV); P.Würz. 16.20 (?) (349); P.Lips. 28.7,27 (381); P.Flor. I 71.722 (IV).

10 SB VI 9608.4 (VI).

11 P.Oxy.X 1311.

12 E.g. Hist.mon.Aeg., Joan.Lyco. 145.

13 P.Jews 1926. 9–11: τῶν ασκούντων καὶ θρησκευόντων ἀποκαλύμματα δεικνύονται.

14 P.Turner 54.1.

15 P.Lond. I 77, S. 235 (um 600): das Testament des Apa Abraham.

16 P.Turner 54 (6. Jahrhundert): Vertrag über Wasserlieferungen an *monasterion* des Apa Joannes; P.Ant. III 202 b 9 (6./7. Jahrhundert): Rechnungen.

17 P.Oxy. X 1311 (5. Jahrhundert): Quittung über das Öl für einen Einsiedler.

18 SB VI 9608 (6. Jahrhundert): Brief über Steuerangelegenheiten; P. Würzb. 16 (349): Gestellungsbürgschaft eines Diakons.

19 P.Herm.Rees 7–10 (5. Jahrhundert): Briefe an Joannes; P.Lips. 28 (381): Adoptionsurkunde; P.Flor. I 71.722 (4. Jahrhundert): Rechnungen; PSI XIII 1342.5,27 = Nald.86 (Anfang (5. Jahrhundert): Brief der Sitologen.

20 P. Jews 1923–1929.

21 P.Herm.Rees 7–10.

22 P.Jews, S. 101–102.

SB VI 9608 (VI) aus Κόμα (Fayum) enthält den Namen eines Θεόδωρος ὁ ἀποτακτάριος (Z.4).

Im P.Turner 54 (VI) finden wir ἄββα Ἰωάννης στυλλίτης (Z. 1).

P.Lond.I 77 ist das bekannte Testament des Apa Abraham, ἀναχωρητής, Bischof von Hermonthis.[23]

P.Ant.III 202 b enthält in Z.9 die Wörter:]αγαϑον ἀναχωρ(ητήν).

Der Herausgeber sieht in αγαϑον einen vollständigen Eigennamen Ἀγαϑός (vgl. P.Würzb. 16.19), was aber nicht die einzige Möglichkeit ist. Es könnte beispielsweise die Endung eines *nomen compositum* sein).

Es ist hier auch die Urkunde eines Ἀντώνιος zu erwähnen. Wegen der angeblichen Seltenheit des Namens sah der Herausgeber in ihr einen Brief des hl. Antonius, und zwar an den aus der *Vita* des Antonius bekannten Ammon (oder Amoun), von dessen Namen allerdings nur 2 Anfangsbuchstaben im P.Lond. V 1658 da sind. Diese Interpretation ist natürlich wegen der Häufigkeit sowohl des Namens Ἀντώνιος wie der von Ammon abgeleiteten Personennamen völlig unverbindlich und aus anderen Gründen sicher abzulehnen. Trotzdem wurde sie 1968 von M. Naldini wiederholt[24].

Welche Hinweise liefern die Urkunden sonst? Es fehlen in den Texten jegliche Informationen über die asketischen Praktiken. Auch über die Personen und Angelegenheiten der Asketen ist äußerst wenig überliefert.

Nach der Meinung des Herausgebers ist P.Herm. Rees 10 als ein Brief des Anachoreten Joannes und der anderen Personen an einen geistlichen Würdenträger zu interpretieren. So sieht auch M.Naldini diese Urkunde, die er unter Nr.85 in seinem Werk wieder veröffentlicht.

Der unvollständige Text lautet am Anfang:

[± 10] Θεῷ μεμελημένῳ

[± 8 Ἰω]άνης παναχωρητής

[ ]ιος καὶ Σόϊς καὶ Πατουμέϑις (M. Manfredi, vgl.BL VI)

In der Lücke am Anfang der Z.3 ergänzt Rees καί, was Joannes, zusammen mit den anderen drei, zum Absender dieser Bittschrift macht. Desungeachtet – und trotz der falschen Benutzung der Nominativform statt Dativform – ist Joannes doch ohne Zweifel der Empfänger des Briefes von (παρά am Anfang der Z.3 zu ergänzen) ...ios, Sois und Patumethis[25]. Diese wenden sich an ihn um Hilfe vor Gericht, da sie dort angeblich falsch angeklagt worden sind (es wäre übrigens überraschend, wenn der Anachoret, der selbst als Empfänger demütiger. Bitten galt, seinerseits zusammen mit anderen eine ähnliche Bitte an eine geheimnisvolle Persönlichkeit richten würde).

Wenn P.Herm.Rees 10 als Autograf eines Asketen ausfällt, bleibt uns P.Würzb. 16 (349), wo aber der ἀποτακτικός nur die Rolle der Schreibers für einen ἀγράμματος (Z.19–23) spielt.

Das späte Testament des Abraham, Anachoret und Bischof von Hermonthis (P.Lond.I 77, S.235, ca. A.D. 600) ist schon vielfach kommentiert worden, u.a. als Beweis dafür, daß der Bischof nur koptisch sprach und darum auch dieser griechische Text in seinem Auftrag formuliert worden ist.

Der Text, in dem ein mit einem εὐαγὲς μοναστήριον verbundener στυλίτης erscheint (P.Turner 54,5,VI), berührt das Problem der Wasserlieferungen, das sich auch im Falle der einzelnen Asketen stellte. Die *Historia monachorum* (XXII.5) bringt darüber eine interessante Geschichte über den Eremiten Amun, der das Wasser (laut Text) für den Fall eines Besuches brauchte. Ein freiwilliger, aber nicht zuverlässiger Lieferant wurde durch übernatürliche Kräfte für die Nicht–Lieferung eines πίϑος Wassers bestraft – sein Kamel fiel sofort den Wölfen zum Opfer.

In manchen Texten finden wir klare Andeutungen auf eine Gemeinschaft (Gruppe) der die dort erwähnten Asketen angehören. Viele tragen die entsprechende Bezeichung als eine Art Ehrentitel, der bestimmt durch (frühere?) asketische Praktiken begründet war. Der Bischof Abraham war höchstwahrscheinlich im Moment der Niederschrift seines Testaments kein richtiger Anachoret mehr (P.Lond.I 77,S.235). In einem Papyrus aus Antinoupolis (P.Ant.III 202 b 9) erscheint der Anachoret in den Kirchen- und Klosterrechnungen.

---

[23] Dazu vgl. M. Krause, *Apa Abraham von Hermonthis: ein oberägyptischer Bischof um 600* (Diss.), Berlin 1956.

[24] M. Naldini, *Il Cristianesimo in Egitto. Lettere private nei papiri dei secoli II–IV*, Firenze 1968, Nr. 42; vgl. G. Ghedini, *Lettere cristiane dai papiri greci del IIIe IV secolo.*, Milano 1923. Vgl. dazu die Kritik der E. Wipszycka, » Remarques sur les lettres privées des IIe–IVe siècles (à propos d'un livre de M. Naldini) «, JJP 18 (1974), 203–221.

[25] Auf eine solche Möglichkeit hat schon J. Rea, Cl.Rev. 16, S. 43 hingewiesen.

Ein Papyrus aus dem Fayum (SB VI 9608.4) erwähnt den ἀποτακτάριος Theodoros zusammen mit einem Hesychios.

Ein zu Öllieferungen berechtigter ἀποτακτήρ aus dem Raum Oxyrhynchos war mit dem Martyrium des Apa Justus verbunden (P.Oxy.X 1311).

Bei PSI XIII 1342.5,27 liegt die Vermutung nahe, daß der ἄπα Σαβῖνος ἀναχωρητής an den sich die Sitologen aus dem *nomos* Hermopolites wenden, wohl ein Archimandrit (oder ähnliches) war. Auch die Texte aus dem 4. Jahrhundert erwähnen klar die Genossen der Anachoreten, und zwar P.Herm.Rees 8.20–22 und 9.16–20. Zu derselben Zeit wirkt ein ἀποτακτικός als Schreiber einer Urkunde (P.Würzb.11).

P.Jews 1925 hat in der Adresse eine von Bell vorgeschlagene *lectio* μ]ονῖς (statt μονῆς) μονα[χῶ]ν.

Diese Lesung benötigt jedoch eine Korrektur. Statt μ]ονῖς usw. ist Πι]όνις μονά[ζω]ν zu lesen. Es ist also das Ende der Adresse mit der Angabe des Absenders.

Als das wichtigste Material müssen wir aber vor allem die in den Briefen erhaltenen Angaben über die Stellung der Asketen in der Gesellschaft des spätantiken und koptischen Ägypten betrachten. Der erhaltene Anachoreten-Briefwechsel, der hier als Quelle benutzt werden kann, besteht aus:

1. Höflichkeitsbriefen verschiedener weltlicher und geistlicher Persönlichkeiten,
2. Briefen vornehmer Personen, die von Anachoreten ständig beraten wurden,
3. Bittschriften verschiedener Art.

Die meisten der Briefe enthalten nichts mehr als eine Reihe von untertänigen Wendungen, Grüßen und Bitten um Gebete für den Absender.

Die Versuche zur Identifizierung der Autoren, vielleicht mit Ausnahme von Αὐσόνιος (P.Jews 1924.2) der an Papnuthios schrieb und tatsächlich mit dem gleichnamigen *praeses Augustamnicae* identisch sein kann, sind alle mißlungen, und es besteht auch wenig Hoffnung auf bessere Ergebnisse in der Zukunf. Wir können trotzdem mit Sicherheit feststellen, daß die Absender der Briefe meistens der sozialen Oberschicht angehörten. P. Jews 1924 (Brief des Ausonius) ist im Stil fast lakonisch und informativ. Die Bitte um Gebete hat eigentlich einen rein formalen Charakter. Ein anderes Fragment des Briefes scheint interessanter zu sein, und zwar die Wörter: μεμνημένος τῶν ἐντολῶν τῆς σῆς θεοσεβίας κτλ. Es ist klar, daß der Brief nur ein Glied in einem Briefwechsel war. Wenn die Identifizierung des

Ausonius richtig ist, so konnten die » Anweisungen « des Anachoreten wohl nicht nur das Privatleben des *praeses* betreffen.

Es bestehen keine Chancen für eine Bestätigung bzw. endgültige Ablehnung der Hypothese Bells, daß P.Jews 1929 wohl ein Brief des hl. Athanasius an Papnuthios ist.

Ein interessanter Fall ist im P.Jews 1926 zu betrachten. Stil, Rechtschreibung und die Schrift einer Frau namens Οὐαλερία beweisen keineswegs ihre hohe Ausbildung. Trotzdem scheint der Inhalt auch auf eine vornehme Schicht der Gesellschaft hinzuweisen. Valeria bittet um Hilfe bei der Krankheit, die sie als δυσποία δεινή bezeichnet.

Auch Herakleides (P.Jews 1928) wendet sich an Papnuthios mit der Bitte um Heilung und deutet auf seine früheren (brieflichen?) Kontakte mit dem Asketen hin: ἀεὶ μὲν σός ὁ καιρὸς τοῦ εὔξασθαι ὑπὲρ ἡμῶν (Z.3) und διὰ τῶν εὐχῶν σου βο[η]θείας δ[εό]μεθα (Z.4).

Es fehlt natürlich kaum die übertriebene byzantinische Stilistik, vor allem im P.Jews 1927, dessen Autor seine Absicht, Papnuthios zu besuchen andeutet.

Auch 2 Briefe aus dem » Archiv « des Joannes bestehen praktisch nur aus höflichen Wendungen und Bitten um ein Gebet (P.Herm. Rees 8;9). Von den anderen beiden bietet der eine (P.Herm.Rees 7 = Nald.82) mehrere Interpretationsprobleme, die mit der sehr fragwürdigen Grammatik im Zusammenhang stehen.

Der Petent wohnte im Dorf Pouchis im *nomos Antaioupolites*, also in einer gewissen Entfernung von Hermopolis. Er bittet um Hilfe zur Befreiung von der Militärdienstpflicht. Er läßt verstehen, daß er schon selbst einige Maßnahmen zu diesem Zweck getroffen hat. Da er aber deren Wirksamkeit bezweifelt, richtet er seine Bitte an Joannes: ἵνα ἀπολύομαι ἐὰν μὴ ἀπολυθήσομαι Z.7–8). Er hat dem Sohn eines Extribuns und seinem Assistenten (βοηθός) Geld (8 Solidi Gold) gegeben. Er berichtet auch, daß wegen des Geldes seine Kinder bei einem Pfandleiher verpfändet sind. Zum Schluß gibt er als Begründung seiner Ansprüche eine Fingerkrankheit (!) an. Er erwartet vom Anachoreten, daß er einen Brief an den Extribun schickt, um die Befreiung zu sichern.

Die Behauptung Naldinis, daß der Extribun » evidentemente amico del monaco « sei, paßt nicht gut zu den Hinweisen des Absenders, an wen und weswegen der Anachoret den Brief schicken soll. Er schreibt auch: ἔλαβες γὰρ παρ' ἐμοῦ ἵνα ἀπολύωμαι καὶ οὐκ ἀπολυσόν μαι (Z.10–11). Rees und Naldini nehmen ἔλαβες wörtlich und behaupten, daß der Petent auch dem Anachoreten Geld überreicht hat. Wenn aber kein Zweifel darüber besteht, daß ἀπολύσον als ἀπέλυσαν, zu verstehen ist, ist wahrscheinlich auch anzunehmen, daß mit ἔλαβες ἔλαβε gemeint ist, was sich auf den Sohn des Extribuns bezieht. *Er* hat das Geld genommen und trotzdem wurde der Petent nicht entlassen. » Ich bitte Gott « — schreibt Psois weiter, » daß ich entweder befreit werde oder es werden mir 8 Solidi zurückgegeben «. Es ist natürlich indirekt die Bitte an den Anachoreten.

Dann kommen — erstaunlicherweise in der Mitte des Briefes — die Angaben des Petenten und eine dramatische Mahnung » aber um Gottes willen zögere nicht, mein Herr «, ἤδη γὰρ τὰ τέκνα μου ἔδωκας ὑποθήκας [τ]ῷ δανι[στ]ῆς διὰ τὸ χρυσάφιν. Rees übersetzt wörtlich: » For *you* have already given my children as securities to the money–lender on account of the gold «. Naldini, der in den Texten die Beweise christlicher Tugenden gern findet, kann selbstverständlich eine solche Version nicht akzeptieren und versteht deshalb ἔδωκας als einen Fehler für ἔδωκα. Auch wenn man diese Tendenz nicht teilt, ist diese Interpretation doch wahrscheinlich die einzig mögliche. Das χρυσάφιν bezieht sich ohne Zweifel auf die obengenannten Gelder, die der Petent, (bisher) umsonst, den Leuten um den Extribun gegeben hat. Um sich dieses Geld (und nicht eine *nicht erwähnte* Summe für den Anachoreten) zu beschaffen, mußte er die Kinder verpfänden. Ob hier wirklich ὑποθήκη παρὰ τοῦ δανιστοῦ der παραμονή gleich ist, bleibt eine offene Frage [26].

Auch der P.Herm.Rees 10 ist eine Bitte um Intervention bei Behörden (Gericht): αἰτ]ήσης τὸν δικαστὴν ἀκοῦ[σαι ἡμῶν]. Im allgemeinen bekommen wir den Eindruck, daß der Apa Joannes eine sehr mächtige und bei den Behörden sehr einflußreiche Persönlichkeit gewesen ist.

In späterer Zeit (Anfang 5. Jahrhundert) sind es die Sitologen κώμης Ἀλαβαστρίνης, die vom Anachoret Sabinus Übersendung des Geldes für die Steuer des Schmiedes Viktor verlangen [27].

Die Papyrustexte bestätigen also eine wichtige Rolle die die ägyptischen Anachoreten in der Gesellschaft, vor allem im 4. Jahrhundert, spielten. Besonders wichtig sind die Zeugnisse die auf ihren Einfluß bei den Behörden Hinweisen.

Dazu finden wir auch in anderen Quellen sehr interessante Angaben. Und zwar berichtet Sozomenos in seiner Kirchengeschichte über den berühmten Eremiten Antonius Folgendes: » Er bemühte sich äußerst fleißig und mehr als jeder andere um Verteidigung der Benachteiligten. Ihretwegen begab er sich öfters in die Städte. Die Menge der Klagenden zwang ihn, ihre Angelegenheiten vor den Magistratsbeamten und den staatlichen Stellen zu vertreten. Denn jeder schätzte es sehr hoch ein, ihn zu sehen, seine Rede zu hören und seinen Befehlen zu folgen, weil er, obwohl er so bedeutend war, darauf bestand, unbekannt zu bleiben und sich in der Wüste zu verbergen. Obwohl er, unter Druck, gelegentlich in die Stadt kam, um den Klagenden zu helfen, kehrte er sofort nach Erledigung der Sache in die Wüste zurück « (Hist.eccl. I 13, 9–10).

Wir finden Ähnliches auch in den koptischen Quellen. Antonius selbst soll nämlich dem Theodoros, Schüler des Pachomius, erzählt haben, daß er von zahlreichen Leuten dazu gezwungen wurde, an die Behörden und Beamten wegen ihrer Klagen zu schreiben (!) [28].

Übrigens hatte Antonius nicht nur lokale Korrespondenten. Der Kaiser selbst bequemte sich, ihm zu schreiben und um seinen Rat zu bitten, was eine andere Stelle bei Sozomenos bestätigt [29].

Ein anderer Nachfolger des Pachomius, Horsiese, wurde dringend gebeten, sich zum Gouverneur zu begeben und für die Berfreiung der zwei Söhne einer Frau zu plädieren [30].

Diese Stellen bei Sozomenos und die anderen Quellen liefern nicht nur interessante Analogien zu den Daten, die wir in den Papyri finden *. Sie beweisen auch die Mobilität der Asketen, die unter Umständen die Wüste verlassen konnten, um in den Städten ihren Einfluß zugunsten Bedürftiger geltend zu machen.

---

[26] Naldini, *Il Cristanesimo...*, Nr. 82, S. 324.

[27] PSI XIII 1342.5,27.

[28] *Vies coptes de saint Pachôme et de ses premiers successeurs*, trad. L.Th. Lefort, Louvain 1943 (*Bibliothèque du Muséon* 16), 270.

[29] Sozomen., Hist.eccl. 13.1.

[30] *Vies coptes...*, S. 402.

* A d d e n d u m : Auch P.Haun. II 26 (VI–VII) bietet einen interessanten Hinweis auf Briefwechsel eines ἐγκλειστος (Z.3), der sich zum κάστρον τῶν μαύρων (Z.2) begab und jemanden zum theologischen Gespräch εἰς μέσον τόπον (Z.5) einladen wollte. Φιλων ist in diesem Zusammenhang nicht als Personenname, sondern als Ortsname (Philae) zu verstehen. Es ginge also um τὸ κάστρον τῶν μαύρων τὸ πλησίον Φιλῶν, d.h. "das Lager der *Mauri* in der Nähe von Philae".

COPTIC STUDIES

Leslie S. B. MacCoull

Coptic Papyri in the Duke University Collection

The Duke University papyrus collection, housed in Perkins Library, contains 123 inventory numbers of Coptic documentary papyri. They were acquired over time by both donation and purchase, both in Egypt and from emigrés to the United States. Nearly one-half of that number, about sixty inventory numbers, are tiny fragments no bigger than one square centimetre, bearing perhaps one or two letters of inscription, and hence too small to identify or place. Of the remainder of the documentary pieces, over thirty-five are letters, six are accounts, two are *asphaleiai*, one is a *logos mpnoute* document, and seven or eight are literary. The *logos mpnoute* piece, inv. C.4 which contains the *incipit* of the Gospel of Matthew, and inv. C.58, which appears to be a literary text mentioning Anthimos of Trebizond who was deposed from the see of Constantinople in 536 and became a Monophysite culture hero, are being published by myself in the *Bulletin of the American Society of Papyrologists*.

Of the letters, always the most numerous genre of Coptic writing, most are readily classifiable in the light of the new and most useful work of Dr Biedenkopf-Ziehner on epistolary formulary. As expected, they contain personal and place names that will eventually need to be incorporated into a prosopography and gazetteer of Late Antique Egypt. We encounter an unnamed patriarch, Anoup the gardener, the monastery of Apa Apollo (see J. Gascou in ZPE 49 [1982]) *, Paul the teacher, and the usual assortment of abstract forms of address and emotional expressions of greeting and farewell.

A long letter (inv. C.31) addressed to one Saltik mentions the following commodities: three camels, ten camel skins, five *lakane* and five other vessels, sheepskin cloaks, other cloaks, twenty *karamantai*, dates, and a female slave. Inv. C.42 is an account of farm products listing 3 sheep, 6 geese, and 24 bunches of, probably, grapes. Inv. C.46 is a receipt for the *eisbatikon* tax (for shipping goods), mentioned in *P.Oxy.* XIX 2239.21 (A.D. 598) and *P.Lond.* II pp. 333, 393 (vii). One of the most complete texts, or rather a pair of texts, is the letter written on the vertical-fibre side of inv. C.51 from Petre to his brother the *papa* Serene, asking him to intervene in the affairs of one Ammone, and the reply on the other side dictated and signed by Serene himself, in which the ecclesiastic asserts that he has assigned the *ebot n-alhalma*, literally 'month of support', including an artaba of onions and one of lentils (*arshin*). Ammone's case appears to have been a matrimonial one: *analoma* appears in Coptic documents as the technical term for one of the four kinds of matrimonial property.

One of the latest of the documentary pieces appears to be inv. C.75, an *asphaleia* with an oath-clause by Almighty God and signed by Leon the *elakhistos* deacon and John son of Phoibammon. If the last line be correctly read as bearing the year 710 of Diocletian, viz. A.D. 994/5, this document would be a remarkably late Sahidic example of its type.

The Duke collection also includes twenty-five investory numbers of Coptic literary manuscripts, on parchment and paper. Bearing the number 1 is a 109-leaf bilingual Bohairic-Arabic funeral lectionary, dated 14th century (I have not seen the colophon), which will of course be of interest to Fr Ugo Zanetti in his work of untangling the immensely complicated system of liturgical lections is use at different periods. Number 12 may possibly, from its hand, be from the White Monastery (Prof. Orlandi will know): it is a bicolumnar leaf bearing a homiletic text, or possibly the praise of a saint. It

---

*And in Anagennesis 1 (1981), 219–230.

contains the striking phrase ⲭⲓⲣⲟⲕⲣⲁⲫⲟⲛ ⲉⲛⲉ ⲩⲛⲟⲃⲉ a "*cheirographon* (note the legal loan-word) of our sins"; and mentions "the necessity of death for all flesh, (even) if it happens to a poor man..." The writer declares, "I wept for him, upon his honoured ⲗⲉⲓⲯⲁⲛⲟⲛ (relics)": interesting light upon the veneration of relics (and cf. *P. Lond. V* 1698 and *P. Cair. Masp.* II 67151). And he apostrophises, in phrases reminiscent of the Coptic epitaphs we know from Hall and Cramer, 'O death, the destroyer of all *techne*, "O death the *reftounos* (lifter-up) of weeping ⲣⲓⲙⲉ and pain (*lype*)...". We can hear the note of lamenting personification so often found in funerary inscriptions.

As might be expected, the majority of the literary pieces are late and liturgical. Number 17, perhaps 16th century, is two leaves containing the litany of commemorations in the mass: our holy orthodox fathers, ... Alexander, Timothy, Cyril, Dioscorus ⲡⲉⲛⲥⲁϩ, Gregory the Theologian, "who spoke with the Holy Spirit". And the usual formulae of the incarnation are found, viz. that Christ took flesh, died, and rose. The same phrases are found in the late and garbled Number 20, which contains invocations of Christ "who gives life, having taken flesh of the Virgin, as the prophet Isaiah said, saying, Behold, a virgin shall (conceive etc.)" 20 also commemorates Melachias the *prostates* (of the religious community that produced the MS?), Mark the apostle, "the cherubim and seraphim and all the *tagma*(*ta*) in Sion".

Outstanding in the literary group is number 25, two parchment leaves bearing the text of a homily on how to distinguish true dreams and visions that come from God from false *phantasiai* that are unscriptural and diabolical. It has been suggested (by Dr D. Spanel) that the work may be by Shenoute; but this attribution will need exhaustive stylistic analysis by specialists in that field. There are possible parallels in Synesius (and Porphyry) and in Syriac sources that will repay comparative study.

Also kept in the care of Duke University, though they are the property of the University of Mississippi collection, are thirty-three numbered and unnumbered Coptic documentary papyri and two literary fragments. Fifteen of the documents are letters, containing the expected assortment of personal and place names, economic transactions, and greetings. Fragment I C 3 is a letter closing with the formula "Farewell in the power of the Holy Trinity", hitherto attested mostly in the region of Thebes (Biedenkopf, *Briefformular*, p. 253). In a folder numbered "5" is a contract signed by one Andreas son of Paule, fortified by oaths by the Pantocrator, the "throne of ...", and "upon the great *louterion*", witnessed by Pshapshe the priest (serving as *epitrope*), and dated Pharmuthi 12, indiction 15. Two of the papyri are tax receipts, for *diagraphe* and *andrismos*, the latter dated by a coming eleventh indiction. Perhaps relevant to the procedure of conscription of sailors in the Aphrodito area in the 8th century is number I C 24, a receipt from Psate the ⲥⲁϩ and *kalaphates* (caulker), from the *topos* of Apa Apollo: its third-indiction date may correspond to A.D. 719. Also from monks of Apa Apollo named Ersenouphi and Theodore comes number I 20, an account for *demosion* (undated). Finally, number I C 3 bis contains a prayer: "O God, do not show forth to me according to my worthiness; O God do not make me a stranger (Lit. 'be to me in strangerhood'); O God, protect my soul from shame before your fearful tribunal; O God, save me from blame at your great judgement on that day". We shall probably never know the identity of this Coptic forerunner of the *Dies Irae*.

There are of course also Greek papyri in the Duke collection that are of interest for the cultural history of Late Antique Egypt. P.Robinson 29 is an opisthograph literary papyrus that contains a *kanon* on the Virgin Mary, possibly seventh-century, and constructed with all the awareness in the *kanon* form of allusions to the scriptural canticles (Hannah's ode, the song of Habakkuk) as well as the Lucan text of the Magnificat. (For help with this text I am most gretreful to Dr Eva Topping). The poetic text ends with a *proskynesis* to the Trinity and an apostrophe to the Virgin: δόξα σοί, ἡ ἐλπις τῶν ψυχῶν ἡμῶν. Study of texts of this type and date will do much to increase our understanding of the Egyptian roots of liturgical poetry.

One hopes that one day there will be a complete publication of the Duke Coptic texts. In the meanwhile I am grateful to Professors Kent Rigsby, John Oates, William Willis, and Orval Wintermute for giving me permission to work on them and help in making them known to the scholarly community.

COPTIC STUDIES

Giancarlo Mantovani

Illumination et illuminateurs : à la recherche des sources de l'Apocryphon de Jean

Il n'est presque personne qui ne regarde comme la partie plus sûrement païenne de l'AJ ce qui concerne la spéculation sur les quatre illuminateurs. C'est surtout à H.M. Schenke que revient le mérite d'avoir dégagé la caractéristique « sethienne » de cette mythologème, q'on retrouve dans plusieurs écrits de Nag Hammadi, de type non valentinien. Toutefois on doit reconnaître que les éléments de cette spéculation sur la tétrade des φωστήρες ne peuvent pas tous s'éclairer par rapport à une gnose dont la doctrine de révélation est d'inspiration non chrétienne. En particulier, le thème de l'investiture christique (BG : 30,9–31,5) avec le fait de souligner l'excellence du Christ, considéré un et trin (unique autogénéré et trin parce que nous–vouloir–logos), et enfin l'étroite relation établie entre le Christ–autogénéré et les quatre illuminateurs devenus aspects et qualifications du Christ–lumière, donnent à la structure du monde divin de l'AJ un caractère fort christocentrique. De l'analyse des diverses attestations mentionnées dans d'autres écrits apparentés à l'AJ, on peut alors essayer de distinguer les différents éléments qui composent cette spéculation sur les quatre illuminateurs. De toute évidence, c'est dans l'AJ que nous trouvons la forme la plus développée de la tétrade des φωστήρες qui, en développant le symbolisme originaire d'une doctrine angélologique juive, a réinterprété des doctrines gnostiques plus archaïques pour le modifier avec certains traits valentiniens. Cette combinaison de thèmes sotériologiques divers est encore visible dans la double présentation du quaternion vérifiable dans les blocs parallèles de l'AJ et de l'Évangile des Égyptiens. Ces deux schémas, des origines divines et de la fin eschatologique, présentent dans l'É. Égypt. un processus moins christianisé. Ici, des quatre éons luminaires partent toutes les interventions salvatrices dont le but sera de racheter la substance d'en–haut qui est perdue en ce bas–monde. Ce sont en somme les intermédiaires du salut. Dans l'AJ, par contre, ces traditions ont été réinterprétées en fonction d'une nouvelle doctrine du salut, qui se base sur le rôle unique du Christ dans d'œuvre de révélation et d'illumination.

Il est donc nécessaire, par souci de méthode, de commencer par décrire tous les passages où se retrouve le premier schéma – concernant le cadre révélatif du plerome – pour comprendre comment, à l'intérieur de chaque traité, s'explique le thème des φωστήρες, pour enregistrer leurs points communs et surtout leurs divergences.

a) AJ – II 7,22–8,28.
   – II 8,28–9,24.
b) É. Égypt. – III 50,17–22; 52,6–16; 52,19–53,12.
   – III 65,12–26; 69,6.
c) Zostrien – VIII 6,7–7,22; 29,1–15; 51,16–19; 31,15–20; 127,20–27.
d) Melchisédech – IX 6,2–5.
e) Protennoia Trimorphe – XIII 38,33–39,8.
f) Codex Brucianus – éd. Schmidt, p. 264,5–6.
g) Irénée Adv. Haer. – I 29,2

On remarque avant tout dans le texte d'Irénée, parallèle à une partie de l'AJ, une première différence. D'après Irénée I 29,2. l'apparition des quatre éons illuminateurs est mise en relation avec l'Autogénéré : « De Lumine autem, quod est Christus, et de Incorruptela, quattuor emissa luminaria ad circumstantiam Autogeni dicunt ». Cette description aboutit à un schéma ogdoadique, puisqu'on dit que : « Et de Thelemate rursus et aeonia Zoe quattuor emissiones factas ad subministrationem quattuor luminaribus, quas nominant Charin, Thelesin, Synesin, Phronesin ». Cet exposé des quatre illuminateurs figure aussi dans l'É. Égypt. où viennent s'ajouter, comme conjoints, les quatre entités χάρις, αἴσθησις, σύνεσις, φρόνησις ce qui constitue l'ogdoade du Dieu Autogénéré. Puis aux quatre grands luminaires et à leurs noms grecs viennent se joindre une autre ogdoade — non mentionnée en Irénée I 29 — des anges juifs, comme Abraxas, et concepts grecs. Les noms d'Archanges de Gabriel, Gamaliel, Samblo et Abraxas n'apparaissent point dans l'AJ, qui toutefois montre qu'elle part d'une liste identique et la modifie.

L'É. Égypt. offre alors la liste suivante (III 52,8–53,10) :

Harmozel	— χάρις	— Gamaliel	— μνήμη
Oroiael	— αἴσθησις	— Gabriel	— ἀγάπη
Daveithe	— σύνεσις	— Samblo	— εἰρήνη
Heleleth	— φρόνησις	— Abraxas	— αἰώνια ζωή

L'AJ transforme ainsi les deux ogdoades de l'Évangile de manière à aboutir à une dodécade d'éons pour entourer comme un zodiaque céleste la figure du Christ (B.G. 33,7–34,7) :

Harmozel	— χάρις	— ἀλήθεια	— μορφή
Oroiael	— πρόνοια/ἐπίνοια	— αἴσθησις	— μνήμη
Daveithe	— σύνεσις	— ἀγάπη	— ἰδέα
Heleleth	— τελείοτης	— εἰρήνη	— σοφία

Par ces remarques, on peut comprendre comment l'AJ présente une amplification de la tradition connue en Irénée I 29 et une modification substantielle de celle attestée par l'É. Égypt.

Il faut se demander, avant tout, quelle est la signification de cette nouvelle organisation des éons dans l'AJ. Nous donnerons d'abord les arguments suivants pour saisir l'évolution, en étapes successives, de cette liste d'éons :

1. On voit comment, dans Irénée I 29 et dans l'É. Égypt., les noms et les fonctions des entités grecques sont des gloses à terminologie sapientielle introduites pour expliquer les noms sémitiques des archanges, c'est-à-dire des quatre φωστήρες. Cette structure explicative a été oubliée dans l'AJ, qui présente une série de quatre puissances et douze éons à terminologie grecque : expressions hypostatiques du Christ–plérome.

2. Dans l'É. Égypt., on trouve désignés comme conjoints (σύζυγος = É. Égypt. 52.16 : διάκονος) des φωστήρες quatre autres figures de gardiens célestes, tant le grand Gabriel que l'Abraxas souvent invoqué par les papyrus magiques [1]. Ils apparaissent dans d'autres textes gnostiques avec le rôle de tirer du feu les élus et de les introduire dans les lieux d'en-haut, auprès des quatre illuminateurs [2]. Au contraire, l'AJ a inséré, à côté des quatre illuminateurs, douze éons qui sont tout à fait des dénominations abstraites et qui semblent posséder différentes fonctions. Non plus des gardiens célestes ou des envoyés du monde de la lumière, mais des figures conceptuelles qui décrivent la constitution transcendante du Christ. Une telle transposition, qui fusionne ensemble la constellation des φωστήρες et douze entités abstraites, peut trouver appui dans la combinaison du mythe préalable de l'Autogénéré (Irénée I 29) et des quatre illuminateurs avec l'interprétation christologique connue par les exégètes valentiniens. En effet, il semble possible qu'à partir de la division tripartite en Ogdoade, Décade et Dodécade rappelée par Irénée I 1,3, l'auteur de l'AJ ait voulu hiérarchiser les douze éons de la cour du Christ selon le modèle de la Dodécade née d'Anthropos et d'Ecclesia : « Anthropon autem et ipsum emisisse cum Ecclesia Aenonas XII quibus nomina haec donant : Paracletus et Pistis, Patricos et Elpis, Metricos et Agape, Aenos et Synesis, Ecclesiasticos et Macariotes, Theletos et Sophia » (Irénée I 1,2). Cette Dodécade de Pneumatiká évoque d'une certaine façon, le tableau des six syzyges androgynes du Livre d'Eugnoste III 82,7–83,2, où la dernière entité féminine de la liste est la Sagesse, πίστις. Cela représente une constante dans les systèmes valentiniens. Par conséquent, le morceau de Sophia à la fin de la liste donnée par l'AJ doit avoir été introduit dans le document de base, comme le montre la liste parallèle de l'É. Égypt.

---

[1] R. Reitzenstein, *Poimandres*, p. 294.

[2] Révélation d'Adam V 74, 26–76,7; Codex Brucianus (éd. Baynes, p. 97); et autres traditions conservées par les Mandéens.

d'où Sophia est absente. En créant pour lui-même une série de quatre illuminateurs et douze éons, le Christ de l'AJ s'attribue un espace céleste semblable à la cour divine de l'Homme Barbelo. Les entités classées par rang descendant rappellent (la) ⲦⲀϤⲐⲀⲢⲦⲞⳞ Ⲛ̄ⲠⲚⲈⲨⲘⲀⲦⲒⲔⲎ Ⲛ̄ⲈⲔⲔⲖⲎⳞⲒⲀ (III 55,3–4) de trônes, gloires et autres puissances que dans l'É. Égypt. le grand Oint (ⲚⲬⲢ̄Ⳍ̄) va établir « à l'intérieur des quatre éons » (III 54, 22–23), ainsi que les « myriades sans nombre » des anges qui sont « au service » du Fils de l'Homme dans le Livre d'Eugnoste (III 81,1 sq. = le Christ de S.J.C. BG 99, 14–100,3). Il faut remarquer, à ce propos, que comme pour Eugnoste et SJC, ainsi la doctrine valentinienne transmise par Irénée connaît cette terminologie angélologique pour les compagnons du Sauveur Christ : « Paracletum autem misit ad eam (Sophia), hoc est Salvatorem, praestante ei virtutem omnem Patre et omnia sub potestate tradente, et Aeonibus autem similiter, uti in eo omnia conderentur, visibilia et invisibilia, Throni, Divinitates, Dominationes. Mittitur autem ad eam cum coaetaneis suis Angelis » (Irénée I 4,5).

Ces « angeli coaetani » du Sauveur sont aussi appelés vision des Lumières : « Hanc autem Achamoth extra passionem factam concepisse de gratulatione eorum quae cum eo sunt luminum (visionem), hoc est Angelorum qui erant cum eo, et delectatam in conceptu eorum peperisse fructus secundum illius imaginem docent, partum spiritalem secundum similitudinem factum satellitum Salvatoris » (Irénée I 4,5).

A l'instar de ces témoignages, on peut essayer de comprendre au moins un aspect de la connexion, établie par l'AJ, entre le Christ lumière et les êtres qui l'entouraient : appelés φωστήρες et éons. Dans ce contexte nous avons une assimilation du thème juif des quatre anges gardiens du trône de la Merkabah (inspiré en dernier lieu de la vision d'Ézéchiel I 5–21; 10 1–22), avec une doctrine des éons tout à fait particulière. Le but de l'auteur de l'AJ nous semble avoir été de vouloir transposer l'ensemble des triades liées aux quatre grands

anges en concepts angélologiques. Voici d'avance le cadre des questions :

a) d'une part, les traducteurs de l'AJ montrent quelques difficultés dans la caractérisation des φωστήρες, en même temps appelés éons et anges : BG 33, 8–9 « Harmozel qui est l'ange de lumière, dans le premier éon »,
III « Harmozel qui est l'ange du premier éon », II « l'éon lumière Armozel qui est le premier ange »;

b) d'autre part les douze éons, qui évoquent une sorte d'Ecclesia angélologique du Christ, rappellent les aspects de la Sagesse juive, ainsi que des qualifications intellectuelles. Cette dernière imagination des éons renvoie à un arrière-plan platonicien, déjà représenté par Philon qui identifie ἄγγελοι, δυνάμεις, λόγοι, ἀρεταί, σφραγῖδες à ἰδέαι[3].

c) enfin, la structure de ces triades comme dodécade peut bien refléter un schéma valentinien. Or, pour retourner aux traditions concernant les anges « au service » du Christ, qui comme on a pu le constater pour le livre d'Eugnoste, ne sont pas spécifiquement valentiniens, on peut noter que dans le valentinisme la venue du Christ est souvent associée à des anges porteurs de révélation et de gnosis[4]. D'ailleurs on trouve un rapport entre le Sauveur et les anges « satellites » : « ...satellites quoque ei (Salvatorem) in honorem ipsorum eiusdem generis Angelos cum eo prolatos » (Irénée I 2,6).

Dans ce texte, ils sont décrits comme des « gardes du corps », des δορυφόρους semblables à la nature du Christ, appelé ici « l'étoile du plerome ».Tous ces termes techniques peuvent rappeler la description que fait Irénée I 29,2 lorsqu'il dit que les quatre « luminaria » ont été émis par le Christ « ad circustantiam Autogeni », c'est-à-dire dans le sens de l'entourer (= comme un roi) ou de l'assister (= comme gardes du corps). Dans le même contexte, la version du codex III a conservé le terme grec παράστασις (III 11,19), ici synonyme de l'autre expression latine d'Irénée utilisée pour l'Autogénéré : « ad repraesentationem »[5]. Dans ce cas, il n'est pas possible

---

[3] G.C. Stead, « In Search of Valentinus », dans: *The Rediscovery of Gnosticism* I, Leiden 1980, p. 94.

[4] G. Quispel, « Genius and Spirit », dans: H. Krause (éd.), *Essays on the Nag Hammadi Texts*, Leiden 1975, pp. 155–169.

[5] R. Van den Broek, « Autogenes and Adamas. The Mythological Structure of the Apocryphon of John », dans: M. Krause (éd.), *Gnosis and Gnosticism*, Leiden 1981, p. 21.

d'interpréter, comme l'a proposé S. Petrement, cette terminologie dans le sens de « un développement du valentinisme » [6]. Le texte copte des quatre recensions de l'AJ a en effet conservé deux

BG 32,6–7	ⲁϥⲁ︢ⲍⲉⲣⲁⲧϥ ⲉⲣⲟϥ	III 11,3–6	ⲉⲩⲡⲁⲣⲁⲥⲧⲁⲥⲓⲥ
BG 33,2–4	ⲉⲩⲁ︢ⲍⲉⲣⲁⲧⲟⲩ ⲉⲣⲟϥ	III 11,19	ⲉⲩⲡⲁⲣⲁⲥⲧⲁⲥⲓⲥ
BG 34,10–11	ⲉⲧⲡⲁⲣ︢ⲍⲓⲥⲧⲁ	III 12,18	ⲁ︢ⲍⲉⲉⲣⲁⲧⲟⲩ

Il est intéressant de noter ce que les versions parallèles ont essayé de traduire. Et seule la version du codex III montre un texte précis quant à l'usage des termes et des significations. En fait, la terminologie grecque a été conservée pour les deux premiers passages (le substantif παράστασις) et au lieu du verbe copte (ⲁ︢ⲍⲉⲉⲣⲁⲧⲟⲩ) pour le troisième. C'est-à-dire qu'on utilise le nom παράστασις (= manifestation) au regard de l'apparition de l'Autogénéré et des quatre illuminateurs au lieu du verbe παριστάναι (= être préposé) donné aux éons. Dans le dernier des trois passages (BG 34,10–12) on reconnaît bien la distinction, quant à leurs niveaux, entre les φωστήρες, qui entourent le (Christ) Autogénéré, et les douze éons qui « se tiennent près (ⲉⲧⲡⲁⲣ︢ⲍⲓⲥⲧⲁ) de l'Enfant, ce grand Autogénéré, Christ ». On voit le glissement de signification depuis l'être à παράστασις de Dieu, jusqu'à devenir παραστάτες ou « satellites » : c'est-à-dire gardes du corps, comme les anges du Sauveur valentinien. Le sens originaire des termes « ad repraesentationem », « ad circustantiam », ‹ⲉⲩⲡⲁⲣⲁⲥⲧⲁⲥⲓⲥ› c'est alors d'indiquer la manifestation de la Gloire (Kabod, Doxa) de Dieu. L'être « παράστασις » indique donc la participation à la gloire de la nature divine et la fonction de la manifester. Ce n'est pas par hasard que, dans l'É. Égypt. où est particulièrement développée la fonction des quatre φωστήρες, le mot-clé utilisé est « le πλήρωμα des quatre éons » (III 50,23–24). Cette même conception se retrouve dans le dernier élément de la quadripartition temporelle de l'histoire du salut, qui désigne dans l'AJ les âmes repenties : « Dans le quatrième éon furent établies les âmes de ceux qui ignorèrent le Plerome et qui ne se sont pas repentis rapidement, mais qui ont persisté un temps et ensuite se sont repentis. Ils furent près du quatrième luminaire, Eleleth » (II 9,18–24).

diverses utilisations du mot παράστασις/ παριστάναι qui doit être eclairci. Nous avons à ce sujet trois passages où revient le sens « être παράστασις » :

Nous voyons qu'une restitution possible du terme « Pleroma », c'est « manifestation/révélation » : ceux qui ignorent le Plerome sont ceux qui n'ont pas reçu la révélation / Doxa des quatre illuminateurs [7].

En conclusion, diversement d'Irénée I 29 – qui donne une tétrade androgyne où sont associés Harmozel, Oroiael, Daveithe et Eleleth avec Charis, Thelesis, Sunesis et Phronesis – on peut noter comment l'AJ présente la combinaison de deux traditions : d'une part les quatre φωστήρες qui restent près de l'Autogénéré, pour manifester la Doxa divine; de l'autre les douze éons, qui évoquent une structure typiquement valentinienne. On voit encore comme cette synthèse est bien marquée lorsque, dans le morceau final de l'exposition dédiée au Christ, il y a la récapitulation suivante :

« – Voilà les quatre luminaires qui se tiennent près de l'Autogénéré divin, – les douze éons qui se tiennent près (παριστάναι) de l'Enfant, ce grand Autogénéré, Christ » (BG 34,7–12)

3. Nous allons maintenant à la recherche des motifs sapientiels. A ce propos on doit remarquer comment la vision christocentrique de l'AJ présente une harmonisation des références à la Sagesse juive avec une théologie de l'Aion tetraprosopon. Le plerome des éons et des illuminateurs qui représentent le Christ, dans la liste des entités précédemment citée, est dit émaner de la syzyge χριστός – ἀφναρσία (BG 32,19 s.) [8]. Ce commencement dans l'AJ, confirmé par Irénée I 29, constitue le leitmotiv des manifestations successives. La raison théologique de ceci, c'est l'identification du Christ avec la Sagesse de Dieu : identification connue aussi par le Nouveau Testament, mais dans l'AJ surtout dérivée des livres sapientiaux juifs. Ἀφθαρσία, le syzygos de

---

[6] S. Petrement, « Les ‹ quatre illuminateurs ›. Sur le sens et l'origine d'un thème gnostique », *Revue des Études Augustiniennes* (1981), 5.

[7] P.H. Poirier et M. Tardieu, « Catégories du Temps dans les écrits gnostiques non- valentiniens », *Laval Théologique et Philosophique* 37 (1981), 3–13.

[8] R. van den Broek, « Autogenes... », 17.

Christ, décrit en effet la nature profonde de Sophia dans la Sapientia Salomonis, où elle est dite demeurer auprès de Dieu (Sap. Salomonis VI,19). On sait qu'une tradition fixée par la théologie gnostique concerne la théologie gnostique concerne la « coniuctio » Christ / Sophia. Dans la SJC, par exemple, dont une version a été trouvée dans le codex Berolinensis à côté de l'AJ, le Christ céleste apparaît en syzyge avec la Sophia pangeneteira [9]. Dans notre texte, tout le cadre rédactionnel — qui comprend la vision initiale et l'hymnologie finale — présente le Révélateur-Christ dans le vêtement de la Sagesse. Cela est démontré par l'utilisation de la formule ἐγὼ εἰμὶ attestée dans le logion de II 2,12–14 et dans l'hymne placé en conclusion de la recension longue. Le choix de ce type théologique est bien visible dans la section christologique (BG 32,19–34,18), où certaines des entités éoniques ont des noms repris des attributs de la Sophia juive. Et voici les parallèles.

L'utilisation d'abstractions intellectuelles pour caractériser la divinité était connue par les écrits sapientiaux et pauliniens, où nous trouvons souvent une structure ternaire pour définir les éloges de la Sagesse. De fait l'auteur de l'AJ a modifié la liste connue par Irénée I 29 et É. Égypt., fabriquant une table de concordance qui pose dans chaque φωστήρ une triade de noms divins. Tout cela reste très proche du langage des sapientiaux. Dans le chap. VIII des Proverbes la Sagesse énumère ses propres qualités par des triades :

Prov. VIII, 12 ἐγὼ ἡ σοφία κατεσκήνωσα
               βουλήν καὶ γνῶσιν καὶ ἔννυιαν...
         14 εμὴ φρόνησις ἐμὴ δε ἰσχύς
         18 πλοῦτος καὶ δόξα...καὶ δικαιοσύνη
Prov.   II,   2 ... σου εἰς σύνεσιν; II, 3–7

Il en est de même dans Jn 14,6 (Voie, Vie, Vérité) et dans Galates V,22 où le καρπὸς του πνεύματος est nommé ἀγάπη, χαρά, εἰρήνη
Dans la Sap. Salomonis se retrouvent d'autres titres, équivalents du terme même de Sagesse, qui reviennent dans l'AJ :
ἀγάπη — αφθαρσία (Sap. Salom. VI, 18–19)
φρόνησις — ἐπιστήμη (Sap. Salom. VII, 16).
Si l'origine littéraire de ces séries est identifiée à partir d'un milieu sapientiel, la signification de cette organisation par multiplication triadique de chaque élément de la tétrade des φωστήρες est liée à une réinterprétation astrologique des attributs sapientiels.

COPTIC STUDIES

Małgorzata Martens-Czarnecka

Some Known and Some New Features of Nubian Painting on the Murals from House "A" in Old Dongola

The paintings from the House "A" in Old Dongola were already presented by Dr Jakobielski at the International Nubiological Congress in Cambridge.[1] Also Dr Godlewski's contribution at the same Congress covered the subject of iconography of Christ — the most important representation out of that group of paintings.[2]

Here I would like to present some further remarks on the murals from House "A" in Old Dongola as a whole.[3]

As it is known the majority of those paintings comes from the room no 3. In the remaining two rooms only some faint traces were preserved. The room no 3 whose purpose is still the matter of debates, was divided by the thin wall partition into two parts (fig. 1). In the centre of east face of that partition, in the shallow niche, the already mentioned representation of Christ trampling the snake and the lion was positioned (fig. 2). On the north wall of the eastern part of the room two figures of standing angels were depicted. On the south wall there are the figures of St Mercurius spearing Julian the Apostate and St Theodore fighting the snake. The east wall was decorated with the floral design consisting of the branch with big flowers and the guilloche framing the window. The walls in the western part of room no 3 were decorated with crosses.

The state of preservation of the murals is rather poor. Because of the destruction of upper parts of the walls and partly inner surfaces of the remaining walls only fragments of paintings such as for example lower halves of figures, were preserved. Fragments of paintings on numerous pieces of loose plaster found in sand and rubble inside the room were used for reconstruction of some representations that were originally above the height of preserved walls. Thus the representation of Christ was completed and two medallions matched up. In one of the medallions there is the text in Greek which contains fragments of Gospel according to St John (1,1–85; 21,25) (fig. 3), in the other one the bust of a bearded man, his face partly preserved and his hand in the gesture of blessing (probably it represents a Saint) (fig. 4). Both medallions are encircled with the floral ornaments. According to the reconstruction proposed by Dr Jakobielski the medallions were placed on the upper part of the wall partition.[4]

Poor state of preservation makes the interpretation of the paintings very difficult. Nevertheless on the ground of preserved parts of murals and loose pieces of plaster on which fragments of robes, faces, hands and floral decorations can be seen, the analysis of stylistic features of that group of paintings can be attempted. Colouring is rather limited. Black, yellow, white, purple and very little red are the only colours used. On all the paintings different shades of purple are predominant. Those shades range from very dark to pale, intensely watered, verging on pink. Representations of persons are to a great extent flat and schematic. With the exception of standing Christ all the other figures are depicted in the uniform manner (fig. 5).

[1] S. Jakobielski, "Polish Excavations at Old Dongola 1976 and 1978", in: *Nubian Studies, Cambridge Symposium 1978*, Warminster 1982, pp. 116–126; cf. also S. Jakobielski, "Polish Excavations at Old Dongola 1973–74", in: *Études Nubiennes, Colloque de Chantilly, 2–6 Juillet 1976*, Cairo 1978, pp. 139–140; id., "Dongola 1974 (Chronique des fouilles)", *Études et Travaux X* (1978), 415–416; id., "Dongola 1976 (Chronique des fouilles)", *Études et Travaux XI* (1979).

[2] W. Godlewski, "Some Comments of the Wall Painting of Christ from Old Dongola", in: *Nubian Studies*, pp. 95–99.

[3] Cf. also M. Martens-Czarnecka, "Charactéristiques du style 'violet' dans les peintures à Dongola", *Études et Travaux XIV* (in print).

[4] Jakobielski, *Nubian Studies*, pp. 117–118.

1. Room no 3 from the east

2. Christ (drawing by H. Lewak)

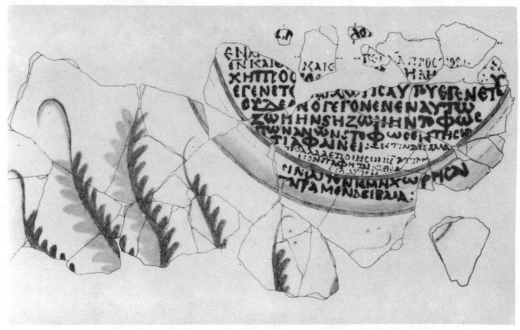

3. Fragment of inscribed circle. Mural no 7a (drawing by H. Lewak)

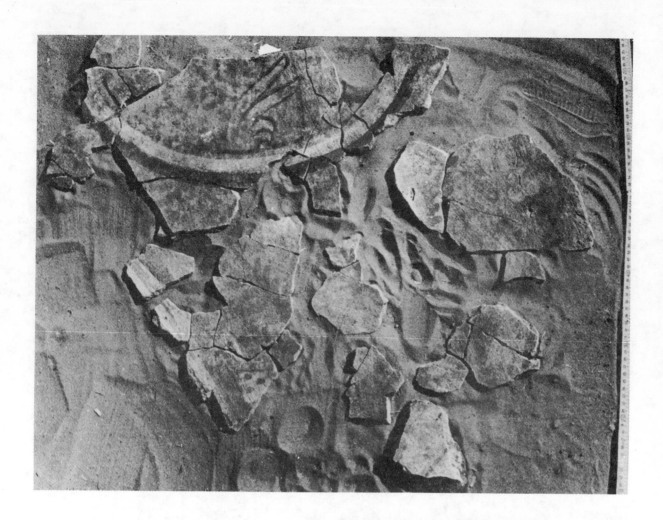

4. Fragment of the circle with bearded man. Mural no 7b (drawing by H. Lewak)

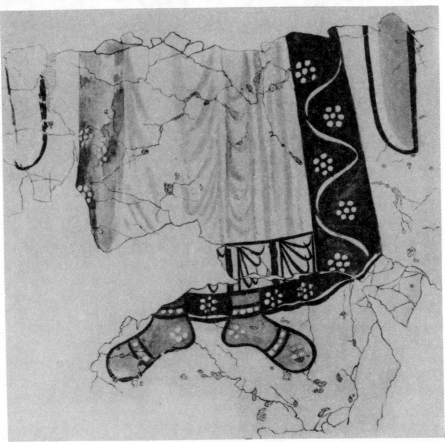

5. Figure of an angel. Mural no 8 (drawing by H. Lewak)

Each of them stands *en face* wears pallium or paludamentum, dalmatic and tunic, and high boots reaching above the ankles. In each case the cloak hangs on both sides of the figures making sort of a background, tunic reaches just above the ankles and shows very little from underneath the dalmatic making the narrow stripe accross the figure. All robes are contured with the black line. Also the colour scheme is uniform for those figures. Very pale purple tunics and dalmatics, slightly darker boots and dark purple cloaks. The only exception from this rule is the yellow cloak of St Mercurius. The way in which folds on vestments are represented is noteworthy. The folds on the cloaks are shown as the thick black vertical lines. On the dalmatics and tunics the folds are finer and shown as the dark purple vertical lines of different thickness with vertical rows of slightly rounded V-shaped lines between them. The way in which the dalmatics fall in folds indicates that they were tied with belts and in the case of St Mercurius, the wider folds on the right hand side of the figure can be probably explained as the result of the vestment being pulled up by the raised hand holding the spear (fig. 6). The folds have to a certain extent natural appearance, however, it is obvious in all painting that they were meant to make considerably decorative composition. Also decoration of robes bears the features of uniformity. The repertoire of decorative motives is rather limited both in colouring and design. The robes of the two Saint Warriors are decorated with the rows of rosettes, each composed of four dots (figs 6, 7). The dots on purple cloaks and dalmatics are white, the ones on St Mercurius's yellow cloak are purple. Angels' robes are decorated with the stylized floral ornament consisting of a "wavy" white line thickened by the black shadow with the rosette of six dots placed inside each bend of the line. One figure has white dots, the other red ones (fig. 5). Shoes in all cases are decorated with rosettes on toes and heels and the rows of white dots between two purple lines on insteps. The way in which faces were depicted can be established on the basis of preserved face of Christ and fragments of others

(figs 8, 9). Wide open eyes with irises close to the upper eyelids predominated over the whole face. The nose was straight, pointed, with narrow nostrils and only left outline, extending into rounded brow, marked. Mouths and chins were marked with straight strokes of a brush in the latter case thickened at the ends. The shape of the ears and beards is also characteristic. The yellow halos encircled with the purple line and long necks in round, decorationless necklines of the robes should also be noted.

All described characteristics such as colouring, facial features, shape and decoration of robes and way of representation of folds on them as well as strictly "en face" position and schematism of the figures, prove, beyond any doubt, that the paintings from House "A" in Old Dongola belong to the so-called Violet style of the Nubian painting, occurring in the 8th and early 9th centuries.[5] Another proof of that classification is of a paleographic nature. In the preserved fragment of one of the mural's legends the letters in the word ⲁⲣⲓⲟⲥ do not form the ligature (fig. 10). This is typical of early inscriptions from Nubia and appears in Faras only in legends of murals belonging to the Violet style.[6] The ornaments of the text in the form of little crosses and four V-rosettes are typical of the inscriptions of that period[7] (fig. 11). Such decoration appears also in the inscription belonging to the representation of Christ.

The paintings from the House "A" in Dongola together with fragments of murals from the Mosque-Building, Cruciform Church and the North Church are the only presently known examples of painting from the territory of Makuria. Presented stylistic analysis of the murals from House "A" confirms once more that the styles established for painting of Nobadia (Faras) in this case the Violet style,[8] are applicable also to the painting of Makuria. In the considered group of paintings however, there is a new factor, so far unknown in the Nubian painting of the 8th or 9th centuries, namely the presence of floral motifs. Those motifs were handled in the different manner than distinctly linear representations of figures.

[5] M. Martens, "Observations sur la composition du visage dans les peintures de Faras (VIIIe–IXe siècles)", *Études et Travaux* VI (1972), 207–236; ead., *Faras VII. Les éléments décoratifs sur les peintures de Faras*, Warsaw 1982, pp. 15–29.

[6] S. Jakobielski, "Inscriptions", in: K. Michałowski, *Faras. Wall Paintings in the Collection of the National Museum in Warsaw*, Warsaw 1974, p. 283.

[7] Jakobielski, "Inscriptions", 284, 285; Martens-Czarnecka, *Faras VII*, p. 25.

[8] Michałowski, *Faras*, pp. 30–33; Martens-Czarnecka, *Faras VII*, pp. 15–32.

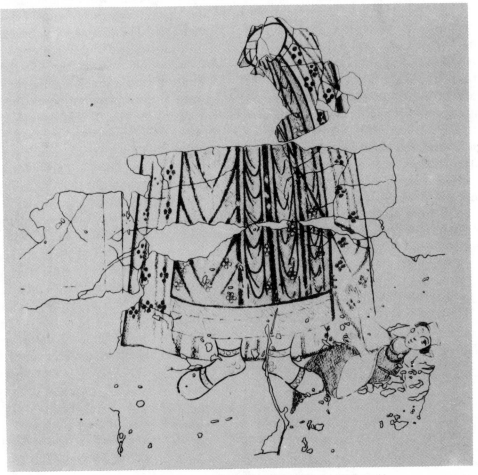

6. Figure of St Mercurius. Mural no 3 (drawing by H. Lewak)

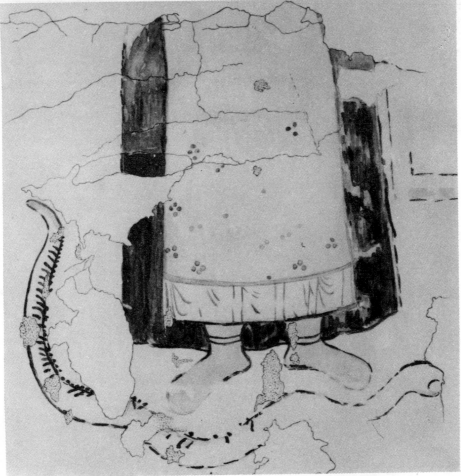

7. Figure of St Theodore (?). Mural no 1 (drawing by H. Lewak)

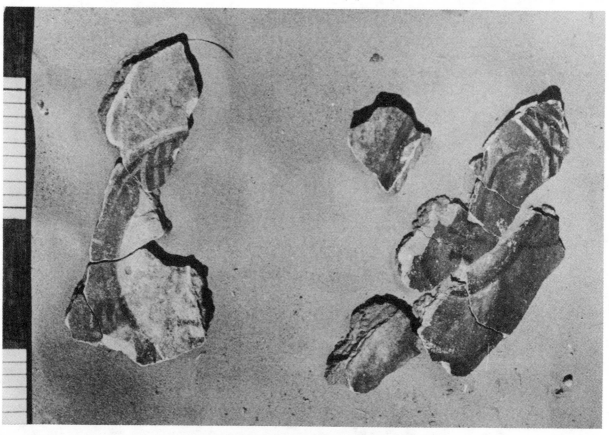

8. Fragment of the face. Mural no 8,8

9. Fragment of the face. Mural no. 7b

10. Fragment of the inscription

11. Fragment of the inscription

The colouring is the same but certain softness of the outlines is apparent. Shading is applied to create three-dimensional apearance and the delicate contours separate particular elements of the design from the bacground and enhance plasticity. One of the fragments of paintings represents the big flower growing out of the branch (traces of the other flower are visible below to the right — fig. 12). Because of the skilful shading the yellow branch with purple contours appears cylindrical and the flower with pointed, black outlined, slightly bent petals in yellow turning red looks nearly three-dimentional.

The floral decoration of the two medallions is executed in the similar manner although with a little less plasticity (figs 3, 4). The thin twig tipped with the little three-petaled flower grows out of the long narrow, jagged yellow and purple leaves.

It seems that such artistic manner of representation of floral motifs in Nubian painting is encountered for the first time, because, known from the later Nubian paintings, floral motifs, such as palm trees and olive trees or branches are linear and schematic.[9] Probably it is so, because they always made the symbol or attribute related to the iconography of particular representation and therefore could be reduced to the simplest and most readable form. On the contrary, on the paintings from House "A" in Old Dongola flowers and branches make the important part of the whole composition, have no meaning but purely ornamental character and add to the decoration of the wall.

Connections of the early Nubian painting of the Violet style with the Coptic art are very well

---

[9] Cf. K. Michałowski, *Faras, die Kathedrale aus dem Wüstensand*, Zürich 1967, figs. 46, 55, 75, 88,89.

12. Fragment of the floral motif. Mural no 12a (drawing by H. Lewak)

known. Their stylistic and iconographic similarities have been proved in many publications.[10] The analysis of style of the group of murals from the House "A" in Dongola adds some new arguments confirming those connections. The same way of representation of faces and entire figures, repertoire of decorative motifs or arrangement of robes, can be easily found in the Coptic painting.[11] The same applies to the iconography. Christ trampling a lion and a snake or Saint Warriors

[10] K. Witzmann, "Some Remarks on the Sources of the Fresco Paintings of the Cathedral of Faras", in: *Kunst und Geschichte Nubiens in christlicher Zeit,* Recklinghausen 1970, pp. 325–340; M. Rassart, "Visages de Faras. Caractéristiques et évolution stylistique", *Études et Travaux* VI (1972), 250–275; ead., "Quelques considérations sur les rapports thématiques et stylistiques entre l'Égypte copte et la Nubie chrétienne", in: *Mélanges Armand Abel* III, Leyde 1978, pp. 200–220; ead., "La peinture copte avant le XIIᵉ siècle. Une approche", in: *Acta ad Archaeologiam et Artium Historiam Pertinentia* IX, Roma 1981, pp. 270–279; Martens-Czarnecka, *Faras* VII, pp. 24–29.

[11] J. Maspero, *Fouilles exécutées à Baouît,* 2, Cairo 1943, pls XXII, XXVIII, XXXIII, L.

spearing a human figure or a snake, reflect the struggle between good and evil and such type of representations is thought to originate from Egypt.[12] Looking for further analogies between the murals from House "A" and Coptic painting one should not neglect the floral motifs so common in the Coptic art. It is enough to mention the floral motifs in the decoration of Chapels in Bawit[13] or Monastery in Saqqara[14] or in Kelia.[15] In Coptic art floral patterns frame the niches and registers with representations of figures as well as door and window openings, twigs with jagged leaves tipped with the three-petaled flower similar to those from House "A" decorate the medallions with busts of angels and Saints. Trees and flowers separate representations of different subjects and finally various floral motifs woven into ornamental "panneau" decorate big surfaces of walls. There is no doubt that the floral motifs on the murals from House "A" in Dongola have the same purely decorative character which adds a new element to the question of connections between Nubian and Coptic painting.

---

[12] Godlewski, "Some Comments ...," 96; M. Rassart, "La peinture copte avant le XIIe siècle. Une approche", in: *Acta ad Archaeologiam...*, IX, Roma 1981, p. 232.

[13] M. J. Clédat, *Le monastère et la nécropole de Baouît* XII, 2, Cairo 1906, pls LXXV, LXXVI, LXXIX, LXIII, CI, XLII, LI, LII.

[14] M. Rassart, "Quelques remarques iconographiques sur la peinture chrétienne à Saqqara", in: *Acta ad Archaeologiam...*, IX, Roma 1981, pp. 208–209; P. van Moorsel, M. Huijbers, "Repertory of the Preserved Wallpainting from the Monastery of Apa Jeremieh at Saqqara", in: *Acta ad Archaeologiam...* IX, Roma 1981, pl. VII.

[15] R. Kasser, *Kellia 1965*, Genève 1967, figs 30, 31, 50.

COPTIC STUDIES

Francisco Javier Martinez

The King of Rūm and the King of Ethiopia in Medieval Apocalyptic Texts from Egypt

Late Christian Apocalyptic produced in the East seems like the Cinderella of apocalyptic studies. Many works, some very important, are not available in critical or reliable editions,[1] and the answer to the many questions raised by the known apocalypses is still far ahead. In this situation, the most urgent task is to edit the relevant texts. Only then some sort of general conclusions on the development of this tradition can be reached, and the background and the purpose of the texts can be properly understood. On the other hand, and simultaneously, preliminary attempts to trace the history of particular themes and motifs will greatly help to clarify the relations between a given group of texts, thus setting some sort of frame in which new ones can be placed. The purpose of this paper is to make a small contribution in this last direction. By studying a motif that appears prominently in several medieval apocalyptic texts from Egypt, it will try to shed some light on the growth of Egyptian apocalyptic tradition in the Middle Ages.

1. The Dossier of Late Egyptian Apocalypses

The apocalyptic production of Egyptian Christianity after the Muslim conquest and dealing with the problems raised by Muslim rule is quite rich.

This is a provisory list of such works, with no claim to completeness:

1. The short apocalypse embodied in the Arabic *Life of Shenute,* cf. E. Amélineau, *Monuments pour servir à l'histoire de l'Égypte chrétienne aux IVᵉ et Vᵉ siècles,* Mémoires publiés par les membres de la Mission Archéologique Française au Caire, IV, Paris 1888, 289–478. The apocalypse is found on pp. 340–46.

2. The *Sahidic Apocalypse of Pseudo-Athanasius* (= *PA*), preserved almost complete in the Pierpont Morgan Codex M 602, ff. 52v–77v, and now edited in F.J. Martínez, *Eastern Christian Apocalyptic,* 247–590, together with the Arabic versions of it.

3. Among the several Arabic apocalypses attributed to Athanasius, the one mentioned in G. Graf, *Geschichte der christlichen arabischen Literatur* (= *GCAL*) I, Studi e Testi 118 (Vatican City, 1944), 277, as preserved in MS Vat. ar. 158, ff. 99v–111v and MS Paris ar. 153, ff. 461v–70v, certainly deals with the Muslims. We call it *PA ar. II,* to preserve the order in which it appears in Graf, and to distinguish it from *PA ar. I* (an apocalypse close to the *Apocalypse of Paul,* with no historical material), and from *PA ar. III* (the Arabic versions of the Sahidic *PA*). The present writer is now preparing an edition of this text.

4. The Arabic *Apocalypse of Samuel of Calamun,* cf. J. Ziadeh, "L'apocalypse de Samuel, supérieur

---

[1] When this paper was delivered, there was no available edition of the Syriac apocalypse of Pseudo-Methodius (*PM*), one of the most influential ever written. Since then, the Syriac *PM* has appeared in an edition by H. Suermann, *Die geschichtesteologische Reaktion auf die einfallenden Muslime in der edessenischen Apokalyptik des 7. Jahrhunderts,* Europäische Hochschulschriften, Reihe XXIII/256, Bern 1985, and another, quite different in its conception, by the present writer, *Eastern Christian Apocalyptic in the Early Muslim Period: Pseudo-Athanasius,* Ph. D. Diss., Washington DC, 1985. This one, as the title indicates, includes also an edition to the Sahidic/Arabic Apocalypse of Pseudo-Athanasius (*PA*), a text less famous than *PM,* but not less important for the Egyptian Church. Works in need of a fresh edition are, among others, the *Bahira Legend,* very deficiently published by R. Gottheil at the turn of the century, cf. ZA 13 (1898), 189–192; 14 (1899), 265–268; 15 (1900), 56–102; 17 (1903), 125–166, and the *Book of the Rolls* (*kitāb al-majāll*), published by A. Mingana from a single Kāršūnī MS; cf. *Woodbrooke Studies III,* Cambridge 1931.

de Deir-el-Qalamoun." ROC 20 (1915–17), 374–404. Cf. also F. Nau, "Note sur l'apocalypse de Samuel," ibid., 405–07. More MSS of the prophecy in GCAL I, 282.

5. The Arabic *Letter of Pisentius,* cf. A. Périer, "Lettre de Pisuntius, évêque de Qeft, à ses fideles", ROC 19 (1914), 79–92, 302–23, 445–46. Cf. also R. Griveau, "Notes sur la lettre de Pisuntius," ibid., 441–43. More MSS in GCAL I, 280.

6. The homily attributed to Patriarch Theophile, cf. H. Fleisch, "Une homélie de Theophile d'Alexandrie," ROC 30 (1935–36), 371–419.

7. The so-called *Fourteenth Vision of Daniel,* preserved in Bohairic and Arabic. Cf. H. Tattam, *Prophetae majores in dialecto linguae Aegyptiacae Memphitica seu Coptica,* II, Oxford 1852, pp. 386–405. The Arabic is to be found in C.H. Becker, "Das Reich der Ismaeliten im koptischen Danielbuch," *Nachrichten von der königlichen Gesellschaft der Wissenschaften zu Göttingen, Philolog.--historische Klasse,* 1915, Heft 1, Göttingen 1916, 5–57. This apocalypse has received unusual attention on the part of scholars, probably because of its attribution to Daniel. Cf. F. Macler, "Les apocalypses apocryphes de Daniel," RHR 33 (1896), 163–76; O. Meinardus, "A Commentary on the XIVth Vision of Daniel According to the Coptic Version," OCP 32 (1966), 394–449; H. Suermann, "Notes concernant l'apocalypse copte de Daniel et la chute des Omayyades," *Parole de l'Orient* 11 (1983), 329–48.

8. According to W. Macomber, "Catalogue of Christian Arabic MSS of the Franciscan Center of Christian Oriental Studies, Mûskî, Cairo", *Studia Orientalia Christiana,* Jerusalem 1984, 33, MS 150, 4°, ff. 148a–159b, contains a "fragment of a prophecy concerning the emperors of Rome, the schism of the Churches, the reestablishment of the union of the Churches, the Christian reconquest of Egypt by the emperors of Ethiopia and Rome, and the end of the world." This is obviously relevant to the main topic of this paper, but I could not examine the text on time for the publication of this paper. It could well be some version of one of the known apocalypses.

9. In the same collection of the Franciscans at Cairo, MS 324, 5° (ff. 116a–143a) contains "Prophecies of Anba Shenuda." A first glance at this text shows that is deals with the "sons of Ishmael." The name of Muhammad is spelled in Coptic on f. 116b as ⲘⲀⲘⲀⲆⲒⲟⲥ.

10. The catalogue of the library of the monastery of St Elijah preserved in the Ostracon IFAO 13315, recto, line 50, mentions a prophecy attributed to Pachomius "de fine communitatis" (ⲈⲦⲂⲈ ⲐⲀⲎ ⲚⲦⲔⲟⲒⲚⲰⲚⲒⲀ), which is unknown among Pachomius' works. Cf. R.-G. Coquin, "Le catalogue de la bibliothèque du couvent de Saint Élite 'du rocher' (Ostracon IFAO 13315)," BIFAO 75 (1975) 207–39. T. Orlandi, in his *Elementi di Lingua e Letteratura Copta,* Milano 1970, 100, suggests a possible connection of this work with the *Letter of Pisentius* and the *Apocalypse of Samuel of Calamun,* but this is not the only possibility, cf. Coquin, "Le catalogue," 229.

There may be other texts to add to the dossier. I was unable, for instance, to examine two other Arabic MSS with apocalypses attrributed to Athanasius: MS Cairo, Coptic Patriarchate 835 (Lit. 214) with a *mīmar li-'anbā 'Athanāsīūs 'an ar-ru'yā 'allatī ra'ahā,* and MS Cairo, Coptic Patriarchate 683 (Hist. 88), containing a *ru'yā 'Athanāsīūs 'indamā ḥaḍara 'ilayhi 'anbā 'Anṭūnīūs,* cf. M. Simaika, *Catalogue of the Coptic and Arabic Manuscripts in the Coptic Museum, the Patriarchate, the Principal Churches of Cairo and Alexandria and the Monasteries of Egypt,* II, Cairo 1942, pp. 376, 313–14. None of these titles seems to correspond to the known pseudo-Athanasian works, but without an examination of the MSS this is impossible to decide, as well as the question whether they have anything to say about the Muslims. Also, there is in Armenian a "vision" of Athanasius, which may or may not be related to the Egyptian apocalypses. Cf. Isaias Daietsi, *S. Ahanasii Alexandriae patr., orationes, epistulae, controversiae,* Venetiis 1899, pp. 493–99. We leave *ex professo* outside the scope of this paper the *kitāb al-majāll,* whose textual history, place of origin and date of composition cannot be elucidated without a critical edition (cf. GCAL I, 283–292). On the contrary, we have included in our study *The Ten Visions of Shenute,* an Ethiopic apocalypse clearly belonging together with the other texts studied here, cf. A. Grohmann, "Die im Äthiopischen, Arabischen und Koptischen erhaltenen Visionen Apa Shenute's von Atripe," ZMDG 67 (1913), 187–267; 68 (1914), 1–46. Although Ethiopic Apocalyptic tradition needs a study on its own merit, at the end of the paper we shall make some suggestions in regard to the date and purpose of the *Kebra Nagast,* as these are enlightened by the study of Egyptian apocalypses.

2. The Motif of the Kings of Rūm and Ethiopia

The texts just listed are quite different in character, and clearly belong to various apocalyptic traditions. There is, for instance, not much in common between the Sahidic *PA* and the *XIVth Vision of Daniel*. Studying the motif of the two kings, which appears in several of them, will help to isolate one of those trends of tradition.

The motif can be broadly described in the following manner: In the description of the final events, the final peace [2] is preceded by a Christian victory over the Muslims, in which both the king of Rūm (i.e., Byzantium) and of Ethiopia take part. As a consequence of this joint campaign, peace is established for the whole Church. In some works, before the beginning of the peace, a conference is held between the two kings on the subject of the orthodox faith, resulting in a divine judgement that sanctions the faith of the Coptic Church as against the Chalcedonian confession held by the Byzantines. After the settlement on the orthodox faith, the king of Ethiopia vanishes. The king of Rūm rules on the earth from Jerusalem and there he hands over his crown to God at the end of the world.

The motif appears in its less developed form in the Arabic *Apoc. Samuel*, the 7th century founder of the monastery of Calamun in the Fayum.[3] The bulk of this work, obviously a composite one, gathering materials from different apocalyptic traditions, is formed by a description of the hardships suffered by the Christians under the Muslims and the state of decay of the Coptic Church under the new masters.[4] Literary dependence on the Sahidic *PA* can be detected at times.[5] It is in the short final section where a sketch is drawn of the final events and where the motif of the two kings finds its way. It describes first the wicked rule of the last Arab king, a certain Lasmarīnī (or Lasmarīsū), followed by the reaction of a Greek king, who, strengthened by a vision of the Archangel Michael, will destroy the Ishmaelites and liberate Egypt from their hands. In this context, the king of Ethiopia is suddenly mentioned for the first time:

> The king of Ethiopia will bring a terrible ruin to the land of their fathers in the East. The Muslims will flee to the desert where they had been before, escaping from the king of Ethiopia coming from the East, and from the king of Rūm, who will fall over the sons of Ishmael and encircle them in the wādī-al-Hafār, the dwelling place of their fathers. He will destroy them from the West.[6]

This is clearly a joint campaign of the two Christian kings against the Muslims. The Byzantine king will attack the Muslims "from the sea",[7] while apparently the Ethiopians will ravage Arabia and come against them "from the East". After their victory, both kings appear again together:

> The king of Ethiopia will marry the daughter of the king of Rūm, and there will be a great peace, reconciliation and agreement all over the earth, for forty years, the like of which had never been on the earth. There will be great joy among the Christians. They will publicly open the doors of their churches, build houses, plant vineyards, build high castles and rejoice in the Lord their God. Woe to the Muslims in those days![8]

After this, the sketch of the final events continues: First, "the wild king" appears, followed by the coming of Gog and Magog. There is then a short

---

[2] The idea of a final peace comes from 1 Thess 5:3, and probably also from passages like Matt 24:37–39.

[3] On Samuel, cf. P. van Cauwenbergh, *Étude sur les moines d'Égypte depuis le concile de Chalcédoine (451) jusqu'à l'invasion arabe (640)*, Paris 1914, pp. 39–50; 80–122. Also J. Simon, "Saint Samuel de Kalamoun et son monastère dans la littérature éthiopienne", *Aethiopica* 1 (1933), 36–40. The Sahidic Life has recently been edited by A. Alcock, *The Life of Samuel of Kalamun by Isaac the Presbyter,* Warminster, England, 1983. For the Ethiopic Version of the *Life,* cf. F.M. Esteves Pereira, *Vida do abba Samuel do Mosteiro do Kalamon,* Lisboa 1894. Cf. also J. Simon, "Fragment d'une homélie copte en l'honneur de Samuel de Kalamoun", in: *Miscellanea Biblica edita a Pont. Inst. Biblico ad celebrandum annum XXV ex quo conditum est Institutum* II Roma 1934, pp. 160a–78. According to the *Arabic Synaxary,* Samuel "pronounced many exhortatory talks and discourses, and prophecied the coming of this nation, namely, the Muslims" (cf. PO III, 408).

[4] Particular importance is given to the decay of the Coptic language, described in dramatic fashion, cf. Ziadeh, "L'apocalypse de Samuel," p. 379, line 14–380, line 18.

[5] Cf., for instance, Ziadeh, "L'apocalypse de Samuel," pp. 378, line 19–379, line 5; 379, line 19–380, line 1; 383, lines 12–18, and compare with *PA* X: 6–8; XI: 3–10 (Martinez, *Eastern Christian Apocalyptic,* pp. 381–84, 536–39; 384–85, 539; 366–74, 525–31).

[6] Ziadeh, "L'apocalypse de Samuel," p. 390, lines 11–14.

[7] "After this, the Lord will remember his people, that was very much despised, and will send against them the king of Rūm, with a great wrath, from the side of the sea," ibid., p. 390, lines 7–9.

[8] Ibid., p. 390, lines 22–26.

interlude of a year and a half by a new king of the Greeks, who will now reside in Jerusalem, and finally the relevation of the Antichrist. "Ten Greek kings will support him, will think like him and make firm his dominion."[9] Here the Apocalypse ends. Of the Ethiopian king, there is no more mention.

The motif of the two Christian kings is found again, in a much more developed manner, in the Arabic *Letter of Pisentius,* a 7th century bishop of Keft.[10] The *Letter* is an apocryphal outgrowth of the "authentic" letter of Pisentius, dealing with the Persian invasion of Egypt, and preserved in the Coptic panegyrics of the bishop.[11] In fact, the Arabic *Letter* is an apocalypse closely related, in form and content, to *Apoc. Samuel.* After a short parenetic section, the Apocalypse begins with an *ex eventu* prophecy of the coming to Egypt of "the Arab nation." We find again passages clearly dependent on *PA.*[12] A difference with *Apoc. Samuel* is that the *Letter* pays some attention, in its final part, to internal developments in Islamic history.[13]

The kings of Rūm and Ethiopia appear in the final, purely apocalyptic section. It describes, first, a military reaction of a king of Rūm named Constantine, who reconquers Egypt from the Muslims, establishes a great peace on the earth and places his son on the throne of Egypt. After a temporary Muslim reaction, involving the death of Constantine's son and his family, Constantine returns to Egypt and chases away the Muslims, this time for good. It is then when the king of Ethiopia is introduced. There is no joint military campaign

this time. Rather, the main concern in the *Letter* seems to be the orthodox faith:

> Then the king of Ethiopia will arise; he will come to meet the king of Rūm. They will sit together for a few days, arguing with one another about the orthodox faith. For, this king of Rūm will follow the faith of the hypocrite Leo, and will honor the doctrine of Chalcedon, while the king of Ethiopia will follow the true religion and will believe in our Nicenian faith, that the fathers, the 318 bishops, have established. Great wars will occur between them, to the point that innumerable persons from both parties will perish.[14]

Finally, the Patriarch of Alexandria has to intervene: "Why is it that you fight with one another, and there are those wars between you both? We all believe in the Father, the Son and the Holy Spirit."[15] He makes a proposal under the suggestion of the Holy Spirit, "so that from now on, there will be no more wars nor dispute between you".[16] What the Patriarch proposes is a sort of ordeal that will settle once and for all their dogmatic differences. The scene is conducted after the model of the divine trial between Elijah and the priests of Baal on mount Carmel (1 Kgs 18): two Masses should be celebrated, and the one on which the holy Spirit comes would have God's sanction. The Spirit comes, of course, upon the altar of the Patriarch of Alexandria, and the king of Rūm, with all his army, converts to the orthodox faith, banning the Council of Chalcedon and the *Thomus* of Leo. The writer comments:

> After this, agreement and great peace will come all over the earth. The Church will be united by the unity of the confession, churches will be built

---

[9] Ibid., p. 391, lines 13–14. The text here shows that the writer is not very sympathetic toward the Byzantines. If the victory over the Muslims is attributed to a king of Rūm, this must be a fact that came to him from tradition.

[10] On the chronology of Pisentius, cf. van Cauwenbergh, *Étude sur les moines d'Égypte,* pp. 159–61; W.E. Crum, in a review of E.A.W. Budge, "Coptic Apocrypha in the Dialect of Upper Egypt", London 1913, appeared in ZDMG 68 (1914), 176–184: cf. pp. 178–181.

[11] For the Sahidic panegyric, cf. Budge, "Coptic Apocrypha", 75–127 (version, pp. 258–321). The Bohairic was published by Amélineau, *Un évêque de Keft au VIIe siècle,* extract from *Mémoires de l'Institut Égyptien* II (1887)) = *Étude sur le Christianisme en Égypte au septième siècle* (Paris 1887). There is an Arabic recension edited by De Lacy O'Leary, "The Arabic Life of Pisentius", PO XXII, 317–487.

[12] Cf., for instance, Périer, "Lettre de Pisuntius", p. 306, lines 14–22, and compare with *PA* IX:9 (Martinez, *Eastern Christian Apocalyptic,* pp. 372–373, 529–530).

[13] These allusions (cf. Périer, "Lettre de Pisuntius", p. 307, line 14–308, line 7) can be cautiously used to suggest a date for the final composition of the *Letter.* The earliest extant MSS go back to the XVth century. The work, however, has to be prior to the Crusades, which are not alluded to. If the Turks —the last Muslim rulers referred to in the *Letter*–were the Ikhshidids (and this is made probable because only of them can be said that "they ruled over the South, from Akka to the borders of Ethiopia", ibid., p.308, lines 4–5), this would place the final redaction of the *Letter* in the second half of the 10th century, a not unlikely date for hopes in a Roman recovery.

[14] Périer, "Lettre de Pisuntius", pp. 309, line 20–310, line 7.

[15] Ibid., p. 310, lines 10–12.

[16] Ibid., p. 310, line 13.

THE KING OF RUM

and restored, and the Lord will rejoice in mankind as He rejoices with the worship of the holy angels (...). There will be upon the earth great peace, as in the reign of Constantine the righteous. It will last for forty years, and the peace of the Lord will rule the earth.[17]

During these forty years there will be ten Roman kings. The tenth king will come to Jerusalem, abdicate his crown upon the Cross, and place Cross and crown upon the altar in the holy Church of the Anastasis. Crown, Cross and altar will be taken up to heaven, and then, a wicked king will immediately precede the coming of the Antichrist. His destruction and the final Judgement are described in the regular apocalyptic order.

A third apocalypse containing the motif is the still unpublished *PA ar.II*.[18] In comparison with the two works mentioned thus far, this is a later work. It has allusions to the Crusaders; the long parenetic developments typical of earlier Egyptian apocalyptic have been substituted by allusive and symbolic lists of kings, in a style which is known from other late medieval productions.[19] A first set deals with Roman rulers, a second with Muslim kings. The apocalyptic section begins with a terrible civil war among the Muslims near the river Euphrates. The angel of the Lord takes care of the battle and exterminates the Muslims. It is then when the kings of Rūm and Ethiopia are introduced:

> The kings of Nubia and Ethiopia will hear (of these revolts) and come out, ruling over the whole land of Yemen, and coming to Egypt. They will find it (= Egypt) devastated, not finding in it anybody, not even a dog barking. There will not be in it a populated village, except the island of Banaqius. This will be shocking for them and they will be very much grieved. Then they will dwell in Egypt and build in it a great temple in the space of thirty days.[20]

The news reaches "the king of the Franks" (*malik al-ifranj*), whose name is Constantine, and who is further characterized as "the lion's whelp." He will enter Constantinople by the sword, and throw all

its horses into the sea. Then he will take the holy Cross and travel to the East, where he will establish the Christian religion and the canons of the Church. Finally he will come to Jerusalem, which he will find devastated as the kings of Nubia and Ethiopia had found Egypt. He will also build in Jerusalem "the holy Temple".[21] After that, the meeting of the two kings is described at length. Here also the main concern is to see whether they both have the same doctrine. Only a warning of the archangel Gabriel prevents war between them. This is the angel's message to the king of Ethiopia:

> The Lord says to you: "There will be no sword nor killing, and you shall not meet one another for war, but you shall make peace, and there shall be love between you."[22]

The same message is addressed to the king of Rūm. To settle the issue of the orthodox faith, they agree to go to the temple in Egypt. The author's remark at this point is important:

> The king of Rūm agreed and travelled with him (the king of Ethiopia) to Egypt, to fulfil the prophecy of David the prophet, when he said prophecying about Kuš: "Ethiopia will precede, and hand over its power to God (Ps 68:31)."[23]

The divine ordeal takes place as in the *Letter* of Pisentius, and then,

> The faith and the divine love will become stable between the kings, the peoples and the nations. They will go to Jerusalem and God will reveal the crown that had come down from heaven. One single king will be established among them, namely Constantine, the lion's whelp. They will present the crown to him and they will establish his residence in Jerusalem. He will stay there for seven weeks, for it is the center of the world.[24]

The motif is completed with a long description of the final peace, and the ten kings coming from the progeny of "the lion's whelp", the last of whom bears also the name of Constantine. The abdication takes place as in *Pisentius' Letter*.

Finally, the motif still appears in the *Ten Visions of Shenute*, an apocalyptic *pastiche* extant in Ethiopic whose editor, A. Grohmann, ascribes it to the

---

[17] Ibid., p. 312, lines 17–313, line 3.

[18] No. 3 in our list above.

[19] Such as the *XIVth Vision of Daniel*, or the Syriac *Apocalypse of Ezra*, cf. J.-B. Chabot, "L'Apocalypse d'Esdras touchant le royaume des arabes", *Rev. Sémitique* 2 (1894), 242–250, 333–346.

[20] MS Vat. ar. 158, f. 107r.

[21] MS Vat. ar. 158, f. 107v. Probably there is here an echo of the first Crusade.

[22] MS Vat. ar. 158, f. 108r.

[23] Ibid., f. 108v–09r. The form of the quote from Ps 68:31 is significant: *al-ḥabašah tasbiqu wa-tusallimu yadahā li-11āhi*. It seems to depend on the Syriac version, where the verse says: *kuš tašlem 'īdā l-'alâhā*. On the meaning of this verse in the Syriac apocalyptic tradition, cf. further below.

[24] Ibid., f. 109v.

14–15th centuries.[25] The work reflects Coptic apocalyptic tradition, with some adaptations to the local environment. Its structure, however, is different from that of the works studied thus far. The so-called *Tenth Vision*, that takes most of the text, is a typical conversation between Shenute and Jesus on the subject of the last judgement and the destiny of righteous and sinners on the last day. Shenute's *Vision of the Church* forms an independent text, perhaps added to the previous one. Shenute has a vision of a big Church that he himself has built and that soon comes under the attack of Satan. St. Michael defends the church, that will stay until the Lord comes. There follows immediately the gathering, in Shenute's church, of the king of Rūm and a king of Ethiopia named Teyōdā,[26] with their troops and their Patriarchs. The gathering follows exactly the pattern of *Pisentius' Letter* and *PA ar. II*. The orthodox faith is established and the Romans throw their books into the sea. Romans, Jews and Muslims convert and are baptized in the name of the Holy Trinity. (The assimilation of the Romans to the Jews and the Muslims shows that the writer does not seem to have a very clear knowledge of what the Romans confess). It is after the conference where the most characteristic features occur:

> 27. Woe to the city of Mecca on that day, because of the multitude of the troops of the king of Ethiopia, the black footsoldiers! They are many, and there is not at hand a stone (for every one), to take it and destroy (them). 28. The standard of this king will be all beauty, straight and high. 29. He will substitute the king of Egypt, take his wife captive with him, and place another instead of him. 30. On his way home, he will come to the river Geyōn, to take the tribute from Egypt and from the kings of Rōmē, and he will rule over Jerusalem. 31. And the standard of this king will be beautiful and high, and he will

bear the sign of the cross in the midst of his chest. 32. Afterwards, all will return to their land. 33. At that time, the demons will be in chains for forty years. 34. Rest, joy and peace will rule over the whole world.[27]

Although local Ethiopian features are clearly visible, by and large the tradition is unmistakably the same: final victory over the Muslims, shared more or less by the two Christian kings, rule of the Roman king over Jerusalem, forty years of peace over the world. The greater emphasis on the role of the Ethiopian king and the foggy description of the Romans hardly call for an explanation.

3. The Origins of a Tradition

That we have to do here with a fixed, traditional motif is obvious. Especially significant is the fact that four Monophysite works, absolutely uncompromising on the subject of orthodoxy, take for granted that the final victory over the Muslims will be achieved by a Greek king. Obviously, a good number of features in the motif are purely Egyptian: the relevance given to Egypt in the struggle with the Muslims, the mediation of the Patriarch of Alexandria in the question of the orthodox faith, etc., bear witness that the motif has developed in Egypt. On the other hand, the motif is altogether absent in the older apocalypses from Egypt dealing with the Muslim invasion. It is not to be found in the Sahidic *PA*, which can be dated about the first two decades of the 8th century, nor in the Arabic versions of it.[28] It does not appear in the vision of Shenute embodied in the Arabic version of his *Life*, a text that may come from the same period.[29] Even in the *Apoc. Samuel* and the *Letter of Pisentius*, the motif appears in the final section, a part which is most probably a later

---

[25] Cf. Grohmann, "Die... Visionen Apa Shenute's", ZDMG 67 (1913), 208 f.

[26] According to Grohmann, "Die... Visionen Apa Shenute's,", ZDMG 67 (1913), 255, Teyōdā is there for king Tēwodros, who ruled from 1411 to 1414, and who appears also in the apocalypse *Fekkārē Iyāsūs*. The name of the king of Rūm was also given, but has disappeared from the extant MSS.

[27] Grohmann, "Die... Visionen Apa Shenute's.., ZDMG 67 (1913), 261–265. For verse 30, three MSS (P2, L2, T) have a different text: "... to take tribute from Egypt, and the king of Rōmē will rule over Jerusalem". This reading is most probably the original one, as the one more in accord with the apocalyptic tradition from which the *Vision* comes. Verse 31 fits also better in the context if one assumes this alternative reading. The editor's suggestion, ibid., p. 263, note 9, that verse 30 may be an addition, originates from the failure to observe this.

[28] For the date of *PA*, cf. T. Orlandi, "Un testo copto sulla dominazione araba in Egitto", in: T. Orlandi and F. Wisse (eds.), *Acts of the II International Congress of Coptic Studies, Roma, 22–26 September 1980*, Rome 1985, pp. 225–33. Orlandi proposes the data 740–750 for the composition of *PA*. I would incline myself for a date somewhat earlier, between the monetary reforms of ʿAbd-al-Malik in 691/692 and the general census under Hishām in 630, cf. Martínez, *Eastern Christian Apocalyptic*, pp. 261–268.

[29] Cf. above, no 1 in the list of Egyptian apocalypses dealing with the Muslims. I would date this apocalypse about the same

addition to earlier works, conceived very much in the spirit of *PA*. Can we determine more precisely where the motif comes from?

I believe we can. Its ultimate origin is not an Egyptian work, but the apocalypse of *Pseudo-Methodius* (= *PM*), a Syriac work dating from the last decade of the 7th century.[30] There, for the first time in a Christian apocalypse, Ethiopia is given a decisive role to play in the final drama. *PM* was written in the convulsions created in the Christian world by the appearance of the Muslim empire, and by the gradual realization that the Muslims were there to stay. This shook the view of history shared by every one in the Syriac speaking Church since the 4th century, and based on the book of Daniel: the four world empires were the Assyrians, the Medes, the Persians and the Romans.[31] After the four world empires, only Gog and Magog, the Antichrist and the eternal kingdom of God were expected. In this view of history, the Muslims appeared as a major disruption, that made necessary a fresh reflection on the whole direction of history.

Is was in this context of utter confusion, when people – *PM* says – had begun to turn toward Ethiopia. The Axumite monarchy was a Christian kingdom too. In the past, the Ethiopians had already come to Arabia to help their Christian brothers. Will perhaps Ethiopia be the final kingdom, after a continuing Roman defeat? All this was more than just wishful thinking. There was a passage in the Syriac Bible to support such a view. It was, of course, the passage in Ps 68:31, usually translated as "Ethiopia will lift up the hands to God." In the Psitta, this had been translated as *kūš tašlem 'īdā l-'alâhā,* using a Syriac idiom (*'ašlem 'īdā*) which usually means "to yield the power," "to surrender." Thus, every Syriac reader of the Bible could read in the Psalms that "Ethiopia will yield the power of God," being in this way prepared to look for a place for Ethiopia in the final events. Moreover, the idiom was the same used by the Syriac translator for 1 Cor 15:24, where it is the Son who, at the end, "will yield the kingdom" to the Father: the apocalyptic connotation of the idiom was therefore sanctioned by the Bible itself.[32]

The Syriac author behind *PM* will choose the tradition. The Romans will still be the final kingdom, but the Ethiopians are not disregarded. Both kingdoms are for him, as a matter of fact, brother kingdoms. This is the whole point of the elaborate genealogy that makes Byzas (the legendary founder of Byzantium) marry an Ethiopian queen (the legendary Kūshat, daughter of Pīl and Alexander's mother).[33] They can therefore cooperate to free the Christian world from the Muslim power.[34] Cleverly, the writer never betrays his christological allegiance, and this fact was certainly one of the reasons for the astonishing success of his work all over the Christian world. The available editions of the Syriac *PM* are based on a single MS (Vat. Syr. 58, ff. 118v–136v, written in the 14th century, of West Syrian origin). There are other MSS known to contain *PM's* text, but they have never been studied. The seemingly very complicated textual history of the text poses still

---

time as *PA* or a little earlier. The last events clearly alluded to are the Muslim attempt "to rebuild the Temple in Jerusalem", and a reference to the monetary reforms, events which have both to be placed in 'Abd-al-Malik's time.

[30] There is a wealth of literature on *PM*. The most valuable contributions to the study of this work are S. Brock, "Syriac Views of Emergent Islam", in: G.H.A. Juynboll (ed.), *Studies on the First Century of Islamic Society,* Papers on Islamic History 2, Carbondale and Edwardsville, Illinois 1982, pp. 9–21; and G. J. Reinink, "Ismael, der Wildesel in der Wüste. Zur Typologie der Apokalypse des Pseudo-Methodius", *Byz. Zeitschrift* 75 (1982), 336–44; "Der Verfassername 'Modios' der syrischen Schatzhöhle und die Apokalypse des Pseudo-Methodius", OC 67 (1983), 46–64; "Die syrischen Wurzeln der mittelalterlichen Legende vom römischen Endkaiser", in: M. Gosman and J. van Os (eds), *Non Nova, sed Nove. Mélanges de civilisation médiévale dediés a W. Noomen,* Groningen 1984, pp. 195–209. For a discussion of the date of composition, cf. Martinez, *Eastern Christian Apocalyptic,* pp. 28–32.

[31] This view is expressed already in the *Vth Demonstratio* of Aphraat *On Wars,* cf. PS I, Paris 1984, cols 232–236, and became traditional in the Syriac Church. On this, cf. my forthcoming paper, "The Apocalyptic Genre in Syriac: The World of Pseudo-Methodius", read to the *IV Symposium Syriacum,* Groningen 1984.

[32] Cf. *PM,* chap. IX (MS Vat. Syr. 58, ff. 125v, bottom -126); and chap. XIV (f. ibid., 135r–v).

[33] Cf. *PM,* chaps. VIII–IX (MS Vat. Syr. 58, ff. 123v–126v).

[34] The cooperation of both kings is only allusively referred to in *PM*. Besides the genealogy linking Byzantium and Ethiopia, there is the passage in which the Greek king comes against the Muslims: "He (the Greek king) who was accounted by them (the Muslims) as dead, will come out against them from the sea of the Kushites" (*PM* chap. XIII. MS Vat. Syr. 58, f. 133r, bottom). Such a move, of course, could not be done without the cooperation of the Ethiopian king. The way this is developed in Egyptian apocalyptic tradition shows also that the text was understood in the sense of a joint military offensive against the Muslims.

many unsolved questions.[35] The Syriac fragments published by F. Nau in 1917 as belonging to *PM*, are probably part of a later work, an apocalypse reworking *PM* perhaps at the end of the 13th century.[36] In any case, we know today that *PM* had been translated into Coptic. Prof. T. Orlandi has recently communicated me that, by reading the Syriac *PM*, he was able to identify a Coptic fragment previously published by him, as containing part of a Coptic version of *PM*.[37] The influence of *PM* on the *Letter of Pisentius* and the *Apoc. Samuel* was already noted by Nau, who had only at his disposal the Syriac fragments just mentioned, and the Greek and Latin texts of *PM*.[38] We are today in a better position to assess this influence. The presentation will follow the apocalyptic pattern of events.

a) The hardships suffered by the Christians at the hands of the Muslims.

> *PM*: A man will go to sleep at night and get up in the morning, and he will find outside his door two or three oppressors and exactors of tribute and money.[39]
> *Apoc. Samuel*: Men will sleep in their houses at night, and every one will find in the morning at the door three officers, every one asking for a kind of loss.[40]
> *Pisentius' Letter*: The Egyptians will sleep at night and will get up in the morning, and they will find at the door of their houses three officials of the Sultan, every one of them making some unjust requisition.[41]

b) The joint attack of the two Christian kings.

> *PM*: Then, suddenly (...), the king of the Greeks will come out against them with great anger (...) He who was accounted by them as dead will come out against them from the sea of the Kushites, and pour desolation in the desert of Yatrib and inside the dwelling place of their fathers.[42]
> *Apoc. Samuel*: (God) will send against them the king of Rūm with great anger from the side of the sea (...) The king of Ethiopia will bring a terrible ruin to the land of their fathers in the East. The Muslims will flee to the desert where they had been before, escaping from the king of Ethiopia coming from the East, and from the king of Rūm, who will fall over the sons of Ishmael and encircle them in the wādī al-Ḥafār, the dwelling place of their fathers. He will destroy them from the West.[43]

The *Apoc. Samuel* develops here what is only suggested in *PM* and, not suprisingly, gives more relevance to the Ethiopian king. In the other Egyptian works, the joint campaign disappears under the growing influence of the conference on the orthodox faith. Still, in the woe to the city of Mecca found in *Shenute's Vision of the Church* (cf. verse 27, in the passage quoted above), one can hear an echo of the original feature.

c) In *PM* the Greek king is accompanied in the fight by "his sons." The feature is taken up by the Syriac fragments published by Nau:

> *PM*: The sons of the king of the Greeks will seize the regions of the desert and will finish by the sword any survivor left among them (the Muslims) in the Promised Land.[44]
> *Nau Fragments*: Then the king of the Greeks will come out from the West, and his son from the South.[45]

---

[35] A. Vööbus, "Discovery of an Unknown Syriac Author: Methodius of Petrā", *Abr-Nahrain* 17 (1976–7), 1–4, mentions three other MSS that have the text of *PM* more or less complete: Mardin Orth. 368 (written in 1365), Mardin Orth. A (written in 1956) and Mardin Orth. 891. All of them are of Western Syriac origin. The merit of identifying the text "discovered" by Vööbus as that of *PM* belongs to Reinink, "Ismael", 337. Even if all the known MSS are West Syrian, it seems clear that *PM* is rooted in Eastern Syrian tradition, cf. Reinink, "Ismael", 344; "Verfassername", 62–64. Reinink thinks of a Nestorian origin for the work. In *Eastern Christian Apocalyptic*, pp. 26–28, I have argued for the possibility of a Melkite living in Northern Mesopotamia, and familiar with Eastern Syrian tradition.

[36] Cf. F. Nau, "Méthodius-Clement-Andronicus", JA, XI Series, 9 (1917), 415–71. The text of this fragment, preserved in two Eastern Syriac MSS, is edited and studied afresh, in the light of the complete text of *PM*, in: Martinez, *Eastern Christian Apocalyptic*, pp. 206–246. Cf. for the problems of dating the text, pp. 210–11, 218–19. There are no grounds whatsoever to assume, as Nau did, a Monophysite origin for these fragments.

[37] I owe this information to a private communication of T. Orlandi. The fragment is found in Orlandi, *Papiri Copti di contenuto teologico*, Österreichische Nationalbibliothek (Wien 1974), no. XX (K 7630), pp. 188–90. The Coptic text corresponds to *PM*, most of chaps VI and VII (MS Vat. Syr., f. 123r-v). Orlandi places the Coptic handwriting in the 8th century. A close comparison of this text with the Syriac and the Greek version will make possible to say whether the version was made from Syriac or from Greek.

[38] Nau, "Note sur l'apocalypse de Samuel", ROC 20 (1915–17), 405–407.

[39] *PM*, chap. XIII (MS Vat. Syr. 58, f. 132r-v).

[40] Ziadeh, "L'apocalypse de Samuel", p. 383, lines 8–10.

[41] Périer, "Lettre de Pisuntius", p. 307, lines 7–9.

[42] *PM*, chap. XIII (MS Vat. Syr. 58, f. 133r-v).

[43] Ziadeh, "L'apocalypse de Samuel", p. 390, lines 8–14.

[44] *PM*, chap. XIII (MS Vat. Syr. 58, f. 133v).

[45] Nau, "Méthodius", p. 427, line 14.

If "the sons" means "the allies", it is perhaps possible to see here, in the context of *PM*, another weiled allusion to the role of the Ethiopian king. At least, this is the way the expression was understood by *Apoc. Samuel*, in the passage quoted above under b).[46] It is worth noticing that the Nau fragments are half way between *PM* and the Egyptian text. In the *Nau fragments*, written in Northern Mesopotamia, the king of Rūm comes from the West, and "his son" from the South. In the Egyptian *Apoc. Samuel*, the king of Rūm comes from the West, and the Ethiopian king from the East.

The feature reappears perhaps in *Apoc. Samuel*, when after the victory of the two kings, we are told, "the king of Ethiopia will marry the daughter of the king of the Greeks."[47] More probably, however, this is a projection in the future of what *PM* had placed in the distant past (the marriage between Byzas and Kūshat) in order to lend support to the idea of a cooperation of the brother kingdoms in the war against the Muslims. The reversal of the sexes (Greek king-Ethiopian princess in *PM*, Ethiopian king-Greek princess in *Apoc. Samuel*) is doubtless significant as to whom the precedence is given in each text. In any case, although no other Egyptian text mentions the marriage, a distant echo of the feature can be heard in the *Letter of Pisentius*. After the king of Rūm has chased the Muslims from Egypt, "he will set up his son, and the husband of his daughter with a few troops in the capital (Babylon of Egypt), and he will return to the capital of the empire (Constantinople) because of the worry for the capital of Rūm."[48]

d) Treatment given to the Muslims by the reconquering Christians.

> *PM*: Fear will fall upon them from all sides. Their wives, their sons, their leaders and all their camps, the whole land of the desert of their fathers will be delivered into the power of the king of the Greeks. They will be given over to the sword, to destruction, captivity and slaughter. Their oppression will be hundredfold stronger than their own yoke. They will be in a hard calamity.[49]

> *Apoc. Samuel*: Great terror and panic will fall upon the sons of Ishmael and all those taking refuge in them. Good will deliver them to the king of Rūm, who will destroy them by the sword and take them captives, because they had destroyed the earth. For this reason God, with a just decree, will deliver them to the king of Rūm, who will oppress them one hundredfold more than they had oppressed. And they will be in poverty, misery, hardships and difficulties, and under the sword.[50]

> *Pisentius' Letter*: (The king of Rūm) will disperse and scatter them at the edge of the sword. They will flee before him, and escape to the land of Cham. Those who will remain will be made captives and submitted to servitude. They will be humiliated and they will have to endure more evils than those they had caused to the sons of men. The sons of Esau will be persecuted and oppressed seven times more than what they had done to the sons of men.[51]

e) We have already mentioned how *PA ar. II* uses the quotation from Ps 68:31, the very text which is the key of *PM*'s developments.[52] Although the context there is quite different from that in *PM*, and the reference to Ps 68:31 in a work concerned with Ethiopia hardly needs justification, yet the form in which the text is given points to the Syriac Bible, and the most likely place from which such a text could have reached *PA ar. II* would be the body of traditions connected with *PM*.

f) The description of the final peace is too general a feature to be significant. When *PA ar. II* says that during that peace, "the living will pass by the dead and be sorry for him, for not living in those excellent days," this has a striking parallel in the *Nau fragments*.[53] Still, one has to be cautious. Such an idea has parallels in different apocalyptic traditions (for instance, in the much earlier *Apocalypse of Elijah* 2:53), and may come ultimately from Qoh 4:2. Nevertheless, the idea of a dependence on the traditions connected with *PM* cannot be completely ruled out.

g) Where the Egyptian apocalypses studied here show more clearly their dependence on *PM* is in the features connected with the Last Roman emperor. That this legend, involving the abdica-

---

[46] Ziadeh, "L'apocalypse de Samuel", p. 390, lines 8–14.

[47] Ibid., lines 22–23.

[48] Périer, "Lettre de Pisuntius", p. 309, lines 7–9.

[49] *PM*, chap. XIII (MS Vat. Syr. 58, f. 133v).

[50] Ziadeh, "L'apocalypse de Samuel", p. 390, lines 15–19.

[51] Périer, "Lettre de Pisuntius", pp. 308, lines 19–309, line 2. "The sons of Esau" is an old Jewish denomination of the Romans. It came to be used for all sort of enemies of God's people.

[52] Cf. MS Vat. ar. 158, f. 108v–109r, quoted above, pp. 11–12.

[53] Cf. MS Vat. ar. 158, f. 109v; Nau, "Méthodius", p. 328, lines 3–4.

tion of the last Roman emperor in Jerusalem, originates in *PM* is today an established fact.[54] According to *PM*, the Roman emperor, as soon as the Antichrist is revealed, comes to Jerusalem, to the Golgotha, and abdicates his crown "handing over the power to God" (and fulfilling in this way Ps 68:31 and 1 Cor 15:24). The royal crown and the cross are taken up to heaven.[55] The whole scene is a dramatization of the main idea of *PM*, namely, that the Byzantine empire will last to the very end. The Roman emperor acts on the earth as a deputy of Christ, in whose name he "hands over the power to God" once all enemies are vanquished. Who this Roman emperor is, we are not told in *PM*. It could well be the same who had chased the Muslims. In any case, the abdication scene takes place after the final peace, the coming of Gog and Magog, and the appearance of the Antichrist.

Apoc. Samuel summarizes greatly the information in *PM*. After the final peace, that here lasts forty years, Gog and Magog ravage the earth for five months. Only then we are told that "the king of the Greeks will rule over the earth for a year and six months. He will place his residence in Jerusalem. After this, God will abolish kingship from the earth, and the wild beast will appear, namely, the false Messiah".[56] In the *Letter of Pisentius* and *PA ar. II* we are at the same time farther away and closer to *PM*. On one hand, the motif suffers

several transformations. The king who had chased the Muslims and reunified the Churches is not surprisingly named Constantine. Perhaps to fill the gap between the time of the victory over the Muslims and the abdication scene, ten Roman kings are introduced after Constantine, the last of whom is the one who abdicates. According to *PA ar. II*, the name of this last king will also be Constantine.[57] On the other hand, the abdication itself is narrated in very similar terms in *PM*, in the *Letter of Pisentius* and in *PA ar. II*, with only few minor divergences.[58] It is worth noticing that *PA ar. II* shows some features in common with the version of the abdication in the *Nau fragments*: only in them, the crown and the cross are taken up to heaven by the angel Gabriel; only in them, the crown is characterized as "the crown that came down from heaven."[59] In *PA ar. II*, besides, it is said that Jerusalem is "the center of the earth", another central idea in the conceptual world of *PM*.[60]

4. On the Historical Development of a Motif: Some Suggestions

At this point of our inquiry, a literary dependence of the four works studied here from the Syriac *PM* seems established. Much further than that we cannot go. We do not know yet which way *PM*

---

[54] Cf. especially, P.J. Alexander, "Byzantium and the Migration of Literary Works and Motifs. The Legend of the Last Roman Emperor", *Medievalia et Humanistica* 2 (1971), 47–68; "The diffusion of Byzantine Apocalypses in the Medieval West and the Beginnings of Joachinism", in: A. Williams (ed.), *Prophecy and Millenarism. Essays in Honour of Marjorie Reeves*, Burnt Hill, Harllow, Essex, 1980, pp. 55–106; G. J. Reinink, "Die syrischen Wurzeln", 195–209.

[55] *PM*, chap. XIV, (MS Vat. Syr. 58, f. 135r-v).

[56] Cf. Ziadeh, "L'apocalypse de Samuel", p. 391, lines 9–12.

[57] MS Vat. ar. 158, f. 110r.

[58] Cf. *PM*, chap. XIV (MS Vat. Syr. 58, f. 135r-v); Périer, "Lettre de Pisuntius", p. 313, lines 4–10; *PA ar. II*, MS Vat. ar. 158, f. 110r. Compare also with Nau, "Méthodius", 432–33.

[59] *PA ar II*, MS Vat. ar. 158, f. 109v: (After the settlement over the orthodox faith, the kings) "will go to Jerusalem, and God will reveal the crown that came down from heaven". In the *Nau fragments*, "Méthodius", pp. 432, lines 18–433, line 2, "when he (the king of the Greeks) will go up (to Golgotha) with the Cross in his hand, the crown that came down from heaven over the head of Jovinian, the first king, will pass on top of the Cross, and he will lift up the Cross and the crown toward heaven". The reference is, of course, to the crown of Nimrod, "the first king" (cf. Gen 10:8–10). In Syriac tradition Nimrod's crown had come down from heaven, and had passed through the four world empires until it will return to heaven at the end of the world. Cf. C. Bezold (ed.), *Die Schatzhöhle. Zweiter Teil: Text*, Leipzig 1888, p. 128, lines 1–3. This whole legend about Nimrod's crown is developed in a still unpublished Syriac tract preserved in MSS Brit. Mus. 922 (Add. 25.875), ff. 58v–77v and Vat. Syr. 164, ff. 79r–109r. If the *Nau fragments* mention Jovinian, this is an interference from the crowning of Jovinian in the Syriac *Romance of Julian*, cf. J.G.H. Hoffmann (ed.), *Julianos der Abtrünnige. Syrische Erzählungen*, Leiden 1880, pp. 200–201.

[60] The idea was already central for the *Cave of Treasures*, one of the sources of *PM*. Cf. Bezold, *Die Schatzhöhle*, pp. 22, lines 8–13; 30, lines 12–15; 84, lines 7–18; 112, lines 4–14; 116, line 13–118, line 10; 146, lines 12–148, line 2; and 254, lines 9–255, line 12. *PM*, chap. X (MS Vat. Syr. 58, f. 126v), will link this theme with 2 Thess 2: 6–7. What "restrains" (*mā d-'ahīd*) the Son of Perdition, and "has to be taken from the 'center' (*men msʿata*) before he can be revealed, is the holy Cross, that was erected in the "center" (*msʿata*) of the earth, and the kingdom of the Romans, "who has taken refuge (*'ahīdā gawsā*) in the Cross". All these thoughts are woven together in the abdication scene in *PM*.

travelled to Egypt, nor if there were intermediary links in passing the tradition. What is clear, however, is that the influence of *PM* did not confine itself to Byzantium and the Latin West, but spread through Egypt and reached Ethiopia.

And yet, even at this preliminary stage of research, with so many unsolved issues, some suggestions on the historical development of the tradition can be offered. If our analysis is correct, one has to distinguish in both the *Apoc. Samuel* and the *Letter of Pisentius* an older apocalypse in the style of PA, more genuinely Coptic, and a historical apocalypse inspired by *PM* and added to the previous works. In dealing with questions of date and historical background, the two sections may perhaps be treated separately. As regards the section depending on *PM*, *Apoc. Samuel* is the one that has it in its less developed form. As for *PA ar. II*, it represents the definitive introduction in Egypt of a foreign style in apocalyptic writing, much closer to Syriac models and conceptions than to the older Egyptian apocalyptic tradition. It is the same tendency that can be observed in the *XIV Vision of Daniel*.

Besides, the way *PM*'s was understood by the Egyptian apocalypses helps to understand *PM* itself. The whole motif of the two Christian kings constitutes in a certain sense a Monophysite exegesis of *PM*. The widespread influence of *PM* in Egypt (even the existence of a Coptic version of *PM* as early as the 8th century) may perhaps strengthen the hypothesis of a Melkite origin for *PM*, or at least, of an interest of the empire in the diffusion of *PM* all over the Christian world. Behind the motif of the two kings in the Egyptian apocalypses there is a polemical point which is best understood as a response to Melkite propaganda, an instrument of which was perhaps *PM*. The reaction pays hommage to the influence of such propaganda.

In this connection, we would like to make a suggestion which seems already supported by our study. We have seen that the motif of the two kings, as was developed in Egyptian apocalyptic, had come to Ethiopia. In an article of 1976, I. Shahîd

argued for the early date of composition of the Ethiopian epic known as the *Kebra Nagast*.[61] The rediscovery of the Syriac *PM* by the byzantinist P. J. Alexander gave prof. Shahîd another argument in favor of his thesis. He suggested that the Ethiopian theme in *PM* was dependent on the *Kebra Nagast*, which he considered to be a 6th century Coptic work.[62] In the light of recent research on the Syriac *PM*, and of what we have seen of its influence on Egyptian apocalyptic, such a dependence is highly unlikely.

First, there are no hints of *PM* knowing Ethiopian tradition. *PM*'s interest in Ethiopia is self-explanatory, caused by the chaotic historical situation and the need to explain a difficult passage in the Syriac Bible. Second, the reconstruction of prof. Shahîd goes not without difficulties. For instance, it is not so clear that a strong interest in Byzantium indicates an early date.[63] The apocalypses studied in this paper are all late, and their concern for Byzantium *as a kingdom* is a feature prominent in all of them, in a way closer to the sort of concerns in the *Kebra Nagast* than to the ways of thinking about Byzantium in earlier Egyptian works. It is difficult to imagine a Copt writing a political theory for the Ethiopian monarchy in the sixth century. A Copt was then a citizen of the Roman empire, and the legitimacy of that empire was never put into question before the Muslim conquest. A neat division of the world between the two kingdoms like that proposed by the *Kebra Nagast*, based on dogmatic grounds, would be unthinkable at such an early date. Such a speculation, besides being most dangerous to Byzantine interests in Egypt, has left no traces whatsoever in Coptic literature or tradition. As is the case with Byzantium, concern for Ethiopia *as a kingdom* does not appear in Egypt until after the Muslim conquest, and always in dependence on *PM*. The whole colophon in the *Kebra Nagast*, with the data about the successive translations from Coptic to Arabic, and from Arabic to Ethiopic is most probably a literary device to lend authority to the final edition of the work in the 14th century.[64] Finally, there are a few elements in the *Kebra*

---

[61] I. Shahîd, "The *Kebra Nagast* in the Light of Recent Research", *Le Muséon* 89 (1976), 133–78.

[62] Ibid., 174–76.

[63] Cf. ibid., 135–36. 140–41. For the passages in the *Kebra Nagast* concerning Byzantium and Ethiopia, Cf. C. Bezold, *Kebra Nagast. Die Herrlichkeit der Könige*, Abhandlungen der königlich bayerischen Akademie der Wissenschaften, Band XXIII, 1, München 1095, chaps 19, 20, 72–73, 93, 95, 113, 117.

[64] Cf. Bezold, *Kebra Nagast*, p. 138.

Nagast that seem to be dependent, in the last resort, on the body of traditions originating in *PM*. One such element is the emphasis on the fact that, if Byzantium has the Cross, Ethiopia has the Tabernacle of the Law and the Chariot. The very interest in showing that Ethiopia is superior to Byzantium, and that Ethiopia will last to the end while Byzantium will fail, looks too much like an effort to counter Byzantine speculations in the contrary direction. Such speculations did not arise in Byzantium until the influence of *PM* spread out. Sometimes, the dependence appears in minor features, the most conspicuous being the motif of "the vanquisher of the enemy," the bridle made from the nails of the Cross at the time of Constantine: this motif is found in the *Nau fragments*.[65] The meeting of Justin and Caleb in Jerusalem looks also like a development of the motif studied here — only in this case projected in the past.[66] Moreover, the idea that the king of Rūm will take the title of "king of Ethiopia"[67] is a very strange idea, understandable, however, if it is inspirated by the developments in *PM*, where the last Greek king is called "king of Kush" on the basis of its exegesis of Ps 68:31.[68] Again, the renunciation of Caleb to his crown in favor of his two sons is inspired, according to Shahîd, by the *martyrium Arethae*.[69] In the *Martyrium*, Caleb deposits his crown in Jerusalem,

a feature which is known also from Syriac sources, and is embodied by *PM* in the abdication scene of the last Greek king.[70]

To end with this list, we would dare to suggest a hypothetical solution for the mysterious figure of Dĕmātĕyōs (Domitius) of Rome, with whose book the prophecies in the *Kebra Nagast* are said several times to be in agreement.[71] Could not the name Dĕmātĕyōs be a corruption of Methodius? The name Methodius was already mistreated by Syriac writers and copists.[72] In the *Book of the Bee* of Salomon of Baṣrā and in one kāršūnī fragment of *PM*, Methodius is explicitly qualified as "bishop of Rome."[73] If this hypothesis is correct, the mysterious figure would be explained, and we will have found an explicit indication of the role of *PM* as a reference point in the composition of the *Kebra Nagast*.[74]

The interest in studying the development of the Egyptian apocalyptic tradition after the Muslim conquest goes far beyond the concern for classifying texts and describing the wild transmission and migration of motifs. Such a study has a number of immediate consequences for the historian of the Coptic Church.

A closer look into the Egyptian apocalypses will help to nuance current statements on the attitude of the Copts toward the Muslims. The idea of Egyptian nationalism, used to explain the assumed

---

[65] Cf. Bezold, *Kebra Nagast*, chap. 113 (pp. 133–34). Nau, "Méthodius", p. 427, lines 3–11. Cf. also Nau, "Sur la fête de la Croix. Analyse d'une homélie de Moyse bar Cepha et du MS. grec. 1586 de Paris", ROC 19 (1914), 225–46.

[66] Bezold, *Kebra Nagast*, ch. 117 (pp. 136–37).

[67] Ibid., p. 136.

[68] *PM*, chap. XIV (MS Vat. Syr. 58, f. 125v).

[69] On the *martyrium Arethae*, cf. Shahîd, "The Martyrs of Najrân. New Documents", *Subsidia Hagiographica* 49, Bruxelles 1971, pp. 181–231, where the relevant bibliography is given. For the motif of the crown in the narrative of Caleb's renunciation, cf. Shahîd, "The *Kebra Nagast*", 171–72.

[70] Cf. E.A. Budge, ed., *The History of Alexander the Great, being the Syriac Version of the Pseudo-Callisthenes*, Cambridge 1889, pp. 257–58, where Alexander promises to leave his throne in Jerusalem, so that the Messiah might sit on it when He comes. The episode is not to be found in the Syriac Pseudo-Callisthenes, but in a Christian legend about Alexander appended to it, and written as a pamphlet to support Heraclius' policies in Northern Mesopotamia, cf. Reinink, *Das Syrische Alexanderlied*, CSCO 445/Syr. 196, Louvain 1983, pp. 10–11. The motif of the crown had been used before in the *Julian* Romance, cf. Hoffman, *Julianos der Abtrünnige*, pp. 200–01. It is, of course, taken by *PM* in the abdication scene of chap. XIV, and by the Egyptian apocalypses (*Letter of Pisentius*, PA ar. II). Shahîd, "The *Kebra Nagast*", 171, knows these texts, but dismisses them too quickly.

[71] Cf. Bezold, *Kebra Nagast*, chaps 19 and 117. Bezold, ibid., p. 10, tries to identify this figure with Saint Domitius, one of the two Roman brothers of Scetis.

[72] In the Syriac Commentary known as the *Gannat Bussâmē*, Methodius is referred to as Mādīōs, cf. Reinink, "Verfassername", 46–47; and in the tract mentioned above, from MS Brit. Mus 922 (Add. 25.875), ff. 72ra; 73rb, as "Mâr Tādīōs the seer."

[73] Cf. Budge, *The Book of the Bee*, Anecdota Oxoniensia, Semitic Series, I, part II, Oxford 1886, p. 140; and MS Borgia art. 135, f. 20v.

[74] We do not intend here to address all the problems connected with the composition of the *Kebra Nagast*, which may still embody earlier material. But if our suggestions are correct, the *final* composition of the work cannot be placed before the influence of *PM* reached Ethiopia. In this way we come closer to the judgement of J. Doresse, *L'Empire de Prêtre-Jean*, I, Paris 1957, pp. 267–68. The Ethiopic apocalypses mentioned there shuld be studied in the light of the new data.

wellcome given by the Copts to the Muslims, and often considered as the main reason for their rejection of the Chalcedonian creed, is another common place that needs correction.[75] A certain Egyptian chauvinisme and naïve pride cannot be confounded with "nationalism" in the modern sense. In this respect, the apocalypses studied here betray a very sincere longing for Christian unity, and that, independently of spontaneous feelings toward the Byzantines (as the case of *Apoc. Samuel* shows). Of course, one shoud not be deluded by the reasons mixed in such a desire: the *Letter of Pisentius* naïvely confesses that "all the districts around in (Egypt) will give him (Muhammad) tribute, with the only exception of the district of the Romans."[76] Still, factors such as this one are never the determinant element. Nothing shows that better than the whole motif of the joint conference of the two Christian kings on the orthodox faith. No matter how useful the cooperation of the Byzantines could be to get rid of the Muslim yoke, the question of orthodoxy admits no compromise: for a lasting peace to be possible, that question has to be settled, and only God can do it. Centuries before, it was the same stubborn faithfulness of the Copts to their understanding of the Holy Faith and to their tradition that made them resist to the unfortunate policies of the Byzantine administration.

---

[75] Cf., for instance. W.M.C. Frend, "Nationalism as a Factor in Antichalcedonian Feeling in Egypt", in: S. Mews (ed.), *Religion and National Identity*, Studies in Church History 18, Oxford 1982, pp. 21–45.

[76] Périer, "Lettre de Pisuntius", p. 307, lines 5–6.

COPTIC STUDIES

Mark Milburn

Nomads and Religion in the Context of Christian Nubia and Coptic Egypt: an Enquiry

The remark in this short paper, by one at home in the central and southern Sahara, though not in Egypt nor the Sudan, are mostly in the form of queries. They arise from having seen, quite by chance, an observation of A.J. Arkell (1973: 198–199) that... "Tuareg were introduced (into Kordofan) in the time of the kingdom of Meroe to look after the new transport animal, the camel, for which the steppes of Kordofan provide such suitable grazing. Kel Anag to such Tuareg camel--owners will have meant the Meroitic inhabitants of the Nile valley... Although we do not know when the Tuareg passed from Palestine through Egypt into North Africa, their traditions imply that they must have done so".

Note here a suggestion regarding common pasturage of cattle and sheep between Blemmyes and Noubades, made in the 5th century (Skeat, 1977: 162). It looks as though the "Tuareg introduced into Kordofan" will have been capable and willing to cooperate, though perhaps only for so long as it suited them, if this is not to judge them by their history in the Sahara.

This idea of Tuareg so far east is not found in numerous works, some of them for public consumption, on the general subject of "the Tuareg", whose popular ancestors are seen as the Garamantes if not the Sea People, whoever both may have been, in the widest sense of the expression. Having consequently looked further east than is my wont, it seems clear that there were a good many nomads or semi-nomads moving around on business of which we are mostly unaware, some of them evidently nefarious and the cause of much discontent among more orderly factions who suffered from the depredations (cf. Kirwan, 1937a: 71–72, citing a Coptic text). If their misdeeds caused much ink to flow between dignitaries of some of the injured parties, their ability to circulate

far and wide have occasioned culture contact, some of it religious (cf. Michałowski, 1981: 329). I propose to raise a number of questions and will be most grateful to receive comments as a result: even the most farflung and non-specialist ideas may prove helpful, if and when some sort of general picture can be put together. Who can tell where this enquiry may end?

I shall try to spell names of people and places as the individual authors have done, noting some large variations: the Nobatae are a case in point. I wish to look first at the Garamantes and Christianity. When Arabs overran the Fezzan and took prisoner the ruler, who was probably a Garamantian − in the lack of contrary evidence − we hear no mention either then or later of Christian buildings or institutions encountered. It will be recalled that the Garamantes had a sedentary organization in and around their capital, Garama (the modern Germa), with plenty of Roman relics and buildings that have survived the ravages of time.

Thought to have been writing around 547, Cosmos states that Christianity existed among the Nubians and Garamantes: I can see nothing in his wording (McCrindle, 1897: 120) to indicate that there were Garamantes in Nubia, an impression that could be gained from certain authors (Kirwan, 1934: 201, Shinnie, 1954, map 1). Perhaps the idea was floated by MacMichael (1912: 239–241) and well-publicized by Monneret de Villard (1938: 64–65). I have seen no mention of Garamantes by Adams (1984) nor Frend (1984).

We are also told that the Chronicle of Joannes Biclarensis for the year 569–570 records the conversion to Christianity of the Garamantes as well as the Maccuritae, the latter held to live immediately to south of the Nobatae (Kirwan, 1934: 202). Actually a later text (Desanges, 1962:

256–257) puts down the Maccuritae as "unlo-cated" though Shinnie (1954: 2) places the capital of post-Meroitic Makuria at Old Dongola (cf. Michałowski, 1981: 327).

There do nonetheless exist a very few straws at which one can try to clutch. In the last century it was recounted, in Libya, that "the Zuela people, like all other Moors, attribute strange buildings... to the Christians" (Lyon, 1821: 215).

This may not be worth much when compared to the habit of Arabs of northern Kordofan of applying the term "Anaj" ... to ancient Egyptian, Meroitic or Christian ruins (Arkell, 1973: 198).

A less-fragile "straw" is provided in the Kawar region of northern Niger: this is the name Qasr Umm Isa, perhaps corresponding to Ayemma (Lange and Berthoud, 1977: 28), which could have flourished during the dominant period of the Zaghawa, although I have tried to argue elsewhere (Milburn, in press a) that the Zaghawa, whose influence reached up into Fezzan, may have muscled-in on a trade opportunity left vacant by the fall of the Garamantes: thus the place might have been named by Christian Garamantes, unless the converting influence came from the east (?). Via a movement from converts on the same approxim-ate latitude (cf. Trimingham, 1963: 15). One source suggests the possibility of Coptic Christians there (Cuoq, 1984: 23).

In terms of a Garamantian route towards the east, coming from Fezzan, the existence of an ancient way towards Egypt is affirmed by Rebuffat (1970: 10 and 14), who notes that the Garamantes must have been masters of the itinerary passing Augila to reach Siwa. If this is so, how much further east may they have gone and with whom may they have come into contact? Cf. Zayed (1981: 139) for possible earlier use of similar (?) routes by dynastic Egypt.

Some as yet undeciphered inscriptions on a north Libyan building started after 201 A.D., termed "Libyque de Bu Njem" (Rebuffat, 1974–75: 165), appear to have counterparts is Benghazi, in several regions of Fezzan and even in northern Niger (Milburn, 1984a). It is possible that more remain to be discovered: those in Niger suggest movement along the so-called Bornu Route by people who may have been traders, if not necessarily Garamantes.

The problems of identifying differing populations, all termed Garamantes, has been rightly raised by a French Fezzan expedition (Bellair et al., 1953:

97): some are seen as redoubtable nomad warriors, some as agriculturalists and stock-raisers, and others as long-distance traders. Cf. Trimingham (1963: 12).

If we are hampered to some extent by Christian writers with their own particular axe to grind regarding sober historical fact, as was to be the case with some Arab writers later on, I have dwelt at some length on the Garamantes — nearer my own home ground — with a view to suggesting some parallels in and around Nubia. My grasp of Nubian history being embryonic, as in December 1984, a number of diverging views are evident from such literature as I have encountered to date.

In the age-old controversy of nomad or sedentary, the Blemmyes are often portrayed as nomads. They seem, however, to have divided their time between "the desert and the sown, raiding the valley from time to time and sometimes settling, as they did in Lower Nubia" (Kirwan, 1966: 121). It is said of the Noubae and of the Noubades (Desan-ges, 1962: 195–196) that they may have been split up from the beginning into a northern and a southern clan, also that the Ancients could have regarded the Noubae, and possibly the Noubades, as Libyans, which could indicate a long acquain-tance with nomadism.

The Nôba, at some time prior to 350 A.D. lived in settlements of grass huts, also possessing certain towns of bricks, captured from the Meroites: they cultivated the cotton tree (Kirwan, 1937b: 52). The barbarian luxury of Group X kinglets — seen as Nobades or Blemmyes — is recounted in some detail by Leclant (1981: 294). Hakem (1981: 317) recalls that in the last centuries of the Meroitic Kingdom neither Rome nor Meroe were able to defend trade routes against nomadic Blemmyes and Nobades.

I should like to mention here the apparent practice of Ahaggar Tuareg, during medieval times and later, of "protecting" trades passing through their territory. One may surmise that this was tempered with considerations of their own personal safety in the event that the caravan were well-mounted and numerically strong, as also with the estimated likely material gain from robbing instead of "pro-tecting". Perhaps things were the same along the trade routes above-recounted.

Nomads have been obliged to settle in the past from economic necessity, or forced by political contingencies to do so. The departure of a number of Aïr Tuareg to Darfur during the First World

War is a case in point (Fuglestad, 1973). Many Ahaggar Tuareg have recently been encouraged to settle by their national authorities.

The camel seems to have transformed Beja (Blemmye) society and culture by the end of the 3rd century (Adams, 1984: 389), as it is held to have done in North Africa in the same era. This versatile beast provided a vehicle which gave potential raiders a certain degree of immunity: and unwilling settlers could regain their nomad life as desired. One view sees increasing desiccation compelling herders to develop suitable means of transport (Shaw, 1979: 686), though I do not wish to be drawn into the academic controversy as to whether the camel was actually imported afresh or became domesticated through dire necessity.

The Nobades apparently clung to the last remnants of their Meroitic heritage right up to their official conversion to Christianity, about the middle of the 6th century, thereafter persisting in sacrificing humans and animals as hitherto (Kirwan, 1966: 126). The Blemmyes are said to have embraced Christianity — at least nominally — towards the end of the same century, and to have forsaken their ancient gods. It is possible, however, that paganism may not have ceased to exist among them (Kirwan, 1937a: 89 and 91).

I am unable to fathom the true religious leanings of the Beni Kanz — an amalgamation of Arab, Nubian and Beja elements — immediately prior to the Islamization of Makouria (Adams, 1975: 13), though of course my prime interest is in their Beja component.

The same evident hesitancy in fully abandoning old beliefs has been remarked among the Tuareg. Even though the veil is seen by Gast (1975: 13) as a religious attribute adopted by Howara and Lemtouna of central Sahara, there are plenty of superstitions and strange practices alive to-day. Only a few years ago I came across a low stone structure, new-looking and of markedly non--Islamic aspect and was horrified to find bulldozer tracks passing beneath it (Milburn, 1983: 4–5 and fig. 2). In November 1983 I noted a Targui, who had just discovered that a Tenere tomb was Islamic (or islamized?), placing a discreet offering of dates, inside a plastic bag, beside the three small standing stones in its eastern border.

The veil seems to have escaped mention by Classical authors and I have wondered about the implications of "veiled" Blemmyes and Atravan (Fire Priests) noted by Palmer (1970: 95, 114 and 188). Lack of an apparent mouth in rock art of Aïr has been taken as meaning that the persons shown were veiled: it seems that Palmer felt the same about Blemmye pottery (Palmer, 1970: 139).

Many authors have speculated as to whether Tuareg were once Christian. Apart from all that has already been said, one popular "proof" is to take certain words alleged to be part of their language and trace them back to Christian times. The earliest example currently known to me is by Delafosse (1924: 174): Trimingham is sceptical (1963: 15) though the presence of Christians is mentioned in the 10th century in Ouargla, Algeria (Cuoq, 1984: 15).

The only definite Christian-like cross of which I know from literature is that illustrated by Barth (1857, I: 195), reproduced here as fig. 1. This depicts a rider with a cross on his large shield and very small cross just showing between his knees: this will have been fixed to the front of his saddle. I have come across nothing similar, before or since, although the so-called Cross of Agadez and the cross on the camel-saddle exist to-day, though in quite different forms. The "cross", first published around 1905, has been compared to the ankh.

Another symbol apparently enjoying a wide zone of distribution, as well as conserved to-day among peoples of the southern Sahara and the Sahel, is that shown by Palmer (1970: pl. IX, no 5), which I have reproduced as fig. 2: it is apparently taken from Blemmye pottery found at Karanog. Palmer sees it as ressembling the Tuareg shield.

Approximately the same form occurs on pottery from Turkey (Garstang et al., 1937: pl. XXX, no 3). In a modern context, something similar is worn on the forehead or the side of the temple among the Peulh Bororo and some Tuareg (Chesi, 1981: 87, 93 and 94, 94; Fisher, 1984: 156) or as a pectoral by Tuareg (Fisher, 1984: 217).

Arkell (1951a: 210) considers that numerous traces of the cultural influence of Meroe may be found among the modern Tuareg, citing various objects having their likely origin in India (1951b: 37–38). While I feel unable to comment on the sword depicted on the Sun Temple at Meroe, it is a fact that many Tuareg and others dwelling in the Sahel wear their sword slung from one shoulder, as the Beja (formerly Blemmyes) of the Red Sea Hills do to-day (Shinnie, 1967: 163).

MacMichael (1912: 240) mentions a matrilinear system prevailing among the Tuwarek nomads as well as among the Beja. If the Mazices (Tuareg?)

1. Tuareg shield-design and cross on front of saddle (after Barth)

2. Design of Blemy pottery (after Palmer)

who raided Kharga in 436 A.D. had any contact with the Blemmyes and Nobatae, who attacked Philae in the latter half of the reign of Theodosius II (Arkell, 1973: 179), it is possible that all three peoples, probably with a long history of desert environment behind them, would have some similar customs.

Because of a suggestion by Arkell (1973: 177) that Nubians could be descended from the C Group, I feel bound to point out one misapprehension which has clearly arisen. He cites *tumuli* with stone pillars on which are engraved cattle, at Lemqader in Mauritania, noting that it will be of interest to see, when the *tumuli* are excavated, whether there be any cultural connection between them and the C group (Arkell, 1973: 49). In fact three such *tumuli* were opened by Monod (1948: 31–32) and fragments of four individuals found, of which almost no details are stated: such sparse grave-goods as are mentioned were intepreted as neolithic.

During a quick visit to Lemqarder (2047N 1204W) some twelve years ago, I personally noticed only one engraved pillar. Though I have studied the distribution of such structures, limited *grosso modo* to that area (Milburn, 1978a: 7–8), I have grave doubts as to whether a number of carvings and inscriptions on the highest pillar — always at the approximate centre of a line of lesser ones — are always contemporary with the burial(s) in the adjacent tumulus (Milburn, 1978b).

Meanwhile I am still perplexed as to how to relate an apparent neolithic context to a statement by Petit-Maire (1981: 85), to the effect that "by 2000 BP the coast was a desert through which ... nomads passed, leaving ... sometimes odd erect megaliths". An engraved bovid recalls other areas where their kind grazed in profusion during the final neolithic (as late as the early first millenium in parts of Mauritania), though probably not much after about 4500 BP in western Tenere Tafassasset (Smith, 1984: 86) and also probably about the same time near the frontier of Algeria and Niger (Milburn, 1984b: 307).

Conclusion. If the question of whole-hearted Blemmye and Nubian (Nobatae) Christianity in the early period remains enigmatic, the effects and consequences of movement from Coptic Egypt may have had direct and indirect influence on regions even further off than Nubia. One view holds that "radiations penetrated Saharan Berbers and Blacks through political and commercial influence both from the north and from Nubia. "It may have gained some inhabitants of Borku: Ibn Sa 'id is cited as saying that the part of Berkāmi (in Kawar) which touches the Nubians, professes Christianity" (Trimingham, 1963: 15).

This brief look at ancient populations of Nubia plus the central and southern Sahara, as well as medieval and modern peoples, though lacking in depth, may have helped to underline the importance of seeking out religious influences and contacts around the latitude of the modern Nubian desert: and a good distance to westward too, searching though Kordofan (cf. Arkell, 1973: 191–194), Kawar and indeed perhaps as far as the jagged peaks and leafy hamlets of Aï. If this comes to pass, it will mean that Nubian specialists have viewed these notes with a degree of tolerance, as well as interest, and my purpose will have been achieved.

Abbreviations

Adams, W.Y. 1975 = "The Twilight of Nubian Christianity", in: K. Michałowski (ed.), *Nubia. Récentes Recherches*, Varsovie: Musée National, 11–17.

— 1984 *Nubia, Corridor to Africa*, London: Allen Lane.

Arkell, A.J. 1951a = *The History of Darfur. 1200–1700 A.D.*, Sudan Notes and Records XXXII, Part II, 207–238.

— 1951b "Meroe and India", in: W.F. Grimes (ed.), *Aspects of Archaeology in Britain and beyond*. Essays presented to O.G.S. Crawford, London: H.S. Edwards, 32–38.

Arkell, A.J. 1973 = *A History of the Sudan to A.D. 1821*, Westport, Conn: Greenwood Press.

Barth, H. 1857 = *Travels and Discoveries in North and Central Africa*, I, London: Longman.

Bellair, P., Gobert, E.G., Jodot P. and Pauphilet D. 1953 = *Mission au Fezzan*, Tunis: Institut des Hautes Études.

Chesi, G. 1981 = The Last Africans, Woergl: Perlinger Verlag.

Cosmas, see McCrindle.

Cuoq, J. 1984 = *Histoire de l'Islamisation de l'Afrique de L'Ouest des origines à la fin du XVIe siècle*, Paris: Geuthner.

Delafosse, M. 1924 = "Les relations du Maroc avec le Soudan à travers les âges", *Hespéris* V, 153–174

Desanges, J. 1962 = *Catalogue des Tribus africaines de l'Antiquité classique à l'ouest du Nil*, Dakar: Publications de la section d'histoire, Université de Dakar.

Fisher, A. 1984 = *Afrika im Schmuck*, Köln: Dumont.

Frend, W.H.C. 1984 = *The Rise of Christianity*, London: Darton, Longman and Tod.

Fuglestad, F. 1973 = "Les révoltes des Touareg du Niger (1916–17)", *Cahiers d'Études Africaines XIII*, 49, 82–120.

Garstang, J., Phytian Adams, J. and Seton Williams, V. 1937 = "Third Report on the Excavations at Sakje-Geuzi, 1908–1911", *Liverpool Annals of Archaeology and Anthropology XXIV*, 119–140.

Gast, M. 1975 = "Les influences arabo-islamiques dans la société des Kel Ahaggar (Sahara algérien)", *Travaux du Lapmo*, 23 pages.

Hakem, A.A. 1981 = "The Civilization of Napata and Meroe", in: G. Mokhtar (ed.), *General History of Africa. II. Ancient Civilizations of Africa*, London: Heinemann, 298–325.

Kirwan, L.P. 1934 = "Christianity and the Kura'an", *Journal of Egyptian Archaeology* XX, 201–203.

— 1937a = "Studies in the Later History of Nubia", *Liverpool Annals of Archaeology and Anthropology* XXIV, 69–105.

— 1937b = "A Survey of Nubian Origins", *Sudan Notes and Records* XX, Part I, 47–62.

— 1966 = "Prélude to Nubian Christianity", in: M.-L. Bernhard (ed.), *Mélanges offerts à Kazimierz Michałowski*, Warszawa: Państwowe Wydawnictwo Naukowe, 121–128.

Lange, D. and Berthoud, S. 1977 = "Al-Quṣaba et d'autres villes de la route centrale du Sahara", *Paideuma* 23, 19–40.

Leclant, J. 1981 = "The Empire of Kush: Napata and Meroe", in: G. Mokhtar (ed.), *General History of Africa. II. Ancient Civilization of Africa*, London: Heinemann, 278–297.

Lyon, G.F. 1821 = *A Narrative of Travels in Northern Africa*, London: John Murray.

MacMichael, H.A. 1912 = *The Tribes of Northern and Central Kordofán*. Cambridge: University Press.

McCrindle, J.W. 1897 = *The Christian Topography of Cosmas, an Egyptian Monk*, London: Hakluyt Society.

Michałowski, K. 1981 = "The Spreading of Christianity in Nubia", in: G. Mokhtar (ed.), *General History of Africa. II. Ancient Civilizations of Africa*, London: Heinemann, 326–340.

Milburn, M. 1978a = "Some Pre- and Protohistory of the Northwestern Sahara: A Plea for Action", *The Maghreb Review* 3, (9), 7–13.

— 1978b = "Towards an Absolute Chronology of Certain Saharan Rock Art", *Antiquity* LII, 135–136.

— 1983 = *The Tuareg of the Sahara and the Sahel*, London: Young Explorers' Trust at the Royal Geographical Society.

— 1984a = "Sur quelques inscriptions énigmatiques des confins nigéro-fezzanais", *Le Saharien* 91.

— 1984b = "Archaeology and Prehistory", in: J.L. Cloud-sley-Thompson (ed.), *Sahara Desert*, Oxford: Pergamon Press, 291–310.

In press a. "Romans and Garamantes — an Enquiry into Contacts", in: D.J. Buck and D.J. Mattingly (eds), *Town and Country in Roman Tripolitania*, Oxford: B.A.R.

Monod, Th. 1948 = "Sur quelques monuments lithiques du Sahara occidental", *Actas y Memorias*, Sociedad Española de Antropología, Etnografía y Prehistoria XXIII, 12–35.

Monneret de Villard, U. 1938 = *Storia della Nubia cristiana*, Roma: Pont. Institutum Orientalium Studiorum.

Palmer, Sir. R. 1970 = *The Bornu Sahara and Sudan*, New York: Negro Universities Press.

Petit-Maire, N. 1981 = "Aspects of Human Activity in the Coastal Occidental Sahara in the Last 10 000 Years", in: J.A. Allan (ed.), *The Sahara. Ecological Change and Early Economic History*, Outwell: Menas Press, 81–91.

Rebuffat, R. 1970 = "Routes d'Égypte de la Libye intérieure", *Studi Magrebini* 3, 1–20.

— 1974–75 = "Graffiti en 'Libyque de Bu Njem'", *Libya Antiqua* XI–XII, 165–187.

Shaw, B.B. 1979 = "The Camel in Roman North Africa and the Sahara: History, Biology and Human Economy", *Bulletin de l'IFAN* 41, série B, 663–721.

Shinnie, P.L. 1954 = *Medieval Nubia*, Khartoum: Sudan Antiquities Service.

— 1967 = *Meroe. A Civilization of the Sudan*, London: Thames and Hudson.

Skeat, T.C. 1977 = "A Letter from the King of the Blemmyes to the King of the Noubades", *Journal of Egyptian Archaeology* 63, 159–170.

Smith, A.B. 1984 = "Origins of the Neolithic in the Sahara", in: J.D. Clark and S.A. Brand (eds), *From Hunters to Farmers. The Causes and Consequences of Food Production in Africa*, Berkeley, Ca: University of California Press, 84–92.

Trimingham, J.S. 1963 = *A History of Islam in West Africa*, London: Oxford University Press.

Tubiana, M.J. and Tubiana J. 1977 = The Zaghowa from an Ecological Viewpoint, Rotterdam: A. A. Balkema.

Zayed, A. H. 1981 = "Egypt's Relations with the Rest of Africa", in: G. Mokhtar (ed.), *General History of Africa. II. Ancient Civilizations of Africa*, London: Heinemann, 136–154.

COPTIC STUDIES

Mounir Basta

Winged Figures on Wooden Panels

In 1947 the Coptic Museum obtained a valuable collection of carved wooden panels, most of them dating to the 4th and 5th cent. A.D. The Museum devoted part of the Old Wing to the exhibition of these excellent pieces of wooden panels.

This unique collection, which has probably no parallel, forms a remarkable link between ancient Egyptian art, Late Hellenistic art and the beginnings of Coptic art. The carved reliefs on these panels represent Nilotic scenes, which were favoured in ancient Egyptian art — bunches of grapes, crocodiles, swimming naked figures carrying fruit baskets and lotus flowers. The panels were probably meant to decorate the walls of palaces in the Old Coptic periods. Today I wish to speak of the most interesting scenes found upon these panels, that is the figures of winged cupids or angels carrying floral garlands encircling a human bust, a cross, or a rosette. The figures each have two wings and robes that show them to be flying. Some are fully dressed, others are half-naked (figs 1–6).

In the Coptic Museum there are three limestone sculptures in room no 3, the room of "Bawit". One of them represents Christ enthroned on a panel carried by two flying angels; the second shows the bust of Christ in a garland carried by two flying angels; finally, the third represents a cross in a garland also carried by two angels (figs 7–9).

Such a motif was well known in the Christian era, but was originally pagan. A comparative study of these pieces from the Christian era and a limestone sculpture bearing a similar relief dating to the pagan times of the Roman Empire shows that this theme had originally been pagan and had been continued under Christianity as were many other elements. The limestone relief has been interpreted as Ceres, the goddess of agriculture, but, in my opinion, the relief represents the bust of an Emperor holding a sceptre in one hand and a kind of plant in the other. The bust is in a floral garland which is carried by two winged figures, probably Victories, who are exactly similar to the figures carrying the bust of Christ, the cross and the rosette. The other elements of the scenes, that is the curtains and columns carved on both edges of the fragments, are also the same (fig. 10).

I have noticed that the Christ bust carved on wood panels is depicted with two wings; this may be interpreted as the bust of angel as some Coptologists state. I think that, since I have the cross, a symbol of Christ, in a similar relief, I cannot interpret this relief as a figure of an angel, for the cross here represents and replaces the figure of Christ. Thus, we arrive at the conclusion that the busts, although with wings, are the busts of Christ. Probably in early Christianity, when the creed was vague in the minds of the Egyptians, it was believed that Christ could have wings, like the angels, this to facilitate the idea of resurrection. But what of the rosette which is carved in a round medallion similar to that of the bust of Christ and the cross, and also carried by two figures. Has it any relation to Christ? Or the cross? The interpretation is that the artist had wanted to say that Christ is the rosette of the world, or that he wanted to write the letter "X" — Christ combining it with the cross in a decorative motif (fig. 11).

This assumption is emphasized by the reliefs on some limestone funerary stelae which have rosettes carved upon them to indicate their holiness. They are exhibited in the Coptic Museum (figs 12–14). The other conclusion to be drawn from this study is that the angels depicted on the walls of churches, monasteries and other objects, are derived from figures well known in pagan times, representing then the gods Eros and Cupid, or the goddess Victory. The Christians did not hesitate to continue depicting such figures to indicate the idea of angels, mentioned often in the Holy Bible, even though the figures were reminiscent of paganism.

1–3. Panel showing the bust of Christ carried by two angels

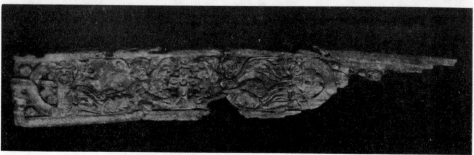

4–5. Panel showing the cross carried by two angels

6. Panel showing a rosette carried by two angels

7. Limestone frieze showing Christ enthroned carried by two angels

8. Limestone frieze showing the bust of Christ carried by two angels

9. Limestone frieze showing the cross carried by two angels

10. Limestone frieze depicting the bust of an Emperor carried by the goddesses of Victory

11. Limestone fragment with a relief of Christ in a floral garland

12. Limestone funerary stela with the relief of a rosette

13. Limestone fragment with the ʿnḥ sign and a rosette

14. Limestone fragment with a rosette in front of the sanctuary façade

COPTIC STUDIES

Mounir Basta

Renovation of the Coptic Museum

It is a great pleasure to be among my colleagues, Coptologists from all over the world.

On behalf of my colleagues in the Coptic Museum and myself I would like to express my gratitude for this invitation. We, Egyptians, are extremely proud of attending this Congress of Coptology, which shows indeed to what extent you, eminent scholars, are interested in the Coptic period of ancient Egyptian history.

Since the Coptic Museum is considered one of the centres for studying Coptology, I wish to speak briefly of the renovation that has taken place in the museum, for the benefit of those of you who had not the chance to attend the inauguration ceremony.

First of all I have to state that, under the sponsorship of President Mubarak and the Minister of Culture Mr Mohammad Abd-el--Ramid Radwan, and in cooperation with Dr Kadry, who is now renowned in Egypt and the world for his enthusiasm in renovating our museums and restoring Egyptian antiquities all over Egypt, the Coptic Museum has had the chance to be renovated in record time thanks to work continuing night and day. As my time is limited, I cannot explain in detail all that has been done, but with the aid of some slides, I would like to give you a brief idea of some of the essential points of interest to Coptologists. Assuming that most of you have visited the Museum or have at least read about it, I will speak on the following main subjects:

1. the method of display,
2. changes in the display made as a result of scientific studies,
3. the re-opening of the old wing (closed since 1966).

Method of Display

Since the limestone pieces of sculpture in the nine rooms on the lower (ground) floor had been mostly fixed to the walls with iron bars, humidity had affected or was about to affect many of them. After long discussions and researches made by the restoration department headed by Dr Shawky and Mr Mohammad Fawzy we arrived at the conclusion that the sculptures should be removed from the walls by some centimetres and that bars coated with plastic should be used in order to protect them from the humidity, which, fortunately, is not very high. This new display method shall remain under constant supervision so that all defects can be promptly discovered and remedied as quickly as possible.

On the Upper Floor we replaced completely the old cases with new ones and illuminated them with artificial lights from above. This kind of light could probably have a bad effect on some exhibits such as textiles or manuscripts. To avoid this, we used a certain kind of glass; still we are doubtful and shall continue inspecting its effect on the exhibits.

The display of objects in the cases was completely changed so as to make it more attractive to visitors, who really appreciated it, especially the Egyptian visitors.

New labels were written in three languages: Arabic, English and French; additional data was given.

This, in brief, are those of the essential changes made in the display method that may be of interest to you.

Changes in the Scientific Arrangement

We all know that the Coptic exhibits had been arranged in the rooms on a chronological basis. We found it logical and reasonable to reorganize some of the rooms. For instance, the contents of room no. 18A (in front of the Manuscript Library) was miscellaneous sculpture of different date. We discovered that it was of no significance to the visitors. Thus, since it lies at the beginning of the tour, it was preferable to have it coincide with the chronological arrangement. For this reason we replaced its contents with a collection of funerary stelae discovered recently in a pagan cemetery of "Abou Billou" west of the Delta, which goes back to the end of the 3rd or the beginning of the 4th century A.D. The stelae are very similar to stelae of the Early Christian period in many things:

a) the raising of the hand,

b) the clothes of the male and the female figures, especially the shroud worn by the women,

c) the frontal carving of the faces,

d) the features of the faces and the manner of carving (figs 1a, b).

All of us agree that the Egyptians who converted to Christianity adopted the same manner of carving, with one exception — the addition of the cross. The new display will help the ordinary visitor understand how Coptic art came into being and realize that the Egyptian art of the Christian era was really the continuity of the art of the ancestors, excluding differences that resulted from changes occurring over the ages. This, in my opinion, is one of the main purposes of the museum.

Another scientific change took place in room no. 2 (on the ground floor). The contents of this room represents the transition from paganism to Christianity, so the objects here have to clarify this idea by mixing elements of both creeds. Our duty was to remove objects which had no relation to this idea and replace them with others bearing this combination. Fortunately, the storages had a number of pieces which we could exhibit in this room, of a great variety, showing clearly the influence of Egyptian paganism on Early Christian art (figs 2a, b).

Of course, I lack the time to multiply examples, but I hope that you will have the oppurtunity to visit the museum one day and enjoy seeing this excellent display.

Besides, we wished to help the visitor easily understand Coptic art, so we collected in room no. 8 all the exbitis with biblical scenes and all the objects with hunting scenes. The visitor can now easily get a good idea of this kind of reliefs and can also follow their evolution through the centuries. Concerning other objects in the new wing of the Museum, such as manuscripts, textiles, icons, ivory

1–2. Two funerary stelae of limestone, one pagan, the other Coptic, showing Coptic Art to be a continuity of Late Egyptian art (room no 18A)

3. Funerary stela showing a lady adoring, placing a
shroud upon her shoulders

4. Funerary stela exhibited in the transitional room 2 in
the New Wing, showing ancient Egyptian influence

and metal work, no essential changes were made, except for the decreasing of the number of exhibits in the cases.

tions. It now contains frescoes, woodwork, pottery and glass (figs 5–8).

The most interesting objects in this wing are the woodwork elements such as the ceilings, mashrabiahs and windows. It is well known that Morcos Simaika, the founder of the Museum, had brought all these wooden elements from the old palaces owned by Copts. Thus, we can say that the old wing is an architectural monument two hundred and fifty years old. Our architects, headed by Dr Kadry, were very aware of this fact and insisted upon restoring the building in order that it exist as long as possible.

The Old Wing

This is the part built by Morcos Semika in 1910. It has been closed since 1966 for architectural reasons (cracks had appeared in some of the walls). We reopened it after strengthening the founda-

5. Two large frescoes extracted from the ceilling of the temple at Abou-Ouda in Nubia (Old Wing)

6. Cases with woodwork elements (Old Wing)

7. Cases with pottery (Old Wing)

8. Cases with pottery plates and vessels (Old Wing)

COPTIC STUDIES

Peter Nagel

The Present State of Work in the Edition of the Sahidic Version of the Old Testament

Four years ago, at the Second International Congress of Coptic Studies in Rome, I read a paper on the intention of a critical edition of the Coptic--Sahidic version of the Old Testament, or, with regard to the underlying Greek text of this version, of the Septuagint, and I made some proposals towards its realization.[1] You have been so generous to give support for that task.[2] Today I feel obliged to give an account on what we have done since the proclamation of our intention.

As you know, there are many editions, careful as well as careless ones, of individual books and manuscripts of the Coptic Septuagint, but no attempt has been made at an edition of the text as a whole based on all available manuscripts.[3] Beside the printed texts, we have at our disposal the check lists of editions until 1960, compiled by Vaschalde[4] and Till,[5] but no documentation of Sahidic manuscripts and fragments with Old Testament texts published or unpublished. Therefore, the first task was to collect all printed texts including the manuscripts that the respective edition is based on. The second task was to pick up and to list all available manuscripts and fragments with Sahidic Old Testament passages not yet published. The preliminary studies resulted in a twofold card-index. The first card-index is arranged corresponding to the biblical references. This index gives full bibliographical data, the catalogue number and/or inventory number of manuscripts, and the quotation of "incipit" and "desinit" of the mentioned passage. The other index lists the manuscripts with catalogue and inventory number, the contents, and bibliographical references. The cards of thix index are arranged according to the depositories of the manuscripts in alphabetical order. The inventory numbers form the subarrangement of this index. The card-index of biblical texts is supplemented by an index of biblical quotations in early Coptic literature. The full text of the quotation is excerpted from the respective edition.

The job of arranging the indices is done by Walter Beltz and the present speaker, following *grosso modo* the bipartite edition of the Septuagint by Alfred Rahlfs.[6] That means that W. Beltz is responsible for the poetical and prophetical books, P. Nagel takes care of the historical and narrative books.

The main problem during and after the documentation of the direct textual transmission is the synopsis of scattered manuscripts, leaves and fragments which belonged originally to one and the same codex, above all the manuscripts of the White Monastery. Two articles by A. Hebbelynck, published in 1911 and 1912 in the journal *Le Muséon*, can serve as a model for the puzzle-play of joining together the complementary fragments

---

[1] P. Nagel, "Aufgaben und Probleme einer kritischen Edition der koptisch-sahidischen Version der Septuaginta", in: *Acts of the Second International Congress of Coptic Studies*, Roma 1986.

[2] Cf. International Association for Coptic Studies, *Newsletter*, ed. by T. Orlandi, no 8 (July 1981), 10.

[3] In some editions of single books that has been done throughout; our intention is directed on an edition of the *corpus* of the Sahidic version of the Septuagint.

[4] A. Vaschalde, "Ce qui a été publié des versions coptes de la Bible", in: *Revue biblique 1919–1922* (Sahidic texts); *Le Muséon* 43 (1930), 409–431; ibid., 45 (1932), 117–156 (Bohairic); *Le Muséon* 46 (1933), 299–306 ("moyen égyptien", i.e. Fayoumic); ibid., 306–313 (Achmimic and Subachmimic).

[5] W. Till, "Coptic Biblical Texts Published after Vaschalde's Lists", *Bulletin of the John Rylands Library* 42 (1959/60), 220–240.

[6] Septuaginta, ed. A. Rahlfs, 2 vols, Stuttgart 1935. Vol. I: *Leges et historiae*, vol. II: *Libri poetici et prophetici*.

from the White Monastery.[7] The present speaker makes an attempt to continue the almost forgotten work of Hebbelynck — not even mentioned in a recent special bibliography of the Septuagint.[8] The first result in following up Hebbelynck's synopsis, in somewhat modified form, was published in the *Zeitschrift für ägyptische Sprache und Altertumskunde* 1983. This article deals with the complementary fragments of Codex Borgianus sahidicus no I–XVI (Genesis — iv Kingdoms),[9] the second one, dealing with Codex no XVII–XXX, is in print in the same journal. The third part of this series is devoted to the famous lectionary of Old Testament lessons, Cod. Borg. sah. no XXXII (in preparation). A subsidiary of the review of catalogues is a synopsis of *Bilingual Greek-Coptic Texts of the Sahidic Old Testament* in press in the congress volume *Graeco-Coptica.*[10]

The preliminary studies for the edition had been based mainly on printed works, editions as well as catalogues. From 1981 onwards, we began to set up a photo-collection of manuscripts, which amounts at present to about 1400 copies in the form of photostats or microfilms. For this basic material we are indebted to many institutions and individuals, among whom I would like to mention above all Professor David W. Johnson from the Catholic University of America, who placed at our disposal not only microfilms and photostats of codices M 566 (Leviticus, Numbers and Deuteronomy) and M 568 (Isaiah) from the Pierpont Morgan Library, but also photos from the collection of the late Henry Hyvernat. If we take into account that some prototypes of

Professor Hyvernat's photo-collection are not at present detectable, those photos gain supreme documentary value.

In December 1983 I was given the opportunity of a four-week sojourn in the National Library of Paris. It was extremely useful to check not only the famous manuscript volumes BN copte 129[1-3], but also the lectionary volume BN copte 129[19] and a number of fragments, especially with regard to the fact that there is no modern catalogue on the Coptica in Paris as a whole nor on the biblical texts comparable to the catalogues of W.E. Crum[11] and W. Till[12] (Porcher's catalogue on vol. 131[1-8] should be mentioned as a praiseworthy exception).[13] Thanks to the collation of a number of crucial texts, I was able to correct some former data or assertions made from second hand in the forthcoming part of the *Studien zur Textüberlieferung...* (cf. note 9).

The preparation of the first volume of the edition is under way. By technical reasons, I cannot start with the books of Genesis and Exody. The first part of volume I (Pentateuchus) is to contain the books of Leviticus and Numbers, whose textual transmission gives rise to a joint edition. The manuscript for the publishers is to be completed by the end of 1985. The books of Genesis and Exody will follow immediately. The first volume will be completed by the edition of Deuteronomy. At present, a young scholar at our department prepares a doctoral dissertation on the interrelationship of the Sahidic manuscripts of Deuteronomy and their relation to the Greek version. The Sahidic version of the Septuagint is to be published

---

[7] A. Hebbelynck, "Les manuscrits coptes-sahidiques du Monastère Blanc: Recherches sur les fragments complémentaires de la collection Borgia. I. Les Fragments de l'Ancien Testament", *Le Muséon* NS 12 (1911), 91–153; II. Les fragments des Évangiles, ibid., NS 13 (1912), 275–306.

[8] S. Jellicoe, S.P. Brock, Ch. Fritsch, *A Classified Bibliography of the Septuagint,* Leiden 1973.

[9] P. Nagel, "Studien zur Textüberlieferung des sahidischen Alten Testaments. Teil I: Der Stand der Wiederherstellung der alttestamentlichen Kodizes der Sammlung Borgia (Cod. I–XVI)", *Zeitschrift für Ägyptische Sprache und Altertumskunde* 110 (1983), 51–74.

[10] P. Nagel, "Griechisch-koptische Bilinguen des Alten Testaments", in: *Graeco-Coptica. Griechen und Kopten im byzantinischen Ägypten*: Wiss. Beitr. Univ. Halle, 1984, pp. 231–257. Among the Coptic manuscripts in the Fisher Rare Book Library (Toronto), St. Emmel identified some new fragments of a leaf with Greek-Coptic Psalter text (r° Coptic Ps 9: 3–10ᵛ Greek Ps 9: 12–20). I express my heartly thanks to St. Emmel for this kind information.

[11] W.E. Crum, *Catalogue of the Coptic Manuscripts in the British Museum,* London 1905. Crum's *Catalogue* will be continued by B. Layton, *Catalogue of Coptic Literary Manuscripts in the British Library Acquired Since the Year 1906,* 1988 I am deeply indebted to Prof. Layton, who gave me the first proof-sheets with Old Testament texts at the occasion of the Warsaw Congress.

[12] W. Till, "Papyrussammlung der Nationalbibliothek in Wien. Katalog der Koptischen Bibelbruchstücke. Die Pergamente", *Zeitschrift für die neutestamentliche Wissenschaft* 39 (1940), 1–57.

[13] M.E. Porscher, "Analyse des manuscrits coptes 131[1-8] de la Bibliothèque Nationale, avec indication des textes bibliques", *Revue d'Égyptologie* I (1933), 105–160; 231–278; II (1936), 65–123.

by the Akademie-Verlag, Berlin, in the series *Texte und Untersuchungen zur Geschichte der altchristlichen Literatur*.

Some remarks should be added concerning the edition itself. The study of manuscripts [14] resulted in an alteration of the original intention which was to take the codex M 566 as basic text and to add the variants of the other manuscripts in the critical apparatus. Apparently, M 566 is no good text, not only with regard to its post-classical language with Fayumic intrusions characteristic of the Hamouli manuscripts, but essentially, the copy is a careless one, disfigured by misunderstandings of the scribe, omissions due to homoioteleuton and other faults.

It would be absurd to print a bad manuscript as basic text and to banish the better readings into the apparatus. The critical text is to be established from the good manuscripts found in the White Monastery, whereas the Hamouli text is reserved to fill up the gaps. The dichotomy of the critical apparatus is to be preserved. Its first section is restricted to purely orthographic variants, the second one lists the textual variants.

If we can continue with our studies, the next report on the work in progress shall be connected, as I hope, with the display of the first part of volume I of the Sahidic version of the Old Testament.

---

[14] In the transcription and/or collation of manuscripts took part: W. Beltz, P. Nagel, B. Seidel, U. Seidel. I am very thankful to my colleagues in Halle for their help and support.

COPTIC STUDIES

Claudia Nauerth

Evidence for a David Cycle on Coptic Textiles

In the course of research on Heracles in Coptic art,[1] I came across a composition of Heracles' labours, so far apparently restricted to the Coptic realm. This unusual pictorial representation of four of Heracles' labours I termed the "medallion draft", since the recurrent iconographic arrangement is always framed by a medallion. The medallion draft occurs on textiles only, where it is relatively common. Examples in Florence,[2] London,[3] Paris,[4] Recklinghausen[5] and Trier[6] are known to me, and surely these numbers could be increased by investigation. First of all, I wish to deal with the pictorial draft, and as a basis for my description I will use the two well-preserved examples in Recklinghausen and Trier.[7]

I. The composition is arranged around the central figure of Heracles:

1) The naked Heracles is taking long strides to the right and is wrestling with the Nemean lion, which seems to stand on its hind legs, the claws of its fore- and hind legs clearly visible. With the right hand Heracles takes hold of the beast's mane. The lion's head is shown in frontal position and gives to the viewer the impression of a mask with its dark surrounding mane, a detail well-documented on the piece in Recklinghausen.

2) In the upper right of the roundel's field king Eurystheus is depicted in a scale smaller than Heracles and with a more aged face than that of the hero. On the fragment in Recklinghausen the king is crouching with bent legs, and because of the position of his hand and the terrified facial expression he conveys an impression of fear: Heracles is shown bringing him the wild boar of Erymanthus. On the piece in Trier and also on several others only the king's head with a halo is preserved; Heracles carries the boar hanging down over his right shoulder. On the specimen in Recklinghausen one can recognize the boar's head with one eye and pointed ears as well as the forelegs. Here, Heracles is carrying the boar and is at the same time wrestling with the lion, thus two of the hero's exploits are combined in a single scene.

3) In the round of the medallion, at Heracles' back, there is a pattern of tendrils or branches, holding flowers or fruits. This can only represent the tree in the garden of the Hesperides, and the dark, barrel-shaped block either in or behind the tree should be identified as the dragon guarding the golden apples. The dragon's head is set off by colour, and on the piece in Recklinghausen there is a serrated line above the head. On the other textiles, which cannot be described here in detail, the tree of the Hesperides and the dragon appear to be an ornament of foliage and flower buds, which could not have been recognized without the two fragments described here. Therefore, the

---

[1] Manuscript, pp. 27 ff; see also "Formen des Herakles. Seine Taten auf koptischen Stoffen", in: *Festschrift Fink*, Köln-Wien 1984, pp. 147–157.

[2] Florence, Archaeological Museum, no cat. 7954: L. Guerrini, *Le stoffe copte del museo archeologico di Firenze,* Roma 1957, no 108, pl. XXXVIII, pp. 89–91.

[3] London, Victoria and Albert Museum, Inv. no 417–1887: A.F. Kendrick, *Catalogue of Textiles from Burying-grounds in Egypt,* vol. III, 1922, pl. VIII, no 631; 1963 exhibited in Essen: *Katalog Koptische Kunst,* Essen 1963, no 345, p. 335.

[4] Paris, Louvre, Inv. no X 4749: P. Du Bourguet, *Catalogue des étoffes coptes* I, Musée du Louvre, Paris 1964, F 179.

[5] Recklinghausen, Ikonenmuseum, Inv. no 581: no illustration known to me, a photo of the SFB Göttingen.

[6] Trier, Museum Simeonstift, several specimens: Inv. no VII. 69; VII. 193; VII. 179; VII. 78: C. Nauerth, *Koptische Textilkunst im spätantiken Ägypten,* Trier 1978, nos 72 and 81, p. 96, note 91.

[7] Example Inv. no VII. 69, exhibited under Catalogue, no. 72.

1. Recklinghausen, Ikonenmuseum, Inv. no 581 (phot. Sonderforschungsbereich der Universität Göttingen)

2. Trier, Museum Simeonstift, Inv. no VII. 69 (phot. courtesy of the Museum)

question must be asked, whether the artisan, when copying the scene onto the textile, understood this particular detail.

4) The same holds true for the fourth and last episode. Heracles is shown in a striding movement, thereby a triangle is created in the lower part of the roundel. It is solely the piece in Recklinghausen, which helps to clarify the subject: there, between Heracles' legs the tips of a bird's wings point vertically into the air, near it, two legs of a bird with claws are spread wide apart. In all probability, it is one of the dead Stymphalian Birds hit by an arrow in the shape of a tree-pronged feather, which is depicted here. On the other textiles, the bird has been turned into a peculiar double leaf, which could not be recognized without the accompanying details and the meaning of which had been lost to the artisan working on the textile.

Thus, in the medallion composition four of Heracles' labours are portrayed: the strangulation of the Nemean Lion, the capture of the Wild Boar of Erymanthus, the adventure with the Golden Apples of the Hesperides and the overpowering of the Stymphalian Birds.

II. The medallion draft with these four labours of Heracles is commonly found together with another mythological subject, which — also framed by a medallion — represents Apollo and Daphne. On several textiles [8] these roundels with Apollo and Daphne are placed side by side, alternating with two half-roundels with antithetic riders. This composition covers mainly red--ground textiles in a continuous pattern. I do not wish to discuss now the problems of this design,

instead of it, I will present some other, rarer pendants to the Heracles' scenes.

Apart from the Heracles' roundel, an already mentioned textile fragment in London [9] displays four half-medallions with antithetic riders and an additional complete, though at the edges slightly damaged medallion with a definite scene. In the collections at Baltimore,[10] London,[11] and Trier [12] there are parallel textiles, on which the order of figures is sometimes reversed. This fact is of no importance for the iconographical interpretation. The pictorial representation conveys immediately that the scene concerns a child or youth. In the centre, between two grown-ups, a middle-sized figure is standing. One of the adults, clad in tunic and pallium, appears to escort the child. The latter is advancing towards an aedicula with a pointed gable, under which a third figure is seated on a throne with his feet resting on a suppedaneum. The enthroned person is wearing a wide flowing mantle and raises his hand in such a way that he touches the support of the aedicula, a detail distinctly marked on all textiles. The three persons, the enthroned, the escort and the child or youth, are provided with a halo.

In order to arrive at an interpretation for this scene I draw my parallels from the well-known silver plates discovered in Cyprus. The nine plates are decorated with episodes from the life of David and are dated to the seventh century A.D.[13] On one of the plates, now in the Metropolitan Museum of Art in New York,[14] king Saul is shown seated under an arcade in the centre and is receiving the youthful David, whom he has invited to come to see him. The same subject occurs on Coptic textiles

---

[8] This is the case with textiles in Florence and Paris (see notes 2 and 4) and with two pieces in Trier (Inv. nos VII. 193 and VII. 179); compare also the single orbiculi with Daphne and Apollo in the Louvre (Inv. no AC 825 = F 180 and X 4862 = F 181 in Du Bourguet's catalogue (see note 4). Further examples could certainly be added, i.e. A.C. Lopes Cardozo- C.E. Zijderveld, *Koptische Weefsels*, Haags Gemeentemuseum 1982, no 79 (Inv. OW 62–1936) (The reference by courtesy of Mrs Zijderveld).

[9] See note 3.

[10] Baltimore, Walters Art Gallery, a pendant (!) to Inv. no 83, 727; Gift in memory of Janet E.C. Wurtzburger by Dr and Mrs Robert A. Milch and friends.

[11] London, British Museum, Inv. no 65 662, no illustration is known to me.

[12] Trier, Museum Simeonstift, Inv. no VII. 190.

[13] For the find in general see the catalogue Age of Spirituality, ed. K. Weitzmann, New York 1979, nos 425–433; the article "David", DACL IV, 1 (1920), figs 3623 ff.; the article "David", RBK I (1966), cols 1145–1161 (K. Wessel); M. van Grunsven-Eygenraam, "Heraclius and the David Plates", BABesch 48 (1973), 158–174; St. H. Wander, "The Cyprus Plates: The Story of David and Goliath", *Metropolitan Museum Journal* 8, 1973, 89–104; K. Weitzmann, "Prolegomena to a Study of the Cyprian Plates", *Metropolitan Museum Journal* 3 (1970), 97–111; G. Suckale-Redlefsen, *Die Bilderzyklen zum Davidleben von den Anfängen bis zum Ende des 11. Jh.*, Diss. phil. München 1972, Catalogue no 5, pp. 7 f.

[14] New York, Metropolitan Museum of Art, Inv. no 1917, 17. 190.397; illustrations: Catalogue Age of Spirituality no 427; DACL IV, 1, fig. 3627; Wander, fig. 1; Weitzmann, fig. 10; van Grunsven-Eygenraam, fig. 3.

3. Trier, Museum Simeonstift, Inv. no VII. 193 and VII. 190, (phot. courtesy of the Museum)

4. London, Victoria and Albert Museum. Inv. no 417–1887 (phot. courtesy of the Museum)

in medallion form: David is appearing before Saul, enthroned in the aedicula. The third bearded figure, acompanying young David, could be identified as Samuel the priest.[15] Although on the Cyprian plates the scene has a richer repertory of figures, the basic composition corresponds to that of textiles. Even the spider-like, gripping hand — so pronounced on the textiles — is explained by the raised hand of the seated king Saul. However, the architectural details are different: on the textiles, the building is always narrow and with a pointed gable, while on the silver plate colonnades and a semicircular arch are shown.

With regard to the Cyprus plates, scholars have discussed the question which of the meetings between Saul and David is meant to be illustrated, for there are at least two possible situations. According to 1 Sam. 16:21 ff. Saul summoned David to entertain him with his lyre. According to 1 Sam. 17:31 ff. Saul ordered David to be brought before him and whom he enticed, after a long discussion, to accept the challenge of armed combat with Goliath the Philistine. Since the gestures of speech are vividly expressed on the silver plate, the majority of scholars [16] tend to believe that the second meeting between Saul and David is referred to, which then leads on to the battle with Goliath. On the Coptic textile roundels, the gesturing hand of Saul cannot be overlooked; therefore, one should equally relate the episode to David's second appearance before Saul.

III. The so-called presentation of David to Saul is not the only pendant to the Heracles medallions on Coptic textiles, found on the Cyprus plates. Together with David being presented to Saul, another scene occurs, which is also framed by a medallion and likewise consists of three figures — the Anointing of David. Textile fragments with this scene, although quite badly damaged, are known to me from London [17] and Trier.[18] Again, the centre of the roundel is taken up by a small-sized figure, walking with his left arm outstretched towards another person, while at the same time being lead by a third figure raising his right hand. The raised arms of the two large figures meet exactly above the head of the smaller figure. Unfortunately, it is a section where both textiles are seriously damaged. Nevertheless, it is most likely that there was the place of the horn of oil as one can deduce from the matching scene on the Cyprus plate.[19] It follows that the person on the left is to be interpreted as Samuel the priest about to anoint the youthful David. The peculiar details which cannot be defined on the textile, could be part of the special priestly dress of Samuel. The third figure is to be identified as David's father Isai who is pointing at his youngest son, whom he had presented to Samuel the priest (1 Sam. 16:11 ff.). Yet another detail can be compared: on the plate as well as on the textile medallion the raised hand of the father, Isai, has been brought into prominence. In this scene, the composition of the figures corresponds exactly with that on the silver plate; in fact, the centre of the plate's illustration is depicted as a section on the textile. On the other hand, the latter lacks any hint of an architectural setting.

IV. With the two pictorial roundels in Coptic textiles identified as episodes from the life of David, it becomes apparent why these scenes can be grouped with a Heracles medallion. During the youth of both these heros, adventures with wild beasts were of great importance, and just at the time, when Saul meets young David, intending to inquire about his prowess, because of the impending battle with Goliath, David explicitly declares that he has killed lion and bear (1 Sam. 17:34 ff.). In fact, the medallion no longer illustrates Heracles' deed, but rather David's achievement. On two of the Cyprus plates,[20]

[15] See Weitzmann, "Prolegomena...", 108.

[16] For example Wander, "The Cyprus...", 89 f.; Weitzmann, "Prolegomena...", 106 f.; van Grunsven-Eygenraam, "Heraclius...", 162 f.; compare Suckdale-Redlefsen, Bilderzyklen..., 46.

[17] London, Victoria and Albert Museum: A. F. Kendrick III, pl. IX, no 632.

[18] Trier, Museum Simeonstift, Inv. no VII. 190.

[19] New York, Metropolitan Museum of Art, Inv. no 1917, 17.190.398: Catalogue Age of Spirituality no 425; DACL IV, 1, fig. 3626; Wander, fig. 4; van Grunsven-Eygenraam, fig. 1.

[20] Animal adventures on silver plates: Lion combat: New York, Metropolitan Museum of Art, Inv. no 1917, 17.190.394; illustrations: Age of Spirituality no. 429; DACL IV, 1, fig. 3622; Wander, fig. 7; van Grunsven-Eygenraam, fig. 5; F. Volbach–M. Hirmer, Frühchristliche Kunst, München 1958, fig. 250. Bear combat: Nicosia, Inv. no J 453; illustrations: Age of Spirituality no 428; DACL IV, 1, fig. 3623; Wander, fig. 8; van Grunsvan-Eygenraam, fig. 6.

5. New York, Metropolitan Museum of Art, Inv. no. 1917, 17. 190. 397 after *Wealth of the Roman World AD 300–700*, ed. by J.P.C. Kent and K.S. Painter, The Trustees of the British Museum 1977, p. 106, no. 181)

6. London, Victoria and Albert Museum, Inv. no: cf.: A.F. Kendrick, *Catalogue of Textiles from Burying-grounds in Egypt*, vol. III, 1922, pl. IX, no 632 (phot. courtesy of the Museum)

7. New York, Metropolitan Museum of Art, Inv. no. 1917, 17. 190. 398 (after *Wealth of the Roman World AD 300–700*, p. 108, no. 183)

David's subdual of the animals is depicted. However, the composition is totally different. In both scenes, David thrusts his knee into the animals' backs and grabs the respective mane and fur with his left hand, while in his right one he wields a weapon ready to bludge on the animal. In contrast, the artisan of the Coptic textile has made use of a different, yet more intricate copy of the lion combat. In view of the great number of iconographical variants of just his subject, the difference should not surprise us. Ultimately, the composition on the silver plate can be traced to its source of a Heracles' theme, other plates help to verify this derivation.[21] If the scheme of the textile with four of Heracles' labours changes into a cycle of David's life, it becomes clear why the other labours of Heracles as well as certain details were considered irrelevant, or were not even understood. In any case, for the image of David, the lion's subduer, they were of no consequence. The textile medal-

lions on the life of David enable us to determine the process, in the course of which an episode from Heracles' labours is modified to a David scene. The image of "Heracles battles the lion" is changed to "David subdues the lion".

So far, there are three scenes on Coptic textiles which relate to episodes in David's life — the presentation of David to Saul, the anointing of David and the lion combat. These subjects are not the only known representations of David on textiles, at least another episode on the medallions bears a clear relationship to David's person, i.e. David the musician.

V. Representations of David playing the lyre — David lyricus — are quite common on Coptic textiles. I have collected the material for another study and so will restrict myself to only a few remarks.[22] The best-known variants of the scene

---

[21] Bear combat on a plate from the Kama region: illustration: Age of Spirituality, fig. 61 on p. 451; Heracles' lion combat on a plate in the Cabinet des Médailles, illustration: van Grunsven-Eygenraam, fig. 7; Volbach-Hirmer, fig. 251; on the subject see Wander, "The Cyprus...", 101, and van Grunsven-Eygenraam, "Heraclius...", 165.

[22] David lyricus, in: "Festgabe für L. Steiger zum 50. Geburtstag 1985", BDBAT 5 (1985), 275–285.

are preserved on textiles in Baltimore,[23] London,[24] and Leningrad.[25] In each case, two persons are depicted. The left figure, nimbed and clad in tunic and pallium, is standing with his right hand raised, while the right figure, also nimbed and dressed in the same way, is seated and holds a lyre to his left side. The seat is worked in a striking manner: the suppedaneum rises upwards in a tilt and merges over an attachment into the cushioned seat of the chair. This elaborate arrangement turns the seat into a throne and, accordingly, emphasizes the seated person's importance. The higher social standing of the two men is expressed by their clothing and nimbus. Remains of letters are visible by the sides of the figures, however, they do not make any apparent sense.

The comparable piece from Cyprus is nowadays exhibited in the Nicosia Museum.[26] On the silver plate, a young man is seen advancing from the left, clad in short tunic, chlamys and boots, while raising his right hand in a gesture of speech and holding a staff in his left one. The second figure is seated on the right, clad in tunic and pallium, and he also gestures with his right hand. In his left hand, he holds the lyre, which apparently was laid to rest on higher ground, covered by a cloth falling in folds. At both men's feet, a sheep is grazing, and a ram is resting. This detail indicates that the lyre player and the messenger are placed in a landscape. Therefore, David should be identified with the right figure, playing the lyre as a shepherd, while the left figure represents the messenger sent to David as described in 1 Sam. 16:12. Thus, the plate depicts the summoning of David.[27] In a raised compartment placed at the top of the plate, a segment of heaven with the sun, moon and several stars is shown, alluding to the divine connotation of the summoning.

When comparing the scene on the silver plate with that on the textile medallions, corresponding details as well as differences are found: the basic composition has been kept, while the grazing animals and the segment of heaven are missing. The rockery seat of the plate has become a chair with leg-rest and cushion, even though the original arrangement can be recognized. The figure seated to the right has been wrapped in his mantle in a manner, which makes the anatomically inconsistent drapery recall a prototype. Only the halos are identically copied. The gestures have been reduced or altered: the messenger is still "speaking" with his hand, and David is placing his right hand in front of his breast. Finally, the heads have been given a different position, both of them are held frontally, yet the eyes are staring intensely to the left.

VI. In view of these changes one has to ask whether the Coptic textile medallion should still be identified with the "summoning of David". Altogether, the picture has become more static, with, possibly, the copying artist not realizing that the scene was to be understood with the background of 1 Sam. 16:12. On the other hand, it must have been common knowledge that David was shown as playing the lyre. In the portrait on the Coptic textile, David is dressed royally, he is seated on a throne and is playing the lyre. One has to investigate whether the second person is meant to represent the messenger, or whether it could be king Saul. Here, one can refer to the episode on the textile in Berlin,[28] which differs in a single detail

---

[23] Walters Art Gallery, Inv. no 83.727; Gift in memory of Janet E. C. Wurtzburger by Dr and Mrs Robert A. Milch and friends. Illustration: A. Kakovkin, "Koptische Stoffe mit David in der Ermitage" (in Russian), Viz. *Vremenik* 44 (1983), 182–183, fig. 3 (I owe this reference to Frau Dr Dorothee Renner who also informed me that there are two additional pieces in Baltimore). The example Inv. no 83.727 is shown in fig. 3.

[24] London, British Museum, Inv. no 65 662; no illustration known to me.

[25] Leningrad, Hermitage, apparently several pieces, Inv. no. 13122a-b.–Ill.: A Kakovkin 1, 2 and 5.

[26] Museum, Inv. no J 454; Ill.: Catalogue Age of Spirituality no 426; DACL IV, 1, fig. 3628; van Grunsven-Eygenraam, fig. 2; Wander, fig. 9; Weitzmann, fig. 10. A.Kakovkin has already pointed out the relationship between the Cyprus plate and the Coptic textile medallions. However, as far as I can judge the matter from his illustrations, he has not realized that not solely this scene, but others from the life of David can be compared with the Cyprus plates. See Kakovkin, fig. 3. (The text is going to be translated).

[27] Wander, "The Cyprus ...", 94 ff.; Suckale-Redlefsen, *Bilderzyklen* ..., pp. 38 ff. gives the type the more neutral definition of "David, the shepherd, receives a message". Van Grunsven-Eygenraam, "Heraclius ...", 161, suggests a different interpretation of the scene: it is Saul, approached by David! (acc. to 1 Sam. 16:21), since crook and nimbus are suitable only for David.

[28] Berlin, Staatliche Museen, Inv. no 4680; ill.: O. Wulff–F. Volbach, *Spätantike und koptische Stoffe aus ägyptischen Grabfunden*. Staatliche Museen Berlin 1926, p. 85 and pl. 105.

8. Baltimore, Walters Art Gallery, Inv. no. 83. 727 (phot. postcard)

9. Nikosia, Museum Inv. no. J 454 (after *Wealth of the Roman World AD 300–700*, p. 111, no. 186)

from the other textiles. The right figure as usual should be identified with David making music, the second figure is holding in his right hand a lance or a javelin. One could argue that the staff of the messenger, who appears before David, has been changed in this manner. Yet, I believe that there should be a different interpretation of the figure and of the scene. Most probably, together with David playing the lyre king Saul is depicted, who, according to 1 Sam. 19:9 f. (and compare 18:10 f. and 16:21 ff.), is attempting to hit the harping David with the javelin. Thus, the motif of David lyricus can be joined to different narratives: the messenger appears before David, the harping shepherd, and Saul is making an attempt on the life of the playing David. It is difficult to determine whether both iconographically related scenes result from independant prototypes.[29] Already when expressing the subject of "David plays before Saul", two episodes might be illustrated: Saul draws his weapon and throws it at David, or Saul is listening quietly to David's performance. If the Coptic textile roundel in Berlin does in fact refer to the act of "David playing before the armed Saul", then the pictorial composition is different from the few other known variants, where Saul is either seated or lying, but never standing.[30]

In view of the differences between the Berlin textile and the silver plate, one has to consider the likelihood that, on other textiles as well, the scene represents "David playing before Saul". Certain iconographical details speak for this interpretation, i.e. the position and the movement of the left figure and the turning of the head and the mantle drapery of the right figure. In the Berlin example — in my opinion definitely referring to Saul and David — another detail of ornament is noticeable: besides the edge of the roundel, the corners of the textile have additional decorations.

On textile roundels in The Hague[31] and Trier[32]

another variant of the scene is found. There also, the textiles have additional corner ornaments and close equivalents in scrolls on the medallion's frame. Just as in the orbiculus from Berlin with Saul and David, the variation of the scene concerns the figure on the left. On the right side, the playing David is as usual seated on a throne, whilst on the left side an apparently unnimbed female person is depicted. David himself being shown more frontally, and together with the female figure, the scene can only be interpreted as David lyricus and a Muse. The composition has numerous prototypes in illuminated manuscripts.[33] Thus, the possible variations of the "David lyricus" theme are also present in the manifold occasions showing David making music.

VII. The episode of David being summoned, as represented on the Cyprian silver plate, has, so far, the only direct parallel on a single textile in Berlin.[34] Its figurative narrative is very abstract and up to the present has not been interpreted. It is only in comparison with the music scene on the Cyprus plate that it can be explained. In the near centre of the textile band, the man playing the lyre is either standing or seated, the instrument and his hand, almost detached from the body, are clearly visible. The figure is depicted at a very odd inclination with apparently an attempt to express perspective. Of the second figure, only the lower part of the body and the feet remain, but near the other figure's head one might discern a fragment of the messenger's staff. When comparing this piece with the scene on the Cyprus plate, there can be no doubt that in the centre, David is playing the lyre seated or standing, whilst on the left, the messenger approaching David is depicted. Some other additional details from the silver plate are observed, which are lacking on the textile medallions. At the bottom right, a four-legged animal is shown,

---

[29] The iconographical affinity between David's summoning and David the musician is also discussed by Wander, "The Cyprus...", p. 100. It is probable that with regard to the summoning on the Cyprus plate, Wander's following supposition is correct: "This scene must be a seventh-century creation joining a running figure and a harping David in order to narrate the episode".

[30] See Suckale-Redlefsen, *Bilderzyklen* ..., pp. 47 f.

[31] Haags Gemeentemuseum, Inv. no OW 51 z.j. — Ill.: A.C. Cardozo, C.E. Zijderveld, Haags Gemeentemuseum 1982, no 80. (I owe this reference to the author Mrs Zijderveld).

[32] Trier, Museum Simonstift, Inv. no VII. 72, Catalogue no 75 and fig. 47.

[33] For example Milano, Bibliotheca Ambrosiana, Psalter MS M. 54 sup. fol III V; Ill.: Wander, fig. 15.

[34] Berlin, Staatliche Museen, Inv. no 6965; ca. 15 × 24 cm; from Achmim; Ill.: Wulff-Volbach, *Koptische Stoffe in Berlin*, p. 126 and pl. 112 (see note 28); G. Bröker, *Koptische Kunst 1844–1969*, ca. 1970, no 173 and colour plate; A. Effenberger, *Koptische Kunst*, Leipzig-Wien 1976, fig. 123 with the explanation "Female saint (?)".

10. Trier, Museum Simeonstift, Inv. no VII. 72 (phot. courtesy of the Museum)

which can be interpreted as the remains of a landscape scene. Also, there is one final reminiscence, above the animal, one can see a large patterned triangle with a small semicircle. Again referring to the Cyprus plate, these seemingly enigmatic additions become clear, they represent the segment of heaven with the sun, moon and stars, having been pulled out of shape on the Coptic textile. In fact, the Berlin piece should be taken as an almost exact replica of David the musician as represented on the Cyprus plate.

VIII. Finally, there is another episode in the life of David, which might have been depicted on textile medallions. In the Trier Museum, there is a rather unusual equestrian picture[35] with its roundel inscribed in the same ornaments as those with scenes from the story of David. In its present state, the textile fragment has fringes on the left edge, but it is not clear, whether on the right edge the ornamentation was carried on in a continuous pattern or whether there were also fringes. In the corners are small ornaments. The rider has raised both arms, with the right on finishing in a dark splash. This detail might be identified as Goliath's head, which David impaled after the combat and brought it home as victor on horseback. Alternatively, the end of the arm might be meant to represent an entirely deformed hand. The finish of the textile does not permit a definite interpretation. If this interpretation of the scene is correct, then there is proof of another illustration from the life of David on Coptic textiles. In point of fact, the image of David returning home from the fight with

[35] Museum Simeonstift, Inv. no VII. 74; Ill. no 54 and catalogue no 77a, according to 1 Sam. 17:54–57.

11. Berlin, Staatliche Museen, Inv. no 6965 (after G. Broker, *Koptische Kunst 1844–1969*, ca. 1970, no 173)

12. Trier, Museum Simeonstift. Inv. no VII. 74 (phot. courtesy of the Museum)

Goliath is not depicted in late antique art and occurs only sporadically in Byzantine illuminated manuscripts.[36] Accordingly, the following episodes appear so far on Coptic textiles:

1) the lion cambat of (Heracles-)David,
2) the presentation of David before Saul,
3) Samuel anointing David,
4) the summoning of David musicus,
5) David musicus with Saul,
6) David musicus with Muse,
7) David the rider with Goliath's head.

IX. In conclusion, I would like to consider the general significance of the David scenes on Coptic textiles. To begin with, it is worthy of note that in Coptic art a David cycle is depicted. Episodes from David's life are altogether rarely found in late antique art and are mostly only fragmentarily preserved.[37]

The identification of the scenes is based on the well-preserved and from the iconographical point reliable silver plates from Cyprus. Yet, the possibility to define the scenes on the textiles according to the silver plates does not mean *a priori* that the reliefs served as prototypes for the particular scenes. Is is only the picture of David musicus on the Berlin textile, which may be taken as an accurate copy of the silver plate. The main reason is to be seen in the additional details, even though the rectangular textile has a different basic form than the circular plate. The remaining variants of David musicus on textiles display a close affinity to the silver plate, but none does conform in full. Actually, several situations can be referred to, e.g., David musicus as shepherd together with the messenger, David musicus before Saul, who is either listening to David's play in silence or is hurling the weapon at him, and finally,

David with a Muse. The textile variations seem to express these different incidents, and as a result, the search for prototypes does not become easier.

With regard to the presentation and anointing of David, it is quite feasible that the composition of the silver plate served as an example for the matching picture of the textiles. However, both might originate from a common prototype, for the rendering of architecture is an ambiguous evidence. The striking gesture in speech of both figures does at least suggest that the same situation is referred to, namely, David's second appearance before Saul according to 1 Sam. 17, which directly proceeds the fight with Goliath.

In the lion combat, the iconographical differences between the textile and the two animal pictures on the plates is of no consequence, since, several pictorial versions are known for Heracles' lion combat and thus potentially also for David's. Indeed, the Coptic textile medallion with the lion's combat illustrates an image of Heracles, which is unknown in antique art, and which has not only been used for Heracles, but is also traceable as a David picture. The prototype of this complex composition should be looked for most likely in a painting or a relief, whereas the round form was apparently inherent to the pictorial draft.

For the last scene, i.e. David with the head of Goliath, no relevant comparisons exist. It is also possible that a general picture of a horse and rider has taken on the same significance in connection with the David cycle. The scenes with David have certainly not been designed in singles or in series solely for the textiles, but the question of individual prototypes will still have to be solved.

The translation into English is owed to Dr Renate Rosenthal-Heginbottem

---

[36] See Suckale-Redlefsen, *Bilderzyklen* ..., p. 57.

[37] Besides the David plates, one can enumerate the fragments of the wooden door in Milano, the frescoes of chapel III in Bawit, and the frescoes from Dura Europos — all of them very damaged —, and finally in manuscript illumination the fragments of the Itala of Quedlinburg, see Suckale-Redlefsen, *Bilderzyklen* ..., p. 1, 5 ff., 24 ff., 74 ff., 80 ff., 95 ff.

COPTIC STUDIES

Lucia Papini

A Lease of Land from Aphroditopolis

In some notes, written by the hand of H.I. Bell, concerning unpublished papyri of the British Museum, which he had examined to do a concise catalogue,[1] we read about inv. 2849: "Lower part of a Coptic contract, slightly imperfect on left. Might be from Aphrodito".

The papyrus contains a lease of land, that maybe was cultivated with date–palms (1. 12: ⲙⲡⲛⲕⲁⲣ ⲡⲟⲥ ⲛⲛⲉⲃⲏⲛⲉ). It comes almost surely from Aphroditopolis, since one of the contracting parties is coming from that village (1. 13: ⲙⲡⲓⲧⲓⲙⲉ ⲛⲟⲩⲱⲧ ϫⲕⲱⲟⲩ). The beginning of the papyrus is lacking, as Bell says, but also a little strip on the left containing probably 4 or 5 letters. As for the date an inner one is lacking, and we may say only that, regarding the writing, the papyrus may be ascribed to the sixth century. This hypothesis will be corroborated, as we shall see, by some remarkable resemblances with the formulary of other Coptic sixth-century papyri from Aphroditopolis.

The deed had to be directed by the lessee to the lessor, as it happens in the majority of cases in the Byzantine age. Since the beginning of the deed is lacking, we do not know the name of the lessor but we may only infer that they were more than one person, because in the body of the deed there is always used the word ⲛⲏⲧⲛ . We know the name of the lessee from the signature at the end of the deed, even if it is full of blanks: he is Colluthus, son of ⲁⲡⲁ ⲥⲓⲁ .The name is followed by the formu-

la ϩⲓⲧⲟⲟⲧ ⲁⲛⲟⲕ ⲙⲁⲣⲕⲟⲥ ⲡϣⲉⲣⲉ ⲙⲡⲙⲁⲕⲁⲣⲓⲟⲥ ⲫⲟⲓⲃⲁⲙⲙⲱⲛ , from which one may infer that the latter is acting on behalf of Colluthus, as his representative. We find the same formula in P. Vatic. Aphrod. Copti 1,[2] a sale of a wagon of the first half of the sixth century, in which the mother, a widow, is acting on behalf of the son, the seller. But in this papyrus we find the formula in the body of the deed, where the seller declares that he has received the money for the sold property: ⲧⲓⲧⲓⲙⲏ ⲛⲟⲩⲃ ⲁⲓϫⲓⲧⲥ ⲁⲛⲟⲕ ⲡⲉⲧⲧⲓ ⲉⲃⲟⲗ ⲇⲁⲩⲉⲓⲧ ⲡϣⲉ(ⲣⲉ) ⲛⲭⲣⲓⲥⲧⲟⲫⲱⲣⲟⲥ ϩⲓⲧⲟⲟⲧ ⲁⲛⲟⲕ ⲧⲥⲩⲣⲁⲥ ⲧϣⲉⲉⲣⲉ ⲛⲥⲁⲃⲓⲛⲉ ⲧⲉϥⲙⲁⲁⲩ. The signature of the deed is unfortunately full of blanks: ⲁⲛⲟⲕ ⲇⲁⲩⲉⲓⲧ ⲡϣⲉ(ⲣⲉ) ⲛⲡⲙⲁⲕⲁⲣⲓⲟⲥ ⲭⲣⲓⲥⲧⲟⲫⲟⲣⲟⲥ ⲙⲧⲟϥ . . . . . .ⲕ ϩⲁⲣⲟϥ ⲧϥⲙⲁⲁⲩ ⲧⲓⲥⲧⲏⲭ(ⲉⲓ) ⲉⲧⲓⲡⲣⲁⲥⲓⲥ.

ⲙⲧⲟϥ . . . . . .ⲕ ϩⲁⲣⲟϥ we know that ⲙⲧⲟ is the Coptic equivalent of πρόσωπον (cf. Crum 193 A). ϩⲁⲣⲟϥ (= ὑπὲρ αὐτοῦ): its reading is not sure but it might be the typical formula which means the legal representation,[3] in this case of the mother, a widow, towards her son (maybe a minor?). On the verso we read the address in Greek: πρᾶ(σις) γεναμμ(ένη) τοῦ Δαυειδ χριστόφορος διὰ Τσύρας μητ(ρὸς) αὐτοῦ...ἅμαξαι.

The mother appears always as representative, even if David is the seller. Unfortunately the papyrus begins with the name of the purchaser,

---

[1] Maybe these papyri are the same about which he says, in his article "An Egyptian Village in the Age of Justinian, in *Journal of Hellenic Studies* LXIV (1944), 22: "Some twenty years after the original discovery [of Dioscorus' archive in 1905] the British Museum acquired further papyri from this site, which are still unpublished and only superficially examined, but do not seem likely to add much of importance to what is already known". Now most of these papyri are no more in the British Museum, but at the Universities of Yale and Michigan. Among those still in the British Museum, some are Coptic (this lease of land and some letters) and others are Greek (they will be studied by Dr Pintaudi).

[2] Cf. my articles "Formulary of Coptic Documentary Papyri", BSAC XXV (1983), 83–9, and "Annotazioni sul Formulario giuridico di documenti copti del VI secolo", *Atti del XVII Congresso Internazionale di Papirologia*, Napoli 1984, 768–76.

[3] Cf. M. San Nicolò, "Das ⲉⲓⲣⲉ ⲙⲡⲣⲟⲥ ⲱⲡⲟⲛ als Stellvertretungsformel", *Byzantinische Zeitschrift* XXIV (1923), 336–45.

and the part which deals with the name of the seller is lacking. So we do not know in which quality the mother was acting on behalf of the son : if it was a matter of legal representation, it is strange the fact that the expression ⲉⲓⲣⲉ ⲙⲡⲣⲟⲥⲱⲡⲟⲛ [4] does not appear, and we can say the same thing about P. British Museum 2849. In the similar cases which I could examine, when ⲉⲓⲣⲉ ⲙⲡⲣⲟⲥⲱⲡⲟⲛ is in the beginning of the deed, generally it is repeated in the signature, too.

As for ⲋⲓⲧⲟⲟⲧ A. Steinwenter, in *Das Recht der Koptischen Urkunden* (Monaco 1955), in chapter XIII about "Stellvertretung" p. 43, n. 5, declares that ⲋⲓⲧⲟⲟⲧ is the Coptic equivalent of διά. [5]

I have found in other papyri a formula like the one which I have examined, but it is always in the beginning of the deed and not in the signature, as it is in our case.

CPR IV 117, a seventh-century lease of land from Ashmunein: ⲉⲓⲥⲋⲁⲓ ⲙⲡ]ⲇⲓⲕ[ⲁ]ⲓⲟⲛ ⲛⲡⲁⲭⲟⲉⲓⲥ ϥⲁⲅⲓⲟⲥ ⲑⲉⲟⲇⲱⲣ[...]ⲉ ⲋⲓⲧⲟⲟⲧⲱ̄ ⲛⲁⲡⲁ ⲃⲓⲕ ⲧⲱⲣ ⲡⲉⲩⲗᵀ⸗ ⲛⲇⲓⲁⲕ, [ⲁⲩⲱ ⲡⲉϥⲣⲟ]ⲛⲧⲓⲥⲧⲏⲥ

P. Ryl 164, a lease of land from Ashmunein: ⲋ̣ⲓⲧⲟⲟⲧⲕ ⲁⲡⲁ ⲡⲉⲋⲏⲩ ⲡⲉϥⲣⲟ[ⲛⲧⲓⲥⲧⲏⲥ

P. Ryl 181, a receipt for the rent of a lease of land from Ashmunein : ⲡⲇⲓⲕⲁⲓⲟⲛ ⲛⲡⲑⲩⲥⲓⲁⲥⲧⲏⲣⲓⲟⲛ ⲉⲧⲟⲩⲁⲁⲃ ϥⲁⲅⲓⲟⲥ ⲅⲉⲱⲣⲅⲉ ⲋⲓⲧⲟⲟⲧ ϣⲉⲛⲟⲩⲧⲉ ⲡⲣᵉ ⲉⲓⲥⲋⲁⲓ. But in these three cases, as we have seen, ⲋⲓⲧⲟⲟⲧ ·refers to the representative of the δίκαιον of a monastery which leases a peace of land to someone, while on the contrary in P. British Museum 2849 it is a private citizen who leases a peace of land from someone.

In two other instances on the contrary the expression appears in the signature, but the context is once more different from that of P. British Museum 2849, since the subject acts on behalf of some heirs.

CPR II 80 = CPR IV 141, a receipt for a seventh--century lease in Sahidic dialect :ⲡⲉⲕⲗⲏⲣⲟⲛⲟⲙⲟⲥ ⲛⲡⲙⲁⲕⲁⲣ, ⲕⲟⲗⲗⲟⲩⲑⲉ ⲋⲓⲧⲟⲟⲧ ⲁⲛⲟⲕ ⲡⲥⲟⲛ ⲧⲛ̄ⲥⲧⲟⲓⲭⲉⲓ (the same expression is at the beginning of the deed too, and refers to the lessor).

BKU III, 435, a ὁμολογία (maybe an arbitration ?) from Ashmunein: ⲁⲛⲟⲛ ⲛⲉⲕⲗⲏⲣ⸗, ⲛⲡⲙⲁⲕⲁⲣ, ⲧⲁⲩⲣⲓⲛⲉ ⲛⲉⲣⲱⲙⲉ ϣⲙ̆ ⲋⲓⲧⲟⲟⲧ ⲁⲛⲟⲕ ˙ϥⲟⲓⲃᵈ

ⲧⲓⲥⲧⲟⲓⲭⲉⲓ ⲉⲧⲓⲋⲟⲙⲟⲗⲟⲅⲉⲓⲁ (the beginning of the deed is lacking).

It is interesting to point out that all these examined instances have in common the place of origin, Ashmunein, except one which has an unknown origin. So we may think to an use of ⲋⲓⲧⲟⲟⲧ referring to the legal representation, peculiar to Middle Egypt (Ashmunein, Aphroditopolis). We have to remember that Aphroditopolis' papyri testify, in the eighth century, another peculiarity :[6] the use of ⲡⲣⲟⲥⲱⲡⲟⲛ without the verb ⲉⲓⲣⲉ having the meaning of "representative", either of public officers or of private citizens.

Proceding now the other elements of the deed, the phrase concerning the period of validity of the lease is in lacuna. We know that the rent is fixed in money ϥⲟⲣⲟⲥ and exactly in three Lolocottinos and one trimesion. The lessee declares himself willing for the yearly payment of it (? the papyrus here is full of blanks): the word ⲕⲁⲧⲁⲃⲟⲗⲏ is used (even if the last two letters are in lacuna, the restoration seems to be certain), which means exactly the payment of an instalment and which I have found with this meaning in papyri either Greek or Coptic. In Dioscorus' archive cf. e.g., P. Michael. 43, 19, a lease of land of A.D. 526. Among Coptic documents which I could examine, I noticed that the use of this word is different as for time and area : in fact in the eighth-century papyri coming from Djeme the word is found in various types of deeds but not in leases, and is always related to πρόστιμον. On the contrary, in the seventh-century papyri coming from Middle Egypt the context is different and more similar to that of our document.

Crum, Coptic Mss British Museum 1022, a lease of land from Ashmunein: ⲕⲁⲧⲁⲃⲟⲗⲏ ⲉⲩⲁϫⲓⲧⲟⲩ ⲛⲧⲟⲟⲧⲕ.

CPR II 80 = CPR IV 141 (I have already quoted it before): ⲉϥϣⲁ[ⲛ]ⲟⲩⲁⲣ ⲧⲕⲁⲧⲁⲃ[ⲟⲗ]ⲏ ⲛⲧⲓⲣ ⲟⲙⲡⲉ.

In lines 10–11 of P. British Museum 2849 we read of a loan which the lesses has received (probably from the lessors) and which he undertakes to return :]ⲱⲡⲉ ⲛⲧⲟⲟⲧ ⲙⲡⲣⲟⲭⲣⲉⲓⲁ ⲉⲩϣⲁⲛⲙⲓⲥⲉ ⲥⲟⲩϣⲱⲡⲉ ⲛⲁⲓ ⲉⲩϣⲁ[.... ⲁⲡⲟⲗⲟ]ⲣⲓⲍⲉ ⲛⲏⲧⲛ ⲡⲣⲟⲥ ⲑⲉ ⲛⲧⲁⲥⲇⲟ⳨ⲉⲓ.

---

[4] Cf. ibid., 340.

[5] About διά in this meaning cf. L. Wenger, *Die Stellvertretung im Recht der Papyri*, Lipsia 1906, pp. 9–11, and J. Herrmann, *Studien zur Bodenpacht im Recht der Graeco-Aegyptischen Papyri*, München 1958, p. 61.

[6] Cf. San Nicolò, op. cit., p. 343.

We find a similar phraseology, in Dioscorus' archive, in P. Mich. 666, a sixth-century lease of land,[7] which shows remarkable analogies with P. British Museum 2849, as we shall see later on, too: 11.28–30 ὀφείλω ὑπὲρ τῆς προχρείας τῶν βωικῶν ζόων τοῦτ᾽ ἔστιν χρυσοῦ νομισμ(ά)τ(ια) ὀκτὼ ἕκαστων παρὰ κεράτιον ἕν ταῦτα λογίσασθαί σοι ἕν καιρῷ τελειώσεως τοῦ χρόνου τῆς παρούση⟨ς⟩ ἐγγράφου μισθώσεως πρὸς τὰ δόξαντα. And in line 34 ἀπολογίσασθαί σοι κριθὸν ἀρτάβας πέντε πρὸς τά δόξαντα. Similarly PRyl 144, a lease of land from Ashmunein, attests the same meaning of δοκεῖν 'to be convenient': ΕΠΕΙΔΕ ΤΑΙΤΕ ΘΕ ΝΤΑϹΔΟΞΗ. On the contrary the sense is less clear in PRyl. 174, a lease of land from Ashmunein, which is full of blanks: ΔΙΑΚΟ, ΑϹΔΟΞΗ ΤΑΡϕ.

As for the term ΠΡΟΧΡΕΙΑ I have not found examples of it in the Coptic documents which I could examine, in a context similar to that of P. British Museum 2849. The only example which I found is a declaration about the duty of giving back some προκρεῖαι, a eighth-century deed from Ashmunein: CPR II 50 = CPR IV 100. On the contrary in Greek the word is often found in leases, having the meaning of 'loan which the lessor has granted to the lessee',[8] among the documents of Dioscorus' archive cf. P. Mich. 666 (that sixth--century lease of land which I have already quoted), P. Michael. 43 (a lease of land of A.D. 526), and 44 (a loan of corn of A.D. 527. As for the meaning, it seems to me that 'loan' is more suitable than 'payment in advance',[9] considering that in the following line we find the word ΑΠΟΛΟΓΙΖΕ 'to give back'.

After this declaration, in line 11 we read the *stipulatio* in the form ϹΟΥΧΝΟΥΙ ΤΑϨΟΜΟΛΟΓΕΙ that is to say expressed with the conjunctive. We find it in the same form once again in line 8, and then finally in line 14, before the signatures of the lessee and the witnesses. In line 11 the formula is followed by a cross and then the locution ΤΝΤ ΑΥΟ ΟΝ ΜΠΙΚΑΙϢΑΧΕ[, which is attested by P. Vatic. Aphrod. Copti 1 and 5 too.[10] P. Vatic. Aphrod. Copti 1,31 ΧΕ ΑΙΤΑΥΟ ΝΕϢΑΧΕ ΤΗΡΟΥ ΝΤΙϨΕ (following the *stipulatio* expressed with the first perfect); P. Vatic. Aphrod. Copti 5,32 ΤΙΤΑ ΟΝ ΜΠΙΚΑΙϢΑΧΕ ΝΤΙϨΕ (following the *stipulatio* expressed with the first perfect), and 5,35 ΧΕ ΤΙΤΑΥΟ ΟΝ ΝΠΙΚΕϢΑΧΕ ΝΤΙϨΕ (following the *stipulatio* expressed with the conjunctive). The last instance is the most similar to that of P. British Museum 2849, since the *stipulatio* has the conjunctive and the following phrase the first present. This phrase which follows the *stipulatio* seems to serve the purpose of adding new agreements, as it happens e.g. in the above quoted P. Mich 666, in which after a first ἐπερωτηθεὶς ὡμολόγησα we find δηλονότι followed by a further agreement, and then again the *stipulatio*. But I have not found examples like that of P. British Museum 2849 among Coptic published papyri which I could examine.

In line 14 we have the definitive *stipulatio*: ϹΟΥΧΝΟΥΙ ΠΑΛΙΝ ΤΑϨΟΜΟΛΟΓΕΙ. We have a similar phrase in P. Vatic. Aphrod. Copti 1,34 and P. Vatic. Aphrod. Copti 5,35 and 43. I have found a Greek example in Dioscorus' archive, just in P. Mich. 666 which I have so frequently mentioned, lines 36–37: πάλειν ὡμωλόγησα.

As for the form of the *stipulatio*,[11] the one expressed with the conjunctive is of more recent use in comparison with the one expressed with the first perfect, according to what Till says,[12] placing the moment in which the use changes in the second half of the eighth century. But now we see that in P. Vatic. Aphrod. Copti 5 (A.D. 521/522 or 536/537) we have in line 32 ΑΥΧΝΟΥΙ ΑΙϨΟΜΟΛΟΓΕΙ but in lines 35–36 ϹΕΝΧΝΟΥΙ ΠΑΛΕΙΝ ΤΑϨΟΜΟΛ

---

[7] The papyrus may be dated more exactly A.D. 512 or A.D. 527, owing to a comparison with P. Vatic. Aphrod. Copti 5, in which the same person, Colluthus son Christophorus, syntelestes, appears: cf. note 4 of my article cit. "Annotazioni sul formulario giuridico di documenti copti del VI secolo".

[8] Cf. J. Herrmann, *Studien*..., p. 131.

[9] Cf. P. Lond. IV 1397, a fragment of letter from Aphroditopolis concerning extraordinary taxes and dated A.D. 709: in note to line 7 Bell says "προχρεια(ς); the meaning of this word in the present context is not quite clear. Its earlier meaning of 'loan' or 'advance' (BGU 439–443, P. Amh. 149) will obviously not suit here; but a comparison of 1412, 17 etc., as well as of 1360 concerning a προτέλεια suggests that it means prepayment, a very natural extension of the original sense".

[10] Cf. above note 2.

[11] An interesting example of *stipulatio* in an anomalous form is testified in a sale of wine for future delivery (coming from Heracleopolis and datable to the sixth-seventh century), which is written on a wooden tablet belonging to the Vatican Library and will be soon published by Prof. Sijpensteijn. The *stipulatio* is expressed there by the conditional followed by the first present called habitude: ΕΥϢΑΝΧΝΟΥΙ ϢΑΙϨΟΜΟΛΟΓΕΙ. This form of the *stipulatio* was not yet testified, as far as I know.

[12] Cf. "Die koptische Stipulationsklausel", Orientalia XIX (1950), 84.

οτει. In P. Vatic. Aphrod. Copti 1, which is later than 5 (we do not know how much later, but probably a few years), we have on the contrary the phrase expressed with the first perfect, in both examples in which the *stipulatio* appears. This alternation in the use of conjunctive and first perfect points out, in my opinion, the beginning of the change in the first half of the sixth century. P. British Museum 2849 has the form with the conjunctive in all three cases, and this makes me think that it is later than P. Vatic. Aphrod. Copti 1 and 5. But I think that, in consideration of the remarkable resemblance existing among P. British Museum 2849 and P. Vatic. Aphrod. Copti 1 5, with regard to the formulary of the *stipulatio* and the phrase which follows, the distance in time should not be very long. And moreover I should have been inclined to think that the three deeds had been written by the same notary, who repeated his typical expressions, if the *completio* were not a proof that the notaries were different. In fact in P. British Museum 2849 line 24 we read δι'ἔμοῦ Γεωργίου σὺν Ϡ(εῷ) ταβελλ(ίωνος), while in P. Vatic. Aphrod.Copti 5 δι'ἔμοῦ Ιωσήφου σὺν Ϡ(εῷ) ταβ(ελλίωνος) ἔγρ(άφη). In P. Vatic. Aphrod. Copti 1 the notary's *completio* is lacking, and we find only a further attestation of a witness, but a Greek Ιακὼβ τοῦ Γεωργίου μαρτυρ(ῶ) ὡς πρόκ(ειται).

The notary called George is not mentioned until now in any other deed coming from the area of Aphroditopolis; as well as either Colluthus son of Apa Sia or Marcus son of the late Proibammon are not identifiable with persons already known in Aphroditopolis' prosopography. The same thing we may say about witnesses, 4 in number: Promauos son of the late Petros, Aurelios Heracleios son of the late Apollos, a presbuteros whose name I could not read, and Eustatios Petros (maybe a mistake for 'son of Petros'?) περ (maybe another mistake for 'presbuteros'?). It is to be wished that some news about these persons are going to be issued in the revision of the Aphroditopolis' prosopography which is in preparation.

COPTIC STUDIES

Piotr Parandowski

Coptic Terra-cotta Figurines from Kôm el-Dikka

The set of Coptic terracottas from Kom el-Dikka in Alexandria counts nearly 300 figurines and fragments. Although the "repertoire" is, of course, not so rich as this of Graeco-Roman terracottas, however they merit a careful study.

With no risk of exaggeration one can define them as Cinderellas among other archaeological finds. Coptic terracottas exist on the marginal, neglected place, are treated badly by the scholars, as well as by the antiquarians of Egypt. One has to dig them from the deepest corner. It results from the lack of interest and as a matter of fact they were none as skillfully made and not so "artistical" as their Graeco-Roman counterparts. They are considered as more "ugly".

The Coptic terracottas were studied neither as the complementary material, nor as the subject in itself. With some exceptions: K.M. Kaufmann introduced them into the repertoire of the Graeco-Roman and later terracottas of Egypt.[1] Some part of the Coptic figurines from Kom el-Dikka was elaborated by M. Czarnecka-Martens.[2]

In order to bring the subject nearer we shall list the main characteristics without pretending to produce any final conclusions, only to suggest some probable ascertainments together with the facts.

1. 90% of the figurines were found in the sondage M XVII. There was a large dumping area between the external wall of the theatrical building and its corridor. They were tangled, mixed together with a great number of the Late Roman sherds dating from the 6th century, St Menas ampoulae, thousands of work-shop rejects, animal bones and so on. This dumping area was rather of urban character, with loose or no relation with the theatre. The rest comes from different spots of Kom. The discoveries of Mr M. Rodziewicz[3] in the quarter "R" point to the 6th century (without excluding the possibility of some regress to the end of the 5th century) as a period of the largest development of this industry.

2. The following *types* and compositions can be distinguished:

a) head-pots (fig. 1);

b) figurines of standing women with child (fragments of bodies and heads, mostly crowned with diadems) (fig. 2);

c) standing women with other attributes as bunch of flowers, birds, cradle..

d) masculine heads — parts of standing figurines of St Menas? Harpocrates?...

e) horse-riders (fig. 3);

f) separate figurines of the animals: birds, camels with saddle-bags, swines, gazelles;

g) a sitting personage holding a vessel;

h) a woman mounting the throne with a child and a crocodile (fig. 4);

i) a group of the terracottas representing orants and women holding the children. They are made of red-brick clay;

j) some inexplicable fragments.

3. Technique of execution. For the most part, the figurines issued from two moulds (heads, bodies). Some of the trunks of the animals were fashioned on the wheel. Hand-moulded were: hands, ribbon-like diadems, Phrigian horse-riders' caps, horse's tails.

---

[1] K.M. Kaufmann, *Aegyptische Koroplastic,* Cairo 1913; id., *Die Ausgrabungen der Menas Heiligtumer,* vols I–III, Cairo 1906–1908; id., *Ikonographie der Menasampullen,* Cairo 1910; P. Labib, "Fouilles du Musée Copte à Saint Ménas (Ière campagne)", Bull. Inst. Eg. (1951–52).

[2] M. Martens, "Les figurines en terre-cuite coptes découvertes à Kôm el-Dikka (Alexandrie), BSAA 43, 1975, 53–77.

[3] M. Rodziewicz, *Les habitations romaines tardives d'Alexandrie à la lumière des fouilles polonaises à Kôm el-Dikka,* Varsovie 1984, 229, 234, 235 and pls 60–62.

A

D

1. Head-post (ampoulae). Two variants

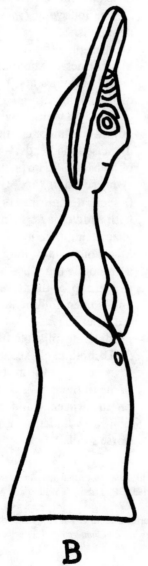

A

B

2. The most frequent types: woman holding a child and woman
with hands resting on belly

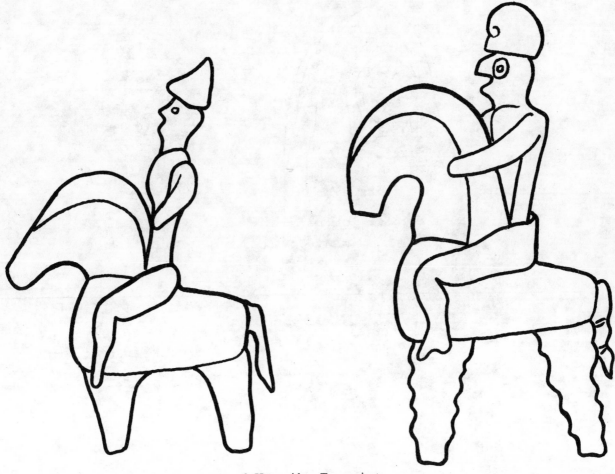

3. Horse-riders. Two variants

The only figurine made without hand-moulded details was the woman mounting the throne. This fact is not without significance: a developed composition which, no doubt, represented the Holy Virgin with Child in the native Egyptian conjunction with a crocodile ranged among the most popular. It was standardized like oil-lamps, St Menas ampoulae, head-pots. *Colours*: red, white (especially for the ground), light-green, ochre, blue and sometimes black (?). The same colours were applied in wall painting of the 6th century in Coptic Egypt.

The figurines were made of light yellow clay, characteristic for the Mareotic industry.

The characteristics we mentioned above would be hardly sufficient for an elementary classification of the Coptic terracottas. They must be examined from the stylistic point of view. It is especially fruitful when it concerns the types represented by large number of figurines. In order to focus the attention on the main features and tendencies let us confine ourselves on one type, namely on *heads-pots*. This group of terracottas can be, after all, recognized as representative for the whole industry and also for the method we applied.

We can distinguish several *stylistic* variants within a type. But, it does not mean that we necessarily detect some chronological, successive development or the regress. The modifications could be a result of the parallel existence of the numerous subtypes, samples of which were executed better or worse, in close relation to the prototype or without of it.

We paid particular attention to: 1° general cubic form and its frontal outline; 2° plasticity and picturesqueness of the face.

On this ground we singled out four stylistic variants. Variant "A" represents a well-known "Hellenistic" type of an ephebe. The form of a human head is fully developed and proportional as well in the relation to the face, the neck with a

4. Woman mounting the throne
(des. M. Michałowska)

circular base, as to the neatly shaped cylindrical pot which seems to be really carried upon the head's top. The composition is harmonious and subordinated to the axial divisions. In the distinct contrast to that, the variant "D" is characterized by the flattened form of head. The widening of its volume effects the widening of the pot which assumes the shape of a flattened funnel. The neck becomes short and large. More important is the far advanced flatness of the face. We can hardly resist the idea that the enlarging of the faces was intentional. Small face — typical of variant "A" with detailed plasticity of the minute features was very difficult object for *painting*. A potter, serving himself with a brush appropriate rather for painting bigger pots failed to follow the delicate relief, even if he only tried to underline it. More often he simply covered it, particularly the eyes. The relief almost disappeared under the thick white ground and of the layers of the paint. On the contrary, the flattened and, as if, unfolded facial surface gave enough place for painting. At the cost of the correct anatomical (classical) proportions the heads gained a lot of picturesqueness. Of course, they were, in general, carelessly executed, mass of hair, pot and base roughly coated with paint, with just one exception: the *eyes*. According to the character of Coptic art, the potters really applied their skill to the design of eyes. One thing is certain: large, expressive design of eyes was in harmony with the size and proportions of the face.

We can say that while the heads of variant "A" are examples of the reminiscences of Hellenistic art and were rather awkwardly adapted to the Coptic "pictural needs", the flattened heads of variant "D" are very Coptic creations. They stand on the borderline between the sculpture and the wall painting.

The same tendencies can be observed among other iconographical types. Some figurines of standing women are rather compact then puffed out, some are nearing to the proportions of woman's body, other have more spacious, flaring cubic form, prived of the bodies' convexities. The secondary but distinctive features are the relatively small hands made of ribbons of clay and simply attached to the volume. They are ovally shaped and devoid of any sharp edges.

The sharp edges, compact form and more careful rendering of the details are features of variant "A". The eyes are smaller, cheeks and chins singled out. The variant "B" is represented by ovally shaped forms, but its main feature consists of a relation of the diadem to the face. It is distinctly larger, especially in upper part and is not only the frame but the predominant element of the composition. The effect is also achieved by the inclination of the diadem: the face gets all the more subordinated to it.

The variant "B" of the figurines of women characterized also by large eyes and rich ornament of the diadem belongs to the same kind of industry which created the heads of variant "D". The stylistic analogies are not limited to two types. The similar distinction is to be observed among the figurines of horse-riders, just as if they were products of the different centres of the craftsmen. Of course, they were not. The same clay, colours and patterns testify to one centre which was, no doubt, Abou Mina. [4]

---

[4] Z. Kiss, "Les ampoules de St Ménas découvertes à Kôm el-Dikka (Alexandrie)", *Études et Travaux* I, V, VII, IX.

COPTIC STUDIES

Birger A. Pearson

Two Homilies Attributed to St Peter of Alexandria

The Coptic Manuscript Collection of the Pierpont Morgan Library in New York includes two ninth-century vellum mss (M 602 and M 611) containing unpublished homilies in Sahidic Coptic attributed to the "Seal of the Martyrs," Peter I, seventeenth patriarch of Alexandria (d. 311). These mss are part of a very large manuscript discovery made in 1910 by fellahin digging for sabakh at the site of the ancient monastery of St Michael at Hamouli, on the southern edge of the Fayyum. The entire lot of more than fifty volumes was purchased in 1911 by J.P. Morgan.[1] My student, Tim Vivian,[2] and I have transcribed and translated the afore-mentioned homilies attributed to Peter of Alexandria, and we hope eventually to publish the fruits of our study.[3] This paper is intended as a preliminary account, necessarily brief, of the contents of these interesting texts.

M 611,1 (folios 1r–18r) is an Epiphany homily, completely preserved. Other copies of the same homily are attested in Coptic fragments from the White Monastery now kept in Paris.[4] The superscription of the homily reads,

> A homily (*kathēgēsis*) delivered by the holy Abba Peter, Archbishop of Alexandria and martyr, concerning the day on which our Savior received baptism in the Jordan river by John the Baptist, which is the eleventh of Tobi. In the peace of God. Amen.

We have divided the text of the homily into paragraphs, numbered 1 to 44. The text falls into two main parts, consisting of an exposition of the gospel text and paraenesis. The following outline shows how the homily is structured:

1. Proemium (paragraphs 1–3; fol. 1r, col. a–2r,a)
2. Exposition of Matt 3:13–17 (4–20; 2r,a–8r,b)
3. Paraenesis (21–40; 8r,b–16r,b)
4. Peroration (41–43; 16r,b–18r,a)
5. Doxology (44; 18r,a-b).

The homily is very artfully constructed, and obviously reflects considerable rhetorical skill on the part of the author. After an enthusiastic proemium, in which the homilist refers to the joy of the entire world on the occasion of the baptism of the Lord and the light shining throughout the city on the eve of the festival, the exposition of the gospel text opens with an apostrophe of John the Baptist (4–8), in which John is directly addressed and invited to teach the congregation. The next section describes the marvels which attended the baptism of Christ (9–17), and opens as follows:

> Do you wish to know about the marvels which happened by the Jordan? Listen, I will teach you. Only listen to me not with the exterior ears only but with ears of the heart and soul ..." (9; 3v,b).

One of the marvels attending the baptism is the turning-back of the Jordan river:

[1] See H. Hyvernat, *A Check List of Coptic Manuscripts in the Pierpont Morgan Library,* New York 1919; id., "The J.P. Morgan Collection of Coptic Manuscripts", JBL 31 (1912), 54–57; id., *Bibliothecae Pierpont Morgan Codices coptici photographice expressi ...,* Roma 1922, esp. vols 25 and 31 (for M 602 and M 611).

[2] Mr Vivian is currently finishing a dissertation on Peter of Alexandria: *Saint Peter of Alexandria, Bishop and Martyr* (Ph. D. diss., University of California, Santa Barbara, 1985). He is also joint-author, with D.B. Spanel, of an article on Peter, forthcoming in the *Coptic Encyclopaedia* (ed. Aziz Aitya et al.).

[3] We wish to acknowledge gratefully a travel grant received from the Academic Senate Committee on Research of the University of California, Santa Barbara, which enabled us to spend a week in the Pierpont Morgan Libary in New York in September of 1983, studying the two mss. We are grateful, too, to Mr William Voelkle, the Associate Curator of Manuscripts, and his staff for putting the mss and the facilities of the Library at our disposal during that time.

[4] See Tito Orlandi, "La raccolta copta delle lettere attribuite a Pietro Alessandrino," *Analecta Bollandiana* 93 (1975), 127–132, esp. 129. On the fragments see Enzo Lucchesi, *Répertoire des manuscrits coptes (Sahidiques) publiés de la Bibliothèque Nationale de Paris,* Genève 1981. The fragments in question are P 131 [1], 51–58v; 131 [5], 116v–119; 132 [1], 62. I have recently heard from Dr Lucchesi that he is preparing an edition of this homily which will include the Morgan ms as well as the Paris fragments.

And immediately the Creator of the waters walked down to the Jordan, that he might receive baptism in it. The Jordan stirred and cried out for joy, desiring to flee. Then David the Psalmist came into the midst. He rejoiced and was glad. He sang, saying, "The sea looked and fled; the Jordan turned back. The mountains skipped like the hinds, the hills like the lambs of sheep. What is it with you, O sea, that you looked and fld? O Jordan, that you turned back? O mountains, that you skipped like the hinds? O hills, like the lambs of sheep? The earth moved in the presence of God." (15; 6r,a-b, quoting Ps 113 (114): 3–7).

The motif of the turning-back of the Jordan river, interestingly enough, is found earlier in an Alexandrian Gnostic text, the *Testimony of Truth* (Nag Hammadi Codex IX, 3: 30,20–23), a text which is also addressed "to those who know to hear not with the ears of the body but with the ears of the mind" (ibid., 29,6–9).[5] The motif of "spiritual hearing" doubtless has a long history in Alexandria, and is inherited from Alexandrian Judaism, of which Philo is a prime representative.[6]

The exposition of the gospel concludes with a section on the purpose of Christ's coming (18–20), i.e., to effect salvation. This salvation is offered anew in the flesh and blood of the Eucharist, to which the homilist invites his congregation.

The sacraments of Baptism and the Eucharist constitute the basis for the moral exhortation found in the paraenetical section (20–40). Here, again, evidence of traditional exegesis rooted in Alexandrian Judaism is to be noted, as the following passage illustrates:

Therefore, then, let us not offer sacrifice to God with animals that are crippled or blind or maimed or (with) the tongue cut, or with any blemish on it. For God does not accept their sacrifice, nor does he pay heed to them (25; 10r,a-b).

As the preceding context makes clear, the reference is to moral defilement and impurity, as symbolized by the maimed sacrificial animals referred to in

Leviticus 22:22. The same kind of exegesis of Leviticus 22:22 is found in Philo of Alexandria.[7] The concluding paragraph of the paraenesis (40; 16r,b–17r,a) was eventually lifted from our Epiphany homily and used, also with attribution to Abba Peter of Alexandria, as a separate *kathēgēsis* for the morning office of the fourth day of Holy Week. As such, it is attested in a number of Bohairic mss.[8]

Apart from the superscription, attribution of the Epiphany homily to Peter is internally indicated. In the context of a discussion of the holiness of the altar in the worship service, with the invisible presence of Christ, the true high priest, the following "autobiographical" passage occurs:

For I also told you this on another occasion, at the time when I drew back, (choosing) not to sit upon the throne because of the fearful thing which I saw in the holy place resembling a flame of fire. Because of this my conscience blames me, and I also fear to advance toward (the throne) because I am disgraced on account of my sins. O my children, he who sits in that place is not a man like me, but he is the living God. (29; 11v,b)

This passage reflects a piece of hagiography associated with St Peter of Alexandria: he humbly refused to sit upon his episcopal throne, choosing to sit instead on the footstool. But after he was dead his people placed his body upon the episcopal throne before burying him.[9]

If Peter is the real author of this homily, it would presumably be our earliest-attested Epiphany homily (assuming that the Epiphany homilies attributed to Hippolytus and to Gregory Thaumaturgus are spurious).[10] But it is more likely that is was written some time after Peter's death and piously attributed to him.[11] In terms of content it clearly reflects an Alexandrian provenience, and could possibly go back to the late fourth century in its original Greek form.

The other homily is M 602,1 (folios 1r–13r), a discourse on riches and on the Archangel Michael.

---

[5] See Birger A. Pearson, *Nag Hammadi Codices IX and X*, NHS 15, Leiden 1981, esp. pp. 122–125.

[6] See e.g. Philo, Decal., 35.

[7] See Philo, Spec. Leg. I, 166–167.

[8] See O.H.E. Burmester, "The Homilies or Exhortations of the Holy Week Lectionary", *Muséon* 45 (1932), 21–70, esp. 50 f. (Bohairic text) and 68 f. (ET).

[9] This story is found in the *Passio Petri*. See e.g. J. Viteau, *Passions des Saints Écaterine et Pierre d'Alexandrie*, Paris 1897, 83; also Paul Devos, "Une passion grecque inédite de S. Pierre d'Alexandrie", *Analecta Bollandiana* 83 (1965), 175 f.

[10] PG 10, 851–862; PG 10, 1177–1190.

[11] On the problem of attribution of patristic literature in Coptic see T. Orlandi, "The Future of Studies in Coptic Biblical and Ecclesiastical Literature", in: R. McL. Wilson (ed.), *The Future of Coptic Studies*, Leiden 1978, 143–163, esp. 152–153. Cf. p. 153, note 46: "Some homilies attributed to Peter of Alexandria and Theophilus of Alexandria (scil. in the Morgan collection) may be authentic only in part".

An entire quire of eight leaves (16 pages of text) is missing from the Morgan ms, but fortunately the entire homily is preserved in an unpublished Bohairic version in the Vatican Library (Vat. 61,3). Fragments of the Sahidic version from the White Monastery exist in Paris, Vienna, and Naples; there are fragments of the Bohairic version in Leipzig and Leningrad; and there is a small fragment of the Sahidic version from the Amherst collection of papyri in the Morgan Library in New York.[12] We have utilized all of these resources in preparing our translation, and hope eventually to publish a complete edition of both versions of this homily.

This homily presents a considerably more complicated picture than the Epiphany homily, as can be seen from the superscription:

> A discourse (*loso*) delivered by the blessed Apa Peter, Archbishop of Alexandria, concerning those who set their hearts on wealth and their money and their possessions and their power, depriving themselves of the eternal things, setting their hearts on the temporal things only. And he spoke also about the resurrection which will happen to all creation. He said also that man (can) not teach himself, nor is it possible for kings or rulers to give him (instruction). And he spoke also about those who pervert judgment for the sake of a gift, teaching these great ones everywhere to love the poor. And he said a few (words) also at the end of this discourse concerning the archangel Michael. In (the) peace of God. Amen.

From this superscription it can easily be seen that the homily is devoted to two main subjects: on the temptations of wealth and the eternal threat it poses, on the one hand, and on the Archangel Michael on the other. Indeed the homily, as it now stands, was intended to be read on one of the festival days of St Michael, the Twelfth of Athōr (Nov. 22). It is sometimes referred to as an "Encomium on the Archangel Michael",[13] but this is misleading in that the material devoted to Michael is limited to a small and distinctive section of the text. Analysis of the document as a whole has driven us to the conclusion that the encomiastic material on Michael is an interpolation added to an earlier homily on riches. The structure of the entire homily can be seen from the following outline [14] (referring to our numbered paragraphs):

1. Proemium (1–13; fol. 1r, col. a–3r,b)
2. Address to the rich (14–54; 3r,b–9v,b +)
3. Address to the poor (54–69)
4. Special application to church leaders (70–74)
5. On judgment and the resurrection (75–81 and 118–119; 12v,b–13r,a)
6. Interpolated Encomium on the Archangel Michael (82–117; 10r,a–12v,b)
7. Peroration and doxology (120–121; 13r,a-b)

The Michael encomium is interpolated into a discussion in the pre-existing homily of judgment and resurrection,[15] and expands on a quotation from 1 Thessalonians 4:16 ("by a voice of the archangel, by a trumpet of God") with a discussion of the identity of the archangel in question: "Who, indeed, among the angels is he whom the Lord will entrust with this fearful judgment and this great declaration?" (par. 82). The encomium contains material on Michael's role in the judgment and resurrection at the end of time (82–96), a rationale for identifying Michael as the archangel in question based on an interpretation of Daniel 10 (97–99), a polemic against the doctrine that Michael was installed as the chief archangel in the place of the fallen Satanael (100–101),[16] a report of

---

[12] For a complete list of mss see A. Hebbelynck and A. van Lantschoot, *Codices Coptici Vaticani Barberiniani Borgiani Rossiani*, Città Vaticana 1937, vol. 1, 420–421. W.E. Crum published the papyrus fragment, but erroneously associated it with four other fragments of an unidentified sermon. See his *Theological Texts from Coptic Papyri*, Anecdota Oxoniensia; Oxford 1913, no 10, fol. 5 (pp. 56 f.). We were able to study this fragment in New York, and concluded that our fragment is not only not from the same text as the other four fragments but also not inscribed by the same hand !

[13] "Encomio di Michele arcangelo"; see T. Orlandi, "La raccolta", 129.

[14] The missing pages from the Morgan ms constitute the material from the middle of our paragraph 52 to the middle of par. 103. We have been able to fill out this part of the homily on the basis of a transcription of the Vatican ms (Bohairic) 61,3 (82r–116v) kindly supplied to us by Dr Donald B. Spanel, made by him from photostats in the Griffith Institute of the Ashmolean Museum, Oxford. Fragments of the Sahidic version have also been utilized: Borg. Nat. Neap. 1B 14,461 (= Zoega Catal. 288), for paragraphs 83–91 (part); Paris BN 131 [5], 38, for paragraphs 99 (part) — 102 (published by Crum, JTS 4 (1903) 395–397). We are grateful to Dr David Johnson of the Catholic University, Washington, D.C., for supplying us with photostats of these and other fragmentary mss of our homily.

[15] A treatise *On the Resurrection* is attributed to Peter of Alexandria in the Syriac tradition. For the Syriac fragments see J.B.C. Pitra, *Analecta Sacra*, vol. 4, Paris 1883, 189–193 (Syriac), 426–429 (Latin).

[16] See esp. C.D.G. Müller, *Die Bücher der Einsetzung der Erzengel Michael und Gabriel*, CSCO 225–226: Scriptores Coptici 31–32; Louvain 1962, esp. vol. 32, pp. iii–iv, for a discussion of our text. Cf. also Müller, *Die Engellehre der koptischen Kirche*, Wiesbaden 1959, pp. 13–16, 174–175; and W.E. Crum, "Texts Attributed to Peter of Alexandria", 387–397, esp. 395–397 (on

Theonas' teaching on Michael's three Old Testament appearances on the Twelfth of Athōr (102–108, based on Genesis 18:1–9; Joshua 12:24, cf. 5:14; and Daniel 6:22), and another report of Theonas' teaching, concerning the destruction of the idol *Bōōh* (=Buchis) by Michael and the establishment of his festival on the Twelfth of Athōr in the days of Abba Eumenios, the seventh archbishop after Mark (109–117).

The rest of the material in our homily can properly be entitled *On Riches*. The basic theme is the proper use of wealth, and the attitudes which should be adopted by the wealthy, on the one hand, and the poor on the other, on the grounds that it is God who has created both the rich and the poor, and it is God who will reward the righteous, rich and poor alike, and punish the wicked, both rich and poor. But in reading the text one easily gets the impression that it has been subject to considerable editorial expansion.[17] Such expansions may include the special admonitions to fellow clergy found in the unusually lengthy proemium focusing originally on Solomon (3–12, which includes in paragraph 10 a quotation from the *Apostolic Canons*)[18] and in a special section after the address to the poor (70–74). Another such expansion may consist of the references to the legendary sweet-smelling beast, the *Alloē* (44–46), and the foul-smelling dung-beetle (49), introduced to illustrate the fragrance of good works and the foul smell of selfishness. This "bestiary" material may be taken from an Egyptian recension of the *Physiologos*.[19]

What remains, after removal of the suspicious interpolations and expansions, is a rather well constructed discourse which, in its original Greek form, could easily have been written by a fourth-century Alexandrian church leader. It picks up certain themes already sed forth by Clement of Alexandria in his famous sermon, *Quis dives salvetur* ("Who is the Rich Man who will be Saved?"). The opening passage in our homily's address to the rich is a good example of this, in which our author addresses, in diatribe style, an imaginary wealthy opponent:

> You will say to [me], "God is the one who gave me this wealth. Yes, I [say] to you, [God] is the one who gives [wealth] and poverty. But [he did not give you wealth in order for] you [to spend it wickedly)kakōs)] but (rather) benevolently (kalōs). (14; 3r,b).[20]

With this statement we can compare Clement's remarks:

> (Riches) have been prepared by God for the welfare of men. ... You can use (wealth) rightly (kalōs); it ministers to righteousness. But if one use it wrongly (kakōs), it is found to be a minister of wrong.[21]

Other examples of similarity between our homily and Clement's consist mainly of the use of the same scriptural passages to make similar points (Matt. 19:29; Matt. 10:42; Matt. 5:13; 1 Cor. 15:52).[22] A nautical metaphor also occurs in our text which is reminiscent of a similar nautical metaphor used by Clement.[23] To be sure, the more prominent gospel passages dealt with in our homily are Luke 16:19–31(29–29) and Luke 12:16–21(30–31), texts ignored by Clement, whose main gospel text is Mark 10:17–31.

Is our homily from the pen of Peter? Apart from the interpolated Michael encomium, with its use of the stock phrase, "my father Theonas who reared me,"[24] the following passage, occurring in a section of the proemium about which we have already raised some suspicions, is clearly a reference to Peter:

> We do not teach with mean-pleasing devices nor with vain ordinances, teaching some to [be] fearful before us, [as] I heard in [the] place where I am hidden [on account of] the severity

---

Paris 131 [5], 38). This interesting tradition is obviously developed out of ancient Jewish apocryphal traditions, e.g. *Vita Adae et Evae* 12–16. The name Satanael (for Satan; our text reads erroneously "Sanatael") occurs e.g. in *2 Enoch* 18:3; 29:4; 31:4, in contexts dealing with the fall of Satan.

[17] Cf. Orlandi's comment, quoted above note 11.

[18] Canon 19 in the Coptic version. See Paul de Lagarde, *Aegyptiaca*, Göttingen 1883, p. 216.

[19] See W.E. Crum, "Texts Attributed to Peter of Alexandria", 394–395, on Paris 130 [5], 102.

[20] Lacunae in the Morgan ms have been restored with reference to the Bohairic version.

[21] Q.d.s. 14, Butterworth's translation in the Loeb edition.

[22] Par. 51, cf. Q.d.s. 21–22; 52, cf. Q.d.s. 31; 74, cf. Q.d.s. 36; 80. cf. Q.d.s. 3.

[23] Cf. par. 57 and Q.d.s. 32.

[24] 102, 109. This phrase is found in other texts attributed to Peter, e.g. British Museum Or. 3581, published by Crum, JTS 4 (1903), 392.

of the persecution of the [lawless] emperors who have [risen] against the Church, concerning some leaders [in] the [provinces, that] they beat [men and] women, that they should only be fearful before them.[25]

This passage, referring to Peter's flight from persecution,[26] could be part of an editorial expansion intended to make more explicit a traditional attribution of the homily *On Riches* to Peter of Alexandria. That Peter is the real author of the original homily cannot be proven, of course, but cannot be ruled out either.

Much more could be said about these two homilies attributed in the Coptic tradition to the seventeenth patriarch of Alexandria, but it is hoped that what has here been presented will convey something of the challenge that they pose to the scholar and, certainly not least, the intrinsic value of their contents.

---

[25] Par. 9; 2v,a. Lacunae in the Morgan ms have been restored with reference to the Bohairic version, and the Sahidic fragment Paris 131 [5], 43. There follows in par. 10 the quotation from Canon 19 of the *Apostolic Canons*. Cf. note 18.

[26] Cf. also the fragment from another homily attributed to Peter, Paris 130 [5], 123 f., edited by C. Schmidt, *Fragmente einer Schrift des Märtyrerbischofs Petrus von Alexandreia,* TU 20 [6], Leipzig 1901, esp. pp. 5 (Coptic text) and 6 (German translation): "You know that, for a long time, I have been fleeing from place to place for fear of Diocletian and his persecution" (my translation). Despite Schmidt's belief in the authenticity of this fragment, it can hardly by genuine. See e.g. John Barns and Henry Chadwick, "A Letter Ascribed to Peter of Alexandria", JTS 24 (1973), 443–455, esp. 444.

COPTIC STUDIES

Krzysztof Pluskota

Early Christian Pottery from Old Dongola

Archaeological research carried out by the Polish Mission since 1964 provides us with quantities of ceramic material every year. The greatest part of the surface of the concession, as it can be seen on other archaeological sites in Nubia or in Egypt, is covered with fragments of burnt bricks and potsherds from the Christian period. During the exploration of individual structures such as churches,[1] the Mosque,[2] dwelling houses[3] and graves,[4] have been found vessels and fragments representing: hand-made utility wares, decorated fine wares, and liturgical vessels. Wares dated back to the Classic, Post-Classic, and Late Christian periods (850–1350 A.D.) are most frequent and correspond mainly to the types occurring at the sites in Lower and Upper Nubia. Their quantity and quality seem to confirm the significance of Dongola, as the capital of the Christian Kingdom, producing and importing goods. This first aspect, local production, is still not completely analysed, because of lack of traces of workshops or pottery kilns among discoveries. However, the presence of considerable quantities of fine, red ware in Classic Christian structures allow us to assume, that they were made in local workshops. We hope to solve this in the course of the next seasons, which too, may lead us to discovery of Meroitic pottery, which has not been found yet in Old Dongola. Unlike Classic Christian wares, pottery dated to the Transitional and Early Christian periods is not so frequent so far. It was collected at two sites:

1. Old Church (under the Church of Granite Columns). This structure was excavated since 1964 till 1971. Especially important (concerning Early Christian pottery) was findspot between the floors of the Old Church in the room no 9, under the staircase.[5]

2. Building X (under the Church of Stone Pavement). During exploration of the 1983 and 1984 seasons carried out at the complex of the stratyfied structures of the Cruciform Church and the Church of Stone Pavement, under the foundations of this last one, traces of an older building were found. In order to establish its plan several trial pits were executed and pieces of pottery were found at each layer. The stratigraphy of the fragments was demarcated by the pavement of the new discovered Building X and the floor of the Church of Stone Pavement.

Pottery found at these two sites consists mainly of fragments and several almost completely preserved vessels. Even superficial observation permits us to ascertain that vessels of both are contemporary, moreover easy recognizable styles of decoration and forms indicate the Transitional period.[6]

Small semiglobular bowls are prevalent form and among them these decorated with a simple painted embellishment in which design is executed in black and the filling in white or cream paint.[7] Although that style is outgrown from X-Group tradition, but one can detect in simple patterns of nos 1–7

---

[1] S. Jakobielski, "A Brief Account on the Churches of the Old Dongola", in: *Proceedings of the Colloquium on Nubian Studies, The Hague 1979*, – Leiden 1982, pp. 51–56.

[2] W. Godlewski, "The Mosque Building in Old Dongola", in: *Proceedings of the Coloquium on Nubian Studies, The Hague 1979*, Leiden 1982, pp. 21–28.

[3] S. Jakobielski, "Dongola 1976", *Études et Travaux* XI, (Warszawa 1979), 229–244.

[4] Jakobielski, "A Brief Account...", 55.

[5] S. Jakobielski, "Polish Excavations at Old Dongola 1970–72", in: *Nubia. Récentes Recherches*, Warszawa 1975, p. 72.

[6] W.Y. Adams, "An Introductory Classification of Christian Nubian Pottery", KUSH X (Khartoum 1962), 252; id., "Progress Report on Nubian Pottery" I, KUSH XV, (Khartoum 1967–1968), 11.

[7] Analog. for form and decor.: M. Pelicer, M. Llongueras, *Las Necropolis Meroiticas del Grupo "X" y Cristianas de Nag-el-Arab (Argin, Sudan)*, Madrid 1965, Lam. VIII, 4.

stylized signs of cross or monogram.[8] A bowl no cat. 3 apart from that conventional painted decoration, has scratched (by the owner) representations of animals and inscriptions not decifered so far. Noticeable is that inscriptions are provided with crosses, so frequent in private inscriptions scratched on plasters of Nubian Churches.

Decoration of the others fragments of this ware seems to be devoid of any symbolics, nos cat. 5, 9–11. Similarly ornamental quality has embelishment of ledge rims of bowls nos cat. 12–14 belonging to the Classic X-Group Ware (400–600 A.D.).[9]

High standard of technology represent fragments of bowls decorated with a white design executed on black collar band no cat. 15–18. Their paste is slightly more bright and harder, layers of the slip and paints are very thin and consolidated in firing. Two bowls nos cat. 19,20 represent rare form with a subtle modelled rim and slightly flattened bottom. Their paste is homogeneously grey and surface has natural colour or pinkish selfslip. Decorative patterns of both occurred in Early Christian period.[10]

Generally, remarkable are frequent signs of cross painted on vessels from this period. Even if design on fragments nos cat. 1–7 and 20 can be acknowledged as only geometric patterns, in the case of the vessels nos cat. 21–23 and 26 Christian symbolics of the decoration is unquestionable. Therefore, conclusion drawn about Early Christian pottery in Wadi Halfa region by prof. W.Y. Adams: "there is nothing in the pottery to reflect the Christianisation of Nubia which took place at this time"[11] in Dongolese pottery is not confirmed.

Other fragments of vessels belong to the imported wares or made under foreign influences. Fragments of rims of pots nos cat. 24 and 25 and of large bowl no cat. 26 have a common decorative element, i.e. wavy ornamentation stuck below the rim.[12] The bowl is decorated with four crosses painted radially on inner surface. Samian ware is represented by several fragments of rims of small bowls and plates, nos cat. 27 and 28. The red-brown paste differs them from rather orange Upper Egyptian wares.

Two fragments of amphorae were found in the foundation level of the Building X. Fragment no cat. 29 belonged to amphora of Imported Brown Utility (T) ware, form P 2.[13] Characteristics of the second one no cat. 30, i.e. light beige paste, no slip, shape of a rim and a section of the broken handle permit to classify this vessel as a form P 3, Imported White Utility (T) ware.[14] Occurrence of this ware in Nubia is limited to a very short period of the first half of the 6th century A.D. Therefore, that fragment has a great importance for the precise dating of whole collection.

All wares described above, represent rather narrow variety of forms, determined probably by the character of the findspots, i.e. ecclesiastic structures. Some of them, semiglobular bowls are of undeniable local production. Others even if made in Nubia reflect distinct foreign influences, that has come in Nubia from or through Egypt. Generally, they give evidence of both importation and specialized local production. The latter achieved in Classic Christian period a summit in the variety of forms and decoration, typical of Nubian wares.

Catalogue

1. Bowl with rounded bottom, rim diam. 10 cm. Paste: red-brown, dense, medium hard, no temper. Creamy paint inside and outside.
Red-brown, polished, slipped collar band below the narrow, black rim strip intersected by three checked rectangles.
Single body grove.
Findspot: Old Church, room no 9, under the staircase.
Figs 1. 2

2. Bowl with a rounded bottom, rim diam. 10 cm. Characteristics: as above.
Findspot: as above.
Fig. 1.

---

[8] L. Török, "Abdallah Nirqi 1964, Finds with Inscriptions", in: *Acta Archaeologica Academiae Scientiarum Hungaricae* 26, Budapest 1974, p. 371, inscr. 22.

[9] Adams, "An Introductory ...", KUSH X, 252, fig. 11.

[10] For no cat. 20 cf. Pelicer, Ilongueras, *Las Necropolis...*, Lam. VIII 5; figs 17, 9.

[11] Adams, "Progress Report...", KUSH XV, 11.

[12] Analog. decor.: F.J. Presedo Velo, *La Fortaleza Nubia del Cheikh-Daud*, Madrid 1964, fig. 14, I.

[13] Adams, "An Introductory...", KUSH X, 275.

[14] Ibid.

1. Nos cat. 1 and 2

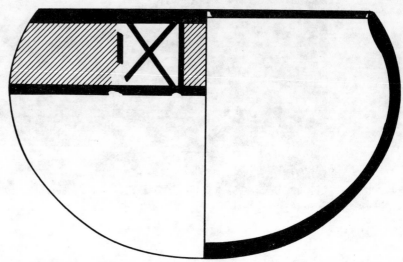

2. No cat. 1

3. Bowl with rounded bottom, rim diam. 10 cm.
Paste: brick-red, fine, rather soft, micaeous. Mat, light pink slip shadowing to white outside and the same inside.
Painted decor.: as above.
On the collar band representations of following animals scratched: camel, cat, donkey(?), goat. On two panels inscriptions scratched.
Findspot: Old Church, under the foundations, narthex. Now in National Museum in Khartoum.
Figs 3, 4.

4. Fragment of bowl, rim diam. 10 cm.
Characteristics: as nos 1 and 2.
Findspot: as nos. 1 and 2.
Figs 5, 6.

5. Fragment of bowl.
Paste: as above.
Decor.: black painted pattern on white-pinkish surface.
Below the red brown slipped collar band.
Findspot: as above.
Figs 5, 7.

6. Fragment of bowl.
Paste: as above.
Decor.: as nos 1, 2, 3.
Findspot: Building X, under the pavement.
Figs 5, 8.

7. Fragment of bowl, rim diam. 10 cm.
Paste: as above.
Slip: as above.
Decor.: as above.
Findspot: trial pit in apse of Cruciform Church (Building X?).
Figs 5, 9.

8. Fragment of bowl, rim diam. 10 cm.
Paste: red-brown, slightly porous, with sand temper. Red-brown polished surface.
Black rim strip and black painted decor. on orange surface (monogram?).
Findspot: as no 1.
Figs 5, 10.

9. Fragment of bowl, rim diam. 10 cm.
Paste: red-brown, hard, dense.

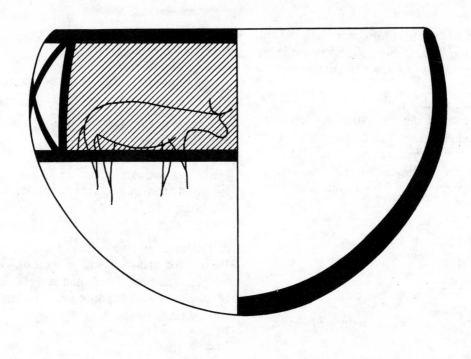

3–4. No cat. 3

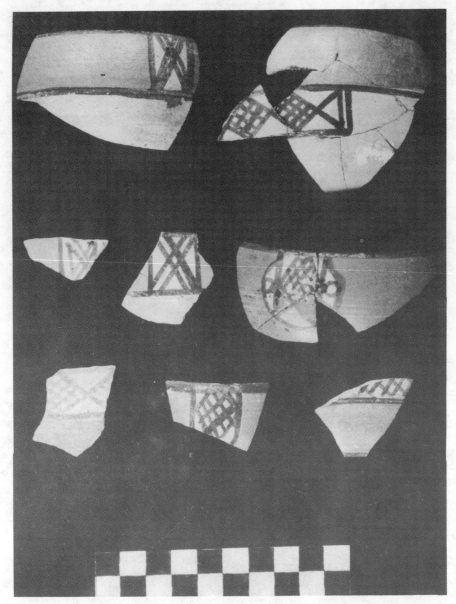

5. Top: nos cat. 4 and 5: middle: nos cat. 6, 7, 8; bottom: uncatalogued, no cat. 9, uncatalogued

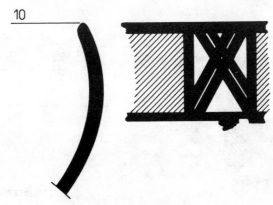

10

6. No cat. 4

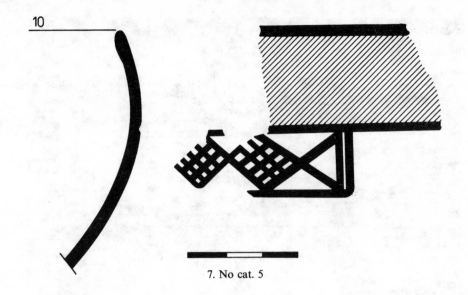

7. No cat. 5

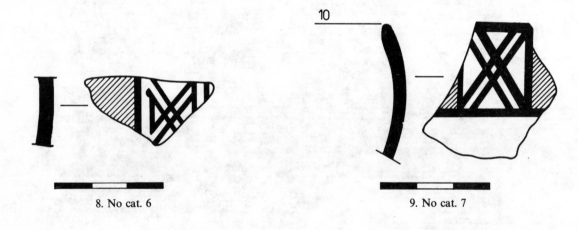

8. No cat. 6

9. No cat. 7

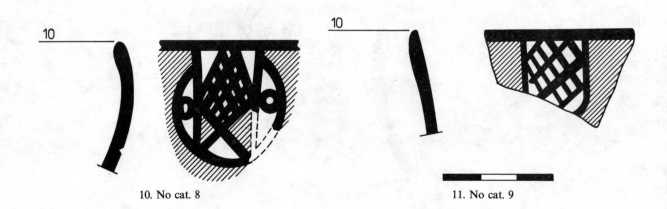

10. No cat. 8

11. No cat. 9

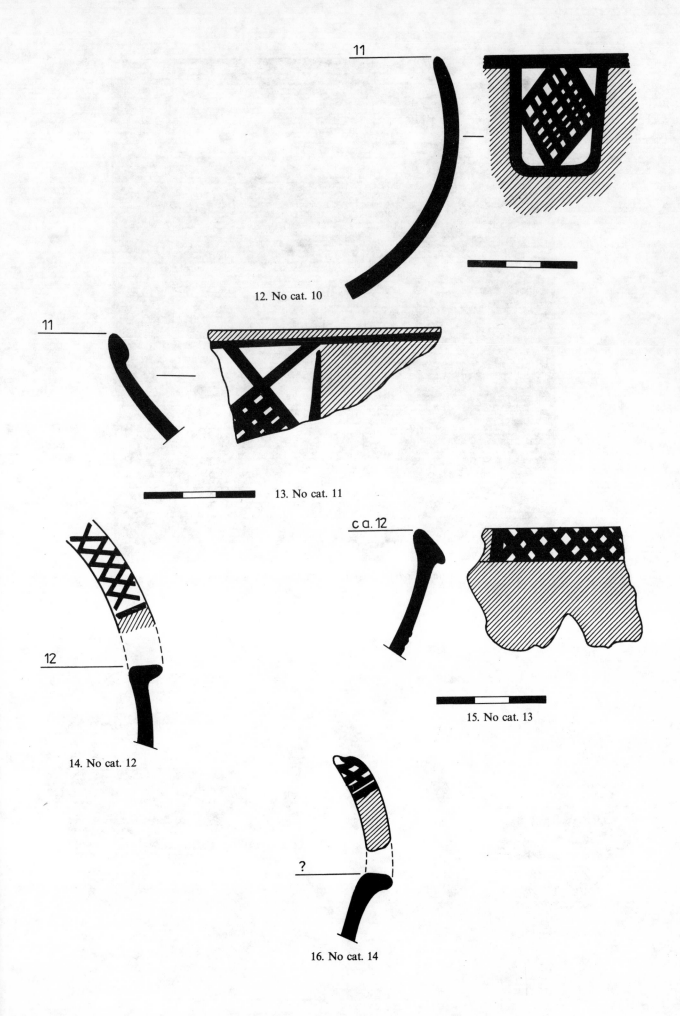

11

12. No cat. 10

11

13. No cat. 11

c a. 12

15. No cat. 13

12

14. No cat. 12

?

16. No cat. 14

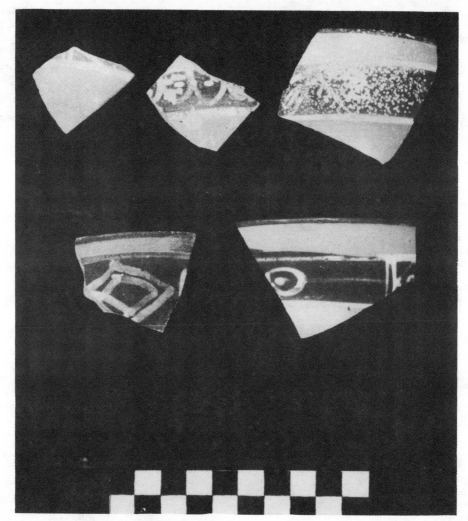

17. Top: uncatalogued, nos cat. 15, 16; bottom: nos cat. 17, 18

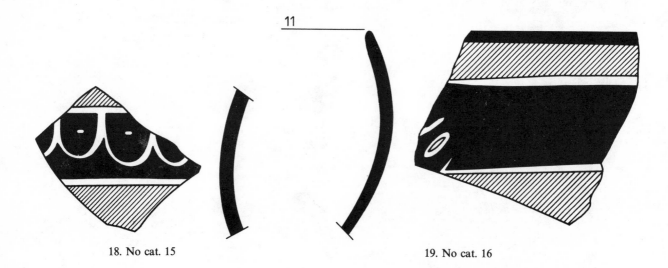

18. No cat. 15

19. No cat. 16

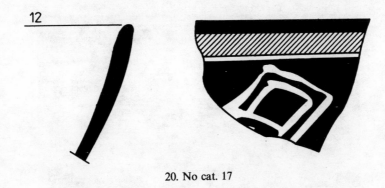

20. No cat. 17

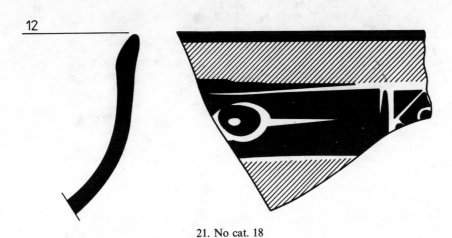

21. No cat. 18

Decor.: black rim strip and pattern black on white below.
Findspot: Building X, under the pavement.
Figs 5, 11.
10. Fragment of bowl, rim diam. 11 cm.
Paste: light brown, hard, dense.
Brown, lustrous slip on both sides.
Decor.: as no. 9.
Findspot: Cruciform Church, trial pit, S-wall of diaconicon.
Fig. 12.
11. Fragment of bowl, rim diam. 11 cm. Thickened rim.
Paste: red-brown, dense, hard.
Slip: red-brown.
Decor.: geometric pattern, black on white.
Findspot: Building X, under the pavement.
Fig. 13.
12. Fragment of bowl with ledge rim diam. ca. 12 cm.
Paste: light red-brown, fine, medium hard, micaeous.
Red-brown slip on both sides, polished.

Ledge rim decorated with cross-pattern of dark brown on light cream.
Findspot: Old Church, rock levelling.
Fig. 14.
13. Fragment of bowl with ledge rim.
Paste: as above.
Decor.: as above.
Findspot: Old Church.
Fig. 15.
14. Fragment of bowl with ledge rim.
Paste: as above.
Decor.: as above.
Findspot: Building X, above the pavement.
Fig. 16.
15. Fragment of bowl.
Paste: red-brown, hard, with sand particles.
Red-orange slip.
Decor.: white, transparent paint on black surface.
Findspot: Old Church.
Figs 17, 18.
16. Fragment of bowl, rim diam. 11 cm.
Paste: as above.
Decor.: as above.

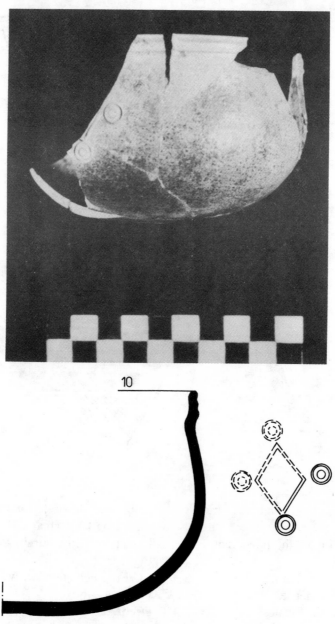

22–23. No cat. 19

Findspot: Old Church, room no 9.
Figs 17, 19.
17. Fragment of bowl, rim diam. 12 cm.
Paste: red-brown, hard, dense.
Decor.: as above.
Findspot: Building X, under the pavement.
Figs 17, 20.
18. Fragment of bowl, rim diam. 12 cm.
Paste: light red-brown, hard, dense.
Slip: light red-orange, polished.
Decor.: as above.
Findspot: Church of Granite Columns, trial pit
situated in staircase.
Figs 17, 21.

19. Fragment of bowl, rim diam. 10 cm. Modelled
rim.
Paste: very fine, grey, hard.
Slip: like surface done by firing.
Decor.: stamped.
Findspot: Old Church, room no 9.
Figs 22, 23.

20. Fragment of bowl, rim diam. 10 cm. Rim as
above.
Paste: grey, dense, medium hard.
No slip, brown stylized cross (?), brown rim strip.
Findspot: Building X, under the pavement.
Fig. 24.

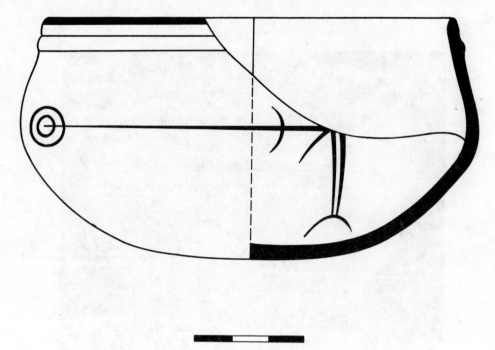

24. No cat. 20

21. Bowl, rim diam. 10,5 cm.
Paste: grey-yellowish, hard, no temper. Yellowish, polished on both surfaces. Black and red painted decor. outside (cross in a frame).
Findspot: Old Church, room no 9.
Figs 25–26.

22. Fragment of vessel (bowl?).
Paste: creamy, hard, dense.
Creamy slip on both surfaces.
Decor.: black painted design and red filling (cross with pendants between arms).
Findspot: Building X, under the pavement.
Figs 27, 28.

23. Fragment of bowl.
Paste: cream-buff, dense, rather hard.
Light orange slip on both sides. Two groves below the rim.
Decor.: black painted cross with red filling.
Findspot: Church of Stone Pavement, under the floor.
Figs 29,30.

24. Fragment of pot, rim diam. 20 cm.
Paste: red-brown, porous, medium hard.
Decor.: inside, below the rim white on black ledge band. Wavy ornamentation stuck outside below the rim.
Findspot: as above.
Fig. 31.

25. Fragment of pot, rim diam. 19 cm.

Paste: as above.
Decor.: wavy ornamentation as above.
Findspot: as above.
Figs 31, 32.

26. Fragment of large bowl, rim diam. 49 cm.
Dark to orange creamy paste, rather porous, sand particles.
Decor.: four red-brown painted crosses inside. Wavy ornamentation, as above.
Findspot: Old Church, room no 9.
Figs 33, 34.

27. Fragment of bowl, rim diam. 20 cm.
Paste: red-brown, dense, hard. Red-brown slip.
Findspot: Building X, under the pavement.
Figs 35, 36.

28. Fragment of bowl.
Paste: as above.
Slip: as above.
Findspot: as above.
Figs 35, 37.

29. .Fragment of amphora.
Paste: brown, porous, hard. Ribbed outer surface, resinated inside.
Findspot: Building X, under the pavement.
Fig. 38.

30. Fragment of amphora.
Paste: light beige, porous, medium hard.
No slip.
Findspot: Building X, under the pavement.
Figs 38, 39.

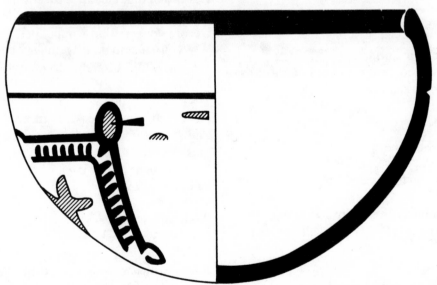

25–26. No cat. 21

27–28. No cat. 22

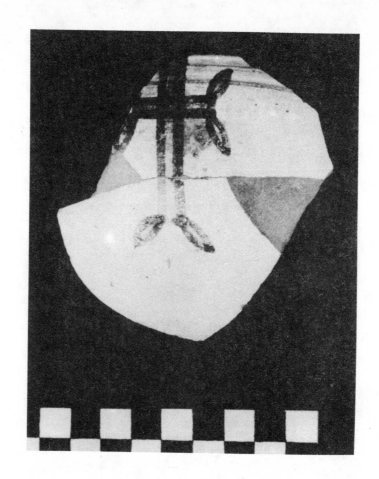

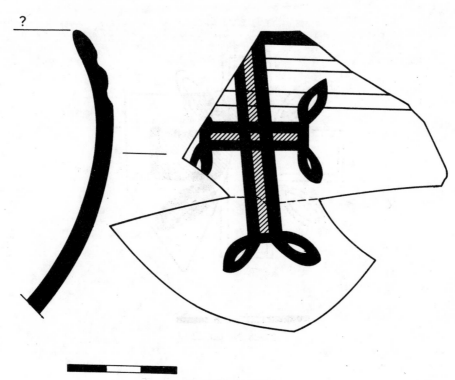

29–30. No cat. 23

31. Top: no cat. 24, bottom: no cat. 25

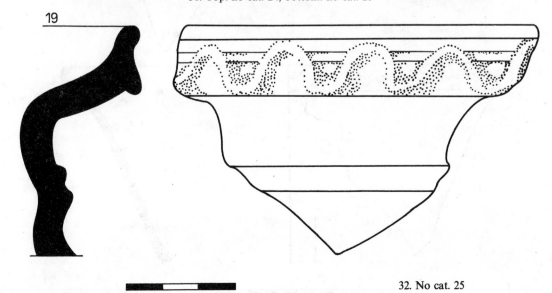

19

32. No cat. 25

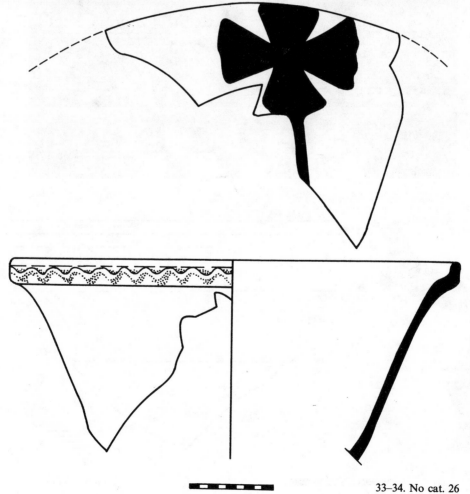

33–34. No cat. 26

35. Top: no cat. 27, uncatalogued; middle: no cat. 28, uncatalogued, uncatalogued; bottom: uncatalogued both

36. No cat. 27

37. No cat. 28

38. Top: no cat. 29; bottom: no cat. 30

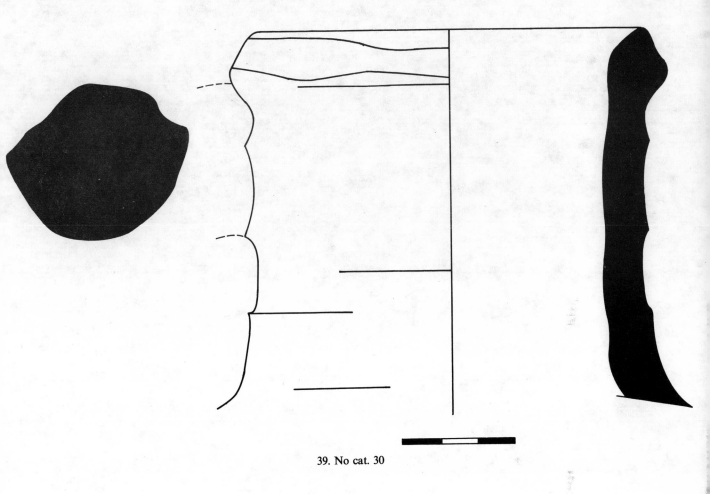

39. No cat. 30

COPTIC STUDIES

Nina Pomerantseva

Spread of the Traditions of Ancient Egyptian Art on the Iconography of Coptic Ritual Sculpture (4th–6th centuries A.D.)

While treating this subject which is limited to the monuments of sculpture, we should exclude other categories of Early Christian art, such as textiles, which although they permit us to raise fundamental questions of date and origin, are unsuitable for a consistent tracing of Early Christian style and iconography. The problem of correlation of ancient Egypt with the Christian World is assuming special topicality in connection with the new investigations in the field of Coptic art. Such correlations find their expression in the philosophical-religious concept, symbolic meaning and stylistic structure of monuments. This subject has at last become the central object of interest. Contemporary research is moving increasingly deeper into the study of this problem. About forty years ago the Soviet art historian A.S. Strelkov pointed out in his book *The Fayum Portrait* that the Egyptian imprint can be found in different aspects of Christian symbols and in pure dogmatic doctrine.[1] The Soviet scholar, academician M.A. Korostovsev, devoted to the problem of Egypt and Christianity a special chapter of his latest book *The Religion of Ancient Egypt*.[2]

Such parallels between ancient Egyptian and Christian outlooks can be traced in the transformation of some Egyptian gods, their images and symbols into Christian ones. These features emerged at the stage when the culture of ancient Egypt, through Rome, got into touch with the Christian World.

Thus the Egyptian artistic means of execution came into contact with the Christian iconography and gradually built up a system of certain rules and fixed principles – namely, the canon. The canon includes a wide range of meanings – the composition of monuments, iconography of images, artistic means of expression and the religious system which is its philosophical bases.

Early Coptic ritual stelae do not display all the components of the canon. Among all its components the proportions of Coptic stelae do not form an orderly system; they are based on the golden section, but some stelae which have an analogous composition also vary in proportional structure. This structure was not purely abstract; it was a theologian's concept as much as an artist's. It was the Copts who were considered the traditions of ancient Egypt as their local ones. Those traditions met their own aesthetic ideals – the inclination towards conventionality which found its expression in a very flat manner of execution. The style of Coptic funerary stelae combines the concrete visualization and irrefutable logic of the Roman school with the philosophical mysticism and abstract outlook of the Alexandrian one. It is such convention, coupled with an increasing use of primitive technique, that transformed Alexandrian art into Coptic in Egypt.

The corporeal palpability on the one hand, and abstraction of images on the other, are well typified in the Coptic sculpture of the 4th–6th centuries. Its images have no spirituality. To make them more expressive, a Coptic master uses the deformation as an artistic method – see for example the votive figure of a woman in the orant – posture from Behnaza, funerary stele of Isismyste from Schêch Abâde and the like.[3]

The Coptic sculpture of the 4th–6th centuries as a rule uses the Egyptian canonical types of composi-

---

[1] A.S. Strelkov, *Fayumskiĭ Portret*, M–L 1936, p. 56.

[2] M.A. Korostovsev, *Religia Drevnego Egipta*, M. 1976, gl. XXXVIII, pp. 285–297.

[3] K. Wessel, *Koptische Kunst*, Recklinghausen 1963, Taf. IV, V.

tion. One distinction between them we note at once is the increased significance of the head. It is the head but not the face that dominates Coptic statues. Christianity in the mature period of its development will make the face the main theological category of its doctrine—the face in the Christian icon is the realization of a unvisual image of God in its visual representation. But the images of Coptic funerary stelae are indifferent to their prototype, to personal individuality.

All of them have similar features: protruding large open eyes impart great expression to the images; though the other features of a face are flat — cheeks, lips and so on, see for example the bust of a woman with a palm branch from Recklinghausen Museum [4]; it has the butten-like eyes with almond-shaped sockets, highlighted according to the Egyptian tradition, by protruding edges, eyebrows and eyeballs. The other features of the face are modeled generally — a low forehead, thick cheeks. The execution of the head is the main task for a master. The expression of a glance is a step toward the dematerialization of an image and predomination of spirituality in it. But the technique of execution for the overwhelming majority of early Coptic sculpture is not of a high quality. Some details are rendered, such as hairs, brows, chaplet, drapery and some attributes, also include the ornamental means of representation. We can observe similar trends in the latest Fayum portraits (fig. 1) and funerary masks (fig. 2) in which stylized and hieratic features have been increasing gradually and then the portrait images are displaced with the typified ones.

Thus the ways of representation constitute the style. It evolves from one epoch to another. The style limited by its time is the stamp that raises a real work of art above mere representation; it consists of rhythm and proportions wrought into the work by following tradition.

Order and correlation of proportional values for the definite parts of a body or a face constitute the basis of the iconography of images. Constant distribution of proportional values constitutes the style of iconography. This style provides not only unity of adequate structure but also the consistency that lends a lithe vitality to the whole image.

The overwhelming majority of Coptic statues and stelae of the 4th–6th centuries (among them Isis-myste, woman's bust and the like) are represented in a frontal altitude. But in spite of borrowing of ancient Egyptian canonical types the Coptic monuments are considered to be Christian. Large-scale figures are characteristic of the composition of Coptic stelae. Instead of complicated compositions, full of figures or some other details, a Coptic master prefers to portray isolated persons. He adheres to the old principles of simplicity and clarity.

The style of Coptic sculptures is really two-dimensional: the background is merely a conventional surface, or limits the action of figures in relief to one plane. On the other hand flat modeling is characteristic of the figures rendered in high-relief. The ancient Egyptian culture did not introduce verbal portrait into practice; exphrasis, as a poetic form is absent. Exphrasis is really intrinsic to Christian literature. [5] A lack of portrait representation is evident in the use of certain archetypes, generalized in the composite type of a young man, woman and so on. The iconographical archetype embodies in visual form some canonical patterns which were corroborated for every type of representation.

Ancient Egyptian monuments are predecessors for certain types of Christian images. Succession of traditions appears in identical compositions but not in the iconography of faces.

Ancient Egyptian art has a harmonious balance of forms and proportions: the Coptic images are characterized by the deformation as means of expression.

The Coptic faces look upon the world with immense eyes expressing the idea of intrinsic spirituality of images. The heads of most of the monuments are enlarged out of proportion, for example the votive figure of a praying woman from Behnaza. [6] The figure is represented in the posture of an orant — that is all that links this image with the Christian iconography of the orant. The posture of praying in itself is not new in Christian art — the remote prototype of it is the ritual Ka, statues of ancient Egypt, but their philosophical conception is quite different.

The woman figure from Behnaza is executed in a

---

[4] Ibid., Taf. III.

[5] M. Riemschneider, *Der Still des Nonnos — aus der byzantischen Arbeit der DDR*, I, Berlin 1957, pp. 48 ff.

[6] Wessel, *Koptische Kunst*, Taf. IV.

1. Portrait of Maiden holding vessel. Distemper, 3rd cent. Pushkin Fine Arts Museum, Moscow

2. Funeral Mask. Plaster of Paris, beginning of 3rd cent. Pushkin Fine Arts Museum, Moscow

very schematic way and without elegance. This motif seems to have been rather popular in Coptic stelae (fig. 3); see also for example two praying figures — a father with his daughter, funerary relief from Kom Abu Billu (limestone, Recklinghausen, Iconenmuseum).[7]

Unlike the typical ancient Egyptian way of representation the head is in full face, the torso in the frontal position while the legs are literally in profile. The feet of the woman in question are spread in different directions. Other parts of the body of this figure do not follow normal proportions. The propositions of Coptic funerary stelae belonging to similar types of composition have no constant canonical system in contrast to the Egyptian canonical representations. Let us compare for example some similar compositions — the round statue of the judge of Bes (XXVI dyn.

Gubbencian, no 158, Portugues, pl. 4) and the stele of Isismyste, which we mentioned earlier. Both sculptural monuments are executed in the canonical posture of a sitting figure with the left knee standing upright. The prototype of this canonical sculpture is the statues of the VIth dynasties — for example, the statue of the nobleman Neeanchre (VIth dyn. Carro, no 6138).[8]

In spite of the traditional posture proportions of the figure of Isismyste do not coincide with the canonical system. His figure is massive, heavy, some parts of the figure are not proportionately related to the whole — the feet are clumsy and too short, the hands are too tiny. The head is exaggerated in size, the torso is shortened.

The same way of representation we can observe in the funeral stele of Isismyste from Schêch Abâde (Antinoë) which is dated back to the 4th century —

[7] Ibid., Abb. 75.
[8] K. Lange, M. Hirmer, *Ägypten,* München 1967, Taf. 78.

3. The funeral stele of a woman. Limestone, Pushkin Fine Arts
Museum. Stele from Fayum

4. The round statue of the judge of Bes XXVI dyn. Gubbencian, Lisbon (draught)

$OB = r$ $r''' = \frac{1}{4} AO = BO'$
d of the face $= 2 r' = \frac{2}{3} 40 = \frac{1}{7} \sqrt{3}$

$\frac{AB}{OB} = \frac{OB}{AO} = \Phi$

$r = \frac{1}{2} OB$
$r' = \frac{1}{5} \sqrt{3}$, $r'' = \frac{1}{2} \sqrt{3}$
$h_{head} = \frac{1}{2} \sqrt{2}$

5. The stele of Isismyste. Recklinghausen, Iconenmuseum (draught)

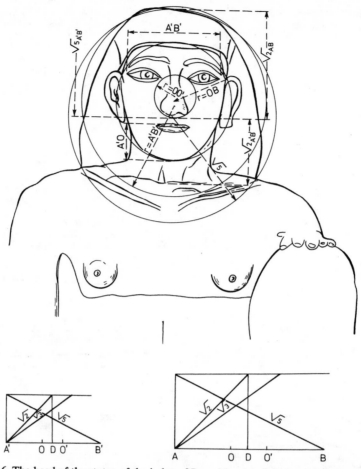

6. The head of the statue of the judge of Bes with geometrical constructions
(draft)

painted limestone.[9] This stele is executed according to the same proportional pattern. The young boy who was devoted to the cult of Isis Goddess has some iconographical features like Harpokrat. These two figures of Isismyste are executed in the same posture, which we can consider to be ritual one. The deformation is used as the intentional way of expression.

The proportions of the above figures are based on the golden section. The height of the head of Bes-statue (fig. 4) is $\frac{2}{3}$ of the small segment ($\frac{2}{3}$ AO). The head of Isismyste (fig. 5) equals $\frac{1}{2}\sqrt{2}$. Up to the level of eyebrows the figure is within the circumference with the radius $\frac{1}{2}\sqrt{3}$, just when the canonical figure of Bes with its upper limit at the

top of the nose and the lowest at the lying knee is within the circle of radius AO (the small segment of section AB in the golden section).

So the borrowing of a traditional type does not mean an adherence to canonical rules as a system. The interval between the outer corners of the eyes (AB) is the basis of all geometrical constructions (figs 6, 7). This interval (the departure of construction) is narrow for Isismyste's face; the same interval of the Bes statue is correspondingly larger due to the cosmetic lines running from the eyelids. The features of Isismyste's face are generalized but they are too concrete and recognizable to be just symbols or the signs, and at the same time they are too abstract to be a portrait. As for the meaning of attributes, they were ultimately adopted by Christian art — the bird and grape are both the symbols of ancient Egyptian art and of Coptic art. The grape is the symbol of Osiris — of Resur-

---

[9] M.W. Müller, *Die Ägyptische Sammlung des Bayerischen Staates*, München 1966, ÄS 4860, 103.

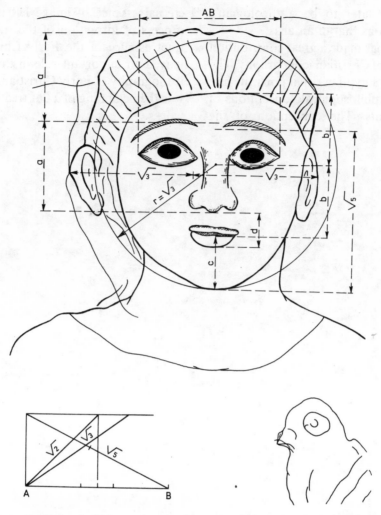

7. The head of Isismyste's stele with geometrical constructions (draft)

rection, the bird may be associated with the Horus image — the son of Isis; the Goddess Isis is the patroness of the deseased, her name is part of the name of Isis — myste. The chaplet on the head of the woman with a palm branch is identical with the ritual wreath of the Fayum portraits.

The transformation of Egyptian religious imagery and symbolism presents invaluable material as far as "contacts" between the pre-Christian era and the Christian world are concerned.[10] That is why I analyse the character of the interaction between Egyptian artistic modes of expression, including the canon, and Christian iconography.

The faces of the overwhelming majority of Coptic stelae are not the portraits, although some of them are executed in the same proportions as the ancient Egyptian faces of the classical epochs — see for example the head of the female Coptic bust — the size of its head is $2\sqrt{3}$. It has a round face within the circle of radius $\sqrt{3}$ — it is the canonical size. In spite of the canonical structure of proportions the face of the Coptic bust lacks the expression of the ancient Egyptian portraits and the spirituality which is the characteristic feature of Christian monuments of the mature period.

Early Coptic ritual stelae did not follow the Egyptian canon very closely: the proportions of stelae do not make up a regular system. The golden section still forms the basis of the composition of stelae. It was not a purely theological system

[10] N. Pomerantseva, "The Iconography of the Christian Paintings of Nubia (Frescoes of Faras 8th–10th cent. A.D.)", in: *Nubian Studies*, Cambridge 1978, pp. 198, 203.

therefore, it turned later to be a theologian's abstraction as much as that of an artist.

Thus Coptic Egypt has made a great contribution to the development of Christian iconography. The traditions of ancient Egyptian ritual portraits had greatly affected the philosophical conceptions of Christian monuments. The conception of the eternal essence of image left its imprint on the process of formation of the transcendental, abstract essence of the Early Christian icon which played an important role in the formation of the iconography of Early Christian ritual sculpture; it was the beginning of a flat treatment of sculptural works.

COPTIC STUDIES

Marguerite Rassart-Debergh

Les peintures des Kellia (Missions de 1981 à 1983)

Comme on le sait depuis quelques années déjà, la région maréotique (au sud d'Alexandrie) constitue l'un des foyers du monachisme égyptien primitif [1] (figs 1–2).

Depuis 20 ans, des fouilles (parfois interrompues à cause de la situation politique au Proche-Orient) ont été menées sur le site des Kellia, à mi-chemin entre les couvents de Nitrie et ceux de Scété [2]. Malgré leur nombre, les peintures découvertes dans les différents monastères n'ont guère suscité l'enthousiasme. Il faut bien avouer que la peinture copte antérieure aux IXe/Xe siècles a toujours été quelque peu négligée : on ne retint, à Baouît ou à Saqqara par exemple, que les scènes figurées, et plus spécialement les fameuses absides où l'on voit la Vierge et l'Enfant (avec des fondateurs, des saints, les archanges Michel et Gabriel, les Apôtres) et la *Maiestas Domini*. Pour le reste, motifs géométriques ou floraux, et humbles portraits de moines ont à peine retenu l'attention. Que dire alors des peintures des Kellia ? Lorsque le regretté Abbé Leroy entreprit la publication du *Corpus* de la peinture copte, auquel son non reste attaché [3], il décida de ne pas s'attacher à cette peinture de « caractère généralement funéraire et traitée selon les lois de la peinture hellénistique et romaine » (p. XVI). Il bâtit donc son programme de recherche en « négligeant les barbouillis qui, ici et là, font leur apparition sur les murs de certains monuments, comme aux Kellia ou dans les ermitages d'Esna, œuvres qui témoignent plus de la piété que de l'habileté artistique de leurs auteurs », s'en tenant « uniquement aux représentations visiblement faites selon les lois iconographiques retenues » (p. XV).

Ayant obtenu du professeur Kasser la généreuse autorisation de dresser un *corpus* des peintures des Kellia, je fis part de cette intention à l'Abbé Leroy qui marqua malgré tout quelque intérêt pour ce répertoire des premières peintures coptes, pont entre le paganisme et le christianisme.

[1] Evariste Breccia qui était, au début de ce siècle, directeur du Musée Gréco-Romain d'Alexandrie insistait sur la richesse de l'endroit et écrivait : « la région maréotique n'est pas riche en monuments imposants, mais elle est parsemée de ruines qui présentent un réel intérêt « (cf. E. Breccia, *Le Musée gréco-romain d'Alexandrie 1925–1931*, Rome 1970, éd. anast. de l'éd. de Bergame 1932, 56). Dans ce sens, il fit de nombreux sondages dans la région, effectua une fouille à Abou Girgeh, ainsi qu'aux Qouçoûr Isa et s'intéressa à Abou Ménas, cf. E. Breccia, *Rapport sur la marche du Service du Musée en 1912*, Alexandrie 1912, 3–14 ; id., *Alexandrea ad Aegyptum. Guide de la ville ancienne et moderne et du Musée Gréco-Romain*, Bergame 1914, 285–286. On verra également M. Rassart-Debergh, « Peintures coptes de la région maréotique : Abou Girgeh et Alam Shaltout », dans : *Annuaire de l'Institut de Philologie et d'Histoire Orientales et Slaves*, Bruxelles, 26 (1982), 91–107.

[2] *Kellia I. Kom 219. Fouilles exécutées en 1964–1965*, sous la direction de F. Daumas et A. Guillaumont, fasc. 1, Le Caire 1969 (cité : *Kellia I, Kom 219*) ; *Kellia 1965. Topographie générale, mensuration et fouilles aux Qouçoûr el-Abîd, mensurations aux Qouçoûr el-Izeila. Première expédition archéologique de l'Université de Genève au site copte appelé Kellia, en Basse-Égypte* occidentale, sous la direction de R. Kasser, Genève 1967 = *Recherches Suisses d'Archéologie Copte*, I (cité : *Kellia, Recherches I*) ; *Kellia, Topographie* par R. Kasser, Genève 1972 = *Recherches Suisses d'Archéologie Copte II* (cité : *Kellia, Recherches II*) ; *Kellia. La poterie copte. Quatre siècle d'artisanat et d'échanges en Basse-Égypte*, par M. Egloff, 2 vols, Genève 1977 = *Recherches Suisses d'Archéologie Copte*, III (cité : *Kellia, Recherches III*) ; *Survey Archeologique des Kellia (Basse-Égypte). Rapport de la campagne 1981*, 2 vols Louvain–Leuven 1983 = *EK 8184. Projet International de Sauvetage scientifique des Kellia. Mission Suisse d'Archéologie Copte de l'Université de Genève*, sous la direction de R. Kasser (cité : *Kellia, Survey, 1981*) ; R.G. Coquin, « Campagne de fouilles aux Kellia. Rapports préliminaires », dans : *Bulletin de l'Institut Français d'Archéologie Orientale 80* Le Caire (1980), 347–368 ; (1981) 159–188 ; 82 (1982), 363–377 (cité : Coquin, *Rapports préliminaires*).

[3] Jules Leroy, *La peinture murale chez les Coptes, I : Les peintures des couvents du désert d'Esna*, Le Caire 1975, MIFAO XCIV ; id., II : *Les peintures des couvents de Ouadi Natroun*, Le Caire 1983 (= MIFAO CI).

Son œuvre est maintenant poursuivie par ses collaborateurs et Paul van Moorsel qui présentera, à ce Congrès, le programme des volumes à venir.

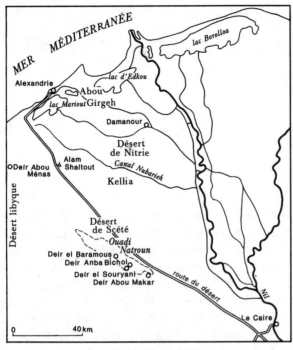

1. Carte de la région maréotique

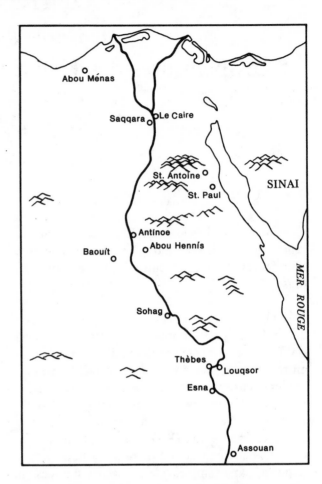

2. Carte d'Égypte avec les sites mentionnés (d'après K. Wessel, *L'art copte*, Bruxelles 1964, p. 242)

Les trois dernières campagnes de fouilles[4] ont confirmé les premières constatations et hypothèses et, en même temps, ont élargi considérablement le registre des iconographies attestées aux Kellia.

Aux Kellia, comme à Abou Ménas où fouille notre collègue Peter Grossmann[5], la présence de spécialistes de la peinture marque une volonté d'aborder d'une manière totalement renouvelée cet important chapitre de l'histoire de l'art copte. Notre volonté est de nous pencher autant sur les aspects « humains » (thèmes, style, interprétations historique et théologique) que techniques. Ces découvertes récentes, comme celles de Grossmann à Abou Ménas, permettent une nouvelle approche de la peinture copte : une vision technique qui jusqu'ici a été complètement

---

[4] La campagne de 1981 a déjà été publiée (cf. supra, note 2 : *Kellia, Survey,* 1981). Le rapport de celle de 1982, basé sur les mêmes principes de *Survey* est prêt à partir à l'imprimerie. Des articles ont signalé immédiatement les principales découvertes de 82 : les premiers ont paru dans la *Tribune de Genève* du 10 décembre 1982, p. 11 et dans le *Journal d'Yverdon* du 4 janvier 1983, p. 6. On verra aussi M. Rassart-Debergh, « Des sables de l'Égypte renaît un art chrétien », dans : *Connaissance des Arts,* 382, Lausanne, décembre 1983, 62–67 (cité : Rassart-Debergh, *Connaissance des Arts*); M. Rassart-Debergh, « Le thème de la croix sur les peintures murales des Kellia : entre l'Égypte et la Nubie chrétiennes », dans : les actes de la Fifth International Conference of the Society for Nubian Studies Heidelberg, 20–25th September 1982, Nubische Studien 1986, 363–366.

Un colloque vient de se tenir à Genève afin de faire la mise au point de nos connaissances, mais aussi des nombreux problèmes que soulève le site (les actes du colloque devraient paraître au printemps 1985); à l'occasion de cette rencontre, un petit volume a été publié : *Le site monastique des Kellia (Basse-Égypte), Recherches des années 1981–1983,* Louvain 1984.

[5] Si les publications ont été nombreuses dès le début des fouilles, on est peu renseigné sur les peintures qui ornaient les divers édifices de cet ensemble monumental. La plupart sont encore inédites et les ouvrages généraux de C.M. Kaufmann n'en parlent guère. Je dois à l'amitié de Peter Grossmann de connaître leur existence, d'avoir vu le maximum des photos prises au fur et à mesure des découvertes, ainsi que les fragments conservés dans le musée du site.

Dieter Ohlhorst est occupé à séparer les couches superposées (parfois au nombre de 4), à nettoyer les fragments, à tenter de les reconstituer et de les consolider. On verra la mise au point que P. Grossmann publie dans l'encyclopédie copte en cours d'élaboration (s.v. « Saint-Ménas »).

négligée. Généralement les ouvrages consacrés à la peinture murale antique ne donnent que de maigres indications sur la peinture copte [6]; on suppose que les Coptes poursuivent la façon de faire de la période pharaonique [7], à laquelle s'ajoutent les apports gréco-romains [8]. Aux Kellia on a la possibilité d'étudier sur pièce les matériaux, la manière de les traiter, les ustensiles...

Sans doute, J. Clédat [9] et A. Gayet [10] avaient déjà émis quelques considérations, tandis que P. van Moorsel et M. Huybers notaient diverses constatations à propos de peintures provenant du couvent de St Jérémie à Saqqara [11].

Aux Kellia, comme ailleurs, les peintures souffrent sitôt qu'elles retrouvent l'air libre, vent et soleil s'allient pour altérer la couche picturale : le vent l'écaille, le soleil dessèche les liants, les sels affleurent sous l'effet de l'humidité de l'aube et la chaleur de la journée [12].

L'analyse de quelques fragments ramassés sur le sol est actuellement en cours à l'Institut Royal du Patrimoine Artistique à Bruxelles, afin de déterminer la matière des liants, des pigments et des supports [13].

Déjà, une simple vision au binoculaire aide à déterminer les types de pinceaux et de spatules, et à comprendre la préparation de l'enduit (dans de rares cas, la couleur appliquée sur le fond encore humide a produit une réaction chimique, de sorte que l'on pourrait parler de « fresques accidentelles »); on constate aussi la multiplication des nuances soit par la superposition de couleurs, soit par un subtil mélange de teintes de bases; quant au fond, tantôt il a été simplement brossé, tantôt au contraire, il a soigneusement été taloché [14] (fig. 3). A ces remarques faites en laboratoire, s'ajoutent celles faites directement sur place. Ainsi peut-on remarquer l'existence par endroits de plusieurs couches superposées. Ce n'est certes pas une nouveauté; Clédat [15], tout comme Gayet [16] avaient constaté qu'au cours des occupations successives des cellules, les moines avaient parfois recouvert la peinture initiale, en totalité ou partiellement [17], d'un lait de chaux pour y peindre ensuite de nouveaux motifs; la chose est fréquente aux Kellia également [18].

Une étude attentive des motifs floraux et géométriques conduit à des affirmations plus neuves et

---

[6] P. Mora et P. Phillipot, *Technique et conservation des peintures murales,* Rome 1977, notamment pp. 90–92, 116 et 126.

[7] A. Lucas, *Ancient Egyptian Materials and Industries,* Londres, 4ᵉ éd. revue par Harris, 1962, 338–366; A. Mekhitarian, *La peinture égyptienne,* Genève 1954.

[8] Une mise au point des apports de ces différentes techniques a été tentée par R.J. Forbes: R.J. Forbes, *Studies in Ancient Technology* III, Leyde 1955, pp. 202–255, not. 238–243 et 247–248.

[9] J. Clédat, *Le Monastère et la nécropole de Baouît* 1, Le Caire 1904, (MIFAO 12), par exemple p. 33.

[10] A. Gayet, *L'art copte. École d'Alexandrie — Architecture monastique. Sculpture–Peinture, Art Somptuaire,* Paris 1902, 254–286, not. 254–259.

[11] P. van Moorsel et M. Huijbers, « Repertory of the Preserved Wallpaintings from the Monastery of Apa Jeremiah at Saqqara », dans: *Coptica = Acta ad Archaeologiam et Artium Historiam Pertinentia* IX, 1981, 125–186, not. 179–180 (Some remarks about technique and colours).

[12] Quelques essais ont été faits sur le site afin de tenter de préserver les peintures (cf. Dieter Ohlhorst, « Wissenschaftliche Grabung und Restaurierung », dans: *Kellia, Survey,* 1981, cité note 2, pp. 67–70). Les peintures détachées et traitées ont été transportées au Musée Copte du Caire.

[13] Ce m'est un agréable devoir de remercier ici Madame Masschelijn, actuelle conservatrice et Messieurs Kockart, Marijnissen et Savko grâce à qui ces recherches sont possibles.

[14] Un premier aperçu a été présenté au cours du Colloque de Genève: M. Rassart-Debergh, *Les grands thèmes de la peinture Kelliote; ses sources d'inspiration, sa place dans la peinture copte antérieure au Xᵉ siècle.*

[15] Il remarque à propos de la chapelle VII: « les restaurateurs n'avaient fait que recouvrir les fresques d'un lait de chaux qui, nettoyé avec soin, laissait reparaître les peintures tout aussi fraîches et tout aussi brillantes de coloris que si elles n'avaient reçu aucun enduit. Ce procédé de restauration a été employé dans diverses salles et s'il peut être critiqué, il vaut certainement mieux que celui qui a pour but d'enlever le premier enduit de plâtre peint pour en placer un nouveau qui n'a conservé que sa couleur blanche. Dans le procédé de blanchissement à la chaux, on peut, avec un peu de patience, faire revenir à la lumière des fragments de peinture qu'on chercherait vainement à faire revenir de l'autre... », cf. Clédat, *Le Monastère...* (cité note 9), p. 33.

[16] « Sur les vieilles fresques de l'église primitive à peine écaillée (*sic*) le beau zèle de quelques dévots posa une couche d'enduit, sur lequel s'étendit une nouvelle composition. Cette seconde fresque, qu'elle ait été ou non l'œuvre d'un maître, commençait-elle à pâlir, un autre dévot croyait faire œuvre pie, que de la recouvrir à son tour, si bien qu'aujourd'hui, il est difficile, pour ne pas dire impossible, de rétablir l'heure de la pose, aux Iᵉʳ s. de l'ère copte... », Gayet, *L'art copte...* (cité note 10), p. 256.

[17] Le même procédé apparaît au Monastère de Saqqara, dans la cellule A: M. Rassart-Debergh et J. Debergh, « A propos de trois peintures de Saqqara », dans: *Coptica* (cité note 11), pp. 187–204, not. 187–192.

[18] Notre collègue Jan Partyka a constaté qu'aux Kellia, ce sont avant tous les personnages qui ont été recouverts d'un lait de chaux; ils ont parfois aussi été martelés ou grattés. Ces faits l'ont amené à se demander si on n'était pas face à des preuves

3. Kellia, Qouçoûr er-Roubâ'îyât, kôm 306, salle 5, mur est; détail
montrant la préparation du support (d'après diapositive de l'auteur)

éclaire d'un jour nouveau les connaissances techniques des artisans[19]. Ainsi, à maints endroits, on
s'aperçoit qu'un motif qui se répète tout au long
des parois a été réalisé au pochoir; il s'agit d'une
frise de triangles évidés, séparés par des plantes :
une même portion est reproduite sans aucune
variante (fig. 4). Ailleurs le dessin préalable
apparaît soit incisé soit peint; ainsi, les lignes
maîtresses : verticales et obliques, déterminent-
-elles le mouvement des veines dans les vastes
panneaux imitant les plaques de marbre (fig. 5). Ou
encore, le centre de cercles a été marqué à l'aide
d'une pointe (fig. 6); l'artisan a-t-il utilisé une sorte

de compas, ou plus simplement a-t-il fixé une
pointe d'où partait une corde, ce qui lui permettait
de tracer des cercles réguliers? En vérité, les deux
méthodes se retrouvent dans nos peintures.
Ces quelques constatations montrent que le
peintre connaissait bien les matériaux, qu'il dispo-
sait de divers outils dont il usait en fonction du
résultat souhaité; elles témoignent d'une certaine
maîtrise de la matière, ce qui a déjà été constaté en
architecture.
Abandonnons l'aspect technique pour passer rapidement en revue les motifs.
En deux mots, on peut dire que le mode de

d'iconoclasme. C'est là une séduisante hypothèse de travail qui mérite de plus amples recherches. On verra, à propos de cette
crise que traversa l'Empire Byzantin entre 726 et 843, la remarquable synthèse d'André Grabbar : A. Grabbar, *L'iconoclasme
Byzantin. Le dossier archéologique,* Paris 1957; 2ᵉ éd. revue et augmentée, Paris 1984 (coll. *Idées et Recherches* dirigée par F.
Bonnefoy).

[19] S. Favre, *L'artisanat aux Kellia* dans les actes du Colloque de Genève. Par ailleurs, on consultera avec profit les nombreux
articles relatifs aux travaux que nos collègues polonais ont consacrés aux peintures de Faras. Rappelons que près de la moitié
ont été nettoyées et restaurées ici et sont conservées dans une aile, qui leur est totalement consacrée, du Musée National de
Varsovie.

4. Kellia, Qouçoûr el-'Izeila; frises de motifs géométriques et floraux (calques de l'auteur, d'après Kellia, Survey 1981, p. 312, pl. CLXXVI)

5. Kellia, Qouçoûr el-'Izeila, kôm 45, « église »; plaque peinte imitant des marches (calque de l'auteur, d'après Kellia, Survey 1981, p. 304, pl. CLXVIII)

20 cm

6. Kellia, Qouçoûr el-'Izeila, kôm 11, salle 00; motif géométrique avec cercles marqués à l'aide d'une pointe (d'après Kellia, Survey 1981, p. 324, pl. CLXXXVIII)

décoration auquel on avait recouru habituellement, est sans conteste la peinture. Selon une technique fréquente dans l'art hellénistico-romain [20], elle sert à évoquer, par des jeux de lignes et de couleurs, les pierres précieuses ou rares (comme le marbre) que les moines ne pouvaient se procurer qu'avec difficulté. Elle remplace les mosaïques auxquelles elle emprunte d'ailleurs nombre de motifs et dessine des tapis sur le sol des pièces ou sur les tablettes des niches. Elle est présente dans presque toutes les pièces. Là, elle souligne le soubassement rouge pompéien de lignes, frises géométriques ou tresses. Ailleurs, elle évoque une flore et une faune variées [21].

Baouît et Saqqara nous ont laissé l'impression que la faune et la flore étaient rares dans les peintures. L'une ou l'autre gazelle, des paons à Baouît, ou encore quelques feuillages séparant les files de moines [22]; moins encore à Saqqara: un aigle sur des feuillages, quelques plantes autour d'une croix [23]. Les Kellia offrent au contraire un répertoire extraordinaire et d'une énorme recherche. La flore variée mêle les éléments réels (pampres de vigne — fig. 7 — palmiers, grenades, cactées, succulentes) et inventés. La faune méritera des recherches ultérieures, lorsque le *corpus* complet sera terminé, afin de voir si on peut recréer le contexte animalier dans lequel évoluaient les moines. A côté de sujets communs à tout le monde chrétien et dont la symbolique est bien connue: paons ou colombes, seuls ou affrontés autour d'un canthare ou d'une croix, sujet déjà connu à Baouît [24] et surtout dans les ermitages d'Esna [25], on trouve également des perdrix, des perroquets, des chevaux, des girafes, des camélidés, des cer-vidés, des lions, des lièvres, des poissons de tout type (fig. 8).

Les personnages ne sont pas absents de nos peintures: guerriers, moines et saints dessinés d'un trait rapide dans la plupart des cas. Cet ensemble atteste un art populaire, souvent plein d'humour, qu'on néglige souvent de voir, préoccupé que l'on est de rechercher les scènes en connection avec la théologie, le culte... Les rapports de fouilles de Baouît et de Saqqara mentionnent nombre de peintures rapides, « mal faites » qui ne furent même pas documentées [26]. Les Kellia sont donc la seule possibilité d'appréhender cet art où les moines aiment se représenter dans leurs occupations journalières.

Des peintures qui satisfont d'avantage l'historien d'art et le théologien furent également trouvées au cours des différentes campagnes: têtes de saints ou du Christ en médaillon (fig. 9) (la chose est bien connue à Baouît et à Saqqara), saints en pied comme le célèbre Ménas dont le couvent est voisin, ou comme les saints militaires proches par l'iconographie du beau guerrier de Faras (Georges?) conservé au Musée de Varsovie [27]. Pas de Vierge à l'Enfant jusqu'à présent, mais les fouilles ne sont point terminées.

Deux motifs toutefois sont particulièrement bien représentés aux Kellia: les bateaux et la croix [28]. Il n'est pas nécessaire de rappeler ici la signification eschatologique du bateau. Dessiné dans la niche orientale de l'oratoire, il revêt évidemment un aspect symbolique. Mais d'autres vaisseaux sont peints à larges traits rapides ou au contraire avec un luxe de détails tel qu'on en pourrait déterminer le type [29].

---

[20] M. Rassart-Debergh, « Survivances de l'hellénistico romain dans la peinture copte (antérieure au IXᵉ s.) » dans: *Graeco-Arabica*, II, Athènes 1983, 227–247 (= Actes du *First Internationnal Congress on Greek and Arabic Studies — June 19–24, 1983*).

[21] J'ai déjà insisté maintes fois sur la richesse et la variété de la faune et de la flore, cf. Rassart-Debergh, *Connaissance des Arts* (cité note 4).

[22] Par exemple dans les chapelles XVII et XXXVII. M. Rassart-Debergh, « La peinture copte avant le XIᵉ siècle. Une approche », dans: *Coptica* (cité note 11), pp. 221–285, not. 251–255, avec bibliographie antérieure.

[23] Dans la chambre 728: M. Rassart-Debergh, « La décoration picturale du Monastère de Saqqara, Essai de reconstitution », dans: *Coptica* (cité note 11), pp. 9–124, not. 94–97 et figs 45–46.

[24] Ainsi dans la chapelle XIX où des paons s'affrontent autour d'une croix et où des pampres de vigne hissent des canthares cf. Clédat, *Le Monastère*... (cité note 9), fasc. 2, pls LXXIX–LXXX II.

[25] S. Sauneron, J. Jacquet et al., *Les ermitages chrétiens du désert d'Esna*. I *Archéologie et inscriptions*, Le Caire 1972 (= FIFAO XXIX, 1), not. pp. 72–77, figs 42–44, pl. XXVII.

[26] M. Rassart-Debergh, « Quelques remarques iconographiques sur la peinture chrétienne à Saqqara », dans: *Coptica* (cité note 11), pp. 207–220, not. 219; ead., « La peinture copte... » (cité note 22), p. 279.

[27] *Le site monastique*... (cité note 4), pp. 29–38, not. figs 21–22.

[28] J'ai déjà eu l'occasion de présenter à Heidelberg, en 1982, les types de croix des Kellia. Les trouvailles postérieures n'ont en rien modifié ce que l'on savait déjà, cf. Rassart-Debergh, « Le thème de la croix... » (cité note 4, not. figs 16–18).

[29] *Le site monastique*... (cité note 4), not. fig. 20.

7. Kellia, Qouçoûr el-'Izeila; motifs floraux et pampres (calques de l'auteur, d'après Kellia, Survey 1981, p. 310, pl. CLXXIV)

8. Kellia, Qouçoûr er-Roubâ'îyât, kôm 306, salle 2, mur sud (reconstruction des décors par l'auteur sur des élévations de Giorgio Nogara)

Il importe de noter la profusion de croix aux Kellia. Elles apparaissent partout. Avec un sens prophylactique, la croix se place sur une voûte, une réparation peu sûre, fragile, par ex. près d'une porte... Signe de piété, elle accompagne, précède ou conclut, les nombreuses inscriptions [30]. Surtout, elle orne la niche orientale des oratoires où elle se substitue aux fameuses représentations de Baouît et de Saqqara [31], étudiées de manière pénétrante par le prof. van Moorsel [32].

Notons encore que la niche des Kellia est mise en valeur par une exubérante végétation, où se mêlent boutons pourpres et tiges verdoyantes (fig. 10); un tel décor est absent à Baouît et à Saqqara.

A quelques exceptions près, les croix des Kellia sont toutes des croix de procession et se dressent fièrement sur un haute hampe.Elles sont également gemmées et parées de joyaux qui les rehaussent de mille feux, tout comme les pendentifs (clochettes, encensoirs, lampes, ...) aux couleurs chatoyantes que des chaînettes d'or maintiennent suspendus à leurs branches. En cela, elles se distinguent des croix de Baouît [33], de Saqqara [34] et d'Esna [35], et se rapprochent par contre des croix de Nubie.

Je voudrais d'ailleurs terminer par l'analyse plus particulière de deux ensembles qui trouvent leur parallèle direct en Nubie.

La conque de la niche orientale de l'oratoire du Kôm 14, aux Qoucoûr el-ʿIzeila, présentait une peinture déjà quasi détruite lors de la découverte. Une étude patiente et un assemblage minutieux

m'ont permis d'identifier un Christ en buste bénissant d'une main et tenant le livre saint de l'autre. Ce motif, courant à Baouît et à Saqqara [36], est jusqu'à présent, un *unicum* aux Kellia [37]. Sur les parois latérales, on voyait des moines (peut-être des fondateurs ou les titulaires?) à la tête bouclée, aux longs vêtements blanc et or et aux pieds chaussés de noir. Sur la paroi du fond se détachaient, devant un portique, trois légionnaires que l'auréole encandrant les boucles brunes de leur chevelure identifient sans nul doute comme des saints militaires [38] (fig. 11).

Si ces derniers sont légion dans le monde copte, ils diffèrent ici du schéma traditionnel qui se plaît à les montrer à cheval, terrassant le Mal sous son aspect animal ou humain [39]. Ils sont ici debout, appuyés sur leur lance, vêtus du costume romain classique [40] et ne tuent ni menacent un quelconque ennemi. Je ne connais qu'un exemple analogue, malheureusement fort abîmé: un saint provenant d'Abou Girgeh, non loin des Kellia, et conservé au Musée Gréco-Romain d'Alexandrie [41].

La représentation la plus proche, c'est à Faras que nous la trouvons: un saint Georges (?) en pied, portant le même vêtement militaire. Mais ce dernier renoue avec l'iconographie classique car, de sa lance, il transperce un démon [42] (fig. 12).

Le second ensemble est constitué par des croix aux branches formées de palmes et à l'intersection desquelles se trouvait un médaillon [43]; l'état de ce dernier ne permet point de dire avec certitude si

---

[30] Ibid., figs 25–28.

[31] *Le site monastique*... (cité note 4), pp. 29 et 32, figs 16–18; M. Rassart-Debergh, « Fouilles récentes aux Kellia. Leur apport à la connaissance de l'art copte », dans: *Annales d'Histoire de l'Art et d'Archéologie* de l'Université Libre de Bruxelles VI, 1984, pp. 23–44, not. 38, voir aussi supra, note 28.

[32] P. van Moorsel, « The Coptic Apse-Composition and Its Living Creatures », dans: *Études Nubiennes. Colloque de Chantilly, 2–6 juillet 1975,* Le Caire 1978, pp. 325–333 (= Bibliothèque d'Étude IFAO, 77).

[33] Les croix ne sont pas nombreuses à Baouît, elles sont encadrées d'oiseaux (supra, note 24) ou de fleurs (chapelle 5 par ex. cf. J. Maspero, *Fouilles exécutées à Baouît*; *notes mises en ordre et éditées* par E. Drioton, Le Caire 1943 (= MIFAO 52,2) not. pl. XIV.

[34] P. van Moorsel, « The Worship of the Holy Cross in Saqqara: Archaeological Evidence », dans: *Theologia Crucissignum crucis — Festschrift für Erich Dinkler zum 70 Geburstag,* Tübingen 1979, pp. 409–415; M. Rassart-Debergh, « Quelques remarques... » (cité note 26), pp. 218–219.

[35] Sauneron, Jacquet et al., « Les ermitages... » (cité note 25), pp. 64–72.

[36] Supra, note 32.

[37] On a trouvé plusieurs figures de Christ mais celle-ci est la seule à orner la conque de la niche orientale de l'oratoire. Supra note 27, not. fig. 21; Rassart-Debergh, « Fouilles récentes... » (cité note 31), pp. 40–41.

[38] Supra, note 27, not. fig. 22.

[39] Rassart-Debergh, « La peinture copte... » (cité note 22), not. 276.

[40] S'il n'y avait pas d'auréole, on les prendrait pour des militaires de haut rang, non pour des saints.

[41] Rassart-Deberght, « Peintures coptes... » (cité note 1), pl. II, b, fig. 2,2 et p. 100. A Baouît, sur une colonne était peint un saint Georges, militaire, mais le geste qu'il a de la lance invite à penser qu'il menaçait un ennemi (cf. Leroy, *La peinture murale...,* cité note 3), pl. IV, B.

[42] K. Michałowski, *Faras Wall Paintings in the Collection of the National Museum in Warsaw,* Varsovie 1974, pp. 116–118.

[43] *Kellia, Survey,* 1981 (cité note 2), pls CL XXXIV–V.

9. Kellia, Qouçoûr er-Roubâ'îyât, kôm 306, salle 2, mur est; Christ en buste (cliché M.S.A.C. Genève)

10. Kellia, Qouçoûr er-Roubâ'îyât, kôm 258, salle 4, mur est (cliché M.S.A.C. Genève)

11. Kellia, Qouçoûr el-'Izeila, kôm 14, mur est de l'oratoire: détail des saints militaires (cliché M.S.A.C. Genève)

13. Kellia, Qouçoûr er-Roubâ'îyât, kôm 219, chambre XII: Christ d'après Kellia I, kôm 219, pl. XXXIXC

12. Faras, Cathédrale: saint militaire
(cliché J. Debergh)

14. Faras, Cathédrale: Théophanie nubienne (d'après
K. Michałowski, Faras, Die Kathedrale, p. 87)

l'intérieur était ou non orné d'une figure. Mais il n'est pas inutile de rappeler que c'est aux Kellia que fut trouvé un motif qui me paraît l'ancêtre des théophanies nubiennes. C'est certes avec raison que des chercheurs, parmi lesquels on mentionnera tout spécialement Paul van Moorsel[44], ont rapproché les fameuses croix de Nubie des absides de Baouît et de Saqqara, ainsi que d'ampoules syro-palestiniennes. Mais la croix trouvée il y a près de vingt ans aux Qouçoûr er-Roubâîyât s'y apparente également et constitue, dans la peinture copte, un intéressant *hapax*.

Au centre d'une croix gemmée, que drape un tissu pourpre, se trouve le Christ en buste, tenant le livre et bénissant[45] (fig. 13). Il s'agit là d'un motif extrêmement rare dans l'ensemble du monde chrétien : je ne connais que trois représentations proches, mais non identiques. Deux sont des mosaïques, respectivement des VIe et VIIe siècles, la troisième une peinture qui leur est contemporaine.

Sur la mosaïque de la conque absidale de Sant'Apollinare in Classe à Ravenne[46], le visage d'un Christ barbu, auréolé de perles, apparaît au centre d'une croix gemmée. A Santo Stefano Rotondo, à Rome, dans la chapelle des saints Prime et Félicien, on voyait, au-dessus d'une croix scintillante de pierreries, le buste du Christ[47]. Dans les deux cas, la croix et le Christ sont associés, mais leur représentation diffère fortement de ce que l'on voit aux Kellia et en Nubie.

Plus proches sont les deux peintures ornant l'oratoire des Quarante Martyrs (égyptiens) à Santa Maria Antica sur le Forum romain : les croix gemmées et parées de guirlandes contiennent une couronne dans laquelle s'inscrit la tête du Christ[48].

Si ces trois représentations peuvent être rapprochées des théophanies nubiennes, on notera toutefois qu'en Italie, seuls le visage et le haut des épaules du Christ apparaissent dans le médaillon, alors qu'aux Kellia, c'est le Christ bénissant tel qu'il figure dans la mandorle portée par les Quatre Vivants au centre des croix nubiennes[49] (fig. 14). J'espère avoir, par cette modeste contribution, attiré l'attention sur un aspect des peintures des Kellia, comme charnière entre les arts copte et nubien.

---

[44] P. van Moorsel, « Une théophanie nubienne », dans : *Miscellanea in onore di E. Josi*, I (= Riv. di Arch. Christ 42 (1966), 267–316.

[45] *Kellia I, Kom 219*, p. 24, 47–49, pl. XXXIXC.

[46] E. Dinkler, *Das Apsismosaik von S. Appolinare in Classe*, Cologne 1964, pp. 50, 77–100; G. Bovini, *Edifici di culta d'eta paleocristiana nel territorio ravenate di Classe*, Bologne 1969, pp. 76–79, fig. 24.

[47] G. Matthiae, *Le chiese di Roma dal IV al X secolo*, Bologne 1962, pp. 210–211, fig. 109.

[48] W. de Gruneisen, *Sainte Marie Antique*, Rome 1911, pl. LVII.

[49] K. Michałowski, *Faras, Wall Paintings...* (cité note 42), pp. 234–240.

COPTIC STUDIES

Michel Roberge

Chute et remontée du *Pneuma* dans la *Paraphrase de Sem*

La *Paraphrase de Sem*, premier traité du septième codex de Nag Hammadi [1], développe dans ses vingt-quatre premières pages une cosmogonie dont on a souligné à bon droit l'originalité, mais dont on n'a pas encore tout à fait réussi à démêler l'écheveau d'épisodes qui la composent. Les chercheurs qui se sont jusqu'à présent intéressés à ce texte ont préféré s'attaquer à des problèmes d'ordre plus général, comme par exemple les relations entre la *Paraphrase de Sem* et la *Paraphrase de Seth*, traité auquel renvoie Hippolyte et qu'il semble citer dans la première partie de sa notice sur les Séthiens (*Elenchos*, V, 19–22) [2], le genre littéraire de l'écrit et les différents aspects de sa composition [3], ses rapports avec le judaïsme, le christianisme ou le paganisme [4]. On a aussi abordé quelques points particuliers, tels la figure du Rédempteur [5] ou la polémique antibaptismale [6].

---

[1] Cf. *The Facsimile Edition of the Nag Hammadi Codices* published under the auspices of the Department of Antiquity of the Arab Republic of Egypt in conjunction with the UNESCO, Codex VII, Leiden 1972. Édition du texte copte et traduction allemende par M. Krause, « Die Paraphrase des Sêem », dans: *Christentum am Roten Meer*, ed. F. Altheim und R. Stiehl. Zweiter Band, erstes Buch: *Neue Texte*, 1. Kapitel, Berlin 1973, pp. 2–105; traduction anglaise par F. Wisse, *The Paraphrase of Shem* VII, 1, dans: *The Nag Hammadi Library in English*, General Editor J.M. Robinson, San Francisco 1977, pp. 308–328. Pour une présentation générale du traité cf. « Berliner Arbeitskreis für koptisch-gnostische Schriften, Die Bedeutung der Texte von Nag Hammadi für die moderne Gnosisforschung », dans: *Gnosis und Neues Testament*, éd. K.-W. Tröger, Berlin 1973, pp. 57–59; H.-M. Schenke, « Zur Faksimile-Ausgabe der Nag Hammadi Schriften », ZÄS 102 (1975), 123–138.

[2] Cf. F. Wisse, « The Redeemer Figure in the Paraphrase of Shem », NT 12 (1970), 130–140 (notamment 138 s.); C. Colpe, « Heidnische, jüdische und christliche Überlieferung in den Schriften aus Nag Hammadi II », JAC 16 (1973), 106–126; D.A. Bertrand, « Paraphrase de Sem et Paraphrase de Seth », dans: *Les textes de Nag Hammadi: Colloque du Centre d'Histoire des Religions de l'Université des Sciences Humaines de Strasbourg* (Strasbourg, 23–25 octobre 1974), éd. J.-É. Ménard, NHS VII, Leiden 1975, pp. 146–157; J.-M. Sevrin, « À propos de la Paraphrase de Sem », *Le Muséon* 88 (1975), 69–96; M. Krause, « Die Paraphrase des Sêem und des Bericht Hippolyts », dans: *Proceedings of the International Colloquium on Gnosticism* Stockholm, 20–25 août 1973, Stockholm 1977, pp. 101–110; M. Tardieu, « Les livres mis sous le nom de Seth et les Séthien de l'hérésiologie », dans: *Gnosis and Gnosticism: Papers read at the Seventh International Conference on Patristic Studies*, Oxford, 8–13 septembre 1975, éd. M. Krause, NHS VIII (Leiden 1977), 204–210.

[3] Cf. Wisse, « The Redeemer... », 130; B. Aland, « Die Paraphrase als Form gnostischer Verkündigung », dans: *Nag Hammadi and Gnosis: Papers Read at the First International Congress of Coptology*, Le Caire, 8–18 décembre 1976, éd. McLachlan Wilson, NHS XIV (Leiden 1978), 75–90; L. Abramowski, « Notizen zur 'Hypostase der Archonten' », éd. Bullard, ZNW 67 (1976), 280–285 (285). Sur la *Paraphrase de Sem* comme apocalypse, cf. P. Perkins, « The Rebellion Myth in Gnostic Apocalypses », dans: *Society of Biblical Literature 1978 Seminar Papers*, éd. P.J. Achtemeier, Missoula 1978, pp. 15–30; M. Krause, « Die literarische Gattungen der Apokalypsen von Nag Hammadi », dans: *Apocalypticism in the Mediterranean World and the Near East. Proceedings of the International Colloquium on Apocalypticism*, Uppsala, August 12–17, 1979, éd. D. Hellholm, Tübingen 1983, pp. 621–637; G. Macrae, « Apocalyptic Eschatology in Gnosticism », ibid., 317–325,. Sur le caractère composite de l'écrit, cf. Sevrin, « A propos de la Paraphrase... », 69–71.

[4] Cf. Wisse, « The Redeemer... », 137–140; E.M. Yamauchi, *Pre-Christian Gnosticism*, Londres 1973, pp. 115 s., Colpe, « Heidnische, jüdische... », K. Rudolph, « Coptica-Mandaica », dans: *Essays on the Nag Hammadi Texts. In Honour of Pahor Labib*, NHS VIX, éd. M. Krause, Leiden 1975, pp. 191–216; Sevrin, « A propos de la paraphrase... », 75–96.

[5] Cf. Wisse, « The Redeemer... ».

[6] Cf. Sevrin, « A propos de la Paraphrase... », 89–96. Schenke, « Zur Faksimile... », 126 s.; F. Morard, « L'Apocalypse d'Adam du codex V de Nag Hamadi et sa polémique antibaptismale », RevScRel 51 (1977), 214–233; E.M. Yamauchi, « The Apocalypse of Adam Mithriasm, and Pre-christian Gnosticism », dans: *Etudes mithriaques*. Actes du 2e Congrès International, Tehéran, du ler au 8 septembre 1975, Acta Iranica 17, Leiden 1978, 537–563, (notamment 541 s.); L. Koenen, « From Baptism to the Gnosis of Manichaeism », dans: *The Rediscovery of Gnosticism. Proceedings of the International Conference on Gnosticism at Yale*, New Haven, Conn., March 28–31, 1978, vol. 2 (Suppl. to Numen XLI), éd. B. Layton, Leiden 1981, pp. 734–756 (notamment 749 s.); K. Koschorke, « Die Polemik der Gnostiker gegen das Kirchliche Christentum », NHS 12 (Leiden 1978); J.-D. Dubois, « Contribution à l'interprétation de la Paraphrase de Sem », à paraître dans *Cahiers de la Bibliothèque copte*, Louvain.

Quant à la cosmogonie du traité, elle a fait l'objet d'une présentation sommaire dans un article de K. M. Fischer [7] et dans l'étude de B. Aland sur la paraphrase comme genre littéraire propre à la proclamation gnostique [8].

K.M. Fischer est d'avis que la dernier rédacteur du traité n'a pas voulu présenter une suite logique d'épisodes, ni même décrire une cosmogonie au sens propre. Il a plutôt mis sous les yeux du lecteur une suite d'images aptes à décrire symboliquement l'expérience gnostique de l'existence. Ainsi le début de la cosmogonie présente trois ébauches du même processus, soit 2, 10-3, 29; 3, 30-4, 18; 4, 18-32. Il serait vain d'y chercher une suite logique; les images ne font que refléter le drame intérieur du gnostique avec son inquiétude, sa haine du monde et son espérance d'en être un jour délivré. On aurait donc là un ensemble de métaphores valant pour elles-mêmes, et dont la fonction fondamentale serait d'exprimer l'anthropologie gnostique [9].

B. Aland, de son côté, cherche la clé d'interprétation de l'écrit dans son titre : La paraphrase de Sem. Ce titre se trouve en effet complété de la façon suivante : « Paraphrase au sujet de l'Esprit inengendré », c'est-à-dire au sujet de l'Esprit qui vient de la Lumière et qui, tombé dans la Ténèbre, doit en être délivré. Tout le traité ne fait que redire ce thème sous différentes images. Les six premières pages, entre autres, lui fournissent une bonne illustration de ce procédé. Le thème exposé une première fois en 1, 16b–35 se trouve repris en quatre variations, soit : en 1, 35b-3, 29; 3, 30-5, 2; 5, 2-36; 6, 1-35. Inutile de chercher dans ces « variations » une suite chronologique ou logique d'épisodes. Le traité serait donc appelé « Paraphrase », non au sens habituel et classique d'interprétation libre d'un passage déterminé, mais au sens de reprise constante sous différentes images d'un même thème fondamental [10].

Dans un article sur le rôle du Noûs dans la Paraphrase de Sem [11], nous avons pris la contre-partie de ces positions et cherché à dégager une trame narrative cohérente dans les sept premières pages du traité. Nous nous proposons ici d'étendre notre investigation aux vingt premières pages, c'est-à-dire jusqu'à la fin du passage qui traite de la création du ciel et de la terre (20, 29), et d'y analyser le thème de la chute et de la remontée du Pneuma. Une telle tentative comporte certes une bonne part d'hypothèse. Cela est dû en partie au fait que le traducteur de ce texte se trouve constamment confronté à des pronoms aux antécédants problématiques et qu'il doit faire son choix en fonction de l'interprétation qu'il entend donner au passage. Mais, comme vient de la rappeler R.McL. Wilson dans sa note à la traduction anglaise du livre de K. Rudolph, Gnosis : « Dans l'état actuel de la recherche sur les textes de Nag Hammadi, il n'est pas mauvais que nous ayons une variété de traductions différentes, afin de bien laisser voir les différentes possibilités d'interprétation » [12]. Nous n'aborderons pas non plus le texte par le biais de la critique littéraire. On peut sans doute admettre pour notre traité l'emploi de sources et l'intervention de rédactions multiples, mais nous pensons qu'il est aussi méthodologiquement justifié d'en faire une lecture synchronique en nous situant au niveau du dernier rédacteur [13].

Nous essaierons donc de montrer la cohérence des vingt premières pages de la Paraphrase de Sem en étudiant comment s'y trouvent décrites : I. L'harmonie originelle, II. La chute du Pneuma, III. La remontée du Pneuma.

I. L'harmonie originelle (1, 16b–2, 19a)

La révélation que Derdekeas communique à Sem s'ouvre sur la description des trois puissances ou racines (ⲚⲞⲨⲚⲈ) [14] qui existaient dans les origines :

---

[7] Cf. K.M. Fischer, « Die Paraphrase des Seem », dans : Essays on the Nag Hammadi Texts, pp. 255–267.

[8] Aland, « Die Paraphrase... », Voir aussi M. Tardieu, « Ψυχαιος σπινθηρ. Histoire d'une métaphore dans la tradition platonicienne jusqu'à Eckhart », RevEtAug 21 (1975), 225–255 (sur la Paraphrase de Sem, pp. 234–238.

[9] Cf. ibid., 263 s.

[10] Cf. ibid., 78–81.

[11] Cf. M. Roberge, « Le rôle du 'Noûs' dans la Paraphrase de Sem », dans : Colloque international sur les textes de Nag Hammadi, Québec, 22–25 août 1978, éd. B. Barc, Québec-Louvain 1981, pp. 328–339.

[12] Cf. K. Rudolph, Gnosis. Translation ed. by R. McLachlan Wilson, Edinburgh 1983, p. 7.

[13] Sur l'aspect littéraire du traité cf. Sevrin, « A propos de la Paraphrase... », 69–71; Roberge, « Le rôle du Pneuma... », 328–330, 337.

[14] Cf. 2,7. Sur les rapprochements de ce terme avec la littérature mandéenne, cf. Rudolph, Gnosis, pp. 201 s.; avec la littérature manichéenne, cf. H.-Ch. Puech, Le manichéisme, Paris 1949, pp. 169 s., n. 285.

Il y avait de la Lumière et de la Ténèbre
et il y avait un Esprit (ΠΝΕΥΜΑ) entre elles.
(1, 25b–28a)

Cette doctrine des trois principes à l'origine de toute réalité apparente la *Paraphrase de Sem* à la *Paraphrase de Seth* (*Elenchos* V, 19-22)[15]. Toutefois, la *Paraphrase do Sem* y ajoute une description détaillée des éléments du chaos :

Et la Ténèbre
était vent dans des eaux.
Celle-ci possédait le *Noûs*
recouvert d'un feu agité

(1,36b–2, 3)

Pour comprendre le langage du traité dans les développements qui vont suivre, il faut essayer de se représenter la disposition de ces éléments les uns par rapport aux autres. On peut s'aider de ce que le texte dit de la Ténèbre plus loin : « Mais ayant pu contenir sa malice, elle restait couverte d'eau ». On peut donc penser que l'auteur imagine les éléments associés à la Ténèbre comme des régions superposées : l'eau au sommet, ensuite le feu ou le vent, puis, tout en bas, la Ténèbre avec son *Noûs*. Or cette représentation du chaos originel se retrouve dans un vieux traité d'astronomie syriaque du VIe siècle, que cite F. Cumont dans son étude sur la cosmogonie manichéenne d'après Théodore Bar Khoni[16]. On y enseigne que « sous la terre se trouve la mer redoutable des eaux nombreuses, sous les eaux le feu, sous le feu le vent, sous le vent les ténèbres ». Selon une terminologie que l'on remarque également dans les textes manichéens[17], et qui va aussi s'appliquer au *Pneuma*, notre traité parlera donc de régions (μέοος) mais aussi de membres (μέλος) de la Ténèbre[18]. Et lorsque celle-ci voudra aller voir ce qui se passe au-delà de son royaume, elle devra monter[19] (ЄΙ ЄℤΡΑΙ) ou élever (ⅩΙCЄ) son *Noûs*[20].

La présence du *Noûs* au sein de la Ténèbre ne manque pas d'étonner. Le texte ne mentionne aucun acte d'agression antérieur de la part de la Ténèbre en vue de s'emparer du *Noûs*. Il ne dit pas non plus que le *Noûs* se trouve dans la ténèbre parce qu'il y serait tombé. Alors que dans la *Paraphrase de Seth*, le *Noûs* n'apparaît qu'après la création du ciel et de la terre, engendré par le vent et l'eau qui retient déjà en elle une part de lumière et de *pneuma*[21], dans la *Paraphrase de Sem*, le *Noûs* est associé à la Ténèbre dès les origines et donc présenté comme un élément du chaos.

La position du *Pneuma* comme principe intermédiaire rappelle le texte de *Gen.* 1, 2, qui présente la Ténèbre au-dessus (ἐπάνω) de l'abîme et également le *Pneuma* au-dessus (ἐπάνω) de l'eau[22]. La *Paraphrase de Sem* se démarque du texte biblique en situant la Ténèbre en-dessous des eaux (cf. 1,36–2,1; 2,17b–19a, 30–31). Il est en effet important pour le narrateur d'indiquer que le *Pneuma* ne peut à l'origine entrer en contact avec la Ténèbre. C'est pourquoi le texte continue en parlant des racines :

Elles régnaient en elles,
elles seules, et elles étaient cachées les unes aux autres (ΝЄΥℤΟΒЄC ЄΝЄΥЄΡΗΥ)[23] chacune dans sa puissance.

(2,7b–10a)

Les trois racines constituent donc d'après notre texte trois royaumes qui ne communiquent pas entre eux, et cette absence de communication ou de mélange se fonde sur l'ignorance mutuelle.

Cette ignorance ne concerne cependant pas la racine supérieure, car celle-ci connaît la bassesse de la Ténèbre :

---

[15] Sur l'origine de cette doctrine, cf. W. Bousset, *Hauptprobleme der Gnosis*, Göttingen 1907, pp. 121–123; Colpe, Heidnische, jüdische... », 110; Krause, « Die Paraphrase... », 109; Sevrin, « A propos de la Paraphrase... », 76 s.; Tardieu, « Les livres... », 210; J. Montserrat-Torrents, « La notice d'Hippolyte sur les Naassènes », dans: *Studia Patristica* XVII, éd. E.A. Livingstone, Part one, Oxford 1982, pp. 231–242 (notamment 231).

[16] Cf. F. Cumont, *La cosmogonie manichéenne d'après Théodore Bar Khoni* (Recherches sur le manichéisme I), Bruxelles 1908, p. 12. L'opuscule a été publié par M. Kugener dans les *Actes du Congrès des Orientalistes d'Alger*, Paris 1907, 2e section, p. 177. Le traité refléterait dans son ensemble « de vieilles doctrines chaldéennes à peine modifiées par quelques éléments grecs », p. 143, n. 3.

[17] Cf. Cumont, *La cosmogonie...*, 9. Voir aussi H.-Ch, Puech, dans: *Annuaire du Collège de France* 63 (1962–63), 198–291.

[18] Cf. 3, 11–13; 3, 22; 4, 10–12 (μέρος). 3, 9, 12; 4, 10–12; 9, 21–23; 14, 1–2 (μέλος).

[19] Cf. 2,31.

[20] Cf. 3,7–8.

[21] Cf. *Elenchos* V, 19, 13–15.

[22] καὶ σκότος ἐπάνω τῆς ἀβύσσου, καὶ πνεῦμα θεοῦ ἐπεφέρετο ἐπάνω τοῦ ὕδατος (LXX).

[23] Nous traduisons « étaient cachées les unes aux autres » plutôt que « se couvraient mutuellement » (Krause, Wisse).

Or la Lumière,
puisqu'elle possédait une grande
puissance, connaissait la bassesse
de la Ténèbre et son désordre,
car la racine n'était pas égale.
                              (2,10b–14)

La Ténèbre, au contraire, reléguée dans la région inférieure du chaos, ignore complétement qu'il existe une racine supérieure (2,10b–17a); tant qu'elle reste couverte d'eau, l'harmonie règne (2,17b–19a).

II. La chute du *Pneuma* (2,19b–3,29)

La chute du *Pneuma* est décrite en trois étapes :

1. *Agitation de la Ténèbre et montée de l'Esprit* (2,19b–28). L'harmonie originelle est d'abord soudainement rompue par l'agitation de la Ténèbre (ⲁ̄ⲩⲱ ⲁⲩⲕⲓⲙ)[24]. Effrayé par le bruit, le *Pneuma* s'élève jusqu'à son Lieu et c'est de là que, par sa Pensée, il aperçoit l'eau ténébreuse et s'en dégoûte. Il se rend compte aussi que la mauvaise racine ne se soucie pas de la Lumière infinie.

2. *Division des eaux et montée de la Ténèbre et de son Noûs* (2,29–35a). Par la division de l'eau qui recouvre la Ténèbre (2,18–19a), la puissance supérieure suscite alors la montée de la Ténèbre et de son *Noûs*. Le but de cette initiative est la libération du *Noûs* :

Or, par la volonté de la grande Lumière,
l'eau ténébreuse se divisa
et la Ténèbre monta,
revêtue de l'ignorance mauvaise,
afin que (+ δέ) le *Noûs*
se séparât d'elle, car celle s'enorgueil-
lissait de lui.

                   (2,29–35a)

3. *Chute du Pneuma* (2,35b–3,29). Comme le laissent entendre les dernières lignes citées, la Lumière va se servir de l'orgueil de la Ténèbre pour atteindre son but. La Lumière du *Pneuma* se révèle à la Ténèbre et celle-ci dans son orgueil veut

s'égaler à cette puissance qu'elle ignorait et qui lui est supérieure. Elle élève donc son *Noûs* vers ses membres ou ses régions supérieures et le rend en partie semblable aux membres du *Pneuma* (3,11–13a; cf. 3,21–22a)[25] dans une vaine tentative pour s'égaler à lui. Toutefois, en se révélant à la Ténèbre, le *Pneuma* a perdu une partie de sa lumière au profit du *Noûs*. Celui-ci s'élève donc et illumine d'une *lumière de feu* l'Hadès tout entier (3,23–24a), ce qui manifeste d'une part la dispersion et le mélange de la lumière du *Pneuma* avec un élément du chaos et, d'autre part, l'égalité de la lumière du *Noûs* avec celle du *Pneuma*, ce qui fonde son droit au salut[26]. Le passage qui décrit cette chute est délimité par une inclusion (2,35b–3,1 et 3,28b–29), qui souligne, au plan formel, que c'est bien en se révélant que le *Pneuma* a perdu une partie de sa lumière :

2,35b   Mais, après qu'
elle (la Ténèbre) se fût agitée, la Lumière du *Pneuma*

3,1   se révéla à elle.
L'ayant vue, elle s'étonna :
elle ne savait pas qu'il y avait une autre puissance au-dessus d'elle. Aussi, quand

5   elle vit que son image était
ténébreuse face au *Pneuma*, elle éprouva de la douleur,
et dans sa douleur elle éleva
son *Noûs* vers les membres
supérieurs de la Ténèbre — celui-ci

10   était l'œil de l'amertume de la malice —.
Elle rendit son *Noûs* en partie semblable aux membres du
Pneuma. Elle pensait, car elle voyait sa malice,
qu'il pourrait

15   s'égaler au *Pneuma*. Mais il n'en fut pas capable. Car il voulait faire
quelque chose d'impossible, et cela n'arriva pas. Toutefois, pour que ne fût pas réduit à néant le *Noûs* de la Ténèbre,

20   qui est l'œil de l'amertume de la malice,
puisqu'il avait été établi dans une ressemblance
partielle, il s'éleva et illu-
mina d'une lumière de feu
l'Hadès tout entier, afin que fût

---

[24] L'agitation et le bruit caractéristiques des puissances inférieures. Cf. *Poimandres* 4.

[25] En rapprochant 3, 11b–13a de 3, 21–22a, on peut corriger ⲙⲉⲗⲟⲥ pour ⲙⲉⲣⲟⲥ et ⲙⲉⲣⲟⲥ pour ⲙⲉⲗⲟⲥ dans le premier passage et traduire : « Elle rendit son *Noûs* en partie semblable aux membres du *Pneuma* ». Sur la confusion entre μέλος et μέρος, cf. Liddle and Scott, p. 1099; Stern, 33; Crum, 80b.

[26] Cf. 3, 24b–26a. Dans ce passage ⲩⲱⲩ signifie probablement « égalité ». Mais le terme peut aussi signifier « dispersion » (cf. Crum, 605. S'emploie spécialement à propos des parfums et des odeurs). Voir *Elenchos* V, 19,4 : « ...le souffle... répand en tout sens sa bonne odeur » (ἐκτείνεται καὶ φέρεται πανταῇ on serait tenté de garder au terme le double sens de dispersion et d'égalité.

25   manifestée l'égalité de la Lumière
sans déficience. En effet, le *Pneuma*
avait trié parti de toutes les formes
de la Ténèbre, parce qu'il
3,29   s'était révélé dans sa grandeur.

Il est intéressant maintenant de comparer notre texte à celui de l'*Elenchos* où se trouve rapportée la chute de la lumière :

> La lumière, comme les rayons du soleil, fait naturellement descendre ses traits sur les ténèbres qui sont au-dessous d'elle, et de son côté le souffle, qui occupe le milieu, répand en tout sens sa bonne odeur... Puisque telle est la puissance des trois principes, la puissance de la lumière et celle du souffle se trouvent à la fois dans les ténèbres situées au-dessous (V,19,4)[27].

Dans ce texte, la chute est présentée de façon intemporelle, comme la diffusion naturelle des rayons lumineux et des effluves du *Pneuma*. Dans la *Paraphrase de Sem*, au contraire, le récit prend un tour dramatique. La chute de l'élément lumineux intermédiaire entre dans le plan de la grande Lumière en vue de dépouiller la Ténèbre du *Noûs* dont elle s'enorgueillit. En permettant qu'une image du *Pneuma* se disperse dans le *Noûs*, la Puissance supérieure déclenche le processus qui va aboutir à la libération du *Noûs*. Le récit de la *Paraphrase de Sem* apparaît donc comme un développement de celui de la *Paraphrase de Seth* et se situe davantage dans la ligne du mythe manichéen d'après lequel l'Homme primordial et ses cinq fils s'offrent en pâture comme un poison aux cinq fils de la Ténèbre[28].

Nous ne pensons donc pas que dans le traité du codex VII la chute de la lumière soit présupposée à la description du chaos[29]. Elle n'est pas non plus insinuée en 2,23, lorsque le *Pneuma* voit l'eau ténébreuse et s'en dégoûte[30] et pas davantage en 5,16, lorsque le *Noûs* s'entrechoque avec le *Pneuma*, puisque cette action suppose que le *Noûs* possède déjà une image issue du *Pneuma* (cf. 5,18–19)[31].

III. La remontée du Pneuma (3,30–20,29)

On aborde ici la partie la plus développée et la plus complexe de la cosmogonie. La processus de remontée se complique du fait que *Pneuma* doit remonter en même temps que le *Noûs*. Certains épisodes ne concernent que le *Noûs*, d'autres seulement le *Pneuma*, d'autres à la fois le *Pneuma* et le *Noûs*. Les épisodes qui traitent de la remontée du *Pneuma* s'arrêtent en 20,9, après la création du ciel et de la terre. Ceux qui concernent le *Noûs* se prolongent jusqu'en 24,2, après la création des hommes stériles et des femmes stériles. A partir de là, on passe de la cosmogonie à la sotériologie[32]. Étant donné l'ampleur du texte, notre exposé restera surtout descriptif et s'attachera à montrer l'enchaînement des différents épisodes. Ceux-ci sont délimités par les interventions du Sauveur qui à chaque fois utilise un moyen différent pour effectuer la libération du *Noûs* ou rassembler la lumière du *Pneuma*.

Première intervention du Sauveur (3,30–7,10a)
Le Sauveur se révèle d'abord au *Pneuma* dans l'image du *Pneuma* et cette révélation déclenche le processus de libération du *Noûs*. Plusieurs étapes marquent le déroulement de cette première intervention :

a) La Lumière supérieure se révèle au *Pneuma* (3,30–4,13a)
Par son Fils, Derdekeas[33], la Lumière supérieure décide de se révéler au *Pneuma* dans l'image de *Pneuma*, afin de libérer le *Noûs* de l'Hadès :

> Moi, j'apparus. C'est moi
> le Fils de la Lumière
> immaculée, infinie.
> J'apparus dans l'image
> du *Pneuma*. Car c'est moi
> le rayon de la Lumière universelle
> et sa manifestation. Cela
> pour que le *Noûs* de la Ténèbre
> ne demeurât pas dans l'Hadès
>   (4,1–10a)

b) Formation de la Matrice et engendrement d'un *Noûs* semblable au *Pneuma* (3,30–5,12a)
L'apparition du Fils suscite aussitôt la formation de la Matrice par l'action du Noûs :

>   Moi, Sem, lorsque
> j'apparus...

---

[27] Traduction d'A. Siouville, *Philosophoumena*, Paris 1928, p. 184.

[28] Voir par exemple la présentation du mythe chez Théodore Bar Khoni. Cf. M. Tardieu, *Le menichéisme*, Paris 1981, pp. 94–101 (notamment 96).

[29] Cf. « Berliner Arbeitskreis..., 57; Aland, « Die Paraphrase... », 77.

[30] Cf. Wisse, « The Redeemer... », 132.

[31] Cf. ibid.

[32] Cf. Sevrin, « A propos de la Paraphrase... », 77.

[33] Cf. 1,5; 8,24.

....

le *Noûs* tira le feu agité
—celui-ci était recouvert d'eau—
entre la Ténèbre et l'eau.
Puis, hors de la Ténèbre, l'eau
devint une nuée, et
à partir de la nuée la Matrice prit forme.

(4,12b–13a, 18b–25a)

Selon une conception courante d'l'époque, notamment parmi les Stoïciens[34], la Nature est présentée comme une gigantesque matrice d'où vont sortir tous les éléments de l'univers. Cette analogie va en même temps servir à l'auteur pour exprimer son rejet absolu de toute sexualité. La Matrice ayant donc été formée, le feu agité s'y rend et séduit la Ténèbre[35]. Celle-ci s'unit alors à la Matrice et expulse en elle son *Noûs* car, précise le texte : « il était semence (σπέρμα) de la Nature, issue de la racine ténébreuse » (4,37b–5,2). Grâce à cette semence, chaque image prend forme dans la Nature. Mais l'image du *Noûs* qui alors prend forme dans la Nature ressemble au *Pneuma* (5,3–8) :

> Et lorsque la Ténèbre
> engendra pour elle-même l'image du *Noûs*,
> il resembla au *Pneuma*
> (5,6–8)

c) Formation des quatre nuages (5,12b–6,13a)
Dès que la Matrice eût enfanté le *Noûs* dans la nuée[36], il s'entrechoqua (ἐντινάσσειν) avec le *Pneuma*, puisqu'il possédait une image issue de lui (5,18b–19a)[37]. Le choc du *Noûs* avec le *Pneuma* provoque aussitôt la division de la nuée en quatre nuages ou sphères[38] :

> Et aussitôt la Nature
> se divisa en quatre parties.
> Elles devinrent des nuages d'apparence différente.
> On les appela :
> Hymen, Chorion[39]
> Puissance, l'Eau.
> (5,22–27)

Cette division de la Nature en quatre sphères

superposées va permettre au *Noûs* de s'en retourner vers sa puissance, c'est-à-dire vers le *Pneuma*, qui avait été mélangé (ⲉⲣⲧⲱⲥ ⲛ̄ⲙⲙⲁ϶) à lui dans la Ténèbre (6,1–6).

d) Réaction du *Pneuma* (6,13b–30a)
La pesanteur du *Noûs* provoque l'etonnement (θαῦμα) chez le *Pneuma*. Cette puissance de l'Étonnement secoue (ⲛⲟ϶ⲟ϶ⲍ)[40] Le *Noûs*-fardeau, qui retourne vers sa chaleur. Le *Noûs* se revêt alors de la lumière du *Pneuma* et la puissance de l'Étonnement adhère (κολλᾶν) au nuage de l'Hymen.

e) L'image du *Pneuma* est portée hors de l'Hadès (6,30b–35a)
Par la volonté de la Grandeur, le *Pneuma* regarde en direction de la Lumière infinie pour qu'on ait pitié de sa lumière. L'image du *Pneuma* est alors portée hors de l'Hadès (ⲁ϶ⲉⲓⲛⲉ ⲙ̄ⲡⲓⲛⲉ ⲉ϶ⲣⲁⲓ ϶ⲛ̄ ⲉⲙⲛ̄ⲧⲉ) (6,34b–35). D'après ce qui sera raconté plus loin, en 9,10–25, il semble que l'image du *Pneuma* sorte de l'Hadès, c'est-à-dire de la région ténébreuse, mais reste quand même dans l'eau.

f) Le *Noûs* reçoit l'insufflation du *Pneuma* supérieur et prend forme (6,35b–7,10a).
Ce premier épisode se termine par l'insufflation du *Pneuma* supérieur sur le *Noûs*. Le souffle puissant de Derdekeas divise les nuages, parvient jusqu'au *Noûs* et lui donne de prendre forme (ϫⲓ ⲉⲓⲛⲉ) :

> et
> après que le *Pneuma* eut regardé, je déferlai,
> moi, le Fils de la Grandeur,
> comme un flot de lumière
> et comme un ouragan du *Pneuma*
> immortel. Et je soufflai dans
> le nuage de l'Hymen sur l'Étonnement
> du *Pneuma* inengendré. IL (le nuage)
> se divisa, il illumina les nuages.
> Ceux-ci se divisèrent...
> ....C'est pourquoi le *Noûs*
> prit forme
> (6,35b–7,10a)

---

[34] L'assimilation du cosmos à un corps humain était classique à l'époque. Elle est commune à presque toute l'école stoïcienne. Cf. G. Verbeke, *L'évolution de la doctrine du pneuma du stoïcisme à S. Augustin*, Paris–Louvain 1945, pp. 11–173.

[35] La Ténèbre étant considérée comme l'élément mâle, on devrait peut-être traduire ⲡⲕⲁⲕⲉ par l'Obscur afin de sauvegarder l'analogie sexuelle.

[36] Le texte identifie Nuée, Matrice et Nature, cf. 4,24, 30–32; 5,3–12.

[37] C'est-à-dire le *Pneuma* situé en son Lieu (cf. 2,22), mais qui a dispersé une partie de sa lumière dans la Ténèbre.

[38] Ces nuages semblent représenter pour l'auteur les différentes sphères du cosmos, cf. 41,9 s.; 47,20–31.

[39] Le Chorion, c'est-à-dire l'enveloppe extérieure du fœtus. Cf. Aristote, *De la Génération des Animaux*, II, 7, 739b, 745b, 746a.

[40] Il est possible que le verbe ⲛⲟ϶ⲟ϶ⲍ utilisé en 6,17 pour décrire la réaction du *Pneuma* traduise le verbe grec ἀποτινάσσειν, qui correspondrait alors à ἐντινάσσειν employé en 5,16.

Il est tentant de voir dans ce passage une relecture de *Genèse* 2,7, analogue à celle que présente Philon dans le *Legum Allegoriae* :

> ...Mais il faut réfléchir que l'homme de terre, c'est l'intelligence (νοῦς) au moment où Dieu l'introduit dans le corps, mais avant qu'elle y demeure introduite. Cette sorte d'intelligence serait en vérité semblable à la terre et corruptible, si Dieu ne lui insufflait pas une puissance de vie véritable...
> (Leg. Alleg., I,32. Trad. Cl. Mondesert, Paris, 1962)

G. Verbeke commente ainsi ce passage : « Il y a d'abord la formation de l'homme terrestre, comprenant un corps et une intelligence également terrestre et périssable. Ce νοῦς était évidemment passif et informe; mais il a été transformé totalement par la collation du pneuma divin, qui a élevé son pouvoir intellectif et lui a donné l'immortalité » [41].

Dans la *Paraphrase de Sem* également, le principe inférieur, le *Noûs*, doit recevoir l'insufflation du principe supérieur, le *Pneuma*, pour prendre forme. Chez Philon, toutefois, le *Noûs* provient de la terre, alors que dans la *Paraphrase de Sem* il origine de la Ténèbre. Le dualisme est ainsi plus fortement marqué.

Intermède. Description des quatre nuages (7,10b--30)

Le scénario de la libération du *Noûs* est interrompu par la description des quatre nuages: l'Hymen, le Chorion, la Puissance et l'Eau. Divers passages du traité nous permettent de préciser la topographie des nuages ou sphères célestes (cf. 47,20–31), ainsi que leur nomenclature [42] :

1. *L'Hymen* : est « un nuage qu'on ne peut saisir, un grand feu » (7,12–13). Appelé aussi simplement le Lieu (cf. 8,3; 11,27; 35,30) ou lieu de l'Hymen (35,28b–29). L'étonnement du *Pneuma* est uni au nuage de l'Hymen.

2. *Le Chorion* : c'est « le nuage du Silence. C'est un feu majestueux » (7,15–16). Appelé simplement le Silence (cf. 13,3,7; 14,26 s.; 16,37; 17,6,19 s.) ou le Lieu (14,28).

3. *La Puissance* : « Elle aussi était un nuage de la Nature » (7,18–19). Appelé le *Millieu* (cf. 13,4,16 s.;

14,27 s.; 16,7,13,25; 17,20 s.; 18,9 [bis], 20, 29), « le nuage du Milieu » (33,16 s.; 47,30), « le Milieu de la Nature » (43,8). Le *Noûs* est mélangé à ce nuage (ef. 6,11–13; 18,9–11; 7,7–19).

4. *L'Eau* : « Et l'Eau ténébreuse était un nuage de crainte » (7,22–24).

Deuxième intervention du Sauveur (7,31–9,33a)

Derdekeas, le Fils de la Grandeur, remonte à son lieu implorer la Lumière supérieure afin que la puissance du *Pneuma* augmente dans le Lieu [43] et se remplisse de sa Lumière (ⲙⲟⲩ︤ϩ︥ ⲉ︤ⲛ︥, cf. 8,3,10; 9,5,11), sans la puissance de la Lumière infinie (9,5–7). Il se manifeste donc une seconde fois. Mais, pour confondre la Nature il revêt son vêtement de lumière et vient sous l'apparence du *Pneuma* (8,31b–9,1a). Alors, selon la volonté du Souveur :

> Le *Pneuma*
> s'éleva (ϫⲓⲥⲉ) par sa puissance.
> On lui accorda sa grandeur,
> pour qu'il se remplît de sa lumière
> et qu'il sortît de toute la pesanteur
> de la Ténèbre
> ....
> ....Et
> le *Pneuma* se réjouit parce qu'il avait été préservé de l'eau terrifiante.
> (9,8b–13a; 15b–17a)

Et le texte ajoute : « lorsque le *Pneuma* s'éleva au dessus de l'eau, son image noire se révéla » (9,24–25). L'épisode se termine par une prière d'action de grâce du *Pneuma* à l'adresse de la Lumière supérieure (9,26–33a).

Intermède (9,39b–12,15a)

Un second intermède suit cette intervention du Sauveur. A deux reprises, le Révélateur s'adresse à Sem en style direct, en 9,33b–34 et en 11,34–35. Au plan littéraire, le morceau semble composite, mais on peut le diviser assez facilement en deux parties. Une première partie qui va de 9,33b à 11,6 concerne la Pensée (ⲙⲉⲉⲩⲉ) ou l'Ennoia que conçoit le *Pneuma*, et présente surtout des considérations sur les épisodes antérieurs. La seconde partie, qui s'étend de 11,7 à 12,15a rapporte le chant de jubilation de la lumière de l'Étonnement dans le nuage de l'Hymen.

---

[41] Cf. Verbeke, *L'Évolution...*, p. 242.

[42] Au plan littéraire, ces lignes se présentent comme une paraphrase. Cf. Roberge, « Le rôle du Pneuma... », 357.

[43] C'est-à-dire le Lieu du *Pneuma* au-dessus de la sphère de l'Hymen (cf. 2,22; 47,23).

Troisième intervention du Sauveur (12,15b–18,1a)
Le récit de la troisième intervention du Sauveur s'étend sur près de six pages, soit de 12,15b à 18,1a. On y raconte la libération de la lumière du *Pneuma* dans les trois nuages de l'Hymen, du Silence et du Milieu.

a) Libération de la Lumière dans le nuage de l'Hymen (12,15b–14,31)
Par la volonté de la grande Lumière, Derdekeas descend dans le nuage de l'Hymen sans son vêtement universel (cf. supra 8,33–35). Il y reçoit un vêtement trimorphe pour qu'il puisse se révéler dans le nuage comme s'il était revêtu de la lumière du *Pneuma* (12,15b–30a; cf. 13,29b–31a). Lorsqu'il apparaît, le nuage de l'Hymen laisse d'abord échapper une partie de lumière qui traverse le nuage du Silence et va se mélanger au nuage du Milieu (12,31b–13,23a). Quant à la Lumière restée dans L'Hymen, elle entreprend de se libérer (13,23b–14,25):

> Or la lumière qui était dans l'Hymen
> fut troublée par ma puissance et
> elle arriva à mon milieu.
> Elle se remplit de la pensée
> universelle. Et, dans le Logos
> de la lumière du *Pneuma*, elle se tourna
> vers son repos. Elle prit
> forme dans sa racine. Elle resplendit
> puisqu'elle était sans déficience.
> (14,17–25)

Ce n'est cependant pas toute le lumière de l'Hymen qui est libérée, puisqu'une partie descend se mélanger au nuage du Silence (14,26–31).

b) Prière de la Lumière égarée dans la Milieu (14,32–16,34a)
La partie de Lumière séparée de l'Étonnement (cf. 12,31b; 13,23a) et descendue dans la Nature s'est revêtue de l'oubli. Grâce à cette lumière du *Pneuma*, la Nature est devenue puissante (14,32––15,16a). Une lumière descend alors dans le chaos et fait remonter de l'Eau la lumière ainsi que la Matrice. Puis celle-ci est de nouveau refoulée dans l'Eau (15,16b–16,23). La Lumière du Milieu tourne alors son regard vers la Lumière supérieure et lui adresse une prière:

> ...Seigneur, aie pitié de moi,
> car ma lumière et ma peine
> se sont égarées. En effet, si ta bonté
> ne me redresse, je ne sais vraiment pas
> où je suis.
> (16,30b–34a)

c) Derdekeas libère la Lumière du Silence et la Lumière du Milieu (16,34b–18,1a)
Derdekeas apparaît d'abord dans le nuage de l'Hymen, puis dans le nuage du Silence sans son vêtement saint. Il rend hommage à son vêtement trimorphe et, dans le Silence, il revêt la lumière qui s'y trouve (16,35–17,16a). Il dépose ensuite son vêtement dans le nuage du Silence et pénètre dans le Milieu pour y revêtir finalement la Lumière qui s'y trouve (17,16b–18,1a).

Quatrième intervention du Sauveur (18,1b–19,26a)
Derdekeas enlève à nouveau son vêtement de lumière. Il revêt un vêtement de feu qui lui a été préparé dans le Milieu et qui provient du *Noûs*. Pour le revêtir, il descend dans le chaos. Grâce à ce vêtement le Sauveur se prostitue avec la Nature:

> Or mon vêtement de feu, selon la
> volonté de la Grandeur descendit
> vers ce qui est puissant et vers la
> partie souillée de la
> Nature, celle que la Puissance
> ténébreuse recouvrait. Et mon vêtement
> caressa la Nature de son
> étoffe, et sa
> féminité impure devint puissante
> (18,27–35a)

Sous l'action de cette caresse la Matrice expulse le *Noûs* hors de l'eau tel un poisson et rejette en même temps ce qu'elle possède encore de Lumière.

> Et
> la Matrice, en colère, monta.
> Elle mit le *Noûs* au sec
> comme un poisson, lui qui possédait
> une étincelle de feu et
> une puissance de feu. Mais, lorsque
> la Nature eût rejeté le *Noûs* loin
> d'elle, elle fut troublée et
> pleura. Lorsqu'elle fut dans la douleur et
> dans ses larmes, elle rejeta
> la puissance du *Pneuma* loin d'elle.
> Elle s'arrêta comme moi, qui avais revêtu
> la lumière du *Pneuma*. Et je
> me reposai avec mon vêtement à la
> vue du poisson.
> (18,35b–19,13a)

L'image du poisson appliqée au *Noûs* peut paraître au premier abord surprenante. Elle doit, semble-t-il, s'interpréter dans le contexte de la polémique antibaptismale que le traité développe un peu plus loin, (30,21b–32,26). En effet, dans la symbolique chrétienne baptismale, le poisson apparaît en général dans un contexte baptismal. Ainsi chez Tertullien: « Mais nous, petits poissons, qui tenons notre nom de notre ἰχθύς Jésus-Christ, nous naissons dans l'eau et ce n'est qu'en demeurant en elle que nous sommes sauvés » (*De Bapt.*, I, 3)[44] et chez Ambroise : « Mais il t'a été réservé que les eaux te régénèrent pour la grâce comme elles ont engendré les autres à la vie. Imite ce poisson... » *De Sacram.*, III, 3[45]. La *Paraphrase de Sem* rejette ce symbolisme. C'est paradoxalement hors de l'eau que le *Noûs*-poisson trouve son salut ! Expulsé par la Matrice et jaillissant hors de l'eau, il devient dès lors l'archétype du gnostique, lequel n'a pas à chercher son salut dans un rite lié à un élément essentiellement mauvais.

Cet épisode se termine par la description de la naissance des bêtes, fruit de la fornication du Sauveur avec la Matrice (19,13b–26a) :

Et afin que
fussent condamnées les œuvres
de la Nature à cause de son aveuglement, plusieurs
formes de bêtes sortirent
d'elle, selon le nombre des vents
qui soufflent...

(19,13b–18a)

Cinquième intervention du Sauveur (19,26b–20,29)
Pour obtenir la création du ciel et de la terre et par là permettre que toute la lumière remonte à sa racine, Derdekeas va finalement revêtir la Bête :

Je revêtis
la Bête et lui adressai
une grande demande :
qu'elle créât un ciel et une terre,
afin que s'élevât
toute la lumiere.
Car d'aucune autre manière, la puissance
du *Pneuma* n'aurait pu être délivrée du lien
à moins que je ne lui apparaisse
sous un déguisement de Bête.

(19,26b–35)

La Nature, qui vient de produire les bêtes, acquiesce alors à la demande du Sauveur comme s'il était son fils. Le ciel et la terre sont créés. La terre produit aussi la nourriture suivant le nombre des bêtes ainsi que la rosée, les vents et toutes les semences (19,36–20,20b).

Puis le vêtement de feu de Derdekeas s'élève au milieu du nuage de la Nature et brille sur la création jusqu'à ce qu'elle soit asséchée. La Ténèbre, qui était le vêtement de la Nature, est rejetée dans les eaux, et le Milieu se trouve enfin purifié de la Ténèbre (20,20b–29).

Les dernières pages de la cosmogonie racontent l'établissement du *Noûs* sur la création (20,30–23,8) et la naissance des femmes stériles et des hommes stériles (23,9–24,2a). Mais il n'est plus question de la remontée de la lumière du *Pneuma*, puisque, comme le souligne le texte :

La lumière du *Pneuma* a été rendue parfaite en trois nuages.

(21,8–9a)

Nous concluons notre exposé, espérant avoir démontré que ces vingt premières pages de la *Paraphrase de Sem* ne présentent pas seulement une suite d'images symboliques ou des « variations » sur un thème fondamental, mais bien une véritable cosmogonie fondée sur un mythe de chute et de remontée. Dans ce mythe, le *Pneuma* joue le rôle de sauveur sauvé. Grâce à la lumière qu'il communique au *Noûs*, celui-ci peut entreprendre de se libérer de la Ténèbre. Toutefois, en se révélant à la Ténèbre, le *Pneuma* a perdu une partie de sa puissance et ne peut plus par lui-même rassembler sa lumière dispersée. Derdekeas, le Fils de la Lumière supérieure viendra alors au secours du *Pneuma*. Son activité salvifique consistera d'une part à rassembler par son vêtement la lumière dispersée du *Pneuma* et à la rendre parfaite en trois nuages, en sorte que le *Pneuma* puisse se remplir (ⲙⲟⲩϩ ⲅ̄ⲛ̄) de toute sa lumière et briller par sa propre puissance; elle consistera d'autre part à faire en sorte que le *Noûs* passe de la Ténèbre dans la Matrice, soit expulsé des eaux de la Martice et puisse finalement régner sur la création par sa puissance.

Pour obtenir son salut, le gnostique sera invité à revêtir ce *Noûs* (43, 25 s.) sauvé de l'eau ténébreuse plutôt que de recourir à un quelconque rite baptismal utilisant l'eau, puissance essentiellement méprisable.

---

[44] Traduction M. Drouzy, *Sources Chrétiennes* 35 (Paris 1952), p. 65.

[45] Traduction B. Botte *Sources Chrétiennes*, 25bis, (Paris 1961), p. 93. Les peintures des catacombes apportent aussi de nombreux témoignages sur ce lien du poisson et de l'eau baptismale. Cf. J. Danielou, « Le symbolisme de l'eau vive », RechScRel 32 (1958), 335–346; *Les symboles chrétiens primitifs*, Paris 1961, pp. 49–63; C. Vogel, « Le repas sacré au poisson chez les chrétiens », RevScRel 40 (1966), 1–26 (la note 1 à la p. 1 donne les principaux ouvrages consacrés au symbolisme du poisson).

COPTIC STUDIES

Marian Robertson

A Coptic Melody Sung Interchangeably in Different Languages: Comparisons thereof and Proposed Dating therefor

At present there are certain melodies of the Coptic Church services that are sung interchangeably in different languages, namely, Greek, Coptic, and Arabic.[1] This practice arose from the desire and need of the congregation to understand the text. Since Arabic has become increasingly prevalent in these holy rites, scholars have expressed fear that changing the language may inevitably bring change to the music as well. Thus one question at hand is that of what really happens to a melody as it goes from one language to the other. Does it remain essentially intact, or is it altered to fit the individual characteristics of each language?

A second question upon which some small light may be shed by examining the relations of the languages to the music is that of dating the numerous melodies in the Coptic ritual observances. It is well known that the Copts have preserved their music over the centuries by means of an oral tradition, and that hence there are no manuscripts bearing notation to guide musicologists in their attempts to establish a chronology for this tradition.[2] However, if some dates were to be found for some of the texts meant to be sung, there might at least be a clue as to the antiquity of certain songs.[3]

A beautiful melody from Holy Week services stands forth as an ideal subject for a linguistic/musical study. Sung as a response during the Morning Offering of Incense on Maundy Thursday, and again as another response during the Sixth Hour on Good Friday, it has two completely different texts: one in Greek and Coptic, and the other in Greek and Arabic, texts which date, according to Anton Baumstark, from the seventh or eighth century.[4] A rather simple, but subtle little tune, devoid of extended ornamentation, it is metrical, and is composed of two phrases, each of which is four measures in length. In both the Maundy Thursday and Good Friday services, as the song proceeds from beginning to end, this melody is repeated many, many times.

Because the Good Friday version is simpler than that of Maundy Thursday, it will be discussed first. Performed by the chorus (choir of deacons), the song has six verses: three in Coptic followed by three in Greek,[5] and is the plea to Christ from the thief on the Cross.[6] It may be identified by its opening phrase, "Remember me..." (Coptic: ⲁⲣⲓⲡⲁⲙⲉⲣⲓ ...; Greek: μνήσθητί μου...).[7] However, before comparing the melody as it is sung in these two languages, it is advisable, as a

---

[1] In recent years, Copts residing in Europe and America have begun to use French, German, and English in their services. The analysis of these languages and their influence on Coptic melody could be the subject of another study.

[2] There are a few manuscripts extant (British Museum, Bibliothèque Nationale à Paris, Collection of the Rylands Library at Manchester, the Insinger Collection at the Leiden Museum of Antiquities) which bear strange markings and dots that may or may not be some discarded form of musical notation. They are as yet undeciphered.

[3] It has been proposed, for example, that Coptic melodies having Greek texts were probably in existence before the Arab conquest of Egypt. Cf. René Ménard, "Note sur la mémorisation et l'improvisation dans le chant copte," *Études grégoriennes* III (1959), 143.

[4] Anton Baumstark, "Drei griechische Passionsgesänge ägyptischer Liturgie," *Oriens Christianus* III (1929), 76.

[5] This is the order of the languages as the song is presently performed. There is no indication as to the proper chronology.

[6] Luke 23:42.

[7] A. Baumstark has reconstructed and edited the Greek text with nine added verses, farced with the Coptic refrain, ⲁⲣⲓⲡⲁⲙⲉⲣⲓ .... Baumstark, "Drei griechische ...", 69–77. This extended text has been adapted into Arabic, and is now sung immediately after the song under discussion; but the melody thereto is entirely different.

control measure, to determine what happens when it is sung in but one language and merely repeated over and over. Verses one and two of the Coptic text have been chosen for this comparison (the first and second times around for the music).

Note: In all of the following comparisons, three elements basic to the melody are examined: 1) pitch (actual pitch and interval relationships), 2) rhythm, and 3) ornamentation (embellishments). Another important element to be considered, which, however, cannot be transcribed, is the style of singing.

I (See transcription):[8]

A. Pitch: The actual pitch of verse two is one-quarter tone higher than that of verse one. However, the interval relationships are identical, even to the quarter-tone, cf. measure two, beat three going into measure three; measure three, beats one, two, and beat three going into measure four.

B. Rhythm: Note that the tempo of verse two is faster than that of verse one, cf. the metronome markings, measures one and four. However, the basic beat remains unchanged in both verses.

C. Ornamentation: Indeed, the embellishments are slightly different, but the basic notes of the melodic line are maintained, cf. measures one and five. It is interesting to observe the prevalence of the embellishment figure of measure two, beat one, which appears in all of the examples.

The above comparisons show that even when the language remains the same, the melody exhibits some change in details of pitch, rhythm, and ornamentation, change due primarily to repetition, certainly not language. Despite these differences of detail, it is obvious, however, that the basic melody stays intact. It may be noted in passing that the general tendency of the music to get almost imperceptibly higher and faster as it proceeds is a characteristic of much Coptic singing.

The next logical step of this study is to examine the melody as it is sung in Coptic and Greek. The Coptic text, verse three (third time around for the melody) and the Greek text, verse three (sixth time around for the melody) have been chosen for comparison.[9]

II (See transcription):

A. Pitch: The Greek version (of which the transcription shows the actual pitch) is heard as one-half step higher than the Coptic. However, as was the case above, the interval relationships remain identical, even to the quarter-tone, cf. measure two, beat three going into measure three. One small variance thereof may be noted in measure three, beat three going into measure four.

B. Rhythm: The tempo of the Greek version is appreciably faster than that of the Coptic, cf. metronome markings, measures one and five. There is no change in the basic rhythm.

C. Ornamentation: Some variances are evident, but the basic notes of the melody and their relationships to each other are kept intact, cf. measures one, five, and six.

From Example II it can be seen that although the language changes, the differences in the melody are those of detail, and are no greater than those found in Example I. The higher pitch and faster tempo of the Greek may be attributed to the repetition of the melody rather than to the change in language (see Example I).

When sung during the Maundy Thursday service, this melody has an entirely different text, one of some thirty-one verses, of which seventeen are in Greek, and fourteen in Arabic, with the Arabic being a translation of the Greek. It treats the

---

[8] The criteria of transcription are as follows: 1) "A" above "Middle C" equals 440. 2) A minus sign (−) above a note indicates that the note is sounded one quarter-tone lower, conversely, a plus sign above a note (+) indicates that the note is sounded one quarter-tone higher. 3) The notes actually sound one octave lower than notated. (All singing is done by men only). 4) To facilitate comparison of the melodic line in Examples II, III, and IV, both versions have been transcribed in the same pitch, which has involved transposing one line in each case. The original interval relationship has been scrupulously maintained everywhere. 5) Broken lines drawn between the two staves indicate those notes of the melody which are the same, but which might not be so identified at first glance. 6) Measures are indicated by bar lines, but no rhythmic signatures (3/4, 2/4, etc.) are used because the number and value of the beats in each measure may change. 7) All beats are aligned vertically, one beneath the other.

All examples have been transcribed from recordings of the Holy Week Services, made at the Institute of Coptic Studies under the supervision of Ragheb Moftah, 1983 ca.

[9] The sequence of the texts to verses two and three is reversed in the Coptic and Greek versions, with Coptic verse two, ⲁⲣⲓⲡⲁⲙⲉⲅⲓ ⲱ ⲡⲁⲟⲩⲣⲟ... being the equivalent of Greek verse three, μνήσθητί μου δέσποτα and Coptic verse three, ⲁⲣⲓⲡⲁⲙⲉⲅⲓ ⲱ ⲫⲏⲉⲑⲟⲩⲁⲃ..., being the equivalent of Greek verse two μνήσθητί μου ἅγιε...

I   Comparison of melody when repeated with no change in language

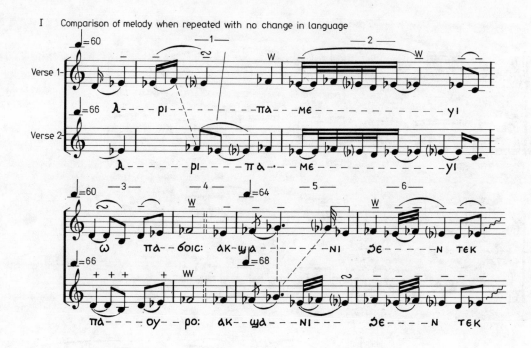

II   Comparison of melody sung in Coptic and Greek

1. Good Friday: "Remember me..." (Coptic: Αριπαμεγι ...; Greek: μνήσθητί μου...)

2. Maundy Thursday: "Judas..." (Greek: Ιούδας..., Arabic: Yahūzā...)

betrayal of Christ by Judas Iscariot, and may be identified by its opening lament, "Judas, Judas..." (Greek: Ἰούδας, Ἰούδας...; Arabic: Yahūzā, Yahūzā...). It is performed not by the chorus (as was the song on Good Friday), but rather by different soloists, each of whom has his own individual singing style (feeling for pitch, rhythmic eccentricities, patterns of embellishment, not to mention musicianship and voice quality). These soloists have a freedom and spontaneity, especially in embellishment, that makes "Judas, Judas..." sound quite different from "Remember me..."[10] For comparison of the melody as it is sung in Greek and Arabic, the opening verse of "Judas, Judas...," which is repeated at intervals throughout the song as a sort of refrain, has been chosen. The Greek transcription is the fifth tim around for the melody, with the Arabic being the twenty--second.

III (See transcription):
A. Pitch: The Arabic version (of which the transcription shows the actual pitch) is higher than the Greek by a diminished fifth. As to the interval relationships, there seems to be a difference in that the Greek may sound as "major" to the Western ear while the Arabic may sound as "minor". However, this dissimilarity is more apparent than real, for the use of the quarter-tone in Coptic music introduces intervals that are not commonly recognized in the Western musical tradition. One finds, for example, that the interval of the third, which in the West is always classified as either "major" or "minor," often lies half-way between these two designations, and thus is neither one nor the other, cf. measure one, beat three; measure four, beat one; measure four, beat three going into measure five; measure three and four combined.[11] B. Rhythm: In the "Judas, Judas...," whether sung

in Greek or Arabic, the rhythm is decidedly freer (more rubato) than in the "Remember me...," but basically it remains unchanged.
C. Ornamentation: Whether the language is Greek or Arabic, the basic melodic line is kept, but the ornamentation obviously displays the individuality of each soloist.

From Example III it can be seen that the main difference between the Greek and Arabic renditions is that of the "major" (Greek) and "minor" (Arabic), a difference more apparent than real. Whether the change from Greek to Arabic is in itself responsible for this variance would be difficult to say. (It may be noted that the entire "Remember me..." is heard as "minor"). In fact one would be hard put to pinpoint any variations in the melody caused specifically by the change of language.[12]

However, at this juncture, some important observations about all of these languages and their relationship to the melody should be mentioned. Throughout every version of the song, whether the text be Coptic, Greek, or Arabic, the words have been fit to the needs of the music. Vowel quantity (long or short) is largely ignored, cf. Example II, Greek, measure one, beat three; entire measure three; Example III, the setting of the word "Judas" in both languages; Greek, measures seven and eight; Arabic, measure six, beat three, and measure seven, beat three; but there is correlation between the Greek written accent and the melodic stress, cf. Example II, measures one, two, three, five; Example III, measure seven; Example IV, two and six.

Further evidence of the requirements of the Greek text being ignored may be seen in many verses of "Judas, Judas....," wherein the musical phrase often ends not only at the beginning of a Greek phrase, but even in the middle of a word, cf.

---

[10] Not only because "Judas, Judas..." is performed solo while "Remember me..." is choral, but also because each song expresses such different emotions, the melody is not readily recognized as being the same for both. However, a beat-by-beat comparison of the notes and intervals reveals that there is indeed but one melody involved. Further evidence of this fact is that Ernest Newlandsmith transcribed the identical melody, in its basic form, for both texts. Ernest Newlandsmith, *Holy Week Hymns*, Vol. II, i.e., Vol. VII of his complete collection of transcriptions (unpublished manuscripts compiled in Cairo 1926–1932, under the aegis of Ragheb Moftah, available on microfilm at the University of California at Santa Barbara), 120, 128.

[11] This apparent indifference to the Western "major" and "minor" distinctions is quite common in Coptic music. Cf. Hans Hickmann, "Quelques observations sur la musique liturgique copte des Coptes d'Égypte," *Atti del congresso internazionale di musica sacra* (Rome, 1950), pp. 105–106; and Marian Robertson, "The Reliability of the Oral Tradition in Preserving Coptic Music, Part II," *Bulletin de la Société d'Archéologie Copte* XXVII (1985), 73–85.

[12] Concerning the influence of Arabic upon the music in Coptic services, there are still many questions demanding much further study and analysis, as, for example, the relationships of Coptic and Arabic music over the years, whether, when, and how much one tradition may have affected the other, etc.

Example IV, measures seven and eight.[13] Such treatment of the words and discrepancies in the phrasing of the text and music indicate that the melody was certainly not composed for the text in question, but rather, that this text was set to a melody already in existence and probably well known.

In view of the above, mention must be made, however, of two verses in "Judas, Judas..." which are striking exceptions to the rest of the song. In Greek verse fifteen and its Arabic counterpart, which is a translation of Greek verses fifteen and sixteen, the music is definitely adjusted to the text. To enhance the meaning and intensify the feelings of exultation evoked by the words, "He is risen" (Greek: 'ανεσῖη; Arabic: qāma), the rhythm becomes very rubato and the melodic line is extended with ornamentation. In many respects, this setting marks the "high point" of the entire song, cf. Example IV, especially measure two. It is interesting to observe that the Arabic need for each syllable to begin with a consonant + vowel is incorporated into the Greek text, cf. Example IV, measures two, three, and four.

Summary and Conclusions:

1. Changes in this melody occur primarily because of repetition and individuality of the various soloists. Changing the language does not by itself bring change to the melody.
2. Despite change in pitch (higher) and tempo (faster), and despite individual differences in ornamentation, the basic melodic line and rhythm remain intact.

Proposed Dating for the Melody:

Determining the antiquity of this melody is impossible without notated manuscripts for documentation. However, the following facts may be noted:
1. Different recordings of this melody[14] and earlier transcriptions thereof[15] have been compared. These studies show that the melody has been kept basically intact for at least sixty years, and it is reasonable to assume that it has remained thusly for a much longer period of time.

2. Extensive studies by ethnomusicologists have shown that melodies preserved by an oral tradition do not change essentially over long periods of time, centuries even.[16] The attitude of the Copts vis à vis their liturgical music, which they have long held as sacred and not to be changed, and their tradition, which has persisted unbroken from the beginnings of the Church, would tend to accentuate this situation.[17] In addition, studies show that Coptic music has tended to remain distinct over the centuries.[18]

3. As was mentioned, Anton Baumstark has dated both Greek texts from the seventh or eighth century. Whether this melody, in its basic form, comes from the same period cannot, of course, be definitively proven. However, its tenacity and resistance to change — whatever the language — are evident. Therefore, in view of the internal, comparative, and ethnomusicological evidence, it is not unreasonable to suggest that this little tune may possibly be as old as the Greek text, if not perhaps older.

---

[13] Examples of such disregard for the Greek text are to be found in verses two, three, four, six, nine, twelve, thirteen, fourteen, fifteen, and sixteen. They have not been included herein because they do not bear directly upon the topic under discussion, and for reasons of space.

[14] *Holy Week Services,* recorded at the Institute of Coptic Studies under the direction of Ragheb Moftah, 1980 ca. and 1983 ca.

[15] Newlandsmith, *Holy Week...,* 120, 128.

[16] Ilona Borsai and Margit Toth, "Variations ornementales dans l'interprétation d'un hymne copte," *Studia Musicologica Academiae Scientiarum Hungaricae* (henceforth referred to as *Studia*) XI (1969), 91–105.

[17] Ilona Borsai, "Die musikhistorische Bedeutung der orientalischer christlicher Riten," *Studia* XVI (1974), 4–14.

[18] Ilona Borsai, "Le tropaire byzantin 'O Monogénes' dans la pratique du chant copte," *Studia* XIV (1972), 329–354.

COPTIC STUDIES

James M. Robinson

The First Christian Monastic Library

The first Christian monastic order was founded in Upper Egypt by Pachomius early in the 4th century. What was left of its library was buried when the order was near extinction as a result of the Calcedonian-Monophysite schism in the 6th or 7th century. It was discovered in 1952 and is known to scholars as the Bodmer Papyri. It is the information leading to this conclusion that is here to be summarized. It will be presented in more detail in a book being prepared for publication at Fortress Press in Philadelphia.

The term Bodmer Papyri derives from the series of *editiones principes* published by the Bibliothèque Bodmer and entitled *Papyrus Bodmer I* (1954) through *Papyrus Bodmer XXIX* (1984), plus a few texts that were published in the Corpus Scriptorum Christianorum Orientalium and the journal *Museum Helveticum*, all of which manuscripts are at the Bibliothèque Bodmer in Cologny near Geneva (except for P. Bodmer VIII and a few scattered fragments) and are thought to come from the same manuscript discovery (except for P. Bodmer XVII, generally agreed to come from another discovery). By extension, the term 'Bodmer Papyri' has come to be used, as here, to refer to all the manuscripts of that discovery, thus including such materials that happen to be at several other repositories, but excluding P. Bodmer XVII. In Upper Egypt the discovery is known not as the Bodmer Papyri, but as the Dishna Papers.

1. The Dishna Papers

The discovery of the Dishna Papers was made late in 1952 by Ḥasan Muḥammad al-Sammān and Muḥammad Khalīl al-Azzūzī, both of whom come from Abū Manāʿ "Baḥrī." This hamlet is on the right bank of the Nile in the area where it flows from east to west, and hence literally on the north bank. Abū Manāʿ lies some 4 km from the river's edge, near the foot of the cliff Jabal Abū Manāʿ, which is 12 km east of the Jabal al-Ṭarīf where the Nag Hammadi Codices were discovered. It is 5 km northeast and in full view of Fāww Qiblī, ancient Pabau (Greek) or Phbow (Coptic), the site of the headquarters of the Pachomian Monastic Order, and 5.5 km northwest of Dishnā, the larger town at the river with a railroad station, thus playing the role in this discovery corresponding to that of the town Nag Hammadi in the case of the Nag Ḥammadi Codices. Abū Manāʿ itself is 10 km east of Ḥamrah Dūm, the hamlet that controls the site of the discovery of the Nag Hammadi Codices, much as does Abū Manāʿ in the case of the Bodmer Papyri.

Hasan and Muhammad were digging for *sabakh* some 300 meters out from the foot of the Jabal Abū Manāʿ at al-Qurnah ("the corner"), when Ḥasan uncovered a large earthen jar containing the books. He broke the jar with his mattock, leaving the sherds where they fell. Some fragmentary parts of the find were burnt on the spot, and others were given away to passersby, who incidentally terrified Ḥasan with the idea that they were books of giants. Yet he carried the bulk of the discovery home in his *jallabīyah,* the typical peasant ground-length robe; Muḥammad took for his part a wooden plank variously interpreted as a cover, a mirror, or a catalogue of the library's contents.

Hasan lived in his wife's family home, presided over by her father Umar al-Abadi. Her brother, ʿAbd al-Āl, trafficked in the books, unsuccessfully at first, since they could not even be bartered for sugar. Some leaves of a large papyrus book were crushed up and used as fuel to light their water pipe; parchment burnt like an oil lamp. Rural electrification reached the hamlet only in 1980.

ʿAbd al-Āl worked in the Dishnā jewelry shop of the goldsmith Subḥī Qusṭandī Dimyān, to whom he sold a book. Subḥī showed it to the Dishnā priest "al-Qummuṣ" Manqaryūs, who was related to the priestly family of al-Qaṣr through whose hands Nag Hammadi material had passed, to inquire if it were equally valuable. "Al-Qummuṣ" Manqaryūs told him it was worthless, hoping thus to be able to acquire it himself. But Subḥī's son Jirjis taught at the same Coptic parochial school at Dishnā as did the member of that al-Qaṣr family who had sold Nag Hammadi Codex III to the Coptic Museum in Cairo for £250, Rāghib Andarāwus "al-Qiss" ʿAbd al-Sayyid. Jirjis showed his father's book at the Coptic Museum, where it was confiscated and he threatened with jail, until a powerful friend persuaded the Museum to return his book and press no charges. Jirjis sold the book to Zakī Ghālī, an antiquities dealer in Luxor, for a price said to be £400.

ʿAbd al-Raḥīm Abū al-Ḥājj, Umar's nephew, was a village barber going from house to house to ply his trade, as well as a share-cropper working fields belong to a Dishnā goldsmith, Riyāḍ Jirjis Fām. Riyāḍ began dirt poor, the son of a peasant who eked out a living making baskets from reeds taken from the edge of the Nile, but scrounged his way up to the role of the ruthless strong-man of Dishnā. When he heard of the discovery, he took another goldsmith with him, Mūsā Fikrī Ashʿīyah, and went to the house of ʿAbd al-Raḥīm in Abū Manāʿ. The latter was afraid of the accompanying stranger and refused to deal with them, but on a subsequent visit when Mūsā Fikrī was not present sold Riyāḍ three or four books.

"Al-Qummuṣ" Manqaryūs became involved with Riyāḍ's acquisitions, along with Mūsā Fikrī and another goldsmith, Shākir Ghubrīyāl. They thus created some kind of partnership, the priest providing a semi-educated assessment, ecclesiastical connections, and a haven free of police searches, whereas the goldsmits no doubt provided the capital and Riyāḍ also the entrepreneurship.

Accompanied by his son Nuṣhi, Riyāḍ returned to Abū Manāʿ and went directly to the house of Umar al-Abadi, where he bought out the rest of what the family held. He was able to leave the hamlet with the loot only with the armed escort of Umar's sons as far as the paved highway. He went straight to the home of "al-Qummuṣ" Manqaryūs, where he counted out to him "thirty-three books." Though this figure recurs repeatedly in the story, it is not clear whether it is meant to include the books Riyāḍ had already acquired, and whether it included material usually distinguished from the "books," namely ten small rolls the size of one's finger, three or four large rolls some 25 cm or more high, and a few triangular-shaped leaves some 15 cm high. If the counting procedure was for the sake of monitoring how much material was entrusted to the priest, lest some of it not be returned, it must have included everything in that transaction. In spite of such ambiguities, the figure does tend to indicate roughly the extent of the discovery, perhaps as much as three times that of the thirteen Nag Hammadi Codices.

Muḥammad, irritated at having been excluded from the sales and profits, reported the discovery to the police, who found concrete evidence with Masri ʿAbd al-Masīḥ Nūḥ, who had acquired the wooden board from Muḥammad. He implicated the others. Charges were not brought against the priest, but Riyāḍ and Mūsā Fikrī were charged. And, by a case of mistaken identity, Shafīq Muḥārib Bisharun was charged instead of Shākir Ghubrīyāl. Also charged were Ḥasan and the brother of ʿAbd al-ʿĀl, as well as Abū al-Wafā Aḥmad Ismāʿīl, who had acquired a triangular parchment leaf. By a combination of threats and bribes Riyāḍ prevented them from testifying against him in their effort to exonerate themselves. His defense lawyer, Ḥilmī Bandarī, argued unsuccessfully before Judge Rabāʿ Tawfīg that the possession of antiquities was not illegal, they were ignorant of what they had acquired, and there was no incriminating evidence. All eight were sentenced to a year in jail. Engaging Aḥmad ʿAlī ʿAllūbā "Pasha", a Conservative Party politician from Cairo as their attorney, Riyāḍ appealed the case at the Court of Appeals in Qinā. Six were acquitted, but two were sentenced to six months in jail; Masri's sentence was suspended and only Ḥasan served time.

During this trying time "al-Qummuṣ" Manqaryūs was concerned that his house be searched. The books were being kept in his home, no doubt on the assumption that a police search of a priest's home was less likely than of a goldsmith's home. The box in which they were kept was hidden at times under the floor, no doubt the dirt floor of the patio, at times behind rafters in the ceiling. But as the pressure mounted, he secreted them in a cubboard built under his divan and asked his neighbour, Saʿīd Diryās Ḥabashī, if he could sun the divan in his patio, where there was more sun than in his own, to free it of fleas. When he recuperated the divan he found the best book missing. Saʿīd Diryās denied having taken it, saying he was unaware of the divan's contents, otherwise he would have taken them all. Riyād traced the book to Fāris, a tailor of Dishnā, who is reported to have paid £ 30 for it and then to have sold it for £ 700 to Phokion J. Tano, the Cypriote antiquities dealer of Cairo who had acquired most of the Nag Hammadi Codices, where Riyād later saw it.

Riyād retrieved the material from "al-Qummuṣ" Manqaryūs, apparently except for a few fragments. For ʿAzīz Suryāl Aṭiyah has reported that the priest's son "al-Qummuṣ" Ṭanyūs showed him a fragment at his home in the posh Cairo suburb Maadi. And Saʿīd Diryās has reported that a Spanish priest obtained some material about 1966 from the priest's son "al-Qummuṣ" Ṭanyūs. The parish diary of the Franciscan Church adjoining the Sugar Factory near Nag Hammadi records that a José O'Callaghan Martinus of Barcelona with passport number 95912 came "to look for papers" on 14–20 November 1964 and for a second visit beginning 1 February 1965. The widow of "al-Qummuṣ" Manqaryūs thought there were fragments in the home when I interviewed her on 18 December 1976 but she could not find them.

Riyād was under virtual house arrest. For he was not permitted to go as far as Cairo, but was limited in his movements to the region from Luxor to Sohag, for trips up to ten hours, and then only with police permission. So he turned to a lifelong friend, Fatḥallah Dāʾūd, who had gone on pilgrimage to Jerusalem with him in 1945 (as their identical tattoos validate), to take books to Cairo to market. Though Fatḥallah Dāʾūd was instructed to report to "al-Qummuṣ" Manqaryūs, Mūsā Fīkrī and Shākir Ghubrīyāl a lower price than he actually received, so that their proportion of the profit would be correspondingly less, he actually told them the truth. Having his own profit thus appreciably reduced, Riyād plotted revenge to recuperate his loss. He hired members of the Abū Baḥbūḥ family to break into Fatḥallah Dāʾūd's house and kidnap a son to be held for the equivalent ransom. In the dark of night they by mistake took a daughter, Sūsū. Rather than paying the ransom, Fatḥallah Dāʾūd appealed by telegram to Nassar. Within a week police sent from Cairo secured the release of Sūsū unharmed. Riyād himself seeks to put a good (or less bad) light on the incident by maintaining that the Abū Baḥbūḥ family were planning to kill Fatḥallah Dāʾūd for their own reasons, but Riyād had talked them out of that unprofitable venture in favor of a slightly less (?) inhumane and in any case more profitable procedure.

Riyād made friends with the two police guards posted at his home, plying them with alcohol on Saturday evenings until they were in a drunken stupor in time for him to catch the midnight train to Cairo. There he would take a few books at a time to Tano's home, receiving profits he has reported in the thousands of pounds, and return Sunday night in time to get into his home under the cover of darkness before dawn Monday.

The death of Riyād's son Wasfi in a brawl some years later, which Fatḥallah Dāʾūd interpreted as divine retribution, led Riyād to move to Cairo, where he lives on the top, fifth floor of a large modern duplex apartment house in Heliopolis which he has purchased.

2. The Acquisition of the Bodmer Papyri

Martin Bodmer had visited Egypt as early as 1950, when he approached Tano to secure manuscripts for his library. Father L. Doutreleau, S.J., one of the editors of the series *Sources chrétiennes* in Lyon, was at the time stationed in Cairo. He provided Bodmer with an expert assessment of manuscripts Tano showed him for this purpose (and provided me with the information here reported with his permission). Tano exported material at times through the diplomatic pouch, at times through a friend who worked at the customs office in Alexandria. He spent summers in the family home of Cyprus, where he stored materials he had available for sale and where he could correspond freely about his business affairs and maintain regular hard-currency banking procedures. From there he went to Geneva in September 1955. It was about that time that P. Bodmer II and III reached Geneva.

Bodmer himself was in Cairo at the end of January 1956. On 8 October 1956 Gilles Quispel was told by Ludwig Keimer, an Austrian in Cairo who was close to Doutreleau and Tano, that Bodmer had bought from Tano P. Bodmer XIV–XV (Luke-John) and much of XXV–IV–XXVI (Menander) at the beginning of February 1956. These codices reached Geneva shortly thereafter. Bodmer's secretary, Odile Bongard, visited Tano in Cairo in March or April 1956. A rather steady stream of acquisitions was interrupted by the Suez crisis in October 1956. Efforts to reactivate Tano were unsuccessful, except for several leaves of Menander Tano showed to Doutreleau in 1958. They were deposited at the Tunisian Embassy in Cairo for export, but then delayed several years by a breaking of diplomatic relations between Egypt and Tunisia, with the shipment finally reaching Geneva, with part of it missing.

A minority of the material held by Tano was acquired by Sir Chester Beatty (then of London, later of Dublin), who usually spent the winters in Cairo and was a long-standing customer of Tano: Ac. 2555 = a fragment from P. Bodmer II, 139/140 (John 19:25–28, 30–32) and a fragment from P. Bodmer XX, 135,13–16/136, 14–17; ac. 1389 = two-thirds of P. Bodmer XXI; and ac. 1390 = mathematical exercises in Greek followed directly by John 10:8–13:38 in Sub-Achmimic. Probably of the same provenience are also ac. 1493 = Apocalypse of Elijah; ac. 1499 = a Greek grammar and a Graeco-Latin Lexicon on Romans, 2 Corinthians, Galatians, and Ephesians; ac. 1501 = 4 sheets of one Psalms codex and 1 leaf of another Psalms text, perhaps an amulet; and various Coptic fragments, of which those from the Book of Jannes and Jambres would seem most appropriate; and perhaps ac. 2554 = P. Beatty Panopolitanus = an unbound, largely uninscribed codex with a few tax receipts of 339–347 A.D. from Panopolis (Achmim), constructed secondarily from two rolls containing the correspondence of the Strategus of the Panopolite nome dated to 298–300 A.D.

Minor segments, some passing through the hands of other middlemen and dealers, reached other repositories:

The University of Mississippi, Oxford, Mississippi, acquired through David M. Robinson and William H. Willis from the Cairo "Art Gallery Maguid Sameda" Mississippi Coptic Codex I (the Crosby Codes) for $ 3000, of which some fragments were also acquired by the Bibliothèque Bodmer; Mississippi Coptic Codex II (half of P. Bodmer XXII) for $ 1,500; P. Robinson inv. 38 = a fragment of leaf 55/56 of P. Bodmer XXVI (Menander's *Aspis*, lines 487–98, 524–32); and P. Duke. inv. L 1 (ex P. Robinson inv. 201) = a fragment of Cicero *Ad Catilinam* 1–2 from P. Barcinonenses inv. 149–61.

The Institut für Altertumskunde of the University of Cologne acquired P. Colon. inv. 904 = P. Köln 3 = a fragment of P. Bodmer XXVI that joins the fragment that came to the University of Mississippi; and perhaps four fragmentary texts that Cologne acquired in the same lot as that which included the fragment of P. Bodmer XXVI: P. Colon. inv. 902 = P. Köln 40 = fragments from Books 3–4 of the Odyssey and hence perhaps related to P. Bodmer I, XLVIII and XLIX, as well as three fragmentary texts that join fragments acquired by the University of Mississippi from the same dealer who sold the University of Mississippi the two codices shared with the Bibliothèque Bodmer: P. Colon. inv. 906 that joins P. Rob. inv. 32 (scholia to Odyssey 1), P. Colon. inv. 901 that joins P. Rob. inv. 35 (Achilleus Tatios) and P. Colon. inv. 903 that joins P. Rob. inv. 37 (an ethnographic or philosophical treatise).

The Fundacio "Sant Lluc Evangelista" of Barcelona acquired P. Barcinonenses inv. 149–61 = Cicero, *Ad Catalinam*; Psalmus Responsorius; Greek liturgical text; and *Alcestis*.

Perhaps to be included is the codex acquired by the Palau Ribes Collection of the Seminario de Papirologia of the Facultad Teologica de San Cugat des Valles of Barcelona: P. Palau Ribes 1 81–83.

There are probably further materials from the same discovery at some or all of these repositories that have not thus far been identified as such, just as some of those listed as probably or merely possibly of the same provenience may in fact not be. And, to judge by certain similarities with known Bodmer Papyri, some of the material may have reached still other repositories not otherwise known to have acquired parts of Bodmer Papyri, such as P. Yale Inv. 1779 = Psalms 76–77 in Coptic, acquired by Yale University, New Haven, Connecticut, around 1962 from H.P. Kraus, the leading rare book dealer of New York; and a small parchment roll in a private German collection containing the Pachomian Abbot Theodore's Letter 2.

Some of this material secondarily reached other repositories:

P. Bodmer VIII was presented to Pope Paul VI and is at the Vatican Library.

The holdings of the University of Mississippi were acquired in 1981 by H.P. Kraus. Mississippi Coptic Codex I (the Crosby Codex) was then acquired for $ 290,000 by the Pax ex Innovatione Foundation of Vaduz, Liechtenstein, through the good offices of Winsor T. Savery, after whom the

Foundation has named it. It is now on loan for reconservation, display and editing at the Institute for Antiquity and Christianity of Claremont Graduate School. Mississippi Coptic Codex II is in a New York bank vault of H.P. Kraus awaiting sale for $ 150,000. The Mississippi fragment of P. Bodmer XXVI and the Mississippi fragment of P. Barcinonenses inv. 149–61 now belong to the Library of Duke University in Durham, North Carolina.

Fragments of P. Barcinonenses inv. 149–61 that were located at the Bibliothèque Bodmer were given to the Fundacio "Sant Lluc Evangelista," which gave a fragment of P. Bodmer XXV it held to the Bibliothèque Bodmer.

The Bibliothèque Bodmer also located and passed on fragments of Melito of Sardis, On the Passover, from the Savery Codes.

3. The Inventory

The total quantity of material involved (not counting the Pachomian material), including the quite fragmentary and the uncertain items mentioned above, would involve what remains of some 40 books. They consist of 9 Greek classical papyrus rolls (numbers 1, 2, 17, 24, 25, 34–37), 1 small papyrus Sahidic Christian Old Testament roll in *rotuli* form (number 40), and 30 codices (numbers 3–16, 18–23, 26–33, 38, 39). The codices are subdivided as follows: 23 are on papyrus (numbers 3–6, 8, 10, 12, 14–16, 18, 20, 23, 26–33, 38, 39), 5 on parchment (numbers 7, 9, 11, 13, 19), and of 2 the Bibliothèque Bodmer has not divulged the material (numbers 21, 22). 11 are in Greek (numbers 3, 5, 6, 8, 15, 16, 18, 29, 30–32), 1 in Latin (number 38), and 1 in Greek and Latin (number 28). 17 are in Coptic (numbers 4, 7, 9–14, 19–23, 26, 27, 33, 39), of which 10 are in Sahidic (numbers 9–14, 19, 27, 33, 39), 2 in Bohairic (numbers 4, 23), 1 in Paleo-Theban (number 7), 2 in Sub-Achmimic (numbers 20, 26), and of 2 the Bibliothèque Bodmer has not divulged the dialect (numbers 21, 22). 2 are non-Christian (numbers 5, 32), 25 Christian (numbers 3, 4, 6–15, 18–23, 27, 29–31, 33, 39), and 4 partly each (numbers 16, 26, 28, 38). 15 contain something from the Old Testament (numbers 4, 6, 7, 9, 10, 12–16, 19, 23, 29, 30, 33) and 9 something from the New Testament (numbers 3, 4, 6, 8, 11, 21, 26, 33, 39).

What follows is an inventory in terms of books, rather than merely in terms of the rather arbitrary numerations under which texts have been published. The inventory includes, in addition to the identification of the texts in each book to the extent they are at least in part extant, a listing of the form (roll or codex), material (papyrus or parchment), and language, when they are not Greek papyrus codices. The bibliographical entries are basically limited to the *editiones principes,* though the first English and German translations are also included. Publication information is itemized except for the series *Papyrus Bodmer* I, etc., which is published at Cologne--Geneva: Bibliothèque Bodmer (beginning with XXIX: Fondation Martin Bodmer) except for P. Bodmer III, VI, XXVII, XXVIII, XLV and XLVI. For items not yet published, the information is derived from the repositories of the material and from published preliminary reports that are also included.

1. Homer, *Iliad,* Book 5 = P. Bodmer I, a Greek papyrus roll, with the text on the verso of a roll of documentary papyri = P. Bodmer L. *Papyrus Bodmer I. Iliade, chants 5 et 6.* Published by Victor Martin, Bibliotheca Bodmeriana 3, 1954. P. Bodmer L is unpublished.

2. Homer, *Iliad,* Book 6 = P. Bodmer I, Greek papyrus roll, with the text on the verso of a different segment of the same roll of documentary papyri = P. Bodmer L. *Papyrus Bodmer I. Iliade, chants 5 et 6.* Published by Victor Martin, Bibliotheca Bodmeriana 3, 1954. P. Bodmer L is unpublished.

3. Gospel of John = P. Bodmer II = P 66 + a fragment of Chester Beatty ac. 2555, *Papyrus Bodmer II. Évangile de Jean, chap. 1–14.* Published by Victor Martin, Bibliotheca Bodmeriana 5, 1956. *Papyrus Bodmer II. Supplément. Évangile de Jean chap. 14–21.* Published by Victor Martin, 1958. *Papyrus Bodmer II. Supplément. Évangile de Jean chap. 14–21. Nouvelle édition augmentée et corrigée avec reproduction photographique complète du manuscrit (chap. 1–21).* Published by Victor Martin and J.W.B. Barns, 1962. The second *Supplément* includes in Plates 135/36 Chester Beatty ac. 2555, a fragment containing John 19:25–28, 30–32. Unpublished fragments from the cartonnage of a rebinding in Late Antiquity consist of remnants of Luke 4:1–2; 5:37–39; John 12:49–13:10; 14:27–15:10 rendered legible by the conservation carried out by the British Museum; they are to be published in P. Bodmer L.

4. Gospel of John and Genesis 1:1–4:2 = P. Bodmer III, a Bohairic papyrus codex, *Papyrus Bodmer III. Évangile de Jean et Genèse I–IV, 2 en bohaïrique.* Edited and translated by Rodolphe Kasser. Corpus Scriptorum Christianorum Orientalium 177–78. Scriptores Coptici 25–26, Louvain: Secrétariat du CorpusSCO, 1958.

5. Menander, *Samia, Dyskolos, Aspis* = P. Bodmer XXV, IV, XXVI + P. Barc. 45 + P. Colon. inv. 904 = P. Köln 3 + P. Robinson 38. Ramon Roca-Puig, "Fragment de 'La Samia' de Menandre, Papir de Barcelona, inventari no 45." *Boletin de la Real Academia de Buenas Letras de Barcelona* 32 (1967–68),

5–13. Ramon Roca-Puig, "Un Fragmento de 'La Samia' de Menandro: P. Barc. 45," *Estudios Clasicos* 12 (1968), 375–83. *Papyrus Bodmer XXV. Ménandre: La Samienne.* Published by Rodolphe Kasser with Colin Austin, 1969. *Papyrus Bodmer IV. Ménandre: Le Dyscolos.* Published by Victor Martin, 1958 [1959], E.W. Handley, *The Dyskolos of Menander,* London: Methuen and Co., 1965. Hans Joachim Mette, *Menandros, Dyskolos,* Göttingen: Vandenhoeck und Ruprecht, 1960, 2nd improved edition 1961. Max Treu. *Menander Dyskolos: Griechisch und Deutsch mit textkritischem Apparat und Erläuterungen herausgegeben,* Tusculum-Bücherei. Ed. H. Färber and M. Faltner, Munich: Ernst Heimeran, 1960. Walther Kraus, *Menanders Dyskolos mit einem kritischen Kommentar.* Österreichische Akademie der Wissenschaften, Philosophisch-historische Klasse, Sitzungsberichte, 234, Band, 4. Abhandlung. Vienna: Hermann Böhlaus Nachf., 1960. Reinhold Merkelbach, "Wartetext 2: P. Colon. inv. 904: Komödienfragment" (from the *Aspis*). *Zeitschrift für Papyrologie und Epigraphik* 1 (1967), 103–04. *Papyrus Bodmer XXVI. Ménandre: Le Bouclier. En appendice: compléments au Papyrus Bodmer IV. Ménandre: Le Dyscolos.* Published by Rodolphe Kasser with Colin Austin, 1969. Bärbel Kramer, "Menander, Aspis 482–497; 520–535," *Kölner Papyri* (P. Köln) 1, Papyrologica Coloniensia 7.1. Opladen: Westdeutscher Verlag, 1976, pp. 18–20.

6. Nativity of Mary or Apocalypse of James (Protevangelium of James); Apocryphal Correspondence of Paul with the Corinthians; Odes of Solomon 11; the Epistle of Jude; Melito of Sardis' Homily on the Passover; a fragment of a liturgical hymn; the Apology of Phileas; Psalms 33–34; 1 and 2 Peter = P. Bodmer V; X; XI; VII; XIII; XII; XX; IX; VIII + a fragment of Chester Beatty ac. 2555. *Papyrus Bodmer V. Nativité de Marie.* Published by Michel Testuz, 1958. *Papyrus Bodmer X–XII. X: Correspondance apocryphe des Corinthiens et de l'apôtre Paul; XI: Onzième Ode de Salomon; XII: Fragment d'un Hymne liturgique. Manuscrit du IIIᵉ siècle.* Published by Michel Testuz, 1959. Othmar Perler, *Ein Hymnus zur Ostervigil von Meliton?* (*Papyrus Bodmer XII*). Paradosis: Beiträge zur Geschichte der altchristlichen Literatur und Theologie 15, Freiburg, Switzerland: Universität, 1960. *Papyrus Bodmer VII–IX. VII: L'Épître de Jude; VIII: Les deux Épîtres de Pierre; IX: Les Psaumes 33 et 34.* Published by Michel Testuz, 1959. *Papyrus Bodmer XIII. Meliton de Sardis, Homélie sur la Pâque. Manuscrit du IIIᵉ siècle.* Published by Michel Testuz, 1960. Stuart George Hall, *Melito of Sardis, On Pascha and Fragments,* Oxford Early Christian Texts. Oxford: Clarendon, 1979, including also (on p. 85) P. Bodmer XII. *Papyrus Bodmer XX. Apologie de Philéas évêque de Thmouis.* Published by Victor Martin. With an *Essai de reconstruction du texte original grec* bound separately, 1964. The *editio princeps* includes from Chester Beatty ac. 2555 a fragment of P. Bodmer XX, 135, 13–16/136, 14–17.

7. Proverbs = P. Bodmer VI, a Paleo-Theban parchment codex. *Papyrus Bodmer VI. Livre des Proverbes.* Edited and translated by Rodolphe Kasser, Corpus Scriptorum Christianorum Orientalium 194–95. Scriptores Coptici 27—28. Louvain: Secrétariat du CorpusSCO, 1960.

8. Gospels of Luke and John = P. Bodmer XIV–XV = P 75. *Papyrus Bodmer XIV. Évangile de Luc chap. 3–24. Papyrus Bodmer XV. Évangile de Jean chap. 1–15.* Both published by Victor Martin and Rodolphe Kasser, 1961.

9. Exodus 1:1–15:21 = P. Bodmer XVI, a Sahidic parchment codex. *Papyrus Bodmer XVI. Exode I–XV, 21 en sahidique.* Published by Rodolphe Kasser, 1961.

10. Deuteronomy 1:1–10:7 = P. Bodmer XVIII, a Sahidic papyrus codex. *Papyrus Bodmer XVIII. Deuteronome I–X,7 en sahidique.* Published by Rodolphe Kasser, 1962.

11. Matthew 14:28–28:20 + Romans 1:1–2:3 = P. Bodmer XIX, a Sahidic parchment codex. *Papyrus Bodmer XIX. Évangile de Matthieu XIV, 28–XXVIII, 20; Épître aux Romains I, 1–II,3 en sahidique.* Published by Rodolphe Kasser, 1962.

12. Joshua = P. Bodmer XXI + Chester Beatty ac. 1389, a Sahidic papyrus codex. *Papyrus Bodmer XXI. Josué VI, 16–25, VII,6–XI,23, XXII,1–2,19–XXIII,7,15–XXIV,23 en sahidique.* Published by Rodolphe Kasser, 1963. *Joshua I–VI and Other Passages in Coptic, edited from a Fourth-Century Sahidic Codex in the Chester Beatty Library,* Dublin. Edited by A.F. Shore, Chester Beatty Monographs 9, Dublin: Hodges Figgis, 1963.

13. Jeremiah 40:3–52:34; Lamentations; Epistle of Jeremy; Baruch 1:1–5:5 = P. Bodmer XXII + Mississippi Coptic Codex II, a Sahidic parchment codes. *Papyrus Bodmer XXII et Mississippi Coptic Codex II. Jérémie XL, 3–LII,34; Lamentations; Épître de Jérémie; Baruch I, 1–V,5 en sahidique.* Published by Rodolphe Kasser, 1964.

14. Isaiah 47:1–66:24 = P. Bodmer XXIII, a Sahidic papyrus codex. *Papyrus Bodmer XXIII. Esaïe XLVII,1–LXVI, 24 en sahidique.* Published by Rodolphe Kasser, 1965. Texts from the cartonage are to be published in P. Bodmer L.

15. Psalms 17–118 = P. Bodmer XXIV. *Papyrus Bodmer XXIV. Psaumes XVII–CXVIII.* Published by Rodolphe Kasser and Michel Testuz, 1967.

16. Thucydides; Suzanna; Daniel; Moral Exhortations = P. Bodmer XXVII, XLV, XLVI, XLVII. Antonio Carlini. "Il papiro di Tucidide della Bibliotheca Bodmeriana (P. Bodmer XXVII)." *Museum Helveticum* 32 (1975), 33–40, plates 1–3. Antonio Carlini and Annamaria Citi, "Susanna e la prima visione di Daniele in due papiri inediti della Bibliotheca Bodmeriana: P. Bodm. XLV e P. Bodm. XLVI." *Museum Helveticum* 38 (1981), 81–120. P. Bodmer XLVII is unpublished.

17. A satyr play on the confrontation of Heracles and Atlas = P. Bodmer XXVIII, a Greek papyrus roll. Eric G. Turner, "Papyrus Bodmer XXVIII: A Satyr-Play on the Confrontation of Heracles and Atlas." *Museum Helveticum* 33 (1976), 1–23.

18. Codex Visionum = P. Bodmer XXIV–XXXVIII. *Papyrus Bodmer XXIX. Vision de Dorotheos.* Published by André Hurst, Olivier Reverdin, Jean Rudhardt, 1984. P. Bodmer XXX–XXXVIII are unpublished.

19. Song of Songs = P. Bodmer XL, a Sahidic parchment codex. Unpublished.

20. The Acts of Paul, Ephesus Episode = P. Bodmer XLI, a Sahidic papyrus codex. Unpublished. Rodolphe Kasser, "Acta Pauli 1959," *Revue d'histoire et de philosophie religieuses* 40 (1960), 45–57. Though not an *editio princeps* (see p. 45, note 4), the text is summarized on pp. 50–52 and paraphrased, indeed in part translated, on pp. 54–56. Rodolphe Kasser, "Anfang des Aufenthaltes zu Ephesus (nach einem bisher noch nicht edierten koptischen Papyrus)." Edgar Hennecke, *Neutestamentliche Apokryphen in deutscher Übersetzung.* Third edition

by Wilhelm Schneemelcher. 2. *Apostolisches: Apokalypsen und Verwandtes.* *Tübingen*: J.C.B. Mohr (Paul Siebeck), 1964, pp.268–70. English translation: "The Beginning of the Stay in Ephesus." *New Testament Apocrypha. 2. Writings Relating to the Apostles; Apocalypses and Related Subjects.* Ed. by R. McL. Wilson, Philadelphia: Westminster, 1964, pp. 387–90.

21. 2 Corinthians = P. Bodmer XLII, a Coptic codex, information as to dialect and material not divulged by the Bibliothèque Bodmer. Unpublished.

22. An Apocryphon in Coptic = P. Bodmer XLIII, a Coptic codex, information as to dialect and material not divulged by the Bibliothèque Bodmer. Unpublished.

23. Daniel = P. Bodmer XLIV, a Bohairic papyrus codex. Unpublished.

24. Fragments of the *Illiad* = P. Bodmer XLVIII, a Greek papyrus roll. Unpublished.

25. Fragments of the *Odyssey* = P. Bodmer XLIX, a Greek papyrus roll. Unpublished.

26. Mathematical exercises in Greek and John 10:8–13:38 in Sub-Achmimic = Chester Beatty ac. 1390, a Greek and Sub-Achmimic papyrus codex. An edition is in preparation by William Brashear, Wolf-Peter Funk, James M. Robinson and Richard Smith.

27. The Apocalypse of Elijah = Chester Beatty ac. 1493 = P. Chester Beatty 2018, a Sahidic papyrus codex. Albert Pietersma and Susan Turner Comstock, with Harold W. Attridge, *The Apocalypse of Elijah based on P. Chester Beatty 2018.* Texts and Translations 19. Pseudepigrapha Series 9, Chico: Scholars Press, 1981.

28. A Greek grammar and a Graeco-Latin lexicon on Romans, 2 Corinthians, Galatians, Ephesus = Chester Beatty ac. 1499, a Greek and Latin papyrus codex. Unpublished. An edition is in preparation by Alfons Wouters, with the title *The Chester Beatty Codex Ac. 1499. A Greek Grammar and a Graeco-Latin Lexicon on St. Paul.*

29. Psalms 72:6–23,25–76:1; 77:1–18,20–81:7; 82:2–84:14; 85:2–88:2) = Chester Beatty ac. 1501 = Chester Beatty Biblical Papyri XIII = Rahlfs 2149. Albert Pietersma, *Two Manuscripts of the Greek Psalter in the Chester Beatty Library Dublin.* Analecta Biblica 77, Rome: Pontifical Biblical Institute, 1978.

30. Psalms 31:8–11; 26:1–6,8–14; 2:1–8 = Chester Beatty ac. 1501 = Chester Beatty Biblical Papyrus XIV = Rahlfs 2150, a Greek papyrus, perhaps an amulet. Albert Pietersma, *Two Manuscripts of the Greek Psalter in the Chester Beatty Library Dublin.* Analecta Biblica 77, Rome: Pontifical Biblical Institute, 1978.

31. Book of Jannes and Jambres. Unpublished. An edition is in preparation by Albert Pietersma. It is to be published as P. Chester Beatty XVI.

32. Two rolls contaning tax receipts of 339–47 A.D. from Panopolis (Achmim) and a codex constructed from these rolls with correspondence of the Strategus of the Panopolitan nome of 298–300 A.D. = P. Beatty Panopolitanus = Chester Beatty ac. 2554. T.C. Skeat. *Papyri from Panopolis in the Chester Beatty Library Dublin.* Chester Beatty Monographs 10, Dublin: Hodges Figgis, 1964. L. C. Youtie, Dieter Hagedorn and H.C. Youtie, "Urkunden aus Panopolis II. Tax Receipts." *Zeitschrift für Papyrologie und Epigraphik* 8 (1971), 214–234.

33. Melito of Sardis On the Passover; 2 Maccabees 5:27–7:41; 1 Peter; Jonah; a homily or hymn = Mississippi Coptic Codex I (the Crosby Codex) = the Savery Codex, a Sahidic papyrus codex. William H. Willis, "The New Collections of Papyri at the University of Mississippi." *Proceedings of the IX International Congress of Papyrology.* Oslo: Norwegian Universities Press, 1961. pp. 381–92 and Plate 5, reproducing p. 104 (numbered in Coptic p. 30), and Plate 6, reproducing p. 96. Stuart George Hall, Melito of Sardis, *On Pascha and Fragments.* Oxford Early Christian Texts, Oxford: Clarendon Press, 1979. Variant readings are published in Latin translation. The Coptic text is unpublished. An edition is in preparation under the auspices of The Institute for Antiquity and Christianity, Claremont Graduate School, Claremont, CA.

34. *Scholia* to the *Odyssey* 1 = P. Rob. inv. 32 + P. Colon. inv. 906, a Greek papyrus roll. Unpublished.

35. Achilleus Tatios = P. Rob. inv. 35 + P. Colon. inv. 901, a Greek papyrus roll. Unpublished.

36. An ethnographic or philosophical treatise = P. Rob. inv. 37 + P. Colon. inv. 903, a Greek papyrus roll. Unpublished.

37. Fragments of *Odyssey* 3–4 = P. Colon. inv. 902 = P. Köln 40, a Greek papyrus roll. Bärbel Kramer, "Odyssee gamma 87–94; 460–472; 489–496; delta 18; 20, 21; 106–111; 135, 138–140; 164–177; 199–206; 230; 257–264; 339–342, 344, 346–354." *Kölner Papyri (P. Köln)* 1. Papyrologica Coloniensia 7.1. Opladen: Westdeutscher Verlag, 1976, pp. 89–97.

38. Cicero, *Ad Catilinam*; Psalmus Responsorius; Greek liturgical text; Alcestis = Codex Miscellani = P. Barcinonenses inv. 149–61 + P. Duke inv. L 1 (ex P. Robinson inv. 201), a Latin and Greek papyrus codex. Ramon Roca Puig, *Himne a la Verge Maria: "Psalmus Responsorius," papir 11ati del segle IV,* Barcelona: Asociacion de Bibliofilos de Barcelona, 1965. William H. Willis, "A Papyrus Fragment of Cicero." *Transactions and Proceedings of the American Philological Association,* edited by Donald W. Prakken, 94 (1963), 321–27. Ramon Roca-Puig, Cicero, *Catalinaries (I et II in Catilinam).* Papyri Barcinonenses. Barcelona, 1977. The Greek liturgical text is unpublished. Ramon Roca-Puig, *Alcestis. Hexàmetres Llatins: Papyri Barcinonenses, inv. no. 158–161.* Barcelona: Grafos, 1982.

39. Gospels of Luke; John; Mark = P. Palau Ribes 181–183, a Sahidic papyrus codex. Hans Quecke, *Das Lukasevangelium saïdisch. Text der Handschrift PPalau Rib. Inv.-Nr. 181 mit den Varianten der Handschrift M 569.* Hans Quecke, *Das Johannesevangelium saïdisch. Text der Handschrift PPalau Rib. Inv.-Nr. 183 mit den Varianten der Handschrift M 569.* Hans Quecke, *Das Markusevangelium saïdisch. Text der Handschrift PPalau Rib. Inv.-Nr. 182 mit den Varianten der Handschrift M 569.* Papyrologica Castroctaviana. Studia et textus 6, 7, 4, directed by José O'Callaghan, S. J. Barcelona: Papyrologica Castroctaviana, 1977, 1983, 1972.

40. Psalms 76–77 = P. Yale inv. 1779, a small roll in rotuli form. Joseph Vergotte and George M. Parássoglou, „Les Psaumes 76 et 77 en Copte-Sahidique d'après le P. Yale inv. 1779", *Le Muséon* 87 (1974), 531–41.

4. The Pachomian Archive

A distinct part of the discovery consists of archival copies of official letters of early Abbots of the Pachomian Monastic Order. All these letters, previously completely unknown or known only in Jereme's Latin translation of 400 A.D., have emerged at the same time and (possibly with one exception) at the same repositories as did the Bodmer Papyri. Most of them are apparently what Riyād referred to as the small rolls, which Tano told him contained letters. In one instance the repository has a record ascribing its Pachomian material to the Nag Hammadi region, which was Tano's favorite vague but advantageous designation of the provenience of the Bodmer Papyri. At least two of the repositories acquired their Pachomian material in the same acquisition with other Bodmer Papyri. The site of the discovery is in full view of the Pachomian Order's headquarters Monastery at Fāww Qiblī 5 km away. These considerations make it probable that the Pachomian archive and thus the discovery as a whole made up the archives of the Pachomian Monastic Order. Perhaps these relics were buried for safe keeping in connection with the imposition of Chalcedonian orthodoxy on the traditionally Monophysite order in the 6th or 7th century, as the dating of the materials might suggest.

1. Pachomius' Letter 11b = P. Bodmer XXXIX, a small Sahidic parchment roll. Armand Veilleux, *Pachomian Koinonia*. Vol. 3. *Instructions, Letters, and Other Writings of Saint Pachomius and His Disciples*, Cistercian Studies Series 47. Kalamazoo, MI: Cistercian Publications Inc., 1982, pp. 77–78. English translation only. The Coptic text is unpublished. An edition is in preparation by Tito Orlandi, Adalbert de Vogüé, Hans Quecke and James Goehring in a volume entitled *Pachomiana Coptica*.

2. Pachomius' Letters 9a, 9b, 10, 11b in Sahidic = Chester Beatty Glass Container No. 54 = Chester Beatty ac. 2556, a Sahidic papyrus codex. Hans Quecke, "Ein neues Fragment der Pachombriefe in koptischer Sprache." *Orientalia* 43 (1974), 66–82.

3. Pachomius' Letters 1–3, 7, 10, 11a = Chester Beatty Ms. W. 145 + P. Colon. inv. 3288 = P. Köln 174 = three fragments from Letter 7, a small Greek parchment roll in *rotuli* form. Hans Quecke, *Die briefe Pachoms: Griechischer Text der Handschrift W. 145 der Chester Beatty Library, eingeleitet und herausgegeben*. Textus Patristici et Liturgici 11, Regensburg: Friedrich Pustet, 1975. Cornelia Römer, "Aus dem siebten Brief des Pachom: Fragmente zur Pergamentrolle der Chester Beatty Library." *Kölner Papyri (P. Köln) 4*, Papyrologica Coloniensia 7.4. Opladen: Westdeutscher Verlag, 1982, pp. 90–98.

4. Theodore's Letter 2 = Chester Beatty ac. 1486, a small Sahidic parchment roll in *rotuli* form. Hans Quecke, "Ein Brief von einem Nachfolger Pachoms (Chester Beatty Library Ms. Ac. 1486)." *Orientalia* 44 (1975), 426–33 and plate 42. Armand Veilleux, *Pachomian Koinonia*. Vol. 3. *Instructions, Letters, and Other Writings of Saint Pachomius and His Disciples*. Cistercian Studies Series 47. Kalamazoo, MI: Cisterian Publications Inc., 1982, pp. 127–29. English translation only. Adalbert de Vogüé, "Epîtres inédites d'Horsièse et de Théodore." *Commandements*

du Seigneur et Libération évangélique, Studia Anselmiana 70. Rome: Editrice Anselmiana, 1977, pp. 244–57, esp. 255–57. French translation only.

5. A second copy of Theodore's Letter 2 in a private German collection, a small Sahidic parchment roll in *rotuli* form. Martin Krause, "Der Erlassbrief Theodors." Studies Presented to Hans Jakob Polotsky. Ed. Dwight W. Young. Beacon Hill, East Gloucester, MA: Pirtle and Polson, 1981, pp. 220–38 and Plate 6.

6. Horsiesios' Letter 3 = Chester Beatty ac. 1494, a small Sahidic papyrus roll. Armand Veilleux, *Pachomian Koinonia*. Vol. 3. *Instructions, Letters, and Other Writings of Saint Pachomius and His Disciples*, Cistercian Studies Series 47. Kalamazoo, MI: Cisterian Publications Inc., 1982, pp. 157–60. English translation only. Adalbert de Vogüé, "Epîtres inédites d'Horsièse et de Théodore." *Commandements du Seigneur et Libération évangéliqué*. Studia Anselmiana 70. Rome: Editrice Anselmiana, 1977, pp. 244–57, esp. 245–49. French translation only. The Coptic text is unpublished. An edition is in preparation by Tito Orlandi, Adalbert de Vogüé, Hans Quecke and James Goehring in a volume entitled *Pachomiana Coptica*.

7. Horsiesios. Letter 4 = Chester Beatty ac. 1495, a small Sahidic papyrus roll. Armand Veilleux, *Pachomian Koinonia*. Vol. 3. *Instructions, Letters, and Other Writings of Saint Pachomius and His Disciples*, Cistercian Studies Series 47. Kalamazoo, MI: Cisterian Publications Inc., 1982, pp. 161–65. English translation only. Adalbert de Vogüé, "Epîtres inédites d'Horsièse et de Théodore." *Commandements du Seigneur et Libération évangélique*, Studia Anselmiana 70. Rome: Editrice Anselmiana, 1977, pp. 244–57, esp. 250–54. French translation only. The Coptic text is unpublished. An edition is in preparation, by Tito Orlandi, Adalbert de Vogüé, Hans Quecke and James Goehring in a volume *Pachomiana Coptica*.

8. Pachomius' Letter 8 = P. Colon. inv. 3246 = P. Colon. Copt. 2 = P. Köln ägypt. 8, a small Sahidic parchment roll. Alfred Hermann, "Homilie in Sahidischem Dialekt." *Demotische und koptische Texte*. Papyrologica Coloniensia 2. Wissenschaftliche Abhandlungen der Arbeitsgemeinschaft für Forschung des Landes Nordrhein-Westfalens. Cologne and Opladen, 1968, pp. 82–85 and Pl. 3. Hans Quecke, "Briefe Pachoms in koptischer Sprache: Neue deutsche Übersetzung." *Zetesis: Album Amicorum... aangeboden aan E. de Strijcker*, Antwerp and Utrecht: De Nederlansche Boekhandel, 1973, pp. 655–63. German translation only. Dieter Kurth, Heinz-Josef Thissen and Manfred Weber, *Kölner ägyptische Papyri (P. Köln ägypt.)*. 1. Abhandlungen der Rheinisch-Westfälischen Akademie der Wissenschaften, Sonderreihe Papyrologica Coloniensia 9, Cologne and Opladen: Westdeutscher Verlag, 1980, pp. 100–02.

9. Pachomius' Letters 10–11a = P. Colon. inv. 3287 = P. Colon. Copt. 1 = P. Köln ägypt. 9, a small Sahidic parchment roll. Angelius Kropp, O. P., "Ein Märchen als Schreibübung." *Demotische und koptische Texte*. Papyrologica Coloniensia 2. Wissenschafliche Abhandlungen der Arbeitsgemeinschaft für Forschung des Landes Nordrhein-Westfalens. Cologne and Opladen, 1968, pp. 69–81 and Pl. 1–2. Dieter Kurth, Heinz-Josef Thissen and Manfred Weber, *Kölner ägyptische Papyri (P. Köln ägypt.)* 1. Abhandlungen der Rheinisch-Westfälischen Akademie der Wissenschaften, Sonderreihe Papyrologica Coloniensia 9, Cologne and Opladen: Westdeutscher Verlag, 1980, pp. 103–08.

COPTIC STUDIES

Barbara Ruszczyc

Die Ausgrabungen in Tell Atrib (Kom Sidi Youssuf)

Die im Jahre 1969 auf dem Kom Sidi Youssuf in Atrib unternommenen polnisch-koptischen Ausgrabungen hatten zum Zweck das Suchen der Kirche, die der Jungfrau Maria geweiht war und die uns aus den Schriftquellen bekannt ist. In den Überlieferungen finden wir eine Beschreibung ihres Aussehens und der Art ihrer Verzierung. Verschiedene Legenden sind mit diesem Bauwerk verbunden. Der lokalen Tradition nach, stand die Kirche an dem heutigen Hügel Kom Sidi Youssuf. Die Kirche erlitt das Schicksal vieler anderer Bauten dieser Art in Ägypten.

Nach einer 10-jährigen Unterbrechung wurden die Ausgrabungen im Jahre 1979 wiederaufgenommen und sind bis heute, jeden Herbst, fortgesetzt. Mein Auftritt soll kein ausführlicher Bericht über alle Abschnitte unserer Untersuchungen sein, sondern eine kurze Zusammenfassung der bisher erreichten Resultate.

Das uns interessierende Gelände ist ein flaches Gebiet, in dessen nördlichem Teil sich ein kleiner Hügel, mit den Resten einer stark beschädigten arabischen Grabanlage auf seiner Spitze befindet. Vom Norden und Osten ist der Hügel von Feldern, und vom Westen durch die, in letzter Zeit errichteten, Wohnhäusern begrenzt. Der Hügel befindet sich im östlichen Viertel einer römischen Stadt. Da man die Grabanlage auf seiner Spitze nicht beseitigen darf, haben wir unsere Arbeiten auf den vier Hänger des Hügels unternommen, ohne sein zentraler Teil und das vom Osten angrenzende Gelände zu berühren. Ein Testschnitt wurde auch auf den vom Norden angrenzenden Feldern angelegt. Die wichtigsten Schnitte waren: vom Osten Schnitt C und vom Norden Schnitt D, wobei die auf dem Flachgelände und auf den Feldern angelegten Suchschnitte auch von einer grossen Bedeutung sind. Sie haben uns ermöglicht die Ausdehnungsgrenze der antiken Bebauung auf diesem Gelände zu bestimmen. Im Schnitt C wurden spätantike Badeanlagen entdeckt und es ist uns gelungen die Ausdehnung ihrer Bebauung festzustellen. Sie erstreckt sich unter dem meisten Teil des östlichen Geländes, reicht bis zum heutigen, nördlich des Hügels liegenden Friedhof und zieht sich unter dem grosseren Teil des Hügels hin. Im westlichen Teil des Geländes haben wir bis heute keine Spuren von Bebauung gefunden.

Während der Ausgrabungen haben wir zahlreiche Münzen, zum größten Teil aus 4. bis 5. Jahrhundert gefunden. Zu den sehr wichtigen Funden gehört die in den Schnitten C und D, entdeckte Schuttschicht in welcher sich Dekorationselementen eines zerstörten Baues befinden. Es sind Elemente des architektonischen Ausputzes, wie auch Verzierungselemente des Innenraumes, die mit Ziegeln, durchgeglühtem Putz, verkohlten Holzelementen und ähnliches vermischt waren. Es wurden viele, leider sehr schlecht erhaltene, Metalelemente gefunden. Die überreste des architektonischen Ausputzes bestehen aus Bruchstücken von der aus Stuck, Marmor und anderem Gestein hergestellten Kapitellen. So wie aus Bruchstücken von Säulensockeln und glatten, wie auch spiralgedrehten Säulenschaften. Ausserdem haben wir auch sehr viele Marmorverkleidungen gefunden, wobei besonders beachtenswert sind vor allem die verzierten Bruchstücke von Pilasterkapitellen, wie auch Fragmente aus farbigen Marmor und anderem Gestein waren. Elemente, welche aus weissen Marmor oder aus Stuck hergestellt waren, konnten bemalt oder im Falle der Marmorelemente mit einer dünnen Schicht vergoldung bedeckt sein. Zahlreiche vergoldete Bruchstücke wurden von uns gefunden. Im Falle der Säulenschaften wurde das Gold im Schachbrettmuster augelegt. Die von uns gefundenen Bruchstücke stammen eher von Teilen der Innenarchitektur. Ausser den oben erwähnten Elementen wurden auch Fragmente von Säulchen und Platten gefunden, welche zur Verzierung einer cancella gehörten und mit einem, im Kreise angebrachten gleicharmigen Kreuz

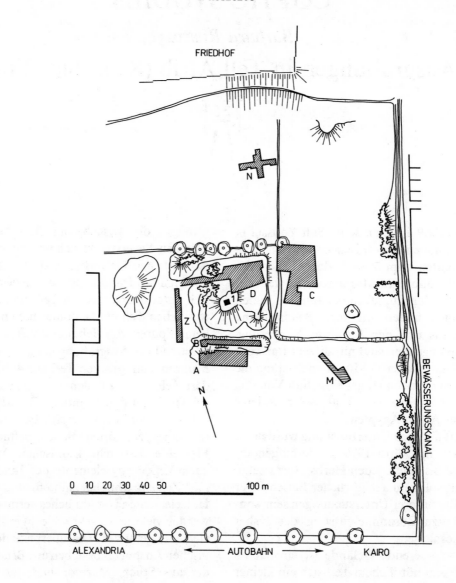

verziert waren. Dasselbe Dekorationsmotiv befindet sich auch auf Bruchstücken der nicht aus Marmor hergestellten Kapitellen. Wir fanden auch Bruchstücke von Fussbodenplatten. In der Schuttmasse haben wir auch zahlreiche, aber leider sehr kleine, Fragmente von Wandmosaiken gefuden.

Ausser den strikt architektonischen Elementen wurden auch Gegenstände der Ausstattung gefunden, wie z.B. die von Frau K. Dmowska identifizierte und rekonstruirte Teile von bronzenen Hängelampen des Policandilontypus. Auch eine grosse Zahl von Glasslampenbruchstücken sowie viele zur Türverzierung und zu anderen Holzgegenständen gehörende Metalelemente befanden sich unter den Funden.

Einleitend kann man heute sagen, daß die von uns gefundenen Elemente des architektonischen Aus-schmucks aus dem 4. bis zum 6. Jahrhundert stammen und wahrscheinlich eine Gruppe von Dekorationselementen des vornehmsten Teiles des sakralen Baues darstellen. Während der Aus-grabungskampagne im Jahre 1983 ist es uns gelungen die Stratigraphie des nördlichen Teiles des Hügels und insbesondere drei Hauptschichten zu bestimmen:

1. Die obere, durchmischte Schicht die einer Menge von losliegender Ziegeln und verschie-denartiger Keramik;

2. Die Schicht darunter, die aussergewöhnlich viel Scherben der spätrömischen und koptischen Keramik enthält. Die koptische Keramik ist reichlich verziert und zeigt viele tierische und menschliche Darstellungen. In dieser Schicht haben wir eine grosse Zahl von bizantinischen Münzen aus des 6. bis zum 7. Jahrhundert, so wie

islamische Nachbildungen von bizantinischen
Münzen des Heraklius und seines Sohnes
gefunden;

3. Unter dieser, oben erwähnten Schicht befindet
sich eine Schuttmasse die Asche und Bruchstücke
architektonischer Elemente enthält. Unmittelbar
auf ihrer Oberfläche ist es uns gelungen die Spuren
von 4 oder 5 Bestattungen festzustellen, diese
waren aber in so einem schlechten Zustande, daß
es unmöglich war ihre genaue Zahl zu bestimmen.
Die Leichen waren in Ost–West Richtung nie-
dergelegt. Bei einem Schädelfragment befand sich
ein Münzenschatz, der 16 Münzen aus dem Ende
des 6. Jahrhunderts enthielt. Die Schuttmasse
bedeckt Überreste von Bauanlagen, die sich unter
dem östlichen Teil des Hügels befinden.

Die Aufgabe diesjährigen Ausgrabungen wird in
der Untersuchung des noch nicht ausgegrabenen
Teiles der Schuttmasse so wie der Bestimmung
ihres Bereiches bestehen. Da der Charakter der
von uns gefundenen Bruchstücken auffalend mit
den, in den Schriftquellen beschriebenen Ausputz-
ungselementen der von uns gesuchten Kirche

übereinstimmt (d.h. Mosaiken, Verkleidungen aus
farbigem Marmor, der goldenen und silbernen
Säulen) liegt die Vermutung nahe, daß die
erwähnten Bruchstücke zu der Innenausstattung
dieses Baues gehören könnten. Offen bleibt immer
noch die Frage, woher diese auf dem Kom Sidi
Youssuf sich befindenden Bruchstücke herkom-
men, es ist doch sicher, daß sie von einer anderen
Stelle hierher gebracht wurden.

Alle Angaben die wir bis heute festgestellt haben,
führen uns zu der Folgerung, daß der Bau, dessen
Verzierungsreste wir gefunden haben, sich selbst
ausserhalb des Koms Sidi Youssuf befand. Diese
Tatsache würde ein Suchen auf dem angrenzenden
Gelände bedürfen, wahrscheinlich im Bereiche der
Felder, was aber aus verschiedenen Gründen zur
Zeit nicht möglich ist.

Somit möchte ich meinen kurzen Bericht schliess-
en. In meiner Aussage wollte ich Ihnen einen
Überblick über die Richtung unserer Forschungen
und ihre bisherigen Resultate vorstellen und
beschränke mich einstweilen auf die erwähnten
Tatsachen.

COPTIC STUDIES

Marie H. Rutschowscaya

Fouilles du Musée du Louvre à Tôd (Haute Égypte) Structures et matériel

Localisation des fouilles à partir de 1980

Un quadrillage du site fut établi par un topographe en 1979 couvrant une superficie d'environ 230 m sur 110 m par des carrés de 10 m sur 10 m. C'est à partir d'un point 0 situé sur le sol de la chapelle-reposoir de Thoutmosis III que furent prises les côtés de niveau (à 44 cm plus haut de celui établi par F. Bisson de la Roque sur le seuil du pronaos du temple de Montou).

Les fouilles se sont réparties selon trois secteurs :

— A l'arrière et sur les côtés du reposoir de Thoutmosis III : secteurs 1, 2, 3, 4 (époque moderne à l'époque romaine). Fouilles commencées en 1980.

— A l'ouest du temple de Montou ; au voisinage de la mosquée : secteur 10 (époque moderne à l'époque copte). Fouilles commencées en 1981.

— Au sud–est du temple de Montou : secteurs 7 et 8 (XIXᵉ siècle). Déblayage de surface en octobre 1981.

Structures

Matériaux : brique crue avec des remplois de blocs de calcaire, de grès ou de granite pharaoniques et coptes : murs, sols, fondations. Brique cuite utilisée en assises ou pour renforcer les points fragiles ou portants des constructions : fondantions, seuils, dallages. Des vases de céramique (particulièrement des canalisations), des tessons pilés pouvaient servir de fondation à certains murs ou être employés en bourrage de sols avant nivellement. Des murs de brique crue ainsi que certains sols présentent un enduit blanc (*mouna*) qui pouvait être peint.

Les constructions mises au jour jusqu'ici appartiennent à des bâtiments modestes qui s'empilent les uns sur les autres sans aucun plan d'ensemble, comme le pratiquent encore les paysans de nos jours. La lecture en est d'autant plus difficile que les inondations successives ont bouleversé le site (écroulements de murs, glissements de terrain).

1. Derrière le reposoir de Thoutmosis III (fig. 1) a été dégagée une couche stérile entre les strates islamiques et coptes, indiquant un arrêt d'occupation. La présence de dallages, de bases de silos en place et de seuils permet de déterminer plusieurs niveaux d'occupation copte qu'il est cependant difficile de dater. Des ostraca datés des VIᵉ–VIIᵉ siècles et la découverte de nombreuses céramiques attribuées à cette période permettent de dégager, à partir de ce niveau, une chronologie realtive des couches stratigraphiques.

Principales structures

a) Plusierus structures circulaires, délimitées par des briques cuites, contenaient des cendres. L'une de ces aires (fig. 2) était mise en relation avec un système de canalisation composé d'une poterie tubulaire cannelée incluse entre deux rangées de briques cuites ; le reste de la canalisation manque, mais il subsiste encore des éléments de « tuyau » disséminés de part et d'autre de la structure ainsi que trois pots de *saqqieh* alignés et retournés (niveau +35/+10). Après nettoyage de la couche plâtreuse blanche (environ 11 cm) mêlée à des fragments de poterie, fut mis au jour un dallage en briques cuites. La destination de ces aires n'a pas pu être déterminée : la dernière structure pourrait appartenir à un four à chaux (?). Il pourrait s'agir aussi d'aires de malaxage de l'argile (?).

Une structure identique fut retrouvée à un niveau plus bas au nord–est de la chapelle de Thoutmosis III, en relation avec une construction en briques cuites d'époque romaine (datée par des monnaies du IVᵉ siècle) : aire circulaire en briques cuites reliée à une autre aire plus petite d'où est issue la canalisation qui s'enfonce sous la construction (−95/−123) ; elle contenait de nombreux réci-

1. Secteur à l'arrière du reposoir de Thoutmosis III en avril 1981
   (phot. J.L. Bovot)

2. Aire circulaire avec canalisation et pots de *saqqieh* retournés
   (phot. J.L. Bovot)

3. Canalisations fichées verticalement et formant une aire
   circulaire (phot. J.L. Bovot)

5. Puits du secteur 10 (phot. D. Bénazeth)

7. Pièce dallée du secteur 10 (phot. M. Kurz)

4. Dallage de dalles en terre cuite disposées en quincone (phot. J.L. Bovot)

6. Porte du secteur 10 (phot. J.L. Bovot)

pients et tessons mêlés à de la cendre : four de potier(?).

b) Système de canalisations emboîtées horizontalement ou fichées en terre verticalement selon un plan circulaire ou semi-circulaire (fig. 3) : la découverte d'une poche de sable dans l'une de ces structures avait conduit à l'hypothèse d'un puisard.

L'une des canalisations était constituée de six tuyaux sur 2,50 m de longueur. Des éléments semblables avaient été découverts à Médamoud par F. Bisson de la Roque en 1930 qui pensait d'ailleurs à un remploi de tuyaux fabriqués à l'époque romaine [1].

c) Dallages limitant deux pièces voisines sur deux niveaux différents (−11, −58) en briques cuites : l'un est constitué de briques rectangulaires en forme de chevrons, l'autre de dalles de 0,25 m de côtes disposées en quinconce (fig. 4).

Le même type de dallage à briques rectangulaires fut mis au jour dans le même secteur à −54 cm, en limite de fouilles et se poursuivant donc probablement sous le kôm, ainsi qu'au voisinage de la chapelle (+40/−60).

2. Du côte de la mosquée, un sondage fut pratiqué le long de la paroi de limite de fouilles, ce qui permit de mettre en évidence plusieurs niveaux d'occupation et particulièrement la présence de silos en terre crue fichés dans le sol.

Au centre du secteur (fig. 5), un puits en briques cuites, visible dès le début des fouilles, coupe les structures, ce qui autorise à penser qu'il fut creusé à l'époque islamique. Les couches présentent un pendage d'ouest en est (de la mosquée vers le temple) dû au glissement du terrain de par sa situation en lisière du kôm.

Principales structures :

a) Porte inclinée d'ouest en est (fig. 6) faite de montants de briques cuites s'intégrant dans des murs de briques crues. Elle est ornée d'un seul côté de deux colonnettes engagées également en briques cuites. Entre ces deux colonnettes a été découverte une base de colonne en calcaire dont il est difficile d'affirmer qu'elle se trouve *in situ*. Les fondations de la porte sont constituées de cinq assises de briques cuites surmontées d'un petit muret. D'un côté, cette porte donnait accès à un espace de terre battue, de l'autre, à une pièce dallée

dont les briques de terre cuite venaient buter contre la dernière assise (+1,76 m).

b) Cette pièce en forme de L (fig. 7), dallée en chevrons, possédait deux autres ouvertures beaucoup plus sobres. C'est sur ce dallage que reposait cinq silos (quatre en terre crue, un terre cuite) ainsi qu'une colonnette copte couchée, en calacaire, manifestement en remploi.

c) La dernière mission en mars-avril 1983 s'est essentiellement attachée à dégager des silos en terre cuite, des canalisations (jusqu'à −0,60 m) et à effectuer un sondage transversal sur 2,70 m de profondeur.

Matériel

1. Céramique. Matériel le plus abondant retrouvé sous forme de conglomérats de tessons pour aplanir les sols ou de pièces cassées ou entières dont les ensembles se présentaient parfois comme des dépôts (fig. 8). Des rebuts et déchets de cuisson attestent la présence d'une fabrication locale de céramiques.

Les pâtes et les techniques sont extrêmement variées, allant de la poterie commune à des exemplaires très raffinés de type sigillés ou ornés de motifs appliqués ou peints. La céramique fut employée aussi bien dans la construction (canalisations, reforcement de murs) que pour l'usage domestique : silos (*dolia*), fours à pains (?) [2], supports de zirs, jarres à vin, vaisselle à cuire, à boire et à manger ; ou pour la fabrication de lampes et de figurines.

Trois plats à cupules entiers et une douzaine de fragments ont été retrouvés sur le site. Deux d'entre eux (fig. 9), comprenant six cupules entourant la cupule centrale plus grande, étaient disposés l'un dans l'autre à l'intérieur d'un grand silo de terre crue qui contenait, entre autre, une coupe, trois briques cuites et des tessons mêlés à de la cendre (+47 cm). L'un de ces exemplaires fut donné en partage au Musée du Louvre en 1982 (fig. 10). Un troisième plat à quatre cupules était situé devant la porte du secteur 10 à +2,04 m. Ces documents offrent un décor peint semblable à ceux qui sont connus par des publications [3] : cupules

---

[1] F. Bisson de la Roque, « Fouilles de Médamoud (1930) », FIFAO, (Le Caire 1931), 14–15.

[2] Par analogie avec les trouvailles faites aux Kellia, cf. M. Egloff, *Kellia, la poterie copte*, Genève 1977, pp. 167–169.

[3] A. Hermann, « Kernos oder Tryblion ? », *Jahrbuch für antike und Christentum* 8/9 (1968–69), 203–213 ; M. Krause, « Koptische Tonschalen des 6/7 Jahrhundert », *Jahrbuch für Antike und Christentum* 11/12 (1968–69), 76–82 ; J. L. Schrader, « Antique and Early Christian Sources for the Riha and Stuma Patens », *Gesta* XVIII, 1 (1979), 152–153.

8. Dépôt de céramiques (phot.
J.L. Bovot)

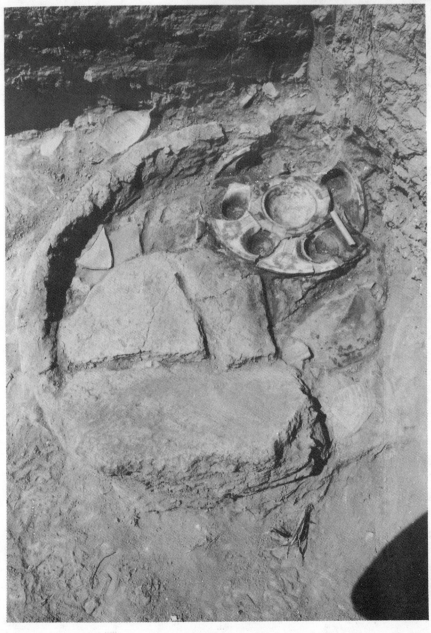

9. Plat à cupules *in situ* (phot.
G. Lecuyot)

11. Conque en grès trouvée à l'ouest de la mosquée (phot. M. Kurz)

10. Plat à cupule en partie restauré (phot. J.L. Bovot)

13. Bracelet en or *in situ* (phot. M. Kurz)

12. Meules(?) en granite (phot. J.L. Bovot)

14. Bloc inscrit (phot. M.H. Rutschowscaya)

séparées par des éléments végétaux (arbre, rosette) et des points. Leur utilisation n'a pas pu être déterminée ; datés par plusieurs chercheurs entre le VIe et le VIIe siècles, ils ont été tour à tour considérés comme plats à offrandes en comparaison avec les *kernoï* de la Méditerranée orientale, comme plats à manger communs à plusieurs convives, comme supports de plats ou comme plats de service.

2. Sculpture. De nombreux blocs sculptés en calcaire et en grès, provenant d'églises, avaient déjà été retrouvés par F. Bisson de la Roque. Les secteurs fouillés depuis 1980 ont essentiellement livré des fragments épars ou des blocs remployés dans la construction des murs : colonnettes et chapiteaux de type « palmiforme » parfois timbrés de la croix ; tête en calcaire mi-humaine mi-animale provenant problement d'un élément de soutien (corbeau ?).

Une conque en grès (fig. 11), portant encore des traces de peinture, fut extraite de la bordure du kôm opposée à la zone de fouilles du secteur 10, à l'ouest de la mosquée. Cette trouvaille confirme bien la présence en cet endroit d'une église dont déjà Mr. J. Vercoutter avait retrouvé des vestiges en été 1949 [4], mais dont la fouille avait dû être abandonnée en raison de la proximité de la mosquée.

3. Objets en pierre. Peu d'objets d'usage domestique furent mis au jour : signalons quelques mortiers et pilons.

Des blocs circulaires en granite sont apparus en plusieurs endroits du chantier (fig. 12) : constitués de deux éléments indépendants, dont l'un vient s'emboîter par un tenon dans la perforation centrale du second , ils étaient manifestement destinés à tourner l'un contre l'autre ; des encoches situées sur la tranche de l'élément perforé permettaient sans doute de transmettre la rotation : meules servant à pétrir ou à broyer l'argile (?) [5].

4. Objets en métal. Un gobelet, un réflecteur de lampe et un vase circulaire reposant sur trois pieds, muni d'une chaînette, sont les seuls objets en bronze d'importance ; notons également un *simpulum* d'époque romaine dont la forme et l'utilisation se poursuivront à l'époque copte. En revanche, un bracelet en or (fig. 13) à jonc torsadé fut découvert en mars 1981 cerné de fragments de briques cuites et de tessons dans le sectur 2 à + 3 cm. (Diamètre intérieur 7,9 cm ; 231,8 g.). Ce bracelet ou armille de dimensions imposantes présente des branches terminées par deux têtes de serpent stylisées décorées de motfis spiralés en filigrane ; le fermoir est constitué par un minuscule clou d'or passé à travers trois anneaux fixés à la guelle des serpents. Le contexte de découverte n'a pas permis de dater ce bijou ; mais les nombreux parallèles établis avec des exemplaires conservés dans les musées, dont les plus proches demeurent ceux du British Museum [6], permettent d'avancer la date de la fin du IIe ou de la I^e moitié du IIIe siècle après J. C.

5. Verre. Nombreux fragments de flacons et coupelles dont aucun n'a pu être reconstitué en entier.

6. Os. Peu de vestiges de cette technique : fusaïole, stylet à kohol, cuilleron, bracelet en forme d'anneau. Deux plaquettes fragmentaires sont sculptées d'un personnage masculin nu, debout, s'appuyant sur une lance (?) dont l'iconographie et le style sont proches des ivoires dits « alexandrins ».

En conclusion, à part les céramiques, peu d'objets d'usage domestique et quotidien ont été mis au jour. Si certaines structures semblent indiquer qu'il pourrait s'agir de zones d'habitation, il existait en tout cas également des espaces d'entrepôts et de fabriques de céramiques attenant à une église.

Documentation épigraphique

Étudiée par M. G. Roquet qui vint en mission à Tôd au printemps de 1983. Il se pencha sur les graffiti inscrits sur des blocs *in situ*, sur des blocs exhumés de la fouille, des vases céramiques et des ostraca. Aucun papyrus n'a été pour l'instant retrouvé.

— Un bloc de calcaire, extrait des fouilles,

---

[4] J. Vercoutter, « Tôd (1946–1949) – Rapport succinct des fouilles », BIFAO L (1952), 83–84.

[5] Il semble que c'est le même type d'objet qui est photographié dans l'article d'A. Vernhet et L. Balsan, « La Graufesenque », *Les dossiers de l'archéologie* 9 (Mars–Avril 1975), 26.

[6] E. Vernier, *Bijoux et orfèvrerie*, Catalogue Général du Musée du Caire, Le Caire 1927, pl. XII, n° 52101 et pl. XIII, n°s 52097, 52099, 52103 ; F. H. Marshal,l, *Catalogue of the Jewellery in the Departments of Antiquities*, British Museum, London 1911, n°s 2801–2802 ; B. Segall, *Katalog der Goldschmiede Arbeiten*, Museum Benaki, Athen 1938, n° 190.

mentionne un certain David, prud'homme de Tiklbëounë (fig. 14).

— Deux vases portent l'un le nom de Daniel (amphore), l'autre une inscription fragmentaire débutant par l'invocation à Jésus-Christ (*dolium*). Les ostraca grecs et coptes (VIe–VIIIe siècles) sont particulièrement intéressants puisqu'ils attestent l'existence d'un *topos* « église, monastère » à Tôd et qu'ils nous renseignent sur des denrées stockées dans des réserves : orge, blé, plants de vigne, dattes, couvertures, sésame, onguent.

Cette documentation épigraphique vient donc heureusement corroborer ce que le site a livré en structures et en matériel : un ensemble de magasins et d'ateliers afférant à l'une des églises de Tôd dont il reste à mettre au jour le deuxième exemplaire.

COPTIC STUDIES

Ida Ryl-Preibisz

Decorative Elements of Capitals in Christian Nubia and Coptic Motifs

I am limiting myself in this contribution to the capitals made of local stone in Nubian workshops between the end of the 6th and the middle of the 8th centuries.[1]

The variability of capitals is mostly confined, leaving aside obvious structurally determined shape classes, to the selection and the mode of execution of ornaments. Studying the decorative elements it is possible to distinguish alien influences and borrowings, in their number Coptic influences, versus the original invention and specific character of local workshops. Here most relevant are the sandstone capitals, those from the First Cathedral in Faras among them. Granite capitals decoration does not contribute specific decorative elements apart from the central cross motif in its over twenty varieties.

I would like to present some decorative elements of Nubian capitals.

The most important of them are *leaves* (pl. I).

1. Large smooth leaves with simple edges narrowing upwards are placed on corners of most of capitals in Christian Nubia (pl. I,1). Their mode of execution is varied (figs 1–6): wide, slightly curved leaves, supporting the corner volutes, make an impression of slenderness; thick ones, stemming immediately from the neck, form volutes under the abacus; and only slightly marked flat leaves on granite capitals.

Smooth-sided leaves without details on their surface have widespread distribution in time and space.[2] They occur frequently in Asia Minor, Syria, Palestine and Egypt. Such leaves were becoming increasingly popular both in Byzantine and Coptic art.[3] Smooth-sided leaves of Nubian capitals and similarly executed leaves on some Coptic ones are obviously related to the Egyptian palm column heads.[4]

2. Simple leaf with differentiated surface and marked stalk and blades—representing a palm leaf, traditional in Egypt and Nubia (pl. I,2; figs 7–11). This type is less frequent than smooth leaves. The same motif, but more triangular and executed with more care occurs in both places in Ptolemaic-Roman composite capitals.[5] This pattern in Coptic capitals with slightly different geometricized modelling was found in Saqqara and Assuan.[6] In Nubia palm leaves are in use on some capitals before (fig. 7) and after the conversion to Christianity (figs 8–11).[7] One can trace the

[1] I. Ryl-Preibisz, "On the Type of Capitals in Christian Nubia", notes 1, 2, 3, (Heidelberg—symposium 1982 in press).

[2] R. Kautzsch, *Kapitellstudien*, Leipzig 1936, pp. 22 ff., 36, 210, nos 23, 24, 26, 32, 34, 38, 149–151, 841, 844; G. Severin, "Problemi di scultura tardo antica in Egitto", in: *XXVIII Corso di Cultura sull'Arte Ravennate e Bizantina 1981*, pp. 238 ff., figs 13–18; V. Scrinari, *I capitelli romani di Aquilea*, Padova 1952, nos 40–43; U. Monneret de Villard, *Il monastero di S. Simeon presso Aswan*, Milano 1927, p. 157, fig. 148; *Eglises de Village de la Syrie du Nord* (Album), Paris 1980, figs 115, 123, 145, 179, 225, 236, 252.

[3] G. Duthuit, *La sculpture copte*, Paris 1931, pl. 50 a–c; U. Hölscher, *The Excavation at Medinet Habu*, vol. V—*Post Ramessid Remains*, Chicago 1954, pl. XLVI; A. Badawy, *Les premières églises d'Égypte*, Le Caire 1947, pls 10, 11; U. Monneret de Villard, *La Nubia medioevale*, T. I–IV, Cairo 1935–1957. T. II, pl. 2.

[4] J. Strzygowski, *Koptische Kunst*, Vienne 1904, pp. 78, 79; A. Badawy, *L'art copte, les influences égyptiennes*, Le Caire 1949, p. 15; J.E. Quibell, *Excavations at Saqqara III (1907–1908)*, Cairo 1909, pl. XXII 4, 5, XXVII 2.

[5] G. Jequier, *Les temples ptolémaïques et romains*, Paris 1924, tab. 22, 3; F. Daumas, La civilisation de l'Égypte pharaonique, Paris 1965, pl. 175, 181; Fl. Griffith, "Oxford Excavations in Nubia", LAAA XIII (1926), p. XXIX, 4—capital from Faras.

[6] E. von Mercklin, *Antike Figuralkapitele*, Berlin 1962, no 51; Kautzsch, *Kapitellstudien*... no 855; Monneret de Villard, *Il monastero di S. Simeon...*, figs 149, 150; Strzygowski, *Koptische Kunst...* pl. IV, 1.

[7] I. Ryl-Preibisz, "Un châpiteau de la période des Nobades à Faras", *Études et Travaux* III (1969), pl. 1 a–b; C.J. Gardberg, *Late Nubian Sites*, Stockholm 1970 (SJE vol. 7), pl. 56, 2; Griffith, "Oxford Excavations...", LAAA XIV 1927, pl. 78, 3; H.D. Schneider, "Abdallah Nirqi", in: *Kunst..., und Geschichte Nubiens*, 1970, p. 102.

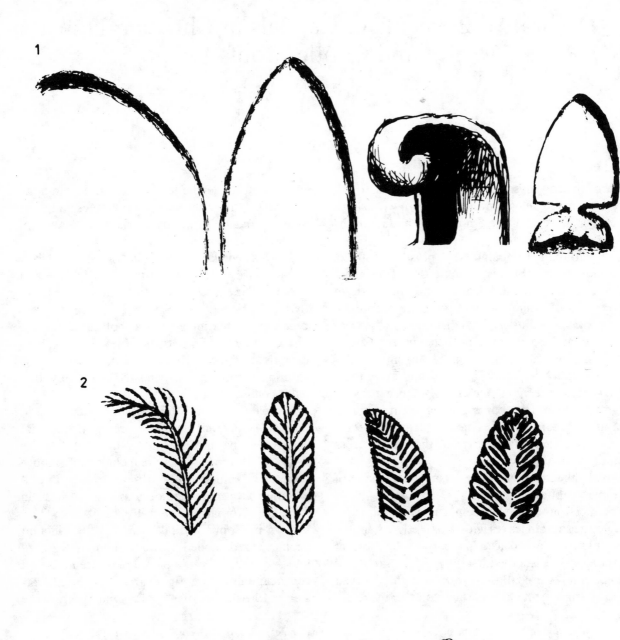

I. Decorative elements of capitals

1. Capital from Faras (FA 103 63/64)

2. Capital from Faras (Inv.no 234071 MN)

3. Capital from Faras (Inv.no 234682 MN)

4. Capital from Faras (Inv.no 234681 MN)

5. Capital from Faras (FA 98 62/63)

6. Capital from Dongola (DA 8, a 65/66)

7. Capital from Faras (Inv.no. 234739 MN)

8. Capital from Faras (Inv.no. 149764 MN)

9. Capital from Dongola (DB 4 69)

10. Capital from Dongola (DA 8, b 65/66)

11. Capital from Dongola (DA 23 67/68)

12. Capital from Faras (FA 101 63/64)

13. Capital from Faras (FA 104 63/64)

14. Capital from Faras (Inv. no 234685 MN)

15. Capital from Faras (Inv.no 234686 MN)

16. Capital from Dongola (DA 5 65/66)

17. Capital from Faras (after Griffith, LAAA XIII, tab. XXXVII,2)

18. Capital from Faras (FA 92 63/64)

19. Capital from Faras (FA 130 63/64)

20. Capital from Faras (FA 103 63/64)

transformation of this motif evolving from softly coiled in volutes on corner – to stiff, schematic, and further – to marked by incisions only on some granite examples (figs 10–11).

3. Some capitals bear above their neck a crown of small leaves (pl. I,3; figs 1, 4,12–17, 20). These rounded leaves are either smooth (figs 4, 13) or framed and incised, imitating palm leaf blades (figs 1. 12, 17, 20) or decorated with spiral (fig. 15) or hemispherical bead perforated at centre (fig. 14). On Coptic capitals (e.g., Philae) there are some-

times one or two rows of such leaves pressed tightly against their bodies.[8] This is most probably reminiscence of a bunch of stems or of lotus flowers in Egyptian composite capitals. These leaves were sometimes decorated with different geometric ornaments.[9] The hemispherical perforated bead is unknown in Coptic capitals, while very popular in Nubia, also in granite examples as well as in other architectural elements (fig. 16).

Another group of decorative elements on Nubian

[8] Monneret de Villard, *La Nubia medioevale* II, pl. II, 9, 6, 60; Duthuit, *La sculpture copte...*, pl. L a, b; Strzygowski, *Koptische Kunst...*, no 7356.

[9] Kautzsch, *Kapitellstudien...*, nos 149, 150; H.G.Lyons, *A Raport of Island and Temples of Phile*, Cairo 1896, pls 60, 61.

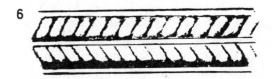

II. Running ornaments and individual motifs

capitals are *running motifs* around neck and abacus (pl. II). Several patterns of that kind occur in Nubia.

1. One of them is vine motif (pl. II,1; figs 1, 12, 15, 20). That ornament inherited from the Graeco--Roman Dionysiac symbols won an extraordinary popularity during Christian period, assuming new symbolic meaning.[10] Commonly employed in innumerable varieties in Byzantine and Coptic art, particularly as an ornament of architectural friezes, capitals, niche frames, door jambs etc. Multiple examples are known from Oxyrynchos, Bawit, Saqqara and others. It occurs frequently in other media: woodwork, ivories and textiles. The vine pattern usually consists of an undulating stem with complicated course of numerous plaits and loops, with or without grape bunches, sometimes with intertwined animals, birds, rosettes, crosses, etc. Rendering of leaves and grape bunches changes from naturalistic to very stylized, though care taken to achieve an overall surface decorative effect is always clear.[11]

Vine motif on Nubian capitals is schematic and consists of rhythmically repeated elements of grape bunches and leaves placed in meanders of a double band (figs 1, 12, 15, 20). Leaves are elongated with 5 blades separated by clear rounded incisions and with oval attachment. Sometimes a straight runner, hooked at its end trails along the leaf and the grape bunch (fig. 15). The design of these geometricized elements is characteristic and unknown outside Nubia. The only similarly mo-

delled pattern occurs in Aswan on several architectural fragments.[12]

Vine patterns in Nubia are known already in the Late Meroitic period as a result of Graeco--hellenistic influence.[13] This motif undergoes a specific evolution, observable on numerous architectural fragments from Faras.[14] Its general composition bases on rhythmical repetition of motif, emphasizing shape and function of the decorated architectural member. In course of time leaves and grape bunches remain unchanged, leaving aside some variability and simplification in their mode of execution. It seems therefore, that this pattern, adopted in past, was long time repeated with purely decorative aims in Nubian sandstone carving. It is worth noting, that as far as I know, such form does not appear on pottery or in murals and seems to have been forgotten in Nubian repertoire of motifs later than the beginning of 8th century, together with the decline of carving art.

2. Another ornament is the *guilloche* — it is ubiquitous in Christian Nubia in carved stone, pottery or mural painting[15] (pl. II,2,3; figs 13, 14, 18). A motif very popular and longlasting in decorative art of different cultures. Widespread in Roman world — —stemming from Greek-Oriental repertoire — —appears as the border design on mosaics of imperial and Byzantine date, as well as on other decorated objects.[16] Commonly used among Copts — in decoration sculptured in stone and wood, woven textiles and painted in manuscripts.[17] In Nubia *guilloche*, used for decorating

[10] H. Leclerq and F.D. Cabrol, *Dictionnaire d'Archéologie Chrétienne et de Liturgie*, Paris 1907–1953, XV, 2, p. 3114; e.g. H.C. Butler, *Early Churches in Syria*, Princeton 1929, fig. 250; *Eglises de Village...*, fig. 283; *Age of Spirituality (ed. K. Weitzmann)*, New York 1979, p. 450, fig. 60, p. 559; E. Drioton, "Art syrien et art copte", BSAC III (1937), 32.

[11] Duthuit, *La sculpture copte...*, pls 36 c,d, 34 a,b, 43 c, 56 d; Quibell, *Excavations...*, pls XXX, XXXI; Ev. Breccia, "Municipalité d'Alexandrie", *Le Musée gréco-romain 1925–1931*; Bergame 1932 pl. XLIII, 153, pl. XLV, 161; E. Drioton, *Les sculptures coptes du Nilomètre de Rodah*, Le Caire 1942, pp. 26 f.; O. Wulf, *Altchristliche und mittelalterliche, byzantinische und italienische Bildwerke*, Berlin 1909, no 119, p. 46; H. Zaloscer, *Une collection de pierres sculptées au Musée du Vieux-Caire*, Le Caire 1948, pp. 37 f., pls II–V, X; A. Badawy, *Coptic Art and Archaeology*, London 1978, pp. 138 f., 186–188.

[12] Monneret de Villard, *Il monastero di S. Simeon*, figs 149, 151; Lyons, *A Report...*, pl. 67.

[13] W. K. Simpson, "Toshka and Arminna 1963", JARCE III 1964, pl. XI, 5; S. Wenig, *Meroitische Kleinkunst*, Leipzig 1978, Tab. 19; W.Y. Adams, "An Introductory Classification of Meroitic Pottery", Kush XII (1964), 144, figs 11, 13.

[14] Griffith, "Oxford Excavations...", pl. 38; B. Idzikowska, "La décoration des portes des édifices de Faras", *Études et Travaux* XII (1983), figs 7–11.

[15] Griffith, "Oxford Excavations...", LAAA XIII, pls 37, 52, 53, LAAA XIV, pl. 95; K. Michałowski, *Das Wunder aus Faras*, Essen 1969, fig. 89; id., *Faras, die Kathedrale aus dem Wüstensand*, Zürich 1967, pls 31, 55, 84; W.Y. Adams, "Medieval Nubian Design Elements", in: *Studies in Ancient Egypt, the Aegean, and the Sudan*, Boston 1981, fig. 3; M. Martens-Czarnecka, *Les éléments décoratifs sur les peintures de la Cathédrale de Faras*, Varsovie 1982, tab. I, j.

[16] O. Asher, *Geometric and Floral Patterns in Ancient Mosaics*, Rome 1980; O.M. Dalton, *Byzantine Art and Archaeology*, Oxford 1911, figs 31, 247; R. Farioli, *Pavimenti musivi di Ravenna paleocristiana*, Ravenna 1975, figs 74–76; A. Deroko, "L'entrelacs en Serbie et en Croatie au Moyen Age", *Vjestnik za Arheologiju i Historiju Dalmatinsku*, 1954–57, pp. 253 ff.

[17] Zaloscer, *Une collection...*, p. 47; Wulff, *Altchristliche...*, nos 93, 235; Duthuit, *La sculpture copte...*, tab. 65, 67; K. Wessel, *L' art copte*, Bruxelles 1964, fig. 85; *Koptische Kunst, Villa Hügel*, Essen 1963, no 528; L. Guerrini, *Le stoffe copte del Museo Archeologico di Firenze*, Rome 1957, no 59; M. Cramer, *Koptische Buchmalerei*, Recklinghausen 1964, p. 87 tab. 12, 13; W. E. Crum, *Catalogue général des Antiquités du Musée du Caire*, Le Caire 1902, no 8586.

the neck and abacus of capitals is the favourite pattern, in Faras in particular (figs 13, 14, 18). It is frequent as architectural decoration, but known also on pottery of Early and Classic Christian periods and it is often found as the secondary ornament in mural painting.[18] This motif should be considered as an ornament common particularly in the Christian epoch, adopted in its simple form directly from the Coptic ornamentation.

Both these patterns — vine motif and *guilloche* — — repeatedly occur on capitals, but the first one is confined mainly to Faras (plus a few fragments from Qasr Ibrim),[19] while the *guilloche* is more often represented on many other sites (Philae, Serre, Debeira etc.).[20]

3. Other running ornaments are sporadically found on individual objects (pl. II,4–9). In one case the band of crosses alternating with rosettes occurs on the neck of sandstone capital (pl. II,4; fig. 17). Such repetitive use of crosses and rosettes in an ornament is customary among Copts, for example there exists similar composition on the frieze from Bawit.[21] Both motifs are common in Christian art and show up often friezes, pilasters etc., together or alternately.[22] The rosette belonging to the basic repertoire of Classical art is frequently treated as an equivalent of the cross in Chrisian art.[23] In addition to that, various forms of crosses are found in Nubia on later capitals but always as central, individual motifs.[24]

4. No exact counterpart in Coptic art exists for the horizontal band of linked lotos flowers found on necks of two identical sandstone capitals from Faras (pl. II,5; fig. 19). The motif adapted from typical Egyptian ornaments is popular in ancient world.[25] It is willingly used by Copts, due to the traditional symbolism, but it seems that never in such a composition.

5. The same two capitals have their abaci decorated with very schematic narrow palm leaves (pl. II,6; fig. 19) — two leaves grow from the corner and meet in centre of abacus side. This pattern reminds the herring-bone motif — it belongs, however, to the indigenous art repertoire.[26] It recurs on Coptic stelae, architectural elements, etc.,[27] but the Nubian version has the stalk marked like on other capitals with palm leaves and varies from the pure geometrical pattern of Coptic running ornaments.

6. Another zonal pattern occurs on the abacus of several sandstone capitals. It consists of recurring knobs in circular or polygonal frames, divided by two vertical lines (pl. II,7; fig. 18). This refers to astragal, so often used in ancient world, found also on Roman and Byzantine mosaics as border pattern, on ivories etc.[28] Judging from the type of capitals where it does occur, it seems that it was used in earlier capitals only. Such ornament does not exist on the capitals of the First Cathedral at Faras.

There are two other individual motifs used to decorate column heads of the First Cathedral at Faras (pl. II,8,9). One of these is placed on the flat surface of large corner leaves. It has a shape of affixed schematic branch with two pairs of connected leaves (pl. II,8; figs 1, 12, 14, 17, 20). The other represents a palm tree with thick trunk and three branches (pl. II,9; fig. 19). The origin of these motifs is difficult to ascertain. Both are unknown in that form in Coptic and Byzantine art. The palm tree motif could simply have been taken from the surrounding indigenous vegetation, but the styl-

---

[18] Idzikowska, "La décoration des portes...," fig. 5; Adams, "Medieval Nubian..."; Martens–Czarnecka, *Les éléments décoratifs...*

[19] J. M. Plumley, "Some Examples of Christian Nubian Art from Excavations at Qasr Ibrim," in: *Kunst und Geschichte Nubiens*, 1970, fig. 97.

[20] G. S. Mileham, *Churches in Lower Nubia*, Philadelphia 1910, pls. 6a, 26a; B.G. Trigger, *The Late Nubian Settlement at Armina West*, New Haven 1967, pl. XI; Lyons, *A Report...*, pl. 60; and also notes 15, 18, 19.

[21] Duthuit, *La sculpture copte...*, pl. LIVc; *Koptische Kunst, Villa Hügel*, no 79.

[22] Wulf, *Altchristliche...*, pp. 73–75, nos 220, 229, 230; Duthuit, *La sculpture copte...*, pl. LVIIIa–b; E. Drioton, "Art syrien et art copte," BSAC III (1937), 29–40; Breccia, "Municipalité..." (1931–1932), pl. XXXIV, 97; Wessel, *L'art copte*, p. 28, fig. 27; Plumley, "Some Examples...," figs 82, 83, 95; Griffith, "Oxford Excavations...," pl. LI, 1; Idzikowska, "La décoration des portes...," figs 2–6.

[23] Drioton, *Les sculptures...*, p. 55; M. Cramer, *Archäologische und epigraphische Klassifikation koptischer Denkmäler*, Wiesbaden 1957, pp. 1–11.

[24] I. Ryl-Preibisz, "Chapiteaux en granit de Nubie," *Etudes et Travaux V* (1971), pl. XIII.

[25] Asher, *Geometric and Floral...*, p. 171; F. Hintze, *Alte Kulturen in Sudan*, Leipzig 1966, fig. 94; Idzikowska, *La décoration des portes...*, fig. 6; M. Rodziewicz, "Terakotowe kraty okienne z Faras," RMNW IX (1967), 143–174.

[26] Asher, *Geometric and Floral...*, p. 105; Kautzsch, *Kapitellstudien...*, nos 522, 523, 548, 673, 707.

[27] Strzygowski, *Koptische Kunst...*, nos 7356/1, 7299; Badawy, *Coptic Art...*, p. 218.

[28] Kautzsch, *Kapitellstudien...*, nos 240, 368, 601; M. Wegner, *Ornamente kaiserlicher Bauten Roms*, Köln 1957, pp. 47ff; Asher, *Geometric and Floral...*, p. 122; E. Kitzinger, *Byzantine Art in the Making*, Cambridge 1977, nos 144, 84; 176.

ized branch is entirely ornamental. Comparing it with various stylized Sassanian motifs (e.g., stucco decoration at Ctesiphon), [29] where different forms of tree and palmette were frequently used, one can risk a hypothesis that these ornaments were in some part influenced by Sassanian models.

*

Summing up the review of decoration of this set of capitals it is possible to note that Nubian stonemasons adopting foreign patterns, Coptic in particular, assorted, arranged and executed them in their own specific way. Some elements were rejected, other traditional in that region were developed, repeated and transformed.

At variance with the Coptic capitals, [30] there are no classical acanthus leaves in the decoration of Nubian column heads. There are, excluding a single example from Dongola, no basked capitals. There are no Christian capitals with representations of animals, birds, with masks, etc.

Such motifs as palm leaf with marked blades or the vine pattern, had remained in use since the Meroitic period and underwent here specific evolution. Of these, the vine pattern disappears after a zenith of architectural decoration is reached in 7th century. The *guilloche* seems to have been borrowed from the Copts and is popular mainly during the Christian epoch (in sandstone but not in granite). Crosses and rosettes as a zonal ornament have been taken over from Copts, but on the granite capitals they occur as autonomous and main decorative element in numerous original varieties and compositions unknown to Coptic art (cf. note 24).

Moreover, the character of all sculptured decoration in Nubia is different. On Coptic friezes or capitals complicated intertwining vines and geometrical motifs cover the whole surface. [31] Here the ornaments are simple, schematic and through their horizontal and vertical zones the body shape of capital is emphasized. Rhythm and symmetry are more important for decoration than diversity and freedom of composition. This is possible to note when studying many other architectural members (friezes, lintels or door jambs) but it is particularly relevant to the capitals of sandstone (from the First Cathedral at Faras), where by selection of suitable motifs it was attempted to emphasize the individual parts of the column head. Such attitude relates in general outline to the classical aesthetic feeling.

Nubia sees in 7th century lively development of sculptured architectural decoration in the Faras centre, with numerous and varied remains found. This happened probably under influence of intensive building activities related to the erection of the Cathedral, and decorative role of carved stone before the introduction of mural painting. Sculptural tradition of long standing and established workshops must have existed there. Otherwise such a task would be impossible to achieve. This explains also why there were no slavish imitations of models, certainly introduced for such a large investment.

The capitals from the First Cathedral at Faras form an original set of remains, which have influenced whole Nubia in their time. Like the basked column heads in Coptic and Byzantine art of 6th century they are beyond doubt an innovation, introduced on peripheries of official art centres at the moment of incorporation of new area into the general current of art and culture of Christianity.

[29] H. Schmidt, "Expédition de Ctésiphon," *Syria* XV (1934), 1–23, pls 1a–b, 2g, 3d; Michałowski, *Faras, Die Kathedrale...*, p. 56.
[30] Cf., e.g. Badawy, *Coptic Art...*, pp. 204–209; Duthuit, *La sculpture copte...*
[31] Cf., e.g. Badawy, *Coptic Art...*, pp. 139, 169, 171, 176, 184, 185, 187, 188.

COPTIC STUDIES

Ashraf Iskander Sadek

Les fêtes personnelles au Nouvel Empire

Nous nous intéresserons dans cette petite étude aux fêtes religieuses ayant un caractère privé, c'est à dire aux célébrations distninctes des fêtes répertoriées et célébrées « officiellement », à l'échelon national ou local.

Nous disposons en effet d'une documentation assez riche, provenant principalement des sites thébains de Deir el Bahari et de Deir el Medina, qui met en évidence l'existence de fêtes (ḥb) célébrées à titre privé par des individus ou de petits groupes, en dehors (ou « en plus ») des festivités officielles: c'est ce que nous appelons les « fêtes personnelles ».

A partir de ces documents nous avons pu établir deux tableaux:

—d'une part un « calendrier des fêtes personnelles datées » (tableau principal);

—d'autre part une « liste récapitulative des fêtes personnelles non datées », classées par type de documents (tableau complémentaire).

C'est l'étude de ces tableaux qui nous permettra de répondre à un certain nombre de questions concernant ces fêtes personnelles:

—où se déroulaient-elles (temples thébains et autres);

—qui les célébraient (ouvriers, contremaîtres, scribes... familles, confréries?);

—en quoi consistaient-elles (offrandes, libations, détente);

—à quelles occasions les célébrait-on (événements familiaux, vacances, voyages);

—à quelles divinités s'adressaient-elles (Hathor... et d'autres).

Ces réflexions nous permettrons bien sûr de compléter notre connaissance de la religion égyptienne, mais elles seront aussi l'occasion de pénétrer un peu plus dans la vie quotidienne et la mentalité de l'Égyptien moyen, ainsi que de situer de façon plus précise le rapport individu–religion–société. « Dis-moi ce que tu fêtes, je te dirai qui tu es » !

Les fêtes personnelles à Thèbes

A. Deir el Bahari, Temple d'Hathor

Le visiteur-type de ce temple est le scribe, généralement accompagné d'une femme—son épouse, ou parfois sa « petite amie »[1] qui se trouve être, le plus souvent, une chanteuse (par ex. une chanteuse d'Amon).

Parfois ces visites au sanctuaire d'Hathor avaient lieu à l'ocasion d'une grande fête publique (le plus souvent la fête de la Vallée, pour Amon, le 2 šmw), mais dans la majorité des cas elles se passaient en dehors des périodes de festivité officielle.

Dans les deux cas, la visite se déroule à peu près selon le même schéma: les visiteurs font des offrandes (wdn) à Hathor, probablement au moins des offrandes de pain et de bière, puis ils implorent ses faveurs.

Ces fidèles sont issus des rangs moyens de la société égyptienne: peu de « grands hommes » publiques ou politiques, beaucoup de scribes ordinaires[2].

B. Deir el Medina

Les matériaux ici sont plus riches, plus variés; ils permettent d'apprécier avec plus de précision le comportement de certains dignitaires de l'État.

Tout d'abord, le calendrier des dates de célébration des fêtes personnelles (tableau principal, ci–joint) ne coïncide pratiquement jamais avec celui des fêtes chômées connues[3]. On peut en

---

[1] M. Marciniak, *Deir el Bahari*, I, Varsovie 1974, n° 29 (cf. tableau principal, 32); note 31 (un homme et sa femme?). Cf. aussi notre traduction: A. Sadek, *Göttinger Miscellanies* 71 (1984), 88–89.

[2] Cf. tableau principal, 32 et 33.

[3] Dans le tableau principal, on trouve la date de 1 *prt* 20, qui peut être une date commune à une fête personnelle et une fête générale (stèle J. J. Clère. R. d'É. 27, 1975, p. 76; fête de Meretseger et de Rennenout). C'est un cas assez rare.

conclure que les fêtes personnelles ne font pas partie des grandes festivités, mais qu'elles sont vraiment le fait d'individus ou de petits groupes privés.

Du point de vue terminologique, deux mots permettent de repérer cette catégorie de fêtes : ḥb (particulièrement dans ḥb.f ; p3y.ḥb) et wdn, « offrir ». La documentation rassemblée à partir de ces mots-clé permet de brosser un tableau assez complet.

1. Les fêtes individuelles

Il s'agit des fêtes célébrées par un homme ou une femme seuls, ou éventuellement accompagnés d'un ami ou d'un membre de leur famille.

Prenons le texte 2 du tableau principal : l'entrée en matière, « Khons, sa fête », ne nous en dit pas bien long ; mais lorsque nous voyons ensuite un certain Pendoua « buvant avec Khons », le même jour (tab. princ.,2), nous pouvons en déduire qu'il s'agit d'un homme, Khons, qui célèbre sa ḥb en buvant avec son ami.

On trouve des références similaires et plus explicites à des personnes qui chacune « brasse [la bière] pour sa fête » (tab. princ., 12, 17, 20).

Dans deux cas, nous trouvons quelqu'un « brassant pour Hathor » (tab. princ., 25, 36). Dans le texte 25, il s'agit d'Amenemope et d'un collègue qui, le jour après la fête, « offrent à Hathor » (wdn n Ḥtḥr) ; dans le texte 4 du même tableau, Rahotep accomplit un rite identique.

On peut en conclure pour l'instant qu'un homme pouvait obtenir « des congés » afin de brasser de la bière fraîche pour lui-même et le lendemain pour son dieu (par ex. Hathor). La bière était offerte à la divinité puis bue le jour de sa fête par le fidèle, accompagné, s'il le souhaitait, d'un ami. C'est donc cela que signifiait pour Wennefer « offrir à son dieu » (tab. princ., 39)[4]. Le congé pouvait occasionnellement durer 2 jours au lieu d'un seul (tab. princ., 2).

Hathor n'est pas la seule divinité concernée par ces fêtes[5]. En effet nous trouvons aussi « sa fête de Ptah » (tab. complémentaire, I. 3), « sa fête de Touéris » (tab. compl., II. 2), « sa(fém.) fête de Tou(éris ?) (tab. princ., 8), « ma fête d'Amon de la Joyeuse Rencontre » (tab. compl., IV. 5), aussi bien que « sa fête d'Hathor » (tab. princ., 1) et « ma fête d'Hathor (tab. compl., IV. 5) ; un homme « offre à Sébek » (tab. princ., 43), un autre à Aménophis I (tab. compl., V. 3).

Les éléments fournis par les listes récapitulatives (tableau complémentaire) et les documents qui s'y rapportent semblent indiquer que d'autres dieux pouvaient également être honorés à ces occasions. D'autre part, les provisions fournies aux fêtes d'Hathor, de Touéris, d'Isis, de Meretseger, d'Anoukis et même de Re sont pratiquement semblables sur chacune de ces listes, qu'il s'agisse de « sa fête » ou simplement de « la fête » d'une divinité.

En ce qui concerne les offrandes, on voit, toujours d'après les listes du tableau complémentaire et les documents qui s'y rapportent, que ces fêtes personnelles exigeaient des offrandes alimentaires plus importantes qu'un simple pot de bière. On constante aussi que souvent les offrandes alimentaires étaient à peu près identiques (en particulier pour les fêtes des déesses), à quelques détails et à quelques exceptions près. Ainsi, en ODM 230 (tab. compl., II), on a apporté pour chacune des 2 fêtes de Touéris et également pour celle d'Isis 5 pains sšrt et une jarre mnt de srmt de Qode (?) ; Anoukis a le même pain, mais pas de srmt ; le régime de Ptah est différent de celui des déesses, avec une botte de légumes et deux jarres de bière.

On retrouve presque les mêmes éléments dans Ostraca Liverpool 13625 (tab. compl., III) : pour chacune des fêtes de Touéris, Hathor et Meretseger il y a de nouveau 5 pains — sšrt (mais pas de boisson), puis une offrande de graisse fraîche et d'autre chose dont on a perdu le nom.

A son tour Ostraca Michelides 48 (tab. compl., I), confirme cette constatation : pour la fête de Ptah et d'un autre il y a chaque fois 10 pains sᶜb et deux jarres de haricots (pry, « fèves »)[6].

On peut donc penser à partir de ces comparaisons qu'il y avait pour les fêtes personnelles certaines quantités de pain, de boisson et d'autres aliments selon les époques. Les offrandes aux déesses étaient les plus importantes.

---

[4] L'expresion m–c ntr. f, « avec son dieu » (tab. princ., 24), en parlant de Khons, est peut–être une variante de cette formule.

[5] W. Helck semblait supposer qu'il en était ainsi, dans JESHO 7 (1964), 163 ; en effet, dans les pp. 163–164, il distingue simplement entre les fêtes d'Hathor et les fêtes de famille.

[6] De même, dans le tableau complémentaire, V, on voit une femme rendre un culte à Touéris, ou Aménophis I, entre autres dieux, en offrant 10 pains, ou 5 + 5 pains, et 1 pot (dont le contenu n'est pas précisé).

L'utilisation de la phrase *rdyt n.f* « donné à lui » ou *rdyt n. s* « donné à elle » à l'occasion de telle ou telle fête, soulève la question de l'identité du donneur (cf. tab. princ., 85 ; O. Liverpool 13625) : se pourrait-il que ce soit les autorités qui gouvernaient et entretenaient le village qui donnaient aux ouvriers, en plus des congés, les provisions nécessaires aux offrandes, lors des fêtes individuelles ? On tend naturellement à supposer plutôt que les particuliers devaient fournir eux-mêmes, les provisions pour ces fêtes, à partir de leurs biens personnels domestiques. Toutefois il reste deux exemples où l'offrande représente vraiement une grosse dépense : il s'agit dans le premier cas (tab. princ., 34) de « l'égorgement d'un taureau pour Ptah », et dans le deuxième cas (tab. princ., 20, 20a) également, d'un ouvrier égorgeant son taureau ou celui de quelqu'un d'autre pour des raisons non spécifiées.

Enfin, il apparaît clairement que ces fêtes personnelles avaient lieu non seulement à l'occasion de congés ou comme actes de piété personnelle envers un dieu, mais aussi en relation avec les événements familiaux [7].

Ainsi, Nakhy, en congés avec le contremaître Hay, célébra « sa fête [pour ?] sa fille » (tab. princ., 13) ; un autre eut une « fête de [ou pour] une femme Honneroy » (tab. princ., 41). Le motif de la célébration — naissance, mariage, décès ? — — n'apparaît pas clairement ici.

Par contre, deux autres exemples suggèrent ce type d'événement. Dans O. Gardiner 61, on parle de la mort de la sœur de quelqu'un, ainsi que de la fête d'Hathor de quelqu'un (peut-être de Telmont, ligne 4), avec des offrandes alimentaires pour chacun de ces événements (tab. princ., 1) [8].

Dans la liste collective des fêtes, l'Ostraca Michaelides 48 (tab. compl., I) comprend ausssi un début de phrase intéressant : « la purification de sa fille » suivi d'une liste endommagée de provisions, dans laquelle on voit 2 fois 5 $^c n$(= ?), 10 pains $s^c b$, et un autre objet, perdu. Il pourrait s'agir d'une offrande accompagnant ou suivant le rite de purification d'une femme après son accouchement [9].

Ainsi que l'a signalé Helck, les ouvriers pouvaient recevoir des congés pour les naissances, décès, enterrements, etc... survenant dans leur famille, et sans qu'il ait été question de rites [10].

En ce qui concerne les cultes familiaux du souvenir, nos documents mentionnent de façon répétée l'usage des *w3ḥ-mw*, « libations », pour l'accomplissement desquelles on pouvait aussi recevoir des congés (tab. princ., 6 et 15, Nakhet-Min). On peut citer les 2 phrases d'introduction successives et très claires, sur Nefer'Abou « embaumant son frère » un jour et « faisant des libations sur lui » le lendemain (tab. princ., 14,15). On peut en déduire que Sa-Ouadget et Paser sont aussi en train d'honorer la mémoire de parents décédés et de leur rendre un culte, lorsqu'ils font des libations, l'un pour son père, l'autre pour son fils (tab. princ., 14, 15) — et, dans l'un des cas, pendant trois jours successifs. Ces rites se sont peut-être déroulés dans la chapelle funéraire de famille, ou encore dans la maison, devant une stèle *3ḫ-ikr* du défunt ?

Il ne reste qu'à ajouter que le fait « d'offrir » (*wdn*) à son dieu n'était pas l'apanage des individus de Deir el Medina. Il existe un curieux « calendrier » des jours où il est recommandé d'offrir à son dieu, et de ceux où il vaut mieux s'en abstenir [11]. Ce calendrier précise même les jours où l'on doit offrir aux dieux et pas aux déesses !

2. Les fêtes de groupes

Il arrive parfois que certaines fêtes sont célébrées non plus simplement par une ou deux personnes, amis ou parents, mais par un groupe de 3 à 6 hommes, pendant un ou plusieurs jours.

Dans ce cas la formule utilisée n'est plus *wdn n nṯr.f* « offrir à son dieu », mais *wdn n p3 nṯr*, « offrir au dieu », ainsi qu'on le voit dans le texte 9, 10 du tableau principal : le premier jour c'est un groupe

---

[7] Comme l'a mentionné Helck, JESHO 7 (1964), 164, au sujet des femmes.

[8] Cf. encore W. Helck, *Materialien zur Wirtschaftsgeshichte des Neuen Reiches*, 1963, p. 663. Voir aussi notre tableau complémentaire, V, 1.

[9] Cf. les 14 jours de purification pour Roudgedet dans le Papyrus Westcar, ainsi que les lois hébraïques anciennes (1 semaine, 33 jours pour un garçon, 2 semaines, 66 jours pour une fille, puis une offrande) en Lévitique 12 dans l'Ancien Testament.
[10] Helck, JESHO 7 (1964), 105.

[11] Cf. A. Gardiner, *Calendar, Days of Any Month*, Ostraca 109. Voir aussi S. Allam, *Hiert. Ostraca und Papyri der Ramzeit*, pls 40–41.

de 5 hommes qui « offrent au dieu » ; le lendemain c'est un homme seul [12].

Il est probable que ces fêtes célébrées par de petits groupes de personne se déroulaient à peu près de la même façon que les fêtes individuelles : offrandes à la divinité, puis repas, suivi d'un temps de détente--boisson.

Dans un autre cas, on voit quatre hommes « offrant » un jour puis deux le lendemain, et un autre un troisième jour (tab. princ., 26–28). Ailleurs, trois hommes sont réunis, l'un d'entre eux pour la fête « [de] son chef » (càd de son contremaître) [13].

Il arrive aussi que deux hommes ou plus se réunissent pour accomplir certains rites particuliers. Ainsi, Kha'emtir et Nefer'Abou « enterrent le dieu » ensemble le 4 $3ht$, 17 (tab. princ., 7), soit un jour environ avant le début des festivités rituelles des temples de Sokar-Osiris [14]. Il s'agit peut-être d'une référence à la fabrication d'un « Osiris végétant » — ce qui consistait à enterrer des graines dans un moule en forme d'Osiris, empli de terre, que l'on arrosait pour les faire germer et symboliser ainsi la résurrection du dieu. Un exemple beaucoup plus remarquable est celui où l'on voit cinq ou six hommes engagés — apparemment tous ensemble — dans une cérémonie de purification pour la déesse Touéris, le 3 prt 7 ou 8 (tab. princ., 22). Cet acte ($NN\ dit\ w^cb\ sw\ T3wrt$) n'apparaît semble-t-il nulle part ailleurs, et le sens exact du rite accompli reste obscur.

Ces célébrations accomplies par des groupes de personnes agissant de concert posent la question des associations de culte ou des « confréries » à Deir el Médina. B. Bryère avait en effet supposé qu'il existait à Deir el Médina des groupes religieux disposant de chapelles particulières, dédiées à une divinité, et pratiquant un culte populaire dans ces sanctuaires [15]. Cette opinion a été remise en question par le fait qu'il n'y avait à cette époque aucune trace d'organisation financière, législative ou représentative au niveau de ces groupes. Il n'en reste pas moins que les chapelles en question existent, avec leurs sièges destinés à des célébrants dont nous savons aussi qu'ils appartenaient à la communauté des ouvriers, qui jouaient donc lors des célébrations le rôle de prêtres et officiants [16].

Or, nous venons de voir que des fêtes pouvaient être célébrées par des groupes : ceci semble confirmer l'existence non pas de « confréries » semblables à celles de la Basse Époque, qui étaient de véritables sociétés religieuses organisées, mais quand même des groupes religieux possédant déjà certains rites et peut-être certaines règles et que l'on pourrait qualifier de précurseurs par rapport aux confréries qui leur ont succédé.

Il nous reste enfin à voir la question des pèlerinages, définis comme des déplacements accomplis par des gens dans un but religieux. Ainsi que l'a souligné avec justesse M. Jean Yoyotte [17], les vrais pèlerinages, compris dans ce sens sont assez rares dans l'Égypte ancienne ; il s'agit le plus souvent de personnalités qui visitent Abydos (ou un autre site) et qui profitent de cette visite pour accomplir leurs dévotions. On peut ajouter d'autres exemples à celui de M. Yoyotte. Ainsi, la stèle de Turin 1465 est dédiée conjointement à Osiris et Isis d'Abydos par Mahou et Youpa, administrateurs des temples de Ramsès II, respectivement à Héliopolis et à Thèbes [18], et qui s'étaient probablement rencontrés à Thèbes pour d'autres affaires.

Parmi les auteurs des graffiti de l'époque ramesside que l'on peut lire sur le temple hathorique de Thoutmosis III à Deir el Bahari, on reconnaît quelques visiteurs non-thébains, qui se rendaient au sanctuaire au cours de leurs voyages [19], ou à la veille d'une grande fête comme la Fête de la Vallée d'Amon [20], ou encore pendant cette fête. Toutefois ces visiteurs sont en très petit nombre.

Quelquefois il semble que certaines personnes envoyaient un don ou une offrande par une

---

[12] Le fidèle concerné, Sa–Ouadget, était peut–être un homme particulièrement religieux — ou alors il agissait par obligation, ou encore il affectionnait les congés : il apparaît en effet deux fois, et chaque fois ses offrandes et ses libations durent plus longtemps que celles de ses collègues (tab. princ., 9–10 et 14–15).

[13] Cf. Ostraca CGC 25, 532 (J. Cerny, *Ostraca Hiératiques*, p. 30).

[14] S. Schott, *Altäg. Festdaten*, p. 89, note 60, avec les rites de la « plantation des graines » (tombe 50).

[15] B. Bruyère, *Rapport sur les fouilles de Deir el–Medineh* (1931–1932), pp. 56–60.

[16] OBM 5634, Černy–Gardiner, *Hier. Ostr.*, I, pls 83–84 ; (KRI, III 517–522).

[17] Cf. J. Yoyotte, « Les pèlerinages », *Sources Orientales* 3, Paris : Seuil 1960, pp. 22–24, 34, 37–38 ; 39, 43.

[18] Publié par J. Ruffle, dans : Ruffle, Gaballa, Kitchen, *Glimpses of Ancien Egypt*, 1979, pp. 56–57, pl. III ; cf. aussi KRI, III, p. 444.

[19] C'est par ex. le cas d'un prophète d'un temple d'Horus ; cf. DB n° 119 ; cf. aussi A. Sadek, GM 72 (1984), 81.

[20] Ainsi, Hori, scribe du temple de Min à Panppolis(?), DB n° 28 ; Sadek, GM 71 p. 88.

personne intermédiaire, pour une divinité ou un sanctuaire d'une autre ville. On voit ainsi, à Deir el Médina le contremaître Khons confier un âne au chef de la police Montoumois, avec cette écriture : « envoyé au sud, portant des offrandes (n3 wdnw) pour [la déesse] Raᶜt-tawy », c'est-à-dire certainement à Armante, au sud de Thèbes [21].

Černý = J. Černý, Ostraca Hiératiques non-littéraires de Deir el Médineh I–V, VIII (VII, par S. Sauneron; VI non publié), Le Caire 1935–1959, 1970.

Černý, Gardiner HO, I = J. Černý, Sir A. H. Gardiner, *Hieratic Ostraca* I, Oxford 1957.

CGC = Catalogue géneral du Musée du Caire, avec les numéros officiels donnés par le musée aux monuments et publiés dans le catalogue principal.

DB (n.) = Deir el Bahari, graffiti numérotés, dans : Marciniak, *Deir el Bahari* I, Varsovie 1974.

DM = Deir el Médina ; pour les publications, voir BDM.

GM = *Göttinger Miszellen*,

Goedicke, Wente, OM. = H. Goedicke, E.F. Wente, *Ostraca Michaelides*, Wiesbaden 1962.

HO = voir Černý, Gardiner.

JEA = *Journal of Egyptian Archaeology*.

JESHO = *Journal of the Economic and Social History of the Orient*.

KRI = K.A. Kitchen, *Ramesside Inscriptions* I–IV, Oxford

Lopez = J. Lopez, *Ostraca ieratici*, Turin 1978.

ODM = voir Černý, Ostraca Hiératiques, Le Caire 1935.

Rd'É = *Revue d'Égyptologie*.

Abréviations

BDM (n. ..) = B. Bruyère, Rapport sur les fouilles de Deir el Médineh (1922–1923), à (1948–1951), Le Caire 1924–1953.

BM (n. ..) = British Museum (le monument est indiqué par son numéro).

BM (ouvrage) = The British Museum : Hieroglyphic Texts from Egyptian Stelae etc., 9 vols en 10 Londres 1911–1970. Cité par volume, planche, et numéro dans le musée.

1. Tableau principal : Calendrier des fêtes personnelles datées

Date	Fête	Précisions	Références
1	2	3	4
3ht			
1. 1.A, 1	Hathor	Mort de l'épouse de quelqu'un (vivres pour veillée mortuaire ?) + « sa fête Hathor » + vivres et 21 hommes	OG 61 (Č–G, HO, I, pl. 60²) [R. III]
2. 1.A, 14, 15	— (non précisé)	Khons, « sa fête » + Pendoua, « buvant avec Khons » (le 14)	OBM 5634 (HO, I, pl. 83/84) (KRI, III, 522 : 7–8, 517 : 1–2) [R. II, An 40]
3. 2.A, 3	—	« [x] dans sa fête; [Neb] semen dans sa fête; Routa dans sa fête. »	O CGC 25793 : 2–4 (Č, OH, p. 112) [Saptah]
4. 2.A, 6	—	« Rahotep a offert (wdn) à Hathor. »	O CGC 25779, rº 14(Č, OH, p. 98) [Amenmès, An 1]
5. 2.A, 14	(Hathor)	Prière de demande par P3[...], Prophète du temple d'Horus	DB n. 119 (Marciniak, Deir-el Bahari, I) [An 23, R. III ?]
6. 3.A, 17	—	Qen, « Faisant des libations » (w 3h mw)	O CGC 25779, vs 19. (C, OH, p. 101) [An 2 d'Amenmès]
7. 4.A, 17	—	« Enterrer le dieu » (krs p3 ntr) par Khaᶜ emtir et Nefer'Abou	OBM 5634 (HO, I, pl. 83/84) (KRI, III, 518 :9 et 10. et 520 :15/16) [An 40, R. II]
8. 4.A, 29	T 3 [wrt ???]	« Ce qui lui a été donné pour sa fête de T3 [...] » (rdyt n. st n p3y s hb n T3[...] « [...] bière, 1 pot-mnt	OG 50 (HO, I, pl. 27:2) C. 7 [An 3 de n]
Prt			
9. 1.P, 14	—	« offrir aux dieux » (wdn n p3 ntr) par : Sa-Ouadget, Apehty, Wennefer, Paherypedget, et Rahotep	OBM 5634 (HO, I, pl. 83/83); (KRI, III, 516/7 :5–6; 519 :7/8; 578 :11/12; 520 :3/4; 522 :15/16) [An 40, R. II]
10. 1.P, 15	—	« offrir au dieu » (wdn n p3 ntr), par Sa-Ouadget.	Dito, KRI, III, 516:5/6
11. 1.P, 15	—	« qui était en congés pour brasser » Neferhotep (nty wsf. nᶜth) et Qaha avec lui	O CGC 25³²¹ rº 9 (ČOH p. 22) [An 1, Saptah]

---

[21] O. Gardiner 140, dans : S. Allam, *Hiert. Ostraca und Papyri der Ramzeit*, pl. 42.

1	2	3	4
12. 1.P, /18/20/	–	[x–hotep], « brassant (pour) sa fête », ^{c}th, tw ⟨n⟩ p3y.f hb	O CGC 25^{521}, v° 9(Č, OH, p. 24) [Saptah, An 2]
13. 1.P, 21	–	« Qui était en congés avec (le contremaître) Hay : Nakhy (pour) sa fête [de?] sa fille » (N3hy, p3y. f hb [n?] t3y.f šrit); « ... Kha'emseba, (pour) sa fête », (... x chômant avec lui?)	O CGC 25^{521}, r° 11–12 (Č, OH, 22) [Saptah, An 2]
14. 1. Prt, 24	–	Sa-Ouadget, « faisant des libations pour son père » (w3h mw n it.f)	OBM 5634, r° 4(HO, I, 83/84) KRI, III, 516:5/6
15. 1 Prt, 2'5'	–	Sa-Ouadget, dito; Nakht-Min « faisant des libations » Paser, « faisant des libations pour son fils »	dito (KRI, III, 519:3/4 et 523:1/2) [R. II, An 40]
16. 1 Prt, 2/6/	–	Sa-Ouadget, dito	(ibid., 516:5/6)
17. /1.P, 27/29/	–	[x], ^{c}th p3y. f hb, « brassant (pour) sa fête »	O CGC 25^{521}, v° 16(Č, OH, p. 25) [Saptah, An 1]
18. A l'intérieur /1.P, 28/2.P, 4/	–	« Khamy était (a) sa fête »	ibid., r° 21 (ibid., p. 23) [dito, date]
19. 2.P, 5	–	« Telmont absent; sa fête; ...[x], [absent?], (sa) fête »	OG 37 (HO, I, pl. 26^3) r° 9–10 [R. III]
20. 2.P, /7/8/	–	« [Neb]semen [était absent], pour égorger le taureau de Hoynefer; Harnoufer était absent pour brasser pour sa fête; ^{c}Apehty, sa fête. »	OG 37 (HO, I, pl. 26^3), v° 3–5 [R. III]
20^a. 2.P, 11	–	« Pashed fils de Pennouh, absent, pour égorger son taureau »	ibid., v° 7–8
21. 2.Prt. 17	–	Hoy, brassant (17 et 18) Merouaset, brassant	OBM 5634 (HO, I, pl. 83/84) KRI, III, 518:13/14; 523:13/14 [R. II, An 40]
22. 3. Prt, 8–x :	Touéris	[...x...] dit w^{c}b sw T3wrt; (« (se) rend pur pour Toueris? »)* Hrm-wi3 dit [w^{c}b sw T3] wrt; 3h 3dit w^{c}b sw [T3.wrt]; [...] k3a3?; R^{c}htp dit [w^{c}b sw T3wrt]; R^{c}ms dit w^{c}b sw T3 wrt; Bw knt.f dit w^{c}b sw T3wrt	O. CGC 25, 505, r° 4–8 (C, OH, p. 4) Amenmès/Séthos II (*Ou bien : « Touéris l'a rendu pur? »)
23. 3.P, 13	–	Jour de la visite rendue par le Chef Gardien des Écritures, Penamon	DB n. 96 (Marciniak) [An. 2, règne inconnu]
24. 4.P, 8	–	Khons, M-^{c}ntr.f « avec son dieu »	OBM 5634 (HO, I, pl. 83/84) KRI, III, 522:7/8 [R. II, An 40]
25. 4.P, 27, 28	Hathor	Aménémope a brassé (^{c}th) pour Hathor. Aménémope a offert (wdn) à Hathor); Pendoua, malade Pendoua a offert à la Dame du Vent du Nord (Nbt-mhyt) Aménémope, pareillement Le dessinateur Neferhotep, dans sa fête	O CGC 25782, r° 4 (C, OH, p. 103) O CGC 25780, 7–8 (ibid., p. 102) O CGC 25782 r° 7–8 (ibid., p. 103) [An 3, Amenmès]
Šmw 26.1.Sh, 24	–	Hoy, fils de Hoynefer : offrant (, wdn); Rahotep, offrant;.....; Nebnakht fils de Nakhtmin, offrant; Nakhy fils de Bouqentef, offrant	O CGC 25782, v° 17–23 (C, OH, p. 104) [An 3, Amenmès]
27. 25	–	Nakhy, dito, offrant;.....; Qaha (Harnoufer), offrant;..	
28. 26	–	Anouy, offrant	
29. 1.Sh, 27	–	Paser, brassant	OBM 5634 (HO, I, pl. 83/84); KRI, III, 523:1/2 [An. 40, R.II]

1. Tableau principal: Calendrier des fêtes personnelles datées

1	2	3	4
30. 2. Sh, ? dans (« Pa-oni »)	–	*didi̯.f r db3, m p3yf hb,* m [ḫrs??] 1. « Ce qu'il a donné en échange, dans sa fête, soit 1 [botte]	O CGC 25598, r° 8–9 (C. OH, p. 57) [R.V., An 4]
31. 2. Sh, 7, 8	–	(7: Nefer^CAbou embaumant son frère *wt sn. f*) 8: « faisant des libations pour lui » *w3ḥ n.f mw*	OBM 5634 (HO, I, pl. 83/84); KRI, III, 520: 15/16 [R. II, An 40]
32. 2.Sh, 16, 18 19,23	Hathor (DB) avant la F/V d'Amon	16. Invocation à Hathor par le Scribe Pakatgen, pour obtenir la faveur de sa bien-aimée; (graffito) fait pendant l'offrande (*wdn*) à Hathor de Djeseret	Marciniak, DB, n. 29 [An 7, règne inconnu]
	–	18. Amenmèse, Scribe du grenier	M. DB, n. 70 [An 3, règne inoconnu]
	Hathor (DB)	19. Invocation à Hathor, par Houri, Scribe du temple de Min	ibid., n. 28 [An 4, règne inoconnu]
	Hathor (DB)	23. Ashakhet, Scribe du Temple de Khons, « chanteuse » venue pour offrir (*sm 3^c*) à Hathor de Djeseret, pendant le festival de la Vallée	ibid., n. 31 [An 22, R. III]
33. 3.Sh, 3	Hathor (DB)	Invocation à Hathor pour obtenir des bienfaits, par le Scribe [...], quand il est venu pour offrir (*wdn*) à Hathor de Djeseret	ibid., n. 71 [An 2 de x]
34. Sh, 7	Ptah	Égorger un taureau (*sm 3 iḥ/k3 n Ptḥ*) pour Ptah	O. Turin, 57033, v° 9 (Lopez, I, pl. 22a) [R. III]
35. 3.Sh, 21	–	Dessinateur Neferhotep, faisant des libations (*w3ḥ mw*) (et peut-être, Nebbakht, et Aménémope ?)	O CGC 25784, 5–6 (C, OH, p. 109) [An 4, Amenmès]
36. 3.Sh, 25	Hathor	[x] brassait pour Hathor	O CGC 25533, r° 8(C, OH, p. 31) [R.I]
37. 3.Sh, 28	–	Khacemseba était absent, pour sa fête (*^cḥ^c nḤ^c-m-sb3, hb.f*	ODM 209, v° 2(Č, OHNL, III, pl. 8) [An 2 d'Amenmès]
38. 3.Sh, 29	–	Ipoy, Nakhtsou, offrant (*wdn*)	O CGC 25784, 16/17 (OH, p. 109) [Amenmès, An 4]
39. 4.Sh, 4	–	*wdn n ntr.f*, « offrant à son dieu » (Wennefer)	OBM 5634 (HO, I, pl. 83/84) KRI, III, 518: 11/12 [R.II, An 40]
40. 2.Sh, 18	–	*^ch n Pndw3, n p3y. f hb* « Pendoua était absent pour sa fête »	ODM 209, r° 7 (Č, OHNL, III, pl. 7) [Amenmès, An 2]
41. 4.Sh, à l'intérieur /25, 26, 27	–	[...] *ḥḥ n Ḥwnwry* « ...fête de/pour la femme Honneroy »	O CGC 25533, v° 12 (Č, OH, p. 31) [R. IV]
42. 5 jours « Epagomènes »	(RIEN)	(RIEN)	(RIEN)
43. non daté	Sébek	« offrant à Sébek », emprunte des vêtements	P. DM 3 (Č.-Pos., Pp. DM, I, pl. 18)

2. Tableau complementaire: listes récapitulatives des fêtes personnelles ou assimilables (non datées)

I. O. MIHAELIDES 48	II. ODM 230	III. O. LIVERPOOL 13625	IV. O.QC 1115	V. P. DM2, V°
Goedicke, Wente, pl. 71; KRI, III, 556–7 (R. II)	Černý, OHNL III, pl. 18; KRI, III, 559 (R.II)	R° 1–6, Č–G, HO, I, pl. 63:3 (Meremptah)	Č–G, HO, I, pl. 31:1 (= R.IV)	C. Pos, Pp DM, I, pl. 17
1. [F. de X?]: [vivres]	(etc.)	« Fête de Touéris »: vivres	« ma fête d'Amon* de la Joyeuse Rencontre »: vivres [= 2 *Prt* ??]	« mort de son père, Fête du Nouvel An »: vivres
2. « [F. de] Mertseger »: vivres	*« sa Fête de Touéris »: vivres	« Fête d'Hathor »: vivres	« Pen-Amenhotep »: vivres [= 3. *Prt* 3]	(mois) « allant à Horus »: vivres (4 *Sh.*)
3.*« [S] a Fête de Ptah »: vivres	2^ei « F. de Touéris »: vivres	« F. de Meretseger »: vivres	« Naissance d'Isis » (? enfant):vivres [= 4 *Prt*]	« sa (f) fête d'Aménophis: vivres
4. [F. de Y?] vivres	« Fête d'Isis »: vivres	(« de nouveau on lui a donné...»): vivres	« Pen-Khons »: vivres [= 1. Sh]	« sa fête de Touéris »: vivres
5. *« sa fête »: vivres	[Fête de ?] « Anoukis »: vivres	(« de nouveau, on lui a donné... »): vivres	*« ma fête d'Hathor »: vivres [= 2 *Sh* ??]	« sa fête de Touéris »: vivres
6* « la purification de sa fille »: vivres	« Fête de Ptah »: vivres		(« de nouveau, il a reçu... »): vivres [= 3. *Sh* ??]	« de nouveau, sa (f) fête de [...]: vivres
7. 2e: « Fête de Ra »: vivres			(« de nouveau, il a reçu...»): vivres [= 4 *Sh* ??]	3 *Prt*, 30: vivres
8. 2^ei « Fête d'Hathor »: [? vivres, etc.]				« de nouveau, allant à Horus »: vivres (2 : le père et elle)

* = fêtes personnelles

COPTIC STUDIES

Helmut Satzinger

On the Prehistory of the Coptic Dialects

Dialect variation is the result of numerous spontaneous changes that have sprung up in limited areas. They may have remained restricted to their places of origin, but may also—for social and historical reasons—have intruded into the idioms of neighbouring or even more remote areas. In the course of time very complicated patterns will result from such spontaneous changes and their mutual influence in all directions.

In an area like the Egyptian Nile Valley, however, we may expect a less confusing pattern to result. The Nile Valley is not, in this respect, two-dimensional, but rather one-dimensional. Influences on a given idiom are not exerted from any direction, but rather from either north or south; in this particular case there will be influence from one direction only at the southern extremity, since this is the end of the Egyptian speaking area.

In the following paper I want to discuss phonetic divergences only, these being the result of local sound-changes and their eventual spreadings. I shall leave apart morphology, syntax, and lexics. In particular, the aim of this paper is to discuss the possibilities of determining a date for some of these sound changes on the basis of historical studies in the Egyptian language (for the most important of recent contributions to this subject see Osing 1976: esp. I, 10 ff.)

1. The date of the most recent sound-change can be narrowed down to a certain time range in the shift from x to h in *LSMF*, but not in the extreme South (esp. *A*) and North (esp. *B*): ⲍⲟⲩⲛ : ⳓⲟⲩⲛ : Ⳓⲟⲩⲛ According to Spiegelberg 1915:9 (18) the use of Demotic ḥ signs for etymological ḫ or ḫ₂ (i.e. ḫ in words that did not undergo the shift from x to š in *LSMFB*, like *S* ⳓⲣⲟⲟⲩ 'voice') is attested in Roman period Demotic only. Other evidence may be gained from one of the Old Coptic texts, the Michigan horoscope (pMichigan 6131, see W.H. Worrell 1941). Although this text of the 2nd cent.

A.D. is evidently written is *F*, it has the *B* ⲃ sign as opposed to ⲍ . This means that—in the *F* speaking area—the shift x > h was not yet manifest in the 2nd cent. A.D. It may, however, by then have originated in another area, e.g. in the relams of later *L* and (or) *S*. In the *F* speaking area, the shift x > h must have occurred about the end of the 2nd cent. or the beginning of the 3rd cent. A.D., since we find it already in the oldest *F* texts.

2. Another very important feature separates *B* from all other major dialects: *B* is the only idiom that has preserved the two categories of Egyptian stops, whereas in the other dialects they have collapsed. The two categories of Egyptian stops are generally thought to be voiced vs voiceless, although there is an heretic tradition that would prefer to distinguish the two categories by the criterion of emphasis (see esp. Roessler 1971). In the Coptic dialect of *B*, however, the two categories are distinguished by absence vs presence of aspiration. Spiegelberg 1925: 10 f. (no 24) points out that Egyptian *d* and *t* were distinguished in Aramaic transcriptions (circa 6th to 3rd cent. B.C.) of Egyptian proper names by using Ⲗ *ṭet* and Ⲃ *tau*, respectively.

In Roman period Demotic, "voiced" signs are occasionally used for "voiceless" signs and vice versa, although a complete merging is not attested. My guess, therefore, is that the couples *d* and *t*, as well as *ḏ* (= *ǧ*) and *ṯ* (= *č*), *g'* and *k'*, and *g* and *k*, ceased to be distinguished in the Valley dialects (excluding perhaps the Memphis area: see Satzinger, forthcoming, note 12) around the 1st cent, B.C. (Note that *b* could not, as a rule, merge with *p*, since it had become a voiced fricative ([β] or [v]) at a very much earlier date.)

3. The pre-Coptic palatalization comprises in fact two steps or degrees:
1) postpalatals > palatals (k > k'; x to ç)
2) palatals > palato-alveolars (k' > č; ç to š)

Centuries:	Dialects: A	I	P	L	S	M	F	B	< Egyptian
2nd A.D.?	x	x	x	h	h	h	h	x	< $\underline{h}$, $\underline{h}_1$
1st B.C.	t	t	t	t	t	t	t	th	< t
5th/4th B.C.	k'	k'	k'	k'	k'	k'	k'	č,čh	< g_2,k_2
	x	č?	ç?	š	š	š	š	š	< $\underline{h}_2$
7th/6th B.C. (Upper Eg.:	e	e		a	e	e		a	< ĭ, ŭ
6th/5th B.C.)	a	a		o	a	a		o	< ă
8th/7th B.C.??	r	r			r		l	r	< r
10th/9th B.C.?	o:	o:			ɔ:		o:		< ā
	u:'	o:'			o:'		o:'		< ā'
	i:'	e:'			e:'		e:'		< ū'
14th B.C.	o'	o'			a'		*a'		< ă'

Note: innovations underlined

Fig. 1

and development is different with stops and fricatives.

Stops: the first step we find in all dialects although the extreme South seems to be reluctant in this: cf. Kasser 1980: 75 [dialect *A*]; Satzinger 1980: 86 f. [non-literary dialect of Elephantine]). The second step is accomplished in *B* only: *ALSMF* k' (ϭⲁⲙ, ϭⲟⲙ 'power'); *B* č, čh (ϫⲟⲙ 'power', ϭⲱⲙ 'garden').

Fricatives: the first step is not accomplished in *A*; it is attested by two minor idioms (*I,P*) whereas all others have taken the second step:

A × (ϩⲱⲡⲉ): *IP* ç (?) (ϣⲱⲡⲉ, ϩⲱⲡⲉ); *LSMFB* š (ϣⲱⲡⲉ, ϣⲟⲡⲉ, ϣⲱⲡⲓ), (cf. Kasser 1980–81: II 275).

This palatalization cannot be dated but indirectly; see the following.

4. Short stressed vowels assumed a relatively backward articulation in some pre-Coptic idioms that are reflected in *S* and *B*, among the major dialects: ā remained an A sound in *ALMF* ⲥⲁⲛ 'brother', but became an O sound in *SB* ⲥⲟⲛ ⁺ī and ⁺ŭ, which had merged in ⁺ě, remained E sounds in *ALMF*, cf. ⲃⲉⲗ , but became A sounds in *SB*, cf. ⲃⲁⲗ .

For a historical explanation of this patterning see Satzinger, forthcoming: my belief is that this sound-change originated in the Delta and (or) Memphis area. One such new a/o-dialect — it was most probably, for historical reasons, that of the capital Memphis — was imported into Upper Egypt as a sociolect of the ruling class. It may have been from the continuous contact of this sociolect with the indigenous dialect of the (later) *L*-speaking area that historical *S* emerged.

The shift from ě to ă is already attested in Neo-Babylonian transcriptions of Egyptian proper names, for the first time in the reign of Cambyses (529–522 B.C.); see Edel 1980: 43. The corresponding shift from ă to ŏ is attested for the first time in Greek transcriptions in the work of Herodotus (ca. 450 B.C.; see Edel. loc. cit.), whereas earlier cuneiform transcriptions constantly have *a* (cf. Edel, loc. cit.; Zadock 1983: 73 ff., Vittmann 1984: 65 f. [note that *Ḫar-ri-ú-ṣu* is misread; so Edel in personal communication]; Satzinger 1984: 89). The alternative in cuneiform would, however, have been an U grapheme, which is perhaps not a very suitable device for rendering a sound that may have been similar to what is noted as [ɔ] (cf. also Edel. loc. cit., who thinks of a transitional pronunciation, which he renders å). Actually, both shifts are part of one phenomenon, namely a backward movement of the articulation area, and it may be assumed that they occurred at the same time, though not suddenly, but rather in a lengthy development. This may have commenced in the Saite period, 7th to 6th cent. B.C., and may have ended in the early Persian period, mid-5th cent. B.C. (cf. Satzinger, 1986). The Coptic dialects prove, however, that it affected the idioms of some regions only, while the others adhered to the older articulation of e and a, respectively.

Dialects S and B show that those shifts did not occur when consonants like ^{c}, ḥ, ḫ, and ẖ followed, e.g.:

S ογααB	< *wắ^{c}b	(< *wắ^{c}b‿w)
S ογα2=	< *wắḥ=	(< *wắꜣḥ=)
B ϥα2ep	< *pắḥr	(< *pắḥr‿w)
S cα2=	< *sắḥ=	(< *sắḥꜣ‿w)
S πα2=	< *pắḥ=	(< *pắḥꜣ=)

Now this is true even in cases where ḫ has become palatalized in Coptic, i.e., ϣ; e.g.:

| S ογαϣ= | < *wắḫ= | (< *wắḫꜣ=) |
| S αnαϣ | < *^{c}nắḫ | (< *^{c}‿nắḫ) |

This proves beyond doubt that even the first step of the pre-Coptic palatalization was taken later than the backward shift of short stressed vowels occurred. As both phenomena seem to have spread from the North to the South, it is to be assumed that they originated in more or less the same area. Therefore, palatalization cannot have influenced S and B a considerable time-span later than it had eventually come into existence somewhere else. Of course one may as well assume that palatalization did not affect stops and fricatives in the same time. If so, it is rather the fricatives that came first, as they display the second degree of palatalization in most dialects, whereas stops show the first degree, except in B. (Osing 1980: 986, however, claims that the stops were palatalized much earlier, namely between the New Kingdom and the Late Period).

5. The most conspicuous feature of F is its "lambdazism". I think I have found evidence of the date of its origin, though in one word only: S ογ2op 'dog' has no Egyptian etymology, but it is attested as a component of Egyptian proper names of the Late Period. Vycichl 1951: 21 has adduced a Berber etymology for this word, and this is why we may assume that it was introduced into Egypt during the Libyan Period, XXII to XXIV dynasties, or 10th to 8th cent. B.C. Unfortunately, no true F attestation of this word seems to

have been noted, but S dialectal forms with λ seem to prove that there existed a F *ογ2αλ (cf. Satzinger 1982: 223). This would mean that F lambdazism was effected after Berber -whar spread into Egypt (and changed its meaning from 'fox' to 'dog'), hence rather after, than before, 9th cent. B.C. But it may quite well be much younger, as this is a post quem argument. More accuracy may be achieved by scrutinizing studies in the Greek transcriptions of Egyptian proper names.

6. Another very conspicuous vowel shift must have occurred between the time of Ramesses II (13th cent. B.C.) and the first Neo-Assyrian renderings of Egyptian proper names (8th cent. B.C.): $\bar{a} > \bar{o}; \bar{u} > \bar{e}$. These shifts are attested in all Coptic idioms. In M, however, unconditioned Egyptian $\bar{a}$ is not realized as ω, but rather as o, which is duly thought to render long open o [ ] in this case. Thus, M is the most conservative of all Coptic dialects in this case. If, on the other hand, a long stressed vowel is followed by a glottal stop, M has ω, H (like most other dialects), whereas A is now the most progressive dialect by going one step further: it has-, in this case, ογ, and ι respectively:

*ḥā^c	'to place'	> LSMFB kō', khō'	> A kū'
*ḥū^c	'being placed'	> LSMFB kē,' khē'	> A kī'
*ḥū(t)	'body'	> LSMFB hē', xē'	> A xī'

7. A typical feature of AL seems to go back to the beginning of the New Kingdom since it is claimed to be attested in the cuneiform of the Armarna Letters. Unlike ME, AL has o instead of α in connection with vowel-doubling and at the end of a word; cf. ⲧⲟⲟⲧ⸗ 'hand', 2o 'face'. Thus, AL vocalism coincides with S and B in these cases. But whereas the o of SB goes back to the shift a > o of the 7th–6th cent. B.C. (which did not affect AL!), the shift under discussion has its origin at a much earlier date. It is conditioned by the presence of a following glottal stop (deriving from Egyptian sounds like ꜣ, r, t, etc.). Unfortunately, the evidence is based on one single word. The Coptic month-name of ⲭⲟⲓⲁ2ⲕ is derived from the Egyptian festival kꜣ-ḥr-kꜣ (which is to be vocalized kaꜣ ḥirkaꜣ). For the XVIII dynasty, a pronunciation ka'iḥka' may be expected for this. Nevertheless, the cuneiform transcription kuiḥku rather points to an Egyptian kôꜣjeḥko' (see Osing 1976: II 348) which would display a shift ka > ko under influence of the glottal stop. Actually, the forms for ⲭⲟⲓⲁ2ⲕ found in A and L texts have an O vowel in the first syllable, just like S and B, whereas

F ⲕⲁⲓⲁⲅⲕ has preserved the *A* sound; cf. *ALS* ⲧⲟⲟⲧ″ with *F* ⲧⲁⲁⲧ″ .

Some observations.

1. It seems quite interesting to note from what parts of the country phonetic innovations have sprung up and spread at a given period.

a) In the Saite and Persian periods (7th to 4th cent. B.C.), the Delta and (or) Memphis created innovations that were to influence the South: stressed vowels a, o instead of e, a; palatalization of post-palatal stops and fricatives. There can be no doubt that Memphis and the Delta were, at that time, the areas of political and social importance. Thebes had been the stronghold of Kushite resistance up to 655 B.C., and with the collapse of their rule it lost its rank. It is not astonishing to note that innovations of the North influenced the South, and not vice versa.

b) In the late Ptolemaic period it was in Upper Egypt and (or) Middle Egypt that the two categories of stops merged. In the Roman period, Middle Egypt was obviously the area where the articulation of x was generally weakened, with the result of a merging with h. Still, Memphis and the Delta were of much greater political and social importance than the South; but the spirit of this society was not that of traditional Egypt. During a period of foreign rule, of paramount Hellenistic influence, when the enchoric Egyptian language was deprived of its role as a main medium, innovations of this language could not issue any more from the centres of power and economy. It seems that the South had become, by then, the refuge of traditional — and traditionalist — Egyptian society. It was from there that phonetic innovations of the indigenous language radiated.

2. Apart perhaps from the *F* lambdazism, all major Coptic dialect variation goes back to a time not earlier than the 7th-6th century B.C.; many significant differentiations are even considerably later. A very conspicuous feature — the merging of x h — is of such a late date that it cannot possibly have antidated the origin of any one of the historical dialects. This may explain why the Coptic dialects do not considerably differ from

each other. On the other hand, we have evidence for much more dialect variation in earlier times (see Osing 1975: 1074 f.; Vycichl 1958: 176). The comparably uniform character of Coptic ist most probably the result of the rule of the Saite dynasty and its social and political effects on the entire Egyptian territory.

Not much indeed of the evidence presented here is, in fact, new. What I want to show is, in the main, that the prehistory of the Coptic dialects can be based on historical phonology only. Structural analysis of Coptic phonology is an indispensable tool for this task, but it cannot, by its very nature, yield historical results.

References

E. Edel (1980), *Neue Deutungen keilschriftlicher Umschreibungen ägyptischer Wörter und Namen.* (=Österreichische Akademie der Wissenschaften, Sitzungsberichte 375).

R. Kasser (1980–81), "Prolégomènes à un essai de classification systématique des dialectes et subdialectes coptes selon le critère de la phonétique" I, *Le Muséon* 93, 53–112; 237–297; 94, 91–152.

J. Osing (1975), "Dialekte", in: *Lexikon der Ägyptologie* I, pp. 1074 f.

J. Osing (1976), *Der spätägyptische Papyrus BM 10808* (=Äg. Abh. 33).

J. Osing (1980), "Lautsystem", in: *Lexikon der Ägyptologie* III, pp. 944–949.

O. Roessler (1971), "Das Ägyptische als semitische Sprache", in: F. Altheim – R. Stiehl, *Christentum am Roten Meer* I, pp. 263–326.

H. Satzinger (1980), "Sudan-Ägyptisch und Elephantine-Koptisch", in: *Société d'Égyptologie Genève*, Bull. 4, pp. 83–87.

H. Satzinger (1982), (review of:) W. Westendorf, "Koptisches Handwörterbuch", WZKM 74, 220–224.

H. Satzinger (1984), "Zu den neubabylonischen Transkriptionen ägyptischer Personennamen", GM 73, 89.

H. Satzinger (1986), *On the Origin of the Sahidic Dialect. Acts of the II International Congress of Coptic Studies*, Rome 1986.

W. Spiegelberg (1925), Demotische Grammatik.

G. Vittmann (1984), "Zu einigen keilschriftlichen Umschreibungen ägyptischer Personennamen", GM 70, 65 f.

W. Vycichl (1951), "Eine vorhamitische Sprachschicht im Altägyptischen", ZDMG 101, 67–77.

W. Vycichl (1959), "A Late Egyptian Dialect of Elephontine", Kush 6, 176–78.

W.H. Worrell, "Notice of a Second-Century Text in Coptic Letters", AJSSL 58, 84–90.

R. Zadock (1983), "On Some Egyptians in Babylonian Documents", GM 64, 73–75.

COPTIC STUDIES

Hans-Martin Schenke

Bemerkungen zur Apokalypse des Allogenes (NHC XI, 3)

Es ist die Absicht dieser Bemerkungen, die Aufmerksamkeit der gelehrten Welt auf eine besonders wichtige und schöne, aber noch wenig bekannte Schrift aus dem Funde von Nag Hammadi zu lenken, von der Arbeit derer, die an ihrer Erschließung wirken, Mitteilung zu machen und weiterführende Hinweise aus benachbarten Disziplinen zu erwirken. Es bedarf nämlich durchaus der Hilfe vieler, um die Tücke der Materie, die uns diesen komplizierten Text nur mäßig erhalten präsentiert, mit Methode und Scharfsinn zu überlisten. Es handel sich, kurz gesagt, beim » Allogenes « (so lautet der Untertitel dieser Schrift in der Handschrift) um ein Dokument, wahrscheinlich das Leit-Dokument, der philosophisch orientierten sethianischen Gnosis, das zudem zu der Bibliothek der gnostischen Herausforderer des Plotin in Rom gehörte (Porphyrius vita Plotini Kap. 16). Und zwar darf wohl angenommen werden, daß unser » Allogenes « (in dem es ja um eine Offenbarung geht, die zwar der Allogenes allein empfängt, die er aber » seinem Sohn « Messos weitergibt, damit dieser sie verkündige) in vit. Plot. 16 unter der Bezeichnung (ἀποκάλυψις) ᾿Αλλογενοῦς καὶ Μέσου erscheint.

Bei der — im wesentlichen noch nicht in die Öffentlichkeit gelangten — Arbeit an der Erschließung dieser Schrift haben sich vier Personen besondere Verdienste erworben: John D. Turner (University of Nebraska, Lincoln), Charles W. Hedrick (Southwest Missouri State University, Springfield), James M. Robinson (Claremont Graduate School) und Karen L. King (Brown University, Providence).

Turner hat sich am ausführlichsten mit dem » Allogenes « beschäftigt. Er ist ja auch der für diese Schrift Zuständige im Coptic Gnostic Library Project. Entsprechend stammt (im wesentlichen) von ihm (wenn auch unter Mitwirkung von Orval S. Wintermute) die englische Übersetzung des » Allogenes « in The Nag Hammadi Library in English,[1] die, zusammen mit dem betreffenden Teil in The Facsimile Edition of the Nag Hammadi Codices,[2] bisher den einzigen allgemeinen und direkten Zugang zum Ganzen dieser Schrift vermittelt. Turner hat insbesondere Bahnbrechendes geleistet in der Aufbereitung des koptischen Textes mit einer die Möglichkeiten voll ausschöpfenden Erschließung dessen, was in den Lücken des Papyrus einst gestanden haben mag. Darüber hinaus hat er sich schon in drei großen Zugriffen um die Einordnung dieses neuen Textes in die Geistesgeschichte der Spätantike bemüht.[3] Hedrick trägt jetzt Verantwortung für den Text des Allogenes als volume-editor desjenigen, noch in Vorbereitung befindlichen, Bandes der Coptic Gnostic Library, der der wissenschaftlichen Edition des Inhalts der Nag Hammadi Codices XI, XII und XIII gewidmet ist, nachdem er schon vorher (neben Stephen Emmel) einer der Hauptakteure des Coptic Gnostic Library Teams bei der

---

[1] Ed. James M. Robinson, San Francisco 1977, S. 444–452

[2] *Codices XI, XII and XIII*, Leiden 1973, pl. 4, 51–75.

[3] Diese Arbeiten sind im einzelnen: » The Gnostic Threefold Path to Enlightenment «, *Novum Testamentum* 22(1980) 324–351; *Gnostic Sethianism, Platonism and the Divine Triad* (vom Dezember 1982, geschrieben für das Working Seminar » Gnosticism and Early Christianity «, das vom Department of Religious Studies der Southwest Missouri State University vom 29. März bis 1. April 1983 in Springfield, Missouri, veranstaltet worden ist (135 Schreibmaschinenseiten nebst 12 Seiten Anmerkungen); *Gnosticism and Platonism: The Platonizing Sethian Texts from Nag Hammadi in Their Relation to Later Platonic Literature* (als Beitrag für The International Conference on Neoplatonism and Gnosticism an der University of Oklahoma, 18.–21. März 1984), 45 Schreibmaschinenseiten.

langwierigen papyrologischen Grundlagenarbeit (eben auch für den » Allogenes «) im Koptischen Museum zu Kairo war.

Robinson ist es, der — abgesehen von seiner dem Team-Leiter gebührenden Zuständigkeit für das Ganze — in einem Vortrag auf dem International Colloquium on Gnosticism in Stockholm (20.–25. August 1973) als erster auf eine direkte Querverbindung zwischen dem » Allogenes « und neuplatonischen Konzeptionen hingewiesen hat.[4] Karen King schließlich hat unter Billigung und Förderung von Robinson, Hedrick und Turner den » Allogenes « zum Gegenstand ihrer Dissertation gemacht und vorerst (als Grundlage für einen geplanten Sach-Kommentar) unter Benutzung der druckfertigen Textfassung für die CGLib-Edition eine eigenständige, ausführlich eingeleitete und mit vollständigem Register versehene Sonderedition dieser Einzelschrift geliefert.[5]

Was nun, nach dieser Einleitung, die angekündigten Bemerkungen selbst anbelangt, so seien sie nacheinander Problemen der Sprache, des Rahmens und des Inhalts gewidmet.

I. Probleme der Sprache

Nachdem, so kann man wohl sagen, im großen und ganzen klar ist, wovon im » Allogenes « die Rede ist, hängt der Fortschritt des Verständnisses entscheidend von der exakten Erfassung der Struktur der einzelnen Aussagen ab, also von einer eingehenden sprachlichen Analyse des Textes und seiner Elemente.

Wie unmittelbar die Analyse der Form das Verständnis des Inhalts tangiert, kann man am besten an einem Begriff demonstrieren, der so etwas wie der Zentralbegriff des » Allogenes « ist. Dieser heißt auf koptisch ⲡⲓϣⲙⲛ̄ⲧϭⲟⲙ. Turner versteht das (gefolgt von z.B. Robinson) als » the Triple Power « und der in diesem Begriff gefundene Kraft-Aspekt bestimmt tiefgehend das Gesamtverständnis des » Allogenes « bei Turner. Aber dies Verständnis ist eben nicht richtig. Schon die Nicht-Kongruenz von Artikel und dem

(zweiten) Nomen zeigt an, daß in diesem Syntagma nicht die gewöhnliche Hierarchie im Verhältnis von Zahlwort und Substantiv vorliegt. Man kann solchen » Herrschaftswechsel « verschieden zu beschreiben und zu erfassen versuchen.[6] Hier könnte man z.B. folgendes sagen:

statt » *die* dreimalige *Kraft* « (= » die drei Kräfte « oder eben » die dreifache Kraft « bzw. » the Triple Power «).

heißt es » *der Dreimalige* an Kraft « (= » der Dreimalkräftige/mächtige/gewaltige « bzw. » the Triplepowered One «).

Ganz offenbar jedenfalls ist der koptische Ausdruck die Übersetzung eines griechischen τριδύναμος.

Im übrigen möchte ich hier nur Zeugnis davon geben, daß eine solche Analyse von Karen King durchgeführt worden ist und in ihrer Dissertation präsentiert wird. Von ganz entscheidender Bedeutung dabei war übrigens die Identifikation der Satzgrenzen. Vielmehr möchte ich von den dabei gewonnenen Erkenntnissen solche mitteilen, die für die Koptologie allgemein von Interesse sein könnten.

1. Analogiebildung zur Extraposition der Konjugationsbasis des Verbalsatzes beim Ausdruck für » haben «. So jedenfalls könnte man das in unserer Schrift gleich zweimal vorkommende Phänomen nennen.

Vgl. p. 49,31–34: ⲉⲟⲩⲛ̄ⲧⲉ ⲧⲙⲛ̄ⲧⲱⲛ︤ϩ︥ ⲟⲩⲛ̄ⲧⲉⲥ ⲛ̄ⲧⲙⲛ̄ⲧⲁⲧⲟⲩⲥⲓⲁ ⲙⲛ̄ ⲧⲙⲛ̄ⲧⲉⲓⲙⲉ » zugleich besitzt die Lebenskraft die Wesenlosigkeit samt dem Erkenntnisvermögen «;

p. 67,25–28: ⲭⲉ ⲟⲩⲛ̄ⲧⲉ ⲡⲓⲁⲧⲥⲟⲩⲱⲛ︤ϥ︥ ⲟⲩⲛ̄ⲧⲁϥ ⲛ̄ϩⲉⲛⲁⲅⲅⲉⲗⲟⲥ ⲟⲩⲧⲉ ϩⲉⲛⲛⲟⲩⲧⲉ » ob der Unerkennbare Engel oder Götter besitzt «.

2. Kurze Form des affirmativen Energetischen Futurs bzw. Apodotisches *efsōtm*. Eine Form, die u.E. als die von Ariel Shisha-Halevy entdeckte Kategorie gedeutet werden muß, kommt einmal wirklich (p. 49,11), und dreimal in Ergänzungen (Turners) vor (p. 46,23. 27.33). Der sehr schwierige Satz mit der wirklich erhaltenen Form lautet folgendermaßen:

ⲭⲉ [ⲉϣⲱ]ⲡⲉ ⲉⲩϣ[ⲁⲛ]ⲣ̄ⲛⲟⲉⲓ ⲙ̄ⲙⲟϥ ⲙ̄[ⲡⲓⲣⲉ]ϥϫ̄ⲓⲟⲟⲣ

---

[4] *The Three Steles of Seth and the Gnostics of Plotinus*, Proceedings of the International Colloquium on Gnosticism, Stockholm, August 20–25, 1973, Stockholm 1977, S. 132–142. Vgl. zu dieser Problematik jetzt auch L. Abramowski, » Marius Victorinus, Porphyrius und die römischen Gnostiker «, ZNW 74(1983), 108–128.
[5] The Quiescent Eye of the Revelation: Nag Hammadi Codex XI. 3 » Allogenes « : A Critical Edition, Ph.D. diss., Brown University, 1984.
[6] Vgl, für ein analoges Phänomen OLZ 74 (1979), 20.

ⲛ̄ⲧⲙⲛ̄ⲧⲁⲧⲛ̄ⲁⲣ[ⲏⲭⲉ̄] ⲛ̄ⲧⲉ ⲡⲁϩⲟⲣⲁⲧⲟⲛ ⲙ̄ⲡⲛ̄ⲁ̄
ⲉⲧⲕⲏ ⲛ̄ϩⲣⲁ[ⲓ̈] ⲛ̄ϩⲏⲧϥ̄
ⲉⲥⲕⲱⲧⲉ ⲙ̄ⲙⲟ<ⲥ> ⲉⲣ[ⲟϥ]

» Denn [we]nn sie ihn begreifen als den 'Fähr[ma]nn' der Grenzenlo[sig]keit des unsichtbaren Geist[es, der sich] in ihm befindet,
wird sie (die Erkenntnis) ⟨sich⟩ [ihm] zuwenden «.

(p. 49,7–11).

Als Tempus der Apodosis bei Konditionalsätzen erscheint sonst amhäufigsten der Aorist I oder II (p. 48,33; 56,33.[35].36; 57,8. 17; 61,18; 66,20.21), aber auch der Imperativ (p. 59,19.31.33.37), eine Infinitiv-Konstruktion (p. 48,6 f.) und – worauf es mir hier ankommt – das (volle) Energetische Futur (p. 46,17[?]; 48,18; 56,17.18). Innerhalb der zuletzt genannten Kategorie ist die Stelle p. 48,18 insofern besonders interessant, als die futurische Aposdosis zu einer (verkürzten) Cleft Sentence transformiert (das Energetische Futur somit in Relativform) vorliegt:

ⲛ̄ⲧⲟϥ ⲉ[ⲧⲉ]ϥⲉϣⲱⲡⲉ » er selbst ist es, d[er] werden wird. «

3. Die Form ⲉⲁϥⲥⲱⲧⲙ̄ *funkioniert* in unserem Text konkurrenzlos *wie* ein zweites Perfekt (d.h. erscheint als *glose* der substantivischen Cleft Sentence) und *ist* also hier das Perfekt II.[7] Es sind zwei Stellen, die das zeigen (p. 50,11–15; 66,30–33). Sie lauten:

ⲉⲧⲃⲉ ⲧ̄ⲥⲃⲱ ⲉⲧⲛ̄ϩⲏⲧⲟⲩ
ⲉⲁⲡⲓⲙⲉⲉⲩⲉ ⲉⲧⲛ̄ϩⲏⲧ
ⲁϥⲡⲱⲣⲭ̄ ⲛ̄ⲛ̄[ⲏ] ⲉⲧϫⲟⲥⲉ ⲉ[ⲡ]ϣⲓ ⲙⲛ̄
ⲛⲓⲁⲧ[ⲥ]ⲟⲩ[ⲱ] ⲛⲟⲩ

» It is because of the teaching which is in them, that the thought which is in me
seperated tho[se] who are exalted beyond [mea]sure and those who are un[k]no[w]able. «
(Übers. King).

ⲉⲃⲟⲗ ϩⲙ̄ ⲡⲏ ⲉⲧⲁϩⲉⲣⲁⲧϥ̄ ⲛ̄ⲟⲩⲟⲉⲓϣ ⲛⲓⲙ
ⲉⲁϥⲟⲩⲱⲛϩ̄ ⲉⲃⲟⲗ ⲛ̄ϭⲓ ⲟⲩⲱⲛϩ̄ ⲛ̄ϣⲁ ⲉⲛⲉϩ

It is from that one who stands at every time, that eternal life appeared. (Übers. King).

4. Unser Text verwendet im Rahmen seiner negativen Theologie als terminus technicus ein bisher unbekanntes koptisches Verb von offenbar negativer Wertigkeit. Das Wort heißt ϣⲱⲭϩ̄ und kommt an folgenden Stellen und in folgenden *status* vor:

ϣⲱⲭϩ̄	(v.tr.) 62,16; 63,25 f. 26
ϣⲁϩⲭⲉ ϣⲁⲭϩ⸗ :	
ϣⲁϩⲭϥ̄	62,26; 67,32
ϣⲁⲭϩϥ̄	62,7
ϣⲁϩⲭⲟⲩ	62,27
ⲁⲧϣⲁⲭϩϥ̄	63,27 f.

Als Anschauungsmaterial sei der Satz gewählt, der – im Schema: weder–noch–aber auch nicht die Negation – das Wort gleich dreimal enthält (p. 63,25–28):

ⲟⲩⲧⲉ ⲉⲛⲥⲉϣⲱⲭϩ̄ ⲙ̄ⲙⲟϥ ⲁⲛ
ⲟⲩⲧⲉ ⲉϥϣⲱⲭϩ̄ ⲛ̄ⲗⲁⲁⲩ ⲁⲛ
ⲟⲩⲧⲉ ⲛ̄ⲛⲟⲩⲁⲧϣⲁⲭϩϥ̄ ⲁⲛ ⲡⲉ

In Turners Übersetzung ist als Bedeutung » diminish « vorausgesetzt; entsprechend erscheint die Bedeutung » vermindern « (?) im Register von F. Siegert.[8] Leider führt nun auch die Etymologie nicht direkt zu einem eindeutigen Resultat für die Bedeutung. Es gibt allerdings nur ein ägyptisches Wort, und zwar ein *hapax legomenon*, das als Vorläufer von ϣⲱⲭϩ̄ in Frage kommt; ein Wort, das erst J. Osing mir, auf Anfrage, zur Kenntnis gebracht hat,[9] aber auch dessen Bedeutung kann nur geraten werden. Es handelt sich um das Verb śdḥ in p. Sallier I 5,8.[10] das im Wörterbuch der Ägyptischen Sprache.[11] in der Verlesung śꜣḥ erscheint. Es steht (in diesem Schultext des Inhalts, daß man seine Arbeit nicht zugunsten von Vergnügungen vernachlässigen darf) im Pseudopartizip und in der Verbindung ỉw nꜣ j.f ỉrj.w śdḥ.j n ỉb.šn. Als Bedeutung sowohl für śdḥ. dort als auch für ϣⲱⲭϩ̄ hier schlägt Osing nun » beschränken, einschränken « vor. Der betreffende Satz im p. Sallier I würde dann lauten: » Mühsame Arbeit ist vor ihm, wo ihm doch kein Diener Wasser bringt, keine Frau ihm Brot berei-

---

[7] Vgl. H.J. Polotsky, *Études de syntaxe copte*, 1944, § 148 (= Collected Papers, 1971, 152 f.)
[8] Nag-Hammadi-Register, WUNT 26 (Tübingen 1982), 156.
[9] Brief vom 16.1.1984.
[10] A.H. Gardiner, *Late Egyptian Miscellanies*, Bibl. Aeg. VII, Brüssel 1937, S. 82; R.A. Caminos, *Late Egyptian Miscellanies*, Oxford 1954, pp. 313 f.
[11] Band IV, 22,6.

tet, *und seine Gefährten beschränkt sind für ihr Herz* « (d.h. nur für sich selbst sorgen). Und als Übersetzung des oben zitierten Satzes aus Allogenes ergäbe sich:

> » wie er ja weder beschränkt *wird*,
> noch irgendetwas (seinerseits) beschränkt;
> noch ist er unbeschränkt «.

5. In diesem Dokument begegnet uns zweimal der seltsame Nominalausdruck ⲡⲓⲟⲩⲁⲧⲟ (p. 50,2.32). Was er im großen und ganzen bedeutet, ergibt sich nun aus der Parallele von p. 50,30–32 und p. 64,2–4:

ⲛⲏ ⲉⲧⲉ ⲛⲛⲁⲧⲥⲟⲩⲱⲛⲟⲩ ⲙⲡⲓⲟⲩⲁⲧⲟ

> » die (Dinge), die unerkennbar sind für... «

... ϩⲉⲛⲗⲁⲁⲩ ⲛⲉ ... ⲛⲛⲁⲧⲥⲟⲩⲱⲛⲟⲩ ⲛⲁⲩ ⲧⲏⲣⲟⲩ

> » irgendwelche Dinge, die unerkennbar sind für alle «.

D.h., wie ⲛⲁⲩ ⲧⲏⲣⲟⲩ einem griechischen (τοῖς) πᾶσιν entspricht, dürfte ⲙⲡⲓⲟⲩⲁⲧⲟ wohl das Äquivalent für (τοῖς) πολλοῖς sein und das bedeutet wiederum, daß darin das wohlbekannte Nomen ⲁⲧⲟ » Menge « stecken dürfte. Das ist offenbar auch die Meinung von Turner, der » the multitude « übersetzt, und auch die von Siegert, der die eindeutige der beiden Stellen unseres Textes eben unter ⲁⲧⲟ nennt.[12] Allerdings notiert er sie als XI 50,{32}, hält den Text hier also für nicht in Ordnung; verständlicherweise, denn » the multitude « würde ja nur ein ⲡⲓⲁⲧⲟ voraussetzen. Was aber ist ⲟⲩ? Schreibversehen, sekundärer Zuwachs am Wortanfang, oder etwa einfach der unbestimmte Artikel? Es wäre dies ja nicht der einzige Fall im Koptischen, daß ein nominaler Ausdruck mit zwei Artikeln versehen erscheint; vgl. z.B. ⲛⲓⲡⲧⲏⲣϥ̄ (in unserem Text p. 59,3; 62,21) und etwa ⲟⲩⲡⲉⲧⲛⲁⲛⲟⲩϥ sonst. Nun ist der Ausdruck, der uns hier beschäftigt, tatsächlich auch noch anderswo einmal belegt, nur mit dem normalen bestimmten Artikel (statt des demonstrativen) und im status constructus (statt des status absolutus), und zwar in der fayumischen Übersetzung der Epistula Jeremiae V. 12.[13] Die Übersetzung von ἐκμάσσονται τὸ πρόσωπον αὐτῶν διὰ τὸν ἐκ τῆς οἰκίας κονιορτόν ὅς ἐστιν πλείων ἐπ᾽ αὐτοῖς lautet da ⲩⲁⲩⲃⲱϯ ⲇⲉ ⲙⲡⲉⲩϩⲁ ⲉⲃⲁⲗ ⲛⲧⲉⲛ ⲡⲟⲩⲁⲧⲉ ⲩⲁⲓⲩ ⲛⲧⲉⲛ ⲡ ⲏⲓ ⲉⲧϩⲓⲱⲟⲩ. Dabei gib

ⲡⲟⲩⲁⲧⲉ ⲩⲁⲓⲩ die Verbindung ὁ κονιορτός, ὅς ἐστιν πλείων wieder, und zwar so, als hätte sie gelautet ὁ πλείων κονιορτός. Wenn man nun fragt, welches Element in dem koptischen Ausdruck dem πλείων entspricht, so muß die Antwort lauten: (nicht ⲁⲧⲉ-, sondern) ⲟⲩⲁⲧⲉ-. Man wird nach alledem die Sache so sehen dürfen: Der von ⲁⲧⲟ » Menge « abgeleitete Ausdruck ⲟⲩⲁⲧⲟ/ⲟⲩⲁⲧⲉ- » eine Menge (von) « = » Vieles «, » Viele « bzw. » viel... «, » viele... « ist (in manchen Bereichen des Koptischen) so lexikalisiert worden, daß er seinerseits mit dem bestimmten Artikel versehen werden konnte, um » das Viele «, » die Vielen « bzw. » der (die, das) viele... «, » die vielen... « zu bezeichnen. Der im » Allogenes « begegnende Nominalausdruck ⲡⲓⲟⲩⲁⲧⲟ würde demgemäß tatsächlich » die Vielen « heißen.

II. Probleme des Rahmens

Der literarische Rahmen, in dem der Inhalt der Schrift » Allogenes « erscheint, ist kunstvoll und kompliziert. Und so ist es kein Wunder, daß er sowohl bei Porphyrius als auch bei K. Rudolph[14] zu Mißverständnissen führen konnte.

Was klar ist und inzwischen allgemein bekannt sein kann, ist folgendes: Der wirkliche Autor läßt die Schrift *von* einer Person namens Allogenes *für* eine andere Person namens Messos, die Allogenes mein Sohn nennt, geschrieben sein, damit dieser ihren Inhalt unter denen, die dessen würdig sind, verbreite. Und was Allogenes mitteilt, besteht im wesentlichen aus zwei Teilen. Es handelt sich um zwei Offenbarungen, die Allogenes im Abstand von hundert Jahren zuteil geworden sind: die erste im wesentlichen eine Audition und durch ein weibliches Himmelswesen namens Jouel vollzogen, die zweite im wesentlichen eine Vision in Entrückung und durch die sogenannten Kräfte der Erleuchter vermittelt. Sowohl Jouel als auch die Kräfte der Erleuchter gehören dem Pantheon der sethianischen Gnosis an.

Die Schwierigkeit bzw. das, was man vielleicht über das Wohlbekannte hinaus noch sagen kann, liegt in bzw. kommt aus manchen Einzelheiten. Ich möchte, was mir auf dem Herzen liegt, vom

---

[12] Nag-Hammadi-Register, 5.
[13] É. Quatremère, *Recherches critiques et historiques sur la langue et la littérature d'Égypte*, Paris 1808, S. 234.
[14] Die Gnosis, Leipzig bzw. Göttingen [1]1977, 53; [2]1980, 54; richtiggestellt in der englischen Übersetzung, Edinburgh 1983, 48.

alleräußersten Rahmen ausgehend und dann zum Inneren fortschreitend zur Sprache bringen.

Während der Schluß der Schrift mit dem Verkündigingsauftrag an Messos gut genug erhalten ist, um mit Wahrscheinlichkeit rekonstruiert werden zu können, fehlt der Anfang ganz. Aber, was fehlt, sind nur 5 3/4 Zeilen; und mit dem Ende von Z. 6 sind wir schon mitten in der Rede eines Offenbarers an Allogenes. D.h., die Exposition der Schrift (Vorstellung des Allogenes, Erscheinen des Offenbarers, Einführung des Themas der Offenbarung, etc.) muß sehr knapp gewesen sein. Daß die Schilderung des Erscheinens des Offenbarers so knapp gewesen sein muß, ist dabei vielleicht am wenigste auffällig. Denn auch sonst werden in unserer Schrift die Erscheinungen der jeweiligen Himmelswesen, die dem Allogenes die Offenbarungen bringen — auffälligerweise — überhaupt nicht ausgemalt, sondern lediglich — und zwar in knappster Form — konstatiert. Gerade in diesem Zusammenhang nun finde ich eine Erwägung von Karen King sehr interessant. Sie stellt nämlich fest, daß hinsichtlich der konsequent durchgehaltenen Komplexität des Rahmens » Allogenes « innerhalb der Bibliothek von Nag Hammadi nur mit der Epistula Jacobi Apocrypha (NHC I,2) verglichen werden kann, und wird so zu der Vermutung geführt, daß auch » Allogenes « als Brief des Allogenes an Messos konzipiert gewesen ist und man sich also als Anfang ein entsprechendes Briefpräskript vorzustellen habe.[15] Mit dieser Theorie wurde sich eben auch die auffällige Kürze des Eingangs der Schrift, das sofortige Zur--Sache-Kommen gut erklären.

Weiter im Inneren des Rahmens verdienen zwei bzw. drei Suffixe unsere Aufmerksamkeit: Im vorderen Teil des Textes in dem Satz » [Ich habe] diese (Worte) *von dir* gehört « die 2. Pers. sgl. m. in dem Präpositionalausdruck ⲈⲂⲞⲖ ⲚⲦⲞⲞⲦⲔ̄ (p. 50,10f.) und gegen Schluß (zweimal) die 3. Pers. sgl. m. in dem Satz ⲚⲀⲒ ⲆⲈ ⲚⲦⲈⲢⲈϤϪⲞⲞⲨ ⲀϤⲠⲰ ⲢϪ̄ ⲈⲂⲞⲖ ⲘⲘⲞⲒ » Als *er* dies aber gesagt hatte. schied *er* von mir « (p. 68, 23–25). Das aber heißt: vorn (vor p. 50, 10 f.) spricht *noch nicht* die im übrigen den ersten Teil beherrschende *weibliche* Offenbarergestalt der Jouel, und hinten (vor p. 68, 23–25 und irgendwo auf dem verlorenen oberen Teil dieser Seite beginnend) schon *nicht mehr* die Kräfte der Erleuchter, die sonst die zweite Hälfte beherrschen. Übrigens kann das Du von p. 50,10 f.

nicht (als Stück des Briefrahmens) auf Messos gehen, sondern dürfte zu einer Antwort gehören, die Allogenes dem Sprecher der vorhergehenden Offenbarung gibt. Mir erscheint es nun wahrscheinlich, daß der Sprecher des Anfangs und der Sprecher am Ende der Gesamtoffenbarung ein und dieselbe Person ist. Dieses Himmelswesen scheint dem Allogenes irgendwie besonders nahezustehen. Hinten verspricht er dem Allogenes, ihm den gesamten Inhalt der erfolgten Offenbarungen zu diktieren: » Schrei[b' auf, w]as ich dir s[ag]en un[d] woran ich dich erinnern werde « (p. 68,16–19). Zur Komplexität des Rahmens unserer Schrift gehört eben auch, daß der Autor nicht einfach den Allogenes sozusagen aus der Erinnerung das von ihm Gehörte und Gesehene niederschreiben läßt, sondern noch dieses Himmelswesen dazwischenschaltet, der die Worte des Textes authentisch diktiert haben soll. Vorn kommt die Zuständigkeit dieses Wesens für Allogenes in folgendem Hendiadyoin zum Ausdruck: » Der Beschützer, den ich (dir) [ge]geben habe, ⟨ist es,⟩ [der] dich belehrt hat; un[d] die Kraft, die in dir [wo]hnt, ist es, die sich (dir schon) oftmals [zur Re]de gede[hnt] hat « (p. 45, 9–12).

Mit Hilfe dieses Topos können wir nun wahrscheinlich doch noch dieses Wesen, dessen Name und Erscheinung uns mit den ersten fünf Zeilen der Schrift verlorengegangen ist, identifizieren. Wo nämlich Jouel die Rolle des Offenbarers übernimmt, sagt sie zu Allogenes — diesen Topos, wie es scheint, noch einmal aufnehmend —: » Du wurdest bekleidet mit einer großen Kraft, (nämlich mit) jener, mit der dich der Vater des Alls, der Ewige, bekleidet hat, bevor du zu diesem Ort kamst, damit du die (Dinge), die schwer zu sondern sind, sonderst und damit du die (Dinge), die unerkennbar sind für die Vielen, erkennst und du dich (so) rettest zu dem (Ort), der dir gehört « (p. 50,24–34). Der dem Allogenes so nahestehende Offenbarer am Anfang und am Ende der Schrift ist also wohl » der Vater des Alls « (das ist übrigens ein Ausdruck, der nur dieses eine Mal vorkommt; auch das bloße Wort » Vater « kommt nicht noch einmal vor), und das wiederum könnte eine Bezeichung des himmlischen Adamas sein, der ja als Helfer und Offenbarungsmittler für Allogenes, der doch sein im Irdischen befindlicher Sohn Seth ist, auch am richtigen Platz ist.

Daß der Name » Allogenes «, den die Haupt-

---

[15] The Quiescent Eye..., S. 56 f.

person unserer Schrift trägt und der auch als (Kurz-)Titel (am Ende) des Buches fungiert, eine Bezeichnung der aus der israelitischen Tradition stammenden Seth-Gestalt ist, daran braucht hier nur erinnert zu werden. Es ist also kein anderer als der legendäre Heros der Sethianer selbst, der hier die Offenbarungen empfängt. Worauf man aber noch kurz hinweisen könnte, ist, daß das Motiv der hundert Jahre, um die die beiden Offenbarungsblöcke voneinander getrennt sind (p. 56,21 f.; 57,31; 58,8), vorzüglich zu dieser Identifikation paßt und sie seinerseits unterstützt. Nur bei einem solchen Wesen der Vorzeit, das ja nach der Tradition ein Lebensalter von 912 Jahren erreicht hat, ist eine Pause solchen Ausmaßes plausibel. Also, wer Allogenes ist, ist klar! Wer aber ist sein Sohn Messos? Die Forschung sagt: Niemand weiß es! Aber vielleicht kann man das Geheimnis doch mehr oder weniger lüften — im wesentlichen mit Hilfe dessen, was hier von diesem Messos gesagt oder vorausgesetzt wird. Messos kann nicht als *direkter* leiblicher Nachkomme des Allogenes verstanden werden. Dem widerspricht die Art und Weise, wie dies Buch in seine Hände kommen soll, die einen erheblichen zeitlichen Abstand voraussetzt: Allogenes deponiert es auf einem Berge und unterstellt es dem Schutz des dort herrschenden schrecklichen Berggeistes, bis einst die Zeit gekommen sein wird, daß Messos den Berg besteigt und der Schreckliche es ihn nehmen läßt oder es ihm gibt: » Und du sollst dieses Buch auf einem Berg deponieren und d(ess)en H'ute[r] herbeirufen (mit den Worten): 'Komm, du Schrecklicher!' « (p. 68,20–23). Messos kann aber auch nicht als Repräsentant der Sethianer dieser letzten Generation gelten. Es fehlen nämlich bei dem Bergmotiv alle eschatologischen Züge, wie besonders ein Vergleich mit dem Ende des Ägypter-Evangeliums ergibt (vgl. besonders NHC III p. 68, 10–20: » Dieses Buch hat der große Seth... geschrieben.... Er deponierte es auf dem Berge, ..., damit es in den letzten Zeiten und Fristen ... hervorkomme und kundgemacht werde... «). Messos ist kein Letzter, sondern offenbar ein » Mittlerer «, wie schon sein Name sagen könnte, falls der genauso sinnhaltig sein sollte wie der des Allogenes. Der Sinn des Bergmotivs an sich dürfte wiederum sein, das empfindliche Buch (p. 68,21) vor einem seiner beiden Feinde, dem Wasser (der großen Flut) zu bewahren: Der

Berg ist so hoch, daß die Wasser der Flut nicht bis zu seinem Gipfel reichen. Dann ist Messos vorgestellt als eine nach der Sintflut lebende Gestalt der sethianischen Geschichtsvorstellung. Soviel kann man m.E. mit Bestimmtheit sagen. Das letzte Wort in dieser Sache dagegen hat für mich selbst zunächst nur den Charakter einer gedanklichen Versuchung. Dieser versuchliche Gedanke ergibt sich, wenn man zu dem gerade Ausgeführten noch das Allerauffälligste, nämlich die — im Text nur gerade eben berührte — Vorstellung von dem Schrecken verbreitenden Gott dieses Berges hinzunimmt. Dabei kann sich dann die Frage aufdrängen, ob der Messos unseres Textes nicht einfach eine sethianische Adaption und Verfremdung des Mose, der auf dem Sinai von Jahwe die Heilige Schrift empfängt, ist.

III. Probleme des Inhalts

Was den Inhalt des » Allogenes « anbelangt, so ist es das erste, was man deutlich sieht, daß von sethianisch-gnostischem Charakter ist. Die typisch sethianische Nomenklatur und Mythologie kommt Zweifel ausschließend zur Sprache. Das zweite, was gleich danach auffällt, ist der Reichtum an philosophischer Fachterminologie. » Allogenes « gehört zu einer besonderen Gruppe innerhalb des sethianischen Schrifttums (die übrigen drei Schriften sind » Zostrianus «, » Die drei Stelen des Seth « und » Marsanes «), die von einer intensiven Begegnung zwischen sethianischer Gnosis und spätantiker Philosophie zeugt. Und zwar ist » Allogenes «, wie Turner mit guten Gründen gezeigt hat, wohl die älteste Schrift und zugleich der Leit-Text dieser Gruppe, für die Turner deswegen den Terminus » Allogenes-Gruppe « geprägt hat. Als mutmaßliche Abfassungszeit setzt Turner ca. 200 n.Chr. an.[16] Das Sach-Thema, um das es in dieser Schrift geht, d.h. der Gegenstand, der im fiktiven Rahmen der Offenbarungen vom wirklichen Verfasser abgehandelt wird, ist sehr speziell und diffizil. Es ist die Metaphysik bzw. Ontologie der höchsten Sphäre der göttlichen Welt. Dabei wird die Spitze des sethianischen Pantheons: Unsichtbarer Geist, Barbelo mit ihrem, Äon und die drei Emanationsstufen bzw. Gestalten καλυπτός, πρωτοφανής und αὐτογενής, auf seine philosophischen

---

[16] *Gnostic Sethianism*, 86; ähnlich K. King: *First quarter of the third century* (The Quiescent Eye..., S. 58).

Implikationen hin ausgelegt. Der Unsichtbare Geist ist das Eine, das absolut transzendente wahrhaft Seiende; Barbelo und ihr Äon ist der in mehrfacher Hinsicht dreifaltige Bereich des göttlichen Nous bzw. die Welt der Ideen. Besonders bemerkenswerte und identifizierbare philosophische Schul-Konzeptionen, die irgendwie dem Mittleren Platonismus entlehnt sein müssen, sind dabei:

1. Die dreifache Modalität im Bereich des göttlichen Nous als ὕπαρξις/εἶναι, ζωή/ζῆν und νοῦς/νοεῖν an sich und in wechselseitiger Durchdringung.[17]

2. Die dreifache Gliederung bzw. Stufung von Kräften im Bereich des göttlichen Nous in οἱ ὄντως ὄντες παντέλειοι (von Turner auf die paradigmatischen Ideen bezogen), οἱ ὁμοῦ ὄντες παντέλειοι (nach Turner die mathematischen Ideen) und οἱ καθ᾽ ἕνα ὄντες τέλειοι (von Turner als die Ideen der Einzeldinge gedeutet).[18]

3. Die Lehre vom individuellen δαίμων eines jeden Menschen.[19]

4. Die Auffassung von der philosophischen Notwendigkeit der Selbsterkenntnis, wonach im Grunde die Erkenntnis der Tiefe des Selbst mit der Erkenntnis des Höchsten Seins identisch ist.

Was also im » Allogenes « behandelt wird, ist im großen und ganzen klar. Das Problematische am Inhalt des » Allogenes « ist das W i e. Während die mythologisch-konkreten Partien auch in dieser Hinsicht noch ziemlich verständlich sind, kommt es im philosophisch-abstrakten Bereich zu erheblichen Verständnisdefiziten. Das ist ja auch leicht einzusehen; denn gerade in philosophischen Sätzen und Passagen kommt es ja auf die Beziehung der Begriffe, ihre Verknüpfung und die Hierarchie der Teile entscheidend an.

Diese Problematik ist also eine solche, der man vor allem mit exegetischer Kleinarbeit zu Leibe gehen muß; und es ist zu hoffen, daß der von K. King geplante Kommentar, von dem im Ansatz schon manches in der Einleitung ihrer Textausgabe zu erkennen ist, genauere Aufschlüsse bringen wird. Gleichwohl darf man von ihm nicht alles erwarten. Denn es gibt erhebliche objektive Hindernisse: die vorausgesetzte Mythologie und die philosophische Deutung sind nicht völlig zur Deckung zu

bringen. Wir haben nur diesen einen Textzeugen und können also Textverderbnisse, wie sie in jeder Überlieferung vorkommen, nicht durch Textvergleich erkennen und korrigieren. Dieser Textzeuge ist zudem eine Übersetzung und muß also auch im besten Fall, wenn nämlich der Übersetzer sein Original voll verstanden hat, das Gemeinte verunklaren. Und schließlich hat unser Textzeuge ja große Lücken, die gerade das Verständnis diffiziler Einzelheiten und — gegebenenfalls — ungewöhnlicher Gedanken belasten bzw. unmöglich machen; zentrale Aussagen beginnen mitten im Satz bzw. hören mitten im Satz auf, so daß man oft nicht einmal weiß, *von wem* oder *wovon* eigentlich das Gesagte gesagt wird.

Vielleicht aber kann Hilfe von außen diesen Mangel ausgleichen oder mildern. Wenn es nämlich richtig ist, daß in dieser Schrift ein Sethianer redet, der seinen Glauben philosophisch auslegt und untermauert, darf man bis zum Erweis des Gegenteils annehmen, daß er in der philosophischen Interpretation weniger aus Eigenem schöpft, als Fremdes *irgendwoher* übernimmt. Nun gibt es im » Allogenes « so etwas wie philosophische » Fingerabdrücke «, gemeint sind ganz individuelle, prägnante und spezifische, und doch zugleich rätselhafte Aussagen oder Ausdrücke, die (wenn sie, wie gesagt, nicht vom Autor selbst stammen) im Prinzip zur Identifikation seiner *direkten* philosophischen Quelle führen müßten. Und von dieser Quelle her könnte noch Licht auf manches fallen, was sonst dunkel bleibt.

Es sind fünf Aussagen, die ich in diesem Zusammenhang zum Schluß unterbreiten möchte. Und zwar geht es um die Metaphern vom Fährmann, vom Steuermann und vom Haus, um den Terminus » das stille Auge der Offenbarung « und um die Vorstellung von der Komplementarität von, wie man zunächst übersetzen wird, » Erstoffenbarung « und » Offenbarung «. Die betreffenden Stellenn lauten folgendermaßen:

» Denn [we]nn sie ihn begreifen als den 'Fähr[ma]nn' der Grenzenlo[sig]keit des unsichtbaren Geist[es, der sich] in ihm befindet, wird sie (die Erkenntnis) ⟨sich⟩ [ihm] zuwenden, um zu erfahren, was [jener] ist, [d]er in ihm ist, und wie er [ex]istiert «. (p. 49, 7–14)[20]

---

[17] Vgl. Robinson, *The Three Steles...*, 140 f.; Turner, *Gnostic Sethianism*, 40–42.

[18] Vgl. Turner, *Gnostic Sethianism*, S. 83.

[19] Vgl. King, The Quiescent Eye..., S. 65 f.

[20] Der erste Abschnitt wurde unter sprachlichem Gesichtspunkt schon in Teil I herangezogen.

>> [Und] unbewegt bewegte sich der, der dort in dem Steu[e]rmann ist, um nicht unterzugehen in dem Grenzenlosen (, und zwar bewegte er sich) durch eine andere Wirksamkeit des Erkenntnisvermögens. Und er hielt Einkehr bei sich selbst und offenbarte sich als jegliches Begrenzen. << (p. 53,9–17)

(Vom transzendenten Gott) >> Er ist einerseits etwas Körperliches, das sich an einem (bestimmten) Platz befindet, er ist andererseits etwas Unkörperliches, das sich in einem (ganzen) Hause befindet, weil er ein dem Werden nicht unterworfenes Dasein besitzt. << (p. 65,30–33)

(Von dem, der ungeziemend über den transzendenten Gott gedacht hat, gilt:) >> Er war blind, (weil er) fern von dem stillen Auge der Offenbarung (war). << (p. 64,30–33)

>> Ich wurde erfüllt mit einer Offenbarung durch eine Erstoffenbarung des Unerkennbaren. << Und: >> Hindere nun nicht mehr die Unwirksamkeit, die in dir ist, durch die Suche nach jenen unerreichbaren (Dingen), sondern höre von ihm — wie es (allein) möglich ist — mittels einer Erstoffenbarung und einer Offenbarung! << (p. 60, 37–61,2 und 61,25–32; der Begriff >> Erstoffenbarung << auch noch p. 61, 9 f.) [21]

---

[21] Zum Verständnis dieser letzten beiden Stellen müßte man vor allem erst einmal wissen, welche griechischen Begriffe hinter den beiden koptischen Ausdrücken stecken. Vielleicht waren diese einander gar nicht so ähnlich, wie es nach dem Koptischen scheint. Man könnte sich durchaus so etwas wie πρωτοφάνεια gegenüber φωτισμός vorstellen. Die gleiche Erwägung hinsichtlich des ersten Begriffs findet sich auch bei L. Abramowski, >> Marius Victorinus... <<, S. 119.

COPTIC STUDIES

Einar Thomassen

Unusual Second Tense Forms
in the *Tripartite Tractate* (NHC I, 5)

The fifth tractate of Nag Hammadi Codex I is an unusually difficult text to read and translate. Conceptual abstruseness and linguistic idiosyncrasies in combination impede the access to this precious piece of Valentinian theology. In order to clear the way to an understanding of this document it is therefore necessary to be armed with the tools of both historical exegesis and grammatical analysis. Consequently, although my own interest in this text has been essentially with its contents, I have been impelled also to consider the linguistic problems. The following remarks, then, represent the exegete's thoughts on some aspects of the grammar of the *Tripartite Tractate*; but it is hoped that they may serve to indicate the interest which this text offers for the study of the Coptic language in general.

I shall concentrate on certain peculiarities relating to the Second Tenses. What I have to say falls into two parts: first, the interpretation of some unusual conjugation forms; secondly, the use of a Cleft Sentence with adverbial predicate as an alternative to a Second Tense.

Before I start let me note that the dialect of this text is basically Subakhmimic, with, as far as I can see, a remarkably large component of Akhmimic forms (Thomassen 1982, pp. 36–61).

1. Unusual Conjugation Forms

The forms in question have been dealt with previously by Kasser, in a special article (1967) and in the introduction to the edition of the text (Kasser et al. 1973, 29). Apart from this they seem to have attracted no attention. What follows may

be regarded, then, as an attempt to correct and supplement what has been said by Kasser on the subject.

1.1. The Form ⲉⲁⳇ.

ⲛ̅ϣⲱⲛⲉ· ⲛ̅ⲇⲉ· ⲉⲛⲧⲁⲩⲟⲩⲁϩⲟⲩ ⲛ̅ⲥⲱϥ· ⲉϩⲟⲩⲛ
ⲛ̅ⲧⲁⲣⲉϥϣⲱⲡⲉ ⲛ̅ⲥⲁ ⲛⲃⲁⲗ ⲙ̅ⲙⲁϥ ⲟⲩⲁⲉⲉⲧϥ̅
ⲉⲁϥϣⲱⲡⲉ ⲁⲃⲁⲗ ϩⲛ̅ ϯⲙⲛ̅ⲧϩⲏⲧ· ⲥⲛⲉϥ

'But the sicknesses which afflicted him after he had become beside himself arose from his faltering' (77:28–32).[1]

ⲛⲉⲧⲁϩⲉ͞ⲓ ⲧⲏⲣⲟⲩ ⲁⲃⲁⲗ ϩⲓⲧⲛ̅ ⲡⲗⲟⲅⲟⲥ ⲉⲓⲇⲉ
ⲁⲃⲁⲗ· ϩⲛ̅ ⲡⲓⲧⲁϫⲱ ⲛ̅ⲇⲉ ⲛⲉⲧϩⲁⲟⲩ ⲉⲓⲇⲉ
ϯⲃⲗ̅ⲕⲉ· ⲉⲧϯ ⲟⲩⲃⲏⲟⲩ ⲙⲛ̅ ⲡⲓⲛⲟⲩϩⲟⲩ ⲁⲃⲁⲗ
ⲙ̅ⲙⲁⲩ ... ⲉⲁⲩⲣ̅ ⲁϩⲓⲟⲩ ⲙ̅ⲙⲟⲟⲩ ⲁⲃⲁⲗ ϫⲉ

ϩⲛ̅ϣⲱⲛⲉ ⲛⲉ· ⲁⲃⲁⲗ ϩⲛ̅ ⲛⲓⲇⲓⲁ· ⲑⲉⲥⲓⲥ ⲉⲧⲛⲁⲛⲟⲩⲟⲩ

'All those who have originated from the Logos, either from the condemnation of what is evil, or from the wrath which fought against it and the turning away from it...(all these) have become worthy, because they originate from these good dispositions' (130:13–27).

There can be no doubt that in these passages the form ⲉⲁⳇ in each case introduces the main verb of the sentence. In the index to the edition this form is described as "préf. v. (anormal) du Parfait II (?)" (Kasser et al. 1975, 302). Now it has been known at least since Stern (1880, § 423 end) that the form ⲉⲁⲩ– can occasionally be used in a main sentence in Sahidic. Polotsky (1944, 48–49) tentatively identified it as a Second Perfect. This identification was subsequently accepted by Steindorff (1951, § 341), who also supplied examples from Shenoute.

---

[1] Quotations from *Tri. Trac.* in this article are based on an independent collation of the codex in the Coptic Museum of Old Cairo.

At the present congress, moreover, H.-M. Schenke has drawn attention to the use of ЄАᕼ- as the sole form of the Second Perfect in *Allogenes* (NHC XI,3).

The form may be interpreted as the Circumstantial of the First Perfect, as well as a Second Perfect (cf. Polotsky 1944, 49). In fact, A. Shisha-Halevy has recently made the observation, with reference to Shenoute, that when certain types of adverbial predicate precede the verb in a Cleft Sentence, the Circumstantial of a First Tence, and not a Second Tense, is used, in the Bipartite as well as in the Tripartite Conjugation Pattern (Shisha-Halevy 1975, 475–76; id. 1976, 36–37). However, as with a couple of the previously known·examples of the form ЄАᕼ-, [2] the two instances in *Tri. Trac.* do not conform to the pattern disclosed by Shisha-Halevy in Shenoute since the logical predicate in both cases follows the verb.

There also exist in fact good reasons for interpreting a form such as ЄАᕼ- as a Second Tense. Both in Fayumic and in Middle Egyptian the Second Perfect is formed by prefixing the Second Tense Converter А- or Є- to the Perfect base. The Fayumic Second Perfect is thus ААᕼ-, and the Middle Egyptian form ЄꙆАᕼ- or АꙆАᕼ- (Schenke 1978, p. 49*[95]; Funk 1981, 185). (Incidentally there is one instance of the Second Perfect ЄꙆА- in this text: 134:4.)

1.2. The Form ЄƿЄАᕼ.

ОУ∆Є ᾹТАᕼ ᕼNАꙆIТᕼ ЄN· ᾹПЄТᕼОЄI ᾹМАᕼ·
ОУ∆Є МᾹ КЄОУЄЄI NАꙆIТᕼ Ᾱ6ОNꙄ
АТƿЄ<ᕼ>ꙆПЄ ОУꙆАN· ЄᾹПЄᕼᕼ ЄꙆNЄᕼ· АƿАꙄ
ᾹNОУ∆ЄIᕼ· ЄƿЄАᕼꙆI ЄN ᾹПƿЄᕼᕼ ꙆНТꙄ ᾹᕼꙆПЄ

'Neither will He remove Himself from that in which He is, nor will any other forcibly bring Him to an end without His ever having desired it: He had no one who preceded Him in coming into being' (52:14–20).

ꙆЄ ПЛОГОC ∆Є ... ᾹПЄᕼᕼОУꙆꙄꙆ АТООТᕼ АЄINЄ
А𐎁АꙆ ᾹПƿНТЄ ᾹꙆЄNПƿОВОꙆНОУ ... АꙆꙆА
ЄƿЄАᕼᕼЄINЄ· [ЄВ]ОꙆ <ᾹꙆᾹ>МᾹТ6𐎁В ЄУCА𐎁К·

'For the Logos ... no longer tried to bring forth (offspring) in the manner of emissions ... but he brought forth little weak things' (80:30–81:1).
ꙆА𐎁Н ГАƿ ᾹМАЄIТ' NIM· ЄƿЄАᕼЄI ЄТВННТꙄ ᾹВI ПЄꙆƿНCТОC 'For more than anything else it was for her (i.e. the Election's) sake that Christ came' (122:17–19).

КАN ЄУᕼАNМОУТЄ· АƿАᕼ ᾹNIƿЄN· {ᾹNIƿЄN}
ᾹАТАПОУ ЄƿЄАУꙆООУ АУ6NᕼЄꙆЄ ᾹМАᕼ
ᾹПIƿНТЄ· ЄᕼᾹПCА NꙆƿНÏ ᾹᕼЄꙆЄ NIM· А𐎁𐎁
ᕼᾹПCА ᾹꙆƿНÏ ᾹꙆƿАᕼ NIM

'Even if it (i.e. Baptism) is called by innumerable names, they have (only) been used as a manner of speaking, for it transcends any word, and transcends any voice' (129:17–21).

This form was described by Kasser as "parfait I dérivé" (Kasser et al. 1973, p. 29; 1975, p. 393; Kasser 1967, 427). However, in the first example the form cannot be a First Perfect, since it occurs with the negative (N) ... ЄN. Moreover, in the last example the verb has an object suffix, thus the conjugation must belong to the Tripartite Pattern. The same conclusion can be reached with regard to ЄƿЄАᕼЄI in the third example, since the infinitive of verbs of motion cannot be used in the Bipartite Conjugation Pattern (Polotsky 1957, 229; id. 1960, 396–97). By assuming, as the most economical hypothesis, that all these instances of ЄƿЄАᕼ represent one and the same grammatical category,[3] we may identify it as a Second Perfect.

The existence of a Second Perfect ЄƿЄАᕼ- alongside ЄАᕼ- in this text is perhaps to be regarded in the light of the general pattern of fluctuation in the Converters used before a nominal actor expression in Akhmimic and at least some varieties of Subakhmimic,   i.e. Є : ЄƿЄ, А : АƿЄ and ЄТЄ : ЄТЄƿЄ (cf. Polotsky 1960, p. 419).[4] The reservation of the element -ƿЄ for the function of distinguishing a nominal from a pronominal agent seems to be less firmly established in these dialects. On the other hand, the use of ЄƿЄ- as a Second Tense Converter is not entirely inappropriate in this respect, since a verb conjugated in the Second Tense shares many of its syntactic

---

[2] Lagarde's *Wisdom* 16:1 (Polotsky 1944, p. 49); Shenoute III 150 Leipoldt (Steindorff 1951, p. 159).

[3] In the first and the last example the context raises the question whether ЄƿЄАᕼ may not also conceal a Circumstantial Converter.

[4] The fluctuation between ᕼАᕼ-and ᕼАƿЄᕼ-,МАᕼ- and МАƿЄᕼ- in the Subakhmimic Aorist may also be cited in this context. As can be seen from the index in Kasser et al. 1975, all these variations, with the exception of the Neg. Aorist, are found in *Tri. Trac.*

properties with the noun (Polotsky 1960, §§ 11, 30–31).

Obs. Kasser (1967, pp. 428–29) has drawn attention to a similar form which occurs once in the *Proverbs* text of Bodmer Papyrus VI: ⲉⲣⲁⲍⲉⲓ ⲅⲁⲣ ⲁⲧⲟⲟⲧⲟⲩ ⲛ2ⲙ̄ⲡⲉⲑⲟⲟⲩ ⲉⲧⲃⲉ ⲡⲕ9ⲃⲏⲣ ἥκεις γὰρ εἰς χεῖρας κακῶν διὰ σὸν φίλον (6 :3). Kasser's interpretation of ⲉⲣⲁⲍⲉⲓ as Circumstantial is not likely to judge from the Greek, but the form may well be read as Second Perfect. (As Kasser notes, the Sahidic and Akhmimic versions have ⲁⲕⲉⲓ, Bohairic ⲱⲁⲕⲓ

1.3. The Form ⲉⲣⲉⲛ̄ⲧⲁ⸗.

ⲝⲉ ϯⲡⲣⲟⲃⲟⲗⲏ ⲛ̄ⲧⲉ [ⲛ] !ⲡⲧⲏⲣϥ̄· ⲉⲧⲱⲟⲟⲡ ⲁⲃⲁⲗ 2ⲛ̄ ⲡⲉⲧ[ⲱ]ⲟⲟⲡ· ⲉⲣⲉⲛⲧⲁⲥⲱⲱⲡⲉ ⲉⲛ ⲕⲁ[ⲧ]ⲁ ⲟⲩⲱⲱⲧ ⲁⲃⲁⲗ· ⲛⲛⲟⲩⲉⲣⲏⲩ

'For the emission of the Alls, which is out of the One who is, has not taken place by way of a cutting off from one another' (73 :18–21).

ⲝⲉ ⲡⲓⲥⲁⲃⲧⲉ ⲧⲏⲣϥ̄ ⲙ̄ⲡⲓⲧⲥⲁⲉⲓⲱ ⲛ̄ⲧⲉ ⲛⲓ2ⲓ̈ⲕⲱⲛ ⲙⲛ ⲛⲓⲉⲓⲛⲉ ⲙⲛ̄ ⲛⲓⲧⲁⲛⲧⲛ̄· ⲉⲣⲉⲛⲧⲁⲩⲱⲱⲡⲉ ⲉⲧⲃⲉ ⲛⲉⲧⲣ̄ ⲭⲣⲓⲁ ⲛ̄ⲛⲟⲩⲥⲁⲛⲉⲱ· ⲙ̄ⲛ ⲟⲩⲥⲃⲱ ⲙⲛ ϯⲙⲟⲣⲫⲏ

'For the whole establishment and design of the images, likenesses and imitations has come into being for the sake of those who need nourishment and instruction and formation' (104 :18–23).

ⲛ̄ⲥⲉⲣ̄ ⲡⲱⲃⲱ̄· ⲝⲉ ϯⲉⲍⲟⲩⲥⲓⲁ ⲉⲣⲉⲛⲧⲁⲩ {ⲧ} ⲛ̄2ⲟⲩⲧⲟⲩ ⲁⲣⲁⲥ ⲡⲣⲟⲥ ⲛ̄ⲥⲏⲟⲩ ⲙⲛ̄ 2ⲛ̄ⲟⲩⲟⲉⲓⲱ ⲉⲧⲉⲩⲛ̄ⲧⲉⲩⲥⲟⲩ

'... and they are unaware that it is only for a time and such periods as they have that the power has been entrusted to them' (120 :32–35).

This form Kasser gave the name "parfait II dérivé," evidently interpreting the element ⲉⲣⲉ – here as a Circumstantial Converter. From the context, however, it is clear that the verbs figure here in main sentences. As a Second Tense form ⲉⲣⲉⲛ̄ⲧⲁⲩ– is clearly a pleonasm, the Second Tense Converter ⲉⲣⲉ – having been prefixed to the form ⲛ̄ⲧⲁ⸗ as a double marking of the Second Tense conversion.

It may be noted that in two of the three instances of this composite form a superlineal stroke is placed over the ⲛ. The two Converter morphemes are thereby kept apart by syllable division.

1.4. A Relative Second Perfect

ⲝⲉ ⲡⲉⲉⲓ ⲡⲉⲉⲧⲉⲁⲡ̄ⲛⲥⲱⲧⲏⲣ ⲱⲱⲡⲉ ⲙ̄ⲙⲁⲩ ⲁⲃⲁⲗ 2ⲛ̄ⲛ ⲟⲩⲙⲛ̄ⲧⲱⲃⲏⲣ ⲛ̄ⲱⲱⲡ ⲛ̄ⲕⲁ2· ⲉⲧⲉ ⲡⲉⲧⲁⲩⲱⲱⲡⲉ ⲙ̄ⲙⲁⲩ ⲡⲉ ⲝⲉ ⲉⲣⲉⲛ̄ⲛⲧⲁϥⲟⲩⲱⲛ2 ⲁⲃⲁⲗ· ⲉⲧⲃⲏⲧⲟⲩ 2ⲛ̄ⲛ ⲟⲩⲡⲁⲑⲟⲥ ⲛ̄ⲁⲧⲟⲩⲱⲱⲉ

'For this is what our Saviour became out of willing compassion, which is that which those for whose sake he appeared had become by involuntary passion' (114 :30–36).

The form ⲉⲣⲉⲛ̄ⲛⲧⲁⲩ– was apparently regarded by the editors of *Tri. Trac.* as simply a variant of the form with a single ⲛ. In the translations the words beginning with ⲝⲉ ⲉⲣⲉⲛ̄ⲛⲧⲁϥⲟⲩⲱⲛ2 have been interpreted as forming either a clause of cause (Kasser et al. 1975, 53; cf. Kasser 1967, 428) or an explicative main sentence (Kasser et al. 1975, pp. 115, 153; Attridge and Mueller 1977, p. 87). But contextual interpretation suggests that ⲝⲉ here, as in several other instances in this text (108 :34, 117 :36, 126 :28), is an orthographic variant of ⲛ̄ⲝⲉ (=ⲛ̄61) and that the following word is a substantivized relative clause. The form ⲉⲣⲉⲛ̄ⲛⲧⲁⲩ– seems in fact to combine the Second Tense Converter ⲉⲣⲉ – and the Relative ⲛ̄ⲧⲁ⸗, and it is tempting to attribute the doubling of the ⲛ to the presence of the "article" ⲛ, by which this relative construction is substantivized. This implies that the Second Tense Converter here precedes the substantivizing morpheme, which seems highly irregular. How this apparent irregularity is to be explained — whether there has been a scribal error or confusion on the part of the translator in the rendering of a convoluted sentence, or the morpheme ⲉⲣⲉ – here has properties of which we are ignorant, or perhaps the whole sentence is to be analysed in a different way — is a problem I am unable to solve. In any case I think that the translation given here must represent the intended meaning of the sentence. There seems to exist one more example in this text of a Relative Second Perfect, with the form ⲉⲛⲧ ⲁⲩ–: ⲛⲉⲉⲓ ⲉⲛⲧⲁⲩ ⲱⲱⲡⲉ ⲉⲧⲃⲏⲧϥ̄ ⲕⲁⲧⲁ ⲗⲟⲅ ⲟⲥ ⲉⲛ (81 :11–12). Whereas the combination of Relative and Second Tense is previously documented in the Present system (Stern 1880, § 422; for *Tri. Trac.* cf. 51 :1, 58 :38, 113 :36), I do not know of any instances outside this text of a Relative Second Perfect.

1.5. The Meaning of these Forms

The forms of the Second Perfect surveyed here exist side by side with the cmmon forms ⲛ̄ⲧⲁⲩ–

and ⲉⲛⲧⲁϥ-. Though Kasser (1967, 427–28; Kasser et al. 1975, 29) suggested that the forms with ⲉⲣⲉ- indicate "une nuance de causalité", I must say that I have detected no underlying rule which may explain why one grammatical form of expression is selected in preference to the others in a given context.

2. Cleft Sentences with Adverbial Predicate

Finally I should like to call attention to a series of passages in which a Cleft Sentence is preceded by an adverbial predicate:

ⲝⲉ ⲁⲝⲛ̄ ⲡⲟⲩⲱϣⲉ ⲉⲛ ⲛ̄ⲧⲉ ⲡⲓⲱⲧ ⲡⲉⲧⲁⲩⲝⲡⲟ
ⲙ̄ⲡⲓⲗⲟⲅⲟⲥ ⲉⲧⲉ ⲡⲉⲉⲓ ⲡⲉ ⲟⲩⲁⲉ ⲁⲛ ⲁⲝⲛ̄ⲧϥ̄·
ⲉϥⲛⲁϯ ⲡⲉϥⲟⲩⲁⲉⲓⲉ ⲁⲗⲗⲁ ...

'For it is not without the will of the Father that this Logos was produced, nor, again, was it without it that he should rush forward, but ...' (76:23:27).

ⲁⲃⲁⲗ ⲍ̄ⲛ̄ ⲟⲩϕⲁⲛⲧ [ⲁⲥⲓⲁ] ⲛ̄ⲧⲉ ⲟⲩⲧⲁⲛⲧⲛ̄ ⲙⲛ̄
ⲟⲩⲙⲉ[ⲩⲉ] ⲙ̄ⲙⲛ̄[ⲛ̄]ⲝⲁⲥⲓⲍⲏⲧ· ⲉϥϣ[ⲟⲩⲉⲓⲧ]
ⲡⲉⲧⲉⲁⲩϣⲱⲡⲉ

'It is of a fantasy of imitation and a presumptuous and vain thought that they have come into being' (82:19–22).

ⲍ̄ⲛ̄ⲕⲉⲕⲁⲩⲉ ⲇⲉ ⲁⲛ ⲉⲩⲝⲱ ⲙ̄ⲙⲟ[ⲥ] ⲝⲉ ⲁⲃⲁⲗ
[ⲍⲓ]ⲧⲛ̄ ⲛⲉϥ[ⲁ]ⲅ·ⲅⲉⲗⲟⲥ ⲡⲉⲧⲁϥⲣ̄ ⲍⲱⲃ

'Others again say it is through his angels that he has worked' (112:35–113:1).

ⲉⲛⲡⲉⲟⲩⲁⲛ ⲙ̄ⲙⲁⲩ ⲙ̄ⲙⲉ· ⲝⲉ ⲉϥⲛ̄ⲛⲏⲩ ⲁⲃⲁⲗ
ⲧⲱⲛ ⲏ ⲁⲃⲟⲗ ⲍ̄ⲛ̄ ⲛⲓⲙ ⲡⲉⲧⲟⲩⲛⲁⲝⲡⲁϥ

'... and none of them realized whence he would come or from whom he would be born' (113:28–31).

ⲝⲉ ⲍ̄ⲛ̄ ⲟⲩⲙⲛ̄ⲧⲁⲧⲣ̄ ⲛⲟⲃⲉ· ⲁⲩⲱ ⲍ̄ⲛ̄ⲛ
ⲟⲩⲙⲛ̄ⲧⲁⲧⲧⲱⲗⲙ̄ ⲁⲩⲱ ⲍ̄ⲛ̄ ⲟⲩⲙⲛ̄ⲧ·ⲁⲧⲝⲱⲍⲙ̄
ⲡⲉⲛⲧⲁⲩⲧⲣⲟⲩⲱ̂ ⲙ̄ⲙⲁϥ

'For it was in sinlessness, unpollutedness and undefiledness that he let himself be conceived' (115:15–17). ⲙ̄ⲡⲓⲣⲏⲧⲉ ⲡⲉⲛⲧⲁⲩⲝⲓ ⲥⲱⲙⲁ· ⲍⲓ̈ ⲯⲩ.
ⲭⲏ ⲛ̄ϭⲓ ⲛⲉⲛⲧⲁⲉⲓ ⲛⲙ̄ⲙⲉϥ 'It was in this way that those who came with him received body and soul' (115:29–31).

Normally a Cleft Sentence cannot take an adverbial predicate in Coptic. The equivalent of a Cleft Sentence with adverbial predicate is expressed by the Second Tenses (Polotsky 1944, §§ 16–24). This implies that the Coptic relative clause, which forms the logical subject of the Cleft Sentence, is by nature adjectival in meaning, whereas it is the property of the Second Tense to produce a substantival clause (the equivalent of a verbal noun in the narrow sense) which may function as the logical subject to an adverbial predicate. This difference in structure and meaning between the Cleft Sentence and the Second Tense is ignored in all of these passages: here the relative clause has substantival, not adjectival, meaning, and the Cleft Sentence of which it forms part has an adverbial predicate. The way in which this construction is used as an alternative to the Second Tense is particularly evident in the first and fourth examples, where the Cleft Sentence with adverbial predicate stands parallel to an actual Second Tense within the same sentence.

It will be noted that these passages all share a common structure in that the logical predicate always precedes the subject. In this respect they conform with the regular word order of normal Cleft Sentences with nominal predicate.[5]

Bibliography

Attridge, H.W., and Mueller, D., 1977, Translation of *Tri. Trac.*, in: J.M. Robinson (ed.), *The Nag Hammadi Library in English*, Leiden: E. J. Brill, pp. 54–97.

Funk, W.-P., 1981, "Beiträge des Mittelägyptischen Dialekts zum koptischen Konjugationssystem", in: D.W. Young (ed.), *Studies Presented to Hans Jakob Polotsky*, East Gloucester, Mass.: Pirtle and Polson, pp. 177–210.

Kasser, R., 1967, "Un nouveau préfixe verbal copte?," *Le Muséon* 80, 427–29.

Kasser, R. et al. 1973, *Tractatus Tripartitus: Pars I De Supernis*, Bern: Francke.

---

[5] I wish to thank Gerald M. Browne, Wolf-Peter Funk, Bentley Layton, Richard H. Pierce and Helmut Satzinger for their very helpful comments on the original version of this paper.

Kasser, R. et al. 1975, *Tractatus Tripartitus: Pars II De Creatione Hominis, Pars III De Generibus Tribus*, Bern: Francke.

Polotsky, H.J., 1944, *Études de syntaxe copte*, Cairo: Societé d'Archéologie Copte.

Polotsky, H.J., 1957, Review of Till, "Koptische Grammatik," OLZ 52, 219–34.

Polotsky, H.J., 1960, "The Coptic Conjugation System," Or 29, 392–422.

Schenke, H.-M., 1978, "On the Middle Egyptian Dialect of the Coptic Language," *Enchoria* VIII, Sonderband, 43* (89)–(104) 59*.

Shisha-Halevy, A., 1975, "Two New Shenoute-Texts from the British Library: II Commentary", Or 44, 469–84.

Shisha-Halevy, A., 1976, "Commentary on unpublished Shenoutiana in the British Library", *Enchoria* VI, 29–61.

Steindorff, G., 1951, *Lehrbuch der koptischen Grammatik*, Chicago: Univ. Press.

Stern, L., 1880, *Koptische Grammatik*, Leipzig: Weigel; rpt. Osnabrück 1971: Biblio.

Thomassen, E., 1982, *The Tripartite Tractate from Nag Hammadi: A New Translation with Introduction and Commentary*, Ph. D. diss., Univ. of St Andrews.

COPTIC STUDIES

Barbara Tkaczow

Archaeological Sources for the Earliest Churches in Alexandria

I should like to present some remarks concerning the archaelogical remains of Alexandrian churches from the 4th to the 7th centuries. It is the general opinion that no traces of them are preserved; to reconstitute this problem we have only some information taken from literary sources. Actually we know about 30 of the names of the Alexandrian churches, and we have some indications permitting the localizing of several of them on the plan of the city.[1] But all these formerly established locations — although generally accepted — are more or less doubtful. St Mark's Church has been placed by different authors in 3 different sites, the Church "of Kaisareion" is very often confused with the Church of St Michael, the identification of the "Dimos" Church with the "Kom el-Demas" is purely artificial, and the traditional identification of Theonas' Church and Athanasius' Church with two early Arabic mosques is also quite uncertain. The entire problem of the topography and architecture, and also the chronology of the Alexandrian churches is always treated as a theoretical question — practically devoid of archaeological evidence. But it is not quite true that no traces of Alexandrian churches have survived until our times. These are numerous, but these have been almost ignored by scholars as objects deprived of any definite architectural context (i.e., plan of the buildings). These remains consist to a great degree of fragments of architectural decorations (capitals,

columns, bases, pedestals, frises, architraves, various kinds of decorative slabs, elements of the interior decoration of the churches as for example table tops [mensas], elements of altars, etc.). The greatest ensemble of these objects was found by the Polish Archaeological Mission in Kom el-Dikka (about 1000 objects of various quality),[2] but there are also other sites in the city where the presumed relics of church decoration had been discovered. The objects from Kom el-Dikka are entirely deprived of their original context (there were discovered re-used or in the debris levels); in the other places in the city we can identify some sites where remains of architectural decoration and a few inscriptions are connected with the ruins dated from the 4th to the 7th centuries.

The archaeological remains relating to the ecclesiastical architecture in Alexandria can be elaborated from two points of view: topographical — — because the arrangement of these remains on the archaeological map of the city could also show the arrangement of the churches in the city; so that some new remarks can be ventured on the traditionally accepted locations of some churches; and stylistical — because, although the buildings are entirely gone, the scattered architectural remains can reveal their decoration and even style.[3] Here it is necessary to say that, although a great number of known Alexandrian churches is ascribed to the important personages of the 4th century (as bishop

[1] E. Amelineau, *Géographie de l'Égypte Copte*, Paris 1893, pp. 24–44; G. Botti, *Plan de la ville d'Alexandrie à l'époque ptolémaïque*, Alexandria 1898, pp. 89–103; F. Chabrol and D. H. Leclerq, *Dictionnaire d'archéologie chrétienne*, t. I, partie I^e, Paris 1924, cols 1098–1182; A. Calderini, *Dizionario dei nomi geografici e topografici dell'Egitto greco–romano*, I, 1935, pp. 165–178; A. Adriani, *Repertorio d'arte dell'Egitto Greco–Romano*, serie C, Palermo 1963, pp. 216–217.

[2] I am now in the course of preparing a catalogue of the fragments of architectural decoration from Polish Excavations in Kom el–Dikka, which mainly are dated for period in question, i.e. 4th–7th centuries and a big group of them could be ascribed to ecclesiastical architecture.

[3] It is necessary to say that we have in two nearest examples — undoubtedly Alexandrian, although lying outside of the city, i.e. Abu Mena and el–Dekhela — good examples and analogies to the architecture and architectural decoration of disappeared Alexandrian churches. Among other things they have one feature in common, i.e. a marble architectural decoration, whereas in the rest of Egypt only local stone was used and marble objects were rare.

Athanasius, bishop Theophil etc.), the majority of archaeological remains are dated from the 6th and 7th centuries. It is essential to bear in mind that between the 4th and the 7th centuries there occurred some grave events in the city — earthquakes, fires etc. and each time after these disasters the restorations of old and constructions of new buildings in the city were initiated.

We have about 18 "archaeological sites " and about a hundred objects, either connected with them, or isolated (apart from the ensemble from Kom el-Dikka), which can be ascribed to the remains of churches. [4] These are:

1. The small sepulchral chapel in Gabbari, in area of the presumed martyr's cemetery, where bishop Peter, martyrized in 311, was buried.

2. Site of the so-called "Mosque of 1000 Pillars" from the 9th century, considered as a site of the so-called Theonas' Church built in the end of the 3rd century. But it was not a church transformed into a mosque, but most probably a mosque constructed on the remains of the ruined church. The mosque was demolished in the beginning of the 19th century and we know its plan (typical mosque, without any traces of transformation) and have numerous architectural remains ascribed to the presumed church, now scattered all over the city. For example two columns with incised monograms of Christ are now in the so-called Hospital Garden in the eastern part of the city, several granite pedestals were re-used in modern monuments of the city, and a considerable number of these fragments was conserved in the Franciscan Church occupying now the place of the mosque. The date of totality of these fragments is various — from the 6th to the 7th centuries.

3. This is a vast area comprising the "Byzantine cisterns" and "Byzantine cemeteries"; it is possible looking at the architecture of some of these tombs cutting in the rock, that the old Ptolemaic hypogea, abandoned after the 1st century, were re-used from the beginning of the 4th century. It is possible that all these cemeteries are connected with the above-mentioned remains of the church.

4. This is the Serapeum area. The Christian remains from here are rather unimpressive; we have only some fragments of architectural decoration of modest dimensions and quality. It is not possible to identify here any traces of the churches built by bishop Theophil after the destruction of the pagan sanctuary.

5. To the north–east of Serapeun we have mostly scattered "traces of a Christian church" — a number of big marble columns "with incised crosses" and some big capitals-imposts decorated with a cross. Because columns "with incised crosses" are found very often, it is possible that it is a sign of some type of "blessing" the architectural elements deriving from the pagan temples (?)

6. On Sieglin's plan this is the place of the "Ehemaliger Temple", and on the Neroutzos' plan — the "Mosque of Amrou". Here were discovered relics of the "Byzantine cemetery" and undefined "big foundations" with a number of interesting architectural remains, among others a big marble basket capital, two marble Ionic imposts decorated with a cross in wreath and two fragments of a marble architrave bearing the same decoration. There were also found two inscriptions and some architectural decorations from the 2nd century. It is possible that we have here the relics of a pagan temple converted into a church (?).

7. Near the main street in the centre of the city is the site of the so-called Attarin Mosque (built in 1084[?], demolished in 1830), presumed to be Athanasius' Church, built by bishop Athanasius in 370 "in the place called Mendesion". In *Description de l'Égypte* we have some drawings showing the types of capitals and other elements re-used in this mosque. We have here examples of basket capitals, imposts decorated with a cross, and many variants of the Corinthian order, also bearing a cross-decoration.

8. This is a site on the coast, where were found the ruins of Late Roman baths, and the ruins of a "Christian basilica" with a number of big granite columns, many capitals — Corinthian — dated from the 4th and 5th centuries, the so-called, bell-capitals from the 5th/6th centuries, and twin basket capitals — the same type as on the site 6, but a little smaller.

9. Here we have also remains of a granite colonnade, and it is possible that it is one complex with site 8, and that from these ruins the architectural elements to be re-used in the Attarin Mosque were taken (?). In my opinion it is possible that here,

---

[4] A complete elaboration of mentioned sites, B. Tkaczow, Recherches sur la topographie de l'ancienne Alexandrie. Essai de la reconstruction (in preparation); IIe Partie (Catalogue des Sites), nos 4(1), 7(2), 9–10(3), 15(4), 16(5), 28–29(6), 25(7), 19–20(8), 22(9), 57(10), 102(11), 60(12), 64(13), 112(14), 98–99 (15), 89–90(16), 147(17) and Catalogue des Objets, nos 282, 319, 319a(18).

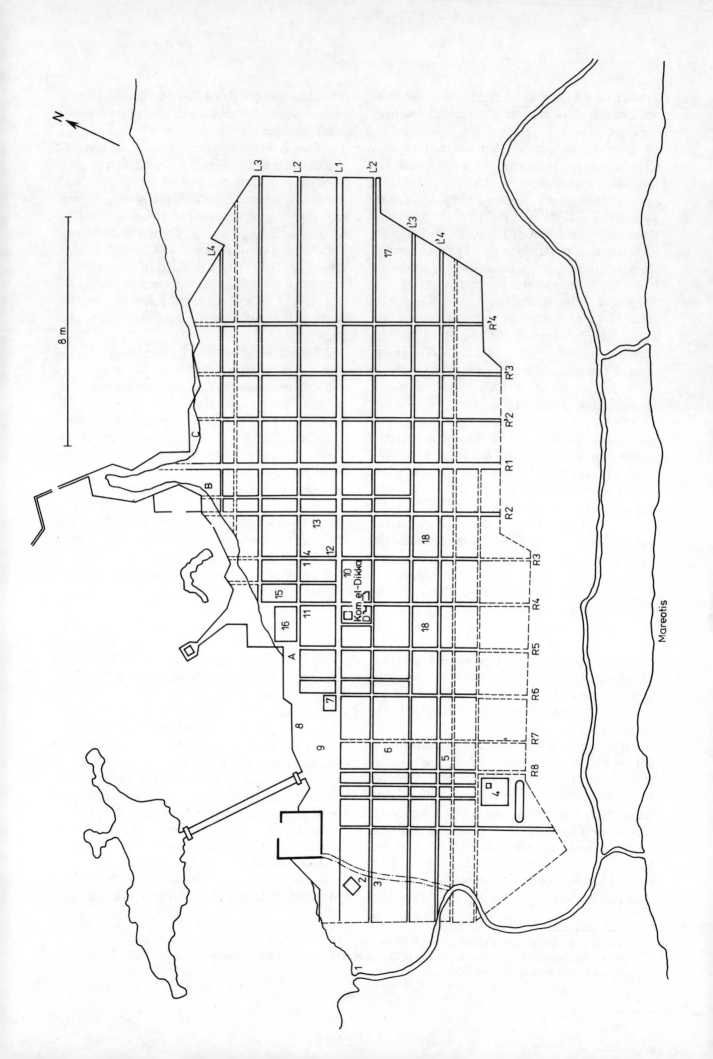

between sites 8 and 9 is the real place of Athanasius' Church, as literary tradition said, lying near the coast (?)

10. Here on the Sieglin's plan are "remains of a Christian church with restes of the colonnade"; in this area were discovered also some isolated architectural remains bearing a cross decoration. Recently (in 1978) the ruins of a 5th-century dwelling (private houses?) were discovered here with a number of architectural fragments, some of them decorated with a cross in wreath. According to Mr M. Rodziewicz it is possible that this house was ruined during the earthquake in 535, and some years after the church was built?

11. In this place the ruins of "church or cloister" were discovered, with many architectural remains — columns of different sizes, capitals, a kind of "obelisk" with an incised cross, and also a quantity of St. Menas' ampoules.

12. On the place where Governor Office now stands, near the main street, but in the eastern part of the city were discovered peculiar relics, considered generally as the remains of the Church of the Archangel Michael, known also as "Bishop's Alexander Church" (converted in 326 from the pagan temple of Kronos). The most important, although undocumented finds are the "substructions with preserved Greek and Coptic inscriptions" and numerous architectural fragments — — capitals, little columns, relief slabs, etc., all decorated "with Christian symbols", i.e. cross (?).

13. In the neighbourhood many columns "with incised crosses" and capitals with the same decoration were found; these capitals are generally described as "Byzantine capitals with cross", i.e. imposts or even basket capitals (?). Unfortunately the documentation of these finds (from sites 12 and 13) is very poor.

14. Here are some Byzantine remains superimposed on the relics of the Ptolemaic, the so-called Polychrome Temple. There are found numerous but dispersed objects from Christian times — some fragmentary inscriptions (one with a dedication of the church?), some capitals, among them a number of imposts and probably basket capitals decorated with cross (according to the description of the finds), fragments of decorative marble panels etc. This place is sometimes considered as a site of St

Theodore Church (lying "on Brucheion") or even of Archangel Michael Church (site 14 is very often confused with site 12).

15. This is the site where, during construction works on the new Coptic Catholic Patriarchate were discovered extensive ruins consisting of well preserved substructions and many architectural elements (columns, capitals etc.) of massive dimensions. Near this site was also found some scattered architectural elements bearing a Christian decoration. The identification of these ruins as relics of the church "of Kaisareion" is evidently erroneus — — a place of a Kaisareion enclosure is a little to the west of this site; here, it should be an episcopal palace (?).

16. This is a right site of Kaisareion (converted into a church in 324). Apart from the remains from earlier times here were discovered numerous architectural elements dated from the 4th to the 7th centuries — marble columns, pedestals, capitals, wall-facing etc. Many of them have traces of fire.

17. In the eastern suburbs, especially in Hadra some traces of small churches or chapels connected with the vast Christian cemetery were found.

18. In the southern part of the city (Moharrem Bey) were discovered some isolated objects deprived of architectural context, as for example a marble base with a Greek inscription consisting of dedication of an anonymous church built in 488 or 588, the huge figural capital decorated with the "masks of the winds" (5th century), some late Roman Corinthian capitals (4th–5th centuries), and recently discovered (in 1983) one big basket capital, the same as in the sites 6, 7 and 8. All these finds were most probably transported here from some other provenance in the city.

The problem of exhaustive analysis of all of these finds from the topographical and stylistical point of view is too extensive question to be discussed in this short article. [5] Here I should like to say only a few words about the group of basket capitals. We have now at our disposal six of these capitals, all from Alexandria — four discovered in the city, now in the Graeco-Roman Museum, [6] the fifth — probably missing and known only from the ilustration in *Description de l'Égypte* (see description of site 7), and the sixth — now in Cairo in the Coptic Museum. [7] There is also a seventh — in Cairo too,

[5] Tkaczow, Recherches sur la topographie..., I[e] partie, chap. 3.

[6] Alexandrie, Musée Gréco–Romain, inv. nos 12070, 13475, 17013 and recently discovered, inv. np 29447.

[7] Cairo, Coptic Museum, inv. no 7352(7178)

in the Nasir Mosque.[8] But while the first six capitals are all nearly identical in the design of decoration, the latter is a little different, and I exclude it from this group. All these capitals are usually compared with the basket capitals from San Vitale in Ravenna but in fact only the capital from Nasir Mosque closely resembles them. In Alexandrian examples all is different — the proportions, the composition of the "basket", and a pattern of a floral panel.

I do not want to enter into discussion on the origin of this type.[9] Assuming that it is a metropolitan invention exported from the Proconnesian quarries along all Mediterranean, it is clear that these six Alexandrian capitals were imported as the half-products and finished in place with an evident modification of a basic pattern. It can also be supposed that these six capitals bearing the identical decoration were finished together as one ensemble. But here the most important is the question of the arrangement of these capitals on the plan of the city, showing that we can ascribe them to 2 or 3 different buildings at least, most probably all churches, erected or re-built after the 1st half of the 6th century. It is possible that there were some new constructions (or reconstructions?) in the city after the great earthquake of 535, or after this (almost legendary) fire in 536, caused by Theodora. So it can be said that this group of capitals testify to the construction of 2 or 3 important, huge and richly decorated churches in Alexandria in the 2nd half of the 6th century, but cannot be identified with any church known from the literary sources. The twin basket capitals from the site 8 are generally considered as the remains of St Mark's Church traditionally located in this place, but this seems rather dubious.[10] The classification of all disponible archaeological material on the archaeological map of the city could show the arrangement of the ecclesiastical architecture in Alexandria in the 4th–7th centuries, but all these sites remain in fact anonymous, except the church "of Kaisareion" (because the place of enclosure was determined by the obelisks), and partially the so-called Athanasius Church.

---

[8] See R. Kautsch, *Kapitellstudien*, Leipzig 1936, no 630, taf. 38.

[9] J. Beckwith, *Coptic Sculpture*, London 1963, p. 21, notes 85, 86.

[10] According to information about destruction of St Mark's Church in the time of Crusades, it is evident that St Mark's Church was placed not in the central, but in the eastern part of the city, in those times lying beyond the fortifications; see J. Faivre, "L'église Saint Sabas et le martyrium de Saint Marc à Alexandrie", BSAC 1937, 67–74.

COPTIC STUDIES

László Török

Notes on the Chronology of Late Antique Stone Sculpture in Egypt

The sculptures exhibited in the so-called Ahnas Room of the Coptic Museum in Cairo may serve as an excellent illustration to the summarizing statement of Ernst Kitzinger: "the history of art in the [Late Antique] period ... is ... dominated by one central and crucial process, namely, the disintegration of the classical canon and the emergence of radically conceptual forms either abstracted from that canon or imposed upon it". [1] The more we forget that no object in the Ahnas Room is dated in any independent way, the less unambiguous the illustration becomes. Indeed, in most works dealing with the art of Late Antique Egypt, we find the art objects arranged in a chronological order so that they describe a gradual process not only of the disintegration of classical canon but also of quality standards usually associated with classical art. Only rarely is the question asked, whether is the illustration in this way realistic, or would it be more adequate to look also in Late Antique Egypt for same illogical and controversial course of development during the 4th and 5th centuries which we find in other, better documented, provinces of Late Antique art? For Late Antique art was characterized not only by the general trend summarized above, but also by "retarding elements, regional factors and the co-existence of different styles depending on subject content" [2] further depending on the actual composition of the workshops that could result in a stylistic poliphony the reasons of which generally escape our understanding. Nevertheless, the fact that the great majority of Late Antique objects from Egypt do not come from scientifically controlled excavations and are thus in no way independently dated, may explain, why does literature prefer to maintain both the general art historical picture and the chronological construction of "Early Coptic art", as Egyptian Late Antique art is generally and wrongly labelled, as they were established by Kitzinger in the late 1930s [3] and to ignore all recent attempts at a more complex explanation and at diverging datings.

In his *Notes on Early Coptic Sculpture* Kitzinger reconstructed a development from the more classically modelled, "soft-style" Oxyrhynchos sculptures through the transitional soft-style Ahnas monuments and through the "hard-style" Ahnas carvings to the Coptic style proper as it is represented in Bawit and Sakkara. On the basis of capitals from the said sites that seemed to have analogies in 5th and 6th century Byzantine architecture he furthermore stated, that one can arrive "at a sixth-century date for most of the fragments from Bawit and Sakkara", secondly, that the latter fragments "are on the whole even more developed than the 'hard' sculptures at Ahnas, and thereby they help to confirm the fifth-century date which... [was] suggested for the latter", thirdly, "that they show the whole development of Coptic sculpture to be one towards an increasing abstraction and rigidity. [4] This chronological scheme was adopted by John Beckwith in a book on Coptic sculpture [5] as well as by other writers of the sixties and the seventies. In 1970 I tried in a very youthful paper to lower the general dating levels of Kitzinger, [6] but until the late seventies and early eighties, when a series of archaeological and

---

[1] Kitzinger 1977, p. 19. Abbreviations used in the following pages are on p. 484.
[2] Kitzinger, 1977, ibid.
[3] Kitzinger, 1937.
[4] Kitzinger, 1937, 191.
[5] Beckwith, 1963, 16–27.
[6] Török 1970.

architectural-historical investigations were carried out and published by Peter Grossmann and Hans-Georg Severin, [7] there was no real chance to challenge the generally accepted results of earlier research by the support of data of non-speculative nature. Besides new data from excavations at Sakkara, [8] the most important result of their investigations is the discovery that the south church at Bawit was in the form as it was excavated, a rebuilt and enlarged fourth century pagan sepulchral building consisting of fourth century walls with original architectural ornaments, further fourth and fifth century ornaments taken from other buildings and finally sixth--century architectural ornaments carved for the sixth-century reconstruction for the purposes of the Christian cult. [9] The fact that the south church at Bawit is not the proof for the stylistic heterogeneity of sixth-century Egyptian art, opens new vistas for the research of this period and further urges the revision of the interpretation and dating of the objects from the preceding centuries. In present paper I shall discuss some observations on fourth-century sculpture inspired or made possible by the above-mentioned works of Grossmann and Severin and I shall try to put them into the context of the stylistic poliphony we have reasons to suppose but the reconstruction of which must still be regarded as hypothetic. Since I deal in the forthcoming mostly with already published objects, long descriptions and analyses will be — as far as possible — omitted. [10]

The paper concerns the following problems: firstly I shall try to demonstrate that the so-called soft and hard styles are contemporaries not only for a short, transitional, period but they are rather stylistic traditions and trends existing side by side for a considerable period of time. The relationship between soft and hard style will raise the question about the chronological situation of Oxyrhynchos, regarded traditionally as the source of soft style also for Ahnas. I shall try to demonstrate that

there were no considerable chronological differences between Oxyrhynchos and Ahnas, either as to the beginnings, or as to the end of the building activity producing the ornaments in question. Furthermore, several stylistic trends observed in the material from these sites occurred contemporaneously also at Ashmunein, Bawit and Sakkara during the fourth century.

While analysing stylistic poliphony, it cannot be left out of consideration that there are not only different stylistic traditions and trends but also qualities. Hard modelling, rudely carved foliages and figures or extremely simplified architectural forms are not necessarily later than soft modelling, naturalistically rendered forms or orthodox architectural members — we must carefully confront within the same stylistic unity its manifestations on a good level with those on a low level of craftmanship.

I shall discuss the carvings arranged into three groups. It seems to me that there are more or less clearly distinct complexes of carvings from the period between the Constantinian age and the turn of the 4th and 5th centuries, each being, however, stylistically pluralistic in a sense that they consist of works of masters with different backgrounds. Analysis and identification of these backgrounds cannot be carried out in the present paper. The individual complexes do not mean, however, clear-cut stages of a process, although they doubtlessly embody a development in time. As we shall see, significant features of the individual complexes existed also in the other ones. As key monument, a handsomely carved acanthus scroll frieze from Ahnas will prove that all diagnostic acanthus forms existed contemporaneously; and, as already mentioned above, similar statement can also be made on stylistic trends in figural sculpture. The three groups were dated on the basis of the capitals belonging directly or indirectly to each of them, for dating is still imaginable first of all on this basis, however also stylistic affinities of the figural

---

[7] Grossmann 1971, Grossmann 1978, Severin 1977,1, Severin 10977, 2, Severin 1981,1, Severin 1981,2, Severin 1983, Grossmann–Severin 1982 (with the literature of earlier excavations).

[8] Grossmann-Severin 1982.

[9] Severin 1977,2.

[10] Researches to the present paper in the Coptic Museum in Cairo (in the following CM) were carried out during winter and spring 1978 and during the winter 1981–1982. Dr Mounir Basta, Director of the Museum, was kind enough to allow me to photograph all stone sculptures in the Museum and granted me access to the basement stores of the New Wing. I am grateful to the Director and the staff of the Graeco-Roman Museum, Alexandria, for the permission to see stone sculptures from Oxyrhynchos in the store rooms of the Museum; however, circumstances did not allow me to take photographs and measures of the pieces. I am therefore forced to reproduce Breccia's plates, without more precise data. Finds from Ashmunein cannot be reproduced here, due to the unfitting quality of the reproductions in Wace-Megaw-Skeat 1959.

sculpture seem to be unambiguous. The earliest capitals found at Oxyrhynchos (figs 15/1, 2) [11] and at Ahnas (figs 12–14) [12] were compared by Kitzinger to dated capitals from Jerusalem (between 380–390) [13] and from Constantinople (425–430). [14] The capitals from Oxyrhynchos were dated accordingly around the turn of the 4th and 5th centuries, those from Ahnas to around 450 A.D. [15] The following details should be considered, however, in connection with these datings. The oldest Oxyrhynchos capital (fig. 15/1, top) is typologically as well as to the acanthus type rather analogous to capitals carved around 300, than to the ones quoted by Kitzinger. [16] Striking are, e.g. the parallels between our capital and the capital from Salona discussed by Kautzsch as starting point of development of the Late Antique Corinthian capital. Although the Ahnas capitals (figs 12–14) are doubtlessly later than the Oxyrhynchos capitals, for the volutes are more covered by their supporting leaves and the helices are as good as omitted, furthermore the acanthi are shorter and wider, they spread out like fans and there are only three tips to each lobe. The carving is much harder, the leaves more angular and their background deeply cut (although not as deeply as at Oxyrhynchos!). Nevertheless, the Ahnas capitals display still the stage of development of the Corinthian capital reached already in the first third of the century, as analogies from Salona and Ostia indicate. [17] It is important to notice that the development of the sharply cut spiky acanthus

starts considerably earlier than put by Kitzinger; the remarkable acanthus leaves of the cornices in the Severan Forum at Lepcis Magna cannot be left out of consideration, either. [18]

As to the extent of time distance between the capitals from Oxyrhynchos and Ahnas, the differences between the Ahnas capital with figural decoration on the abacus (fig. 12) ad the capitals without figural decoration (figs 13, 14) are rather instructive. At first sight the latter seem to be representative of a later stage of development; however, in reality they are both typologically and as to the acanthi entirely identical with the former. Only the modelling is somewhat harder – but to an extent, that we are unable to tell whether is the more angular surface treatment a consequence of a less skilled craftmanship or does it indicate a stylistic concept. As it seems, one of the individual features of the Oxyrhynchos sculpture is generally a soft modelling, while in the Ahnas material we hardly find any attempt at a soft surface treatment. The changes in the form and modelling of the Corinthian capital in Egypt during the first half of the 4th century are illustrated in figs 8–11, and 16. [19] We have no reason to suppose that they are considerably later than their analogies abroad in buildings of tetrarchic, [20] of Constantinian and finally of mid-fourth century date. [21] Within this series the Oxyrhynchos capitals represent an early fourth century date, while the Ahnas exemplars seem to have been made around the end of the first third of the century. This can be confirmed also by

---

[11] Breccia 1933, pl. XLIV figs 111, 112.

[12] Fig. 12: CM 7051 (44069), H = 48, d = 78, D = 90, Monneret de Villard 1923,30 fig. 76. Fig. 13: CM 7349 (7032), H = 35, d = 61, D = 78, Naville 1894, pl. XIV (?), Strzygowski 1904, no 7349. Fig. 14: CM 7348 (7025), H = 35, d = 58, D = 78, Naville 1894, pl. XVI, Strzygowski 1904, no 7348. Inventory numbers in brackets higher than 40,000 are the old Egyptian Museum inventory numbers; other numbers in brackets are earlier or provisory Coptic Museum inventory numbers. H: height, d: diameter at base (of a capital), D: diameter at abacus (resp. width at the abacus of a capital), L: length, W: width, R: radius of a semicircular niche head.

[13] Getshemane church, Kautzsch 1936, 102, no 295, pl. 19.

[14] Golden Gate, Kautzsch 1936, 45, no 155, pl. 11.

[15] Kitzinger 1937, 191.

[16] Cf. Kautzsch 1936, 5 ff., nos 1 ff., pl. 1; further the tetrarchic exemplars quoted by H. Kähler, "La villa di Massenzio a Piazza Armerina", Acta IRN 4 (1969), 41–49, 46 pls XI–XIII; cf. further P. Pensabene, Scavi di Ostia. I capitelli, Roma 1973. Nos 355–368; for the general development see also R. Farioli, "I capitelli paleocristiani e paleobizantini di Salonicco", in: Corsi di cultura sull'arte ravennate e bizantina, Ravenna 1964, 132–177.

[17] For Salona see note 16 above. For Ostia see ibid.

[18] See M. Lyttelton, Baroque Architecture in Classical Antiquity, London 1974, pls 222, 225.

[19] Fig. 8: CM Old Wing garden courtyard, without inv. no. unknown provenance. Cf. Kautzsch 1936, no 10, pl. 2, Salona, mid–fourth cent., no 69, pl. 7; no 98, pl. 7, both Alexandria, 2nd quarter of the 4th cent. Fig. 9: CM 3575, unknown provenance, H = 43, d = 27, D = 52, cf. Kautzsch 1936, 25 f., 28, no 46, pl. 5; nos 61, 69, 1st half of the 4th cent. Fig. 12: CM 7051 (44069), from Ahnas, H = 48, d = 78, D = 90, Monneret de Villard 1923,30 fig. 76. Fig. 16: CM 102 (Old Wing garden courtyard), unknown provenance, H = 41, d = 35, D = 71.

[20] See note 16.

[21] See note 19.

the style of the figural decoration of one of the capitals (fig.12). The local — Egyptian — features of the capitals cannot be overestimated, but the acanthus modelling is doubtlessly more specific. This fact is indicated also by an acanthus base of unknown provenance in Cairo (fig. 7)[22] with leaves of early-fourth-century type the modelling of which foretells the typical modelling starting, as it seems, rather contemporaneously at Ahnas, Bawit[23] and Ashmunein[24] around 330 and going to become, in contrast to other areas of the eastern Mediterranean, the only acanthus type.

Before entering the discussion of the individual groups of sculptures, a few sentences must stand here about a side-aspect of the present investigation. The majority of figural carvings belong at Oxyrhynchos and Ahnas to the decoration of niche-heads. Both niche-heads with semicircular closing and with broken pediment obviously derive from the repertoire of Graeco-Roman architecture. While predecessors of the former type could easily have been found in Egypt (fig.1),[25] Egyptian antecedents of the latter type seemed not

to have existed. Instead, we have supposed, that this particular architectural form was imported some time during the 3rd century from the architecture of another eastern Mediterranean territory.[26] However, the fragments of broken pediments I have recently discovered in the Museum in Alexandria (figs 2–5)[27] may convince us that this hypothesis was wrong. The fragments that originally belonged to miniature niche pediments, dated from the late 1st century B.C. or the early 1st century A.D.[28] indicate that the 4th-century niches with broken pediment derive from an architectural form which must have had some importance in Alexandrian late Hellenistic miniature façade and interior architecture.[29] Although the continuity of this motif between the 1st century B.C. and the 4th century A.D. cannot be proven for the time being, it seems rather probable, that it survived, together with other motifs of late Hellenistic architecture. This is indicated also by the main type of the Oxyrhynchos stelae in niche form with representation of the deceased dating from the period between the 2nd (?) and the late 4th

---

[22] CM forecourt, without inv. no, H = 129, D = 84. For the Hellenistic origins of the acanthus base cf. E. Makowiecka: "Acanthus-Base, Alexandrian Form of Architectural Decoration", Etudes et Travaux 3 (1969), 116–131. A precisely dated acanthus base still *in situ* in Luxor on one of the bases of the tetrapylon erected in 308/9 shows a more classically modelled acanthus. Cf. (for the date) M.–P. Lacau, ASAE 34 (1934), 17 ff., (for the base) J. G. Deckers, "Die Wandmalerei im Kaiserkultraum von Luxor", IdI 94 (1979), 603 ff., fig. 2b. The acanthus bases discovered in the teatre at the Kom el Dikka in Alexandria have Golden Gate-type acanthi, however, without the fleshy modelling of the latter. They seem to date either from the reign of Constantius II (337–361), or from the period after 361; for the ambiguity of their date see K. Michałowski, Alexandria, Leipzig 1971, 16, figs 58–77, esp. fig. 66.

[23] Severin 1977, 2, 121, pl. 38/b. According to H. Torp, "Le monastère copte de Baouît. Quelques notes d'introduction", in: Miscellanea Coptica. Acta IRN 9(1981), 1–8, 2, note 1, the discovery of Severin is "not convincing", but he does not bring any arguments against Severin's well-documented observations. Torp's reconstruction of the architecture of the south church which he proposed already in his "The Carved Decoration of the North and South Churches at Bawit", in: Kolloquium über spätantike und frühmittelalterliche Skulptur 2, 1970, Mainz 1971, 35–41, plans 1, 2, is based on the acceptance of what was maintained by the original excavators, i.e. that the building is result of one single building action. To the problem of the secondary use of architectural ornaments in Egyptian late antique architecture cf. F.–W. Deichmann, "Die Spolien in der spätantiken Architektur", Bayr. Akad. Wiss. Phil. –hist. Klasse Sitzungsber, Jahrgang 1975, Heft 6, München 1975, 53–63.

[24] Wace–Megaw–Skeat 1959, pl. 26/3.

[25] Alexandria Museum 18873, cf. H. Lauter, "Ptolemais in Libyen. Ein Beitrag zur Baukunst Alexandrias", JdI 86 (1971), 149–178, fig. 10. Already Monneret de Villard 1923, 59 ff. quoted late Hellenistic niches in the Wescher catacomb resp. the cemetery of Kom esh Shuqafa as predecessors of semicircular niche–heads from Ahnas. Plastic decoration in the niche–heads poses a more difficult problem. Connections between late antique niches in Egypt and the stucco niches with relief decoration in the 2nd–3rd centuries. Mausoleo dei Valerii in the Vatican necropolis deserve perhaps attention and investigation. The latter are, unfortunately, only in a preliminary form published, see B. M. Apollonj Ghetti et al., Esplorazioni sotto la confessione di San Pietro in Vaticano. (1940–44), Città del Vaticano 1951, pp. 31 f., 50 f., 61 f., 83 f.; J. Ruysschaert, "Necropoli Vaticane", EAA VI, 865 ff.; S. de Marinis, "Stucco", EAA VII, 527 f., figs 630–632, a further niche published in R. Bianchi–Bandinelli, Rome, The Centre of Power, New York 1970, fig. 333.

[26] Török 1970.

[27] Alexandria 3790, H = 26, L = 26, W = ca. 25, L was originally ca. 100 cm. Fig. 5: Alexandria 3785, H = 13,8, L = 34, W = 17. Both unpublished.

[28] For their dating see Lauter, "Ptolemais in Libyen...", (note 25), further cf. H. von Hesberg, "Konsolengeisa des Hellenismus und der frühen Kaiserzeit", RM 24. Ergänzungsheft, Mainz 1980, 68–76. pp.

[29] For Alexandrian miniature architecture see Lyttelton, Baroque Architecture..., (note 18), pp. 40 ff.

centuries.[30] I illustrate here an extraordinarily interesting mid-fourth-century example formerly in the Coptic Museum, now unfortunately lost (fig. 6).[31] It displays several architectural details of Late Hellenistic origin; furthermore, it gives an idea of the architectural context and significance of the 4th-century niche pediments which we know from Oxyrhynchos or Ahnas only uprooted from their original function.[32]

Turning now to figural sculpture, stylistic polyphony in the first third of the 4th century can be well exemplified by two carvings. The first is a frieze fragment with a female figure (fig. 17);[33] the second a fragment of a semicircular niche-head decorated originally with a representation[34] of the birth of Venus (figs 18–20).[35] As to the latter, it reveals rather unambiguously its stylistic backgrounds. Both the face with the curiously rendered beard resembling the porphyry bust from Athribis[36] and the heavy swags of foliage (fig. 20) modelled like the foliage on the fragment from the sarcophagus of Constantine the Great[37] refer to the circle of porphyry sculptures executed in Egypt around 320–340. The identification of the stylistic origin of the former carving is somewhat more problematic. It is rendered possible by the other carvings belonging to the circle of the female

figure: by a relief in Alexandria,[38] a fragment from Antinoe (?) in Paris[39] and a niche-head from Ahnas in Cairo[40] on the one hand, and by a series of mythological reliefs of unknown provenance in Cairo on the other (figs 21–27).[41] The most characteristic feature of the latter — obviously very coherent — group is a specific drapery treatment. The long straight rib-like folds set wide apart from each other and running parallelly or arranged in geometric patterns (see esp. on the bust of the sitting figures on fig. 27), further the treatment of the body behind drapery occurs also on the monumental porphyry statue of an enthroned emperor in Alexandria[42] executed in the first third of the 4th century. The connection between the mythological reliefs and the porphyry statue is certainly not direct, the feature they have in common is, however, specific enough to make a rather close stylistic and chronological connection probable. This is corroborated also by the style of the figures, especially of the faces, which is different from the rigid, geometric style of the porphyry bust from Athribis but which recalls the softer, classicizing trend also existing both in eastern and western sculpture around and after 330.[43] It is a task for further research to investigate the stylistic dichotomy within the porphyry sculpture after 300

[30] For the dating of the Oxyrhynchos niches see recently K. Parlasca, "Der Übergang von der spätrömischen zur frühchristlichen Kunst im Lichte der Grabreliefs von Oxyrhynchos", Enchoria 8 (1978), Sonderband 115–120; cf. also Török 1977, 135 ff.

[31] CM Old Wing garden courtyard, without inv. no (in the stela room). I have photographed the niche in spring 1967; in 1978 the carving could not be found.

[32] To the significance of the niche–heads in pagan sepulchral edifices see Torp 1969, where the erroneous interpretation thereof as parts of Christian churches based on Naville's confusing excavation reports and advocated by Strzygowski and others (e.g. Gayet, Grüneisen, Drioton etc.) is refuted. It is to be noticed that already Kitzinger 1937, 192 f. doubted any Christian context of the mythological representations from Oxyrhynchos and Ahnas.

[33] CM 7276 (7020), H = 19,3, L = 14, probably from Ahnas, Strzygowski 1904, 20, no 7276.

[34] Cf. CM 7047, here fig. 51.

[35] CM 7050, 59 × 46 cm, Török 1970, 174 ff., fig. 1.

[36] Cairo Egyptian Museum, Strzygowski 1904, 6f., no 7257; R. Delbrueck, Antike Porphyrwerke, Berlin 1932, pp. 92 ff.; excellent new photographs by Dieter Johannes, in: G. Grimm and D. Johannes, Kunst der Ptolemäer-und Römerzeit im Ägyptischen Museum Kairo, Mainz 1975, no 29, pls 58–61.

[37] Istanbul Archaeological Museum, see A. K. Vasiliev, "Imperial Porphyry Sarcophagi at Constantinople", DOP 4 (1948), 1 ff., Beckwith 1963, pl. 1.

[38] Duthuit 1931, pl. XXXII/b; cf. Monneret de Villard 1923, fig. 27 and Beckwith 1963, pl. 66.

[39] Louvre AC 107, E. Coche de la Ferté, L' antiquité Chrétienne au Musée du Louvre, Paris 1958, p.88, no 6, fig. p. 15; Effenberger 1975, fig. 13.

[40] CM 7052 (44068), R = 78, Duthuit 1931, pls XXVII/b, XXVIII/a; Beckwith 1963, pl. 62; Effenberger 1975, fig. 18.

[41] Fig. 21: CM 6471, L = 70, H = 36, block with pilaster capital. Fig. 22: CM 7281 (7039), L = 66, H = 27, right–side Victory H = 33; Strzygowski 1904, 24 f., no 7281. Fig. 23: CM 7848, L = 65, H = 35. Figs 24–26: CM 7816, L = 95, H = 35, belongs to same frieze as CM 7848. Török 1977, fig. 14. Fig. 27: CM 7819, L = 81, H = 33, belongs perhaps to 7816 and 7848. A detail was published by H. Zaloscer, Die Kunst im christlichen Ägypten, Wien–München 1974, pl. 34. The whole piece: Török 1977, figs 15/a, b.

[42] Alexandria 5934, Delbrueck, Antike Porphyrwerke, (note 36), 96 ff., pls 40 f.

[43] Cf. Kitzinger 1977, pp. 22 ff. and the ample literature cited there.

1. Stucco niche head, unknown provenance. Alexandria Museum 18873

2. Fragment of miniature pediment, unknown provenance. Alexandria Museum 3790

3. Fragment of miniature pediment, unknown provenance. Alexandria Museum 3790

4. Fragment of miniature pediment, unknown provenance. Alexandria Museum 3790

5. Fragment of miniature pediment, unknown provenance. Alexandria Museum 3785

6. Niche, unknown provenance. Formerly Coptic Museum, without inv.no

7. Acanthus base, unknown provenance. Coptic Museum, forecourt, without inv. no

8. Capital, unknown provenance. Coptic Museum, New Wing, inner court, without inv. no.

9. Capital, unknown provenance. Coptic Museum 2044

10. Capital, unknown provenance. Coptic Museum. Old Wing, garden court, without inv. no.

11. Capital, unknown provenance. Coptic Museum, New Wing, courtyard, without inv. no

and its impact on provincial plastic production in Egypt.

Also CM 7050 (figs 18–20) has its close stylistic analogies. Among these two carvings of unknown provenance (figs 29, 30)[44] representing Daphne resp. a nereid riding on a sea monster seem to be works of the same master. The fragment with Daphne is supposed by Monneret de Villard to have come from Ahnas,[45] which can be confirmed by stylistically related pieces from Ahnas[46] as a frieze with foliage and a bust (Dionysos?) (fig. 31)[47] belonging originally[48] together with a semi-circular niche-head (fig. 32)[49] to the decoration of a richly ornamented room[50] consisting also of a small apsidal part or a semicircular niche of bigger size.

But the connection between CM 7050 and above--quoted reliefs is indicated not only by the figural style but also by the acanthus foliage appearing on them (cf. figs 29, 31). The direct antecedents of the small, flat, rounded lobes arranged along a plastic midrib resp. of the scrolls formed with this kind of acanthus foliage can be found perhaps in Oxyrhynchos (cf. figs 15/3–6)[51] where also the development of the leaf form into the direction of the less and less naturalistic rendering can be

[44] Fig. 29; CM 7061 (7290), 50 × 50 cm, Strzygowski 1904, pp. 34 f., no 7290. Fig. 30: CM 7017 (7289/a), L = 101, H = 52, Strzygowski 1904, 33 f., no 7289/a; Monneret de Villard 1923, fig. 24.

[45] Monneret de Villard 1923, p. 32.

[46] To CM 7061–7017 belong also a frieze fragment formerly in the CM, provisory inv. no 9,11,20,6, Monneret de Villard 1923, fig. 50A (present whereabouts unknown) further two fragments of a peopled scroll allegedly from the Fayum (but probably from Ahnas) in the British Museum, BM 1794, Monneret de Villard 1923, figs 88 f.; cf. furthermore the stylistically related pilaster capital CM 7054 (26,6,20,3), Monneret de Villard 1923, fig. 32.

[47] CM 7060 (45943), L = 45, H = 19, Monneret de Villard 1923, fig. 45.

[48] In the company of a foliage frieze with representation of a wild boar, CM 7060 (11,2,17,3), exhibited formerly together with CM 7060 (see Monneret de Villard 1923, fig. 45).

[49] CM 7008 (44067) (11, 2, 17, 2), R = 50, Monneret de Villard 1923, fig. 50B.

[50] Cf. the architectural ornaments mentioned in notes 46–48.

[51] Figs 15/3, 4: Breccia 1933, Pl. XXXVII. Figs. 15/5, 6: ibid. Pl. XL. Cf. furthermore CM 7334, Strzygowski 1904, p. 65, no 7334, the acanthus scroll frieze in secondary position in the door frieze of the Deir el Ahmar, Sohag, Badawy 1978, fig. 3.123, cf. Deichmann, "Die Spolien...", (note 23), 54 ff.; the acanthus frieze of unknown provenance in the Fogg Art Museum, Badawy 1978, fig. 3.125.

15. Architectural fragments from Oxyrhynchos: 1, 2. Pilaster capitals. 3, 4. Fragments of acanthus scroll friezes. 5, 6, 7. Fragments of peopled acanthus scroll friezes. 8, 9. Fragments of arched friezes. 10. Fragment of frieze. Alexandria Museum, inv. nos (?)

← ⎯⎯⎯

12. Pilaster capital from Ahnas. Coptic Museum 7051 (44069)

13. Pilaster capital from Ahnas. Coptic Museum 7032 (7349)

14. Pilaster capital from Ahnas. Coptic Museum 7348 (7025)

16. Capital, unknown provenance. Coptic Museum 102

17. Fragment of figural frieze, unknown provenance. Coptic
Museum 7276 (7020)

18. Fragment of niche-head from Ahnas (?). Coptic Museum 7050

19. Fragment of niche-head from Ahnas (?), detail. Coptic Museum 7050

20. Fragment of niche-head from Ahnas (?), detail. Coptic Museum 7050

21. Pilaster capital, unknown provenance. Coptic Museum 6471

22. Fragment of figural frieze, unknown provenance. Coptic Museum 7281 (7039)
23. Fragment of figural frieze, unknown provenance. Coptic Museum 7848
24. Fragment of figural frieze, unknown provenance. Coptic Museum 7816

25. Fragment of figural frieze, unknown provenance, detail. Coptic Museum 7816

26. Fragment of figural frieze, unknown provenance, detail. Coptic Museum 7816

27. Figural frieze, unknown provenance. Coptic Museum 7819

28. Fragment of figural frieze from Ahnas. Coptic Museum
7291 (7018)

29. Fragment of niche-head from Ahnas (?). Coptic Museum 7061

30. Niche-head from Ahnas, detail. Coptic Museum 7017 (7289/a)

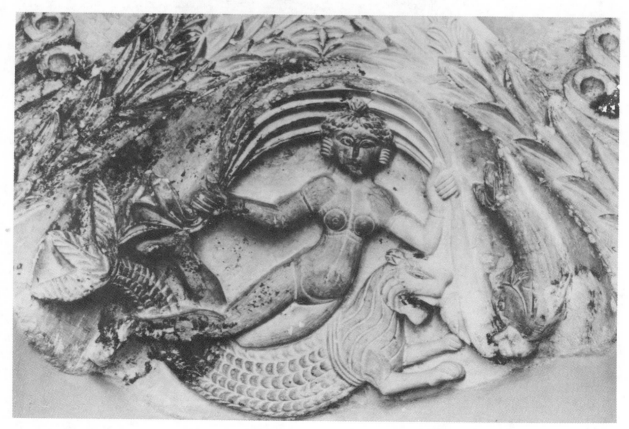

31. Fragment of frieze, unknown provenance. Coptic Museum 7060 (45943)

32. Fragment of niche-head from Ahnas (?). Coptic Museum 7008 (44067)

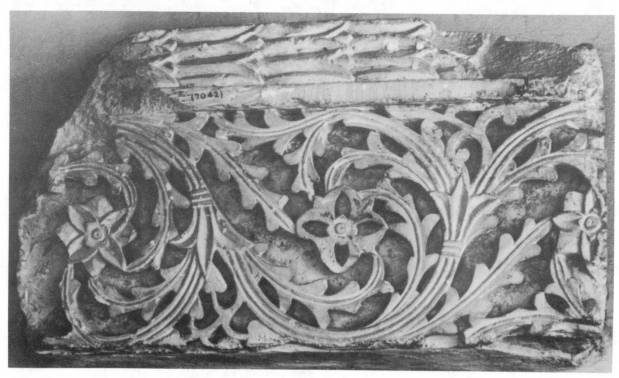

33. Fragment of frieze from Ahnas. Coptic Museum 7042 (7308)

34. Fragment of arched frieze from Ahnas. Coptic Museum 7309 (7009)

35. Fragment of frieze, unknown provenance. Coptic Museum 8078

36. Fragment of frieze from Ahnas. Coptic Museum 7046

37. Fragment of frieze from Ahnas. Coptic Museum
7301

38. Fragment of frieze, unknown provenance. Coptic
Museum 7006 (49658)

followed. The same foliage appears also on the blocks of a frieze from Ahnas (figs 33–35) [52] that was already mentioned in the introduction as having key importance for this investigation.

In the following I shall illustrate resp. quote the fragments preserved from this frieze which, judging on the basis of the size and number of the fragments, must have belonged to the architecture of a building of bigger size. They display four different acanthus foliage types, unfortunately it is unclear, in which way was the seemingly continuous frieze put together from blocks with different patterns. The first type has a plastic

midrib, the lobes are flat and round, as indicated above. Besides the pieces with foliage in Cairo there are further blocks with peopled scroll preserved in Berlin, [53] to these latter belongs also a block with two genii holding in a crown the bust of a Tyche. Furthermore, relief blocks of smaller size with identical decoration are also preserved (fig. 35). [54] The second type differs from the first one only in the rendering of the midrib, the plastic midrib being substituted by a deep incised line (figs 36–38). [55] Also this kind exists on pieces with peopled scroll as, e.g. the fragment illustrated in fig. 38. [56] To the remaining types I return later.

[52] Fig. 33: CM 7308 (7042), H = 38, L = 70, Strzygowski 1904, pp.49 f., no 7308. Fig. 34: CM 7309 (7009), H = 38, L = 73, Strzygowski 1904, pp. 50 f., no 7309. Fig. 35: CM 8078, H = 32, L = 47, unknown provenance, unpublished.

[53] Berlin-East 4453, H = 33, L = 281, Wulff 1909, no 208, Effenberger 1975, fig. 67 (measure without the egg–and–dart).

[54] See further CM 7302, L = 90, H = 36, Strzygowski 1904, p. 46, no 7302, present whereabouts unknown; CM 7317, H = 13,7, L = 76/65, curved frieze from Ahnas, Naville 1894, pl. XVI; Strzygowski 1904, p. 55, no 7317, present whereabouts unknown.

[55] Fig. 36: CM 7046, L = 68,5, H = 38, Strzygowski 1904, pp. 46 f., no 7373; fragment of same frieze: CM 7020, present H = 35, L = 35, Naville1894, pl. XIV, Strzygowski 1904, p. 48, no 7305. Fig. 37: CM 7301, L = 128, H = 36, Naville 1894, pl. XVI, Strzygowski 1904, p. 45, no 7301.

[56] CM 7006 (49658), L = 42, H = 38, unpublished. Monneret de Villard 1923, fig. 49 published a piece which seems to have belonged to the same frieze from the collection of the CM, under the temporary inv. no 11, 9, 21, 22 from Ahnas. It shows identical foliage scroll, with the figure of Heracles and on the corner of the frieze (for it was an outer corner piece) the figure of Dionysos. I could not trace the fragment in the Museum.

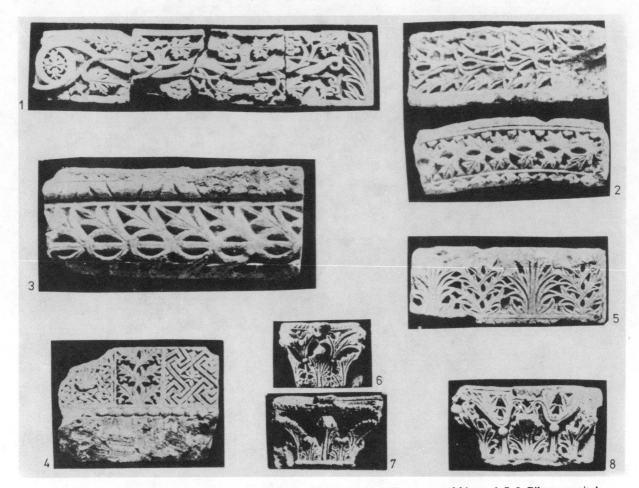

39. Architectural fragments from Oxyrhynchos. 1. Frieze block. 2, 3, 4, 5. Fragments of friezes. 6, 7, 8. Pilaster capitals

We still did not exhaust the sculpture group connected to CM 7050. A frieze block from Ahnas (fig. 40)[57] with the figure of a personification in a foliage wreath displays both the above as first type described acanthus and a new sort with finely modelled lobes. This particular acanthus modelling appears also on a peopled scroll of unknown provenance (fig. 42)[58] and on a frieze block with the representation of Dionysos and a female figure (figs 43, 44).[59] Stylistic closeness of those figures to CM 7050 (figs 18–20) as well as to the personification on CM 7014 (fig. 40) is obvious. The strange treatment of the folds of draperies — which we shall meet also on other reliefs in the following — is known from the porphyry statue of an enthroned emperor quoted above and carved around 330. It

is also striking, that while the figure of the personification CM 7014 has a hard, rigid modelling the figures on the relief block CM 3558 (figs 43, 44) are treated in the style labelled by Kitzinger as soft. In that style is also another frieze block in Cairo carved (fig. 41),[60] the importance of which lies in the fact that it belongs to the same frieze as the hard modelled CM 7014 (fig. 40),[61] as indicated by identical size and the continuous astragal beneath the figures (on fig. 41 not visible).In the knowledge of this fact appear, after all, soft and hard style as two extreme possibilities of one and the same style, of which also the comparison of the hard and soft sculptures closely belonging to the hard-style and to the soft-style relief blocks CM 7014 and CM 7022 (figs 40, 41) may persuade us.

[57] CM 7014, H = 34, L = 32,5, Kitzinger 1937, pl. LXXIV/7.

[58] CM 49659, L = 67, H = 30, unpublished. Another fragment of same frieze: CM 3584, L = 60, H = 30, unpublished.

[59] CM 3558, L = 67, H = 35, L of figural part 40, Kitzinger 1937, pl. L XXIII/7: Ahnas. This acanthus type occurs also in Bawit, on one of the friezes discovered in the south church, see E. Chassinat, "Fouilles à Baouît", MIFAO 13 (1911), pls 22 ff., 29, 32/2, 49, 81/2; cf. Torp, "Le monastère copte...", (note 23), pl. 31/3. Torp interprets this frieze as a high quality variant of the more common spiral acanthus scroll frieze at Bawit and dates both high and low level exemplars to the 6th century.

[60] CM 7022 (26, 16, 20, 4), L = 41, H = 34.

[61] Both seem to have been protruding parts of entablatures over pilasters or over door jambs.

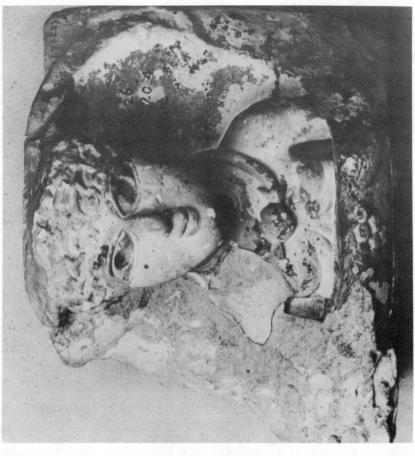

41. Fragment of frieze decorated with bust of personification from Ahnas (?). Coptic Museum 7022 26, 16, 20, 4

40. Fragment of frieze decorated with head of personification from Ahnas (?). Coptic Museum 7014

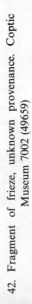

44. Fragment of frieze decorated with figures and acanthus foliage from Ahnas (?), detail. Coptic Museum 3558

42. Fragment of frieze, unknown provenance. Coptic Museum 7002 (49659)

43. Fragment of frieze decorated with figures and acanthus foliage from Ahnas (?). Coptic Museum 3558

45. Keystone decorated with the figure of Orpheus from
Ahnas (?). Coptic Museum 7031

Among the pieces related to the hard-style personification I mention first of all the well-known Nile personification (figs 46, 47)[62] which perhaps belonged to the same building as the two personifications: this carving displays also close stylistic links with the figure on CM 7050 (figs 18–20). Here belongs also a niche-head with bacchic scene (fig. 48),[63] further a niche fragment with representation of Aphrodite (fig. 49).[64] Among the reliefs related to the soft-style personification: a Leda with the swan (fig. 50),[65] a birth of Venus iconographically closely connected to CM 7050 (fig. 51)[66] and a tondo with sea thiasos scene (figs 52–53)[67] deserve mention. The tondo casts a particularly interesting light on the kind of architecture employed in sepulchral buildings in the first half of the 4th century. Finally I illustrate also the well-known Orpheus figure from Ahnas (fig. 45)[68] as belonging to the soft group further as an indication for the probability of the Ahnas provenance of the majority of the above quoted pieces.

Returning to the foliage frieze from Ahnas, its third acanthus type shows small pointed leaflets; they are plastically rendered, in contrast to previous types. Analogies of this type we find in the material from Oxyrhynchos (figs 15/3–6, 54, 55). It is worth mentioning here that the scrolls with this acanthus type appear in Oxyrhynchos in the company of

[62] CM 7021, L = 49, H = 42, decorated on three sides, Duthuit 1931, 34, pls VIII/a, b.–Stylistically closely related is also the niche-head with the figures of Abundance and the Nile in the Brooklyn Museum, inv. no 41.891, H = 38,5, L = 65,5, Beckwith 1963, pls 72 f.

[63] CM 7049, R = 35, Monneret de Villard 1923, fig. 31.

[64] CM 3586, 31 × 32, analogous relief in the British Museum: BM 36143, Badawy 1978, fig. 3.66.

[65] CM 7279 (7026), L = 77,5, H = 34, Monneret de Villlard 1923, fig. 33, a hard-style analogy from Ahnas in Alexandria: Alexandria 14140, Monneret de Villard 1923, p. 30, fig. 35.

[66] CM 7047, 59 × 31 cm, Monneret de Villard 1923, fig. 16.

[67] CM 7015 (12, 1, 30, 26), R = 39, unpublished.

[68] CM 7031, H = 23, L = 18, H of the figure 30, Monneret de Villard 1923, fig. 43.

46. Fragment of projecting entablature (?) decorated with the bust of a personification from Ahnas (?). Coptic Museum 7021 (46726)

47. Fragment of projecting entablature (?) from Ahnas (?), frontal view. Coptic Museum 7021 (46726)

48. Fragment of niche-head with bacchic scene
from Ahnas (?). Coptic Museum 7049

49. Fragment of niche-head, unknown provenance. Coptic Museum 3546

50. Pilaster capital with figural decoration from Ahnas. Coptic Museum 7279 (7026)

51. Fragment of niche-head with figural decoration, unknown provenance (probably from Ahnas). Coptic Museum 7047

52. Fragment of tondo with sea thiasos scene, unknown provenance. Coptic Museum 7015 12, 1, 30, 26

53. Fragment of tondo with sea thiasos scene, unknown provenance, side view. Coptic Museum 7015 12, 1,30,26

54. Fragments of frieze from Ahnas. Coptic Museum 7306 (7013)

55. Fragment of frieze decorated with peopled scroll
from Ahnas. Coptic Museum 8305

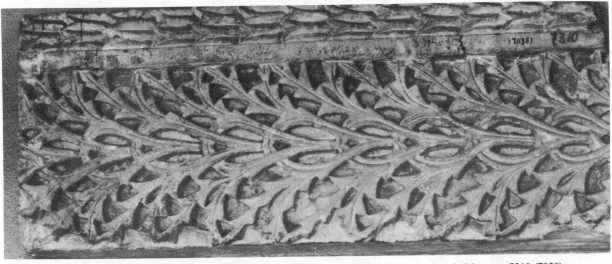

56. Fragment of frieze decorated with interlaced acanthus foliage from Ahnas. Coptic Museum 7310 (7038)

meander decoration (figs 15/7, 8, 10)[69] reminding us that the origins of the Greek key patterns in Bawit in the second half (?) of the century might have been in an older Egyptian tradition surviving from Alexandrian miniature architecture.[70] Further, small but significant details as rosettes in scrolls at Oxyrhynchos and Ahnas indicate that the naturalistic wine foliages frequently appearing on friezes from former site are contemporary with the great acanthus frieze from Ahnas – contemporary evidently in the broader sense of the word (cf. fig. 39/1).[71] The relatively early date of some of these wine scrolls is also indicated by the acanthus dating from around the first third of the 4th century on the frieze illustrated here.

As last type variant in the Ahnas frieze a scroll form must be reviewed here: this is the interlaced acanthus foliage scroll (fig.56).[72] Related interlaced friezes exist also in the material from Oxyrhynhos (figs 39/2, 3, 4, 5).[73] It seems, however, that interlaced scrolls played a less important role in the architectural decoration of Oxyrhynchos. Meander and interlaced acanthus foliage appear together at that site, widening the circle of arguments we have for the mid-fourth century dating of several ornamental carvings discovered in association with the south church at Bawit.[74] Niche heads with closely related Greek key patterns carved in analogous style excavated in Ashmunein[75] demonstrate that the forms and stylistic trends observed in the Ahnas and Oxyrhynchos material are in fact distributed all over the country. As to the simple kind of interlaced acanthus frieze, it appears in the form as we know it from the original decoration of the building which was later to become the south church at Bawit[76] also in Sakkara.[77]

The interlaced scroll from Ahnas has figural relatives, too. Figs 57–60[78] clearly demonstrate that there are no reasons to believe that these carvings would be divided from the carvings quoted as belonging to the other foliage types by a considerable time distance; although they were interpreted in general in this way by Kitzinger.[79] I do not reproduce here CM 7285,[80] for this niche head with the figures of two genii holding the cross in crown belongs to the most frequently reproduced objects from post-Pharaonic Egypt. I remark, however, that on these carvings we find both the spiky, angular interlaced acanthus scroll and the acanthus with plastic midrib and round, flat lobes (cf. figs 29, 31, 33–35).

It is worth mentioning that CM 7055 and 7292/b (figs 58,59) seem to have belonged to the same building. It is perhaps not too bold even to ascribe them to the same master. The sharp geometric

---

[69] Fig. 15/7: Breccia 1933, pl. XXXIX, fig. 102. Fig. 15/8: ibid., pl. XXVIII. Fig. 15/10: ibid., pl. XXXVIII. Fig. 54: CM 7306 (7013), L = 112, H = 36, Strzygowski 1904, 46, no 7306. Strzygowski's fig. 57 shows the left–hand (smaller) fragment of my fig. 54 together with a larger belonging fragment. Monneret de Villard 1923, fig. 84 shows already present situation where the left–hand fragment is associated with a not immediately belonging fragment, which was originally Strzygowski's no 7307, L = 61, H = 36. The other, fitting, fragment disappeared obviously before the transfer of the Ahnas finds to the Coptic Museum. Fig. 55: CM 3767, L = 40, H = 37, its Ahnas origin is rendered probable by CM 7019 (47113), Monneret de Villard 1923, p. 32, fig. 86, a peopled scroll from Ahnas and probably carved by the same master. To CM 3757 seem to belong pieces in the Brooklyn Museum, see Beckwith 1963, pl. 76 and fragments in the Walters Art Gallery, inv. no 26.1, Badawy 1978, fig. 3.127. Further related carving: CM 7003 (20, 1, 34, 3), L = 70, H = 47, Kitzinger 1937, Pl. LXXI/4: Ahnas.

[70] Niches with coffered ceiling make this connection probable, too; cf. Lyttelton, *Baroque Architecture*..., (note 18), 40 ff., Wace – Megaw – Skeat 1959, pl. 25/2.

[71] Breccia 1933, Pl. XXXI.

[72] CM 7310 (7038), L = 100, H = 37, Naville 1894, pl. XVI, Strzygowski 1904, p. 51, no 7310.

[73] Fig. 39/2: Breccia 1933, pl. XXVIII. Fig. 39/3: ibid., pl. XXXIX, fig. 102. Fig. 39/4: ibid., pl. XXXIII. Fig. 39/5: ibid., pl. XXXIX/102.

[74] E.g. Berlin-East 6144–6145, Wulff 1909, nos 1644 f., in general see for the problem Severin 1977, 2. Cf. Breccia 1933, pl. XXXVII.

[75] Wace – Megaw – Skeat 1959, pls. 25/2, 26/7.

[76] Chassinat, "Fouilles à Baouît", (note 59), pl. XLII/3; Severin 1977, 2.

[77] Sakkara: J. E. Quibell, *Excavations at Sakkara (1908–9, 1909–10)*, Cairo 1912, pl. XLII/9. For the 4th century buildings at Sakkara see Grossmann-Severin, 1982.

[78] Fig. 57: CM 7004 (7285), H = 54, L = 170, Monneret de Villard 1923, fig. 61, from Ahnas. Fig. 58: CM 7055, H = 45, original L = 120, Naville 1894, pl. XIV, Monneret de Villard 1923, fig. 42. Fig. 59: CM 7292/b (7044), H = 41, L = 110, Strzygowski 1904, p. 37, no 7292b, from Ahnas. Fig. 60: CM 7012 (44072), 34 × 81 cm, Monneret de Villard 1923, fig. 31, from Ahnas.

[79] Kitzinger 1937, 190 f.

[80] Strzygowski 1904, pp. 28 f., no 7285, H = 38,5, L = 106.

57. Fragment of niche-head
from Ahnas, detail. Coptic Museum
7004

58. Fragment of niche-head
from Ahnas. Coptic Museum 7055

59. Niche-head decorated with bacchic scene from Ahnas.
Coptic Museum 7044 (7292/b)

60. Pilaster base (?) with figural decoration from Ahnas (?).
Coptic Museum 7012 (44072)

plaits of the dress of Orpheus and of the mainad still preserve the particular drapery treatment observed on the porphyry statue of enthroned emperor in Alexandria. [81]

As indicated above, the repeatedly quoted acanthus frieze from Ahnas is significant both stylistically and from the point of view of chronology. Evidently enough, the coincidence of different acanthus scroll types and of different stylistic trends does not mean a wholesale contemporaneity and parallelism thereof. The Ahnas coincidence is composed of different motifs and stylistic tendencies practiced through three or four generations of sculptors, but not through the same three or four generations. A form or trend coincides at the zenith of its career with another form or trend employed perhaps for the last time. The folliage with round flat lobes started its career certainly earlier than the pointed, angular, spiky acanthus and similar must have been also the case of the figural styles, however, here the components are more numerous and less comprehensible.

If we want to translate this coincidence into a chronology, we must be aware of two facts. Firstly of the strong late Constantinian accent of most of the figural sculpture discussed so far. Secondly of the however indirect, but still demonstrable connection of the figural sculpture with a capital type and with acanthus forms that do not display any long process of development. As we saw, capitals associated with the majority of Ahnas sculpture with or without acanthus ornament, either by analogous style of foliage or in an indirect way by a chain of corresponding traits; date from the first third of the 4th century. The chronological range of the figural sculptures we have compared with porphyry sculptures made around 330–340 seems, however, to extend to the middle of the century. A second group of capitals from Oxyrhynchos and

Ahnas and from other sites constitutes on the one hand a terminus *ante quem* for all carvings discussed so far; terminus *ad quem* and *post quem* for carvings to be discussed in the following. It is connected typologically to marble capitals found at Ashmunein [82] and at Ahnas [83] which were executed, in spite of the imported material, probably in Egypt and not in Constantinople; the exemplars executed in local stone were discovered at Ahnas, Oxyrhynchos (figs 39/6–8) [84] Bawit, and Sakkara. [85] The type is characterized by leaves with touching tips, degenerate or entirely omitted cauliculi and remarkably inorthodox proportions (first of all in case of the limestone exemplars). Their most characteristic feature is, however, the acanthus: the uppermost tips of each lobe are curved up to the lowest tip of the next lobe in a way that small elliptical eyes appear between the lobes. But these eyes are not identical with the round, drilled eyes of Constantinopolitan capitals from the first decades of the 5th century and also the plastic treatment of the leaves is still without any sign of the fleshy modelling characteristic of these capitals. [86] Accordingly, the Egyptian capitals in question seem to be earlier than the capitals from the propylaeum of the Hagia Sophia (404–415) [87] or from the Golden Gate (425–430). [88] The existence of a "pre-Golden Gate" acanthus type is also supported by capitals from Jerusalem carved in the last quarter of the 4th century. [89]

Both in the Oxyrhynchos and the Ahnas material capitals with above acanthus form are typologically not very far from the capitals dated above to the end of the first third of the century (figs 38/6–8, [90] cf. figs 12–14, 15/1,2). A capital from Ahnas, now unfortunately lost, [91] with pre-Golden Gate acanthi, has a structure entirely identical with that of the earlier series, further an eagle figure over the central leaf of the crown resp. on the place

[81] See note 42.

[82] CM 7351, H = 65, d = 53, D = 86, Strzygowski 1904, 76f., no 7351; Severin 1977,1, fig. 274/a.

[83] CM 7350, H = 45, d = 51, D = 75, Naville 1894, pl. XVII, Strzygowski 1904, 75 f., no 7350; Severin 1977,1, fig. 274/b.

[84] Fig. 39/6: Breccia 1933, pl. XLIV, fig. 111. Fig 39/7: ibid., Pl. XLIV fig. 114. Fig. 39/8: ibid., pl. XLIV, fig. 115.

[85] For Bawit see Severin 1977,2; for Sakkara Severin 1977,1, fig. 275/b.

[86] Cf. Kautzsch 1936, pl. 9, no 132 (from Egypt), 11, nos 115/a, b (Constantinople, Golden Gate).

[87] A.M. Schneider, "Die Grabung im Westhof der Sophienkirche", *Istambuler Forschungen* 12 (1941); R. Krautheimer, *Early Christian and Byzantine Architecture*, Harmondsworth 1979, fig. 54.

[88] Kautzsch 1936, pp. 44 f.

[89] Kautzsch 1936, pp. 106 f. pl. 20, nos 307 f., cf. also pl. 20, no 305.

[90] See note 84.

[91] Naville 1894, pl. XIV, Strzygowski 1904, pp. 72 f., no 7346, corner pilaster capital, H = 38, L_1 = 30/60, L_2 = 28,5/58.

of the abacus flower.[92] Related capitals were dated by Kautzsch to the second third of the century.[93] Another capital from Ahnas (fig. 61)[94] displays a style of carving that seems to be related to the style of the niche heads with interlaced acanthus foliage. This capital seems to go back on a late Hellenistic type;[95] its further development is illustrated here by an early (?) fifth century capital from Sakkara (fig. 62).[96] In sum, the second group of capitals examples of which were found at Oxyrhynchos, Ahnas, Ashmunein further at Bawit and Sakkara seem to date from the second third, and probably from the latter half of this period. In this way we have a chronological dividing line, however approximate, between the sculptures reviewed so far and the carvings to be discussed in the following.

At Oxyrhynchos pre-Golden Gate acanthus is associated with an ornamental style of special character (figs 63, 64).[97] Foliages, interlaced bands and Greek key patterns appear in a flat rendering; the background is deeply carved but the graphic role of the shadow resp. of the dark deep background is entirely different from the plastic effect of the earlier carvings with interlaced acanthus foliage. In the case of these carvings plasticity is sacrificed for the sake of a linear richness; it is in fact these carvings that reveal for the first time that stylistic trend which is usually regarded as the main trend of Early Christian art in Egypt. The same ornamental style occurs also at Ashmunein.[98] The quality of these carvings is usually rather low; on CM 4475 the figure shows a good level of craftmanship, but the peopled scroll is surprisingly clumsy. Further niche-heads from Oxyrhynchos have their close analogies at Ahnas (figs 65, 66/a,

b).[99] Building resp. activity of sculptors both at Oxyrhynchos and Ahnas continues during the last third of the century and as it seems, at these sites there were pagan sepulchral chapels built even after the turn of the 4th and 5th centuries. In the concluding part of this paper I give a list of carvings from this period; the monuments of later periods at these and other sites discussed above cannot be treated here.[100] But before going to the production of the end of the century, I add some further general remarks to the ones summarized in the introduction. First of all I should like to stress that the appearance of Christian symbols and iconography is not conclusive, as to dating of 4th century carvings. The well-known niche-head with genii holding a cross from Ahnas[101] does not represent a chronological and stylistic dividing line, for production of the workshop carving it continues in the same style also afterwards and making architectural ornament of pagan character. The same can be observed at Oxyrhynchos where Breccia has found a relief representing genii holding a cross which dates from the years around the middle of the fourth century;[102] this piece has also a pagan replica of unknown provenance.[103] It seems that the appearance of Christian symbols at Bawit indicates indeed an *ante quem* for carvings of pagan character; however, the documentation of the site is not less misleading than the notion "carving of pagan character" in the case of ornamental pieces. Still, the age of the semicolumns flanking the north and the south entrances of the south church[104] can probably be established by their motif and style identity with the well-known altar slab in Berlin-East[105] and with the niche--head in the Louvre.[106] If the foundation of the

[92] Cf. Kautzsch 1936, nos 78–80, pl. 6, no 76.

[93] Kautzsch 1936, pp. 30, 39.

[94] CM 7347 (7053), L = 32/39, H = 20, W = 21/24, Strzygowski 1904, pp. 73 f., no 7347.

[95] For capitals with double S volute see Lauter, "Ptolemais in Libyen...", (note 25).

[96] CM Old Wing garden courtyard, without inv. no H = 47, d = 35, D = 64, published by Severin 1977,1, fig. 276/a.

[97] Fig. 63: CM 4475, H = 60, L = 160, Kitzinger 1937, 209, pl. LXXV/1. Fig. 64: Breccia 1933, pl. XLVI.

[98] Wace—Megaw—Skeat 1959, pls 25/3, 27/1, 3B.

[99] Fig. 65: CM 7024 (46246), H = 32, L = 98, Monneret de Villard 1923, fig. 7. Figs 66/a, b: Breccia 1933, pl. XLVII, figs 123, 124.

[100] Cf. Severin 1981,2.

[101] CM 7285, see note 80.

[102] Breccia 1933, pl. XXXVII.

[103] CM 7057, H = 28, original L = 110.

[104] Chassinat, "Fouilles à Baouît", (note 76), pl. 24; Severin 1977,2, pl. 38/a.

[105] Berlin—East 4711, H = 61, L = 85, Wulff 1909, no 237.

[106] Louvre X 5101, H = 60, L = 87, Effenberger 1975, fig. 73.

61. Pilaster capital from Ahnas. Coptic Museum 7347 (7053)

62. Capital from the "grave church", Sakkara. Coptic Museum,
Old Wing, garden court, without inv. no

63. Fragment of niche-head from Oxyrhynchos. Coptic Museum 4475

64. Three niche-heads with figural decoration from Oxyrhynchos. Alexandria
Museum, inv. nos (?)

65. Niche-head, unknown provenance. Coptic Museum 7024 (46246)

66. Fragments of niche-heads from Oxyrhynchos. Alexandria Museum, inv. nos (?)

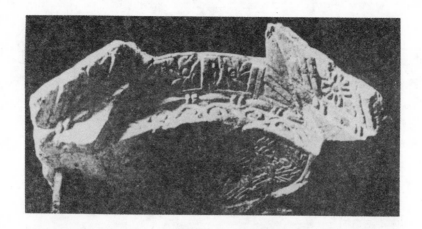

67. a. Niche-head from Oxyrhynchos. b. Fragments of a geison from Oxyrhynchos.
Alexandria Museum, inv. nos (?)

68. Niche-head, unknown provenance. Coptic Museum 4424

69. Niche-head from Ahnas (?). Coptic Museum 3557

Christian monastery really occurred around 390, [107] it would mean that our chronology is not very wide of the mark.

Although the architectural ornaments from Ahnas and the other sites do not originate from excavations, thus their composition is chance, they still render it possible to a certain extent to form a judgement on the character of architecture at these sites. Especially important are from this point of view some niches from Ahnas which are associated with frieze blocks of big size; but equally important are also the fragments revealing rather complicated and rich interior architectural concepts.

Finally I give here a selected list of carvings from the late 4th and early 5th century. A niche-head from Oxyrhynchos (fig. 67/a) [108] belonging originally to a building with homogeneous architectural decoration (fig. 67/b) [109] has a close analogy of unknown provenance in Cairo (fig. 68). [110] A series of semicircular niches (figs 69–73) [111] from different sites — Ahnas, Antinoe (?) among them — — demonstrates the uniformity of architectural ornament in Egypt at this time. Examples from Oxyrhynchos can also be quoted (figs 74/1–3). [112] Three niche-heads (figs 75–77) [113] seem to demonstrate the final phase of the production of the Ahnas workshop. A further niche-head from same period and of same provenance (fig. 78) [114] may illustrate the development of the broken

---

[107] Cf. H. Torp, "Some Aspects of Early Monastic Architecture", *Byzantion* 25/27 (1955/57), 513–538; id., in: *Mélanges d'archéologie et d'histoire* 77 (1965), 170; cf., however, the extreme caution as to the dating in M. Krause and K. Wessel, "Bawit", *Reallexicon zur Byzantinische* Kunst I, Stuttgart 1966, pp. 568–583.

[108] Breccia 1933, pl. XLVII, fig. 122.

[109] Ibid., pl. XXXIII, top.

[110] CM 4424, H = 19, L = 74, unpublished.

[111] Fig. 69: CM 3557, R = 44. Fig. 70: Louvre AC 112 (Antinoe?), H = 61; P. du Bourguet, *Die Kopten*, Baden-Baden 1967, fig. p. 36. Fig. 71: CM 7037, from Ahnas, R = 43, Monneret de Villard 1923, 31, fig. 38. Fig. 72: CM 7058, R = 45. Fig. 73: CM 7059 (44081), from Ahnas, R = 42, Monneret de Villard 1923,31, fig. 23.

[112] Fig. 74/1: Breccia 1933, pl. XXVIII. Fig. 74/2: ibid., pl. XXX. Fig. 74/3: ibid., pl. XXXIX, fig. 102.

[113] Fig. 76: CM 7074 (44070), from Ahnas, H = 27, L = 106, Monneret de Villard 1923, p. 31, figs 8 f. Fig. 76: CM 7068, from Ahnas (?), H = 24, L = 103. Fig 77: CM 7035 (44073), from Ahnas, H = 20,2. L = 94, Monneret de Villard 1923, figs 47 f.

[114] CM 7062 (44071), H = 33, L = 100, Monneret de Villard 1923, p. 31, fig. 4.

70. Fragment of niche-head from Antinoe (?). Louvre AC 112

71. Fragment of niche-head from Ahnas (?). Coptic Museum 7037

72. Fragment of niche-head from Ahnas (?). Coptic Museum 7058

73. Niche-head from Ahnas. Coptic Museum 7059 (44081)

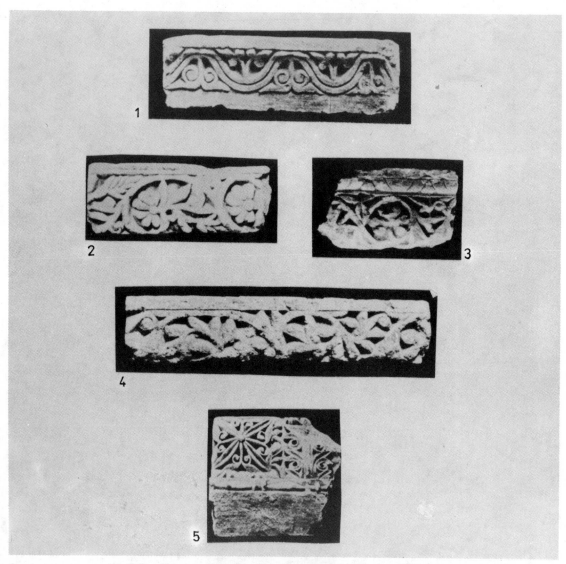

74. Frieze fragments from Oxyrhynchos. Alexandria Museum, inv. nos (?)

75. Niche-head from Ahnas (?), detail. Coptic Museum 7074

76. Niche-head from Ahnas (?). Coptic Museum 7068

77. Niche-head from Ahnas (?), detail. Coptic Museum 7035 (44073)

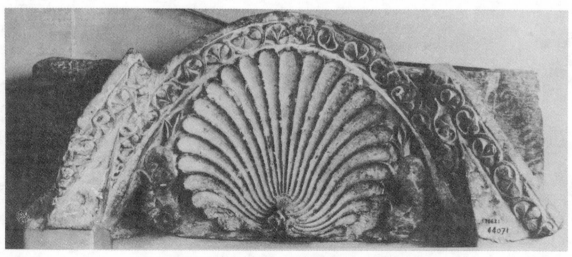

78. Niche-head from Ahnas (?). Coptic Museum 7062 (44071)

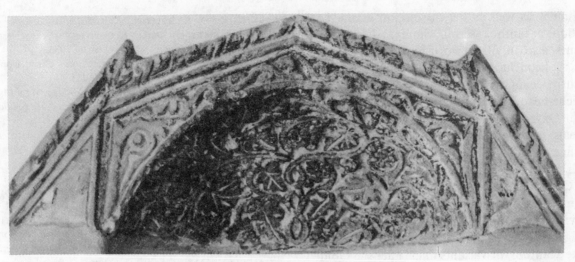

79. Niche-head, unknown provenance. Coptic Museum 3545

80. Niche-head, unknown provenance. Coptic Museum 6503

pediment as well as the dissolution of the Late Antique acanthus scroll. Similar development occurs also in other workshops (figs 74/4, 79, 80). [115] I conclude the list with the mention of two occurrences of the Golden Gate-type acanthus: on a niche-head from Ahnas (fig. 65) and on a cornice from Oxyrhynchos (fig. 74/5). [116] A closer look reveals, however, that neither modelling, nor the outline of the Egyptian exemplars are identical with those of the acanthi from the Hagia Sophia or the Golden Gate. At this point of our investigation we must leave the question open, whether are the Oxyrhynchos and Ahnas acanthi results of indigenous development from the pre-Golden Gate acanthus, or variants made after the Golden Gate type proper.

Abbreviations

Badawy 1978 = A. Badawy, *Coptic Art and Archaeology: The Art of the Christian Egyptians from the Late Antique to the Middle Ages,* Massachusetts 1978.

Beckwith 1963 = J. Beckwith, *Coptic Sculpture 300–1300,* London 1963.

Breccia 1933 = E. Breccia, *Le Musée Gréco-Romain 1931––1932,* Bergamo 1933.

Duthuit 1931 = G. Duthuit, *La sculpture copte,* Paris 1931.

Effenberger 1975: A. Effenberger, *Koptische Kunst. Ägypten in spätantiker, byzantinischer und frühislamischer Zeit,* Leipzig 1975.

Grossmann 1971 = P. Grossmann, "Neue Untersuchungen in der Kirche von Dair Abu Hinnis in Mittelägypten", MDAIK 27 (1971), 157–171.

Grossmann 1978 = id., "Zur christlichen Baukunst in Ägypten", *Enchoria* 8 (1978), Sonderband 89–100.

Grossmann-Severin 1982: P. Grossmann and H.-G. Severin, "Reinigungs-arbeiten im Jeremiaskloster bei Saqqara. Vierter vorläufiger Bericht", MDAIK 38 (1982), 155–193.

Kautzsch 1936 = R. Kautzsch, *Kapitellstudien. Beiträge zu einer Geschichte des spätantiken Kapitells im Osten vom vierten bis ins siebente Jahrhundert,* Berlin–Leipzig 1936.

Kitzinger 1937 = E. Kitzinger, "Notes on Early Coptic Sculpture", *Archaeologia* 87 (1937), 181–215.

Kitzinger 1977 = id., *Byzantine Art in the Making. Main Lines of Stylistic Development in Mediterranean Art 3rd–7th Century,* London 1977.

Monneret de Villard 1923 = U. Monneret de Villard, *La scultura ad Ahnās. Note sull'origine dell'arte copta,* Milano 1923.

Naville 1894 = E. Naville and T. Hayter Lewis, *Ahnas el Medineh (Heracleopolis Magna). Eleventh Memoir of the Egypt Exploration Fund,* London 1894, pp. 32–34, Pls XIV–XVI.

Severin 1977, 1 = H.-G. Severin, "Frühchristliche Skulptur und Malerei in Ägypten", in: B. Brenk (ed.), *Spätantike und frühes Christentum. Propyläen Kunstgeschichte,* Suppl. 1, Berlin 1977, pp. 243–253.

Severin 1977, 2 = id., "Zur Süd-Kirche von Bawīt", MDAIK 33 (1977), 113–124.

Severin 1981, 1 = id., *Gli scavi eseguiti ad Ahnas, Bahnasa, Bawit e Saqqara: storia delle interpretazioni e nuovi risultati. XXVIII Corso di Cultura sull'arte ravennate e bizantina,* Ravenna, 26 aprile/8 maggio 1981, 299–314.

Severin 1981, 2 = id., *Problemi di scultura tardoantica in Egitto,* ibid., pp. 315–336.

Severin 1983 = id., "Egitto 3. Scultura", in: *Dizionario patristico e di antichità cristiana* I, Casale Monferrato 1983, pp. 1120–1125.

Strzygowski 1904 = J. Strzygowski, *Koptische Kunst,* Cat. Gén. Mus. Caire, Wien 1904.

Torp 1969 = H. Torp, "Leda Christiana. The Problem of the Interpretation of Coptic Sculpture with Mythological Motifs", Acta IRN 4 (1969), 101–112.

Török 1970 = L. Török, "On the Chronology of the Ahnās Sculpture", Acta Arch. Hung. 22 (1970), 163–182.

Török 1977 = id., "Notes on Pre-Coptic and Coptic Art.", Acta Arch. Hung. 29 (1977), 125–153.

Wace—Megaw—Skeat 1959 = A. J. Wace, A. H. S. Megaw and T. C. Skeat, *Hermopolis Magna, Ashmunein. The Ptolemaic Sanctuary and the Basilica,* Alexandria 1959.

Wulff 1909 = O. Wulff, *Altchristliche und mittelalterliche byzantinische und italienische Bildwerke* Teil I. Altchristliche Bildwerke, Berlin 1909.

---

[115] Fig. 74/4: Breccia 1933, pl. XXVIII. Fig. 79: CM 3545, H = 28, L = 85. Fig. 80: CM 6503, H = 45, L = 108.

[116] Breccia 1933, pl. XXXVI. Further fragments of the same frieze: ibid., pls XXXIV bottom, XXXV top right, XLV fig. 118 right. It is worth noting that variants of the acanthus scroll of the propylaeum entablature of the Hagia Sophia of Theodosius II seem to occur at Oxyrhynchos, see pls XXIX right column third from top; XLV fig. 118 right, XXXIX, fig. 102 left column second from top. Cf. F.W. Deichmann, *Studien zur Architektur Konstantinopels im 5. und 6. Jh. n. Chr.,* Baden-Baden 1956, figs 9–11, 13, 14.

COPTIC STUDIES

Mieneke van der Helm

Some Iconographical Remarks on St Michael in Sonqi Tino

This mural painting, discovered by Professor S. Donadoni between 1967 and 1969 in Nubia, is now to be found in the museum at Khartoum.[1] The painting shows archangel Michael, who protects a Nubian eparch (or, according to Prof. Michałowski, a royal person) surrounded by the Four Living Beings. Still visible are the lion, up in the left-hand corner, the man, down in the left-hand corner, and the eagle in the right-hand corner.

In addition there are remains of inscriptions:

Near the angels head:
Michael — Samson (pray for us)
You have saved the souls of the just of the Hades
We pray....
Metropolites....
Ecclesias an anthropon....[2]
So far it is all very clear and yet something special to be going on, in my opinion!
A protecting archangel Michael occurs more frequently, but the Four Living Beings with

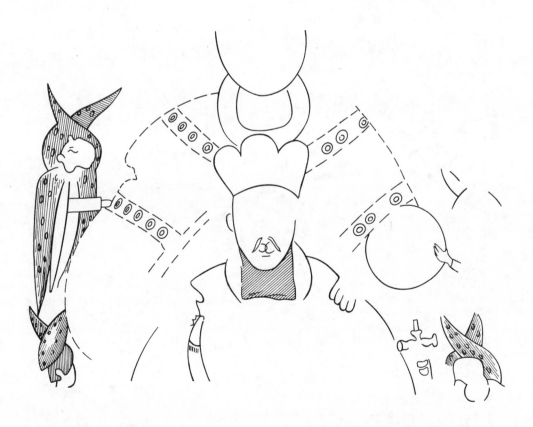

---

[1] S. Donadoni, "Les fouilles à l'église de Sonqi Tino", in: *Kunst und Geschichte Nubiens in Christlichen Zeit*, Recklinghausen 1970.
[2] With thanks to Prof. Donadoni who translated this for me.

Michael are exceptional. Usually these Living Beings only occur with an enthroned Christ. So what are they doing here with Michael?

The solution lies in fact within the mural painting itself and the answer to the question within the fact that beings are not passive, but seem to do something!

When we look at the details, we see how the lion touches Michael's clothing; we see a very small detail of the man, and very slightly in the upper zone on the right, a small hand of the being which must be the bull, holding the sphaira, and the eagle which carries a crozier.

So the Four Living Beings are actually busy with something!

The discovery by Professor J. M. Plumley in Ibrim of a Coptic manuscript does not just lift a corner of the veil but quite a piece of it. The manuscript contains a fragment of a hymn of praise which the archbishop of Constantinople, H. John (Chrysostemos?) is said to have preached with reference to the Four Living Beings.

In this fragment we are told about a very special Michael scene: Michael, shortly after the fall of Lucifer (Archeplasme), is being supplied with his symbols of victory by the Four Living Beings.

COPTIC STUDIES

Paul van Moorsel

The French Project "La peinture murale chez les Coptes"

When in the sixties our Polish hosts, under the leadership of Prof. K. Michałowski, discovered the mural paintings at Faras, the Dutch the paintings at Abdallan Irqi, the Italians the ones at Sonqi Tino, and others made similar discoveries elsewhere in Nobatia, at once the question arose how this pictorial art from Nubia should be defined and localized. Was it to be called Coptic, Byzantine or differently? The first and — sofar — the last to endeavour to answer these questions was Prof. K. Weitzmann with his paper read at the first Symposium about Nubia in Essen in 1969.[1] You know Weitzmann's conclusions. I need not repeat them here. One of the problems Weitzmann had to face in 1969 was that Coptic mural painting had hardly been subjected to serious study. Usually the excavations at Bawit[2] and at Saqqara[3] were referred to as well as the publications about these places which had appeared forty up to sixty years before.[4] El Baghawat,[5] Sohag[6] and other places where mural paintings had been found, were rather ignored, although publications about them were available — think of the publications by Hugh Evelyn White about the Wadi 'N Natrûn,[7] which were certainly of no lower quality than those by Clédat, Maspéro-Drioton or Quibell. Other monasteries, such as those near the Red Sea were ignored completely, because, unfortunately, they had never had the honour of having their paintings published, not even partly. Only some stereotyped pictures were known, like a photo of a greatly restored Theodorus Stratelates from St Anthony[8] or Netchetailov's copy of St Mercurius in the same monastery.[9]

When today, fifteen years after Prof. Weitzmann's lecture in Essen, we know more about Coptic mural painting, we owe this mainly to abbé Jules Leroy and his associates of whom I like to mention Pierre Laferrière. The paintings of both monasteries at Esna were — for the first time — published by Leroy,[10] followed by a publication about the paintings of the monastery of St Macarius and the Syrian monastery in the Wadi 'N Natrûn,[11] as a result of which Evelyn White's study did not

[1] K. Weitzmann, "Some Remarks on the Sources of the Fresco Paintings of the Cathedral of Faras", in: E. Dinkler (ed.), *Kunst und Geschichte Nubiens in christlicher Zeit*, Recklinghausen 1970, pp. 325–340.

[2] J. Clédat, *Le monastère et la nécropole de Baouît*, MIFAO XII, 1, Cairo 1904; MIFAO XII, 2, Cairo 1906; MIFAO XXXIX, 1916; J. Maspéro and É. Drioton, *Fouilles exécutées à Baouît*, MIFAO LIX, Cairo 1931–1943.

[3] J. E. Quibell, *Excavations at Saqqara (1906–1907)*, Cairo 1908; id., *Excavations at Saqqara (1907–1908)*, Cairo 1909, id., *Excavations at Saqqara* (1908–1909, 1909–1910), *The Monastery of Apa Jeremias*, Cairo 1912.

[4] This is why recently our Department has re-published the Saqqara paintings: P. van Moorsel and M. Huijbers, "Repertory of the Preserved Wall-paintings from the Monastery of Apa Jeremiah at Saqqara", *Acta ad Archaeologiam et Artium Historiam Pertinentia* IX (1981), 125–186; M. Rassart-Debergh, "La décoration picturale du monastère de Saqqara. Essai de reconstitution", ibid., 9–124.

[5] A. Fakry, *The Necropolis of el-Bagawat in Kharga Oasis*, Cairo 1951; H. Stern, "Les peintures du Mausolée de l'Exode' à El-Bagaouât", *Cahiers Archéologiques* 11 (1960), 93–119; J. Schwartz, "Nouvelles études sur des fresques d'El-Bagawat", *Cahiers Archéologiques* 13 (1962), 1–11.

[6] U. Monneret de Villard, *Les couvents près de Sohag, Deyr el-Abiad et Deyr el-Ahmar*, 2 vols, Milan 1925–1926.

[7] H. G. Evelyn White, *The Monasteries of the Wadi 'N Natrun*, Part III, New York 1933.

[8] Cf. *Lexikon der christlichen Ikonographie*, vol. VIII, col. 450 ("Wandmalerei des 9. Jh.").

[9] A. Piankoff, "Thomas Whittemore. Une peinture datée au monastère de Saint-Antoine", *Les Cahiers Coptes* **7-8** (1954), 19–24.

[10] J. Leroy, *Les peintures des couvents du désert d'Esna*, MIFAO XCIV, Cairo 1975. Cf. R. Coquin, "Les inscriptions pariétales des monastères d'Esna: Dayr al-Suhada — Dayr al-Fahuri, BIFAO 75 (1975), 241–284.

[11] J. Leroy, "Les peintures des couvents du Ouadi Natroun", MIFAO CI, Cairo 1982.

1. An Enthroned Christ with Apocalyptic Beings in St Paul, A.D. 1333/4

become superfluous but was completed. Between 1974 and 1979 six campaigns to both monasteries near the Red Sea took place, five of which to St Anthony. [12] In 1979 Leroy deceased [13] and in 1981 I was allowed to succeed him. Since then I was enabled to lead two campaigns to St Anthony in order to complete what Leroy had started and in 1984 to lead a campaign to St Paul. Sohag is next on the programme. Although we have certainly not yet finished in St Paul, I can offer some preliminary conclusions of our recent expedition: the mortuary church of the hermit Paul, especially known for its less fine mural paintings made by means of compasses in 1713 A. D., does really contain remains which are older and more apt to please the aesthetic eye. To them belong the remains of the upper zone of what I — together with Leroy [14] — call haïkal D: on the East wall an enthroned Christ, flanked by the four Apocalyptic Beings and by two Angels on the adjacent squinches. On the West side two other angelic beings, Cherubim or Seraphim, of which the one on the South-Western squinch has been well preserved.

The representation on the East wall (Fig. 1) fits completely in the well-known iconography, but betrays a master's hand which differs markedly from the one which worked in e.g., the chapel of the four Apocalyptic Beings in St Anthony. [15]

This painter in St Paul lived in fact later. A date indicates A.M. 1050 (= A.D. 1333/4), whereas I like to date the paintings in the chapel of St Anthony a hundred years earlier. [16]

Unfortunately, only a fragment of the inscription, to which the date belongs, is still readable. The iconography of both Cherubim or Seraphim on the Western squinches of haïkal D is interesting: one can see that they wear six wings studded with eyes. In the right hand the well-preserved specimen holds a sword raised, in the other one something which resembles a cup. [17] And likewise there are other riddles which this, as yet, anonymous master has set to us.

Summarizing the above I like to observe that the abbey of St Paul employed (and remunerated) around 1333/4 a skilled artist, who knew how to give new forms to old themes and who furthermore might have painted more at the spot, together with a contemporary painter, than a visitor or even a monk would now notice at first sight. Even under the products by the painter with the compasses of Anno 1713 older work can be perceived, part of which should possibly be attributed to him. Such double layers may certainly not be called an exception in the mural painting of the Nile Valley. Here in the Faras Gallery of the National Museum there are plenty of examples.

---

[12] Cf. J. Leroy, "Le programme décoratif de l'église de Saint-Antoine du désert de la Mer Rouge, BIFAO 76 (1976), 347–379 and R.-G. Coquin et P.-H. Laferrière, "Les inscriptions pariétales de l'ancienne église du monastère de S. Antoine dans le désert oriental", BIFAO 78 (1978), 267–321. Cf. as well: J. Leroy, "Le programme décoratif de l'église de Saint-Paul du désert de la Mer Rouge", BIFAO 78 (1978), 323–337.

[13] See R.-G. Coquin, "l'Abbé Jules Leroy (1903–1979)", BIFAO 80 (1980), V–XV.

[14] Leroy, "Le programme décoratif de l'église de Saint Paul...", p. 334.

[15] Cf. Leroy, *Les peintures des couvents du désert d'Esna...*, Plates VIII and X.

[16] See R. S. Nelson, "An Icon at M. Sinai and Christian Painting in Muslim Egypt during the Thirteenth and Fourteenth Centuries", *Art Bulletin* 65 (1983), 201–218, esp. 218: "Thus the history of Christian book decoration in Egypt during the thirteenth and fourteenth centuries cannot be seen as a continuous evolutionary development..."

[17] Cf. Leroy, *Les peintures des couvents du désert d'Esna...*, Plates 58–59 and p. 23: "On note encore la présence d'une épée dans la main droite de l'ange et d'un disque [...] dans la gauche. Le séraphin tient de la main gauche un calice [...] et dans la droite un petit drapeau". J. Leroy, ibid., p. 22 gives a date for this wall-painting in Deir al-Fakhoury: A. M. 865 (= A.D. 1148/9).

COPTIC STUDIES

Derek A. Welsby

Excavations at Soba East in Central Sudan, 1983/84

A third season of excavation was conducted by the British Institute in Eastern Africa at Soba East in Central Sudan during the winter of 1983/84.[1] This site, the capital city of the Christian kingdom of Alwa, lies on the east bank of the Blue Nile, 22 km above its confluence with the White Nile at Khartoum. The first season's trial trenching and survey work, directed by Mr C.M. Daniels, has been followed by an area excavation of a small part of the largest mound on the site, mound B, which had been excavated in part by P.L. Shinnie from 1950–52 (Shinnie 1955). Shinnie's excavations revealed a series of large mud brick structures.

The present campaign of excavations concentrating on the western end of the mound, circa 130 metres from Shinnie's excavations, has uncovered a complex of three churches, associated graves and tombs as well as mud brick domestic buildings. An interim report on the second season's work, together with an historical introduction to the site by Sir Laurence Kirwan has appeared in *Azania* (Welsby 1983). In the 1982/83 season two buildings were found, one of which, building A, was extensively excavated. This proved to be a large basilican church, 28 × 24.5 m in size, built throughout of good quality red brick and provided with floors of concrete and later of marble. Unfortunately, the building has been very thoroughly robbed for its bricks.

Lying 4 m to the south of building A another building, B, was partly excavated. Apart from a small area excavated in the south-west angle of building A, the third season's work concentrated on the area to the south, revealing the plan of building B to be another large church 27 × 22.5 m in size. Abutting onto its south wall was a further church, building C, of much smaller size but again built of good quality red brick. A small portion of the mud brick buildings which lay to the south east of building B was also excavated.

Building A

An area in the south-west angle of this building was investigated to ascertain whether there had been an entrance or stairway at this point. No evidence for either of these features was found. At the western end of the building a room had run the full width of the structure. There was no evidence to suggest that there had ever been a tripartite division of this end of the church as was often the case in other Nubian churches.

The building had been constructed throughout of red bricks measuring approximately 44 × 21 cm in size except for in the central section of the west wall of the *narthex* where bricks 28 cm square were used. These square bricks are identical to those employed in the construction of building B and this suggests the possibility that the walling in building A built of these bricks is of a later date than the rest of the walls. The square bricks may have been used to block or reduce the width of a monumental entrance perhaps similar to that provided in building B described below.

[1] The writer would like to thank the many people who have helped to ensure that the excavations progressed with the minimum amount of difficulty, particularly Mrs Judith Filson in London, the staff of the Department of Antiquities in Khartoum and Mr and Mrs Clive Smith of the British Council then in Khartoum. The excellent dig house was, as in previous years, made available through the kindness of the el Kurdi family. The excavation team consisted of L. Brown, S. Butler, D. Crombie, J. Frost, A. Gibson, M. Harlow, C. Tagart, D. Welsby, Babikre Mohammed El Amin, Mohi El Din Abdulla Zaroug and Bedriya Abdulla Hamad.

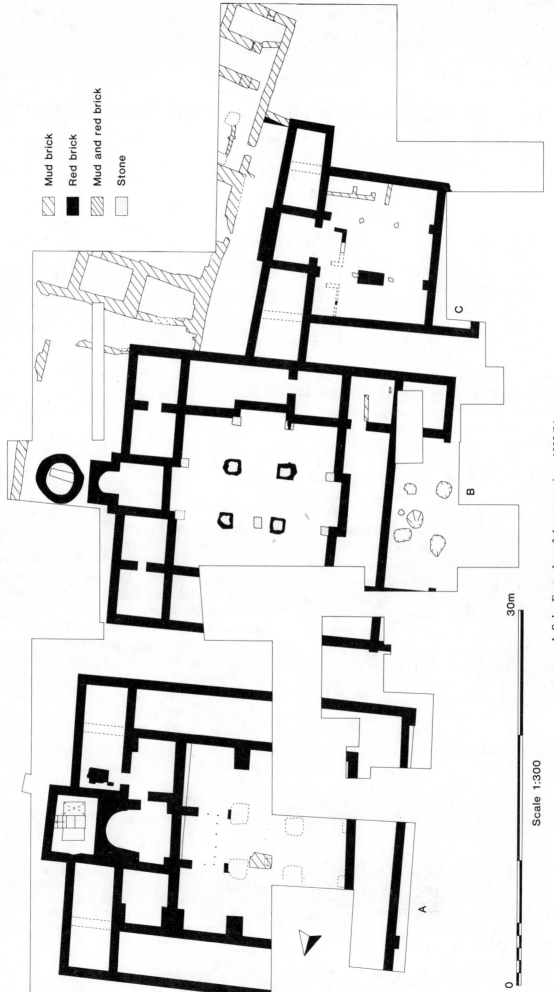

Mud brick

Red brick

Mud and red brick

Stone

C

B

A

0   30m

Scale 1:300

1. Soba East, plan of the excavations 1982/84

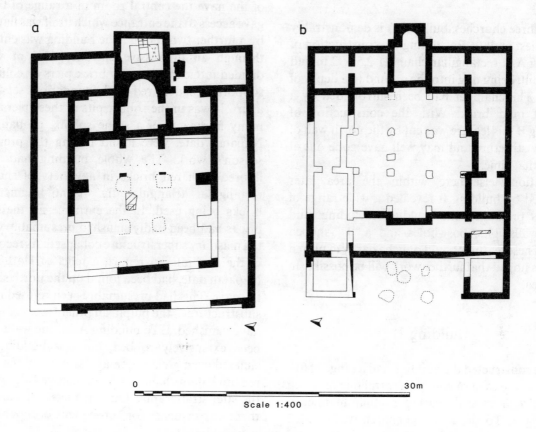

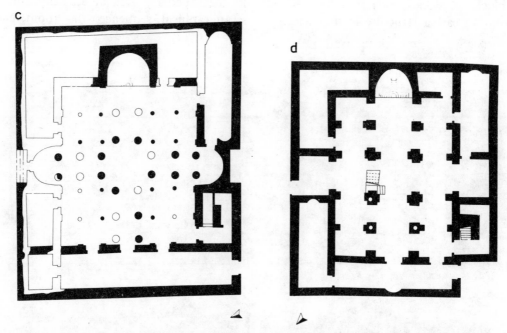

2. Five aisled basilicas: Soba East—buildings A (a); and B (b); Old Dongola—Church of the Granite Columns (after Jakobielski and Ostrasz 1967–68, fig. 6) (c); and Faras—Cathedral of Paulos (after Michałowski 1966, 83) (d)

Pre-Building B Features

Of the three churches, building A is demonstrably the earliest in date. Postdating the construction of building A, a rectangular chamber 2.5 × 2 m had been built, being dug into the ground to a depth of 60 cm. The chamber had been surrounded by a wall of mud brick. With the construction of building B this feature was cut by the north wall of the new structure and may well have gone out of use at that time.

Excavations elsewhere within the area later occupied by building B revealed a wide range of features predating that building, including mud brick walls, pits, post-holes and a "U"-shaped ditch. These features could only be partly explored and it is hoped that further work will be possible in this area.

Building B

As first constructed the building had a range of five rooms at the eastern end, the central one of which projected 70 cm to the east in a similar manner to building A. To the west the church was divided into a nave and two aisles by brick piers supported or large blocks of stone which may have been re-used from an earlier structure in the vicinity.

Four rooms flanked the aisles. At the western end of the nave the central room of a range of three, gave access to the entrance which itself was flanked by a further two rooms. The building was entered through an impressive entrance 11.5 m wide, divided into three bays by brick piers or columns supported on deep red brick foundations set 4.5 m apart. It was in the robber pits of these piers that many fragments of a stone sphinx, probably of Napatan date, were found during the previous season's work. The whole building had been floored with red bricks in a variety of shapes; rectangular, triangular (fig. 4) and fragmentary bricks being used. In the entrance all the floor bricks had been badly smashed presumably when the masonry superstructure collapsed. As recorded in the first interim report, a relief of Hathor, of Napatan date, had been found on the north side of the nave. This had presumably been re-used in the substructure of the pulpit, all other traces of which have vanished. Like building A, all the walls have been extensively robbed, but this building has suffered even greater damage as most of the early red brick floors have also been removed along with the later stratigraphy. Only in a few small areas is there any evidence for subsequent occupation of the building.

In the sanctuary area at an early stage in the stratigraphical sequence, the room had been

3. Soba East, general view of building B looking west

4. Soba East, brick floor in the north aisle of building B

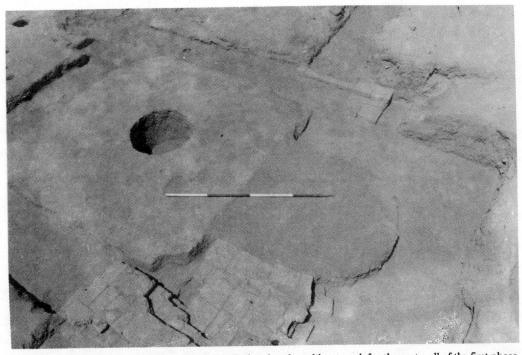

5. Soba East, the sanctuary chamber of building B showing the robber trench for the east wall of the first phase

extended 1.6 m to the east and provided with a small apse (fig. 5). Originally this room had a white lime plaster floor (ephemeral traces suggest that a similar floor may actually have existed throughout the rest of the building) into which were set four red bricks, presumably to support an altar. Subsequently the room was given a floor of rectangular red bricks which was in its turn later buried under another floor of earth with some red bricks set in it. A large circular pit surviving to a depth of 71 cm had been dug in the centre of the room from a level that has been removed by the robbers. In room XIV a mud brick wall 34 cm wide rested directly on the red brick floor. The cathedral of Paulos at Faras, which was of similar plan to building B (fig. 2) had a stairway in the room which occupied a corresponding position in the church, giving access to a gallery or onto the roof and it is quite possible that the wall in building B may have acted as the "newel" for such a stair although no beam holes were noted in it to indicate that it had been so used. Up against the east side of the mud brick wall stratigraphy had survived to a height of 50 cm above the red brick floor. Most of this consisted of a build-up of rubble but there was evidence for squatter occupation at a high level where fires had been lit amongst the rubble.

Building C

Building C abutted on the south wall of building B. This was probably the latest of the three churches and was of a much simplified plan. In its first phase there was again a range of five rooms along the eastern end of the building (as there was in building B and as there had been in an early phase in building A). Later two walls were demolished, leaving two long rooms flanking the central area. The nave had been separated from the aisles by a row of piers, or more likely, by wooden posts resting on the stone post-pads which remain *in situ*. A red brick pulpit was found on the north side of the nave while in the south aisle mud brick walls 20–30 cm thick defined a long, narrow space 1.2 × 4.7 m in size. A *hiqab* built of red brick, which retained traces of the sandy plaster with which it had been rendered and a red brick partition dividing off the eastern end of the north aisle also survived. The entrance to the building presumably lies in the west wall, giving access initially to a

narthex running right across the building. This church had been floored throughout its life with layers of sand. Pre-building features include three charcoal filled pits and a red brick pavement on a different alignment from that of the three churches.

Mud Brick Buildings

To the south-east of building B and to the east of C, extensive remains survived of mud brick buildings, the high standard of preservation of which was the result of the non-reusable nature of mud brick. Under the highest part of the mound walls were found standing to a height of 3 m. Little can be said about the plan of the buildings as only a small portion of them was excavated. They respected the plan of the churches, and in two areas their walls actually abutted the walls of building B, the first course of mud bricks resting directly on top of the construction debris of the red brick building. These buildings had clearly been very substantial; the ground floor walls being well constructed and up to 1.25 m thick. Above first floor level the walls were reduced to 70 cm in width. The first floors, which survived in two rooms, rested on beams of palm set into holes in two of the walls, and on a wide scarcement. A layer of twigs and palm fronds and a further layer of mud completed the floor. In only one room was it possible to excavate below the first floor level which had been burnt but still remained *in situ*. The room had been filled with wind blown sand to within 30 cm of the ceiling before the floor had been destroyed by fire. The original ground floor surface lay 2.3 m below the scarcement level and consisted of a hard layer of earth into which had been dug a shallow "U"-shaped channel. In the occupation material above this floor was found a fine collection of glass.

A number of phases can clearly be seen in these buildings. In the most southerly room excavated, the roof had been supported on four piers constructed of alternating courses of red and mud brick. Subsequently mud brick walls had been built up to two of these piers dividing the room into three. Later still the southern portion of the original room had been used as a rubbish dump and it contained masses of ash, bone and pottery. At this time or later its doors had been blocked, sealing it off from the rest of the structure. These buildings were presumably domestic in character.

The contrast between the dearth of finds in the churches and the large quantity of pottery, bone, glass and clay bungs recovered from the mud brick buildings was very marked.

The Tomb

Lying on the main axis of building B, immediately beyond its east wall, an elaborate tomb was uncovered (fig. 6). This consisted of a grave dug 1.75 m down through the subsoil into the bedrock. The grave itself had been covered by a mud brick barrel vault and the whole had been levelled up with earth. Above ground a circular red brick superstructure 4 m in diameter, constructed of special "voussoir" shaped bricks, had been built and the exterior had been rendered with white plaster. With the collapse of the barrel vault the red brick superstructure had subsided into the resulting void. What remained of the aboveground structure had later been totally robbed out. In the fill of the grave, where it had presumably fallen when the vault collapsed, was an iron cross measuring 26 × 23 cm with a tang at one end for attaching it to a wooden shaft.

A detailed chronology for the buildings excavated to date will have to wait until the finds, particularly the pottery, are studied in detail. Four samples of timber and charcoal from the northern church have, however, been radiocarbon dated. Three of the dates are from structural timbers used in the phase 2 building and are as follows:

A.D. 535 + 120 (GU-1687, 1450 + 120 bp)
A.D. 654 + 55 (GU-1689, 1335 + 55 bp)
A.D. 720 + 75 (GU-1686, 1250 + 75 bp)

These dates suggest that the phase 2 building, providing the timbers were not being re-used, was constructed not later than circa A.D. 760.[2] Building B is later than A though whether it post-dates phase 1 or 2 in the northern church is unclear. Building C, abutting on the south wall of B, could either be contemporary or later than that building. The use of bricks of a different size in building C, however, suggests that a period of time elapsed between the building of the central church and the addition of the sourthern church to the complex.

Building A with its uniaxial plan as reconstructed in phase 2 (the phase 1 plan may well have been similar) is of an earlier form to the biaxial cross in

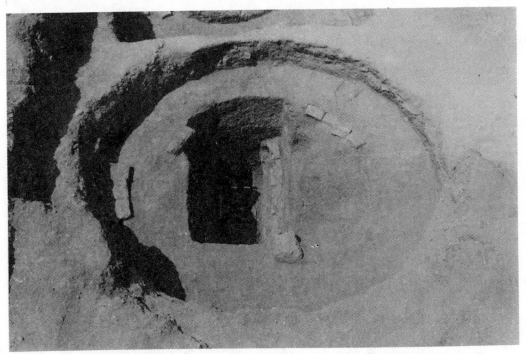

6. Soba East, circular tomb lying immediately to the east of building B

---

[2] The three dates have been calibrated using the curve published by Clark (1975). The brackets in which there is a 95% chance of the dates lying are A.D. 240–760, A.D. 467–763 and A.D. 520–880.

rectangle layout as seen in the Church of the Granite Columns at Old Dongola and in the cathedral of Paulos at Faras (fig. 2). The Faras cathedral is dated to A.D. 707 and the Church of the Granite Columns is of a similar date (Jakobielski and Ostrasz 1967–68, 135). The plan of building B suggests an awareness of the biaxial layout but this is not very marked. The provision of additional roof supports in the Church of the Granite Columns had been dated to the tenth century (ibid., 134; Michałowski 1966, 822 ff.) and may possibly suggest a date for the similar alterations in building A at Soba.

The fourth radiocarbon date was taken from a sample of charcoal found in room H of the northern church. This charcoal formed part of a deposit which was clearly associated with domestic activity within the confines of the church. The date of A.D. 936 + 50 (GU-1688, 1060 + 50 bp) may provide a *terminus ante quem* for the end of the ecclesiastical use of the church. [3]

A total of 19 weeks had been spent on the excavation of 2000 sq. m of mound B by a team of from five to eight archaeologists from England, greatly aided by as many as 70 workmen recruited from the local villages and by an Antiquities officer from the Department of Antiquities in Khartoum. It is now considered desirable to pause while the results obtained are analysed, but it is hoped that excavation by the British Institute in Eastern Africa will resume at Soba in the near future. Clearly with a site covering well over two square kilometres any conclusions drawn from the excavation of the very small portion of the site uncovered to date may have little relevance to the history and development of the settlement as a whole.

Bibliography

Clark R.M. 1975, "A Calibration Curve for Radiocarbon Dates", *Antiquity* 49, 252–266.

Jakobielski S. and Ostrasz A., 1967–68, "Polish Excavations at Old Dongola: Second Season—December 1965–February 1966", Kush XV, 125–164.

Michałowski K. 1966, *Faras—Die Kathedrale aus dem Wüstensand*, Zürich.

Shinnie P. L. 1955, *Excavations at Soba*, Khartoum.

Welsby D.A. 1983, "Recent Excavations at Soba East in Central Sudan", *Azania* XVIII, 165–180.

---

[3] The sample has a 95% chance of dating between A.D. 749 and 1031. This data range, however, may be inaccurate because the charcoal sample was derived from small branches. It has been shown that radiocarbon dates from short lived samples can fluctuate by up to 120 years (Clark 1975, 257).

COPTIC STUDIES

Ewa Wipszycka

Une nouvelle Règle monastique égyptienne

Le titre de mon exposé contient une inexactitude voulue. La Règle dont je vais parler n'est pas un texte inédit. Elle a été publiée au XVIIe siècle et, ayant été réimprimée dans le t. 40 de la PG de J.P. Migne, elle peut se lire dans n'importe quelle bibliothèque. Cependant, elle a été très peu lue et très peu étudiée. La seule recherche systématique qui lui ait été consacrée, celle du bénédictin B. Contzen [1], a été publiée à un endroit très obscur vers la fin du XIXe siècle, donc à une époque antérieure aux recherches modernes sur les Apophthegmes et aux publications modernes de textes coptes et arabes relatifs aux moines d'Égypte; écrivant à cette époque, l'auteur ne pouvait pas savoir grand'chose du monachisme égyptien, si bien que la plupart de ses raisonnements ne sont plus valables aujourd'hui. Il y a plusieurs années, J.-M. Sauget [2] s'est occupé d'une partie de notre texte pour en établir la parenté avec le dossier d'Isaïe; mais le texte en lui-même, sa valeur pour l'historie du monachisme ne l'intéressait pas. Notre Règle est absente de toutes les discussions concernant les formes du monachisme en Égypte, sa mentalité, sa fonction sociale. C'est pourquoi je me sens en droit de la présenter comme une « nouvelle Règle ».

L'intérêt de ce texte résulte d'abord du fait que nous ne possédons que très peu de Règles monastiques égyptiennes: apparemment, la plupart des communautés monastiques en Égypte, n'éprouvaient pas le besoin de fixer par écrit les normes qu'elles observaient dans la vie quotidienne. Deuxièmement, cette Règle est la plus ancienne Règle égyptienne qui ait été conçue pour une laure, et non pour un koinobion.

Troisièmement, il est possible de démontrer qu'elle est née dans la laure de Naqlun, dont parlent des textes littéraires et documentaires et que nous sommes en mesure de situer sur le terrain grâce aux traces qu'on en voit encore aujourd'hui.

L'oubli dans lequel ce texte a été plongé est de tout point de vue injustifié. J'ai l'intention de préparer une étude exhaustive de cette Règle ainsi que du centre monastique pour lequel elle a été créée. La présente communication ne contient que les lignes générales de mon étude future.

Nous ne possédons pas le texte original de la Règle en question. Elle ne s'est conservée que dans une traduction arabe [3], qui a été traduite en latin au XVIIe siècle.

Dans la *Patrologia Graeca* de J.P. Migne, nous trouvons deux traductions latines [4]. La première a été tirée d'un recueil d'œuvres attribuées à saint Antoine et traduites de l'arabe par un érudit maronite, Abraham Ecchellensis. La seconde a été tirée de l'édition du Codex Regularum de saint Benoît d'Aniane, préparée par Lucas Holstenius, mais publiée après la mort de celui-ci. C'est par erreur que cette seconde traduction a été reprise dans la PG de Migne [5]. Elle n'est en effet qu'une première tentative de traduction, faite par le même Abraham Ecchellensis. Au temps où il vivait à Rome, celui-ci transmit cette traduction à Lucas Holstenius, qui s'intéressait à toute sorte de Règles monastiques. L. Holstenius mourut sans avoir achevé son ouvrage, qui devait contenir entre

---

[1] B. Contzen, *Die Regel des heiligen Antonius*, Beilage zum Jahresbericht des humanistischen Gymnasiums Metten für das Schuljahr 1895/96.

[2] J.-M. Sauget, « La double recension arabe des Préceptes aux novices de l'abbé Isaïe de Scété », dans *Mélanges Tisserant* III, Roma 1964, pp. 300–307.

[3] G. Graf, *Geschichte der christlichen arabischen Literatur*, I, Città del Vaticano 1944, pp. 457–458.

[4] PG 40, col. 1065–1074.

[5] Voir Sauget, « La double recension ... ».

autres la traduction de la Règle de saint Antoine, fournie par Abraham Ecchellensis. Lorsque l'ouvrage fut publié, la Règle y fut présentée sans aucune information concernant sa provenance ou l'auteur de la traduction. Préparant cette partie de sa *Patrologia Graeca* sur la base d'un recueil du XVIIIe siècle, J.P. Migne n'a pas regardé le recueil publié par Abraham Ecchellensis, où se trouvent toutes les informations nécessaires. C'est pourquoi son édition donne l'impression fallacieuse qu'il existe deux traductions d'origine différente.

Abraham Ecchellensis a eu en main deux manuscrits arabes, dont l'un contenait les paragraphes 1 – 35 (version brève), l'autre un texte un peu plus long (13 paragraphes en plus, de 36 à 48) ; la doxologie finale se trouvait dans tous les deux manuscrits (dans le premier, après le paragraphe 35). La distinction entre la version brève et la version longue est très importante. Ainsi que J.-M. Sauget l'a démontré, les paragraphes que la version longue possède en plus par rapport à la version brève, proviennent d'un texte attribué à l'abbé Isaïe de Skétis, à savoir de la recension brève des Préceptes aux novices (paragraphes 7–18[a]). Ces Préceptes sont à leur tour des extraits des Logoi de l'Asketikon attribué à Isaïe[6]. Au même dossier il faut ajouter encore un texte publié par Abraham Ecchellensis dans son recueil d'écrits de saint Antoine : les « Admonitiones et documenta varia »[7].

Il est évident que la Règle de saint Antoine était à l'origine celle de la version brève. A un moment que je ne suis pas en mesure d'établir, elle a été incorporée dans un ensemble de textes attribués à Isaïe.

Je n'ai pas l'intention de m'occuper ici du dossier d'Isaïe, dont l'histoire appartient aux problèmes les plus compliqués de la littérature ascétique. C'est la Règle de saint Antoine sous sa forme primitive qui fait l'objet de mes recherches.

Nous ne savons pas si la Règle a été écrite d'abord en grec ou en copte, mais tout ce que nous savons sur l'histoire du monachisme égyptien à l'époque byzantine nous fait pencher vers la seconde hypothèse.

Je n'ai pas trouvé de points de contact entre la Règle d'Antoine et les autres Règles égyptiennes connues (sauf pour l'interdiction de dormir sur la même natte avec un autre moine : mais il s'agit là d'un principe évident, qui a pu être formulé indépendamment dans différentes Régles). Mes recherches dans les textes littéraires concernant le milieu monastique n'ont pas donné de résultats non plus.

Il se peut que deux textes occidentaux du début du Moyen Age se réfèrent à notre Règle[8]. Dans la Vie de Droctovenus (ce saint est mort en 580, mais sa Vie a été écrite vers la fin du IXe siècle), on parle des « normae sanctorum patrum Antonii et Basilii ». Un privilège accordé par le pape Jean IV à un monastère en 641 atteste que les moines vivent « secundum edicta Antonii, Pachomii et haud procul a nostris temporibus Benedicti abbatis ». Mais s'agit–il, dans ces deux textes, de la Règle de saint Antoine ou des principes ascétiques contenus dans la Vie de saint Antoine écrite par Athanase et dont la traduction latine était très lue à l'Occident ? Je ne vois pas le moyen de répondre à cette question.

La localité Nacalon, mentionnée au début de la Règle, doit certainement être identifiée à la localité qui s'appelait en copte Neklone et qui s'appelle en arabe Naqlun. Elle se trouve à 15 km de Medinet Fayoum et à 10 km de el Lahun. Dans le gebel Naqlun, sur son rebord méridional, a existé pendant plusieurs siècles, une des plus anciennes communautés monastiques du Fayoum. Des ruines d'un monastère et des restes d'installations monastiques dans les grottes sont visibles encore aujourd'hui (nous devons à O. Meinardus une description détaillée de ce site[9] ; une étude de la documentation écrite qui le concerne se trouve dans un article de Nabia Abbott sur les monastères du Fayoum[10]).

---

[6] Publié par R. Draguet, « Les cinq recensions de l'Ascéticon syriaque d'abba Isaïe », dans *Corpus Scriptorum Christianorum Orientalium*, 122–123, Louvain 1968.

[7] La traduction latine de ce texte, faite par Abraham Ecchellensis, a été réimprimée dans la PG 40, col. 1073–1100.

[8] Pour Droctovenus, voir les *Acta sanctorum ordinis sancti Benedicti*, I, ed. J. Mabillon (1668), réimpression de 1935, 253. Pour le document du pape Jean IV, voir Ph. Jaffé, *Regesta pontificum Romanorum* I, p. 939, no 278. Cf. B. Contzen, *Die Regel...*, pp. 28–29.

[9] O. Meinardus, « The Laura of Naqlūn », *Bulletin de la Société Géographique d'Égypte* 40, 1967, pp. 173–185.

[10] N. Abbott, « The Monasteries of the Fayum », *The American Journal of Semitic Languages and Literatures* 53, 1956, 13–33, 73–96. Voir aussi P. van Cauwenbergh, *Étude sur les moines d'Égypte depuis le concile de Chalcédoine jusqu'à l'invasion arabe*, Paris 1914, pp. 104–106.

Les débuts de cette communauté sont difficiles à établir, car nous n'avons pas de sources à ce sujet, en dehors d'une légende pleine de motifs fantastiques et dont le héros est le fils du roi perse Aur [11]. Celui-ci, avec l'aide de l'archange Gabriel, aurait fondé la communauté monastique et l'église de Naqlun (c'est pourquoi le monastère portait, entre autres, le nom de monastère de l'ange Gabriel). N. Abbott a cru pouvoir séparer le noyau historique de cette légende et placer, par conséquent, les débuts de la vie monastique à cet endroit aux premières années du IVe siècle. Je suis assez sceptique quant à la possibilité de tirer des informations d'une légende aussi fantastique et qui ne nous est accessible que sous une forme très tardive. C'est pour d'autres raisons qu'on peut admettre la présence d'ascètes à Naqlun au IVe siècle et même, plus précisément, dans la première moitié du IVe siècle. Si l'on tient compte du fait qu'au Fayoum, le mouvement ascétique a commencé très tôt (comme en témoignent les textes concernant saint Antoine), que Naqlun était très proche de Pispir et que sa position géographique favorisait une installation monastique, on reconnaîtra que la datation proposée par N. Abbott a bien des chances d'être juste.

Les données historiques commencent avec Samuel de Kalamun, qui en 630 quitta Skétis et se réfugia dans la communauté de Naqlun [12]. Celle-ci était, à cette époque, déjà un monastère peuplé. Samuel y passa trois ans et demi, habitant cependant dans une grotte et allant au couvent tous les samedis et les dimanches. Quand la persécution de la part de Cyrus, patriarche orthodoxe d'Alexandrie, devint insupportable, il persuada les habitants du monastère, 120 moines et 200 laïcs, d'abandonner le monastère et de se cacher. Nous savons, toujours grâce à la Vie de Samuel, que le monastère avait un économe (nous ne savons cependant pas si, outre l'économe, il y avait aussi un supérieur, ou si celui

qui s'appelait « économe » était lui-même le supérieur).

Le monastère de Naqlun a continué d'exister après la conquête arabe. En témoignent un acte de donation en sa faveur, rédigé en arabe et daté de 947 [13], et une lettre du XIe ou XIIe siècle [14]. Une notice d'Abu Salih [15] nous assure que le monastère, quoique appauvri, existait au XIIIe siècle. En 1672, au moment où P. Vansleb le visite, il vivote encore [16]. Il disparaîtra par la suite, en laissant un kôm imposant à côté de l'église, qui jusqu'à nos jours continue d'être un lieu de pèlerinage.

En lisant la Règle, on sent tout de suite qu'on a affaire à une communauté non structurée [17]. Les moines vivent dans leurs cellules, chacun décide pour son compte à quel moment il doit se mettre à travailler et pour combien de temps, chacun prend ses repas à part. Certes, avant d'accepter un travail, les moines doivent consulter « le père » (§ 32), c'est-à-dire le supérieur ; mais le fait même qu'on ait éprouvé le besoin de mettre par écrit ce principe, prouve que les moines peuvent fort bien décider pour eux-mêmes. Les revenus de leur labeur leur appartiennent, ils sont libres de faire l'aumône soit à d'autres moines (par exemple aux malades), soit aux nécessiteux étrangers à la communauté. Ils peuvent même donner des « banquets », donc inviter des gens, probablement des séculiers. Bien entendu, la Règle condamne ces « banquets » ; mais cela prouve qu'ils sont concevables. Les rapports avec les gens du siècle sont très faciles, les moines reçoivent des hôtes chez eux, ils vont dans les villages. La Règle trouve nécessaire de déclarer que les femmes et les jeunes garçons ne doivent pas entrer dans les cellules. Le « père » de la communauté n'apparaît qu'une seule fois, à savoir dans un passage où il est question de l'organisation du travail. Je ne pense pas, cependant, qu'on puisse tirer de là la conclusion que son rôle était limité à la sphère

---

[11] Le texte copte a été traduit en anglais par E. A. W. Budge, *Egyptian Tales and Romances*, London 1931, pp. 247–267 ; la version arabe a été traduite en français par E. Amelineau, *Contes et romans de l'Égypte chrétienne*, I, Paris 1888, pp. 104–143.
[12] Voir van Cauwenbergh, *Étude sur les moines...*, pp. 39–49, 88–128, 181–188. La Vie copte de Samuel a été publiée récemment par A. Alcock, *The Life of Samuel of Kalamun*, Cambridge 1983.
[13] Publié par Abbott, « The Monasteries... ».
[14] W. E. Crum., *Catalogue of the Coptic Manuscripts in the British Museum*, London 1905, no 590.
[15] Abu Salih, *Churches and Monasteries of Egypt*, éd. B.T.A. Evetts, Oxford 1895, pp. 205–206.
[18] P. Vansleb, *Nouvelle relation en forme de journal d'un voyage fait en Égypte en 1672 et 1673*, Paris 1677, pp. 274–277.
[17] Sur ce genre de communautés monastiques, voir M. Martin, « Laures et ermitages du désert d'Égypte », *Mélanges de l'Université saint Joseph*, Beyrouth, 42, 1966, 181–198, ainsi que son exemplaire publication des restes d'une laure, *La laure de Dêr al Dîk à Antinoé*, Le Caire 1971.

économique. La Règle n'embrasse pas l'ensemble de la vie de la communauté, plusieurs points importants ne sont pas traités (par exemple, le mode d'admission des novices); il serait donc dangereux d'utiliser l'*argumentum ex silentio*.

La Règle insiste que le moine doit travailler[18], mais ne précise pas en quoi consiste le travail. Nous apprenons seulement que les moines partent pour moissonner.

Les moines reçoivent des dons de la part de gens riches. La Règle voudrait qu'en ces occasions, les rapports entre les moines et les donateurs soient limités le plus possible.

Une information intéressante ressort du § 18: « Terram vectigalibus subjectam ne semines et societates cum dominis ne contrahas ». Il faut entendre: « N'ensemence pas une terre grevée de la rente, et ne fais pas de société (contrat de bail) avec des propriétaires ». (Ce que Abraham Ecchellensis a traduit par « vectigal » ne peut pas être un mot signifiant « impôt », car il n'y avait pas, en Égypte, de terres libres d'impôts.) Ce précepte prouve qu'il était concevable qu'un moine prenne de la terre à bail. Ce fait mérite d'être souligné, car nous connaissons plusieurs textes documentaires d'où il ressort que des moines possédaient de la terre, mais nous n'en connaissons aucun qui témoignerait qu'un moine cultivait la terre. Les textes littéraires donnent à ce sujet des témoignages contradictoires. D'une part, ils répètent que le travail agricole ne convient pas aux moines[19]. D'autre part, ils nous apprennent que les champs appartenant à la congrégation pakhômienne et au monastère de Shenouti étaient cultivés par les moines eux–mêmes. Le témoignage de la Règle d'Antoine doit être pris au sérieux malgré son isolement relatif. L'absence de témoignages documentaires ne doit pas nous préoccuper, car si les moines cultivaient directement des terres qui appartenaient à eux personnellement ou à leur communauté, cette activité ne pouvait pas faire naître des documents. Les documents naissent là où des gens entrent en rapport les uns avec les autres et veulent des preuves pour le cas d'un conflit éventuel. L'idée qu'il n'était pas convenable aux moines de travailler sur les champs, sauf pour les moissons, était certainement répandue, mais elle n'était pas en mesure

d'éliminer totalement ce genre d'activité parmi les moines. Si un monastère avait des terres situées dans le voisinage immédiat, les donner à bail devait sembler absurde, d'autant plus que beaucoup de moines étaient des anciens paysans.

La Règle nous fait manifestement connaître la communauté monastique de Naqlun de l'époque où les moines vivaient dans les grottes et où le monastère au pied de la montagne n'existait pas encore. Ce genre de vie, où les moines bougent librement, reçoivent librement des hôtes, où il n'y a pas de repas communs, ni une infirmerie assurant aux malades au moins l'eau, aurait été inconcevable dans un monastère.

Une grotte avait certainement été adaptée aux besoins du culte, et c'est là que les moines se réunissaient chaque nuit pour la prière et qu'étaient célébrées les messes. Mais les moines pouvaient, dans certains cas, descendre vers la zone habitée et aller aux églises des villages, fréquentées par des séculiers. Cela n'allait pas sans danger pour leurs âmes; c'est pourquoi la Règle dit (§ 28): « Ecclesiam ad quam convenit multitudo hominum ne adeas. »

Les moines sont invités à ne pas s'asseoir dans les exèdres, nous pouvons facilement imaginer pourquoi: les conversations qui s'y engageaient ne concernaient pas toujours des sujets pieux.

Un autre précepte encore mérite d'être mentionné (§ 33): pendant qu'ils vont chercher de l'eau (on la puisait dans un canal), les moines doivent lire et méditer. Il me semble qu'il devait être impossible de lire pendant une marche pénible (même si les moines avaient des ânes pour porter les cruches). Peut–être un copiste ou un traducteur, qui ne connaissait plus les conditions de vie dans les laures rupestres, a-t-il déformé le texte. Je suppose qu'en allant chercher de l'eau, les moines ne lisaient pas, mais psalmodiaient et récitaient des textes bibliques.

B. Contzen s'est donné beaucoup de peine pour démontrer qu'il y avait des points communs entre la Règle d'Antoine et la Vie d'Antoine écrite par Athanase. Cet effort a été vain. Les deux textes n'ont pas d'affinité entre eux. Les ressemblances concernent des points très généraux, qui pourraient se trouver dans n'importe quel texte ascétique.

---

[18] Sur les problèmes économiques du monachisme égyptien, voir mon étude: « Les aspects économiques de la vie de la communauté des Kellia, » dans: *Le site monastique copte des Kellia,* Genève 1986, pp. 117–144.

[19] Voir par exemple « le Gerontikon », *Poimen* 22 (PG 65, col. 328): « ce n'est pas une occupation pour un moine ».

Il n'y a pas de doute que saint Antoine n'a jamais songé à écrire (ou à dicter) une Règle. Rien dans sa Vie ni dans les apophthegmes n'indique qu'il ait voulu fixer par écrit son enseignement pratique. La Règle, pour lui, c'était la Bible, qu'il fallait lire et méditer sans cesse. Les préceptes concernant le mode de vie, l'organisation de la vie communautaire, appartenaient à l'enseignement oral[20]. Écrire une Règle aurait été contraire à la logique du comportement de sa génération. Souvenons–nous que ce que nous connaissons comme les Règles de saint Pakhôme a été écrit bien après la mort de Pakhôme et reflète souvent l'état des monastères tel qu'il était plusieurs années après la disparition de leur fondateur. Ces Règles contiennent certainement des enseignements, voire des paroles de Pakhôme lui–même, mais ce n'est pas lui qui a eu l'initiative de leur donner une forme écrite.

Cependant, ce n'est pas par hasard que la Règle qui nous intéresse a été attribuée à saint Antoine. On sait que celui–ci entretenait des rapports étroits avec les moines du Fayoum. Une de ses lettres était destinée « aux frères bien-aimés de la région d'Arsinoé et des environs et à toutes les personnes qui se trouvent avec eux ». Il a rendu des visites aux ascètes de cette région (Vita, 15, 1). Si des ascètes s'étaient déjà installés à Naqlun de son vivant (ce qui est très probable), il a dû séjourner chez eux, d'autant plus que Naqlun est situé sur la piste qui va de Pispir au Fayoum. Certes, il se peut, malgré tout, que les débuts de la laure de Naqlun soient postérieurs à sa mort ; mais même en ce cas, le souvenir de la direction spirituelle excercée par saint Antoine au Fayoum a dû être assez vivant pour qu'on pût facilement avoir l'idée de lui attribuer une Règle dont on ne connaissait plus l'auteur véritable ou dont on voulait augmenter l'autorité.

La Règle doit être postérieure au milieu du IVe siècle, car, comme je viens de le dire, dans la première moitié du siècle, personne ne songeait encore à écrire des textes pareils. D'autre part, elle doit certainement être antérieure à la naissance du monastère, dont l'existence est indirectement attestée pour la première fois en 630 (les 120 moines et les 200 laïcs qui, d'après la Vie de Samuel, vivaient à Naqlun, ne pouvaient pas habiter tous dans des grottes ; même si nous supposons que ces chiffres sont exagérés, nous admettrons qu'il y avait beaucoup de gens, ce qui suppose qu'il y eût un couvent). A l'intérieur de la période qui s'étend du milieu du IVe siècle à l'an 630, rien ne nous permet de dater la naissance de notre Règle de façon plus précise.

Post scriptum (décembre 1988)

En 1986, des fouilles ont été entreprises à Naqlun par une mission archéologique créé par le Centre Polonais d'Archéologie Méditerranéenne de l'Université de Varsovie et dirigée par Włodzimierz Godlewski. Les résultats des quatre campagnes de fouilles qui ont été effectuées jusqu'à présent et qui ont porté aussi bien sur les ermitages que sur le monastère situé au pied du gebel, ont beaucoup enrichi notre connaissance de ce centre monastique. Entre-temps, Michel Breydy a étudié l'histoire du texte et des traductions de la Règle et a préparé une nouvelle traduction de celle-ci ; il a bien voulu me communiquer les résultats de son étude, encore inédite.

Mon article imprimé ci-dessus ne tient pas compte de ces nouvelles données ; il reproduit le texte de la communication que j'ai faite au Congrès.

---

[20] Voir Ph. Rousseau, *Ascetics, Authority and the Church*, Oxford 1978, chapitre « The Written Word ».

COPTIC STUDIES

Cornelia E. Zijderveld

Coptic Textiles in Holland

Coptic textiles are to be found in the collections of ancient textiles at Dutch museums, such as the Museum of Antiquities at Leiden, the Dutch Museum of Textiles at Tilburg and the National Museum in Amsterdam. However, just a few of them are exhibited and if so, only rarely.

Moreover there is quite a number of private collections of Coptic textiles.

Most fragments of the textiles which came to the museums, either by way of donation or purchase, are not ready to be exhibited. The main reason for this is that they are kept in the depots for a long time. It is also due both to the fact that there are not enough specialists in this field, working in the museums and to the fact that the depots are too small or not well locked regarding regulation heat and moist, and the keeping down of dust and moths from the cupboards.

The Municipal Museum of The Hague contains a collection of ninety fragments. This collection happened to become the subject of two university studies at the same time. Having started with some reserve the studies have brought very interesting results, both for the museum and the students.

Thirty fragments were bought in 1936, which purchase has been written down in the inventory as follows: textile bought from Mr Krook, originating from the collection Forrer. Forrer as you know, was the managing Director of the museum of Strassbourg, and has excavated at Achmim in Egypt. But how to prove that these textiles actually come from Forrer? Well, with the textiles we have found a booklet entitled: *Travel letters from Egypt*, written by Forrer in 1895, during the excavations at Achmim. This booklet has been dedicated "to my friend Krook", signed by R. Forrer himself. That is why we suggest carefully that Forrer has found these fragments at Achmim.

Among these 90 textiles of The Hague, we have found rather interesting fragments, e.g. one tabula was really composed of two different fragments. Apparently they tried to repair an incomplete tabula by adding a similar fragment, cat. no 73. Two children tunics, very damaged, one interesting because of the weaving technique and decoration, the other because it has been composed of existing textiles and has been decorated with different applications, cat. nos 84 and 85.

A small fragment of pure silk, the decoration of which is quite identical to a piece in the Victoria and Albert Museum in London, cat. 27; cat. Kendrick 111, pl. XXIX, fig. 840; and also to one in the museum of Fine Arts in Brussels, cat. Errera, fig. 365, p. 165.

A fragment of a pure woollen clavus of a tunic, an identical part of which has been found in the Tropical Museum in Amsterdam. This piece was acquired both by Amsterdam and The Hague in 1959 even in the same month.

While proceeding with my inventory I hope to find still more pieces of this tunic. Of course one ought to take recourse to research in laboratories in order to establish whether place of provenance is identical. With some luck one might assemble quite a part of this tunic, cat. no 31.

As regards the technical aspects one can recognize several weaving methods in this collection, like double weaving, looped weaves, floating warps, reps, sprang, etc.

Concerning the iconography, one finds the interlacing most frequently on monochrome textiles; one comes across vegetative ornaments, Nile scenes, mythological scenes and friezes with animals, etc.

After a thorough study the board of directors has enabled us to prepare an exhibition of the complete collection, 35 years after the acquisition. But how to proceed? How to clean and preserve 90 fragments without a workshop and without a room appropriate for storing the textiles after the exhibition without running the risk of them to deteriorate, and all this in bad economic circumstances.

The Abegg Foundation at Riggisberg in Switzerland, museum and restoration workshop of ancient textiles, offered us their services to clean and preserve the textiles. I myself have been there for 4 months to work in this workshop on the complete collection.

The textiles have been washed in demineralized water and still wet, the warp and weft threads have been put in order very carefully, fixed with pins. After the washing one decides whether the fragment will be sewn on a supporting textile or will be fixed behind glass, this because the textiles are not always good enough to be sewn. For sewing one uses pure silk of a very fine quality and dyed in the same colour as the textile.

Our tunics have been taken care of by the students of the workshop. They have been given a supporting textile and you can see the results of this work of patience. A true metamorphosis, cat. no 85.

The exhibition has been a great succes. From now on the textiles are well kept in new cupboards. Although at first, the textiles were not always ready to be exhibited, they have been preserved very well for centuries; but the question remains: is it due to the kind of soil, or to certain qualities of the balm applied to the corpses at the time.

One has to make a choice: one either leaves the textiles just as they have been found; or one treats them in the manner described above in order to exhibit them well, that is to say, one washes them while running the risk that the textile loses its protective elements. One gives it its freshness, but may take away its durability.

As regards the colours of the textiles, researches have been made by means of infra-red spectrophotometry in the Central Laboratory of Amsterdam. The results can be compared with those obtained by A. Schweppes in the laboratory of the B.A.S.F. in 1976; not pure purple of the *murex brandaris*, but a mixture of *indigo ferotinctoria* and *rubia tinctorum* for the blue colours and just *rubia tinctorum* for the red colour, but also *kermococcus*. Like every one else we have had difficulties with the dating and classification of the textiles. The dates mentioned in the catalogues are all hypotheses. But, fortunately, it will soon be possible to determine the dates fairly accurately.

In some universities it is already possible to apply the ^{14}C tests. It takes a lot of time and one also needs a rather large piece of textile, which is a problem because the fragments sometimes are very small.

For a few years there has been a quicker and more exact method with the so-called "tandem--accelerator" for ^{14}C research. Although a number of laboratories in the world are already working on this research, for example in Zürich and Oxford, little is done on textiles.

That is why the researches in Utrecht in Holland are very important to us. In the Robert van de Graaff laboratory, in collaboration with the university of Groningen, progress is made. For the moment experiments are performed with samples of only 10 mg weight, taken from Coptic textiles. Finally they hope to attain a very high precision of dating.

In 1985 a "Radiocarbon" conference will be held in Trondheim in Norway. The results of all research will then be manifested.

Bibliography

"Radiocarbon", *American Journal of Science*, 25, no 2 (Washington 1983).

Journal of Archaeological Science 11 (1984), 103–117: Academic Press, London.

Archaeometry, research lab. for archaeology and the history of art: Oxford University, 26, part 1, Febr. 1984, 15–21.

DATE DUE

NOV 17 '98			
FEB 1 5 1999			